WIDE AREA networks

Carol Trivedi • DeAnza College

EMCParadigm

USaName: resources
Password: educate

Developmental Editor	Tom Modl
Illustrator	Kevin Trivedi
Editorial Consultant	George Baker
Copyeditor	Julie McNamee
Proofreader	Lynn Reichel
Indexer	Donald Glassman
Text and Cover Design	Jennifer Wreisner

EMCParadigm Publishing Management Team

George Provol, Publisher; Janice Johnson, Director of Product Development; Tony Galvin, Acquisitions Editor; Lori Landwer, Marketing Manager; Shelley Clubb, Electronic Design and Production Manager

The publisher gratefully acknowledges the following instructors for their reviews:

Shannon W. Beasley, Central Georgia Technical College
Michael Stewart, Wake Technical Community College
Rich McMahon, University of Houston, Downtown Campus
Ben Schorr, Kapi'olani Community College

Illustration credits: Figures 3.14, 3.16, 3.17, 3.18, 3.19, 3.20, 3.22, 6.15, 6.16, Black Box Corporation. **Figures 3.21, 4.12, 4.13, 8.17, 11.4, 11.5, 12.5, 12.9, 12.10, 12.11, 12.12, 12.17, 12.18, 12.19, 12.20**, reproduced by EMCParadigm with the permission of Cisco Systems Inc. COPYRIGHT " CISCO SYSTEMS, INC. ALL RIGHTS RESERVED. **Figures 4.6, 4.8, 10.4, 10.14, 14.4**, Copyright " 2003 Novell, Inc. Used with permission. **Figures 6.20, 6.21, 6.22, 6.23, 6.24**, Cubix Corporation. **Figures 9.21, 9.23**, 3COM Corp. **Figure 9.29**, SAAVIS, Inc.

Library of Congress Cataloging-in-Publication Data
Trivedi, Carol.
    Wide area networks / Carol Trivedi.
        p. cm. -- (NetAbility series)
    Includes index.
    ISBN 0-7638-1945-X
    1. Wide area networks (Computer networks) I. Title. II. Series.

    TK5105.87.T75 2003
    004.67--dc21   2002192817

Text w/CD ISBN: 0-7638-1945-X
Order Number: 05600

© 2004 by Paradigm Publishing Inc.
    Published by **EMC**Paradigm
    875 Montreal Way
    St. Paul, MN 55102
    (800) 535-6865
    E-mail: educate@emcp.com
    Web site: www.emcp.com

CONTENTS

Contents

Part Two
Telephony, Transmission, and
Switching   231

PREFACE

Yesterday communication was simple. It started with radio and telephones, moved on to television, and then to fax and e-mail. Today communication is more complicated. It includes the transmission of data, voice, and video across the world on both wired and wireless telecommunications networks. Using the Internet, people today can communicate and transact business electronically. Behind the scenes, a complex wide area network structure supports the devices, media, interfaces, and carrier services needed to connect users to servers anywhere in the world. In this book students are introduced to the history, design, operation, and applications of wide area networks (WANs).

ABOUT THE TEXT

NetAbility Series: Wide Area Networks covers the basic topics students need to know to be able to understand how wide area networks are built and used. This book is ideal as an introductory course in wide area networking technology. The book is divided into four parts: (1) WAN Issues and Trends; (2) Telephony, Transmission, and Switching; (3) WAN Applications and Services; and (4) WAN Architectures, Resources, and Management. In Part 1, the student is introduced to the history, design, and components of WANs, including protocols. In Part 2, they learn the mechanics of how WANs go about transmitting data, with particular emphasis on home office and remote location connections. In Part 3, students learn about how WANs are applied in the real world, for example, in e-commerce. Finally, in Part 4, students are introduced to the exploding use of wireless networks and to the global reach and future of WANs. Each section contains three to four chapters, for a total of fifteen. The text designed to be completed in a 12-week quarter or 16-week semester course.

The study of wide area networking is complicated. In this text each topic is presented in a step-by-step manner, with numerous visual diagrams used to build up an understanding of the concepts. The book teaches how to evaluate different networking technologies, such as satellite, ISDN, VPN, Frame Relay, SMDS, ATM, SONET, and wireless technologies for wide area networks. After each topic is presented, students are encouraged to increase their comprehension by discussing topic review questions. The approach is to provide plenty of practical examples of WAN problems to lead the student through to appropriate solutions. The student's learning success is linked to following instructional objectives that promote understanding of the acronyms and logic associated with the concepts of wide area networking.

At the end of each chapter there is a summary of concepts from the chapter, followed by a review quiz. This is followed by Internet Exercises, in which students are called on to do hands-on research on WAN topics related to the chapter material, and by three Concept Exercises, in which the student is asked to demonstrate comprehension of the chapter concepts by providing answers to narrative, table, and picture exercises based on the chapter text.

Each chapter contains a Case Study. Each Case Study introduces a hypothetical organization that has a particular need or problem related to wide area networks. A solution to the problem is spelled out, and the student is called upon to evaluate the solution and discuss related questions. This activity can be done in class or as a writing assignment. Each chapter also contains a segment of a course-long collaborative project called the Group Term Project. In Chapter 1, the reader learns the particulars of a hypothetical organization. The Group Term Project challenges the students to learn how to design a global e-mail system with locations in Europe, the Asia Pacific region, South America, and the United States. The project is designed to extend throughout the quarter or semester. Each week the students will work with their group to complete a project template at the end of each chapter. The templates are designed to lead the student through all the phases of planning and scheduling the implementation of a wide area network. The ultimate goal is to demonstrate the concepts to the students and have them apply those concepts to the templates provided to solve the global e-mail project.

Each chapter ends with a list of chapter terms indexed to their definition in the text (there is also a comprehensive glossary in the back of the book and on the companion Encore! CD), and a bibliography of both print and Web resources for further study.

EMCPARADIGM ENCORE! CD

NetAbility Series: Wide Area Networks comes with an Encore! Companion CD that provides additional, interactive quizzes and tests with which students can test their knowledge of the concepts in the book. There are two levels of tests, book and chapter, and each level functions in two different modes. In the Practice mode, the student receives immediate feedback on each test item and a report of his or her total score. In the reportable Test mode the results are e-mailed both to the student and the instructor.

The WAN Encore! CD also comes with a comprehensive online glossary, and with key illustrations taken from the textbook. The Student Files function allows students to print out Word file copies of all Review Question quizzes, Concept Exercises, and the templates needed for the Group Term Project.

INSTRUCTOR'S GUIDE ON CD

An Instructor's Guide on CD is available that provides instructors with answer keys for all worksheets and templates, sample syllabi, teaching hints, chapter overviews, and PowerPoint presentations.

NETABILITY SERIES INTERNET RESOURCE CENTER

You can find additional content and study aids for *NetAbility Series: Wide Area Networks* at the NetAbility Internet Resource Center at www.emcp.com. Students will find course information, additional quizzes, and valuable Web links. Instructors will find Instructor's Guide materials (such as syllabi, teaching hints, model answers, and additional assessment tools).

DEDICATION AND ACKNOWLEDGEMENTS

I would like to dedicate this book to my late father, Harry H. Watkins Jr., who always encouraged and inspired me to study, learn, and graduate from his favorite college, the University of Michigan. He encouraged me to keep going chapter after chapter.

Also I would like to acknowledge all of my students from DeAnza College, the University of Phoenix, and the University of Michigan who participated in Wide Area Networking courses I taught. Often they would suggest improvements that should be included in their textbooks. They contributed their ideas and participated in testing several exercises. Thanks for encouraging me to pursue writing this textbook.

A sincere thank you to my son, Kevin Trivedi, for creating over 300 illustrations for this book. The hours you devoted to each detail of every illustration have contributed significantly to the excellent quality of this textbook. I would also like to acknowledge the countless hours that Jennifer Warren devoted to reading each chapter multiple times, offering editing suggestions and assistance with glossary material for each chapter. I would like to extend a special thank you to Tim and Nissa Munroe for their suggestions for incorporating the latest techniques in instructional technology in the Instuctor Guide.

Finally, this book would not have been possible without the dedicated efforts and excellent advice provided by Tom Modl and his editorial staff. A special thank you to Tony Galvin and Janice Johnson for sponsoring the creation of this book.

PART ONE
WAN Issues and Trends

CHAPTER 1
INTRODUCTION TO WIDE AREA NETWORKS

C H A P T E R   O B J E C T I V E S

By the end of this chapter, you should understand the following concepts:
- Characteristics and current technology used for Wide Area Networks (WAN)
- WAN media and alternatives for interconnecting devices such as routers, modems, switches, and leased lines
- WAN issues and economic factors that influence information technology (IT) expenditures
- History of telecommunications from 1850-the present and the events that have impacted it
- Developments surrounding the AT&T divestiture
- Current carrier service trends and new research for wireless initiatives
- Proposed standards for the Next Generation optical networks to be used for wide area networking
- Competition for the "last mile"
- Technology spending patterns and the future direction of the wide area networking industry

INTRODUCING WIDE AREA NETWORKING

Computer networks span the globe to reach millions of people. Messages flow back and forth over miles of telecommunication links so that organizations can share information and resources electronically. Organizations today need information instantly and their global business relationships demand a new level of integration. Information must now be shared beyond the physical borders of the organization. [Webopedia, 1]

The network of telecommunications links and Internet devices that enables communication pathways across countries is called a **backbone**.

Wide Area Networks provide the communications backbone that connects workers, business partners, and consumers. **Wide Area Networks** (**WAN**s) make possible long distance transmission of data, voice, and video information between users in different states and countries, and between different **local area networks** (**LANs**). As mergers and acquisitions have constantly transformed the business environment, the scope of WANs has widened to address the need for a network that provides more and more services.

WAN Characteristics

WANs are not limited by distance, because they span from one side of the world to the other. Links to members of the network are built using services provided by telecommunications providers. These providers offer several alternatives designed to meet different business needs; the services vary by cost, speed, quality, and the number of telecommunications links required. Private leased lines are offered when privacy and confidentiality are required. If access can be shared, then public data communication services offer good performance at a lower cost.

Figure 1.1 shows an example WAN. Two LANs are connected between San Jose and New York. Servers FS1 (File Server #1) and NY_FS01 (New York File Server #1) are connected by telecommunications links over the WAN. Users can share data quickly and easily through that WAN link.

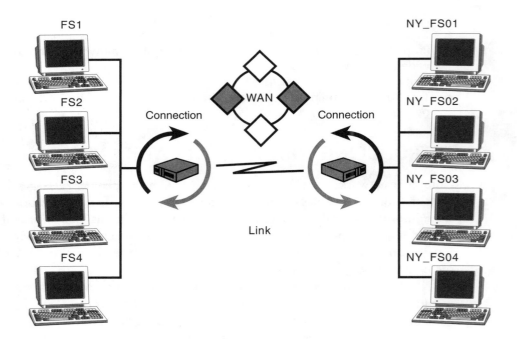

FIGURE 1.1 **Two Connected LANs**

Consumer demand for network services is suddenly increasing and network traffic volumes are exploding. However, budgets are not keeping pace with the demand for network resources. Information Technology (IT) departments are faced with finding ways to minimize bandwidth costs and maximize network availability, efficiency, and performance. To achieve this, they must continually look for ways to consolidate or replace their existing WAN technologies with new services that support new business network applications.

Remote WAN Connections

WANs use several methods, such as dial-up or cable modems, to allow clients to make remote connections to organization headquarters. Today, clients can send and receive mail over mobile telephones or wireless personal digital assistants (PDAs). Figure 1.2 shows several choices for telecommuters: Digital Subscriber Lines (DSL), cable modems, and Fiber to the Home (FTTH). Some organizations have installed videoconferencing to the Desktop for long-distance meetings. In addition, due to IT budget constraints, many companies are beginning to save long-distance costs by routing their voice calls over the Internet at no extra charge.

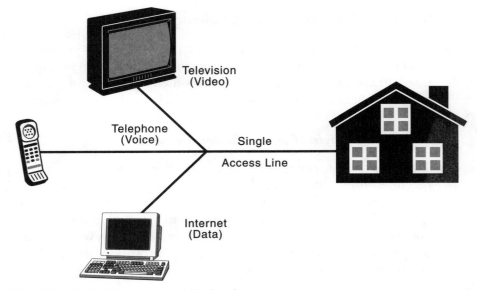

FIGURE 1.2 **Telecommuter Technology**

WAN Media

Wide area networking technologies establish the WAN connection using different types of media, such as metallic circuits, fiber-optic links, or such non-cable media as satellite, microwave, or free-air optic systems. Regardless of the type, media for WANs must be reliable, manageable, and serviceable. As previously mentioned, multiple networking environments often exist (home offices, telecommuter offices, branch offices, regional offices, and so on) and all need access to applications at their organization's headquarters. Different media can be used to establish each connection. At the ends of the media, several devices are used to interconnect users and LANs to the WAN.

WAN Connections

Interconnecting devices such as routers, modems, switches, gateways, multiplexers, bridges, and csu/dsu devices (see Chapter 3) are used to link up to the public telephone network to join independent networks together. Users are often in different locations within an organization and a long distance away from the headquarters facility, so you should consider several factors when planning a secure strategy for accessing the network. You must determine the number of users to be connected per location, the number of hours per day of simultaneous connection, and the type of traffic carried, be it voice, video, or data. [Cisco Systems, 2-3]

WANs and Infrastructure Challenges

In the past year or so, several challenges have moved WANs in new directions to meet the needs of users. These challenges include the growing use of mobile communications, an increase of economic pressures, a decaying infrastructure, new IP protocols, shifts in applications, and the arrival of public network services.

Mobile and Wireless Communication Demands

The use of mobile and wireless communications systems has grown significantly. These systems offer more challenges than copper-based or glass fiber-based systems. With wireless, a network operator tries to manage the electromagnetic spectrum, which is risky because interactions vary within the spectrum and are not always predictable. Nevertheless, because consumers want to use PDAs and cell phones for mobile business applications, network professionals cannot ignore these technologies. [Molta, 1]

Outdated WAN Hardware

Another challenge is outdated equipment that has bandwidth limitations, which hamper performance and speed. As WAN hardware becomes outdated, capital investment is required to replace existing equipment. IT managers are faced with the expense of repairing and maintaining the hardware just to keep it running.

However, investments by organizations in new applications are still moving forward. Over the long term, these applications offer lower costs and inroads into broader markets. Companies desire closer collaboration with suppliers, customers, business partners, and employees. Other areas of investment include installing global LAN e-mail, upgrading network operating systems, consolidating remote access into communications servers, and purchasing new printers as they become outdated or cease to function.

WAN Stability and Security

An effective WAN must upgrade the speed of links to the Internet to accommodate electronic ordering as more customers come online and traffic increases. Public networking services can provide cost-effective connections for WANs, but security becomes an issue. Because of this security issue, Internet-based Virtual Private Networks (VPNs) provide cost-effective secure solutions to network security problems.

Most organizations value a stable infrastructure to maintain their business environments. However, there are always demands for new equipment to be attached to the network to solve business problems. Sometimes it is necessary to find ways to address the latest technology or protocol, for example, IPv6 (see Chapter 4), which requires substantial investment in new equipment. Such equipment must be installed in pairs and changes are required at multiple locations.

Other times, two companies merge their businesses and WAN staff must provide interoperability during the mergers. For example, corporate mergers often require IT to immediately address incompatibilities in e-mail platforms. Other initiatives, such as Disaster Recovery, become too cost prohibitive because of the amount of redundant equipment necessary to provide for continuous business operation. Consequently, many organizations decide to take the risk of not providing any means of disaster recovery other than simply backing up the data.

Often, organizations reduce expenses by closing remote offices and turning sales representatives into telecommuters. When access to corporate data is provided for remote workers, security becomes the organization's most important concern. WAN staff must control access to shared data while still making it easy for the end user to access the data. Security risks need to be weighed against costs to maintain a stable infrastructure.

The scope of WANs has broadened to address workers' requests for faster, lower-cost methods to manage their data, voice, and video needs. IT investments have been directed toward using multiple services to provide access for everyone within an organization.

Economic factors have played a significant role in determining the appropriate technologies to use. Employees today are connected to WANs across the world and are able to easily send and receive information anywhere at any time.

Introducing Wide Area Networking

1. Why do organizations need to use multiple WAN services to provide access for their workers?
2. Is distance limited for certain WAN technologies?
3. What type of media is usually used to establish a WAN connection?
4. What is the impact of not replacing outdated equipment?
5. Why is consumer demand for network services increasing?

HISTORY OF COMMUNICATIONS

Communications technology has found its way into almost every aspect of our lives. When you need to call someone across the country, you just pick up the telephone. Computers are used daily for reading the latest news, browsing the Web, reserving airline tickets, and registering for college classes. Figure 1.3 shows a summary of the evolution of communications over the last 200 years. The years and events have been separated into three periods: the Information Age, the Internet Age, and the Convergence Age.

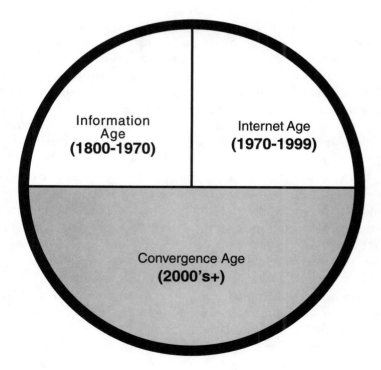

FIGURE 1.3 **Ages of Communication History**

Information Age

The quest for faster methods for sharing information led to innovative ideas and inventions in the Information Age. During this period, from 1800-1970, several experiments with electricity culminated in the creation of the telegraph and the telephone. The ingenuity of scientists during the World War years led to the development of chips and computers to assist in intelligence gathering activities for the military. Each discovery led to other inventions that significantly transformed the way people communicated and shared information worldwide.

Telegraph

Modern telecommunication began with the invention of the optical telegraph in 1793-94 by Claude Chappe. In the 1830s, Samuel Morse theorized that pulses of electrical current could convey information over copper wires. By 1835, he had worked out the elements of a relay system. He eventually developed a coding system for English characters, using combinations of dots and dashes. By 1840, a line had been constructed between Baltimore and Washington D.C. The first telegraph message was sent on May 24, 1844, and read, "What hath God wrought?" [Gorman, 6]

Telephones

In 1876, a communication method was developed that allowed people to transmit their voices over the wires for the first time. Alexander Bell determined that generating a continuous but undulating current could reproduce sound waves. [Gorman, 5] He had developed an apparatus, which he called a "harp," from a series of reeds arranged over a long magnet. Each reed responded to sound waves produced by the voice by vibrating alternately toward and away from the magnet. In June of 1875, Bell asked his long-time associate Thomas Watson to pluck a steel receiver reed with his finger to make sure it was not stuck. When Watson vibrated the reed, the receiver in Bell's room also vibrated even though the switch carrying the current was turned off. Bell realized that the vibration had generated an undulating current, solely on the strength of a slight magnetic field. [Gorman, 5]

As Bell continued to experiment, he studied electrical patterns and observed how they created a variable pattern as a needle moved up and down in a liquid. But this device led to problems with static. He then switched his focus to studying the principles of magnetic induction and had some success. Even though speech had not yet been transmitted, he applied for a patent for the telephone on March 7, 1876. Five days later on March 12, 1876, he and Watson were testing the device and the first words were transmitted. The first phrase Bell spoke to Watson has become legendary, "Mr. Watson – Come here – I want to see you." A year later, Bell developed the first commercial telephone capable of transmitting and receiving on the same instrument. [Fitzgerald Studio, 3]

After this success, Bell was able to obtain financial support from Gardiner Hubbard and Thomas Sanders and the three men formed the Bell Telephone Company in 1877. They expanded, and within three short years had telephone exchanges in most major cities in the United States. They applied for licenses under the name American Bell Telephone Company. Expansion occurred again when the American Bell Telephone Company purchased the Western Electric Company. They were now able to manufacture their own equipment. After the merger, they were able to incorporate as American Telephone and Telegraph Company on March 3, 1885. As the new phone company emerged, it was chartered to build and operate the first long-distance telephone network. [AT&T,1]

Early in the 1890s, necessity prompted Almon Strowger to invent the automatic dial system, which was the precursor to the telephone switching devices used today. Although Strowger was an undertaker, his frustration with a telephone operator caused him to develop the automatic dial system. Apparently, the operator had been transferring Strowger's incoming calls to her husband who was Strowger's competitor. The new automatic dial system eliminated the need for an operator. Telephone companies worldwide quickly adopted this device.

Radio Broadcasting

During this same time period, development had begun on radio broadcasting. A German scientist, Heinrich Hertz, proved the existence of invisible radio waves, which move at the speed of light (186,000 miles per second). Then, in 1901, an Italian scientist named Guglielmo Marconi discovered how to produce and receive waves over long distances. In that same year, after several experiments and demonstrations, he sent a radio signal across the Atlantic Ocean from Britain to Canada. By the early 1920s, music and drama programs were being sent using radio waves all over the United States and Europe. [Jefferis, 6-7]

Early Computers

Computers arrived on the scene as early as 1945 with the construction of the **Electronic Numerical Integrator and Computer (ENIAC),** which was the first operational electronic digital computer. The U.S. Army developed it to compute ballistic firing tables and to crack secret enemy codes during World War II. The ENIAC was enormous; it weighed 30 tons, used 200 kilowatts of electric power, and had 18,000 vacuum tubes and 1,500 relays along with thousands of resisters, capacitors, and inductors. For all its size, however, its computing power was less than that of a pocket calculator. [Webopedia, 1]

The invention of the telephone, radio, and early computers changed our lives significantly. Each development automated and improved the transmission of information, news, and entertainment. Meanwhile, scientists continued to invest more time researching other areas and advancing the progress of the Information Age. The increased availability of such technology, and the power of the companies that controlled it, also led to the creation in 1934 of the **Federal Communications Commission (FCC)** to regulate both broadcasting and telecommunications.

Advances in Computers and Telecommunication Networks

IT escalated rapidly with the development of the microchip in 1959. Many electronic chips could be packed together into an "integrated circuit" on a silicon chip. This integrated circuit technology allowed for the manufacture of new and smaller electronic devices, which were also faster and more reliable. In fact, much of the power of communication equipment today is based on the calculating power of the integrated circuit. [Jefferis, 6-8]

In 1972, Ray Tomlinson devised the first electronic mail (e-mail) system. He devised an addressing method that consists of "this person @ that computer". E-mail use grew steadily, entering the mainframe market with IBM Profs and DEC All-In-One and then moving into the LAN environment in the early 1990s. [Jefferis, 7]

AT&T Divestiture and the Expansion of Telecommunications

For much of its history, AT&T and its Bell Systems telephone network functioned as a legally sanctioned, regulated monopoly. Over the years, AT&T's Bell system had continued to provide the best telephone system in the world. During the 1920s-30s, AT&T made steady progress ensuring that everyone had telephones in their homes. [Miller, 2]

However, as early as 1913, the U.S. government had been monitoring AT&T's business practices. In fact, the Justice Department drafted the **Kingsbury Agreement**, which required AT&T to divest itself of its Western Union holdings and stop the acquisition of independent telephone companies. The agreement also permitted other telephone companies to interconnect to AT&T equipment to provide long distance services. This maneuver assured that although AT&T serviced 83% of American homes, it never controlled more than 30% of the geographical area within the United States.

Later, the Justice Department began to see AT&T's market dominance as an asset, however, and reversed itself by passing the Willis-Graham Act of 1921. This act reversed the Kingsbury Agreement by exempting telephone service from the Sherman Antitrust Act. From there, the monopoly was securely in place until the 1970s. [Farley, 5]

In 1968, the FCC issued a pivotal ruling called the Carterphone Decision, which established the right of telephone company subscribers to connect their own equipment to the public telephone networks, as long as the equipment was not harmful to the network. Tom Carter developed the Carterphone as a device that patched phone calls into two-way radio equipment. AT&T's attempts to prohibit use of this device by filing a complaint with the FCC, were overruled. [Telecom History, 2]

Additionally, in the early 1970s, a federal court mandated that telephone service be defined as the jack on the wall and may not include the telephone itself. This made it possible for consumers to plug in their own answering machines, telephones, and modems. Prior to the court decision, telephone companies owned this equipment. Phone companies were now forced to change their perspective from providing connectivity to providing access. [Frankston, 1]

By the 1970s, the government's reaction to AT&T's business practices was to push for a court-ordered separation of the Bell Operating Telephone Companies from AT&T. The final judgment issued in 1981 decreed that AT&T must divest itself of 22 local Bell Operating Companies (BOCs). [AT&T, 1] This divestiture led to the creation of seven **Regional Bell Operating Companies (RBOC)**, often referred to as the "Baby Bells." The original seven RBOCs were U.S. West (USWest), Ameritech, NYNEX, Bell Atlantic, Bell South, Southwestern Bell, and Pacific Bell (Pacbell) (see Figure 1.4). [Navy Relics, 1]

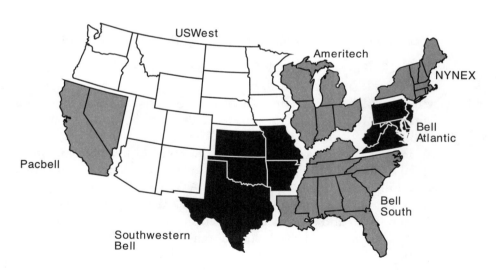

FIGURE 1.4 **The Seven "Baby Bells" [Source: Alliance Datacom, 1]**

RBOCs were under "line of business restrictions" that prevented them from competing with AT&T for long-distance service and manufacturing of hardware. RBOCs were granted rights to provide local phone service, publish Yellow

Pages directories, provide Directory Assistance, use the Bell logo, and direct research and development facilities.

The divestiture also led to the formation of **Local-Access and Transport Areas (LATAs)**. A LATA is a geographic area within which telephone calls can be handled without going through a long-distance carrier. Figure 1.5 shows the LATAs in the United States. [Navy Relics, 2]

FIGURE 1.5 **LATAs in the United States [Source: USA NPA, 1]**

Meanwhile, other major changes occurred in the telecommunications market. Long-distance telephone service became an intensely competitive business. This resulted in AT&T's market share falling from 90% to 50% over the next 12 years. Prices plummeted, dropping by an average of 40% by the end of the 1980s. Better pricing led to increased call volume. In 1984, AT&T carried an average of 37.5 million calls per average business day. By 1989, its volume of calls had increased to 105.9 million, and within 10 years, the volume for all long-distance carriers increased to 270 million. [Infoedge, 1]

The Internet Age

In the Internet Age, technology and information-sharing techniques complemented each other to create a huge network of computers. The Internet is a global network connecting millions of computers in more than 100 countries.

The technology has grown rapidly and today the Internet uses many host servers to interconnect and control the flow of information across its telecommunications links.

Origins of the Internet

Sometime between the 1960s and early 1970s, the U.S. Defense Advanced Research Project Agency developed a large WAN called **ARPAnet** to establish a way for the government and military to exchange messages. Universities involved in military research joined the ARPAnet network, which then became a test-bed for new networking technologies. This WAN is considered the precursor to the Internet. [Webopedia, 1]

The creation of the Internet itself began in 1985, when the National Science Foundation developed a high-speed Internet backbone called NSFNET.

Because it was a public network, the Internet grew exponentially. By 1987, so many users were sending data over this backbone that it became severely congested at a time when the primary traffic on the Internet was text-based e-mails and file transfers. By the early 1990s, it became clear that a public network could not effectively address the escalation in Internet use and the increased use of new types of traffic. In 1995, NSFNET ceased operations and today Internet traffic is carried by privately owned backbones. [Stanford, 1]

Telecommunications Act of 1996

The AT&T divestiture began the deregulation of telecom services, which introduced new problems to solve. The U.S. Congress attempted to address these problems by passing the **Telecommunications Act of 1996**, which allowed Regional Bell Operating Companies (RBOCs) to interconnect directly or indirectly with the facilities and equipment of other carriers. However, the RBOCs were not allowed to install network features, functions, or capabilities that did not comply with specified guidelines and standards. [Infoedge, 1-5] The RBOCs could not prohibit resale of their services and they had to re-establish reciprocal compensation arrangements for transport and termination of telecommunications. In addition, they were required to provide number portability; dialing parity; and access to poles, ducts, conduits, and rights-of-way. [Infoedge, 1-5]

One of the basic principles of the Act was to establish a move toward convergence in which cable, cellular, and satellite companies could offer competitive voice and data services. Deregulation has been slow in the local marketplace; RBOCs have not yet opened up the intra-LATA markets to competitors. [Infoedge, 1-5]

Meanwhile, other organizations have gone to great lengths to avoid using the RBOC's infrastructure. AT&T has forged on with the building of wireless and broadband services by running a separate wire into homes and businesses, completely bypassing the local RBOC. Also during this time, new data communication carriers have emerged with the potential to compete for the "**last mile.**" Owned today by the RBOC, this is literally the last mile to a customer's location from the Central Office switch. The battle for the "last mile" will dictate the fate of a number of telecom providers in the future. [Infoedge, 1-5]

Convergence Age

The Convergence Age is the coming together of technologies that support telephony, computerized data, voice, and video into a united interactive service for consumers. The development of fiber-optic, satellite, and cable modem technologies has provided consumers high-speed access to the Internet. Entertainment, telephony, and computerized data, voice, and video are starting to converge extensively. New equipment and techniques are currently being developed that address integration of information and media of all types.

As the number of Internet users grows, telecom providers and Internet Service Providers (ISPs) must deal with the issues of congestion and bandwidth. Consumer demand for bandwidth increases with every new Web site created. The increases in multimedia content, corporate use of the Internet, and demand for increased bandwidth led to the beginning of the Convergence Age.

TOPIC *review* History of Communications

1. Who discovered that sound waves could be reproduced if one could generate a continuous but undulating current?
2. Why was ARPAnet established?
3. Who had a role in the antitrust case and transformed the way telecommunications services are delivered today?
4. Which government act was passed to increase competition in all aspects of telecommunications?
5. What was the name of the decision published by the FCC in 1969, which established the right of telephone subscribers to connect their own equipment to the public telephone network?

CURRENT TRENDS IN COMMUNICATIONS SYSTEMS

The trends in communications systems today reflect adjustments being made as a result of deregulation, competition, and technological advances. The telecom industry is in a period of transition evidenced by the telecom providers merging and consolidating their assets and employees. In addition, copper wire networks are being replaced by fiber optic and more and more network activity is taking place on wireless networks. Meanwhile, semiconductors and other network hardware are getting faster.

Corporate Mergers

Economic pressures and extremely competitive business practices have resulted in several large mergers between RBOCs. The original seven "Baby Bells" are now reduced to the "Final Four": SBC, Qwest, Verizon, and Bell South. [Verizon, 2] At the same time, the telecom industry in general has suffered significantly in the recent economic downturn. Even major providers have been hit hard. MCI has been investigated by the SEC (Securities and Exchange Commission) for fraud in its accounting practices, which has resulted in massive layoffs and led them toward the brink of bankruptcy. Sprint has been forced to lay off thousands of workers in its wireless division. Williams Communications, a West-coast telecom provider, has filed for bankruptcy. Nevertheless, despite the reduced revenue from telecom equipment and infrastructure, it is projected that the telecom industry will continue to grow and will produce $1.5 trillion in revenue worldwide during 2002. (Big Charts, 1) (Olavsrud, 1)

The Rise of Fiber Optic

Today, we still communicate by transporting analog signals over copper wires in a local loop back to a Central Office switch. Narrow band radio channels are still used over the congested radio spectrum. However, new optical, semiconductor, and wireless technologies are beginning to widen these bottlenecks. For example, a communications channel can remain in optical form over long distances. Optical amplification and wavelength division minimize the need to convert a wide channel into an electrical format. With these new optical technologies, someday every customer and service could each have their own specific optical wavelength. A network operator could then assign one wavelength to an ISP and another to a voice service provider. With the increased use of these technologies, faster, larger, and more powerful networks are now possible.

The spread of the Internet is stimulating demand for instant Internet and other high-speed access data and video services. Organizations that do business via the Web are looking for high-speed access for their intranets and extranets to power e-commerce. More organizations are looking to use the Internet for voice communication to reduce long-distance phone bills.

Telecom providers are faced with an over-abundance of data. ISPs see the optical network as a vehicle for delivering an extensive range of services. Both ISPs and telecom providers want to provide a mega-network that spans the globe. This mega-network would provide access for PCs, PDAs, and cell phones any time of the day or night. Optical network technologies are becoming the preferred technology for reducing costs and time-to-market for new high-speed services. Fiber optic is the only technology that can meet the demand users will place on future networks. Telecom providers who can take advantage of optical networking systems will be able to offer their customers access that is four times faster than non-optic network systems and accrues savings of 60% on equipment costs. [Bell Labs, 1]

Fiber-optic cable can transmit thousands of times more data than a copper wire can transmit. The use of fiber-optic cabling for the WAN will grow approximately 23% by 2005. Telecommunications companies deployed more than 11 million kilometers of fiber in 2000. Copper has some speed limitations; however, it is, and will remain for some time, the dominant way to connect the Desktop to the network. [Assembly, 1]

New technologies have emerged to support users working from home or users when they are away from the office. Mobility, portability, and flexibility are key in these environments. Copper and fiber cables sometimes can be difficult to manage, unlike the wireless alternatives that are appealing because they can be moved easily and taken everywhere. Today, almost everyone has cellular phones to keep in touch with family, friends, and the office.

Wireless Telecommunications

Cellular telephony (mobile telephone service) was actually invented in 1947 by Don Ring, a Bell Labs scientist, who found that wireless technology would allow frequencies to be reused, thus providing wide-ranging communications systems. However, Ring's early concept would not be developed fully until the 1980s. Over time, scientists realized that to provide wide-area coverage they needed to use large cells, or boundaries, for frequency or digital transmission.

Wireless technology now offers anytime access from anywhere for voice, data, and video for your home, your car, and even at the beach. Today, devices allow you to read text e-mail on a cellular handset. The next generation of wireless will have ready access to higher-bandwidth services for multimedia access on wireless handsets.

Designing a modern wireless network is complex because of its wide coverage area. The network is outdoors and needs to be optimized for traffic, geography, capacity, and dropped calls. Other issues are the cost to expand over many different locations and the constantly changing environmental conditions. The main challenge is in building smaller base stations that can be installed on the outside of buildings and atop telephone poles. These smaller base stations can take advantage of smaller microchip technologies available, allowing them to be installed anywhere. [Bell Labs, 5-7]

A major initiative in improving wireless communication is the implementation of a new technology code-named **Bluetooth**. The technology provides low-cost, short-range radio links between mobile PCs, cell phones, and PDAs. Bluetooth radios can replace multiple cable connections via a single wireless link. Because of these technological developments, base stations will continue to shrink, and eventually miniature radios will be both economical and have a range suitable for connecting devices throughout the home. [Bell Labs, 8]

Research and development in wireless technology often is controlled by government mandates. One of the latest FCC regulations orders that wireless 911 calls must be accurately pinpointed. Today, when a customer needs 911 services, the E911 dispatcher cannot immediately determine the location where assistance is requested. With wireless phones, phone numbers are associated with individuals, not location indicators. Currently, the cellular handset's position is determined by using a **Global Positioning System (GPS)**. Bell Labs has developed a new system called **FLEXENT Intelligent Network Determination System (FINDS)**. This technology (see Figure 1.6) is based on GPS satellite data combined with information transmitted from local cell sites to precisely locate a caller. FINDS is a low-cost phone feature that can pinpoint a cell phone user's location with an accuracy of 15 feet outdoors and 100 feet indoors. [Bell Labs, 11&12]

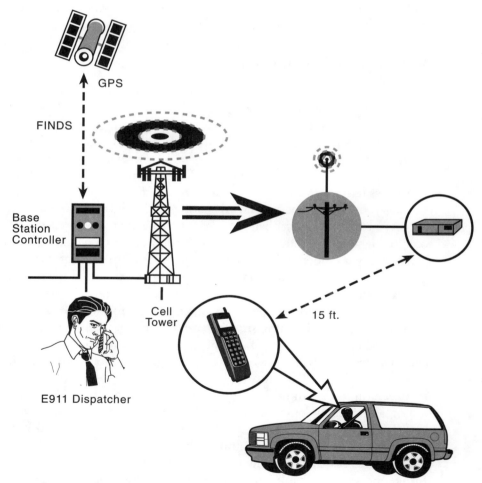

FIGURE 1.6 **FLEXENT Intelligent Network Determination System (FINDS)**

In the United States alone, there are almost 75 million wireless subscribers. Half the population of Finland, Taiwan, and Italy has "cut the cord" and are using wireless phones exclusively. As this technology moves forward, delivery of broadband applications increasingly will be offered both via fiber optics and wireless. WANs need to take into account both kinds of transmission systems. [Plunkett, 21]

Other Emerging Technologies

Scientists designed and introduced transistors, lasers, telecommunications satellites, and microelectronics for use in the twentieth century. The next generation of networks will use the power of photonics (a branch of physics that deals with the properties and applications of photons as a medium for transmitting information) to deliver information at the speed of light through all-optical networks. The latest discoveries in telecommunications (see Figure 1.7) are directed at information bottlenecks in three basic resource technologies: optical, semiconductor, and wireless.

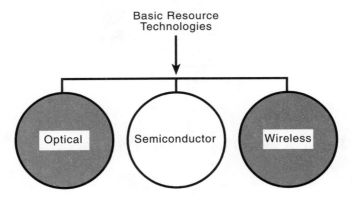

FIGURE 1.7 **Three Major Areas of Telecommunications Innovation**

The first step in solving this problem has been to identify the bottlenecks. In wireless systems, bottlenecks are caused by government control of access to the spectrums. With semiconductor technology, limitations are caused by the properties and limits of silicon. In optical technology, the challenge is creating information channels that are "fat" enough for the Internet.

Research and development efforts today are focused on providing increased speed and capacity in four key areas: the Internet, communications networking, mobile communications, and electronic consumer products.

Chip designers expect unprecedented growth in use of cell phones, game consoles, cameras, set-top boxes, and hand-held electronic organizers. The demands put upon electronics manufacturers will lead to stronger-than-ever demand for faster and more efficient transistors and integrated circuits. Semiconductor manufacturers are developing silicon wafers that improve routing and switching for both electronic and optical signals.

Engineers work feverously to develop new technologies that improve circuitry and transmission rates. At the same time, telecom service providers desire quick deployments because they are trying to overcome Moore's law and retain the increased revenue for as long as they can. Moore's law states that capacity and power double every 18 months (see Figure 1.8) for telecommunications and computer equipment, while costs go down. [Bell Labs, 4]

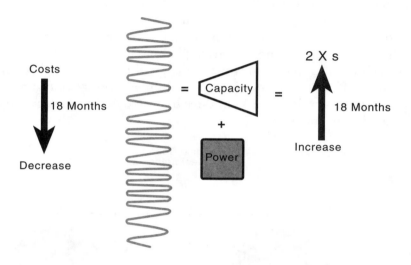

FIGURE 1.8 Moore's Law

The increase in everyday use of the Internet has consumers demanding additional networking services. This demand requires transmission systems that can deliver hundreds of megabits simultaneously to large populations. Research and development engineers are constantly working to remove bottlenecks, solve current problems, and invent new technology to provide WAN services that can deliver terabits of voice, data, and video.

Current Trends in Communications Systems

1. What has caused repositioning and mergers between telecom companies?
2. How does the 911 operator locate a cell phone user?
3. How does the technology called Bluetooth provide for wireless communication?
4. What four areas are researchers investigating to provide increased speed and capacity for WANs?
5. What is Moore's law?

FUTURE PROJECTIONS FOR WANS

No simple guidebook is available to project how the network of the future will look or how each carrier and user will use it. However, we anticipate a future that does not demand "convergence" on a specific technology, vendor, or service concept. As we move forward with optical networking, the various forces at work in business will demand re-thinking of network building principles and service-specific structures. The market that emerges as a result of this re-thinking will determine the fate of wide area networking. [Nolle, 8]

Technology Direction for WANs

WANs provide pathways to everywhere. We use WANs every day to reach several destinations inside and outside an organization. Telecom providers have more than a few services to offer and some of them are better than others. Sorting through all of the services requires a strong understanding of what is offered by each technology. Figure 1.9 shows the multitude of WAN services available today. This section provides brief summaries of these technologies, but throughout this book, you will learn how each technology works, why it should be used, and what type of performance can be expected.

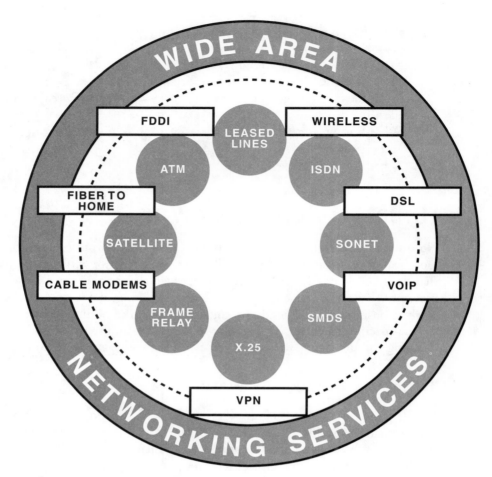

FIGURE 1.9 **Wide Area Networking Services**

Satellite Time

Contemporary networking technology provides the basis for the significant developments that have enhanced WANs. **Satellite** time is now available for purchase by corporations with offices spread across the globe. The use of satellite has become practical for downloading Web pages and streaming video. Satellite is most frequently used for high-speed e-mail access. The development of digital signal processing (DSP) has opened the floodgates allowing data to be moved out of a satellite much faster, in fact at multimegabit transmission rates (see Chapter 6).

Leased Lines

Leased lines have been used for many years as a secure method to connect remote offices. They offer a private dedicated service 7 days a week, 24 hours a day. A leased (T-carrier) line is often used to connect an office to the Internet. Approximately $12.1 billion was spent on leased lines in 2002 (see Chapter 6).

ISDN

Integrated Services Digital Network (ISDN) is used with applications that require bandwidth on demand and flexible digital connections to public switched networks. Many corporations use it for switched LAN to WAN connections. Telecommuters and small branch offices use Basic Rate Interface (BRI). At the corporate office, ISDN Primary Rate Interface (PRI) provides multiple channels to consolidate several BRIs into one unit. The ISDN PRI is connected to the corporate backbone to provide access to corporate servers on the LAN (see Chapter 6).

DSL

Digital Subscriber Line (DSL) uses the existing telephone line to provide "always-on" Internet access. DSL uses the two-wire copper wiring to deliver high-speed data services such as streaming audio/video, online games, application programs, video conferencing, and standard telephone calls to homes and businesses. A DSL link can deliver speeds from 144 Kbps to 6 Mbps (see Chapter 7).

Cable Modems

Cable modems operate over ordinary cable TV, providing high-speed (typically between 3 to 50 Mbps) access to the Internet. The cable modem is connected to your computer via a 10 Mbps Ethernet port. Cable companies can provide high-speed service to thousands of customers in a neighborhood by combining data channels with video, pay-per-view, audio, and local advertiser programs through the cable modem installed in your home (see Chapter 7).

FTTH

Fiber to the Home (FTTH) is just beginning to penetrate the market and its future lies in being able to provide two-way video-based services. Fiber-optic cable is strung all of the way to the customer's home. Usually the city utility company deploys the fiber and many homes in a neighborhood are wired at the same time. A network provider supplies telephone, video, and Internet services to homes. The Internet link provides speeds of 4.5 Mbps upload and 7 Mbps download. Users will soon demand interactive television, distance learning, motion picture video conferencing, and videophones for their homes (see Chapter 7).

Satellite Service

Consumer satellite service uses a single satellite dish antenna for receiving and sending information. It can bring the Internet and hundreds of channels of television all through a single dish antenna into your home. It features "always on" Internet access, which means your high-speed link is available as long as your computer is on. Satellite download speed can reach up to 500 Kbps and current upload speeds range from 40-60 Kbps (see Chapter 7).

VPN

Virtual Private Networks (VPN) are private data networks that run through a public telecommunications network or the Internet. VPNs use encryption and other security techniques to protect the privacy of data. Only authorized users can access the private network. Privacy is maintained through the use of a tunneling protocol. VPN is a private tunnel, or pathway, through the Internet. Organizations favor VPN because it provides cost savings when they use a shared public infrastructure rather than building a private network with T1 leased lines (see Chapter 8).

X.25 Protocol

X.25 is a WAN protocol that uses packet-switching technologies. The X.25 protocol allows computers on different public networks to communicate through an intermediary device to a Packet-Switched Public Data Network (PSDN). A PSDN supports a network in which small packets are routed through a network based on the destination address contained within each packet. The same data path can be shared among several users in the network (see Chapter 11).

Frame Relay

Frame Relay is a fast packet service designed to replace X.25. A fast packet is transmitted without any error checking at points along the route. Frame Relay has a low incidence of error or data loss because it uses fiber-optic media. Companies turn to frame relay to provide high-speed transmission technologies especially for overseas locations. Frame relay provides excellent costs savings over competing technologies such as leased lines (see Chapter 11).

VoIP

Voice over Internet Protocol (VoIP) sends voice information in digital form as separate packets rather than over the traditional Public Switched Telephone Network. A set of facilities is used for **IP telephony** to manage the delivery of voice information using the Internet Protocol (IP). Consumers now can use the Internet as their transmission medium for telephone calls. The clear advantage of VoIP and Internet telephony is that it avoids the tolls charged by ordinary telephone service (see Chapter 11).

FDDI

Fiber Distributed Data Interface (FDDI) is a high-speed backbone technology. The backbone is constructed using a ring topology in which the signal path is modeled in the shape of a circle. It has a dual-ring topology using fiber-optic cable that is used to transmit light pulses to convey information between stations. The optical fiber channel operates at a rate of 100 Mbps and is frequently used in LANs to connect buildings together within an organization (see Chapter 12).

SMDS

Switch Multimegabit Data Service (SMDS) is designed to provide a transport service for organizations that have four or more locations within a city. City governments often use SMDS to connect the city hall, courthouse, police station, and library together for inter-government networking. SMDS offers LAN-like performance to users who need to extend their data communications over a wide geographical area (see Chapter 12).

SONET

SONET (Synchronous Optical Network) is slowly moving forward as a network backbone. SONET transmits synchronous (voice and video) and asynchronous (data) traffic on optical-electrical media. SONET rings are used in metropolitan area networks (MANs) to interconnect offices with each other (see Chapter 3). Optical networking research is looking into ways to design networks that will use fiber optic from the switch to Desktop (see Chapter 12).

ATM

Asynchronous Transfer Mode (ATM) is used when companies need to move large amounts of data quickly. This new telephony infrastructure is built within a circuit, distributed packet, and cell-routing environment. ATM is quickly gaining hold in the marketplace. In fact, ATM is emerging as a worldwide standard for the transmission of voice and digital information. Telephone companies are rapidly deploying ATM technology and it is being used today for video, TV broadcast applications, medical imaging, financial transactions, and seismic analysis for earthquakes (see Chapter 13). [Telecommunications Americas, 1]

Wireless

Wireless communication occurs using electromagnetic waves to carry the signal to the receiver. Wireless technology is rapidly evolving and is playing a greater role in the lives of people throughout the world. Consumers rely on wireless technology for cellular phones, PDAs, pagers, cordless keyboards, cordless mice, and GPS. GPS allows car drivers, ship captains, and airline pilots to ascertain their location anywhere on earth (see Chapter 14).

Spending Patterns/Technology Rollouts

The telecommunications market has been overwhelmed by rapid changes over the past five years. Trends in technology generally reflect the industry's reaction to these changes. The growth of data traffic initiated by the Internet has led global communication service providers to invest billions of dollars in construction and equipment. Capital spending for equipment increased significantly from 1998-2000, while most providers reduced their spending in 2001.

New technologies have emerged to support the need to provide more networking and communications capacity for e-commerce and collaboration projects. Security has become fundamental to the growth of e-commerce. Security breaches such as hacking, viruses, intrusions, data theft, corruption, and denial of service attacks have garnered a lot of attention. Still, organizations are moving forward with e-commerce projects and increasing their security activities by deploying firewalls, mail-filtering programs, shells to restrict access, and private networks as shown in Figure 1.10.

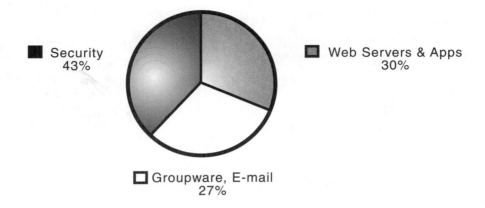

**Security
43%**

**Web Servers & Apps
30%**

**Groupware, E-mail
27%**

FIGURE 1.10 **Global Market Trends 1998-1999 [Source: Data Communications, 1]**

For the past several years, telecom service providers have used ATM to run data over their network cores. Today, almost all carriers use ATM to switch frame relay traffic back and forth across the public network. New network connections can be set up more quickly and less expensively when networks use IP. **Quality of service (QOS)** and security issues must be addressed, however, as many customers have already installed their own IP VPNs. [Telecommunications Americas, 1]

The architecture of the public network must change to meet the drive for application convergence. Standards and forums organizations are now investigating how to provide each carrier and user with quick access to all these new types of media. For the time being, vendors continue to build bigger and faster ATM switches for increasing bandwidth and mileage. The QoS features of ATM make it an ideal transport for audio and video. ATM is still viewed as a strong technology by service providers and carriers and its use in the WAN continues to grow. [Doherty, 4]

The future of wide area networking depends on the cost and complexity of the next generation architecture. The forces that drive business and technology will, of course, influence which products and multi-service architecture is adopted by the industry as a preferred strategy. The strategic goal, however, is clear – vendor independence. This means supporting open architectures in which customers can choose equipment from a variety of vendors to provide a solution that is tailored to their particular needs. New service combinations will increase the value of wide area networking as engineers design innovative approaches to interconnect network and service features. The primary directive will be to offer multi-service architectures that provide lower-priced services to users and faster deployment of new services to the market.

Future Projections for WANs

1. What is a practical use of satellite technology?
2. Which WAN technologies provide "always on" access?
3. When companies need to move large amounts of data, which technology do they consider?
4. How does the architecture of the public network need to change?
5. Describe vendor independence.

CHAPTER SUMMARY

WANs provide a backbone of telecommunications links used to provide long distance transmission of data, voice, and video information. Often, WANs are used to connect users together to share information and resources within an organization. WANs are also used to connect users between states, countries, and different LANs.

The distance of a WAN is unlimited. WAN services are offered by telecommunication service providers and are distinguished by cost, speed, quality, and the number of links required. WANs use several types of media such as metallic circuits, fiber-optic links, satellite, microwave, and free-air optic systems. Devices at each end of the media are used to interconnect users and LANs to the WAN. Several interconnecting devices, such as routers, modems, switches, gateways, multiplexers, bridges, and csu/dsu devices, are used to join independent networks together over the WAN.

Communications technology has been developed over the past 200 years with its history divided into three periods: Information Age, Internet Age, and Convergence Age. During the Information Age (170 years from 1800-1970), scientists invented telephones, radio broadcasting, computers, microchips, and integrated circuits. The Internet Age, a period from 1970-1999, saw the development of ARPAnet, which was the precursor to the Internet. The Internet began in 1985 with the development of NFSNET, which was a high-speed backbone of telecommunications links and Internet devices used for communication pathways across countries. The dawn of the Age of Convergence began in the year 2000, in which scientists developed new technologies to support telephony, computerized data, voice, and video into a united interactive service for consumers.

WANs are used daily to reach the Internet and read the latest news, browse the Web, make purchases, and take classes. The development of fiber-optic, satellite, and cable modem technologies provided high-speed access to the Internet. The current trends in the telecommunications industry are a result of deregulation (AT&T Divestiture), competition (Telecommunications Act of 1996), and technological advances (fiber, semiconductors and silicon).

The growth of the Internet has stimulated demand for high-speed access to data and video services. Telecom providers are faced with an over-abundance of data. ISPs see the optical network as a practical solution for delivering an extensive range of services. Optical networks are becoming the preferred technology for reducing costs and time to market for high-speed services. New technologies have emerged to support users from home and when they are away from the office. Wireless alternatives (cell phones, PDAs, pagers, and GPS) are attractive because you can move them easily and take them everywhere.

The next generation of networks will deliver information at the speed of light through all-optical networks. Innovation now is focused on optical, semiconductor, and wireless technology. Researchers are looking to increase speed and capacity for the Internet, communications networking, mobile communications, and electronic consumer products. Electronics manufacturers are looking for faster, more efficient transistors for cell phones, game consoles, cameras, and hand-held electronic organizers.

Moore's law states that capacity and power double every 18 months for telecommunications and computer equipment while costs go down. Researchers are challenged to develop new technologies to improve circuitry and transmission rates. As optical networking moves forward, organizations will demand convergence and service along with vendor independence.

Services provided by WANs to manage voice, video, and data include satellite, leased lines, ISDN, DSL, cable modems, FTTH, X.25, Frame Relay, VoIP, FDDI, SMDS, SONET, ATM, and wireless. The future of WANs depends on the cost and complexity involved in providing these services and the next generation architecture to the marketplace.

CHAPTER REVIEW QUESTIONS

(This quiz can also be printed out from the Encore! CD that accompanies this textbook. Click Chapter 1, *click* Student Files, *and then click* Chap01review.)
Circle a letter (a-d) for each question. Choose only one answer for each.

1. What type of networking provides for long distance transmission of data, voice, image, and video information between states and countries?
   a. LAN
   b. MAN
   c. VAN
   d. WAN

2. The network of telecommunication links and Internet devices that enables communication pathways across countries is called
   a. World Wide Web
   b. Backbone
   c. Internet Service Provider
   d. ARPAnet

3. Links are built using services provided by
   a. electronics manufacturers.
   b. standards and forums.
   c. telecom providers.
   d. the FCC.

4. Which agreement required AT&T to divest itself of its Western Union holdings and stop the acquisition of independent telephone companies?
   a. Willis-Graham
   b. Kingsbury
   c. Carterphone
   d. Telecom Trade

5. A geographic area in which telephone calls can be handled without going through a long-distance carrier is known as a
   a. BOC.
   b. CPE.
   c. LATA.
   d. RBOC.

6. The appeal of the Convergence Age is that access is
   a. always on.
   b. always off.
   c. always stable.
   d. always changing.

7. When you use a wireless phone, what new system can pinpoint your location within 15 feet?
   a. GPS
   b. Bluetooth
   c. FIND
   d. ISP

8. What will power the next generation of networks and deliver information at the speed of light?
   a. photonics
   b. semiconductors
   c. electronics
   d. magnets

9. Which technology provides an optical network backbone for WANs?
   a. VoIP
   b. FDDI
   c. SMDS
   d. SONET

10. Which is a high-speed Internet backbone formed by the National Science Foundation?
    a. NSSNET
    b. NSFNET
    c. ARPAnet
    d. PARNET

Circle the correct letter (A-E) that corresponds to the descriptions below. Choose only one answer for each.
    A. Cellular Telephony
    B. Moore's
    C. RBOC
    D. ENIAC
    E. Bluetooth

11. A B C D E A record that describes prices, terms, and condition of a telecommunications service offering.

12. A B C D E Mobile telephone service used for communication systems.

13. A B C D E Data communications equipment owned by the company.

14. A B C D E Low-cost, short-range radio links between mobile PCs, cell phones, and PDAs.

15. A B C D E The first operational electronic digital computer.

Circle the correct letter (A-E) that corresponds to the descriptions below. Choose only one answer for each.
    A. Guglielmo Marconi
    B. Tom Carter
    C. Almon Strowger
    D. Heinrich Hertz
    E. Alexander Bell

16. A B C D E Developed the automatic dial system to eliminate the need for an operator.

17. A B C D E Known as the "Father of Radio," he discovered how to produce and detect waves over long distances.

18. A B C D E Developed the first commercial telephone.

19. A B C D E A German scientist who proved the existence of invisible radio waves.

20. A B C D E Sued AT&T to permit connection of his phone patch.

INTERNET EXERCISES

1. According to the Fourth-Generation Mobile Forum, new types of wireless technology are reaching speeds of 4GB. Go to www.4gmobile.com for more information. When and where did the original research begin on 4G technologies?

2. Efforts are underway within the United States and abroad to define the telephone network of tomorrow. The next-generation voice services are referred to as Electronic Numbering (ENUM). Do an Internet search to find which benefits are associated with ENUM technology. List the three primary benefits of ENUM below.
   A. _____
   B. _____
   C. _____

CONCEPT EXERCISES

Concept Narrative
(This narrative exercise can also be printed out from the Encore! CD that accompanies this textbook. Click Chapter 1, *click* Student Files, *and then click* Chap01connar.)*

Read the following description and fill in the blanks with the correct answer.

The government's reaction to AT&T's business practices was to push for a court-ordered _____ of the Bell Operating Telephone Companies from AT&T. The final judgment decreed that AT&T must divest itself of 22 _____ Bell Operating Companies (BOCs).

This divestiture led to the creation of _____ Regional Bell Operating Companies (_____), fondly referred to as the "_____ _____". The original companies were: Bell Atlantic, Southwestern Bell, Nynex, Pacific Bell, Bell South, Ameritech, and US West. The divestiture also led to the formation of Local-Access and Transport Areas (_____s). These are geographic areas within which telephone calls can be handled without going through a _____carrier.

Meanwhile, other major changes occurred in the telecommunications market. Long-distance telephone service became an intensely _____ business. This resulted in AT&T's market share falling from 90% to 50% over the next _____ years. Prices plummeted, dropping by an average of 40% by the end of the 1980s. Better pricing led to increased call volume. In 1984, AT&T carried an average of 37.5 million calls per average business day. By 1989, its volume of calls had _____ to 105.9 million, and within 10 years, the volume for all long distance carriers increased to 270 million.

Concept Table
(This table exercise can also be printed out from the Encore! CD that accompanies this textbook. Click Chapter 1, click Student Files, and then click Chap01contab.)

Read each statement carefully and choose the age of communications history being described. Use only one "X" per statement.

STATEMENT	INFORMATION	INTERNET	CONVERGENCE
1. Samuel Morse discovered that pulses of electrical current could convey information over copper wires.			
2. Development of a high-speed backbone called NSFNET formed by the National Science Foundation.			
3. Access is always on.			
4. Global network with millions of computers in 100 countries.			
5. The right of telephone company subscribers to connect their own equipment to the public telephone networks.			
6. The first operational electronic digital computer.			
7. Integration of information and media of all types.			
8. ISPs deal with congestion and bandwidth issues.			
9. Developed the automatic dial system for phone companies.			
10. Combining entertainment, telephony, computerized data, voice, and video.			

Concept Picture

(This picture exercise can also be printed out from the Encore! CD that accompanies this textbook. Click Chapter 1, click Student Files, and then click Chap01conpic.)

Look at the diagram of Moore's law. Write in the correct answer next to each label A and B.

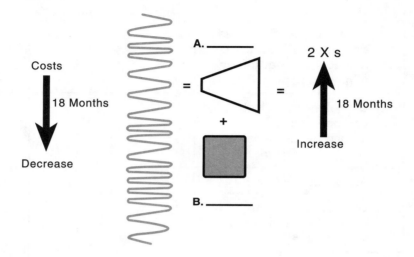

CASE STUDY

A&B PAINT MANUFACTURING

Read the following case study about A&B Paint Manufacturing. Think about the challenge presented to the company and the information solution provided. Then, either by yourself or in a group, answer the case study questions.

Objective:

Determine how to improve performance for remote locations for access to the corporate database. The focus should be on designing a cost-effective solution that provides for higher-speed WAN connections.

Company Profile:

A&B Paint Manufacturing is a traditional paint and wallpaper manufacturer located in Raleigh, North Carolina. A&B uses old-fashioned, tried-and-true methods and only the finest ingredients to manufacture its paint. At the same time, the company is concerned with making sure its paints and wallpapers are environmentally friendly. A&B has been in business for 30 years and has manufacturing plants in Raleigh, North Carolina; Houston, Texas; Sacramento, California; and Bangor, Maine. All of these plants are connected via low bandwidth dedicated leased lines capable of transmitting at 56,000 bits per second (56 Kbps).

Current Situation:

A&B Paint Manufacturing installed a corporate database to provide for planning products, purchasing parts, maintaining inventories, and tracking orders. Since the new system was implemented a year ago, the company's IT department has been receiving complaints about slow performance over the WAN.

Business Information Requirements:

A&B Paint Manufacturing requires faster access to the centralized database at corporate headquarters. Employees need instant access to inventory information so they can better plan the number of stock keeping units (SKUs) per branch. Access to the database must be provided 7 days a week, 24 hours a day. Corporate sales representatives are often on the road traveling to customer locations. They all have laptops and connect via regular phone lines through a dial-up service to the Internet. Currently their dial-up access is not secure.

Communication System Requirements:

Bandwidth demands are rising at a time when the IT budget is tight. The current WAN configuration has very slow connections, which must be addressed. A study has been launched to determine the bandwidth requirements for each location. The goal is to provide higher data rates to remote locations. They also need to provide a solution for Web access over the Internet. However, they are concerned about security and maintaining the uptime required because they cannot guarantee the availability of the Internet.

Information System Solution:

1. A&B upgraded the speed of their leased lines to provide 1.54 Mbps of uninterrupted bandwidth for the four plants in Houston, Bangor, Sacramento, and Raleigh. Because these plants provide mission-critical services and 7-day, 24-hour uptime, dedicated T-carrier leased lines were chosen for their reliability and predictable performance.

2. A&B purchased and installed VPN equipment at corporate headquarters to offer access through a Web browser over the Internet. The VPN solution assures high levels of encrypted security for any client accessing the server. Clients must load VPN software on their laptops to connect to the VPN equipment at corporate headquarters. Once connected, they can log directly into the corporate database.

3. Sales representatives and employees who need to access the corporate database from home all loaded the VPN client software on their laptops. The IT department provided a CD and a set of instructions to each user for easy configuration. They also provided help desk support in case a user could not connect.

4. High speed T-carrier leased lines provide access to the Public Telephone Network and the Internet.

Implementing the corporate database helped manage the availability of material. As real-time data became available, inventories were reduced dramatically. A&B also benefited by using the forecasting features of the database to project the number of SKUs required by each branch.

Mobile users are now able to access the database securely via dial-up lines using their VPN software. They are also able to launch their Web browsers to access corporate e-mail, which saves a lot of time. Sales representatives find it extremely convenient to transmit orders securely over regular telephone lines.

The IT department has decreased its operational costs by 15% within the first 90 days. This 15% drop is attributed to offering Web access to the application over the Internet.

Often several solutions will satisfy the requirements of a case study. This one alternative is presented for class discussion. Examine Figure 1.11 and answer the case study questions. Look in the figure for each circled question number and answer the question.

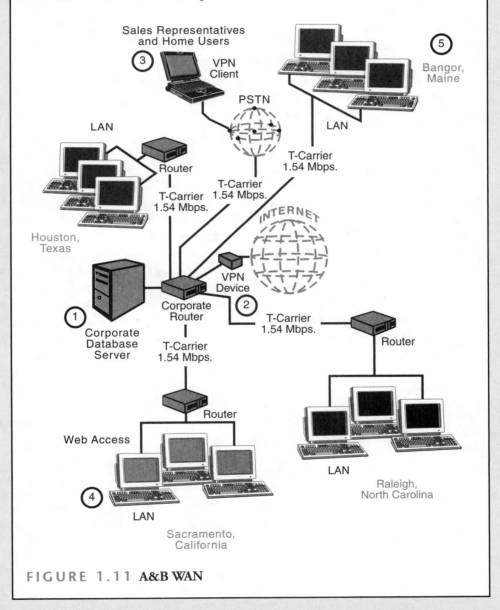

FIGURE 1.11 **A&B WAN**

CASE STUDY QUESTIONS

1. How is the corporate database server connected to the Internet?
2. Does the VPN device have a connection to the Public Telephone Network?
3. How can sales representatives be sure they have a secure connection over the Public Telephone Network?
4. Do the PCs connected to the LAN in Sacramento have access to the Internet?
5. Do the users on the LAN in Bangor have a secure connection to the Internet?

GROUP TERM PROJECT

F&D ENGINEERING, INC.

The group term project offers an opportunity to apply the concepts learned in each chapter to a "real world" example of a WAN project. This is a comprehensive case study that is separated into weekly installments. A different project template is included at the end of each chapter. Each template is also included on the Encore! CD that comes with this textbook. Before each class period, print out the template for the chapter being discussed and bring it to class. The project is designed to be completed during class time with an hour per class dedicated to group discussion. Each template should be turned in at the end of the class period. At the end of the term, each group will assemble all templates together into a workbook. Each group will be responsible for submitting one workbook and a concise diagram of the network solution recommended by the end of the course.

Read the following information about F&D Engineering, Inc. and think about its current situation. Be ready to discuss the business challenges and their impact on the company. Keep in mind that information systems and WANs are constructed to solve business problems. You must thoroughly understand the business problem before you can analyze and solve the case study.

Objective:

Design a global mail system for F&D Engineering, Inc. The information system solution should define the telecommunications links and equipment required at each location worldwide. It should also include solutions for e-mail software, e-mail server hardware, fax services, and remote dial up.

Company Profile:

F&D Engineering, Inc. is a worldwide engineering firm located in Washington, D.C. The firm has offices in 35 countries and employs 20,000 people worldwide. F&D does engineering consulting for federal agencies and specifically for the Department of Energy and the Army Corps. of Engineers.

Current Situation:

The firm requires a client server based e-mail system worldwide. Currently, it has slow data links (56 Kbps) to Europe, Australia, and South America. For the past 10 years, F&D has used a proprietary homegrown e-mail system that runs on F&D's mainframe. The company would like to migrate from this legacy mainframe mail system to a more user-friendly graphical e-mail system. F&D needs to migrate in phases and run parallel with the mainframe mail system for one year. Most of the WAN traffic is text-based e-mail. However, about 30% of traffic is in the form of engineering drawings that are transmitted from overseas locations back to headquarters in Washington, D.C. The WAN hardware used currently is five years old and cannot be upgraded to a newer model. All equipment is out of warranty and a maintenance contract is cost prohibitive.

Business Information Requirements:

F&D requires assistance with the planning and design of a new global network infrastructure. For this phase of the project, the company has allocated $1.5 million for the hardware, software, human resources, startup, capital, and monthly costs during the first year. F&D wants to connect three primary sites in the United States (San Francisco, Houston, and Washington), two sites in Europe (London, England and Frankfurt, Germany), one site in Australia (Sydney), one site in South America (Rio De Janeiro, Brazil), and one site in Asia (Madras, India). Four of the sites are focused on the company's engineering activities: Washington, Frankfurt, Sydney, and Madras.

Communication System Requirements:

F&D has not developed any standards for its office automation platform and, therefore, has a mixture of PCs and Macs. In the Engineering department, Computer Aided Design (CAD) software is run on UNIX as well as PC-based AutoCAD on a Novell 5.0 LAN. F&D also has a substantial amount of existing e-mail stored in the mainframe e-mail system. The total number of users among the 8 sites is 5,000. The breakdown of users per site and their equipment is as follows:

LOCATION	# OF USERS	PC	MAC	UNIX
Washington*	1000	500	200	300
San Francisco	500	300	180	20
Houston	600	400	175	25
London	500	350	125	25
Frankfurt*	600	300	100	200
Sydney*	500	225	75	200
Rio De Janeiro	400	300	75	25
Madras*	900	500	100	300

*Designated as an engineering site

These 5,000 users all use the same cross-platform word processing, spread-sheet, and presentation software for documents. Although use of the mainframe e-mail system varies per site, hundreds of e-mails are sent per day between sites. Because the National Archives and Records Administration has strict guidelines for archiving any engineering drawings and e-mail messages that are government-related, e-mail, documents, and drawings are archived indefinitely.

DAILY NUMBER OF E-MAILS SENT BETWEEN LOCATIONS

Cities	San Francisco	Houston	Wash-ington*	London	Frankfurt*	Sydney*	Rio De Janeiro	Madras*
San Francisco		100	250	100	105	100	108	102
Houston	200		300	150	104	50	100	50
Wash-ington*	200	300		200	210	305	102	500
London	100	125	350		100	125	100	200
Frankfurt*	100	200	275	110		100	125	100
Sydney*	125	150	400	100	200		120	200
Rio De Janeiro	100	100	200	116	125	150		100
Madras*	125	100	300	100	150	200	100	

Average size of text e-mail = 82 KB   Average size of mail with attachment = 286 KB   *Designated as an engineering site

Currently, the engineering sites send their drawings between locations using file transfer protocol (FTP). The daily transfer of drawings between sites is shown in the following table.

DAILY NUMBER OF ENGINEERING DRAWINGS SENT BETWEEN LOCATIONS

CITIES	FRANKFURT	SYDNEY	MADRAS
Washington, D.C.	25	30	100
Frankfurt		15	35
Sydney	10		25
Madras	30	40	

Average size of engineering drawing = 3 MB

A file size conversion chart is provided for traffic calculations.

FILE SIZE CONVERSION CHART

GIGABYTE (GB)	MEGABYTE (MB)	KILOBYTE (KB)	BYTE
1	1,000	1,000,000	1,000,000,000

F&D is trying to determine whether it should install a private data network or whether a public data network would better suit its needs. The daily use of e-mail will likely be about five hours a day per site. Also, F&D needs to provide for fax services through a WAN link and remote dial-in to e-mail for traveling engineers.

F&D is spread across the globe and several of its locations are thousands of miles apart. Air miles are used to calculate WAN services that base their charges on cents per mile.

AIR MILES BETWEEN LOCATIONS

Cities	San Francisco	Houston	Wash-ington	London	Frankfurt	Sydney	Rio De Janeiro	Madras
San Francisco		1651	2449	5371	5693	7408	6629	8640
Houston	1651		1221	4860	5245	8581	5016	9475
Wash-ington	2449	1221		3674	4065	9760	4769	8570
London	5371	4860	3674		394	10562	5708	5106
Frankfurt	5693	5245	4065	394		10251	5893	4722
Sydney	7408	8581	9760	10562	10251		8447	5673
Rio De Janeiro	6629	5016	4769	5708	5893	8447		8650
Madras	8640	9475	8570	5106	4722	5673	8650	

The facilities department has supplied the following information about the number, size, location, number of racks, and electrical outlets required per building.

Location	No. of Buildings.	No. of Floors	Network Room Location	Size (Sq. Ft.)	No. of Equipment Racks	No. of Electrical Outlets
Washington*	2	6	2nd Floor	1,500	10	20
San Francisco	1	5	1st Floor	80	5	6
Houston	1	2	1st Floor	100	6	8
London	1	4	2nd Floor	100	5	6
Frankfurt*	1	3	1st Floor	80	6	8
Sydney*	1	5	2nd Floor	80	5	6
Rio De Janeiro	1	4	2nd Floor	70	4	5
Madras*	2	4	2nd Floor	600	8	18

*Designated as engineering sites

Information System Solution:

F&D Engineering, Inc. requests a project plan detailing the e-mail system objectives, WAN infrastructure objectives, and the project scope. The network plan should include staffing requirements for e-mail installation and post-implementation administration. The project solution should detail expected costs and provide a timeline for the installation. F&D wants to have its users test the global e-mail system before it is rolled out for general use. The company envisions the inclusion of a fallback plan in case the testing is not successful.

Your team will create a recommendation document that describes the solution selected and the advantages and disadvantages of the solution. The Project Review team must perform a walk-through of the project and provide a recommendation review. At the end of the project, your team will create a Post Project Summary that should include comments and recommendations on issues encountered during the project. Finally, your team will create a network diagram that illustrates the placement of telecommunication links, the speed of each link, and the equipment required at each location. You will be doing this work in stages at the end of each chapter.

CHAPTER TERMS

ARPAnet   14
ATM   25
backbone   3
Bluetooth   17
cable modems   23
cellular telephony   17
consumer satellite service   24
DSL   23
ENIAC   10
FCC   11
FDDI   25
FINDS   18
Frame Relay   24
FTTH   23
GPS   18
IP telephony   25
ISDN   23

Kingsbury Agreement   11
LAN   3
last mile   15
LATA   13
leased lines   23
QoS   27
RBOC   12
satellite   22
SMDS   25
SONET   25
Telecommunications Act of 1996   14
VoIP   25
VPN   24
WAN   3
wireless   26
X.25   24

CHAPTER BIBLIOGRAPHY

Book, Magazine, Presentation Citations

Jefferis, David. *Cyber Space Virtual Reality and the World Wide Web*. New York: Crabtree Publishing Company, 1999: 6-8.

Plunkett, Jack W. *Plunkett's InfoTech Industry Almanac 2001-2002*. Houston: Plunkett Research, Ltd.: 21.

Sheldon, Tom. *Encyclopedia of Networking & Telecommunications*. New York: Osborne/McGraw-Hill, 2001:58, 59, 102-111, 674-676, 990-993, 1018-1027.

Web Citations

Alliance Datacom, "RBOC Buyer's Guide," <www.alliancedatacom.com/RBOC/rboc-telco-equipment-suppliers.asp>, (20 June 2001).

Alven, William, "Bill's 200-Year Condensed History of Telecommunications," <www.cclab.com/billhist.htm> (May, 1998).

Assembly, "Global dense wavelength division multiplexing (DWDM) components market size by sales 2000 and forecast for 2001 to 2004," <rdsweb1.rdsinc.com/texis/rds/suite/+JSeAU-BswwwwwFqzvq6mh8xXsxFqo15nG+8XKoFqmRFP> (January, 2001).

AT&T, "A Brief History," <www.att.com/history/history4.html> (13 April 2002).

Bell Labs, "An Outlook for Higher Bandwidth, More Data, Greater Speeds, and Lower Costs," <www.lucent.com/minds/trends> (Volume 4 Number 1 2000).

Bell Labs, "Next-gen Networks Predicted to Advance with the Speed of Light," Lucent Technologies, <www.lucent.com/minds/trends> (Volume 4 Number 2 2000).

Bell Labs, "Technology Predicted to Usher in A Golden Age of Silicon," Lucent Technologies, <www.lucent.com/minds/trends> (Volume 4 Number 3 2000).

Bell Labs, "The Last Mile Shall Be First," Lucent Technologies, <www.lucent.com/minds/trends> (Volume 3 Number 1 1999).

Big Charts, "Market Pulse," <bigcharts.marketwatch.com> (20 April 2002).

Cisco Systems, "What Is Wave Division Multiplexing (WDM)?" <www.cisco.com/warp/public/779/servpro/solutions/optical/docs/whatiswdm.html> (2002).

Cosson, Neil, "The Father of Radio," <www.marconiusa.org/marconi> (12 April 2002).

Doherty, Sean, "The Survivor's Guide to 2002," <www.networkcomputing.com> (December 2001).

Farley, Tom, "Telephone History Page 5 – 1892 to 1913," <www.privateline.com/TelephoneHistory2/History A2.html> (14 April 2002).

FCC, "About the FCC," <www.fcc.gov/aboutus.html> (2 May 2002).

Fitzgerald Studio, "Alexander Graham Bell The Inventor," <www.fitzgeraldstudio.com/html/bell/inventor.html> (6 July 2000).

Frankston, Bob, "Connectivity: What it is and why it is so important," <www.satn.org/about/separateconnectivity.htm> (29 January 2001).

Gorman, Michael, "Alexander Graham Bell's Path to the Telephone," <www.iath.Virginia.edu/albell/introduction.html> (7 December 1994).

Infoedge, "The Last Mile—The March for Victory?" <www.infoedge.com/samples/zona_The%20Last%20Mile.doc> (2 May 2002).

Miller, Clayton, "Whither Unregulated Access Competition?" <www.law.indiana.edu/fclj/pubs/v50/no1/miller.html> (4 May 2002).

Molta, Dave, "Mobile & Wireless Technology," <www.networkcomputing.com> (December 2001).

Navy Relics, "Bell Operating Companies," <www.navyrelics.com/tribute/bellsys/bellopercomp.html> (16 February 2001).

Nolle, Tom, "Emerging Technology: Building Networking's Tower of Babel," <www.networkmagazine.com> (January 2002).

Olavsrud, Thor, "Gartner: Telecom Markets Still Growing," <http://www.internetnews.com/infra/article.php/943851> (2 May 2002).

Stanford University, "Why the Need for Change?" <cse.stanford.edu/class/cs201/projects-97-98/pricing-of-the-internet-1/need_for_change.html> (1997-1998).

Telecommunications Americas, "Global data transmission services market size as revenues in U.S. dollars for each of four ranked types of technology in 2000," <rdsweb1.rdsinc.com/texis/rds/suite/+spezR-BswwwwwFqzvq6mh8xXsxFqo15nG+8XKoFqmRFP2> (March 2001).

Telecom History, "The 1960s (Into a New Age of Technology)," <www.webbconsult.com/1960.html> (14 April 2002).

USA NPA, "USA LATA MAP," <www.611.net/NETWORKTELECOM/lata_map/latatall.htm> (16 February 2001).

Verizon, "Company History," <www22.verizon.com> (13 April 2002).

Webopedia, "Internet," <www.pcwebopedia.com/TERM/I/Internet.html> (10 October 2001).

Webopedia, "ENIAC," <www.pcwebopedia.com/TERM/E/ENIAC.html> (10 October 2001).

Woods, Darrin, "Shedding Light On Sonet," <www.networkcomputing.com> (March 2000).

CHAPTER 2
ELEMENTS OF COMMUNICATIONS SYSTEMS

CHAPTER OBJECTIVES

By the end of this chapter, you should understand these concepts:
- The four basic elements of voice and data communication systems
- The difference between local exchange and interexchange carriers
- The beginning and ending of a local loop and the types and hierarchy of switches used in today's telephone network
- How a long-distance call travels through the telephone network
- How handshaking between data terminal equipment and data communications equipment works
- The difference between LECs, CLECs, ILECs, ITCs, ICP, CAP, and IXP carriers
- How ILECs must provide unbundled access to other carriers
- How the FCC retains regulatory control over interstate and international commerce
- The process of creating an Internet standard and the purpose of the Internet Society and Internet Standards organizations IAB, IETF, and IRTF
- The role that domestic and international standards organizations such as ANSI, EIA, IEEE, ISO, and ITU play in telecommunications

COMPONENTS OF VOICE COMMUNICATION SYSTEMS

When placing a telephone call, communication can begin as soon as another person answers the phone. The caller establishes a connection with the person he wants to speak to using the **plain old telephone service (POTS)** provided by the telephone. POTS is used for all voice transmissions through telephone communication channels. The company that provides phone services to subscribers is known as a local **service provider** or **telco.** To deliver communication, the telco uses several interconnected switching systems around the world. This collection of switching systems is called the **Public Switched Telephone Network (PSTN)**. The PSTN serves as the basis for all WAN connections. [Merit, 1]

A telephone conversation consists of four basic elements: a caller, an interface, a language, and a communications channel or telephone line. The telephone is the caller's **interface** when speaking to the intended receiver. This interface is used to send and receive voice-frequency signals. A signal conveys information in the form of electrical energy. The sender's voice travels over an electronic path known as a communications **channel** or **circuit** to the receiver. At the other end, the person receiving the call answers the telephone and begins communication. To understand each other, both sender and receiver use the same language. Figure 2.1 illustrates the components of a voice communications system.

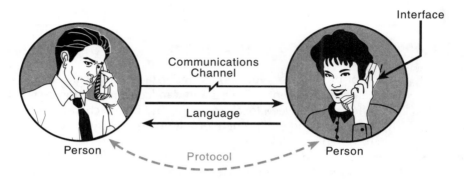

FIGURE 2.1 Components of a Voice Communication System [Infotron, 1.7]

Voice Communications and the Telephone Network

Voice communication via a telephone service is brought to your home through underground cables that can hold a hundred or more pairs of copper wire. A pair of these copper wires runs from a digital concentrator box from your home to the telco's nearest **central office** (**CO**). Another smaller access box is usually located in the basement or on an outside wall of your home (see Figure 2.2). The **access box** also can be referred to as a station protector, entrance bridge, service box, junction box, or demarcation block. [Langhoff, 41]

From the access box, cable lines are run inside your home to the wall jacks where you plug in your phone. [Langhoff, 41] You plug the phone into a telephone jack using a satin wire called a twisted pair cable. A telephone **jack** is where your telephone can be connected or disconnected from the telephone wiring. At the end of the cable, you find a modular plastic piece called an **RJ-11** connector or **plug** (see Figure 2.3). [Langhoff, 43]

No.
Satin is flat not
Twisted

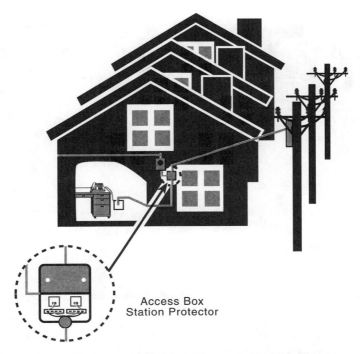

FIGURE 2.2 Access Box to Telephone Network [Langhoff, 41]

Occasionally, you might need to connect multiple devices to the telephone jack such as an answering machine or caller ID box. A **splitter** is used to convert a single outlet into a multiple outlet to accommodate each device (see Figure 2.4). [Langhoff, 54] A splitter is also used when installing a DSL (Digital Subscriber Line); one side of the splitter is connected to your DSL modem and the other side is for your telephone.

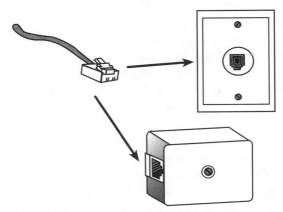

FIGURE 2.3 Modular Plug and Jack for Telephone Connection [Source: Langhoff, 51]

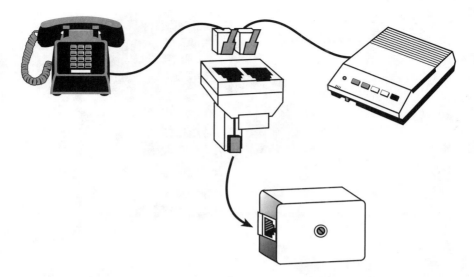

FIGURE 2.4 **Splitter for Multiple Connections [Source: Langhoff, 54]**

In a PSTN (Public Switched Telephone Network), the user or customer is referred to as a subscriber. The **subscriber** is connected via the telephone to the nearest CO equipped with local telephone lines. When the subscriber places a telephone call, it takes a path across a communications channel that is established across a local loop to the CO switch. A **local loop** is the pair of wires that are connected from the subscriber's telephone to the local CO. [Tech Target, 1] This CO building is also known as an **exchange**. In the United States, these local service providers are sometimes referred to as **Local Exchange Carriers (LECs).** A local exchange is the local CO of an LEC. [Tech Target, 1]

Local exchanges are connected to other local exchanges within a **Local Access and Transport Area (LATA).** They are also connected to *Interexchange Carriers* (discussed later in this chapter) for providing long-distance services. For these services, an **access tandem** switch is used to concentrate all trunks from the central office to an interexchange carrier's **point of presence (POP)**. An interexchange carrier can have more than one POP within a LATA. [Parnell, 91] When subscribers makes a local or toll call in their area, they generally do so over a connection to the nearest local exchange carrier. Voice travels across the local loop obtaining access through the distribution plant and eventually moving through a feeder cable into the CO.

The PSTN supports the many switches needed to allow for connections between subscribers and the telco network. These were once electromechanical switches, but today, many are digital. When a subscriber uses a telephone, the conversation is converted into an analog signal, which is transmitted over twisted pair cable to the nearest CO. When it reaches the CO, the analog signal

Explain the digitizing process.

is converted to a digital signal, or **digitized,** at the switch. The resulting digital signal is combined with other signals into large chunks for transmission over high-bandwidth core trunks (for more about analog and digital signals, see Chapter 5). A **trunk** is a line that carries multiple voice or data channels between two telephone exchange switching systems. Channels are used to provide for single or multiple transmission paths through the switch so that signals can flow quickly from the sender to the receiver. When the signals reach their destination, the channels are separated and the digital signals are converted back to analog form and delivered to the receiver's phone. [Tech Target, 1]

The Role of Switches in a Telephone Network

Worldwide telecommunications networks connect millions of users with each other. The center of a telecommunications network is the telecommunications switch. The three types of switches are

- Switches designed to transmit voice only
- Switches that specialize in data only
- Sophisticated switches that handle all types of traffic: voice, data, and video

The switches that connect subscribers and their neighbors are called local exchange switches that are located in telco's CO for that subscriber. In the CO, all subscriber lines terminate in a star configuration at the core switch. Each line is specific to one and only one subscriber. The CO switch completes connections from one local loop to another local loop. (IEC, 1)

Steps → A switch is a simple matrix of pathways. For telephone communications, the pathways are dedicated connections. Once the switch receives a call, it looks for an open pathway to establish a connection. In a digital circuit switch (see Figure 2.5), electrical circuits are opened or closed by transistors that regulate the flow of electrical current through semiconductor material. The subscriber's voice becomes a stream of bytes flowing over the phone line. This stream can then enter the switch and travel from one point to another. When a call is made, a dedicated path is established *Important →* through every switch and transmission line needed to connect the call. No other callers can use this path until the call is ended. Because there is an end-to-end dedicated circuit for the duration of the call, the switch is called a **circuit switch**.

The circuit switch provides the caller with an electronic dedicated path called a **time slot**. A multiplexer, or MUX (see Figure 2.5), manages the time slots for several devices. The user's information is transmitted in a specific time slot and only during that time slot using a method called synchronous transmission. By using a dedicated time slot, a high-quality, error-free transmission for the call is assured. [Bell Labs, 1]

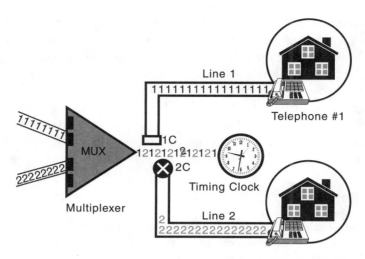

FIGURE 2.5 **Circuit Switch [Source: Bell Labs, 1]**

The use of automated switching equipment along with improvements made in copper and fiber-optic links have increased the speed and enhanced the quality of both local and long-distance calling.

Classes of Switches in the Telephone Network

The PSTN contains five major classes of switches. The classes are numbered 1-5 with Class 1 at the top level and Class 5 at the bottom level of the hierarchy (see Table 2.1). [Merit, 1]

TABLE 2.1 **Hierarchy of Switching Systems [Source: IEC, 3]**

Class 1	Regional Center
Class 2	Sectional/District Center
Class 3	Primary Center
Class 4	Toll Center
Class 5	End Office (CO)

The top level, Class 1, is managed by a Regional Bell Operating Company (RBOC). The only office that is accessible to subscribers is the Class 5 office. A Class 5 office is connected to a Class 4 office via a trunk line. Long-distance calls are routed through a number of switching centers and trunk lines. The exact route a call will take depends on line availability. It doesn't always reach the top of the hierarchy. The call might stop at a primary or secondary switch, depending on where the IXC has its POP. The PSTN is comprised of the entire network hierarchy of switches (see Figure 2.6). [IEC, 1] [Infotron, 3.3]

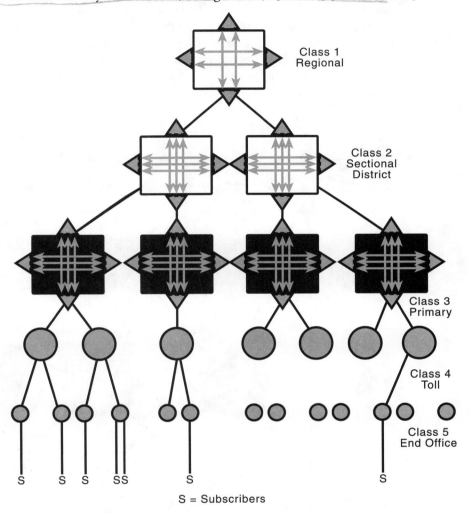

FIGURE 2.6 **Entire Network Hierarchy of Switches [Source: IEC, 3]**

When you place a long-distance call, the local switch accesses a database that contains a record for each phone number connected to the switch. Because there are several different IXCs (AT&T, MCI, Sprint, Qwest, and so on), the database uses a **Primary Interchange Carrier (PIC)** code to find the IXC the subscriber has chosen. The switch looks up the PIC code for the subscriber's number and then connects it to a long-distance switch or POP for the subscriber's IXC. The IXC then routes the call to a local carrier where the call is completed.

Figure 2.7 shows that calls proceed from the Local Exchange to a Transit Exchange. A Transit Exchange eases traffic routing and interconnects the Local Exchanges together. Local and Transit Exchanges route calls to a central switch called a **Signal Transfer Point** (**STP**). STPs are used to setup, manage, and release the voice circuits required to complete a call. The STP is connected to the database that contains a record for each phone number connected to the switch. When calls need to be routed to international locations, a gateway exchange switch is used to connect to a foreign switch on another network.

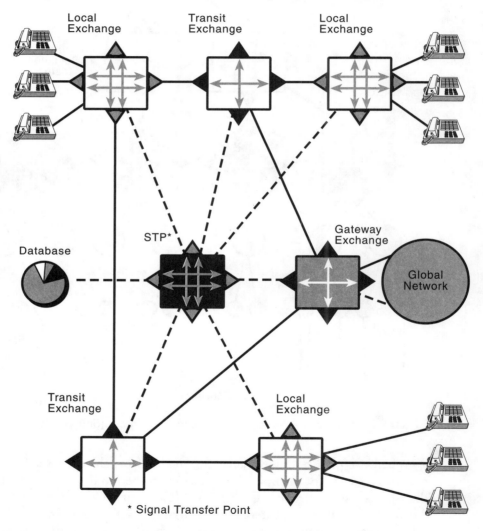

FIGURE 2.7 **User Traffic Path through PSTN [Source: IFLA, A1-2]**

Figure 2.8 shows a typical long distance call traveling through this hierarchy of switches. Paul, who lives in California, would like to call his friend Mary in Michigan. Paul dials 1 indicating to the Local Office that this is a long distance call. The local switch at the CO then connects to the appropriate long distance switch (Toll Center) for Paul's carrier. Paul then dials the three digits of Mary's area code, telling the long distance switch which long distance line to use. Next, he dials her seven-digit phone number. The prefix (first three digits) of this number lets the long distance switch know which CO is needed to make the connection. The long distance carrier (Toll Center) then passes the call onto one of their POP switches (District Center) in Michigan. Next, the District Center switch forwards the call to the Regional Center. The Regional Center in California then sends the call to the Regional Center in Michigan. The call is then forwarded through the District Center and Toll Center in Michigan. Finally the call is sent to the Local Office switch (in Michigan) nearest Mary. The Local Office switch examines the last four numbers of the phone number and routes the call to Mary (Figure 2.8). Regardless of the long-distance carrier used, the call will use the same progression through the switching hierarchy. [Merit, 2]

Circuit-Switched Networks

The first switches used in telecommunications networks were called analog circuit switches. With an **analog switch**, a single connection is set up between two phone lines in the network. A connection is established and lasts for the duration of the call. As each call is placed, it takes a separate electrical path through the switch. This path is also known as a **circuit**. The circuit is formed by a number of conductors that are connected for the purpose of carrying an electrical current. A circuit is capable of providing a number of channels for establishing two-way communications.

A common circuit switch is the **private branch exchange** (**PBX**) or phone switch connected to a desk phone in an office. This circuit switch has two primary functions:

- Allow employees to contact each other by dialing a four number extension
- Provide employees with a communication path to people outside the company

The PBX is connected to a local telco's CO that has a POP to several IXCs. In the telephone network, ordinary phone service is circuit-switched. The telco reserves a specific physical path to the number the subscriber is calling for the duration of the call. This means that no one else can use the physical lines reserved for that subscriber until the call has ended.

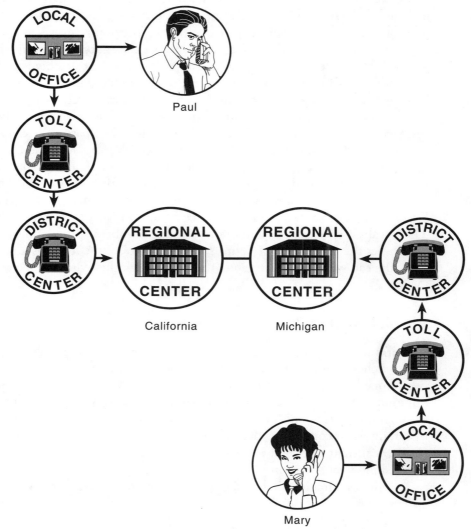

FIGURE 2.8 Paul Calls Mary Long Distance [Source: Infotron, 3.3]

Packet-Switched Networks

Packet switches were developed in 1970 for connecting low-speed data users to corporate data networks. They were designed to handle variable bit rates of burst data transmission. The amount of data and multimedia traffic has increased significantly because of the Internet. In the past, telcos primarily routed voice traffic only. Today, telcos have expanded their services so they can carry greater amounts of data traffic.

When data traffic is broken down into smaller units of data called **packets**, the same data path can be shared between many users in the network. These packets are then routed (using *routers*, which are covered in Chapter 3) through a network based on the destination address contained within each packet. Figure 2.9 shows seven packets numbered P1-P7. Close scrutiny of the figure shows that each packet has traveled over a different WAN link. When they reach the destination, the packets are reassembled in sequence P1, P2, and so on through P7 to represent the original message. From this example, you can see that the communication between the sender and receiver is not dedicated; it is connectionless.

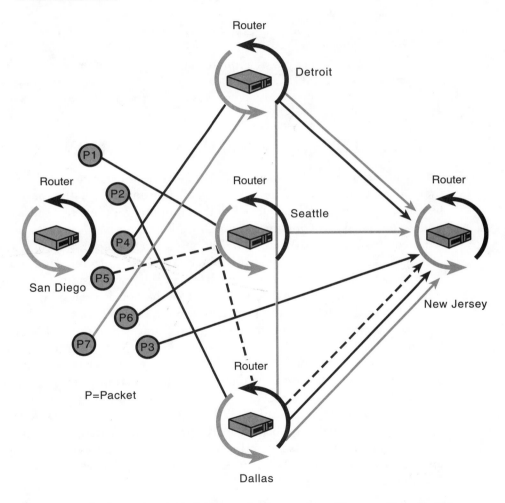

FIGURE 2.9 **Packet-Switch Network Connections [Source: Parnell, 67]**

Both voice and data are currently being routed over packet switches. Packet switches reduce network delays and equipment costs, and provide for more efficient bandwidth use. However, the current POTS still works well for basic services, so many carriers have not abandoned their circuit switches.

TOPIC *review* **Components of Voice Communication Systems**

1. What is the switch called that is used to concentrate all trunks from the central office to an IXC's POP?
2. What is used to provide for single or multiple transmission paths through a switch?
3. Which class of switches in the Public Telephone Network is accessible to subscribers?
4. When a subscriber places a long-distance call, how does the LEC determine who the IXC is?
5. How are both voice and data calls routed through the PSTN?

COMPONENTS OF DATA COMMUNICATION SYSTEMS

All organizations require some type of connectivity for transferring data within their offices or to outside remote facilities. Before any information or data can be transmitted, it must be digitized so the computer on the other end will understand it. Just as with voice communications, four basic elements are required for successful data communications: sender, receiver, medium, and message. The *sender* is known as the source of the transmission. After the information leaves the sender, a *receiver* must accept the transmission. The sender's information is referred to as the *message,* while the signal is carried over a wire referred to as the *medium*. You gain **access** to the data network or LAN and to other organizations' networks through a path connected to the PSTN or the Internet.

To be effective, a data communications system needs to have a reliable method to transfer data between the **data communications equipment (DCE)**. In data networks, a DCE is any device used to interface computer equipment to the communications line. DCEs include modems, csu/dsus, multiplexers, and routers (see Chapter 3). At the source and destination, the computer equipment used to send and receive data is called **data terminal equipment (DTE)**. When the DTE is interfaced to the DCE, it is called the DTE/DCE interface (see Figure 2.10).

Perhaps use the 5 step:
Source
Xmtr
Channel
Rcvr
Destination

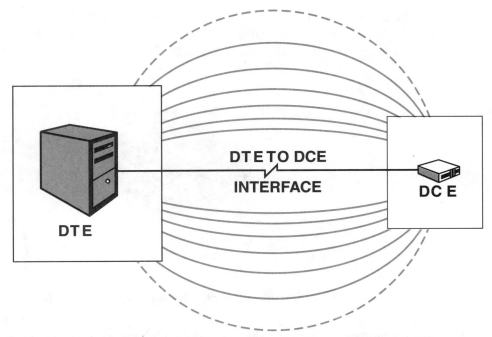

FIGURE 2.10 **DTE to DCE Communication [Source: Infotron, 5.2]**

The interface between the DTE and DCE performs the same function as a telephone does between the sender and receiver. Transmit and receive lines are on both the DTE and the DCE.

After you connect the DTE to the DCE, a data conversation begins. Each device transmits signals to the other with the aim of establishing a session. The two devices essentially let each other know when they are ready to send. The DTE says, "I want to send" and the DCE responds saying, "Go ahead, it's clear." If the DCE does not respond to the send request, it is not clear to send and the session will not begin. This data conversation process is called **handshaking** (see Figure 2.11).

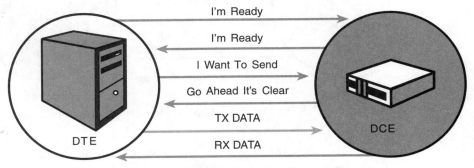

FIGURE 2.11 **DTE to DCE Handshaking [Source: Infotron, 5.5]**

The connection between the DTE and the DCE is defined as a specification called RS232C. RS232C specifies the use of a 25-pin connector wherein each pin is assigned a signal and a function (Figure 2.12).

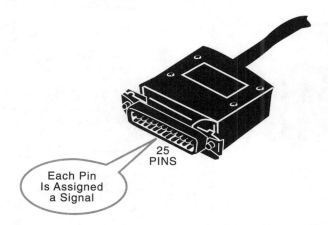

FIGURE 2.12 **RS232C Specification for Cable Connecter [Source: Infotron, 5.7]**

Communication between the DTE and DCE uses predefined **control signals**. These signals are assigned a number. Each number indicates the function to be performed and the control signals to be specified for this RS232C interface. These signals are used by the DTE and DCE to indicate that data communication can proceed. Figure 2.13 shows that data is moved over pin 2 to transmit and pin 3 to receive. The other pins 15, 17, and 24 carry timing signals (clocks) for synchronous applications.

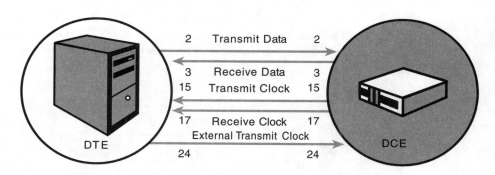

FIGURE 2.13 **RS232 Data and Timing Signaling [Source: Infotron, 5.8]**

In Figure 2.14, the control signals used for communication are 4, 5, 6, 8, 20, and 22. The function of each pin is as follows:
- Pin 4: Request to Send (RTS)

Chapter 2 • Elements of Communications Systems

- Pin 5: Clear to Send (CTS)
- Pin 6: Data Set Ready (DSR)
- Pin 8: Data Carrier Detect (DCD)
- Pin 20: Data Terminal Ready (DTR)
- Pin 22: Ring Indicator (RI)

The conversation begins over pin 6 to determine whether the data set is ready (DSR). Next, the DCE sends a signal over pin 20 to the data terminal (DTE) to inquire whether it is ready to send (DTR). If a positive response is received, then pin 4 inquires with a request to send (RTS). If the response from the DTE is positive, a clear to send (CTS) signal is sent over pin 5. Next, the DCE proceeds to make sure a carrier connection exists and sends a signal over pin 8 (DCD). If a connection is found, then it sends a ring indicator (RI) over pin 22. After all of the control signaling is completed, the actual transmission of data occurs over pin 2 (send) and pin 3 (receive).

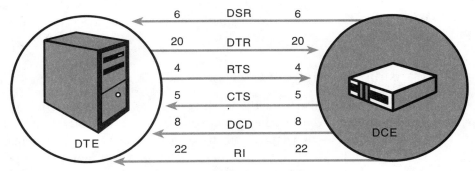

FIGURE 2.14 **RS232C Control Transmission [Source: Infotron, 5.9]**

The primary purpose of data communications is to provide information transfer between users. As described in this section, the process of delivering data is very structured down to the pins in the cable. Several preliminary messages are sent back and forth between sender and receiver to enable communication because the receiver must acknowledge receipt of communication before the sender can send again. This basic process is the core of all data communication and networking.

TOPIC review **Components of Data Communication Systems**

1. What are the four basic elements of data communications?
2. How is the change in voltage defined for digital signals?
3. What type of device do you use to interface computer equipment to a communication line?
4. What is the data conversation process between a DTE and a DCE called?
5. What is a control signal?

CARRIER SERVICES

Carriers, also referred to as service providers or telcos, transport data and voice traffic between customer locations. All of these carriers charge a price for their services. The government regulates where carriers can establish rights of way to lay wires and radio links and also requires carriers to operate under the terms of a tariff.

A **tariff** specifies the exact terms of the service to be provided and the price to be charged. Carriers must initiate **Service Level Agreements (SLA)** with customers to guarantee specific levels of service for throughput, latency, availability, and error rates. **Throughput** is the agreed data rate; for example, 128KB. **Latency** describes delays in transmitting over the WAN. **Availability** is the time period (7 days a week, 24 hours a day) the WAN is accessible. **Error rates** record the incidence of errors involved in transmission. In fact, credits are paid to customers if a carrier fails to meet the agreed-upon service levels. Competition between carriers forces them to meet SLAs. Network downtime translates to lost revenue. Companies often change carriers if they can't meet their SLAs.

Transmission Methods

Most of the transmission methods used by carriers today were originally designed to carry voice traffic. As demand for data traffic increased, voice transmission facilities were adapted to carry data. For example, copper transmission media, developed for voice communication, is now commonly used to interface short-haul (a few miles) transmission media to long-haul (several miles or transcontinental) transmission media.

For short-haul transmission, carriers use two-wire cables. The two-wire cable is a single pair of wires in which one wire is called the "**Tip**" and the other is called the "**Ring**." In the early days of telephone communication, these two wires ended in a plug that was placed into a manual switchboard. When looking at the plug, you see that one electrical contact is at the tip of the plug and the other is at a ring just below it (see Figure 2.15). These plugs were similar in appearance to the stereo phono plug used today in stereo headsets.

Sleeve   Ring   Tip

FIGURE 2.15 **Tip and Ring [Source: O'Reilly, 1]**

Two-wire facilities are often used between a modem and a PBX, between two computers, or between the PBX and the CO. Traffic over this two-wire connection flows in both directions (see Figure 2.16).

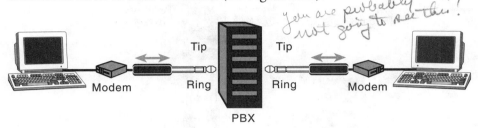

you are probably not going to see this!

FIGURE 2.16 **Two-Wire Metallic Connection [Source: Parnell, 60]**

For long-haul transmission over copper, a four-wire cable is used. This cable is divided into two pairs of wires; the first pair is designated as Tip and Ring and the second pair is called Tip 1 and Ring 1. Transmission occurs in only one direction: sending takes place over Tip and Ring while receiving occurs over Tip 1 and Ring 1. There is little loss or distortion of the signal over four-wire cables, and signals can be carried farther. For this reason, long-distance transmission facilities use four-wire cables. Two-wire and four-wire telephone cabling also can be interfaced together with a four-wire termination set (see Figure 2.17).

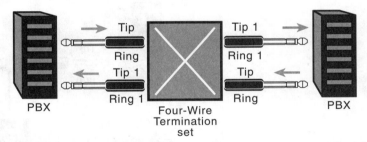

FIGURE 2.17 **Four-Wire Metallic Connection [Source: Parnell, 61]**

In the United States, the existing telecommunications systems consist of copper twisted-pair wiring in the local loop. Transmission components are used to interconnect the wiring and telephone switches. The collection of transmission components, switches, and wiring is known as the **carrier system** (see Figure 2.18).

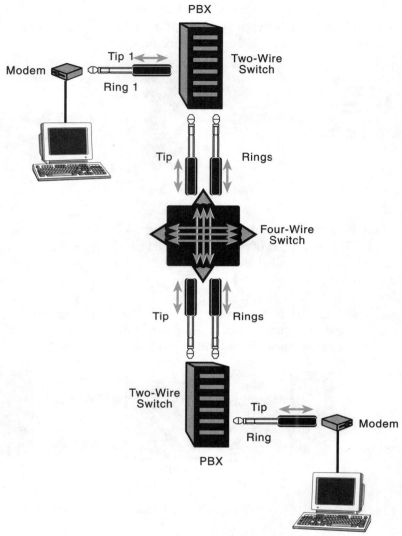

FIGURE 2.18 **Carrier System [Source: Parnell, 62]**

Types of Carriers

Today's telecommunications market is extremely complex because several different types of carriers are available. Each carrier type has a range of services and a geographic limitation defining where they can operate. Some of these exchange carriers have been in business since the days of the AT&T monopoly. Other types of carriers were created as a result of the Telecommunications Act of 1996.

A Local Exchange Carrier (LEC) is a telephone company that operates within a specific geographical area. A LEC has a franchise within a LATA allowing it to provide telephone services. The FCC governs the privileges and restrictions applied to carriers. Local exchange carriers are limited to providing local phone service, producing yellow pages, and selling equipment, and are not allowed to sell long-distance services. [Sheldon, 736]

Incumbent Local Exchange Carriers (ILEC) are the original service providers that were once part of the old AT&T telephone system. When AT&T was broken into separate entities, these service providers became the RBOCs. Many of the original seven RBOCs were allowed to merge as a result of the Telecommunications Act of 1996. Most of these carriers operate across a number of LATAs. [Sheldon, 610]

An **Interexchange Carrier (IXC)** is a telecommunications carrier that provides service between LECs. IXCs provide inter-LATA service. Long-distance carriers such as AT&T, MCI, Sprint, and Qwest are examples of IXCs. The ILECs are required to create a POP so that IXCs can connect to and provide long-distance services for local subscribers.

Competitive Access Providers (CAPs) are carriers who build their own metropolitan SONET (Synchronous Optical Network) rings and offer private WAN services to businesses that can bypass the incumbent carriers. The first CAP was constructed for Merrill Lynch in New York City. A transmission facility was installed in New York to bypass the New York Telephone Company and connect directly to the IXC. [Sheldon, 1134]

Also as a part of the Telecommunications Act of 1996, **Competitive Local Exchange Carriers (CLEC)** were formed to compete with the already established local telephone companies. They were granted the right to build their own network of switching systems to promote competition among local and long-distance service providers. ILECs were required to open up their facilities to the CLECs. This Act also granted that ILECs be required to offer services to CLECs at wholesale prices. CLECs were also granted access to **unbundled network elements (UNEs)** that connect access to the local loop and to the subscribers connected on the other end. [Sheldon, 1134]

Another type of carrier is the **Independent Telephone Company (ITC)**. An ITC operates only in noncompetitive areas not covered by the RBOCs (ILECs) or any other phone company. Many ITCs are located in distant rural areas. These small, independent telephone companies are owned as family businesses, handed down from generation to generation, or these companies have become cooperatives, owned by the community and its customers. [Sheldon, 1134]

Competitive State of ILECs and CLECs

Since the Telecommunications Act of 1996, the viability and nature of the competitive state between ILECs and CLECs has been reexamined. In 1999, the

FCC stated that incumbents (ILECs) must provide to CLECs **unbundled** (offer as separate services) **access** to the following network elements:

- **Loops.** ILECs must offer access to loops, including high-capacity lines such as DSL. They are also required to provide access to dark fiber and inside wire owned by the incumbent LEC.
- **Sub Loops.** ILECs must offer access to sub loops or portions of the loop at any accessible point.
- **NID.** ILECs must offer access to a **network interface device (NID)**, which is used to connect loop facilities to inside wiring.
- **Circuit Switching.** ILECs must offer access to local circuit switching. The one exception to this rule is when switching is used to serve end users with four or more lines in the top 50 metropolitan statistical areas.
- **Interoffice Transmission Facilities.** ILECs must unbundle dedicated interoffice transmission facilities or transport, which also includes dark fiber.
- **Signaling and Call-Related Databases.** ILECs must unbundle signaling links and STPs in conjunction with unbundled switching and on a stand-alone basis.
- **Operations Support Systems.** ILECs must unbundle operations support systems (OSSs) throughout their service territory. This means allowing access to preordering, ordering, provisioning, maintenance, repair, and billing functions supported by ILECs databases.

Internet Service

The service most often requested by companies is Internet access. When compared with other services, there is relatively low expenditure required to obtain Internet service. **Internet Service Providers (ISPs)** provide public Internet access for e-mail and business traffic to travel over a large number of backbone switches. Many corporations are unsure about the quality of performance and the lack of security guarantees for the Internet. Several companies have opted to contract for private IP carrier services in which each customer is assigned a private virtual channel through the telephone network. These carrier services allow traffic to travel independently from the Internet with greater security. [Greenfield, 6]

1. Who regulates where telephone companies can establish rights of way to lay wires and set up radio links?
2. What is the term for the entire collection of transmission components, switches, and wiring?
3. When a subscriber makes a local call to a friend in the same city, which type of carrier will manage the call?
4. What type of CLECs have gained momentum by offering DSL?
5. Which organization has to create a POP so that IXCs can connect and provide long-distance services for local subscribers?

COMMUNICATIONS SYSTEMS, STANDARDS, AND FORUMS

National and international data communications standards organizations work together to facilitate local and global communications. **Standards** are the written agreements that specifically define the rules, guidelines, or definitions of quality required to ensure that materials, products, processes, and services are appropriate for their purpose. They have become the accepted method of applying and using new and existing technology. Published standards are divided into four categories: hardware, software, systems, and processes. [Spohn, 66-67]

Standards provide guidelines to government agencies, manufacturers, and vendors for the development of products for interconnecting different types of equipment for data and voice communications and networking. The standards committees are typically composed of computer scientists from universities and manufacturer representatives who have a special interest in development and implementation of a specific type of technology.

U.S. Standards: The FCC

Standards in the United States are influenced by rulings of the **Federal Communications Commission** (**FCC**) and other government agencies. Their rulings have a direct effect on the standards committees and their focus. The FCC was established by the Communications Act of 1934 to function as a regulatory authority for radio, television, wire, satellite, and cable communications within the United States. It retains regulatory control over interstate and international commerce concerning communications.

The role of the FCC is to
- Review rate and service charge applications for the telegraph and telephone

- Review technical specifications of communications hardware
- Set reasonable common carrier rates of return

The major initiatives currently being debated by standards organizations and the FCC include 3G Wireless, Broadband, Digital Television, and Low Power FM. With each of these initiatives, the FCC strives for a high degree of common design to encourage the use of compatible services worldwide. [FCC, 1]

International Standards: The Internet

The spread of the Internet in other countries has led to the development of standards to support international practices. The Internet Standards process is an activity of the Internet Society that is organized by the **Internet Architecture Board** (**IAB**) and the Internet Engineering Steering Group (IESG). The goals of the Internet Standards Process are:
- Technical excellence
- Prior implementation and testing
- Clear, concise documentation that can be easily understood
- Openness and fairness
- Timeliness

The process of creating an Internet Standard requires a specification to undergo a period of development and several iterations of review by the Internet community. At each stage of the Standards Process, the specification is repeatedly discussed. There are several open meetings during the process of creating a specification, and public e-mailing lists are made available to review the specification. [Bradner, 3]

Four primary organizations conduct the Internet Standards Process: the ISOC, IAB, IRTF, and IETF.

Internet Society (ISOC)

The **Internet Society (ISOC)** is responsible for supporting the IETF and IAB groups that establish Internet infrastructure standards. Membership in the Internet Society spans more than 100 countries with 150 organizational and 6,000 individual members. They share a common goal in maintaining the viability and global scaling of the Internet. ISOC also supports education in developing countries and provides financial support for the Internet Standards process. [ISOC, 1]

Internet Architecture Board (IAB)

The Internet Architecture Board (IAB) is a technical advisory group of the Internet Society. It acts as a source of advice for technical, architectural, procedural, and policy matters pertaining to the Internet. The IAB was set up in 1983 when the Internet was still largely a research activity of the U.S. government. The IAB exists to serve, help, and define the limits of the IETF (see the next section). It is closely linked as a liaison with other Internet standards organizations.

Internet Engineering Task Force (IETF)

The IAB established the **IETF** as the protocol engineering and development arm of the Internet in 1986. Membership consists of a large open international community of network designers, operators, vendors, and researchers. The technical work of the IETF is accomplished by working groups. Each of these groups is organized around one particular concern such as routing, transport, or security. [IETF, 1]

Internet Research Task Force (IRTF)

The **IRTF** is dedicated to the evolution of the Internet. It creates focused research groups that study topics related to Internet protocols, applications, architecture, and technology. [IRTF, 1]

Standards Forums

Today, the rate of development in technology outpaces the ratification of standards. The ratification process is sometimes overwhelmingly slow. Over the years, special interest groups have developed **forums** that attempt to promote standards for new technologies. Forums jump-start the standards process by speeding along the acceptance of new equipment and protocols. The corporations involved in these forums provide the user trials and university test beds necessary to accelerate the testing and acceptance of new technologies. Several prominent forums are influencing the standards process today:

- ATM Forum
- DSL Forum
- Frame Relay Forum
- Network and Service Integration Forum (NSIF)
- National ISDN Council
- Telemanagement Forum

ATM Forum

CPE vendors and CO providers established the **ATM Forum** for the purpose of developing interoperability specifications for ATM hardware and services. Together they focus their efforts toward the convergence of voice, video, data, and images over ATM technology. The specifications they publish are not standards; rather they serve as complementary guidelines to assist in the successful internetworking of equipment provided by many manufacturers. [ATM Forum, 1]

DSL Forum

DSL Forum members share knowledge and the latest and best practices in broadening the adoption of DSL as the world's primary choice for broadband services. They have developed guidelines for auto-configuration, flow-through provisioning, and equipment interoperability for the deployment of DSL. Membership in this forum has grown since 1994 and now has more than 330 participating organizations including telecommunications, equipment, computing, networking, and service provider companies. [DSL Forum, 1]

Frame Relay Forum

The **Frame Relay Forum** is an association of vendors, carriers, users, and consultants committed to the education, promotion, and implementation of frame relay. It was formed and incorporated in May 1991 by DEC, Northern Telecom, Cisco, and StrataCom. Today, they host presentations, and write papers, technical briefs, and tutorials on their Web site. They have published recommendations for flow control, encapsulation, translation, and multicast capabilities over frame relay. [Frame Relay Forum, 1]

Network and Service Integration Forum (NSIF)

NSIF is a non-profit organization that develops end-to-end solutions for multi-technology service delivery. Workgroups are established to address particular technical needs and the resulting recommendation documents are used as specifications for product development and implementation. This forum has published standards documents for bandwidth and fault management, security, SONET, and Multi-technology DCN Integration. [NSIF, 1]

National ISDN Council

Telecommunications service providers and switch suppliers established the **National ISDN Council** to exchange ISDN-related technical information among forum participants. The Council strives to identify the needs of potential ISDN (Integrated Services Digital Network) users to provide input for the development of products for the industry. They investigate connectivity, compatibility, and integrity of ISDN products to offer uniform operation of equipment nationwide. [National ISDN Council, 1].

Telemanagement Forum

The **Telemanagement Forum** offers technical programs, market centers, and catalyst projects for OSS integration and business process automation. Service providers, computing and network equipment suppliers, software suppliers, and customers of communications services make up its 384 members. The Telemanagement Forum also develops strategic guides and products and makes them available to the general public to promote the search for new communications solutions. [Telemanagement Forum, 1].

Official Standards Organizations

Data communications managers and data users are unwilling to risk their organizations on proprietary systems. Many corporations are multinational and, therefore, have a need to interface with data communications equipment in other countries. Users must be sure that the equipment they purchase will interface with that of other vendors. Vendors must realize that if they do not design products around standards, users will take their business elsewhere. Service providers must also participate in the standards-making process to ensure that the vendor's equipment will interoperate. Standards organizations strive to reach consensus between their members. They employ facilitators to lead their meetings toward agreement and assist in resolving conflicts. There are currently five major standards organizations:
- American National Standards Institute (ANSI)
- Electronic Industries Association (EIA)
- Institute of Electrical and Electronic Engineers (IEEE)
- International Organization for Standardization (ISO)
- International Telecommunications Union (ITU)

Each standards organization has a significant history behind its organization. In addition, each organization has evolved along with the discovery of new technologies.

American National Standards Institute (ANSI)

Established in 1918, **ANSI** is a private, non-profit organization. ANSI has served as administrator and coordinator of the U.S. private sector voluntary standardization system for more than 80 years. More than 1,000 companies, government agencies, and institutional members make up its membership. The Institute works to enhance global competitiveness of U.S. business and the American quality of life by facilitating consensus standards and conformity assessment systems in telecommunications. [ANSI, 1]

ANSI does not develop standards itself but works to establish a consensus among qualified groups. It is the official U.S. representative to the International Organization for Standardization (ISO). ANSI has written over 14,650 standards that address critical trends in technological innovation, marketplace globalization, and regulatory reform. [ANSI, 1]

Electronic Industries Association (EIA)

EIA is a non-profit organization that represents 80% of the $550 billion U.S. electronics industry. EIA is organized by market area and around specific electronic products. These sector associations represent consumer electronics, telecommunications, components, government electronics, and semiconductors.

Institute of Electrical and Electronic Engineers (IEEE)

IEEE is a leading authority in computer engineering, biomedical technology, and telecommunications. It is a non-profit professional association that spans 150 countries and includes 377,000 members. The IEEE hosts more than 300 major conferences per year. To date, it has published 860 standards in electrical engineering, computers, and control technology. [IEEE, 1]

International Organization for Standardization (ISO)

ISO was established in 1947 and is a worldwide federation of national standards bodies from 140 countries. Each country has one representative. The ISO publishes international agreements regarding intellectual, scientific, technological, and economic activities worldwide. Its purpose is to remove technical barriers that prevent trade of similar technologies between different countries or regions. Users have more confidence when they purchase products and services that conform to International Standards. [ISO, 1]

International Telecommunication Union (ITU)

As the use of telecommunication and radio-based communication systems increases, the role of the **International Telecommunication Union (ITU)** has expanded from the invention of telephones to the development of radio communications and finally the launch of communications satellites. [ITU, 1] The ITU was founded 135 years ago and was the first organization to establish a spirit of cooperation between governments and the private sector. Today, its membership includes almost all of the world's countries along with over 500 private members, including carriers, equipment manufacturers, funding bodies, research and development organizations, and international and regional telecommunication organizations. ITU's members work through conferences and meetings to negotiate agreements for the operation of global telecommunication services. Because of the efforts of the ITU, users can use the Internet to communicate easily with a person from any country in the world. The work of the ITU benefits everyone who picks up a telephone and dials a number or answers a call on a mobile phone. [ITU, 1]

The ITU is divided into three primary sectors. Each of these meets separately to discuss specifications and operational procedures. Together, they are building and shape the network services of the future. These three sectors are as follows:

- **Radio communication (ITU-R).** ITU-R develops operational procedures for terrestrial and space-based wireless systems and services.
- **Telecommunication Standardization (ITU-T).** ITU-T prepares technical specifications and standards for the operation, performance, and maintenance of telecommunication systems, networks, and services. ITU-T also works to establish tariff principles and accounting methods for providing international service. The mission of ITU-T is to ensure an efficient and on-time production of high-quality standards covering all fields of telecommunications.
- **Telecommunication Development (ITU-D).** ITU-D focuses its work on the preparation of recommendations, opinions, guidelines, handbooks, manuals, and reports that provide developing countries with best business practices for telecommunication network management. [ITU, 1]

Private companies can join one or more of these sectors. Each sector has its own bureau that is responsible for the implementation of the work plan and coordinating activities on a day-to-day basis. Currently, 24 study groups within the three sectors produce around 550 new or revised recommendations every year. The standards published have provided a vital ingredient in the transborder delivery of banking, transportation, tourism, online information, and electronic home shopping. [ITU, 1]

Future of Standards Organizations

Standards organizations are adapting to strive for flexible compatibility. Future standards will be able to operate according to one implementation and then change their operation in response to a request. As telecommunications becomes more of a wireless environment, users need standards that are not constrained. Wireless equipment is completely controlled by software, which means standards need to be more flexible because there is no physical connector to standardize for communication. [Krechmaer, 4]

An open architecture makes practical multiple standards for similar functions. In the future, users will be able to choose which standard to install in their equipment. They will have the flexibility to switch back and forth as needed. For instance, future equipment might automatically switch functions based on the signals received from the equipment at the destination. Standards that support adaptability will be the new foundation for future technology and open communication architecture. [Krechmaer, 4]

TOPIC *review* **Communication Systems, Standards, and Forums**

1. What are the four categories of standards published to manage the data communications market?
2. Which organization works to set reasonable common carrier rates of return?
3. What approach is being used by the IAB to promote awareness of harmful use of the Internet?
4. Which organization works to negotiate agreements for the operation of global telecommunication services?
5. Which organization has published 860 standards in electrical engineering, computers, and control technology?

CHAPTER SUMMARY

Both voice and data communications use four basic elements to establish a voice or data conversation. For voice, the elements are person, interface, language, and a communications channel. Data communications requires a sender, receiver, medium, and a message. Voice communication is provided by POTS over the PSTN. Data communication usually is provided either privately through a digital switch or publicly over the Internet through an Internet Service Provider (ISP).

At the center of the telephone network are devices called switches. Circuit switches are used for voice. Digital switches are used for data. Switches provide for several pathways through the public switched telephone network. The telephone network has five major classes of switches: Regional Center, Sectional/District Center, Primary Center, Toll Center, and End Office. Long-distance telephone calls are routed through a number of switches and several carriers on their way to the receiver.

Today's voice and data networks provide carriers with additional ways to connect offices to the PSTN and the Internet. Deregulation of the industry has added to the complexity of providing local and long-distance telephone services and the laws regarding them. Several new types of carriers emerged: CAP, CLEC, ICP, ILEC, ITC, IXC, and LEC. The major telephone companies have consolidated, merged, and repositioned themselves to compete more effectively with the new carriers that emerged as a result of the deregulation. Because circuit prices and tariffs can be subject to change at any time, the FCC governs the privileges, restrictions, and rates for all carriers. It sets common carrier rates of return and approves applications for telephone and telegraph services.

Standards organizations provide guidelines for hardware, software, systems, and processes. The goal of standards is to promote quality and interoperability between different manufacturers' equipment. Standards provide written agreements that specifically define rules and procedures for the operation of new and existing technology.

The phenomenal growth of the Internet has provided for a whole new group of Internet standards organizations (IAB, IETF, IRTF, and ISOC). Each organization provides specific contributions to support all or some of the policies that guide Internet protocols, applications, architecture, and topology.

Because technology is developing at such a rapid pace, the standards ratification process is not able to keep up. Special interest groups, called forums, have been developed to jump-start the standards process. These organizations (ATM, DSL, Frame Relay, NSIF, National ISDN Council, and Telemanagement Forums) provide testing and quality assurance, and publish reports that are submitted to the official standards organizations (ANSI, EIA, IEEE, ISO, and ITU). The official standards organizations manage conflicts between members, vendors, and manufacturers. When they reach consensus, they publish standards that are adopted worldwide.

CHAPTER REVIEW QUESTIONS

(This quiz can also be printed out from the Encore! CD that accompanies this textbook. Click Chapter 2, *click* Student Files, *and then click* Chap02review.)
Circle a letter (a-d) for each question. Choose only one answer for each.

1. What is the most common wiring used for telephone services in homes today?
    a. Single wire twisted pair
    b. Coax
    c. Fiber
    d. Two-wire twisted pair

2. Which switch is used to concentrate all trunks from the central office to an interexchange carrier's point of presence?
    a. Circuit switch
    b. Access tandem switch
    c. Packet switch
    d. End office switch

3. An Interexchange Carrier (IXC) can have more than one point of presence (POP) within a
   a. PSTN
   b. LATA
   c. telco
   d. local loop

4. When a call is made, a physical dedicated path called a time slot is provided end-to-end for the duration of the call by what kind of switch?
   a. Packet switch
   b. Data switch
   c. Circuit switch
   d. Analog switch

5. When you place a long-distance call, the local switch accesses a database to look for the _____ code to find the long-distance carrier you have chosen.
   a. PIC
   b. POP
   c. PBX
   d. PPP

6. Which type of carrier is limited to providing local phone service, producing yellow pages, and selling equipment?
   a. CAP
   b. IXC
   c. ICP
   d. LEC

7. Which service provider allows inter-LATA service?
   a. LEC
   b. CAP
   c. IXC
   d. ILC

8. Which organization retains control over interstate and international commerce concerning communication?
   a. IETF
   b. FCC
   c. IAB
   d. IRTF

9. Which term describes a special interest group organized to promote standards for new technology and to jump-start the standards process?
   a. Advisory Board
   b. Society
   c. Task Force
   d. Forum

10. The international organization responsible for publishing the ISO standard is the
    a. IEEE
    b. EIA
    c. ISO
    d. ITU

Circle the correct letter (A-E) that corresponds to the descriptions below. Choose only one answer for each.
   A. Access Box
   B. Splitter
   C. Handshaking
   D. Tip
   E. Trunk

11. A B C D E   A data conversation between a DTE and a DCE used to check to see if it is okay to send or receive signals.

12. A B C D E   A line that carries multiple voice or data channels between two telephone exchange switching systems.

13. A B C D E   Used to convert a single outlet into a multiple outlet to accommodate two separate devices.

14. A B C D E   A small box also called a station protector that is usually located in the basement or on an outside wall of the home.

15. A B C D E   The electrical contact at the tip of the plug is used for _____ on your telephone line.

   A. Channel
   B. SLA
   C. Local loop
   D. UNE
   E. Time slot

16. A B C D E   Network services that are separated and granted to CLECs to access the local loop and the subscribers connected on the other end.

17. A B C D E   A communications circuit between two or more devices.

18. A B C D E   A pair of wires that are connected from the subscriber's telephone to the local CO.

19. A B C D E   An electronic dedicated path provided by a circuit switch.

20. A B C D E   A contract between a service provider and a customer.

INTERNET EXERCISES

1. Log on to the Internet and key the following URL:
   http://ld.net/calculator/?uniontel
   Use the U.S. Domestic Rate Calculator and key the following:
   - First six digits of your U.S. Phone number: 408382
   - Interstate Minutes Per Month: 120
   - In-State Minutes Per Month: 300
   Click Perform Calculation.
   A. How many carriers are available?
   B. What is the lowest price available?
   C. What is the highest price available?
   D. Is there a difference in services offered?
2. Now try the International Best Rate Calculator. Key the following:
   - Calling From: USA (48 States)
   - Calling To: Brazil-Sao Paulo
   - Call Duration: 45 minutes
   Click Perform Calculation.
   A. What is the lowest price available per minute?
   B. What is the highest price available per minute?
   C. Do they have any surcharges?
   D. Are credit card payments accepted?

CONCEPT EXERCISES

Concept Narrative
(This narrative exercise can also be printed out from the Encore! CD that accompanies this textbook. Click Chapter 2, *click* Student Files, *and then click* Chap02connar.)*

Read the following description and fill in the blanks with the correct answer.

The telephone is your _____ when speaking to your intended receiver. This interface is used to send and receive voice-frequency signals. A signal conveys information in the form of electrical energy. The sender's

voice travels over an electronic path known as a communications
_____ or _____ to the receiver. At the other end, the person receiving the call answers the telephone and begins his communication. To understand each other, both sender and receiver use the same language.

Voice communication via a telephone service is brought to a subscriber's home through underground cables that can hold a hundred or more pairs of copper wire. A pair of these copper wires runs from a box called a digital concentrator from the home to the telco's nearest _____
_____(CO). Another smaller box called an _____ ____ is usually located in the basement or on an outside wall of the home. The access box also can be referred to as a station protector, entrance bridge, service box, junction box, or demarcation block.

From the access box, cable lines are run inside the home to the wall jacks where the subscriber plugs in a phone. The subscriber plugs the phone into a telephone jack using a satin wire called a twisted pair cable. A telephone ____ is where the telephone can be connected or disconnected from the telephone wiring. At the end of the cable is a modular plastic piece called an _____ connector or ____.

Occasionally, a subscriber might need to connect multiple devices to the telephone jack such as an answering machine or caller ID box. A _____ is used to convert a single outlet into a multiple outlet to accommodate each device. A splitter is also used when installing a DSL line; one side of the splitter is connected to the DSL modem and the other side is for the telephone.

In a PSTN, the user or customer is referred to as a subscriber. As a _____, the customer is connected via the telephone to the nearest CO equipped with local telephone lines. When the subscriber places a telephone call, it takes a path across a communications channel that is established across a local loop to the CO switch. A _____ ____ is the pair of wires that are connected from the subscriber's telephone to the local CO. This building is also known as an _____. In the United States, these local service providers are sometimes referred to as Local Exchange Carriers (____). A Local Exchange is the local CO of an LEC.

Concept Table
(This table exercise can also be printed out from the Encore! CD that accompanies this textbook. Click Chapter 2, *click* Student Files, *and then click* Chap02contab.*)*
Read each statement carefully and choose the appropriate standards organization, forum, or council being described. Choose only one per statement.

STATEMENT	INTERNET STANDARDS ORGANIZATIONS	FORUMS AND COUNCILS	OFFICIAL STANDARDS ORGANIZATIONS
1. Protocol engineering and development arm of the Internet.			
2. An association of vendors, carriers, users, and consultants committed to the education, promotion, and implementation of frame relay.			
3. A leading authority in computer engineering, biomedical technology, and telecommunications.			
4. The first organization able to establish a spirit of cooperation between governments and the private sector.			
5. Creates focused research groups that study topics related to Internet protocols, applications, architecture, and technology.			
6. The primary organization for fostering the development of technology standards in the United States.			
7. An international, non-profit organization formed to expand and advance the use of ATM technology.			
8. Acts as a source of advice for technical, architectural, procedural, and policy matters pertaining to the Internet.			
9. The official U.S. representative to the International Organization for Standardization (ISO).			

Concept Picture
(This picture exercise can also be printed out from the Encore! CD that accompanies this textbook. Click Chapter 2, *click* Student Files, *and then click* Chap02conpic.*)*

Look at the diagram of data communications. Name the four elements of data communications. Write in the correct answer next to each label A, B, C, and D.

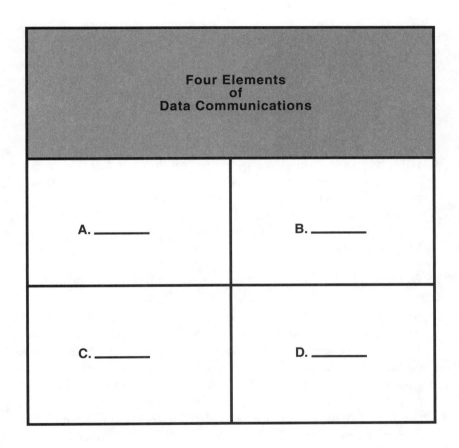

CASE STUDY

ROADSTER INC.

Read the following case study about Roadster Inc. Think about the challenge presented to the company, and the information solution provided. Then, either by yourself or in a group, answer the case study questions.

Objective:

Investigate Roadster Inc.'s telephone and data communications requirements and design a solution for providing better access to vital information.

Company Profile:

Roadster Inc. is a leading automotive manufacturer of passenger and commercial vehicles worldwide. With a global workforce of 329,000 employees, Roadster's manufacturing plants can produce 2,500 to 120,000 vehicles per year. The manufacturing plants and dealerships are located in 35 countries; 60% of vehicle sales occur in the domestic market with the remaining 40% occurring in the international market. Company headquarters is located in Detroit, Michigan.

Current Situation:

Recently, Roadster has become a major sponsor of the "Clean Air Initiative" that proposes to reduce air pollution in large metropolitan cities in the United States and overseas. Research and development efforts at Roadster are focused on evaluating the use of fuel cell technology to build environmentally efficient passenger and commercial vehicles for use worldwide. This initiative requires research and development to collaborate globally on the company's experiments and tests. Roadster currently has a global telecommunications network that has been pieced together using a number of half-circuits from overseas.

Business Information Requirements:

Roadster is concerned about how its products can be adapted to meet local conditions in emerging markets. The company has been trying to attract foreign investment overseas to support its fuel cell technology. Roadster needs to build reliable telecommunications links across continents to seek business opportunities. The company also wants to facilitate the free exchange of information and services among its employees worldwide. The long-term goal is to build a virtual marketplace for fuel cell technology.

Communication System Requirements:

Roadster currently has two international leased lines within Europe. The leased lines radiate out from two main offices in Frankfurt, Germany and Barcelona, Spain and terminate at national hubs across Europe. The hubs then connect to local offices in each country. Roadster is currently building manufacturing plants in Indonesia, China, and India. The plants will be operational within six months. IT management has been researching the best alternatives for carrier service to these locations. Additionally, Roadster is experiencing problems with its present carrier; recently a line was down for six hours in London and Roadster did not receive a credit on its bill until two months later. Within the past 60 days, Roadster has seen prices drop on leased lines about 30% and rumor has it they will drop again by 10% within 10 days. The company would like to find a single carrier with good performance and cost-effective rates for its locations in Europe, Indonesia, India, and China.

Manufacturing plant locations are shown in the following table:

LOCATION	NO. OF EMPLOYEES	PRODUCTION CAPACITY PER YEAR
Detroit, Michigan	5,000	120,000 vehicles
Frankfurt, Germany	1,750	65,000 vehicles
Barcelona, Spain	275	1,000 vehicles
Jakarta, Indonesia	965	3,250 vehicles
Beijing, China	4,000	100,000 vehicles
Bangalore, India	1,500	9,000 vehicles

Information System Solution:

1. Roadster Inc. decided to keep the current leased lines in Europe for Frankfurt and Barcelona. However, the company decided to purchase complete circuits.
2. Through investigation, Roadster found the European Telecommunication Technology (ETT) organization and learned it has agreements with 40 carriers around the globe. Roadster negotiated a single vendor contract with ETT that included lower prices, a help desk, and a single point of contact for resolving all service problems.
3. For the link back to Detroit, Michigan, Roadster contracted for ATM OC-3 service at 155 Mbps. for voice and data communications.
4. In China, Indonesia, and India, ETT found a carrier that handled ATM service to each location from the United States. ETT found it

was more cost effective to use a leased line within each country to interface to the POP in Jakarta, Beijing, and Bangalore.

5. Roadster also discovered that ETT could connect with an ISP in each site to offer Internet mail services.

Roadster Inc. saved considerable time and expense by contracting with ETT to establish the appropriate carrier service for each country. Roadster's IT manager reports that leased lines through ETT are 40% cheaper than the company's previous carrier. It has taken 60 days to change over the leased lines, and these were in place before the connections to Beijing, Bangalore, and Jakarta were established. Users are no longer experiencing any delay or latency in voice or data communications from any of the sites worldwide. The users feel it was worth switching carriers because they have not experienced any downtime.

With overall network performance operating well, the IT department members are pleased with the service level of the new carrier. In fact, they are expecting to increase Internet spending within the next 12 months as a result of their ATM connections overseas. They have been able to reduce the budget spending for the leased lines in Europe and that decrease has helped pay for the ATM service needed in the Asia/Pacific region.

Look at Figure 2.19 while you analyze this solution and answer the case study questions.

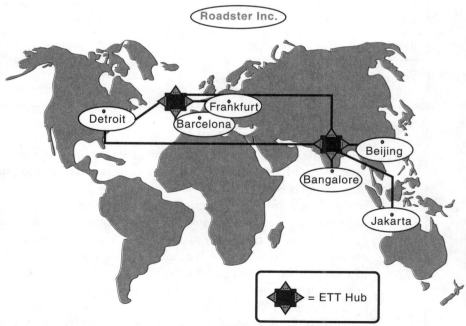

FIGURE 2.19 **Roadster Worldwide Telecommunication Links**

CASE STUDY QUESTIONS

1. Why did Roadster purchase all or part of its current leased lines as complete circuits from one operator?
2. Would it be more cost effective to use leased lines in Indonesia, India, and China?
3. Do you think it made sense to negotiate credits for outages as part of the SLA with the new carrier?
4. Which U.S.-based carriers have telephone and data services to Indonesia, India, and China?
5. Do you think Roadster should have considered ATM technology for voice and data services worldwide?

GROUP TERM PROJECT

WAN PROFILE

The WAN Profile found on the Encore! CD that accompanies this textbook (click *Chapter 2, Student Files, WANProfile*), is a form developed to provide a one-page summary of an organization's current telecommunications environment, and is designed to be used throughout the Group Term Project. The information required for each profile can be gathered from the F&D Engineering, Inc. case study from Chapter 1 (pp. 38–43). Remember that this information is based on what F&D has now, not what it wants in the future. It documents the current situation at the organization at this point in time.

The following is a description of the type of information required for each section of the profile:

- **User Profile.** An audit of the organization is required to determine how many users will be part of the project. List the number of users per department that are part of the project. It is useful also to include the type of users, for example, engineers, financial analysts, and so on.
- **Usage/Applications Profile**. Determine and list which applications F&D uses on a regular basis to accomplish its work.
- **Geographic Profile**. List the locations included in the project and the number of users at each site. Also, indicate what type of facility the company has. Describe the number of buildings and floors per building. Record the square footage for the Computer Room, the number of racks, and the number of electrical outlets.
- **Hardware Profile.** List all the hardware equipment per department. Categorize the equipment as PC, MAC, or UNIX workstations. List the brand, model of equipment, processor speed, amount of memory, total hard disk space, and current amount of hard disk space.

- **Special Requirements Profile**. Each project has requirements that are classified as special because they are unique to this project. For example, some cities require Teflon-coated cable in buildings. If a city inspector dictates this requirement, it must be met to implement the project. List any special needs required in the case study.

During your information-gathering efforts, you obtained the following information from the Human Resources and Facilities departments at corporate headquarters:

F&D Engineering has a large concentration of users and several departments located within its headquarters operation in Washington D.C. that are not in the other locations. These departments are Public Relations, Purchasing, Legal, Economic Development, Labor Relations, Real Estate Planning, and Risk Management. All users in these departments are included in the 5,000 users to be migrated over to the new mail program. The number of employees per department has changed recently due to turnover, so Human Resources does not have an accurate number per department. You need to estimate how many people are currently in each department.

The departments common to all locations are listed in the following table with the number of employees at each location.

Cities	Accounting Payroll	HR	Facilities Mgmt.	Engineering	QA	Sales Mktg.	Shipping Receiving	Executive
Washington	20	12	6	300	25	10	3	6
San Francisco	5	4	3	20	4	5	2	2
Houston	6	5	4	25	5	6	2	3
London	5	4	3	25	5	5	2	2
Frankfurt	6	5	4	200	10	6	2	3
Sydney	6	5	4	200	10	6	2	2
Rio De Janeiro	4	2	2	25	2	4	2	1
Madras	4	5	8	300	20	2	2	4

In addition, two IT system engineers are at each location, except at corporate headquarters where 25 system engineers are split between Telecom, LAN, and WAN. A number of employees in the locations are doing general planning and administrative activities. You must determine how many of each you have at each location.

F&D Engineering purchased new workstations for all employees two years ago. PC desktops have 128 MB RAM, 20 GB hard drives, Pentium III 500 MHz processors, and Windows 2000 Professional operating systems. Apple Macintosh G4 users have 256 MB RAM, 20 GB hard drives, a 400 MHz processor, and version 9.0 of the Mac operating system. R&D also purchased SUN workstations last year for the engineers. These SUN workstations have 128 MB RAM, 20 GB hard drives, and a 400 MHz processor.

Return to Chapter 1 and read the case study to find the other information required for each profile. Each group then should complete one WAN Profile and turn it in at the end of the class period.

WAN PROFILE
F&D ENGINEERING, INC.

GROUP MEMBERS:		DATE:	
GROUP #:			
PROFILES			
I. User Profile			
II. Usage/Applications Profile			

III. Geographic Profile

IV. Hardware Profile

V. Special Requirements Profile

CHAPTER TERMS

access   58
access box   48
access tandem   50
analog switch   55
ANSI   71
ATM Forum   70
availability   62
CAP   65
carrier   62
carrier system   63
channel   48
circuit   51
circuit switch   51
CLEC   65
CO   48
control signal   60
DCE   58
digitized   51
DSL Forum   70
DTE   58
EIA   72
error rate   62
exchange   50
FCC   67
forum   69
Frame Relay Forum   70
handshaking   59
IAB   68
IEEE   72
IETF   69
ILEC   65
interface   47
IRTF   69
ISO   72
ISOC   68
ISP   66
ITC   65
ITU   72
IXC   65
jack   48
LATA   50

latency   62
LEC   50
local loop   50
National ISDN Council   70
NID   66
NSIF   70
packet   57
packet switch   56
PBX   55
PIC   53
plug   48
POP   50
POTS   47
PSTN   47
ring   62
RJ-11   48
service provider   47
SLA   62
splitter   49
standards   67
STP   54
subscriber   50
tariff   62
telco   47
Telemanagement Forum   71
throughput   62
time slot   51
tip   62
trunk   51
unbundled access   47
UNE   65

CHAPTER BIBLIOGRAPHY

Book, Magazine, Presentation Citations

Chase, Maureen and Trupp, Sandy. *Office Emails That Really Click*. Rhode Island: Aegis Publishing Group, Ltd., 2000: 186-187.

Infotron Systems. *How does your network grow?* New Jersey: Infotron Systems Incorporated, 1984: (1.7), (3.1, 3.3), (5.2-5.8), (6.19).

Langhoff, June. *Telcom Made Easy*. Rhode Island: Aegis Publishing Group, Ltd., 2000: 41, 43, 51, and 54.

Parnell, Tere. *LAN TIMES Guide to Wide Area Networks*. Berkeley: Osborne/McGraw-Hill, 2001: 60-67.

PC Magazine, "Email Software Review," (23 April 1995).

Sheldon, Tom. *Encyclopedia of Networking & Telecommunications*. New York: Osborne/McGraw-Hill, 2001: 184, 736, 610, and 1134.

Spohn, Darren. *Data Network Design*. New York: McGraw-Hill, Inc., 1993: 66-80.

Web Citations

ANSI, "About ANSI," American Standards Institute, <www.ansi.org> (2002).

ATM Forum, "The Foundation for Broadband Networking," <www.atmforum.com> (2001).

Bell Labs, "The idea of digital circuit switching," <www.bell-labs.com/technology/network/circuitidea.html> (2001).

Bell Labs, "The idea of digital packet switching," <www.bell-labs.com/technology/network/packetidea.html> (2001).

Bradner, S., "The Internet Standards Process – Revision 3," <www.ietf.org/rfc/rfc2026.rtf> (October 1996).

Cognigen, "Best Rate Calculators," <www.ld.net/calculator> (2002).

Daimler Chrysler, "Company at a Glance,"<www.daimlerchrysler.com/company/company_e.htm> (2002).

DSL Forum, "DSL more than just a phone line...it's a global solution," <www.dslforum.org> (2002).

EIA, "About EIA," Electronics Industry Alliance, <www.eia.org> (2002).

FCC, "Bureaus of the Federal Communications Commission," <www.fcc.gov> (21 May 2002).

Frame Relay Forum, "Welcome to the Frame Relay Forum," <www.frforum.com> (2002).

Greenfield, David, "Global Carrier Survey: New Names, Same Games," Network Magazine, <www.networkmagazine.com> (5 January 2001).

Greenfield, David, "Strategies and Issues: North American Carrier Survey: Tough Enough," Network Magazine, <www.networkmagazine.com> (3 August 2001).

IAB, "IAB Overview," <www.iab.org/iab/overview.html> (May 2002).

IEC, "Fundamentals of Telecommunications," International Engineering Consortium, <www.iec.org/tutorials/fund_telecom/topic02.html> (2001).

IEEE, "About IEEE," Institute of Electrical and Electronic Engineers <www.ieee.org/portal/index.jsp> (2002).

IETF, "Overview of the IETF," <www.ietf.org> (May 2002).

IFLA, "Section A – Public Switched Telephone Network and Integrated Digital Services Network Configurations," International Federation of Library Associations and Institutions, <www.ifla.org/documents/infopol/canada/tsacc1a.pdf> (1999).

ISO, "About ISO," International Organization for Standardization, <www.iso.ch/iso/en/ISOOnline.openerpage> (2002).

IRTF, "IRTF Overview," <www.irtf.org> (May 2002).

ISOC, "Welcome to the Internet Society," <www.isoc.org> (20 May 2002).

ITU, "About Us," International Telecommunications Union, <www.itu.int/home/index.html> (2002).

Krechmaer, Ken, "Technical Standards: Foundations of the Future," <www.csrstds.com/cubit.html> (9 March 1996).

Krechmaer, Ken, "Recommendations for the Global Information Highway: A Matter of Standards" <www.csrstds.com/gih.html> (9 March 1996).

Merit, "Introduction to Internet Networking," <supportnet.merit.edu/m-intint/t-wantec/text/pubswi.html> (8 May 2002).

National ISDN Council, "Welcome to NIC (National ISDN Council)," <www.nationalisdncouncil.com/index.html> (2002).

NSIF, "Network and Services Integration Forum," <www.atis.org/atis/sif/sifhom.htm> (2002).

O'Reilly, "Tip and Ring," <www.oreilly.com/reference/dictionary/trms/T/Tip_and_Ring.htm> (21 May 2000).

PTC, "Building Strong Partnerships," Pacific Telecommunications Council, <www.ptc.org> (2002).

Tech Target, "What is" <whatis.techtarget.com> (8 May 2002).

Telemanagement Forum, "Our Organization," <www.tmforum.org> (2002).

CHAPTER 3

NETWORK DESIGN: NETWORKS, CABLING, AND INTERNETWORKING DEVICES

By the end of this chapter, you should understand these concepts:

- Different types of networks
- Physical topologies available to build backbone structures for WANs
- Various types of cabling and interfaces used for data and voice communications
- Bell and V standards defined for data transmission
- Data compression, error correction, and encryption standards for modems
- Basic network designs using internetworking devices such as repeaters, bridges, switches, gateways, and routers
- Different types of routers used in network design and how their functions affect their use
- Routing algorithms and how they help determine the best path and the least cost
- Multiprotocol Label Switching (MPLS) and how it is used to divert and re-route ISP traffic

TYPES OF NETWORKS

Networks can be configured in many ways. They can extend across a large geographical area or between adjacent buildings within an organization. Networks are divided into three groups: Local Area Networks (LANs), Metropolitan Area Networks (MANs), and Wide Area Networks (WANs). In the past, the key to distinguishing between each type of network has always been the physical distance it spanned. With today's advances in technology, however, distance is no longer the only difference between network types.

Local Area Networks (LANs)

LANs, introduced in Chapter 1, are limited to a relatively small area. In the 1970s, LANs were usually confined to a single building. They were considered local because the physical distance they could reach was limited by the electrical characteristics of the cable used to connect them. Many LANs were designed to allow multiple computers within a department to share the same cable and communication system. By the 1980s, LANs had expanded to include multiple buildings, such as within a campus setting, where the network devices are only a few thousand feet from each other. Today's LANs can be interconnected via WANs and thus span many miles. [Sheldon, 722-724]

Most LANs connect workstations and printers together to allow the organization to share data. The layout of a LAN is called its **topology**. LANs can be arranged in a bus, ring, or star topology. In Figure 3.1, the LAN is constructed in a star configuration with each workstation connecting to one port on the central device called a hub. Using this topology, packets are transmitted through the hub between workstations. [Webopedia, 1]

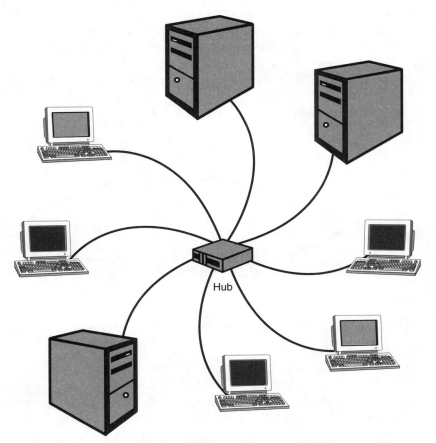

Hub

FIGURE 3.1 **LAN Star Topology [Source: Palmer & Sinclair, 20]**

In contrast to other networks, LANs are privately owned, managed, and controlled by a single organization. LANs are distinct communication systems that contain their own broadcasting and addressing schemes. [Sheldon, 724] LANs also can be connected to other LANs via communications lines and radio waves.

Metropolitan Area Networks (MANs)

A **MAN** connects users over a high-speed network that can span a metropolitan area or an entire city. A MAN is a data communications network that covers an area larger than a LAN and smaller than a WAN. MANs are limited to four locations within a LATA (Local-Access and Transport Area). Typically, fiber-optic cabling is used to connect LANs together within a city. They are used to share networking resources and to support the transfer of data between users within the MAN at a distance of up to 100 miles. The MAN, its communication links, and equipment are owned and operated by a service provider.

Most MANs are constructed in a ring topology. They can be constructed using SMDS (Switch Multimegabit Data Service) or SONET (Synchronous Optical Network) rings that carry ATM (Asynchronous Transfer Mode) traffic. MANs provide new opportunities for research and teaching. For example, in London, England, a MAN connects the Universities of Bath and Bristol with the West of England Universities. When MAN technology was adopted, students, faculty, and researchers gained a fast digital service for e-mail, data, and image sharing within the area (see Figure 3.2).

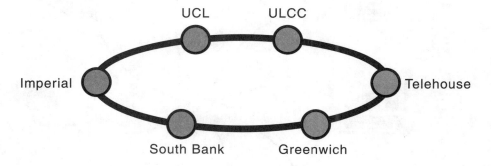

FIGURE 3.2 London Metropolitan Area Network [Source: Lonman, 1]

MANs also can be created using wireless broadband. A piloted, FAA-certified **High Altitude Long Operation** (**HALO**) aircraft provides the hub of this type of network. The aircraft operates at altitudes above 52,000 feet. It flies higher than commercial airline traffic, yet is still 10 to 1,000 times closer to the user than a satellite would be. This allows subscribers within a MAN to exchange video, high-resolution images, and large data files through wireless, broadband, and line-of-sight connections. In Figure 3.3, a dedicated HALO gateway is used to connect to the PSTN (Public Switched Telephone Network) and an ISP to provide access to other networks and the Internet. Users can have connection speeds of 5-, 12.5-, or 25 Mbps. The HALO network remains accessible to customers regardless of obstructions such as foliage, buildings, or local terrain. [Angel, 1]

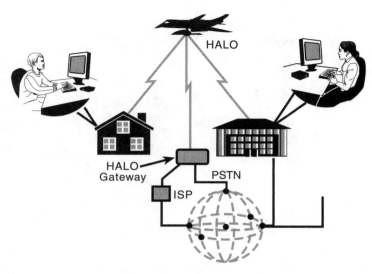

FIGURE 3.3 HALO Super MAN [Angel, 1]

Wide Area Networks (WANs)

As you know, a WAN is a voice, data, or video network that spans a large geographic area. It establishes point-to-point connections between locations using communications circuits from a telco. In the past, most WANs were constructed using dedicated leased lines from telcos. Today, many WAN designers have contracted for virtual circuits through public packet networks in which all of the equipment and lines are owned and managed by a telco.

The service provider exchanges a certain volume of data or voice traffic over the WAN at a QoS (Quality of Service) specified by the customer. Organizations can contract for transmission rates of 2-, 34-, 45-, 155-, or 625 Mbps. However, the type of connectivity offered by the service provider, the transit delay, and the transmission rate may differ depending on the location because the topology of WANs is more complex than that of LANs or MANs.

The typical WAN is usually constructed in a mesh topology with a point-to-point connection between all locations. This provides for more than one link into major locations for redundancy. Figure 3.4 shows that location B has a connection to A, C, E, and F. This means multiple sites have a connection to location B. Location B is serving as an intermediate link between A and C.

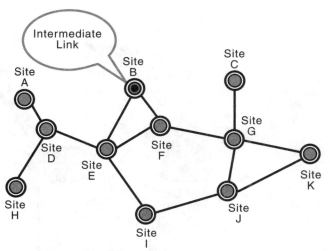

FIGURE 3.4 Mesh WAN [Source: Fairhurst, 1]

A WAN can be designed to combine voice and data networks forming a MultiService WAN. This network can be used to interconnect PBXs (private branch exchanges) for use with IP telephony over a leased line, Frame Relay, or ATM network infrastructure. WAN links make effective use of network bandwidth by integrating IP-based voice and video applications across an organization. In the example shown in Figure 3.5, voice, video, and data traffic have all been routed over the PSTN. The routers at each location have been enabled to migrate voice traffic from the PBXs to on-net voice traffic over the existing WAN infrastructure. (You will learn more about routers later in this chapter.)

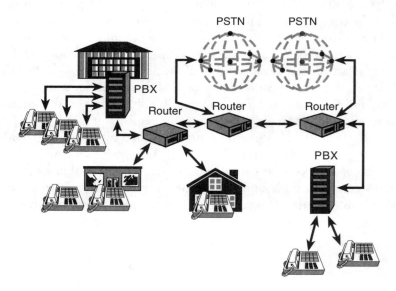

FIGURE 3.5 Voice-Enabled WAN [Cisco, 1]

WANs also can be constructed without point-to-point dedicated leased lines by using Frame Relay, which provides for links between multiple remote sites across a single physical connection. For example, in Figure 3.6, a retail store, a remote branch office, and headquarters have all been connected using Frame Relay. Virtual circuits are established through the PSTN switch to provide pathways between locations.

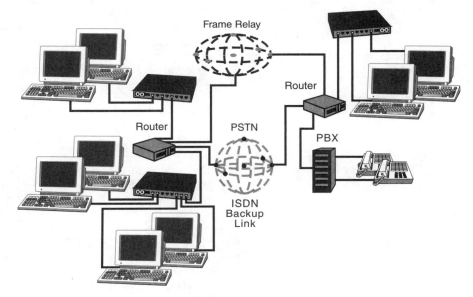

FIGURE 3.6 **Frame Relay WAN [Cisco, 1]**

Shared access can be provided for all types of networks. Figure 3.7 shows how LANs can be interconnected into MANs. The MANs can then be linked to the WAN.

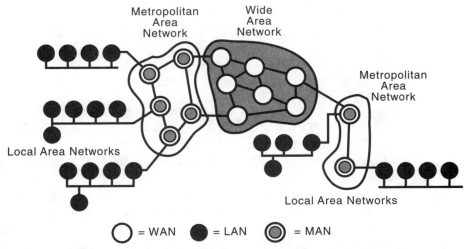

FIGURE 3.7 **Connecting LANs, MANs, and WANs [Source: Fairhurst, 1]**

Table 3.1 shows the similarities and differences among the types of networks. Topologies, cabling, and media are similar but distance and geographic area differ.

CHARACTERISTICS	LAN	MAN	WAN
Geographic Area	Same floor, building, or nearby buildings	Within a city	Within country or between countries
Distance	1/2- to 2-mile range	20-30 miles	Unlimited miles
Type of Media	Primarily data	Voice, data, image, and video	Voice, data, image, and video
Data Transfer Rate	10-, 16-, 100 Mbps	34-, 130-, 155-, 622- Mbps	56-, 64-, 128-, 256-, 384-, 768-, 1.54-, 155-, 622 Mbps
Topology	Ring, Bus, Star, Hybrid	Ring, SONET	Peer-to-Peer, Ring, Star, Tier
Cabling	Twisted pair, coaxial, and fiber optic	Twisted pair and fiber optic	Fiber optic used for leased lines, T1, Frame Relay, and ATM/SONET

TABLE 3.1 **Comparison of LAN, MAN, and WAN Networks**

TOPIC review Types of Networks

1. What is the key difference between each type of network (LAN, MAN, and WAN)?
2. Which type of network is privately owned, managed, and controlled by an organization?
3. You are a network designer who has a consulting agreement to design the network for the next Olympics. What type of network would be most appropriate?
4. What types of connections are used with the HALO super-MAN?
5. Why is the topology of WANs more complex than that of LANs or MANs?

Chapter 3 • Network Design: Networks, Cabling, and Internetworking Devices

BACKBONE STRUCTURES FOR WAN DESIGN

WAN **backbones** are high-speed network structures that connect several locations. The connections between backbone locations can be physical or logical. Physical topology refers to the physical layout of a WAN to the logical topology, which includes establishing pathways or virtual circuits through a packet switch. WAN topology design is usually a trade-off between cost and fault-tolerance. The five basic WAN topologies are [Sheldon, 1332]

- Peer-to-peer
- Ring
- Star
- Mesh
- Tiered

Peer-to-Peer WAN Topology

The simplest WAN topology to implement is the classic leased-line configuration. A **peer-to-peer topology** features a single interconnection for each location. The dedicated circuits are leased from a service provider. The circuit speeds vary, but a continuous connection is assured.

In Figure 3.8, dedicated circuits connect Sites A, B, C, and D. However, no interconnection exists between Sites B and D. Therefore, a user at Site D who wants to send an e-mail to a user at Site B first must send through Sites C and A.

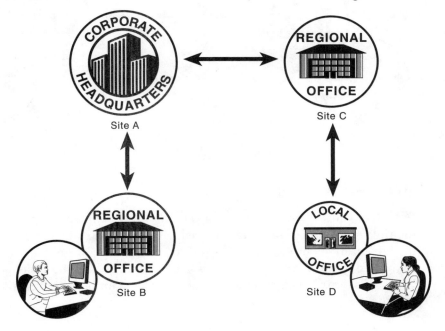

FIGURE 3.8 Peer-to-Peer WAN [Source: Dean, 193]

Ring WAN Topology

Many WANs are constructed with fiber in a ring architecture. **Ring topologies** are simple to implement and have become increasingly popular because they offer an alternative route when other links within the network are down. Ring topologies are built with dedicated circuits and constructed in such a way that each location is connected to two other locations. The physical layout of the WAN forms a complete ring. In Figure 3.9, dedicated links connect all sites A–D together. A direct circuit runs from Site D to Site B to complete the ring. If the link from A to B is down, B can still access A by going through Sites D and C.

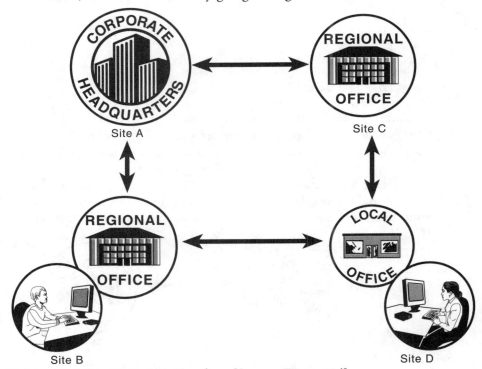

FIGURE 3.9 **WAN Ring Topology [Source: Dean, 194]**

Star WAN Topology

WANs are most often designed in a **star topology**. This layout provides for multiple LANs to be connected through a central site. In Figure 3.10, Site A is the organization's headquarters. Dedicated point-to-point links are in place from headquarters (Site A) to locations B, C, and D. The star topology works in organizations in which the information flows from branch offices to headquarters.

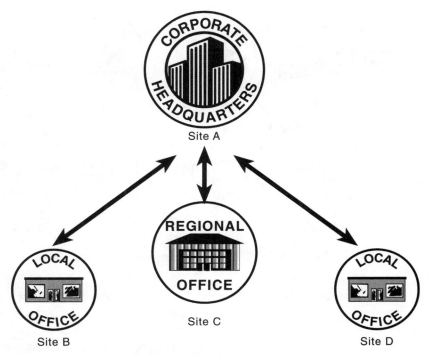

Site A

Site C

Site B

Site D

FIGURE 3.10 **Star WAN Topology [Source: Dean, 195]**

Mesh WAN Topology

With **mesh topology**, several interconnected locations are built in the form of a complex mesh. In these networks, routers are interconnected with other routers so at least two pathways are connecting each location to the others. Figure 3.11 shows a fully meshed WAN topology in which links are established with point-to-point connections between all sites. Even a partial mesh topology has connections to most sites. In Figure 3.11, the only connection missing is between Sites C and D.

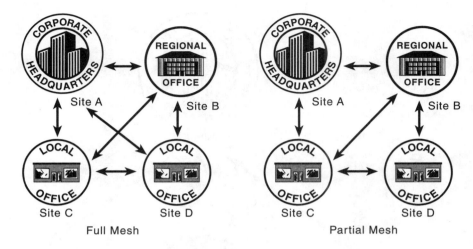

FIGURE 3.11 **Mesh WAN Topology [Source: Dean, 196]**

Companies today are implementing meshed networks so they can run distributed applications over a WAN. A mesh network is appropriate for this because it eliminates the need to route data through a central location. Other companies are using mesh WAN topology for real-time applications such as voice.

Meshed topologies offer organizations the opportunity to build truly responsive networks. On the other hand, implementing a completely meshed network is very expensive.

Tiered WAN Topology

In a **tiered topology**, locations are connected in star or ring formation at different levels. The interconnection points are organized into four layers. This topology is also referred to as the spoke and wheel design. As shown in Figure 3.12, regional centers are set up with high-speed links back to corporate headquarters. Remote branch offices are connected to a regional center, rather than with direct point-to-point connections to corporate. Lower speed links that are less costly can be used for the branch offices (Sites D, E, F, G, H, and I).

Chapter 3 • Network Design: Networks, Cabling, and Internetworking Devices

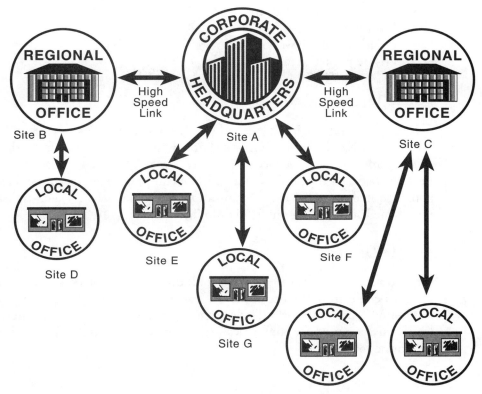

FIGURE 3.12 Tiered Mesh Topology [Source: Dean, 197]

TOPIC review **Backbone Structures for WAN Design**

1. What is the simplest WAN topology to implement?
2. Why have ring topologies for WANs become so popular?
3. What type of information flow is common within an organization that uses a star WAN topology?
4. Why is a mesh WAN the best method to use for distributed applications?
5. What is the benefit of setting up regional sites for a tiered WAN topology?

PUBLIC VERSUS PRIVATE CARRIER SERVICES

A network designer's goal is to determine the least-costly solution to providing an end-to-end path between two sites, networks, or stations. The network designer can choose between the following four basic methods used by carriers for connecting networks with a WAN link:

- Public telephone dial-up
- Private leased lines
- Public packet networks
- Private packet networks

Public Telephone Dial-Up

Telephone dial-up charges are based on time and distance; consequently, organizations that require infrequent and short distance transmission favor the use of this system. If sessions between the devices on a WAN are kept short and connections between the DTEs (data terminal equipment) are local, the dial-up approach makes good sense. Organizations with relatively low data-transfer rates benefit from using public dial-up lines.

Private Leased Lines

Organizations that need to establish multidrop connections on private channels usually benefit from the use of private leased lines. Multidropping a private leased line allows for more effective sharing of the channel between sites. Private leased lines are used for companies with heavy, constant traffic in which delays cannot be tolerated.

Public Packet Networks

Organizations that are spread out over a large geographic area usually find subscribing to a public packet network the most cost effective approach for establishing a WAN. If the data traffic volume is low or moderate, the use of a public packet carrier becomes an attractive solution because charges are based only on volume of traffic and not on the distance between the sites using the network.

Private Packet Networks

When the organization has mission-critical data to be transferred across a large geographic area, it will often use a private packet network to attain greater reliability and better security. Private packet networks can be used for medium- and high-traffic volumes and are more cost effective than dedicated private lines.

Design Considerations

Many network design solutions require a hybrid of both dedicated and switched technologies. The design process needs to include the costs, constraints, and performance requirements of the organization.

Before network designers can determine which method is best to use for the WAN link, they must also examine three main limitations that apply to WAN design: latency, congestion, and throughput.

Recall from Chapter 2 that latency is the amount of time that packets or frames are delayed because of congestion. Congestion occurs when there are too many transmissions over the network. Throughput is a guaranteed data speed measured in bits per second. If latency is excessive or throughput is too slow, the WAN cannot meet the needs of the organization or the user community. After all, communication devices should be able to reach each other over the WAN with some degree of dependability.

TOPIC review — Public versus Private Carrier Services

1. What type of traffic is appropriate for public telephone dial-up connections?
2. Why would an organization decide to use private leased lines?
3. If an organization is spread out over a large geographic area, what type of network is most cost effective?
4. What are the three main limitations applied to WAN design?
5. How does congestion occur on WAN links?

CABLING

Within a building, cables are installed on each floor and wired back to a central place to connect to internetworking equipment. Often the cabling is placed in the ceiling in the space called the **plenum.** This is the same area also used for air circulation in heating and air conditioning systems. This plenum space is used for both telephone and computer cabling. Cabling extends from the plenum area down into telco closets on each floor. From there, it extends to telecommunications equipment housed in separate equipment rooms.

Telco Closets and Equipment Rooms

All telecommunications wiring is channeled through a **telecommunications** or **telco closet (TC)**. Figure 3.13 shows an example TC, which is a closet or room that houses all of the equipment associated with telecom links. The TC contains all WAN and LAN backbone wiring and horizontal wiring for a building. The Customer Premises Equipment (CPE) is contained in a rack inside the TC. TCs have climate control, lighting, and power supplies to protect the equipment and wiring. [Black Box, 4] [Webopedia, 1]

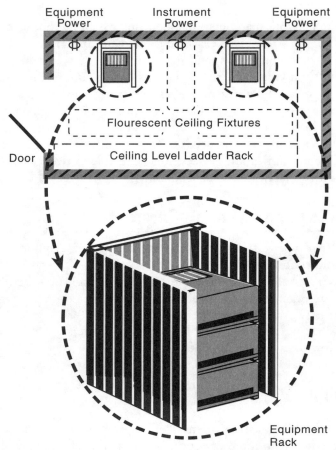

Equipment Power   Instrument Power   Equipment Power

Flourescent Ceiling Fixtures

Ceiling Level Ladder Rack

Door

Equipment Rack

FIGURE 3.13 **Telecommunications Closet (TC) [Source: Black Box, 1307]**

The equipment room is used to house all the telecommunications systems. All the mechanical terminations of a premise wiring system are centralized in this room. **Premise wiring** is a uniform, structured wiring system designed to support multivendor products and environments. It includes telecommunication wiring for telephone and computer outlets in a building. Premise wiring is also used for backbone wiring to connect LAN equipment and WAN equipment between buildings. The equipment room is usually separate from the telecommunications closet because of the complexity of the equipment. Most equipment rooms have PBXs, switches, gateways, and routers installed to establish connection between the LAN and the WAN.

Cabling Standards

A building can be cabled for all its communication needs using common media, connectors, and topology. Cabling currently follows one of three main standards:

- **EIA/TIA 568A**. American standard for structured cabling systems.
- **ISO/IEC 11801**. International standard for structured cabling systems.
- **CENELEC EN 50173**. European standard for structured cabling systems.

These standards govern the performance criteria of the components of a cabling system. [Data Cottage, 2]

Types of Wire Cabling

Cabling provides the communication wire used to connect equipment in a network. An electrical signal carries information from one computer to another on the network over this wiring. As it travels toward its destination, part of the signal is absorbed by the cable. Cables provide physical paths for carrying information between sender and receiver. Several types of cabling are used in LANs, MANs, and WANs today.

As early as 1985, network-cabling designers were striving to develop a single topology, media, and connector for use by all networks. Their goal was to define a generic telecommunications wiring system for commercial buildings. By 1990, a system was developed by the IEEE (Institute of Electrical and Electronics Engineers) called **Ethernet 10BaseT** that supported multiproduct and multivendor equipment. The main advantage of this cabling was that it was inexpensive and easy to install. Today, many types of Ethernet twisted-pair cabling exist and each is assigned a category (CAT). The category defines the design and specification of each cable type.

Twisted Pair

The **twisted-pair** wiring used for telephone systems is connected from the telephone switch to your wall jack where you plug in your phone. It consists of two independent copper wires twisted around one another. Twists occur several times per inch to reduce interference. Copper wire is used for twisted-pair cabling. Sending electrical current through the wires transmits information.

Twisted pair is also used for local area connections within an office. Twisted-pair cable is available for LANs as **unshielded** (**UTP**) or **shielded** (**STP**) cable. STP cables are more expensive than UTP cables but the shielding provides insulation to protect signals from interference.

A twisted-pair cable contains eight wires (four pairs). As Figure 3.14 shows, twisted-pair cable is composed of wire pairs, an insulator, a copper conductor, and a jacket.

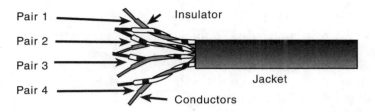

FIGURE 3.14 **Twisted-Pair Cable [Source: Black Box, 252]**

The frequent cabling standard for Ethernet is **10BaseT**. The maximum throughput is 10 Mbps, which is represented as the number "10". "Base" indicates it uses a baseband transmission method. The "T" designates twisted pair. 10BaseT uses two wires at 10 MHz and has a maximum distance limitation of 100 meters. Most organizations have replaced their 10BaseT cable to gain higher throughput rates in the range of 100 Mbps.

As LANs grew larger, the 10 Mbps throughput rate created bottlenecks. The 100BaseT standard was developed to improve response time; it uses baseband transmission and enables LANs to transmit data at 100 Mbps. From this improvement, two standards have emerged: **100BaseTX** and **100BaseT4**. Both use four wires at 100 MHz; however, they differ in the method they use to reach 100 Mbps. For 100BaseTX, the method condenses the time between digital pulses. The 100BaseT4 standard breaks the 100 Mbps data stream into three streams of 33 Mbps each. It uses three pairs of wires to transmit the three data streams. LAN experts prefer 100BaseTX because it can double the bandwidth to 200 Mbps. [Dean, 138-140]

Figure 3.15 shows the color codes for the pairs. The colors of the wires indicate the pair number. Pairs 2 and 3 are used for 100BaseTX and pairs 1, 2, 3, and 4 are used for 100BaseT4.

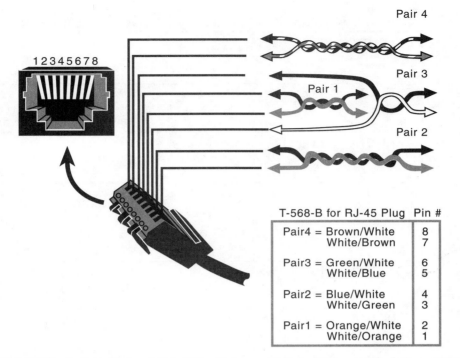

FIGURE 3.15 **Twisted-Pair Wire Colors and Pairs [Source: Black Box, 1323]**

T-568-B for RJ-45 Plug	Pin #
Pair4 = Brown/White	8
White/Brown	7
Pair3 = Green/White	6
White/Blue	5
Pair2 = Blue/White	4
White/Green	3
Pair1 = Orange/White	2
White/Orange	1

Twisted-pair cabling uses a different number of wires based on defined specifications. A specification details how the cable is to be constructed, its distance limitations, and how signals are transmitted over the media. These specifications are each published as a TIA/EIA standard. Several cabling options are available for voice, LANs, and computers. In 1991, the Electronic Industries Alliance (EIA) and **Telecommunications Industry Association (TIA)** defined specifications for twisted pair. Categories (CAT) of UTP cable were also published in Technical Systems bulletin (TSB-36). They established data rates for twisted-pair cable at 20 MHz (**CAT4**) and 100 MHz (**CAT5**) (see Table 3.2).

TYPE	FORM	NO. OF WIRES	FREQUENCY	BANDWIDTH	USAGE
CAT1	UTP	2 wire pairs	___	128 Kbps	Voice communications, not data
CAT2	UTP	4 wire pairs	1.5 MHz	4 Mbps	Too slow for today's networks
CAT3	UTP	4 wire pairs	16 MHz	10 Mbps Ethernet	Data communication to and from desktops
CAT4	UTP	4 wire pairs	20 MHz	10 Mbps Ethernet	Provides greater protection from crosstalk and attenuation
CAT5	UTP	4 wire pairs	100 MHz	100 Mbps Ethernet	Used with Fast Ethernet networks
CAT5E	UTP	4 wire pairs	400 MHz	100/1000 Mbps	Uses higher quality copper, high-twist ratio, and reduces crosstalk
CAT6	STP	4 wire pairs	550 MHz	1/10 Gbps	Foil insulation surrounds copper for shielding against crosstalk and noise
CAT7	STP	Multiple wire pairs	600 MHz	622 Mbps – 2.4 Gbps	Each wire pair surrounded by its own shielding

TABLE 3.2 **Categories of Twisted-Pair Cable [Source: Dean, 136-137]**

Standards have not yet been ratified for **CAT6** or **CAT7**. The transmission frequency reaches 200 MHz with CAT6. Although CAT7 is proposed at 600 MHz using shielded cable, this cabling would require larger connectors than the standard RJ45 used today. Until all network equipment can be manufactured with these larger ports, the network designer must "cycle down" from 600 MHz to 100 MHz (CAT5) to make the connection to the hub or switch.

The newer standards go beyond CAT5 to use the **NEXT (Near-End Crosstalk)** specification. Figure 3.16 illustrates that this specification shows signal interference from one wire pair that adversely affects another wire pair. Some cable manufacturers have begun marketing **PS-NEXT (Power-Sum NEXT)**, which requires a more rigorous crosstalk measurement between all adjacent pairs. PS-NEXT is the official TIA standard for backbone cables with more than four pairs. In terms of performance, PS-NEXT is now the cable of choice for ATM and gigabit networks.

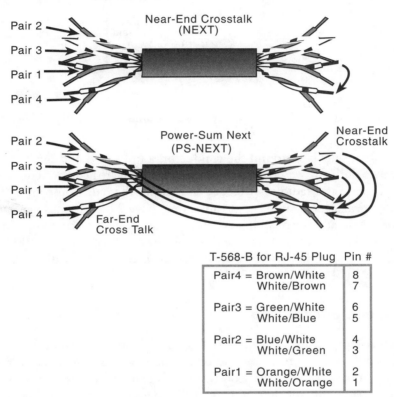

T-568-B for RJ-45 Plug	Pin #
Pair4 = Brown/White	8
White/Brown	7
Pair3 = Green/White	6
White/Blue	5
Pair2 = Blue/White	4
White/Green	3
Pair1 = Orange/White	2
White/Orange	1

FIGURE 3.16 **Near-End Crosstalk [Source: Black Box, 1303]**

Coaxial Cabling

Coaxial cabling (coax) is the primary type used by the cable television industry. Coaxial cable is now also used for multimedia and streaming video transmissions. Web TV services can provide an Internet connection into your home. Coaxial cable is more expensive to implement than standard twisted-pair cable; however, significantly more data can be carried over this medium.

A **coaxial cable** consists of a center wire surrounded by insulation and a shield of braided wire that is grounded. The shield minimizes electrical and radio frequency interference. Coax has two electrical conductors that run along a single axis. The cable components are conductor wire, dielectric, foil shield, braided shield, and jacket. As shown in Figure 3.17, the cable is shaped like a cylinder with concentric layers. [Black Box, 282]

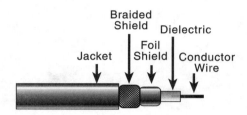

FIGURE 3.17 **Elements of Coaxial Cable [Source: Black Box, 282]**

Two shields surround the conductor: a foil shield and the braided shield made out of woven copper. These shields protect the conductor from electromagnetic and radio interference and reduce the radiation coming from interior electrical signals. Some coax cables even have 24-karat gold plating to ensure better signal transmission and prevent corrosion. The coax used for cable TV is **RG-59U**, which is constructed using a stranded wire with a 100% braided shield (22 AWG). Millions of homes are already wired with coaxial cable for cable TV. [Black Box, 282, 305]

Fiber-Optic Cabling

Fiber-optic cable is favored for high-speed data communications. It serves as the network backbone for telecommunications because it can transmit large amounts of data simultaneously. Fiber is constructed using a glass core, which is a better conductor than copper to eliminate problems inherent in twisted pair, such as NEXT, electromagnetic interference, and security breaches. The speed of transferring data via fiber-optic cable has been doubling every six months. At the same time, the cost of acquiring fiber-optic bandwidth has been dropping by 50% every nine months. As service providers prepare for the future demands of home and office users, their plan is to offer high-speed access from anywhere at any time. Recently, service providers have laid multiple fiber-optic data lines across the United States and have built several SONET rings around large population areas to accommodate more bandwidth for the expected demand. [Plunkett, 8]

Using fiber-optic cable has several advantages, as shown in Table 3.3.

INCREASED BANDWIDTH
Fiber-optic cable has greater capacity for carrying large amounts of information and has greater reliability than copper wire. When used for Wave Division Multiplexing (WDM), more than 2 million telephone conversations can be simultaneously transmitted over a single fiber.
LOW ATTENUATION
Very little signal loss occurs with signals made of light. Data can move at higher speeds and across greater distances.
SECURITY
The signal is not radiated with fiber and is extremely difficult to tap. If tapped, light leaking from the cable causes the entire system to fail, which immediately alerts the personnel who manage the system.
IMMUNITY
The glass acts as an insulator that prevents electric current from flowing through. This makes fiber optics completely immune to interference.
DESIGN
Fiber is slightly more than $1/2$ inch (1.3 cm) in diameter, extremely light, and easy to work with. An armored cable with 12 pairs of fiber can carry 380,000 telephone channels.

TABLE 3.3 **Characteristics of Fiber-Optic Cable**

Reflection and refraction play key roles in fiber optics. **Refraction** is the bending of light and occurs as the light passes through the fiber-optic cable. When the glass core is coated with plastic, it acts as a mirror creating a phenomenon known as total internal reflection. This causes the light to bounce at shallow angles and remain completely within the fiber. The fiber core is as thin as a piece of human hair. When you have a telephone conversation over fiber-optic cable, the signals must be translated from analog to digital. At one end of the fiber cable, a laser switches on and off to send each bit. The laser can turn itself on and off several billions of times per second. Today, multiple lasers of different colors can be used to send multiple signals through the same fiber. [Cassidy, 6] [Brain, 1-2]

Fiber cable can now be manufactured from plastic or glass **silica**. The fibers used in long-distance telecommunications applications are always glass because it has a lower optical absorption rate than plastic. The light used in fiber-optic cable is typically infrared light. [Wikipedia, 1]

As shown in Figure 3.18, fiber is composed of a core, cladding, coating, strengthening fibers, and a cable jacket. The **core** is a single continuous strand of glass or plastic that is measured in microns by the size of its outer diameter. The larger the core, the more light the cable can carry. The **cladding** is a thin layer surrounding the fiber core that serves as a boundary that contains the light waves and causes the refraction necessary to enable data to travel through the length of the cable. The **coating** is a layer of plastic that surrounds the core and cladding to reinforce the fiber core, helps absorb shocks, and prevents excessive cable bends. **Strengthening fibers** can be made of a substance called Kevlar, wire strands, or gel-filled sleeves. They protect against crushing forces and excessive tension during installation. The cable jacket is the outer layer of the cable, and is most often orange (it also can be black or yellow). [Black Box, 272]

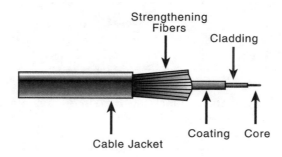

FIGURE 3.18 Fiber Cable Components [Source: Black Box, 272]

Single Mode and Multimode Fibers

The telecommunications industry uses two types of fiber-optic cable: single mode fiber and multimode fiber. Each type of fiber can have various transmission modes. The fibers used today in long-distance telecommunications are single mode because it has only one mode of propagation. Figure 3.19 shows a **single-mode** fiber cable that has a small glass core diameter of 7.1 to 8.5 microns. Single mode can prevent wavelengths of light from overlapping and distorting data. Single-mode fiber has excellent linearity and dispersion behavior, which results in lower loss rates at high speeds. A single-mode fiber can use a pair of strands and send and receive simultaneously to gain twice the throughput of multimode fiber. In fact, single-mode fiber can reach speeds of 40 Gbps on a single wavelength. [Black Box, 272]

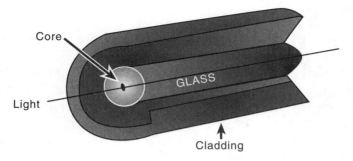

FIGURE 3.19 **Single-Mode Fiber [Source: Black Box, 272]**

Multimode fiber is used for different purposes than single-mode fiber because it has multiple modes of propagation. As shown in Figure 3.20, multi-mode fiber has a glass diameter core of 50, 62.5, or 100 microns. Because of its large size, it can collect light very easily. Several wavelengths of light are used in the fiber core. Different wavelengths of light travel at varying speeds through the fiber. Multimode fiber is not used in long-distance telephone networks because the multiple paths of light can cause distortion at the receiving end, which results in unclear or incomplete data transmission. Multimode fiber is used for applications that require simultaneous, bi-directional data transfer. It can be used for bringing fiber to the desktop or adding existing segments to your existing LAN network. [Black Box, 272-273]

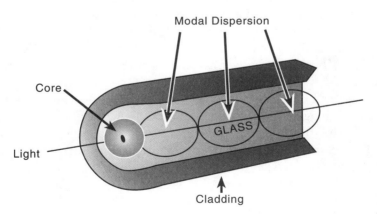

FIGURE 3.20 **Multimode Fiber [Source: Black Box, 272]**

Dark Fiber

Often service providers lay more fiber cabling than is required for an installation. They can save costs by not having to repeat the process every time a customer orders it. The dark strands are called **dark fiber** because they are unused at the time of installation. Dark fiber is dedicated to a single customer. Most customers who own dark fiber networks use them for delivery of Internet service. [Arnaud, 2]

The primary advantage of dark fiber is that no active devices are required in the fiber path. Both small and large businesses can derive significant benefits by acquiring dark fiber. Following are some of those benefits:

- Significant reduction in local loop telecom costs.
- Capability to deploy redundant paths to multiple carriers.
- Relocation of network servers that are speed sensitive to a "server farm." (A "server farm" is a group of servers located adjacent to each other in the same location.)

Dark fiber can be used to support voice, video, and extreme high-speed data to servers. [Webopedia, 1] [Arnaud, 6]

Gigabit Ethernet

The IEEE published the gigabit standard (802.3z) in 1998. Gigabit Ethernet is primarily used for LAN backbones. It provides for high-speed connections between network switches on various floors within a building. As Figure 3.21 shows, the primary purpose of the gigabit switch is to provide faster access to corporate LAN servers. Gigabit Ethernet supports data transfer rates of 1 Gbps (1,000 Mbps). It can use either fiber optic or **CAT5E** twisted pair 100-ohm cable.

Gigabit Ethernet has two flavors: shared and switched. The access method for shared gigabit is Carrier Sense Multiple Access/Collision Detection (CSMA/CD); the access method for switched gigabit is Logical Link Control (LLC). From the data link layer upward, gigabit Ethernet is identical to Ethernet. [Cisco, 1]

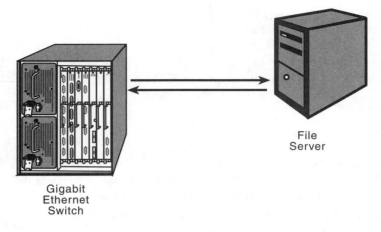

Gigabit
Ethernet
Switch

File
Server

FIGURE 3.21 **Gigabit Ethernet [Source: Cisco, 10]**

Prior to gigabit, data transfer rates had been limited to 100 Mbps. To scale to the higher speed offered by gigabit, the physical interface was modified to take advantage of Fiber Channel technology. The specification for fiber channel allows for 1.062-gigabaud signaling in full duplex mode. When the Fiber Channel connector is used, gigabit Ethernet can support single-mode and multimode fiber. For shorter cable runs, which extend to 25 meters or less, a special shielded 150-ohm copper cable called 1000BaseCX (with a DB-9 connector) can be used. This cable can be used for short-haul data center interconnections between racks and riser closets. With gigabit Ethernet, you can scale the network from 100Mbps to the desktop, connect devices together in a rack with 100 Mbps cable, and connect devices in the data center at 1000 Mbps. [Cisco, 4]

TOPIC *review* **Cabling**

1. What are the problems inherent in twisted-pair cabling?
2. What provided the impetus for the telephone network to increase call-routing capabilities?
3. Why isn't multimode fiber used for long-distance telephone networks?
4. What is the primary advantage of dark fiber?
5. Is gigabit Ethernet predominantly used for LAN or WAN backbones?

INTERFACES

From the desktop to the data center, cabling and networking devices are connected to each other using interfaces to build a high-performance internetwork. **Interfaces** are used to connect devices together. Hardware interfaces are the wires, plugs, connectors, and sockets that are used to provide communication between devices. Interfaces are often called **ports**; for example, almost all PCs have a serial port for connecting to a modem. Connecting a serial cable to a serial port enables transmission between two devices. In technical terms, you connect data terminal equipment (DTE), which is the PC to data communications equipment (DCE), or the modem.

Serial Interfaces

Several types of serial interfaces are used: RS-232, RS-442, RS-449, RS-489, RS-530, and V.35. Figure 3.22 shows that serial interfaces differ in size and the number of pins required for transmission. These interfaces are standardized and will always operate with the same performance if the guidelines are followed.

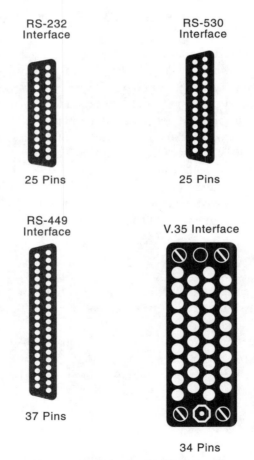

FIGURE 3.22 **Serial Interfaces [Source: Black Box, 1329]**

The following sections examine these serial interfaces to illustrate their differences.

RS-232

The **RS-232** cable is the most commonly and frequently used interface cable for DCE. The latest version—TIA/EIA-232E—uses DB25 connectors to specify the electrical, functional, and mechanical characteristics for interfaces between DTEs (computers, controllers, and so on) and DCEs (modems, converters, and so on). The RS-232 interface is ideal for data transmission at 0-20 Kbps. The maximum cable length is 50 feet (15.2m). [Black Box, 1329]

RS-422

RS-422 is used for serial communications and was designed to replace the RS-232 standard. RS-422 has since been superseded by RS-423. Both support higher data rates when compared to RS-232 and have greater immunity to electrical interference. The RS-422 interface supports multipoint connections, whereas the RS-423 interface supports only point-to-point connections. The RS-422 port found on all Apple Macintosh computers can be used for RS-232C communication. [Black Box, 1329]

RS-449

RS-449 was originally intended to replace RS-232. However, the mechanical and electrical specifications for RS-232 were found to be completely incompatible with RS-449. Instead, RS-449 is usually used with synchronous transmissions. [Black Box, 1329]

RS-485

RS-485 is used for multipoint communications. With an RS-485 connection, one computer can control many different devices. It is similar to RS-422, but it supports up to 64 devices. RS-485 can support more nodes per line because it uses lower-impedance drivers and receivers. [Black Box, 1329]

RS-530

The **RS-530** interface uses the same mechanical connector as the RS-232 but supports higher data rates. It is used to transmit serial binary, asynchronous, or synchronous data at rates from 20 Kbps to 2 Mbps. RS-530 has superseded RS-449 and complements RS-232. [Black Box, 1329]

V.35

V.35 was designed to support high-speed serial connections at greater distances, and specifically for transmission between DTEs and DCEs over digital lines. The ITU (International Telecommunication Union) defined V.35 as a standard for data transmission at 48 Kbps over 60-108 KHz group-band circuits. Actual distances will depend on your equipment and cable quality. Theoretically, the cable has a range up to 4,000 feet (1200m) and a speed of up to 100 Kbps. V.35 is used today to provide a high-speed interface between a DTE or DCE and a CSU/DSU (see below). [Black Box, 1329]

USB

Intel, IBM, Compaq, DEC, and Microsoft developed the **Universal Serial Bus (USB)**, which is a data communication standard for a peripheral bus that provides an interface for computer telephony devices. USB provides a single port for connecting multiple devices such as digital cameras, audio devices, printers, and modems to PCs. Figure 3.23 shows an example of a USB interface compared to a standard RS-232 serial interface. Notice the speed is 12 Mbps for USB's much smaller interface.

25 Pin
Serial

USB
Serial

Speed = 115 Kbps   Speed = 12 Mbps

FIGURE 3.23 **USB Interface [Source: Black Box, 1308]**

USB defines the ports and can provide a bus topology in which connections are formed in a straight line that allows 127 devices to be daisy-chained to a single port. A USB peripheral plugs right into the port and works immediately. A USB interface distributes power so multiple USB devices do not need their own power supply. USB controllers manage the driver software and bandwidth required by each peripheral. Currently, a new specification—USB 2.0—is being developed which will increase speeds to 120 to 300 Mbps. [Sheldon, 1295]

FireWire

FireWire is a high-speed interface for real-time, full-motion video applications. This asynchronous technology provides real-time capabilities because it supports isochronous data traffic. Its high-speed bus supports data transfer rates from 100 to 400 Mb. The standard for FireWire is 1394, which was developed as a joint project between Apple Computer and Texas Instruments. [Sheldon, 526]

FireWire can support up to 63 devices with a maximum cable length of 4.5 meters between devices. FireWire supports a guaranteed data rate free of lags or slowdowns. It lowers costs for connections because applications can use smaller buffers. FireWire is lightweight, flexible, and inexpensive. FireWire is used as a digital interface for consumer electronics and AV peripherals such as digital cameras, scanners, audio recorders, and video recorders. FireWire provides its own bus power for peripherals. [Black Box, 1308]

HIPPI

High Performance Parallel Interface (HIPPI) is an ANSI standard that was developed in 1987 to physically connect devices at short distances and high speeds. The basic standard uses a 50-pin connector and transfers 32 bits in parallel at a data transfer speed of 0.8 Gbps. The Wide HIPPI transfers 64 bits in parallel at a speed of 1.6 Gbps. HIPPI is most frequently used to connect supercomputers together to provide high-speed backbones for LANs. [Webopedia, 1]

TOPIC review Interfaces

1. What is the most frequently used interface cable for DCE equipment?
2. Which interface is designed to support high-speed serial connections between DTEs and DCEs over digital lines?
3. Why are interfaces referred to as ports?
4. Which interface is used with synchronous transmissions?
5. Why does a USB interface distribute power to multiple USB devices?

MODEMS

A **modem** is a device or program that enables a computer to transmit data over telephone lines. Modems allow digital transmissions over analog lines. Computers store and process information digitally as series of 0s and 1s. Because phone lines are analog rather than digital, the information must be converted before it can be transmitted. A modem converts the digital signal to an analog signal so that it can travel over an analog line. (Analog and digital signals are explained in more detail in Chapter 5.)

Modem Operations

When you use a modem to dial up, the information travels over a local loop to the nearest telephone organization central office (CO) and then switched as a routine phone call through the telephone hierarchy of the PSTN to the destination.

Modems are available for computers either as internal or external devices. The RS-232 interface is standard for connecting external modems to PCs. Any external modem can be attached to a computer that has an RS-232 port. Internal modems are on circuit boards that are installed in a PC. An internal modem uses an RJ-11 port to connect directly from the card to the telephone jack in the wall. For laptops, special flat modem (PCMIA Type I) cards are inserted in the side of the laptop. These modem cards have an RJ-11 port so they also can directly connect to the phone line.

Before a transmission can occur, the modems at each end need to negotiate their parameters so transmission can proceed successfully. These parameters are set up within your modem software. Some of the parameters include the data rate (**baud**) and the mode of duplexity. The baud rate is the speed of the data transfer. When you establish the connection, both modems need to be set to the same baud rate. Many modems today are capable of different data rates and can adjust on their own speed to that of the other modem. If you set a modem to full duplex mode, signals travel in both directions at the same time and at the same rate. When you use DSL (Digital Subscriber Line) modems, communication is asymmetrical. The signal speed is faster for downloading information than it is for uploading.

Modems can be asynchronous or synchronous depending on communications requirements. Modems typically used in homes and offices are asynchronous. When you need to dial into a mainframe computer, however, you must use a synchronous modem because the mainframe does not understand asynchronous communication. Asynchronous and synchronous communications are explained in more detail in Chapter 5.

Telephone companies offer DSL modems to use over their Digital Subscriber Lines. Cable companies offer cable modems that operate over cable TV lines. Both of these technologies use broadband communications to provide faster downloads of information. Generally, with an xDSL modem, a user can download a file at 8-32 Mbps. Depending on your geographic area, cable modems can download at up to 2 Mbps. Today, telephone and cable companies can offer higher speed modems than ever before to connect to the Internet. Chapter 7 covers DSL and cable modem technologies in more detail.

Modem Standards

Two sets of standards govern modems: the Bell standards and the V standards. The Bell standards were established in the 1960s and 1970s for use with Bell equipment and lines. The V standards are specified for international use and were established by the ITU. They define the signal-modulation technique, the data rate, compression, asynchronous or synchronous transmission, the mode of duplexity, and whether they can be used for dial-up only or be connected to leased lines. Table 3.4 shows the differences between the various Bell modem standards.

MODEM TYPE	DATA RATE (BPS)	ASYNCHRONOUS SYNCHRONOUS	DUPLEX MODE	TELEPHONE LINE	TYPE OF USE
Bell 103	300	Asynchronous	Full	2-wire dial-up leased	Low demand, infrequent file exchanges
Bell 201B	2,400	Synchronous	Half Full	2-wire leased 4-wire leased	Terminal to mainframe multidrop applications
Bell 201C	2,400	Synchronous	Half	2-wire leased	Dial-up synchronous to mainframe
Bell 208A	4,800	Synchronous	Half Full	2-wire leased 4-wire leased	Connect to mainframe with fewer modems
Bell 2088	4,800	Synchronous	Half	2-wire dial-up	Dial-up connection to mainframe
Bell 212A	1,200	Asynchronous Synchronous	Full	2-wire dial-up	Proprietary; avoids the expense of leased lines.

TABLE 3.4 **Bell Modem Standards [Source: Black Box, 1315]**

The international V standards for modems enable customers from different parts of the world to connect to other modems without compatibility problems. Table 3.5 compares features between V modem standards.

MODEM TYPE	DATA RATE	ASYNCHRONOUS SYNCHRONOUS	DUPLEX MODE	TELEPHONE LINE	TYPE OF USE
V.22	1,200 bps	Asynchronous Synchronous	Full	2-wire dial-up 2-wire leased	Used to access mainframe. Dial up avoids cost of leased lines.
V.22 bis	2,400 bps	Asynchronous Synchronous	Full	2-wire dial-up 2-wire leased	Used for large file transfers.
V.25		Parallel		Dial-up	Specifies an answer tone at 2,100 Hz. Establishes automatic calling and answering circuitry for use of dial-up lines.
V.25 bis		Serial		Dial-up	Performs auto-dialing functions with a V.25 modem.
V.32	9600 bps	Asynchronous Synchronous	Full	2-wire dial-up 2-wire leased	Trellis-encoding modulation enables high data speeds and reduces errors.
V.32 bis	14.4 Kbps	Asynchronous Synchronous	Full	2-wire dial-up 2-wire leased	Use of bis standard increases maximum data rate to 14.4 Kbps.
V.33	14.4 Kbps	Synchronous	Full	4-wire leased	Accesses mainframe at higher data rate of 14.4 Kbps.
V.34	28.8 Kbps	Asynchronous Synchronous	Full	2-wire dial-up 4-wire leased	Automatic fallback to lower speed modems.
V.34+	33.6 Kbps	Asynchronous Synchronous	Full	2-wire dial-up 4-wire leased	Increases data rate to 33.6 Kbps.
V.90	56 Kbps	Asynchronous	Full	2-wire dial-up	Used for high-speed connection to the Internet.

TABLE 3.5 **V Modem Standards [Source: Black Box, 1314]**

Chapter 3 • Network Design: Networks, Cabling, and Internetworking Devices

Even though modems can advertise a data rate of 56 Kbps, the throughput never actually reaches that speed because of rate restrictions, line noise, and cable distance. Impairments can originate at the sender or receiver end of the connection. Generally, the root cause of these problems is the cable's distance from the local phone organization CO. If you are more than 3 1/2 miles from the CO, less usable bandwidth is available to you and this slows down your modem connection. In fact, in parts of the United States, the lines only support 30% of the 56 Kbps data rate. [Hal-pc, 2]

Another factor affecting data transmission through modems is the capability to correct avoidable errors. Industry standards have been developed to govern error correction and compression to ensure the rapid transfer of information. A protocol that is included in modem software called **Microcom Network Protocol (MNP)** provides error-correction capabilities for the communications session. MNP must be implemented in modems at each end of the link. Table 3.6 shows the standards for error correction and data compression that occur at various MNP levels.

PROTOCOL	EXPLANATION OF STANDARD
MNP Levels 1-4	Used for error-free asynchronous data transmission. Microcom Systems developed this proprietary standard. Modems for the sender and receiver must both be set to MNP for successful transmission.
MNP Level 5	A data-compression algorithm is applied which allows the modem to double the amount of data it sends. The compression ratio is 2:1.
V.42	An ITU recommendation for error control that uses two algorithms (LAPM or Link Access Protocol and MNP 1-4). LAPM controls data errors and retransmits "bad" data blocks. No special user action or software is required to establish error control because it is set up automatically. If both modems do not support V.42, they negotiate to use MNP.
V.42 bis	Compression is added to the protocol so more data can be sent in a unit of time. The data compression ratio is 4:1. The size and type of file transmitted affects the compression ratio. V.42 correlates approximately to MNP level 5.

TABLE 3.6 **Error Correction and Data Compression Standards [Source: Black Box, 1315]**

TOPIC
review **Modems**

1. When you use a modem to dial up to the Internet, how does it travel through the telephone hierarchy?
2. What parameters need to be negotiated between modems to set up the transmission?
3. What is the difference between the Bell standards and the V standards for modems?
4. What are the three levels of standards used for error correction and data compression?
5. What is the purpose of the LAPM protocol?

INTERNETWORKING DEVICES

When LANs, WANs, and MANs are connected together, internetworking devices are used to provide for information sharing across the organization or organizations. The challenge of internetworking is to use the various repeaters, bridges, switches, CSU/DSUs (see below), and gateways available in such a way that they form a reliable network architecture. The design must be flexible, allow for growth, and be constructed to provide users with the services they require to perform their jobs.

Repeaters

The simplest device used to tie networks together is the **repeater**. Repeaters also extend the distance of the LAN so that the last workstation connected has as strong a signal as the other workstations. Repeaters are devices that regenerate signals and pass them to other network segments. They receive, amplify, and retransmit packets; however, a repeater cannot filter or error check packets. Repeaters are physical level devices and do not have any algorithms built in to allow them to make any decisions. Their function is limited to digital signal regeneration. In fact, a repeater actually creates a new signal according to the data it receives. Because repeaters restore the signal to its original structure, an issue arises when signals are corrupted because they will be repeated across the network.

Repeaters are also referred to as **hubs**, multiport hubs, or concentrators. The purpose of a repeater is to connect two or more LANs of similar technology and to further extend the distance of a LAN. Repeaters are either local (they connect LANs that are physically close to one another) or remote (they connect two LANs together up to a kilometer apart). Remote connections require a remote repeater at each location and might use fiber-optic cable for distance.

Repeaters are also used to connect workstations to the network. In small offices, small four- to eight-port hubs are used to connect eight workstations to the network. Figure 3.24 shows a standard eight-port hub. Each port on the hub supports a 100 Mbps connection to a desktop or printer.

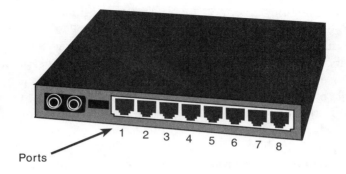

FIGURE 3.24 **Standard Hub with Eight Ports [Source: Black Box, 1151]**

When the number of people expands, then another hub is purchased and stacked on top of the existing hub. Figure 3.25 shows five eight-port hubs stacked on top of each other. These hubs are referred to as stacking hubs. The stack of hubs in Figure 3.25 can support 40 desktop connections.

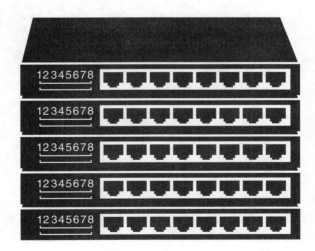

FIGURE 3.25 **Stackable Hubs [Source: Black Box, 1149]**

Bridges

The **bridge** is another device used to interconnect LANs. Bridges differ from a repeater in that they can filter and forward packets by MAC (Media Access Control) address. Local bridges connect LANs that are adjacent to each other and remote bridges connect LANs via a WAN link.

A bridge provides for the creation of a single "logical" LAN longer than any one cable segment. It also offers electrical and traffic isolation between segments. Bridges are protocol independent, which means they can support any protocol on the LAN. The most common use of bridges is for filtering LAN traffic based on MAC addresses. The guiding principle is to use bridges to keep local traffic local on the LAN and only forward traffic on to the WAN backbone when it is required to reach the destination.

Figure 3.26 shows a bridge with a V.35 interface. This bridge also supports a synchronous or asynchronous connection to the WAN.

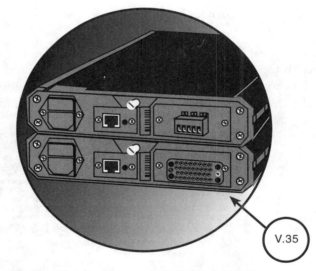

FIGURE 3.26 **V.35 Bridge [Source: Black Box, 1212]**

When a packet reaches a bridge, the packet is examined for the destination address. The bridge then determines whether the packet should be forwarded to another network. If the destination address is not on the LAN, the bridge forwards the packet to a router. The router consults its table and routes the packet across the network to its destination. If the packet destination address is on the LAN, the bridge does not forward the packet to the router, but passes it directly to the destination node.

A bridge learns the network topology and addresses of devices dynamically. The bridge knows the address of every network node because it builds its own

Chapter 3 • Network Design: Networks, Cabling, and Internetworking Devices

bridging table to use when making filtering and forwarding decisions. Unfortunately, when there are many network segments and several alternate routes between hosts, a packet can end up in a loop and never reach its destination. Packets are then bridged using the **spanning tree algorithm**. This algorithm ensures that a packet cannot find itself in an endless loop in the network. Figure 3.27 shows an example of an endless loop. In this example, two parallel bridges labeled BR1 and BR2 are used to connect LAN A and B together. The end user on station K receives two copies of the frame resulting from the loop formed by BR1 and BR2.

With the implementation of the spanning tree algorithm, you can design a single path between any two hosts. In this way, you can avoid duplicate frames and provide more efficient bandwidth use.

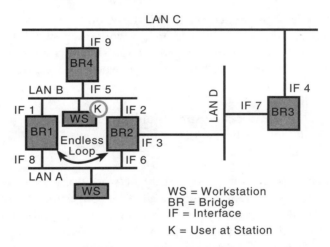

FIGURE 3.27 Spanning Tree Bridge Topology [Source: Bay Networks, 1]

Switches

Switches are used to alleviate network congestion by dividing a network into **virtual LAN (VLAN)** segments. Switches can dedicate more bandwidth to a port or a group of ports. They function at the Data Link layer of workgroups and at the Network layer of network backbones. Switches provide 100 Mbps ports for user connections in switched networks.

Ethernet switches have replaced a number of bridges in large networks. Like a bridge, an Ethernet switch also can filter traffic based on MAC address. However, Ethernet switches have additional capabilities that allow them to manage network traffic better. In fact, today's Ethernet switch can function as a repeater and as a bridge.

The switch fabric of an Ethernet switch works using one of the following techniques:

- **Store and Forward**. Examines incoming frames and filters out bad packets. Each and every packet is examined in its entirety. The packet is not forwarded until the examination process is complete. After the packet has been determined free of errors, it is sent to the destination. This process causes some delay.
- **Cut Through**. Only reads destination addresses to pass frames quickly over the backbone. The forwarding process begins while the packet is being received. The switch takes a quick look at the packet and then forwards it directly to the router. Foregoing the error-checking process increases speed. [Palmer & Sinclair, 103-104]

The size of the switch varies depending on whether it is designed for a workgroup or for the network backbone. A workgroup switch splits a large shared media LAN into smaller workgroups. On the other hand, a backbone switch allows faster connections and is used to relieve congestion between switching devices on the backbone.

Switches do the following:
- Solve network congestion problems
- Load balance heavy users
- Reduce downtime

As an organization grows and the network traffic increases, eventually Ethernet switches replace hubs to alleviate congestion. Most switches today have modular chassis, whose capabilities are increased by adding interface boards. To add a number of fiber ports to increase the speed of a network, for example, a board is added into the modular chassis. Switches can be managed through software to provide for segmenting collision domains within an Ethernet network.

As stated earlier, a switch provides for the creation of VLANs that provide boundaries to keep local traffic local within the VLAN. A VLAN can be created for an entire department or a small workgroup. As shown in Figure 3.28, a LAN switch divides the network into 3 VLANs. Each VLAN has its own hub to support desktop connections for each workgroup. In large networks, often VLANs are created for each floor of a building. The collision domain is limited to each floor.

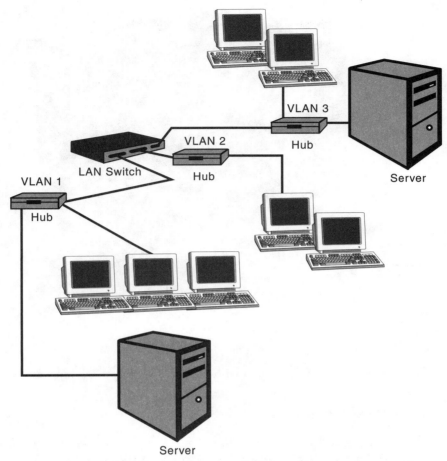

FIGURE 3.28 **LAN Switch Forms VLANs [Source: Black Box, 1324]**

Some users require more bandwidth than others because of their job function. Switches allow a network manager to assign a specific bandwidth to each port on the switch. If, for example, someone needs 100 Mbps to their desktop, the port can be configured to 100 Mbps for that one user. Alternatively, 36 engineers in a department might need to collaborate on drawings. As shown in Figure 3.29, a single interface card at the bottom of the switch has 36 ports, so this card could be configured as one VLAN, called 36-port density configuration.

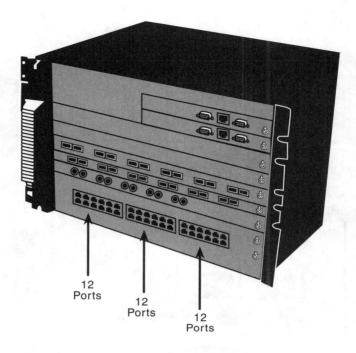

12
Ports

12
Ports

12
Ports

12 x 3 = 36 Ports for 1 VLAN

FIGURE 3.29 **Etherswitch with 36-Port Interface Card [Source: 3Com, 1]**

High-Speed Switches

For larger networks that require faster processing than Ethernet switching, often organizations investigate the capabilities of high-speed switches. A new architecture was designed for these high-speed switches that combines switching and routing functions into one device.

Layer 3 Switches

Ethernet switching allows the integration of mixed-bandwidth workgroups so that bandwidth can be dedicated based on user or workgroup requirements. Recently, routing capabilities have been added to Layer 3 level switches. **Layer 3 switches** use ASIC (Application Specific Integrated Circuit) processors inside that allow the switches to determine paths faster. Layer 3 switches also have expandable memory capabilities to provide for larger buffers to move the data through. Although Layer 3 switches are faster than routers, they support fewer protocols and applications. These switches are generally used in networks that have changing traffic patterns and multiple network segments in larger networks. [Black Box, 1131]

Layer 4 Switches

Layer 4 switches are multilayer switches that have powerful network processors. These switches can classify traffic based on policies and rules that are defined by the network designer for security reasons. Packets are compared to policies and then put into queues based on their classification. A Layer 4 switch examines traffic based on port number, TCP session information, or prioritization tags. The switch examines the packet for application type and packet priority, and can even evaluate URLs to obtain information about destination server directories and file information. The purpose of these switches is to balance the load across servers and balance the delivery of service through prioritization and quality of service. [Sheldon, 888-889]

ATM Switches

Service providers require high-end carrier-class switches to connect throughout the telephone hierarchy. Many service providers use **ATM switches** with SONET/SDH interfaces to accommodate multiple ATM circuits. (SDH is a European equivalent of SONET.) These ATM switches become the backbone architecture of the service provider. Significant amounts of voice, data, video, and image traffic are transmitted through these switches. Redundant switches are required for offering higher total availability and providing alternative paths should the main switch fail. Lower-end concentrators are attached to the switch to provide for lower-speed connectivity.

In Figure 3.30, you see a Cisco ATM switch that has both switching and routing capabilities. This broadband concentrator provides a switch processor to increase routing performance.

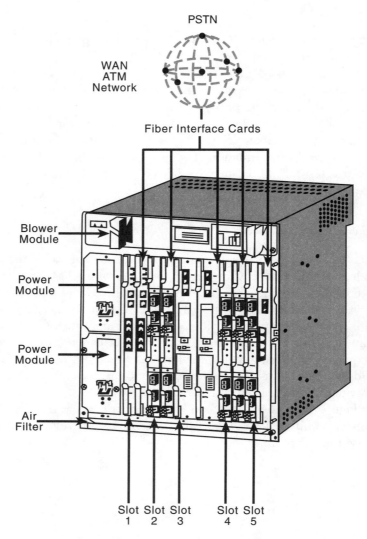

FIGURE 3.30 **Cisco ATM Switch [Source: Cisco, 1]**

Gateways

Sometimes network designers are faced with the challenge of interconnecting two entirely dissimilar networks. In cases such as this, bridges, switches, and routers (see next section) are unable to provide the translation necessary for the networks to communicate to each other, so network designers use *gateways*. The most frequent use of **gateways** is to provide for protocol conversion. When a LAN needs to connect to the mainframe, it uses a 3270 gateway to translate the protocol. The model 3270 is a type of IBM terminal used to connect to an

IBM mainframe. A personal computer or 3270 gateway uses emulation software that changes the PC or gateway so that it acts like a 3270 device to communicate with the IBM mainframe. In Figure 3.31, you see that the 3270 gateway connects to a Front End Processor (FEP). The FEP is Model 3745 and is used to offload communication functions from the mainframe, control communication links, and control the flow of data between devices and workstations.

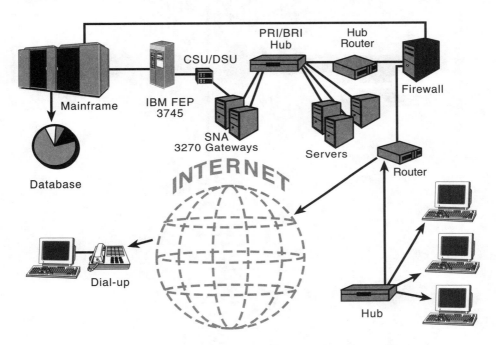

FIGURE 3.31 **Design for 3270 Gateway from LAN to Mainframe [Source: Microsoft, 1]**

LAN gateways are constructed using a synchronous data link control card. This card takes the asynchronous communication from the LAN and converts it to synchronous so the mainframe will receive it appropriately. Another conversion issue arises because the mainframe uses EBCDIC (Extended Binary-Coded Decimal Interchange Code) as the character set and the LAN uses ASCII. In order for the mainframe to understand the characters it is receiving, the emulation software tables in the gateway translate the characters.

Another common use of gateways is for e-mail. A mail gateway provides for synchronization of directories and databases. It also lets users send mail to each other, preserve attachments, and use rich-text formatting. Figure 3.32 shows the position of the mail gateway between sender and receiver. The gateway formats the mail for the appropriate mail system and forwards it on to the mail server.

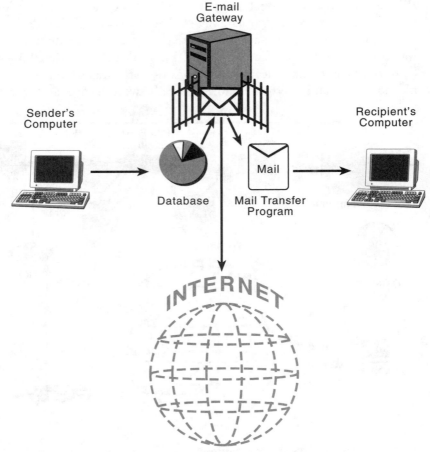

FIGURE 3.32 Mail Gateway [Source: Ruttencutter, 1]

SMTP sends mail as standard ASCII text without any formatting, such as tabs, bold, underlining, and special fonts. Mail translation gateways convert e-mail messages between two completely different e-mail systems. These gateways can preserve the formatting and text wrapping so e-mail messages come through just as they were sent.

Gateways provide one-way mapping of mail messages between proprietary systems. Some e-mail gateways translate between Microsoft Exchange, Lotus Notes, and Novell Groupwise. Gateways for IBM PROFs and other public messaging systems provided by telephone companies are still widely used. This allows companies to continue to use their existing e-mail system for internal use and for the Internet. Most gateways have WAN interfaces for connecting to the Internet. Gateways are usually located at the corporate headquarters and they receive all incoming mail, translate it, and forward it to the corporate mail

Chapter 3 • Network Design: Networks, Cabling, and Internetworking Devices

server. The gateways have a connection to the LAN through their Ethernet card, and they have a connection directly to the WAN. [Symthe, 318]

CSU/DSU

CSU/DSU (Channel Service Unit/Data Service Unit) devices can be separate units or they can be combined into one device. Sometimes, a CSU/DSU is built directly into a router and other times it is a card that is installed inside a phone switch (PBX). The CSU is used to connect for voice calls to reach the local loop. The DSU is used to attach to digital technologies such as Frame Relay. The CSU/DSU can provide either a 56 Kbps or T1 connection to the local loop. The other end of the connection has a CSU/DSU receiving information at your local phone organization. Figure 3.33 shows the front and back of a CSU/DSU device.

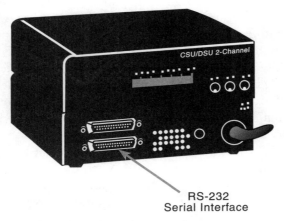

RS-232
Serial Interface

FIGURE 3.33 CSU/DSU [Source: Black Box, 973]

At the bottom of Figure 3.33, the CSU/DSU has a serial connection that can be either RS-232 or, for more speed, a synchronous V.35 interface. Some CSU/DSUs handle multiple channels for asynchronous and synchronous LAN/WAN applications. It can maintain the configured port speed of an application while providing access to higher network speeds over the WAN.

TOPIC
review **Internetworking Devices**

1. Why can't a repeater filter or error check packets?
2. Which device provides for a single "logical" LAN longer than any one-cable segment?
3. What is the primary difference between store-and-forward and cut-through Ethernet switches?

4. What device provides for protocol conversion between dissimilar networks?

5. When and where are ATM switches most frequently used?

ROUTERS

Routers are intelligent, high-level internetworking devices that on their own can determine the best path through a network. A router forms the boundary between one network and another. Routers talk to other routers by exchanging router addresses and protocol information. Their built-in intelligence allows them to examine network traffic and quickly adapt to any changes made to the network. [Palmer & Sinclair, 96-97]

An organization might have several LANs located in different areas of the country. Each of these locations requires a router to establish the connection to the WAN. Each router has a database called a *router table* (p. 140) that is used to retain information about all of the other routers on the organization's network. A router on the same network segment as another router is called a routing neighbor. The distance between the local router and its neighbor is assigned a value called a **hop**. Therefore, the neighbor router might be one hop away from the local router. E-mail messages might travel through several routers before reaching their final destination. A hop occurs each time the e-mail message is forwarded to another router.

Figure 3.34 shows the four routers between San Francisco and Singapore, which means the hop count is four. When there are more hops, it takes longer for data to go from source to destination. Conversely, fewer hops provide faster access and data reaches the destination earlier. [Norton, 1] [Webopedia, 1]

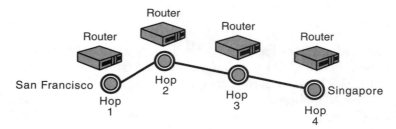

FIGURE 3.34 **Router Hops to Singapore [Source: Fairhurst, 1]**

Router Communication Process

The communication process between routers is based on routing packets. The packet is encapsulated inside of a frame and is then relayed across the network, router by router, until it reaches it destination. When the packet arrives, the router examines the destination address in the packet header field. The router then decides how to forward the packet to the next router.

During this process, the router also searches network status information for available paths. If a path is congested, the router looks for another path. Next, the router must calculate the number of hops it will take for the packet to reach its destination. It then looks in the routing table and determines which interface on the back of the router to send the packets through. [Palmer & Sinclair, 96-97]

Figure 3.35 shows two interfaces, RJ45 Ethernet connections, on the router. Each interface can be connected to a LAN segment, a hub, or Ethernet switch. The interfaces are labeled as EO and E1. Consequently, if the packet needs to travel to a location inside a LAN network, it will be sent through one of these interfaces. [Norton, 1]

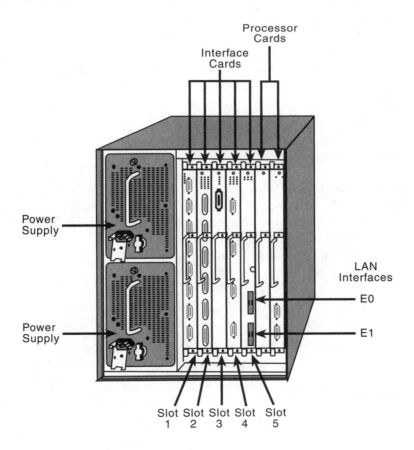

FIGURE 3.35 **Router Interfaces [Cisco, 1]**

Router Table

The **router table** is actually a database of information about an organization's network and is key to routing. It collects information about addresses of other routers and node addresses of devices attached to the network (computers and printers). The table also includes distance calculations, bandwidth capacity, and delay information. A router table can be updated manually (called **static routing**) or dynamically (called **dynamic routing**). [Palmer & Sinclair, 96]

Sometimes an organization will use both techniques. If the organization uses Frame Relay, it will define the pathways to other routers by manually entering the digital link circuit identifiers (DLCI) provided by the telecom provider into the router table. On the other hand, an organization might use the dynamic updating technique in which the routers monitor the network for changes and update their own routing tables. Routers will also reconfigure network paths based on the topology information they receive from other routers.

If a link fails or a router is inaccessible, a dynamic router detects the failure and establishes another path. The new path is based on the network load, the type of line available, and the amount of bandwidth required. A network status database is maintained in each router that stores information about the organization's network topology and the status of the telecommunication links. [Palmer & Sinclair, 97]

Types of Routers

Several types of routers are available that are used for different purposes. Choosing the right type of router requires an examination of the following:
- Interfaces required to connect to the LAN and the WAN
- Protocols to be supported by the router
- Separation required for subnetworks

Table 3.7 lists router types and their functions.

ROUTER TYPE	FUNCTION
Single Protocol Routers	Supports only one network protocol for user data. The entire network has to be set up to use only one protocol worldwide.
Multiprotocol Routers	This device can support multiple protocols for user data. The router can route information by protocol; however, it does not provide translation between protocols. Translation must be provided by a gateway.
Modular Routers	These routers have the capability to add services by inserting an interface card into the router.

	The router is designed like a chassis with slots available to expand to take advantage of more interface ports or the latest technology.
Boundary Routers	The network is configured as a star topology. The boundary router acts as the primary switching agent for the devices located at the spoke-end of the star. The devices can be remote bridges, routers, or low-end routers.
Access Routers	This mid-sized router supports three or four LAN and WAN interfaces, and supports three or fewer network end-user protocols.

TABLE 3.7 **Types of Routers [Source: Smythe, 191-192]**

Organizations with WAN links usually favor modular routers at the corporate headquarters so they can expand to take advantage of new interfaces. However, the types of interfaces available include X.25, FDDI (Fiber Distributed Data Interface), ISDN (Integrated Services Digital Network), T-carrier, leased lines, Frame Relay, SMDS, ATM, satellite links, and microwave links. Most often, the manufacturer can provide a card (interface) that can be inserted in the modular router to add the type of WAN service desired. An important consideration when deciding on a router is the number of slots available because many large organizations support multiple services depending on the availability of services in their area, the type of usage, and number of users at the location. [Symthe, 272]

Routing Algorithms

An **algorithm** is a procedure defined to proceed step-by-step to perform an operation. Routers use algorithms to process information that affects the operation of the network protocol. The two classes of routing algorithms are

- **Distance Vector.** When a router uses this algorithm, it receives the entire contents of neighboring router tables. After retrieving information on the routes available, the router makes decisions based on the number of hops (distance) and a direction (vector). The distance-vector algorithm is alternatively referred to as the Bellman-Ford.
- **Link State.** This algorithm does not send the entire routing table to other routers. Instead, it sends small amounts of update information across the entire network. Each router sends only the section of its routing table that describes the state of its own links. This algorithm is also known as the shortest path first.

The purpose of all these calculations is to find the shortest path that has the least cost, based on the number of hops. Many routers today use the link-state algorithm because it allows them to analyze more information about the network than the distance-vector algorithms. **Distance-vector** routers are limited to the hop count as the gauge to determine the best path. However **link-state** routers can take into account link congestion, transfer delay, and bandwidth availability. Link state is the method preferred by large organizations and ISPs. [Smythe, 274-275]

Multiprotocol Label Switching

The tremendous growth of the Internet has caused a sudden increase in the amount of network traffic that needs to be routed and monitored by ISPs and telecom providers. Today, government, businesses, and home consumers are demanding an unprecedented amount of network bandwidth. The solution offered by telco providers and ISPs for this problem is called **Multiprotocol Label Switching** (**MPLS**).

The MPLS protocol is used to build virtual circuits across IP networks and is designed to overcome the limitations of IP-based networks. MPLS improves IP-packet exchange by simplifying the routing process. Network operators can divert and re-route traffic around link failures, congestion, and bottlenecks. MPLS offers Quality of service (QOS) features to manage data streams based on priority and a service plan. The IETF (Internet Engineering Task Force) based its recommendation for MPLS on label switching approaches designed by Cisco, IBM, and Lucent. [Sheldon, 808] [Webopedia, 1]

At the core of the telco provider or ISP network, a device called a **Label Switch Router** (**LSR**) is used to switch and place outgoing labels on packets. The labels define the corresponding path to take through the network and are assigned by the **Label Edge Routers** (**LERs**), which specify label identifiers. The information contained in the label specifies destination, bandwidth, delay, and QOS metrics. Figure 3.36 shows the architecture of a MPLS network with LERs at the perimeter and LSRs at the core.

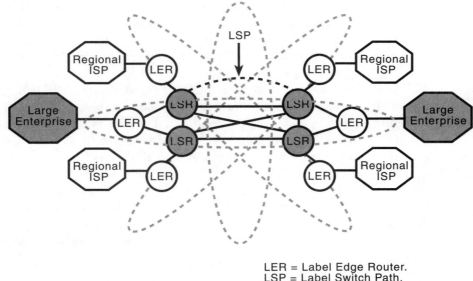

LER = Label Edge Router.
LSP = Label Switch Path.
LSR = Label Switch Router.

FIGURE 3.36 **MPLS Architecture [Source: Sheldon, 8]**

The pathway defined through the telecom provider network is called a **label switched path** (**LSP**), which operates similar to how virtual circuits operate in Frame Relay and ATM. Figure 3.37 shows that when a packet arrives at a MPLS network, the incoming LER receives the packet, examines the packet's IP address, and determines a route. Next, it assigns an LSP and attaches a label. The packet is then forwarded to the LSP and from there it is sent through a series of LSRs until it reaches the outbound LER. At this point, the LER removes the label and the packet is forwarded based on standard IP routing. [Sheldon, 810]

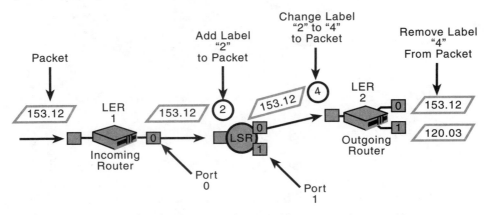

FIGURE 3.37 **MPLS Label Forwarding [Sheldon, 8]**

The IP packet finds its way from the header field on the packet. The source and destination address appear in the header field. The header is examined each time it enters the interface of the next router. The routing tables are built using routing protocols. MPLS devices build label-forwarding tables from the routing information provided by the main router table. LSRs learn about other LSRs' MPLS capabilities through the **Label Distribution Protocol** (**LDP**). The routing and label information is forwarded on to the neighboring routers.

Figure 3.38 shows six routers labeled A-F. The end user is connected to Router A and has sent a message to a user connected to Router C. Using standard IP routing, the path from Router A hops to Router B and then to Router C. MPLS determines that the path between Router A and Router B is congested and calculates the expected delay. Then, MPLS selects the path that is least traveled. This path begins from Router A to Router E, then to Router D, and finally on to Router C. Even though you are hopping over more routers and going a longer distance, the packet will still arrive faster because MPLS avoided the congestion.

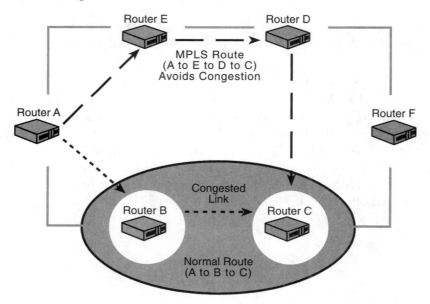

FIGURE 3.38 Route Switching Using MPLS [Source: Woods, 2]

Router Network Architectures

The most commonly adopted model for building a router network architecture is hierarchical with three levels. The levels are access, distribution, and core. This model is scalable, allows for growth, and is easy to maintain. Network designers can use it as a guideline for the layout of their router architecture, which should be designed to customer requirements. ISPs often use advance-switching devices called core switches. Table 3.8 explains the three-level router architecture from the clients on the LAN to the WAN core.

LEVEL	LEVEL TYPE	LEVEL DESCRIPTION
Level 3	Core	Provides for network interconnection functions to provide efficient transfer between sites. Servers that manage the network, such as SNMP (Simple Network Managing Protocol), DNS (Domain Name System), DHCP (Dynamic Host Configuration Protocol), and TFTP (Trivial File Transfer Protocol), are the only ones to be used at this level.
Level 2	Distribution	Consolidates many access paths to provide the best connection to the core. It converts protocols and manages bandwidth between the access and core levels. The distribution device can be either a Layer 3 switch or a conventional router.
Level 1	Access	Provides for functions that need to be close to the end hosts. It is designed to minimize the cost per unit of local bandwidth and cost of connection.

TABLE 3.8 **Model for Router Architecture [Source: Berkowitz, 385]**

Level 1 is the access level provided for users and servers for router architectures to the Internet, as described in Table 3.8. The firewall used to filter and block different types of network traffic is positioned at Level 2. At the top Level 3, Internet access is provided through a high-performance core router.

When designing a router architecture, it is important to match the bandwidth to the expected traffic patterns. The core's basic function is to link sites together, and it can be used to link buildings together or connect to an ISP to reach the Internet. The bandwidth is specified by the speed of the link it is connected to. Traffic patterns need to be analyzed to determine the flow between locations. Normally, traffic does not flow equally to all sites; instead, more traffic volume usually goes in one direction or the other. Larger branch offices produce a significant flow of traffic back to corporate headquarters, for example.

In addition to the router architecture, it is essential to look to other functions that can improve the router's capability to manage the data. Two functions most often considered are data encryption and compression. **Data encryption** protects the data from mischievous hackers. **Compression** reduces the size of the data and saves usage costs on WAN links. Depending on the compression algorithm, savings could reach 50%. [Smythe, 279]

Today's routers also offer other functions used to improve traffic flow. Time sensitive information might need to be assigned to a specific WAN link. A router that supports data forwarding enables administrative control over the flow of forwarding to a specific port on the router. In addition to time-sensitive information, some types of traffic might need to be prioritized. A prioritized service will route information based on classes of data, specific addresses, or even the entry or exit point links to the router. [Smythe, 279]

One factor that always looms in the background is that networks grow with the organization. If your organization merges or acquires another organization, your network architecture will need to change to provide the connection between them. This requires examining the requirements and looking at the architecture model to make performance and cost decisions. Implementing an internetwork with WAN links is not an easy task. The challenge is to support communication within the organization with a reliable, well-managed, effective internetwork. [Cisco, 1-2]

TOPIC *review* **Routers**

1. What type of information is exchanged between routers?
2. What is the purpose of the router table?
3. What do routing algorithms affect?
4. What is the MPLS protocol used for?
5. When designing a router architecture, what factors should be considered in the analysis?

CHAPTER SUMMARY

Network design involves a fundamental understanding of LAN, MAN, and WAN technologies, topologies, internetworking equipment, cabling, and interfaces. Many LANs can be connected together within a MAN or WAN. The key design issues are location of the sites to be connected, distance between sites, and performance required. Building larger networks requires cabling, interfaces, internetworking equipment, and carrier lines.

Network designers study traffic flow within sites and between locations to determine the type of equipment required at each site. They consider how the elements of the network can be matched appropriately for its intended usage. The final design solution requires examining heavy concentration points in the network and then looking for equipment with the capacity to handle the current and future level of traffic expected. The goal is to provide an efficient and easy transfer of information between all sites within an organization.

Selection of the backbone design of the WAN architecture (ring, star, mesh, or tiered) is more critical today because projects are often shared worldwide. Users expect to share information as easily with someone in Singapore as they can with the person in the office next to them. These expectations challenge the network designer to construct and balance network traffic from the edge to the core of the network. Serial interfaces (RS232, V.35, and USB) connect internetworking devices (bridges, switches, gateways, and CSU/DSUs) to provide sufficient throughput between routers in different locations for a smooth running network.

Now, in the Convergence Age, networks must be able to scale in speed and performance to handle multiple types of traffic such as voice, multimedia, and interactive real-time applications. As millions and millions of packets are sent across carrier fiber-optic backbones, network designers have looked to the emergence of Multiprotocol Label Switching (MPLS) to alleviate congestion and more efficiently route traffic over the WAN. MPLS supports multiple paths between end points of the network, traffic prioritization, and Quality of service (QOS). MPLS can offer a higher level of communication for premium customers who are willing to pay for it.

With an MPLS network of many core switches, a service provider can build a network that spans the entire country. Service provider core networks will use MPLS to manage wavelength optical circuits for all of the optical networks of the future. At the edge of the MPLS network, regional ISPs, local telco operators, and private companies will link into the MPLS backbone. Network operators who use MPLS will be able to divert and route traffic based on data-stream type and Internet-access customer.

CHAPTER REVIEW QUESTIONS

(This quiz can also be printed out from the Encore! CD that accompanies this textbook—file name: Chap03review.)
Circle a letter (a-d) for each question. Choose only one answer for each.

1. This type of network is privately owned, managed, and controlled by an organization.
   a. MAN
   b. WAN
   c. LAN
   d. VLAN

2. What type of network is used to interconnect PBXs for use with IP telephony?
   a. VLAN
   b. MAN
   c. LAN
   d. WAN

3. This WAN topology provides dedicated circuits constructed in such a way that each location is connected to two other locations.
   a. Tier
   b. Ring
   c. Star
   d. Mesh

4. With this WAN network topology, routers are interconnected with other routers so that at least two pathways are connecting each location to the others.
   a. Ring
   b. Star
   c. Tier
   d. Mesh

5. Where does all the WAN and LAN wiring for a building terminate?
   a. Telecommunications Closet
   b. Equipment Room
   c. Cable Room
   d. Server Room

6. Which device is used to provide protocol conversion between the LAN and the mainframe?
   a. Switch
   b. Router
   c. Gateway
   d. Bridge

7. What is the communication process between routers based on?
   a. Routing addresses
   b. Routing traffic
   c. Routing hops
   d. Routing packets

8. What protocol is used to provide network operators with the ability to divert and re-route traffic around link failures, congestion, and bottle-necks?
   a. SNMP
   b. MPLS
   c. MLPS
   d. SMNP

9. What type of cable do telcos or service providers use to provide high-speed backbones for the Internet?
   a. Multimode fiber
   b. Single-mode fiber
   c. Coax
   d. Shielded Twisted Pair

10. When designing a router architecture, which elements should you match to provide good performance?
    a. Bandwidth to expected traffic patterns
    b. Time-sensitive information to a specific link
    c. Link to classes of data
    d. Addresses to exit point links

Circle the correct letter (A-E) that corresponds to the descriptions below. Choose only one answer for each.
   A. Algorithm
   B. Distance Vector
   C. Multiprotocol Router
   D. Link State
   E. Dynamic Router

11. A B C D E Each router sends only the section of its routing table that describes the state of its own links.

12. A B C D E Updates the routing table automatically by exchanging address information with other routers and network nodes.

13. A B C D E A procedure defined to proceed step-by-step to perform an operation.

14. A B C D E This router can support and route information by protocols.

15. A B C D E When a router uses this algorithm, it receives the entire contents of neighboring router tables.

   A. Congestion
   B. Refraction
   C. Latency
   D. Switch
   E. Throughput

16. A B C D E The bending of light that occurs as the light passes through the fiber-optic cable.

17. A B C D E A guaranteed data speed measured in bits per second.

18. A B C D E   Slows traffic down and occurs when there are too many transmissions over the network.

19. A B C D E   Devices used to alleviate network congestion.

20. A B C D E   The amount of time that packets or frames are delayed because of congestion.

INTERNET EXERCISES

1. Log on to the Internet and key in the following URL:

   www.globalnetworking.net/fiber.asp

   A. What is an optical transmitter?
   B. What is an optical receiver?
   C. Is fiber-optic cable immune to lightning?
   D. Can fiber-optic cable corrode?

2. Key the following URL: **www.mplsforum.org**

   A. When was the forum started?
   B. What is the purpose of the forum?
   C. What are the three classes of membership?
   D. How much does it cost to join?

CONCEPT EXERCISES

Concept Narrative
(This narrative exercise can also be printed out from the Encore! CD that accompanies this textbook. File name—Chap03connar.)

Read the following description and fill in the blanks with the correct answer.

The MPLS protocol is used to build virtual circuits across IP networks. It was designed to overcome the limitations of _____ networks. It improves IP-packet exchange by simplifying the routing process. Network operators have the ability to divert and re-route traffic around link failures, congestion, and bottlenecks. It offers QoS features to manage data streams based on priority and a service plan. The IETF based its recommendation for MPLS on label switching approaches designed by Cisco, IBM, and Lucent.

At the core of the telco provider or ISP network, a device called a Label Switch Router (_____) is used to switch and place outgoing labels on packets. The labels define the corresponding path to take through the network. The labels are assigned by the Label Edge Routers (_____), which specify a _____ identifier. The information contained in the label specifies destination, bandwidth, delay and QOS metrics. The architecture of an MPLS network places Label Edge Routers at the perimeter and Label Switch Routers are placed at the core.

The pathway that is defined through the telecom provider network is called a label switched path (_____). The label switched path operates similar to how virtual circuits operate in Frame Relay and ATM. When a packet arrives at an MPLS network, the incoming Label Edge Router (LER) _____ the packet. It examines the packet's ___ _____ and determines a route. Next, the LER assigns a label switched path and attaches a label. The packet is then forwarded to the label switched path and from there it is sent through a series of LSRs until it reaches the outbound LER. At this point, the _____ removes the label and the packet is forwarded based on standard IP routing.

The IP packet finds its way from the _____ _____ on the packet, which contains the source and destination address. The header is examined each time it enters the interface of the next router. The routing tables are built using routing protocols. MPLS devices build _____-_____ tables from the routing information provided by the main router table. LSRs learn about others LSRs' MPLS capabilities through the Label Distribution Protocol (LDP). The routing and label information is forwarded on to the neighboring routers. The label information identifies the path that the packet will follow to its destination.

Concept Table
(*This table exercise can also be printed out from the Encore! CD that accompanies this textbook. File name—Chap03contab.*)

Read each statement carefully and choose the type of network being described. Use only one "X" per statement.

STATEMENT	TYPES OF NETWORKS		
	LAN	MAN	WAN
1. The distance limitation of this type of network is 20 to 30 miles.			
2. This network is designed primarily for data.			
3. The geographic area of this type of network is within a country or between countries.			
4. With this network, the most common cabling used to connect desk-tops is twisted pair.			
5. The four topologies used to construct this network are peer-to-peer, ring, star, and tier.			
6. The geographic area of this type of network is within a city.			
7. The distance range of this type of network is limited to $\frac{1}{2}$ to 2 miles.			
8. Recently the telco industry has adopted fiber-optic cabling to establish lease lines, T1, Frame Relay and ATM/SONET.			
9. This network uses only a ring topology.			
10. The distance range for this type of network is limited.			

Chapter 3 • Network Design: Networks, Cabling, and Internetworking Devices

Concept Picture
(This picture exercise can also be printed out from the Encore! CD that accompanies this textbook. File name—Chap03conpic.)

Look at the following diagram of a fiber-optic cable. Name each element of the cable next to the letter (A-E).

Fiber Elements

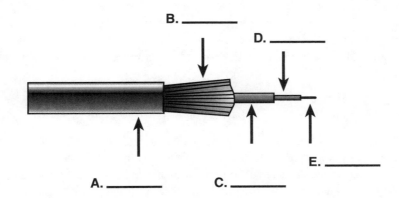

1. _____ A thin layer that surrounds the fiber core.

2. _____ These fibers are made of Kevlar wire strands or gel-filled sleeves.

3. _____ The outer layer of the cable.

4. _____ A single continuous strand of glass or plastic.

5. _____ Layer of plastic that surrounds the core and cladding to rein force the fiber core.

CASE STUDY

ZUMI INC.

Read the following case study about Zumi, Inc. Think about the challenge presented to the company, and the information solution provided. Then, either by yourself or in a group, answer the case study questions.

Objective:

Learn to design a cabling infrastructure and a WAN for a multimedia-rich gaming organization. Study the traffic requirements between locations and within the building to determine the equipment and cabling required to design a high-speed network.

Company Profile:

Zumi is a Japanese-based company that creates advanced entertainment systems and video games. Zumi has designed a sophisticated game console that offers video games, Internet connectivity, e-mail, and chatting services. The soon-to-be released Zumi box has two times the graphics processing power of the fastest Pentium III processor. Sales of the previous Zumi box were astounding with 514,000 units sold in the first week after it was introduced. Zumi Inc. headquarters is located in Tokyo, Japan, and two offices are located in Chicago, Illinois.

Current Situation:

With the prospect of a new more advanced Zumi box, the company needed to increase its workforce and workspace to handle both the existing and newly anticipated products. The current workforce in Illinois is composed of 4,000 users between two locations. Zumi plan to add 1,000 more employees this year. Recently, Zumi located a warehouse in the industrial section of downtown Chicago with a lot of open space and large windows. The warehouse has three floors with a computer room located on the first floor. The company plans to occupy the building within four months and wants to totally redesign the network-cabling infrastructure.

Business Information Requirements:

Currently, Zumi workers use sophisticated simulations, multimedia databases, and customized interactive video applications to design their games for the Zumi box. The programmers, quality assurance testers, technical support team, and marketing department work jointly on each game they design. At this time, engineers located in Tokyo and Illinois need to collaborate on drawings and simulations. They require instantaneous access to all graphic-intensive tools and a drawing library that is only available at headquarters. At present, they have a slow Internet connection to Tokyo and the users have become frustrated with the download times for graphics tools and files.

Communication System Requirements:

The network design should allow for high-speed Internet access so that everyone in the company can quickly send, receive, and download graphic-intensive tools to create interactive computer games. The new network design should also provide increased capacity for data, voice, and video traffic between the company's two locations in Illinois and the headquarters in Tokyo. The quality assurance testing team has two rooms in the existing building in Illinois, which are used for training and testing purposes. When they move to the new facility, they want to set up four rooms in the new warehouse. They must be able to distribute presentations via broadband video to all four rooms simultaneously.

Information System Solution:

1. Within the warehouse building, they designed the backbone between floors for gigabit Ethernet and used Category 6 cabling. The gigabit speed will easily handle the multimedia and graphic-intensive applications used for designing new game programs.

2. Twelve strands of multimode fiber are installed through the inner ducts to the telecommunications closets on each floor. Fire-retardant material was installed in the plenum area of the ceiling, in the walls, and between the floors to minimize the effects of a potential fire.

3. The company has contracted with a service provider for a private WAN using an ATM over SONET connection to Tokyo. The bandwidth of the optical carrier is OC-48 (48 Mbps) between the core switches within the service providers' network. They provide an OC-12 (12 Mbps) to the edge at the Illinois warehouse. The private ATM WAN allows for voice over IP and multicast video applications.

4. For broadcast video to the four quality assurance rooms, they have deployed a fiber-optic based private CATV broadband video network. They currently have 12 channels for their video intranet and have also connected to the ATM backbone to broadcast video to Japan.

The initial cost of installing the CAT6 cabling infrastructure, hardware, and labor was considerable. However, it has provided Zumi with a modular and flexible cabling infrastructure system, which will allow higher data-rate systems in the future. A number of contractors were hired, working just about on top of each other, to allow the project to be completed within the four-month time frame.

For the WAN, Zumi contracted with the service provider for a five-year contract for the ATM network. As part of the agreement, the provider's technicians will oversee the management of the entire network and will stock spare parts and cables on site for speedy repair. Also in the contract, they specified that if there is a cut in the fiber anyplace in the service provider's core switched network, a backup path will be provided so that a single circuit failure will not paralyze the entire network.

Users are pleased with their access speeds to headquarters in Tokyo. They are so pleased, in fact, they are calling technical support to tell them how much faster they are able to download their graphic-intensive applications and tools. With higher-speed access, they have been able to develop virtual libraries with engineers in Tokyo to share multimedia drawings. They have even begun to offer real-time interactive broadcasting sessions between the two locations in Illinois.

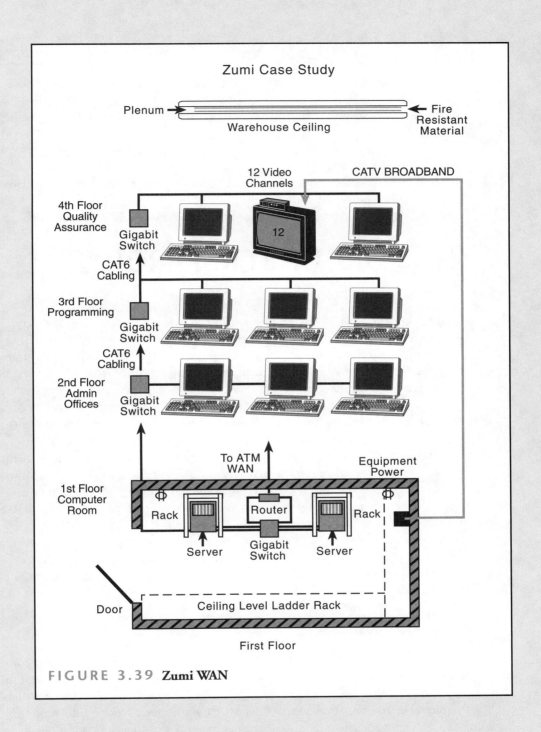

FIGURE 3.39 Zumi WAN

CASE STUDY QUESTIONS

1. What type of cabling infrastructure did they use within the warehouse building?
2. How would you determine the current traffic flow through the Internet to Tokyo?
3. What technology did they use for faster downloading of graphic-intensive tools and drawings from Tokyo headquarters?
4. What type of research would you do to find out how to provide video distribution to the four rooms?
5. What type of routers would you have used for the WAN connection to Tokyo?

GROUP TERM PROJECT

REQUIREMENTS DECISION-MAKING MODEL

F&D Engineering, Inc. has mentioned in the case study that they have some precise requirements for the implementation of the global e-mail system. The requirements decision-making model is used to simplify the identification of requirements. A requirement is a general need or condition that must be met by the system or product to be acceptable by your department. Requirements are grouped into musts and wants. A must requirement is mandatory and must be met for the system or product to be acceptable. A want requirement is desirable, but not mandatory for the system or product to be acceptable. Each requirement is evaluated as to its priority for the project. If there is a tie at the priority level between requirements, then a risk evaluation must be performed. The risk evaluation looks at both requirements and makes an assessment of what could go wrong if one requirement was not met. In other words, what impact does each requirement have on the project or organization?

You will find the requirement worksheets on the Encore! CD that accompanies your textbook (file names *MustRequire* and *WantRequire*). Each group should complete one set of requirement worksheets and turn them in at the end of the class period.

Must Requirements

Print the file MustRequire. Write all your "MUST" requirements in the first column. Score each requirement on a scale of 1 to 10, with 10 having the highest priority and 1 having the lowest priority. Determine the level of importance for each requirement and then evaluate each score by the priority it has for your project.

If you encounter two requirements that have equal importance and priority, perform a risk evaluation. Ascertain the level of impact if this requirement was not met by the project and assign a risk evaluation score based on the same 1-10 scale.

MUST REQUIREMENTS	PRIORITY SCORE	RISK EVALUATION
1.		
2.		
3.		
4.		
5.		
6.		
7.		
8.		
9.		
10.		
11.		
12.		
13.		
14.		
15.		

Want Requirements

Print the file WantRequire. Write all your "WANT" requirements in the first column. Score each requirement on a scale of 1 to 10, with 10 having the highest priority and 1 having the lowest priority. Determine the level of importance for each requirement and then evaluate each score by the priority it has for your project.

If you encounter two requirements that have equal importance and priority, perform a risk evaluation. Ascertain the level of impact if this requirement was not met by the project and assign a risk evaluation score based on the same 1-10 scale.

WANT REQUIREMENT	PRIORITY SCORE	RISK EVALUATION
1.		
2.		
3.		
4.		
5.		
6.		
7.		
8.		
9.		
10.		
11.		
12.		
13.		
14.		
15.		

CHAPTER TERMS

CHAPTER BIBLIOGRAPHY

Book, Magazine, Presentation Citations

Berkowitz, Howard. *Designing Routing and Switching Architectures for Enterprise Networks*. Indianapolis: Macmillan Technical Publishing, 1999: 15, 385.

Black Box. *Network Services*. Lawrence: Black Box Organization, 2000: 4, 252, 272, 273, 282, 305, 973, 1131, 1149, 1151, 1212, 1303, 1307, 1308, 1314, 1315, 1323, 1324, 1329.

Dean, Tamara. *Network+ Guide to Networks*. Canada: Course Technology, 2002: 136-140, 193, 194, 195, 196, 197.

Palmer, Michael and Sinclair, Robert. *Advanced Networking Concepts*. Cambridge: Course Technology, 1997: 20, 96, 97, 103, 104.

Plunkett, Jack W. *Plunkett's InfoTech Industry Almanac 2001-2002*. Houston: Plunkett Research, Ltd.: 8.

Sheldon, Tom. *Encyclopedia of Networking & Telecommunications*. New York: Osborne/McGraw-Hill, 2001: 8, 526, 722, 724, 808, 888, 889,1295.

Smythe, Colin. *Internetworking Designing the Right Architectures*. Cambridge: Addison-Wesley Publishers, Ltd., 1995: 191, 192, 272, 274, 275, 279, 318.

Web Citations

3COM, "Switch 4007," 3COM, <www.3com.com/index2.html> (2002).

AbMAN, "AbMAN Network Topology," University of Aberdeen, <www.abman.net.uk/topology.html > (10 January 2001).

Angel, "HALO," Angel Technologies Organization, <www.angelhalo.com/overview.htm> (2000).

Arnaud, Bill, "Frequently Asked Questions about Customer Owned Dark Fiber, Condominium Fiber, Community and Municipal Fiber Networks," <www/canet3.net/library/papers.html> (1 May 2001).

Bay Networks, "Transparent Bridge Overview – Spanning Tree Algorithm," Bay Networks, <support.baynetworks.com/library/tpubs/html/router/soft1000/bridge/2950A-19.html> (11 April 1996).

Brain, Marshall, "How Routers Work," <www.howstuffworks.com/router.htm> (2002).

Brown, B, "Principles of Communications: II," CIT, <www.cit.ac.nz/smac/dc100www/dc1002.htm> (1995).

CalNews, "Cable Wars: What's It Going to Cost You?" CalNews, <www.calnews.com/Archives/CalNewsOped/ctn071499cable.htm> (14 July 1999).

Cassidy, Daniel, "Types of Optical Media Used in the Communications Industry," TestMark Laboratories, <www.testmark.com/develop/fiber/fiberoptic.html> (15 March 2001).

Cisco Systems, "Frame Relay WAN Network Design" Cisco Systems, <www.cisco.com/warp/public/779/largeent/frame_relay_wan.html> (2001).

Cisco System, "Voice-Enabled WAN," Cisco Systems, <www.cisco.com/warp/public/779/ largeent/design/voice_wan.html> (2001).

Cisco System, " Introduction to Gigabit Ethernet," Cisco Systems, <www.cisco.com> (2001).

Cisco System, "Cisco 7000 Product Overview," <www.cisco.com/univercd/cc/td/doc/product/core/cis7000/7000_him/7000 povr.htm> (1 November 2001).

Cisco Systems, "Internetworking Basics," <www.cisco.com/univercd/cc/td/doc/cisintwk/ito_doc/introint.htm> (2001).

Data Cottage, "Network Cabling Help," Data Cottage, <www.datacottage.com/nch/fibre.htm> (2001).

Fairhurst, Gorry, "Metropolitan Area Networks (MANs)," University of Aberdeen, <www.erg.abdn.ac.uk/users/gorry/eg3561/intro-pages/man.html> (10 January 2001).

Hal-pc, "Expecting 56k (V.90/x2/k56)," Hal-pc, <www.hal-pc.org/~wdg/56k.html> (2 June 2002).

Lonmon, "London Metropolitan Network," London Metropolitan Network, <www.lonman.net.uk/images/map99b.gif> (May 1999).

Microsoft, "Microsoft Host Integration Server 2000 Delivers High-Performance, Reliable Mainframe Integration for Critical Services," <www.microsoft.com/hiserver/evaluation/overview/default.asp> (2000).

Norton, Michael, "Layer 3 Switching – Introducing the Router," O'Reilly Network, <www.oreillynet.com/lpt/a//network/2001/04/13/net_2nd_lang.html> (2000).

Ruttencutter, J. "Mail Gateways," Cornell College, <cornellcollege.edu/~j-ruttencutter/email/mailgateways> (2001).

Webopedia, "Internetworking", Webopedia, <www.pcwebopedia.com/TERM/I/Internetworking.html> (10 October 2001).

Wikipedia, "Optical Fiber," <www.wikipedia.com/wiki/Optical_fiber&diff=yes> (3 March 2002).

Woods, Darrin, "MPLS: A New Traffic Cop for Your WAN," Network Computing, <www.networkcomputing.com/1113/1113ws2.html> (10 July 2000).

CHAPTER 4
WAN PROTOCOLS

By the end of this chapter, you should understand these concepts:
- The difference between a protocol and a protocol stack or suite
- How packets, frames, headers, and trailers control message exchange
- The four categories of protocols
- Mapping protocols and WAN-switching technologies to follow the OSI Model
- TCP/IP network services and their usage
- Formatting and assembling packets as IP datagrams and TCP segments
- The purpose of host names, IP addresses, and DNS
- The implementation of distance vector and link state algorithms
- The role of routing software architecture

PROTOCOL STACKS

A **protocol** is a set of rules that governs data communication. A protocol defines what, when, and how data is communicated. The protocol also determines the format for transmission of data between two devices or networks. For one computer to communicate with other computers, it must first be configured to use the correct protocol. This protocol defines methods for error checking, notification, and acknowledgement.

A **protocol stack** (also called a *protocol suite*) is a set of network protocol layers that work together; a group of specifications are layered in a logical hierarchy. When a new user is connected to a network, a protocol stack is selected for a **network interface card (NIC).** The NIC is an adapter that is inserted in the workstation to provide connections to Ethernet, Token Ring, and other types of networks. After a protocol has been established, workstations and servers that use the same protocol should be able to communicate with one another.

When messages are sent across the network, data must be sent in a specified format. The intervening devices between sender and receiver exchange requests, replies, and event notifications to guide the message to its destination. At every point in the process, the devices know the status (event notification) of the operation. The devices have been programmed through algorithms to either retransmit when there are errors, or, if a device has failed, to bypass it entirely.

Every day, users send messages back and forth across a network or over the Internet. A message is an information unit that is transferred over a network. When a message is sent, it is broken up into smaller units called packets. A **packet** is a piece of a message to be transmitted. Each packet contains the destination address of the recipient user as well as a portion of the message. Packets are transported in **frames**, which are logical groups of information that are formatted as a continuous series of bits. Frames can contain several packets.

Figure 4.1 shows a person using an e-mail application to compose a message. After this user clicks Send, the message is sent from the application to the network. Next, protocol software divides this message into packets. The packets are then grouped and carried across the network as a network frame.

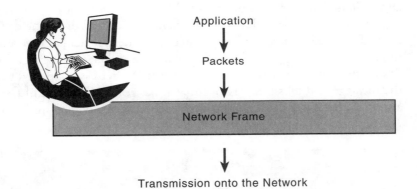

FIGURE 4.1 **The Network Frame [Source: Marney-Petix, 9]**

All the basic functions performed on a network (reading data, retrieving data, writing data, and printing data) involve the use of protocols. The layout of information in each transmitted packet of data is different for each protocol. Figure 4.2 shows three protocols in front of the data. A different protocol is used for each function in a network. If data is requested from a server, a protocol performs the function of connecting to the server. If, on the other hand, a user needs to print to a network printer, a different protocol is used for the connection to the printer. [QuanMongMo, 7] [Novell, 7-2] [Marney-Petix, 12]

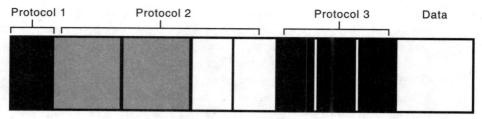

FIGURE 4.2 **Protocol Headers on a Packet [Source: Marney-Petix, 11]**

When data is sent over the network, frames are formatted into *fields*. Within each **field**, a pattern of bits has a specific meaning to be interpreted by the router. Control information—a specific set of instructions and requests for handling the data—is added to the data field.

In Figure 4.3, control information is formatted through the use of headers and trailers that surround the data field. The **header field** is added to the beginning of a message. Each header field contains all of the fields used to perform the function of a specific protocol. The header field also contains instructions about the length of the packet, packet number, synchronization, protocol, destination, and source addressing. The **trailer field** is appended to the end of the message and tells the network that it has reached the end of the packet. It also provides the control information used for error detection. [Marney-Petix, 10-11]

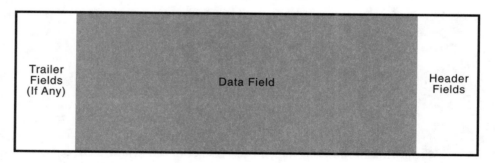

FIGURE 4.3 **Header and Trailer Fields on a Packet [Source: Molta, 1]**

Figure 4.4 shows the fields inside an Ethernet frame. The data has now been formatted with additional control fields used to direct the frame to the destination. The body or data of the packet is referred to as its *payload*. The **payload** is the actual data that the frame delivers to the destination. Figure 4.4 shows that **control fields** precede and follow the data field. These sets of instructions define the start of the frame, the length of the packet, and a frame check sequence (FCS). The FCS is used for error checking to maintain the data integrity of the frame.

802.3 Ethernet Frame

Preamble	Start of Frame	Destination Address	Source Address	Length	Data	Frame Check Sequence

FIGURE 4.4 **Inside a Frame [Source: Spandler, 1]**

To illustrate a packet's journey, this example follows an e-mail packet across the network from Jane to Sarah. In Figure 4.5, Jane composes an e-mail message to send to Sarah over the Internet. In this example, the Internet protocol carrying the packet is **Transmission Control Protocol/Internet Protocol (TCP/IP)**. Each of the packets in Jane's e-mail message is formatted into three parts: header, payload, and trailer. The header contains the IP address of the sender and receiver, the type of protocol, and the packet number. A **packet number** identifies each packet and puts it in sequence to comprise Jane's message. The payload contains the data of the packet. A trailer is added that indicates the end of the packet as well as the error-correction method used. [Brain, 2]

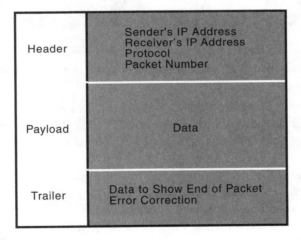

FIGURE 4.5 **Format of a Packet [Source: Brain, 3]**

When all packets are formatted, they are ready to be put into a frame for transmission from the host PC to the Internet. As Figure 4.6 shows, Jane connects to her network access point or router to send the message. The protocol TCP/IP has been added to the packet to match the protocol used by the Internet. The destination address (Sarah's e-mail address) determines the route the e-mail message will take across the Internet to reach Sarah. Routers on the Internet look into the header of each packet to find the destination address. They compare this address with that found in their lookup tables to find out where to send each packet. When the packets reach Sarah's network, the router strips off the header and trailer from each packet and puts the payload data back into its original order, and the entire e-mail arrives intact to Sarah. [Brain, 1]

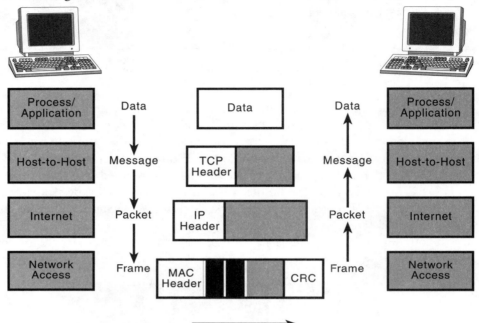

FIGURE 4.6 **Message Transmission over the Internet [Source: Novell, 1-15]**

Note that in Figure 4.6, the error-correction method used on the trailer of the packet is **cyclic redundancy check (CRC)**. This error method uses an algorithm that counts the bits in the packet to ensure that all bits are accounted for. Using this algorithm, the sender's router looks into the data or payload field to find all the 1s, adds them together, and then inserts the total into the trailer as a hexadecimal value before sending. When the packet reaches its destination, a receiving router adds up the 1s in the payload and compares the total to the value given in the trailer. If the two values match, the packet is considered complete and it is delivered to the receiver. If they do not match, the router sends a request to the originating router to resend the packet. [Brain, 1]

A number of elements are required to send a message across a network or the Internet. Many different protocols are used to define the communication process. Some protocols are for LANs only, while others are used for WANs. A number of protocols have been created specifically for the Internet. Additionally, because routers are the key devices used for data transmission, a number of protocols have been developed to speed up and improve the efficiency of the routing process. The four main categories of protocols are LAN, WAN, Internet, and Routing.

Each of the four basic categories of protocols is used at different stages throughout the communication process. Protocols in each category perform one or more basic functions in response to information they find in the packets and frames sent across the network. The links between sender and receiver are WAN communication paths through the carrier network. Before information, messages, or data can be submitted to a network, they must follow a specific format, protocol, and size. New protocols are being developed every day to solve issues with multimedia and other methods of secure data encryption. Programmers who design protocols must adopt standards to ensure they will be able to operate with several operating systems and hardware devices.

LAN Protocols

LAN protocols are used to provide shared access to devices and applications over the LAN. To accomplish this, the protocol is bound to a NIC inside a workstation. When a workstation wants to transmit to another workstation, the protocol information is matched to that of the network to allow for a smooth file transfer. LAN protocols have evolved with the explosion in Internet use, with some operating system developers rewriting their systems to allow for the use of TCP/IP as the single protocol to be used for the LAN and the Internet.

Table 4.1 lists the most common LAN protocols.

PROTOCOL	DESCRIPTION
AppleTalk	This protocol suite provides for file sharing between Macintosh computers. Additionally, a part of the suite is used to connect Macs to PCs, IBM mainframes, DEC VAX, and UNIX systems through interfaces.
Transmission Control Protocol/Internet Protocol (TCP/IP)	This suite of communications protocols connects hosts to the Internet.
Local Area Transport (LAT)	A DEC proprietary Ethernet protocol for connecting terminals or PCs to a LAN. It is used to connect a DEC terminal server and a VAX. LAT is not routable because it lacks a network layer. It must be bridged instead of routed in an enterprise network.
(Netware) Internetwork Packet Exchange/ Sequenced Package Exchange (IPX/SPX)	A proprietary protocol used by Novell Netware operating systems. IPX is a datagram protocol used for connectionless communications. SPX is connection oriented and used for error-recovery services.
Systems Network Architecture (SNA)	A set of network protocols developed by IBM in order to communicate with its mainframes.

TABLE 4.1 **Common LAN Protocols [Teare, 1] [Webopedia, 1]**

WAN Protocols

When organizations connect to the Internet, they are entering the world's largest WAN. Several protocols are used specifically for WAN technologies and services. WAN protocols are used to establish communication paths over WAN links before message exchange occurs. These protocols negotiate the type of connection to be used and provide for efficient exchange after the link has been established. Some WAN protocols are **connection oriented** (for example, Q.921, LAPD, and Q.931). Connection oriented refers to a point-to-point connection in which a path has been set up in advance. With **connectionless protocols** (Internet protocols), on the other hand, each packet is forwarded hop-by-hop toward its destination without a predetermined path. New protocols are also being developed, such as those designed specifically to improve traffic management between ISPs (Internet Service Providers). Table 4.2 lists common WAN protocols.

COMMUNICATON METHOD	PROTOCOL	DESCRIPTION
Mainframe	**High-level Data Link Control (HDLC)**	Used as a transmission protocol. It embeds information in a data frame to allow devices to control data flow and correct errors.
	Synchronous Data Link Control Protocol (SDLC)	A protocol used in IBM's SNA networks. LAN gateways use the SDLC protocol to communicate to an IBM mainframe.
Dial Up	**Point-to-Point Protocol (PPP)**	Used to connect a computer to the Internet over a dial-up link. It sends the computer's TCP/IP packets to a server, which then puts them onto the Internet.
ISDN	**Link Access Procedure for D Channel (LAPD)**	A data link protocol used by ISDN (Integrated Services Digital Network). It also provides a pathway for communication between the components required for internetworking between the Public Switched Telephone Network (PSTN) and IP networks.

COMMUNICATON METHOD	PROTOCOL	DESCRIPTION
	Q.921	Data Link protocol used over ISDN's D channel (LAPD).
	Q.931	An ISDN connection control protocol that manages connection setup and disconnection. It does not provide flow control or perform retransmission.
X.25	**Link Access Procedure Balanced (LAPB)**	(A subset of HDLC) A data link protocol used with X.25 packet switching technology. It is a link access procedure used to control operations over an X.25 link.
	X.25	Allows computers on different public networks to communicate with each other through an intermediary computer.
Frame Relay	**Link Access Procedure for Frame-Mode Bearer Services (LAPF)**	Provides the data link control for Frame Relay networks.

TABLE 4.2 **Common WAN Protocols [Halley, 1] [Freesoft, 1]**

Internet Protocols

Internet protocols are used in both LAN and WAN communications. A suite of communication protocols work together to provide various Internet services to users. The goal of the Internet protocols is to offer diverse connectivity regardless of the hardware or software application being used. To avoid having to support several proprietary protocols to establish communication, a standard protocol is required to transfer data over the Internet. With the tremendous growth in Internet usage over the years, developers are working on new protocols every day to deal with streaming media, XML documents, and other new forms of data. As each new protocol is developed, it is presented to standards committees as a **Request For Comments (RFC)**. The RFC is then published, reviewed, and analyzed by the Internet community to elicit protocol refinements before the final standard is published. [Cisco, 1-2]

Table 4.3 lists and describes the most common Internet protocols currently in use for services such as network time, streaming multimedia, hypertext, XML (Extensible Markup Language), and information services. Because TCP/IP protocols are the foundation of the Internet, they also are considered Internet protocols. However, TCP/IP has an extensive list of additional functions that require comprehensive explanation. Consequently, protocols that comprise the TCP/IP suite are not listed here but are explained and identified later in this chapter.

PROTOCOL TYPE	PROTOCOL	DESCRIPTION
XML	**Blocks Extensible Exchange Protocol (BXXP)**	Used for XML documents on the Internet. An application protocol framework for connection-oriented, asynchronous request/response interactions.
	Data Space Transfer Protocol (DSTP)	Used to index and categorize data using an XML-based catalogue.
Hypertext	**HTTP**	**Hypertext Transfer Protocol.** Used to define how messages are formatted and transmitted over the World Wide Web.
	S-HTTP	An extension to the HTTP protocol that sends data securely over the World Wide Web.
Network News	**NNTP**	**Network News Transfer Protocol.** Used to post, distribute, and retrieve USENET messages.
Network Time	NTP	**Network Time Protocol.** Used to ensure accurate synchronization in milliseconds of computer clock times in a network of computers.
	SNTP	**Simple Network Time Protocol.** Used when full NTP services are not needed.

PROTOCOL TYPE	PROTOCOL	DESCRIPTION
Multimedia	RTP	**Real-Time Transport Protocol.** Used to transmit real-time data, audio, and video as an Internet protocol.
	RTSP	**Real-Time Streaming Protocol.** A proposed standard for controlling streaming data over the World Wide Web.

T A B L E 4 . 3 **Common Internet Protocols [Wack, 2] [Webopedia, 1]**

Routing Protocols

After messages pass through Internet protocols, they arrive at routers used to establish connections to the WAN, which have their own routing protocols. These protocols tell routers the best paths to use through internetworks. Routing tables are used to obtain information from other routing protocols. Routing protocols use algorithms to update the state of changes in the internetwork so that all routers can agree on the paths to be used. A routed protocol enters through an interface on a router and consults the routing table to determine which interface to forward the packets through to the Internet. Routing protocols are discussed in more detail in the "Routing Algorithms and Protocols" section of this chapter. [Norton, 1]

TOPIC review · Protocol Stacks

1. A protocol determines a format for transmitting data; it also specifies methods for which three events?
2. What are the four elements of a message?
3. What are the basic functions performed on a network?
4. What is the purpose of the control fields found inside a frame?
5. What error-correction method is used in the trailer of a packet?

PROTOCOL DESIGN AND THE OSI MODEL

Protocol designers examine the structure of the basic elements of an existing protocol, including its error and flow control, when designing a new protocol. They understand that the communication process needs to adhere to a strict scheme to promote maximum message throughput.

Various theories and tools are used in the development of communications protocols to build the world's computer networks. Several international standards document the formal specification of protocols. Over the years, many of these were developed for proprietary protocols. They were designed for a specific type of hardware or software and would only work in that environment. Developers noted that a more open standards approach to the processes and protocols used for communication was necessary. If protocols could follow specific rules, it would not matter which hardware or software was used.

Support gathered for an open system communication model and eventually the ISO (International Standards Organization) responded with the **Open System Interconnection (OSI)** model for worldwide communication. This model defined a networking framework arranged in **layers** for implementing protocols. Many vendors now support the OSI model, although, on occasion, two or three layers are incorporated into one to satisfy the functionality required. The OSI model is viewed as a teaching model for all other protocols.

Each of the seven layers of the OSI model has a different purpose and can support multiple protocols. The layers are arranged in a hierarchy with the top being Layer 7 and the bottom Layer 1. Some of the layers have been designed to manage user functions, whereas others are specific to network functions. The framework of these layers and their functions are explained in Table 4.4.

LAYER	LAYER NUMBER	FUNCTION
Application	7	Everything at this layer is application-specific. Provides application services for file transfers, e-mail, and telnet. Provides the protocols necessary to perform the specific network service functions.
Presentation	6	Data is transformed into a mutually agreed-upon format (protocol conversion) that can be understood by each network application. Data also is formatted and encrypted and then sent across the network. Data also can be compressed at this layer for sending smaller numbers of packets.
Session	5	Communication sessions are established and managed, and connections are terminated at this layer. Sets up dialogues between the applications at each end and determines which link will transmit first.

Transport	4	Separates the computer network structure from the upper-layer processes. Provides transparent transfer of data between hosts. Responsible for end-to-end recovery and flow control.
Network	3	Moves data to specific locations. Provides switching and routing capabilities and is used to create virtual circuits for transmitting data from source to destination. Other functions include addressing, internetworking, error handling, congestion control, and packet sequencing.
Data Link	2	Bits are organized into data packets and frames. The data packets are encoded and decoded into bits. This layer is divided into two sub layers: Media Access Control (MAC) and Logical Link Control (LLC). (See next section.) The MAC sub layer controls how a computer gains access to the data and permission to transmit it. The LLC sub layer controls frame synchronization, flow control, and error checking.
Physical	1	Conveys the bits as electrical impulses, light signals, or radio signals, depending on the network medium used. Defines the bit transmission timing rules. Specifies the electrical and mechanical specifications for the transmission medium.

TABLE 4.4 **Layers of the OSI Model [Source: Novell, 6-1 to 12-7][Webopedia]**

Control of the data is passed through the layers using headers and trailers. The functions of each layer are embedded into the header and provide services to the layer above. Figure 4.7 shows headers added at each layer except the physical layer (1) and the application layer (7). The packet of data begins at the application layer of Company A and proceeds through the presentation (6), session (5), transport (4), network (3) and data link (2) layers adding a header at each layer. At the other end, Company B, the packet arrives at the physical level with all of its headers. As the packet ascends the OSI hierarchy, it removes a header at each layer. When the packet reaches the top, layer 7, only the original data remains.

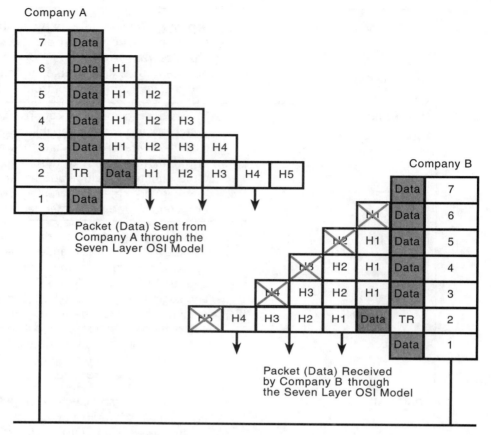

FIGURE 4.7 **OSI Layers with Headers [Source: Teare, 1]**

At each layer of the OSI model, a different name is given to the collection of bits comprising the data. When a user composes a message and sends it from the application layer, it is transported across the Internet as a series of **datagrams**, which are what packets are referred to as in IP networks. (This is discussed in more detail later in this chapter.) At the data link layer, the message is organized into packets and frames. Finally, at the physical layer, the message is sent across as bits (0s and 1s). The following lists layers and their corresponding names:

- Application layer   Messages
- Transport layer   Datagrams and Segments
- Data Link layer   Frames
- Physical layer   Bits

Figure 4.8 shows how the OSI model arranges bits, packets, frames, and datagrams by layer. Note that layers 1-4 are dedicated to network-related functions. Layers 5-7 are involved in presenting the data to the user.

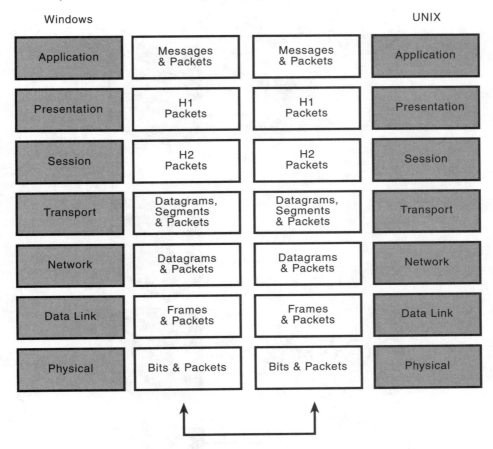

FIGURE 4.8 OSI Model Illustrated as Bits, Packets, Frames, and Datagrams [Source: Novell, 7-2]

Networks running multiple protocols within the LAN and over the WAN are not unusual. The challenge for a network is to support as well as monitor these protocols. Figure 4.9 shows three protocols: AppleTalk (AT), IPX, and TCP/IP. Each has its own addressing scheme, and each network interface must be assigned a network address for each protocol it supports. The router table also must reflect the appropriate method of addressing for each protocol. In this case, a multiprotocol, modular router requires multiple routing interfaces, one for each protocol. At the client side, the network interface card must be configured with drivers required to support multiple protocols.

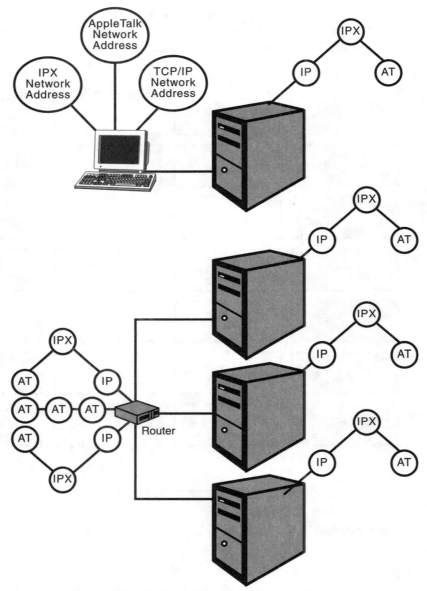

FIGURE 4.9 **Multiprotocols on a Network [Source: Teare, 1]**

Now that the hardware connection has been determined in this multiprotocol scenario, the next step is determining how different protocols map to the OSI model. Some protocols were developed before the OSI model was created, and therefore might not map to it exactly. The OSI model is not a law of communications, but functions as a set of guidelines only, which means that some protocols might not map to it at all.

When the OSI model is used, protocols are divided into lower, middle, and upper layers. At each successive layer, the protocols become more complex and take on additional responsibilities. As shown in Figure 4.10, some protocol stacks combine several functions into one layer. Sometimes a component protocol in one stack performs the same function as a protocol in another stack.

OSI Layer	Apple Computer	IBM SNA	Microsoft	Novell NetWare	TCP/IP Internet
Application Layer 7	Application Programs and Protocols for File Transfer, E-mail, and so on				
Presentation Layer 6	AFP	Transaction Services	SMB	NCP	Telnet, FTP, SMTP, Etc.
Session Layer 5	ASP	Data Flow Control	NetBIOS	NetBIOS	
Transport Layer 4	ATP	Transmission Control	NetBBUI	SPX	TCP UCP
Network Layer 3	DDP	Path Control		IPX	IP
Data Link Layer 2	Network Interface Cards: Ethernet, Token-Ring, ARCNET, StarLAN, LocalTalk,				
Physical Layer 1	Transmission Media				

FIGURE 4.10 **Protocols Mapped to the OSI Model [Source: Lex-Con, 1]**

Because it was developed before the OSI model, the TCP/IP stack does not map exactly layer-to-layer to the OSI model. In fact, TCP/IP does not cover the physical layer of the OSI model at all. To address this, designers have used existing physical standards, which were already developed for Ethernet and LANs. Their goal was to design TCP/IP as a hardware-independent protocol for use with non-proprietary protocols. As a result, TCP/IP is supported by the widest assortment of vendors.

Figure 4.11 shows how the upper layer protocols—FTP, Telnet, and SMTP—perform the same functions as the session, presentation, and application layers of the OSI model. These protocols provide for file transfer and e-mail. Moving down the OSI model, the main transport protocol—TCP—provides addressing services for the network layer. TCP works in connection with IP to move packets across an internetwork. Another protocol, UDP (User Datagram Protocol), accepts and transports datagrams. Like IP, it is a connectionless protocol used for datagram delivery.

In layer 3 in Figure 4.11, the IP protocol operates at the network layer along with routing protocols RIP (Routing Information Protocol) and OSPF (Open Shortest Path First), which are described in more detail later. ICMP (Internet Control Message Protocol) operates at this layer as well because it provides messages about errors during transmission. Finally, ARP (Address Resolution

Protocol) and RARP (Reverse Address Resolution Protocol) are found at the lowest layer in Figure 4.11. These protocols are used to provide address resolution between MAC addresses and IP addresses.

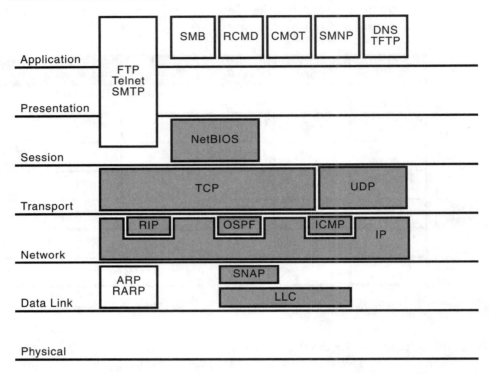

FIGURE 4.11 **TCP/IP Protocol Suite Mapped to OSI Model [Source: Lex-Con, 1]**

Some protocols define the shape of a packet whereas others define the fields within a packet and how they should be interpreted. Protocol suites have rules for an interface to follow between protocols at each successive layer of the OSI model. The primary goal of these rules is to make data exchange possible by compensating for the incompatibilities that can occur between systems.

WAN specifications for protocols are concerned with establishing the connections required over WAN links. The lower layers (physical and data link) operate across physical point-to-point links. The transport layer, on the other hand, operates using end-to-end virtual circuits over packet-switching technologies. WAN protocols are primarily concerned with interfacing functions.

Protocols are also used as core procedures. For example, Figure 4.12 shows that LAPB is the core protocol used for X.25. The LAPB procedure ensures that X.25 packets are successfully transmitted across the link. X.25 uses **packet layer procedures (PLP)** at the network layer to establish and manage the connection setup and disconnection. Because its purpose is to deliver packets error free across the WAN link, LAPB is mapped to the data link layer of the OSI model. [Black, 63]

Data link protocols provide many services for communication between user and network devices: framing, error detection, addressing, flow control, session setup, and termination. Figure 4.12 shows the WAN protocols HDLC, PPP, SDLC, and Frame Relay operating at the data link layer. Some of these protocols are derived from succeeding protocols. HDLC, for example, is a superset of the SDLC protocol. Both of these protocols are used for synchronous communication to the mainframe. The SDLC protocol is used to connect remote devices in either point-to-point or point-to-multipoint connections to the mainframe at a central location. [Sheldon, 305, 306, 581]

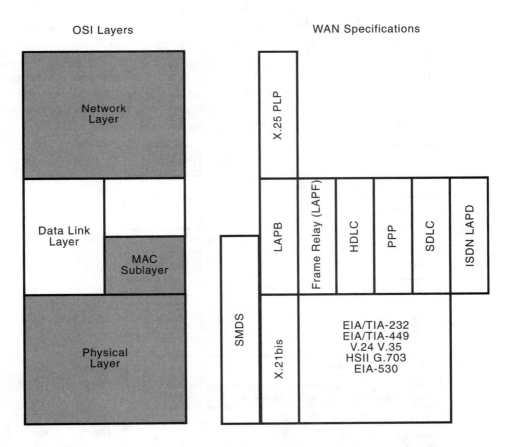

FIGURE 4.12 **WAN Protocols and OSI Model [Source: Cisco, 1]**

Procedures such as HDLC and SDLC were crafted to provide reliable services at a time when terminals could not perform error- or frame checking.

However, the processing power of today's PCs allows these functions to be performed by a NIC in the PC. Services are built into the link access procedures used for ISDN and Frame Relay. In Figure 4.12, notice that LAPD provides the data link control over the D channel of an ISDN connection. LAPD provides physical device addressing, flow control, and frame sequencing. **Link Access Procedure for Frame-Mode Bearer Services (LAPF)**, on the other hand, provides the data link control for Frame Relay networks. [Sheldon, 306] [Sybex, 125] [Sheldon, 728]

Also in Figure 4.12, notice that PPP functions at the data link layer and uses a point-to-point connection to provide Internet connections over dial-up lines. PPP can handle multiple protocols, including TCP/IP, DECnet, AppleTalk, and IPX. PPP also provides router-to-router, host-to-router, and host-to-host connections. At the data link layer, PPP provides a flow of frames into which datagrams are encapsulated and sent across the link.

WAN switching methods function at the first three layers of the model. Figure 4.13 shows circuit-switching functions at the physical layer. With circuit switching, a dedicated physical circuit is established through a carrier network such as AT&T, Sprint, or Qwest. Circuit switching in a WAN is a process similar to a telephone call. It begins with a rapid setup to establish the call. After the call is established, the connection is maintained until the transmission is concluded and disconnected. ISDN is an example of a circuit-switched WAN technology.

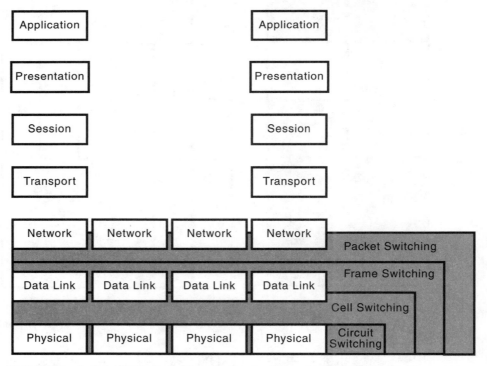

FIGURE 4.13 **WAN Switching Technologies and the OSI Model [Source: Cisco, 1]**

At the data link layer, cell switching operates using ATM technology. ATM creates a virtual circuit between the source and destination locations. These circuits guarantee a specific amount of bandwidth and quality of service. Due to ATM's fixed cell size, it can provide predictable traffic flows at high speeds. Each cell contains an identifier that indicates how the switch should forward the cell. Multiple links can be established between switches allowing ATM connections to be made on the fly as bandwidth is requested. [Sheldon, 65, 74]

Frame switching services are provided at the first two layers of the OSI model as shown in Figure 4.13. At the physical layer, Frame Relay provides point-to-point connections for mesh WAN topologies. Frame Relay provides error detection at the **Logical Link Control (LLC)** sub layer of the data link layer; however, it does not provide for error recovery. Frame Relay assumes that error checking will be performed by higher layer protocols.

Figure 4.13 shows that packet switching operates at the network layer of the OSI model. This WAN-switching method is used to transport packets over a virtual circuit through a packet switch. A single point-to-point path is established between source and destination through a carrier network. Examples of WAN packet-switched technologies are ATM, Frame Relay, SMDS, and X.25.

Along with the functions, protocols, and switching methods, equipment of differing types is used at each layer. Table 4.5 shows that networking equipment is used in the first four layers of the OSI model.

LAYER	LAYER NUMBER	EQUIPMENT
Application	7	N/A
Presentation	6	Gateways
Session	5	N/A
Transport	4	Layer 4 switches
Network	3	Routers, layer 3 switches
Data Link	2	Bridges, switches
Physical	1	Hubs, connectors, cables

TABLE 4.5 **Network Equipment Listed by Layer of OSI Model**

Hubs, connectors, and cables are assembled to perform at the physical layer of the OSI model. These devices, interfaces, and cables are limited to strict technical specifications. The hubs that function at this layer do not have any intelligence built into them, so they cannot make any routing decisions. They simply regenerate or repeat the signal of bits onto the network cable.

The bridges and switches that function at the data link layer are intelligent devices that can filter traffic based on MAC address. To do this, they examine a packet for the MAC address and then consult their dynamic tables to determine whether the packet should stay on the LAN or be routed over the network backbone, and then forward the frame and data accordingly.

Routers function at the network layer, and, like bridges and switches, are also intelligent devices. Routers can filter traffic based on protocols through interfaces. In addition, through their router tables, they can determine the best path to route traffic over the WAN. Layer 3 switches that accomplish both switching services and some routing functions are said to function at the network layer of the OSI model as well.

Layer 4 switches reside at the transport level. Often called application level switches because transport functions are included in the switches themselves, their main responsibility is to ensure reliable communications between the application layers.

Gateways are primarily used for protocol conversion. They actually function at some level at all seven layers of the OSI model. Gateways are often used to translate the TCP/IP protocol used for LANs to the SNA protocol used for mainframes.

TOPIC review — Protocol Design and the OSI Model

1. How is control passed through the seven layers of the OSI model?
2. Which layers of the OSI model contain network functions?
3. What is a protocol suite and how does it function?
4. At what layer of the OSI model do you find Cell Switching?
5. Why are layer 4 switches called application switches?

THE TCP/IP PROTOCOL STANDARD FOR WANS

As early as 1970, the **Advanced Research Projects Agency (ARPA)** had been using TCP/IP to test the viability of packet-switching networks as part of the **ARPAnet** system. TCP/IP was used to facilitate communication across this diverse group of subnetworks. It rose to prominence for two reasons: it had already been adopted as a military standard by the Department of Defense, and it was established as the center of UNIX development at University of California Berkeley. [QuanMongMo, 6, 8]

TCP/IP Services

TCP/IP is a communication architecture used for data exchange, interpretation, and system management. As Figure 4.14 shows, TCP/IP provides several networking services, each with a different function. When the TCP/IP suite is mapped to the OSI model, the application layer protocols are SMTP, FTP, telnet, DNS, RPC, NFS, TFTP, and SNMP; at the transport layer, the protocols are TCP and UDP; and at the network layer, the protocols are RARP, ARP, IP, ICMP, and IGMP.

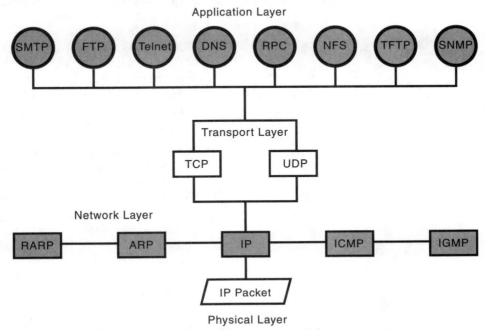

FIGURE 4.14 **TCP/IP Services [Source: Thoresen, 1]**

If organized according to their functions, these services could be grouped into the following categories: transport, routing, network addressing, gateway protocols, and user services. [QuanMongMo, 3-6] Table 4.6 lists the functions of each network service separately by category.

FUNCTION	PROTOCOL	DESCRIPTION
Transport	**Transmission Control Protocol (TCP)**	The primary Internet transport protocol, which is connection-oriented and provides message fragmentation, reassembly, and sequence numbering. It uses TCP acknowledgements to provide error checking and reliable transmission. TCP assigns a connection ID to each virtual circuit through the packet switch over the WAN. [Novell, 13-18]

TABLE 4.6 **TCP/IP Services Listed by Function**

FUNCTION	PROTOCOL	DESCRIPTION
	User Datagram Protocol (UDP)	Accepts and transports datagrams. Like TCP/IP, it is also a transport protocol, however, it is connectionless and does not provide for acknowledgements. Provides a port address as a pointer to a process rather than a virtual circuit connection. Transfers data faster than TCP because it does not need to establish and disconnect connections. [Novell, 13-18]
Routing	Internet Protocol (IP)	A connectionless datagram protocol. A packet-switched network layer implementation that performs addressing and route selection. IP fragments packets into smaller units and numbers them in sequence so they can be reassembled at the destination router. Error checking is performed on the IP header using the checksum algorithm CRC. [Sybex, 110]
	Internet Control Message Protocol (ICMP)	Provides status messages for IP. Functions at the network layer and checks connection services. Notifies IP and upper layer protocols about network-level errors and flow control problems. [Sybex, 111]
	Internet Group Management Protocol. (IGMP)	Establishes host memberships in specific multicast groups on a single network.
	Routing Information Protocol (RIP)	A distance vector routing protocol. Routers using RIP broadcast the entire contents of their routing tables to other routers throughout the network. [Sybex, 112]
	Open Shortest Path First (OSPF)	A link state routing protocol used for route discovery. Provides load balancing and routing based on class of service. Sends only changes to other routers, not the whole router table. [Sybex, 112]

TABLE 4.6 **TCP/IP Services Listed by Function, continued**

FUNCTION	PROTOCOL	DESCRIPTION
Network Addresses	Address Resolution Protocol (ARP)	Converts an IP address into a physical address (MAC or Ethernet address). The physical address comes from the NIC and is located in the source address in a packet.
	Domain Name System (DNS)	A distributed database system used to perform address/name resolution on behalf of client applications. DNS servers maintain databases of domains and hosts for device identification. Consequently, hosts can be identified by logical names rather than by IP addresses. [Novell, 13-18]
	Reverse Address Resolution Protocol (RARP)	The opposite of ARP. Knows the IP address and inquires for the host name. [Sybex, 111]
Gateway Protocols	Exterior Gateway Protocol (EGP)	Transfers routing information for external networks. Provides a method for two neighboring routers located at the edges of their own domains to exchange routing information. [Sheldon, 420]
	Gateway-to-Gateway Protocol (GGP)	Transfers routing information between gateways. One of the first routing protocols developed for use on the Internet, but became inadequate because it could not keep up with all of the dynamic changes on the Internet. [Sheldon, 560]
	Interior Gateway Protocol (IGP)	Transfers routing information for internal networks. The Internet is divided into domains or autonomous systems. IGPs route within a domain. [Sheldon, 609]
User Services	Simple Mail Transfer Protocol (SMTP)	Uses TCP and IP to route mail messages between network hosts. Does not provide a user interface for sending and receiving messages. However, most Internet e-mail applications interface with SMTP. [Sybex, 114]

TABLE 4.6 **TCP/IP Services Listed by Function, continued**

FUNCTION	PROTOCOL	DESCRIPTION
	File Transfer Protocol (FTP)	Transfers files between hosts in an internetwork. Can support file transfers between dissimilar hosts because it uses a generic file structure that is operating-system independent. [Sybex, 113]
	Telnet	Allows a remote computer to emulate a terminal. Users can access host-based applications over the network through remote logins to the host. [Sybex, 113]
	Network File System (NFS)	NFS is a remote file-sharing system used at the application layer. Allows remote file systems and directories on one machine to be mounted on another. Developed by Sun Microsystems. [Novell, 13-19]
	Remote Procedure Call (RPC)	A session layer protocol that enables remote applications to communicate in real time. A software program called a redirector is used to determine whether a request is for the local work-station or files from the network. The redirector handles the call to the net-work and the inter-change is transparent to the user. [Sybex, 114-115]
	Simple Network Management Protocol (SNMP)	Works by sending messages, called protocol data units (PDUs), to different parts of a network. SNMP agents are queried for status. The agents store data about themselves in Management Information Bases (MIBs) and return this data to SNMP requesters. [Webopedia, 1]
	Trivial File Transfer Protocol (TFTP)	Used by servers to boot diskless workstations, X-terminals, and routers. A simple form of FTP.
Other Services	Network Information Service (NIS)	A directory service table used to maintain user accounts across networks. An NIS table contains passwords, user groups, MAC

TABLE 4.6 **TCP/IP Services Listed by Function, continued**

FUNCTION	PROTOCOL	DESCRIPTION
		addresses, and IP addresses. [Sybex, 237]
	Boot Protocol (BOOTP)	Also known as the bootstrap protocol, an Internet protocol that provides network configuration information to boot start a diskless workstation. The boot image provides all of the files required to start the operating system on the computer. BOOTP uses DHCP to derive the IP address for the workstation. [Sheldon, 134]

TABLE 4.6 TCP/IP Services Listed by Function, continued

Addressing on the Internet

Messages are delivered across the Internet based on network addresses. The Internet has a two-level address system that consists of a *host name* and an *IP address*. Every computer attached to the Internet is a host and all hosts have a **host name** that is used to identify the user, application, or workstation.

Each host is recognized by a unique software address called an **IP address**. This address is represented in Dotted Decimal Notation: 142.121.86.132. The IP address is a 32-bit binary number (0s and 1s) composed of two basic parts: network bits and host bits. The address fits into the 32-bit destination and source address fields of the IP headers. Table 4.7 lists the five address classes (A, B, C, D, and E) of IP addresses. Class A addresses are reserved for use by service providers and the military. Class B addresses are used for large companies, such as Microsoft. Class C addresses are limited to 254 hosts and are used for smaller companies. Class D addresses are used for multicasting. Class E addresses are reserved to provide special uses for the Internet.

ADDRESS CLASS	# NETWORK BITS	# HOSTS BITS	DECIMAL ADDRESS RANGE	MAXIMUM NUMBER OF HOSTS
Class A	8 bits	24 bits	1-127	16,777,214
Class B	16 bits	16 bits	128-191	65,534
Class C	24 bits	8 bits	192-223	254
Class D	4 bits	28 bits	224-239	—
Class E	4 bits	—	240-255	—

TABLE 4.7 IP Address Classes

Each of these address classes is allowed a specific number of network bits and host bits. They also have a specific decimal address range. The IP address is divided into 4 octets of 8 bits ($4 \times 8 = 32$ bits). The left part of the IP address points to the network and the right part points to a host. For example, the address 192.171.18.10 is a Class C address, the network portion is 24 bits (192.171.18), and the host portion is 8 bits (.10). For a Class A address, the network would be the first 8 bits or the decimal notation of any address starting with a number between 1 and 126. The address now becomes a Class A, 126.171.18.10.

The **Internet Assigned Numbers Authority (IANA)** was the first organization to coordinate the assignment of official IP addresses and domain names. The IANA also assigned autonomous system numbers, protocol numbers, and port numbers. IANA established the **Internet Network Information Center (InterNIC)** and delegated responsibility to that group for managing the top-level domain names (.com, .org, .net). By the late 1990s, the U.S. government and IANA turned over address allocation to private sector authorities who formed the **Internet Corporation for Assigned Names and Numbers (ICANN)**. The non-profit ICANN organization coordinates the root server system and is dedicated to preserving the stability of the Internet. Currently, Network Solutions, a for-profit organization, provides the actual registration of these IP addresses and assigns class address ranges. [Sheldon, 652]

A hierarchical naming structure called **Domain Name System (DNS)** is used to define official domain names for organizations. The top-level domains are listed in Table 4.8.

EXTENSION	DESCRIPTION	EXTENSION	DESCRIPTION
.com	Commercial	.firm	Business or firm
.edu	Education	.store	Businesses offering goods
.gov	Government	.arts	Culture and Entertainment
.org	Organizational	.rec	Recreational Entertainment
.net	Networks	.info	Information Services
.int	International Treaty Organization	.web	Entities related to the Web
.mil	Military	.nom	For individual nomenclature

TABLE 4.8 **Top-Level Domains**

DNS uses servers with tables of host names and IP addresses to discover and resolve the domain name to a host name and IP address. When an e-mail is sent over the Internet, routing of the e-mail relies on the DNS server to figure out which router to send the mail message to so it will reach its destination. Most ISPs have regional DNS servers strategically located throughout the United States, so fewer router hops are required to retrieve address resolution.

Analysis of IP Datagrams

IP datagrams encapsulate data to carry it across a network. Because IP is a connectionless protocol, it does not require multiple acknowledgements for connection setup. Therefore, the TCP/IP frame is placed inside an IP datagram to enable faster transmission through the network.

The IP datagram contains the information required to provide the router with a destination address for the data to be received. The IP datagram is composed of fields such as type of service, total length, flags, protocol, time to live, identification, and fragment offset. Figure 4.15 shows the placement of each field within the IP datagram. A datagram is a variable length packet consisting of header and data. All the fields described in Table 4.9 are in the header. The data is encapsulated within the IP datagram.

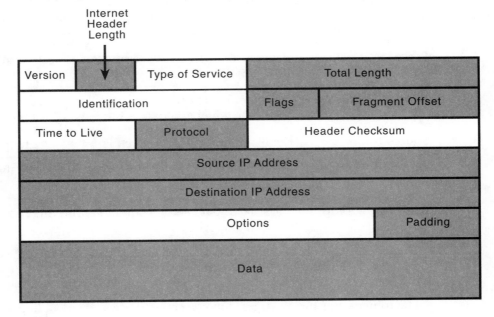

FIGURE 4.15 **Components of an IP Datagram [Source: Dean, 72]**

FIELD	DESCRIPTION
Version	The version number of the protocol.
IHL	Length of the header.
Type of Service	The levels of speed or reliability are specified.
Total Length	The total length of the IP datagram including header. The length cannot exceed 65,535 bytes.
Identification	A value is contained in this field to identify a fragment within a particular datagram.
Flag	A field that indicates whether or not more fragments are coming. If the flag is set to MF, then it indicates this is not the last fragment. Otherwise, if the flag is set to DF, it indicates that the datagram should not be fragmented.
Fragment Offset	Indicates where the datagram fragment fits in the set of fragments.
Time to Live	Tracks total number of passes through the router. With every pass through a router, the counter is decremented.
Protocol	Identifies the transport layer process to receive the datagram.
Header Checksum	Uses an error-detection feature called checksum to determine whether a packet has been corrupted.
Source Address	The IP address of the host sending the datagram.
Destination Address	The IP address of the host identified to receive the datagram.
Options/Padding	A filler field that can be added to ensure the header is a multiple of 32 bits.

TABLE 4.9 **Fields of an IP Datagram**

The router sends the messages along several pathways when guiding them to their destinations. A typical session involves sending packets from a source IP address and a port to a destination IP address and port. The combination of port and IP address is called a **socket**. Packets flow across networks between sockets and end at the destination socket.

TCP Segments

A packet of information that uses TCP to exchange data with its peers is called a **TCP segment**. A TCP segment has a 20-byte header and a variable length data field. The segment is encapsulated into an IP datagram and transmitted across the network. The layout of a TCP segment has 12 fields (see Figure 4.16). The fields in the TCP segment are defined in Table 4.10.

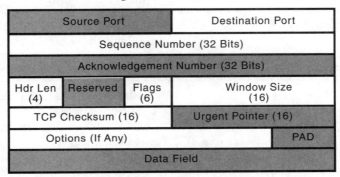

FIGURE 4.16 **Layout of a TCP/IP Segment [Source: Molta, 1]**

FIELD	DESCRIPTION
Source Port, Destination Port	Identifies the port number of the sockets at the source and destination sides of the connection.
Sequence Number	Specifies the number assigned to the first byte of data in the current message. The receiver uses this 32-bit sequential number to identify the data in the TCP segment. The receiver uses the sequence number to reorder any packets that have arrived out-of-order.
Acknowledgement Number	Contains the sequence number for the next segment that the receiver expects to receive. The receiver also uses the Acknowledgement Number to inform the sender when it has already received a packet.
TCP Header Length	Specifies the length of the header.
Reserved	A reserved field.
Sliding Window Size	Indicates to the sender how much space is available in the receiver's buffer. The receiver uses this field to let the sender know it needs to speed up or slow down its transmissions. If the

TABLE 4.10 **Fields of a TCP Segment**

FIELD	DESCRIPTION
	receiver wants the sender to stop transmitting altogether, it can return a segment with 0 in this field.
Checksum	Provides an error-checking value to ensure the integrity of the segment.
Urgent Pointer	Used by the sender to indicate a location in the data where some urgent data is located.
Options	A variable set aside for special options.
Data	A variable-length field that holds the messages or data from applications.

TABLE 4.10 Fields of a TCP Segment, continued

Table 4.11 shows the different kinds of flags that are used by a TCP segment to negotiate communication services.

FLAG	DESCRIPTION
URG	(Urgent) Points to the first urgent data byte in the packet. If this bit is set to 1, information will be found in the Urgent Pointer field of the header.
ACK	(Acknowledgement) Used for acknowledgement and validation. If ACK is set to 1, this indicates that the segment is part of an ongoing conversation and the number in the Acknowledge Number field is valid. If the flag is set to 0 and SYN is set to 1, the segment is a request to establish a connection.
PSH	(Push) A bit set by the sender to request that the receiver send data directly to the application and not buffer it.
RST	(Reset) When set, the connection is invalid for a number of reasons and must be reset.
SYN	Accepts a connection. For a connection request, SYN=1 and ACK =0. When a connection is accepted, SYN=0 and ACK=1. Basically, the process is an acknowledgment of an acknowledgment.
FIN	(Finish) When set, this bit indicates that the connection should be terminated.

TABLE 4.11 Types of Flags Possible in a TCP/IP Segment

TCP uses flow controls, sliding windows, and other techniques when managing sessions. These techniques provide for connection establishment, flow-control management, and congestion control. With each connection, several fields are used to set up and control the connections. The entire process is dedicated to guaranteeing data delivery and providing a reliable service. In an IP environment, TCP provides reliable transmission of data through flow control, full duplex operation, and multiplexing, which are more thoroughly explained in Chapter 5.

Often, Web administrators observe the communication process of IP, UDP, and TCP to diagnose network traffic problems. With the use of a **protocol analyzer**, the administrator can see which protocols are being used for packet transmission and track the communication process from source to destination. The protocol analyzer examines (decodes) all of the fields in the frame and displays the IP packet protocol field and TCP segment port numbers. The protocol analyzer performs frame-by-frame analysis by allowing the administrator to do a network capture of the transmission process. The frame shown in Figure 4.17 (page 196) shows how a network broadcast would appear. The source address is 10.0.0.60, and the destination address is 10.255.255.255. (*255.255.255* means that the packet is a network broadcast.)

Further inspection of the packet reveals all its fields and their values. The version is IP4, the Header Length equals 20, the protocol is UDP, and the checksum value is 0xC538. All of the information about the protocol transmission made available affords an in depth analysis of the communication process.

```
Frame   Time      Src MAC Addr    Dst MAC Addr    Protocol   Description
28      38.016    2400            *BROADCAST      NBT        NS: Query req. for ED1750
```

+ FRAME: Base frame properties
+ ETHERNET: ETYPE = 0x0800 : Protocol = IP: DOD Internet Protocol
  IP: ID = 0x602C; Proto = UDP; Len: 78
    IP: Version = 4 (0x4)
    IP: Header Length = 20 (0x14)
  + IP: Service Type = 0 (0x0)
    IP: Total Length = 78 (0x4E)
    IP: Identification = 24620 (0x602C)
  + IP: Flags Summary = 0 (0x0)
    IP: Fragment Offset = 0 (0x0) bytes
    IP: Time to Live = 128 (0x80)
    IP: Protocol = UDP - User Datagram
    IP: Checksum = 0xC538
    IP: Source Address = 10.0.0.60
    IP: Destination Address = 10.255.255.255
    IP: Data: Number of data bytes remaining = 58 (0x003A)
+ UDP: Src Port: NETBIOS Name Service, (137); Dst Port: NETBIOS Name Service (137);
Length = 58 (0x3A)
  NBT: NS: Query req. for ED1750
    NBT: Transaction ID = 33696 (0x83A0)
  + NBT: Flags Summary = 0x0110 - Req.; Query; Success
    NBT: Question Count = 1 (0x1)
    NBT: Answer Count = 0 (0x0)
    NBT: Name Service Count = 0 (0x0)
    NBT: Additional Record Count = 0 (0x0)
    NBT: Question Name = ED1750
    NBT: Question Type = General Name Service
    NBT: Question Class = Internet Class
+ FRAME: Base frame properties
+ ETHERNET: ETYPE = 0x0800 : Protocol = IP: DOD Internet Protocol
  IP: ID = 0x7530; Proto = UDP; Len: 90
    IP: Version = 4 (0x4)
    IP: Header Length = 20 (0x14)
  + IP: Service Type = 0 (0x0)
    IP: Total Length = 90 (0x5A)
    IP: Identification = 30000 (0x7530)
  + IP: Flags Summary = 0 (0x0)
    IP: Fragment Offset = 0 (0x0) bytes
    IP: Time to Live = 128 (0x80)
    IP: Protocol = UDP - User Datagram
    IP: Checksum = 0xB0C3
    IP: Source Address = 10.0.0.100
    IP: Destination Address = 10.0.0.60
    IP: Data: Number of data bytes remaining = 70 (0x0046)
+ UDP: Src Port: NETBIOS Name Service, (137); Dst Port: NETBIOS Name Service (137);
Length = 70 (0x46)
  NBT: NS: Query (Node Status) resp. for ED1750, Success
    NBT: Transaction ID = 33696 (0x83A0)
  + NBT: Flags Summary = 0x8500 - Resp.; Query; Success
    NBT: Question Count = 0 (0x0)
    NBT: Answer Count = 1 (0x1)
    NBT: Name Service Count = 0 (0x0)
    NBT: Additional Record Count = 0 (0x0)
    NBT: Resource Record Name = ED1750
    NBT: Resource Record Type = NetBIOS General Name Service
    NBT: Resource Record Class = Internet Class
    NBT: Time To Live = 300000 (0x493E0)
    NBT: RDATA Length = 6 (0x6)
  + NBT: Resource Record Flags = 24576 (0x6000)
    NBT: Owner IP Address = 10.0.0.100
- 3 -

FIGURE 4.17 **Broadcast Packet Capture [Source: Wilson, 1]**

Chapter 4 • WAN Protocols

Browser Request to the Internet

Every computer that is connected to the Internet uses Web browsers to look at and interact with information on the World Wide Web. The primary means of transmitting that information over the Internet is TCP/IP and its services.

A Web browser makes a request to a Web server for information or pages. The Web server has a host name and an IP address. A **Uniform Resource Locator (URL)** is used to request a domain name such as http://www.emcp.com. The domain name is "emcp.com". One of the Internet's DNS servers must respond to the request and translate the domain name into its IP address. The IP address is now available to access the URL.

For example, Sarah is requesting a Web page from http://www.emcp.com. She types in the URL in her Web browser and waits for a response. TCP segments are used to set up the connection. Figure 4.18 shows that three segments are required to open the connection. The first SYN bit is set to 1 and sent to the Web server to request a connection. Next, the second segment SYN is sent to open a connection and acknowledges the first SYN message. Finally, an ACK message is returned from the Web server to acknowledge receipt of the TCP segment.

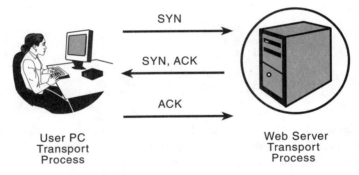

SYN

SYN, ACK

ACK

User PC
Transport
Process

Web Server
Transport
Process

FIGURE 4.18 **TCP Segments Required to Open a Connection [Source: Molta, 1]**

Sarah's PC sends a **Hypertext Transfer Protocol (HTTP)** request, because HTTP is the protocol used for communication between a Web server and a Web browser. Figure 4.19 shows that her **HTTP request** is in the data field of the packet. A header is added to encapsulate the HTTP request within a TCP segment.

After the Web server receives the HTTP request, it sends back an ACK to acknowledge receipt. Next, the transport layer process on the Web server passes the HTTP request along to the Web server application program. The Web server application then creates an HTTP response message to deliver to Sarah's PC. When it is received at Sarah's PC, an acknowledgement (ACK) is sent to verify receipt of the HTTP response which in this case is the Web page for www.emcp.com.

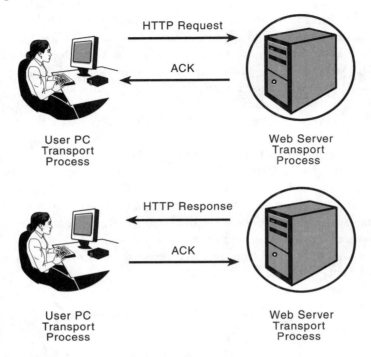

FIGURE 4.19 **HTTP Request and Response [Source: Molta, 1]**

Sarah views the Web page for some time and finally downloads the last file. She then decides to leave the site and close her browser. Figure 4.20 shows that it takes four TCP segments to close the connection. The browser initiates the closing process after the last file has been downloaded. First, the browser sets the FIN bit to 1 to inform the Web server that the connection is going to close. The Web server sends back an ACK response to acknowledge the request to close the connection. Next, the browser sends a second FIN to close the connection. Finally, the Web server responds with an acknowledgment and closes the connection.

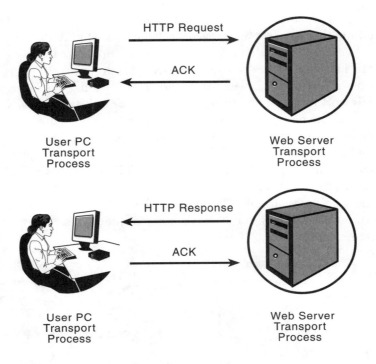

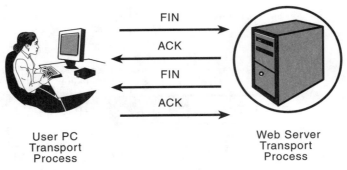

FIGURE 4.20 **Closing the Connection [Source: Molta, 1]**

During the time Sarah spent on the Web, a total of 11 TCP segments were sent back and forth between her PC and the Web server. To summarize this process:

- Three TCP segments were required to open the connection
- Two TCP segments were used by Sarah's PC to send the HTTP request and obtain acknowledgement for each request-response
- Two TCP segments were used to send the HTTP response from the Web server and obtain acknowledgement for each request-response
- Four TCP segments were required to close the connection

This process of repeatedly acknowledging each request and response to ensure that the data has arrived demonstrates why TCP/IP is so reliable.

The next example illustrates the routing processes involved in processing HTTP requests. In this case, the user Antonio wants to request a Web page from a Web server in Italy. In Figure 4.21, Antonio has initiated his request. His workstation finds the router used to connect to the WAN. The router looks to find the best path to the Web server in Italy. It inquires to resolve the destination IP address from a regional DNS server. After the IP address is resolved, the router forwards the HTTP request to the router in Italy where the Web server is located. In Figure 4.21, the HTTP request has been formatted with an IP header that has the IP address of Antonio's PC (source) and the IP address of the Web server in Italy (destination). The Ethernet or MAC address of Antonio's PC and the Ethernet address of the Web server in Italy appear in the frame.

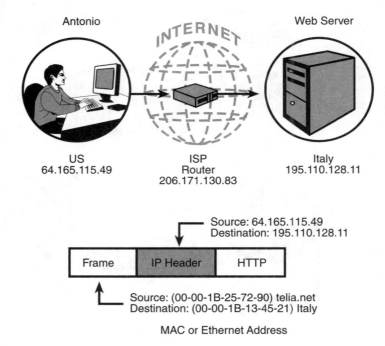

FIGURE 4.21 **Routing a Packet to Italy**

The router table in Figure 4.22 shows the routing path that was determined to connect to the Web server in Italy. Inside the router-forwarding table, the router compares the destination IP address to each row in the table. If the table matches the IP address, the router delivers according to the delivery rule defined for that path. As shown in row 3, the IP address matches and its delivery rule forwards the packet to the router in Italy (195.110.128.1).

IP Address	Delivery
128.165.11.15	Local
0.0.0.0.	Next Hop Router
206.171.130.83	195.110.128.1

FIGURE 4.22 **Router Forwarding Table**

Today's dynamic routing protocols treat all routers as peers (neighboring routers). A router creates a router-forwarding table strictly according to the information retrieved from its peers and any manual entries entered into its table. The router uses the destination IP address of the incoming packet to decide which output port to use to send the packet over the WAN to the next router. Figure 4.23 shows that after the interface has been determined, the packets are sent across the Internet to the Web server in Italy. There, the router consults its table and determines that the IP address of the Web server is inside its network. The router forwards the packets to the hub or switch to which the Web server is attached. Now the HTTP request/response/acknowledgement process begins to deliver the home page of the Web site to Antonio.

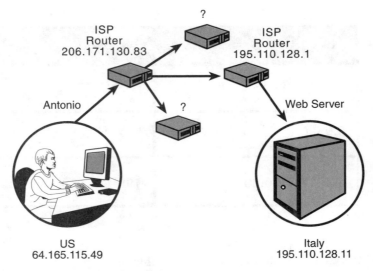

FIGURE 4.23 **Router Forwarding to Web Server in Italy [Source: Molta, 1]**

TOPIC *review* **The TCP/IP Protocol Standard for WANs**

1. Why are TCP packets encapsulated in IP datagrams?
2. What are the combination of port and IP addresses called?
3. What techniques does TCP use to manage sessions?
4. What is the purpose of a router table?
5. How do routers get information for their router-forwarding tables?

ROUTING ALGORITHMS AND PROTOCOLS

Routing is a method of path selection that enables information to find its way from one host computer to another. One feature that all routing protocols share is the **routing algorithm**. A routing protocol uses a routing formula, called an algorithm, to calculate the best path between two networks. The routing protocol determines the algorithm that will be used by the router. The routing protocol then collects information or values used by the algorithm to calculate a routing path. These values are referred to as *metrics*. A **metric** is a number used as a standard of measurement for each link on a network. Each WAN link is assigned a cost (metric) for the amount of bandwidth provided and the cost to use the link to reach the destination.

Routing Algorithms

Today, basically two different algorithms are used by routing protocols: *distance vector* and *link state*. There is a distinct difference in how paths are determined between these two algorithms. The distance vector algorithm uses one metric **hop count**, to calculate the lowest cost between source and destination. Each hop in a path is assigned a hop-count value, which is typically 1. However, a link state protocol uses more than one metric, such as network traffic, connection speed, and network congestion to determine lowest cost.

When a router uses a **distance vector algorithm**, its goal is to determine the best path at the lowest total cost to the destination. Figure 4.24 shows several links between the routers. Each link has been assigned a cost. Costs for links are determined in different ways; some are arbitrary, and others are based on latency or reliability of the link. The WAN administrator determines the assignment of costs. All of the costs are collected and placed in the routing table of the router. The distance vector algorithm calculates the best path from source to destination by adding costs for several links until it finds the one with the least hop count.

Looking at Figure 4.24, two paths are available from Site E to Site G. One path goes from E to F to G. The other path goes from E to B to F to G. The cost for E/F/G is 1+2=3. For E/B/F/G, the cost is 1+2+3=6. The distance vector algorithm calculates for the lowest cost, which in this case is E/F/G because the cost is 3. The router, then, would use this path to send packets from E to G.

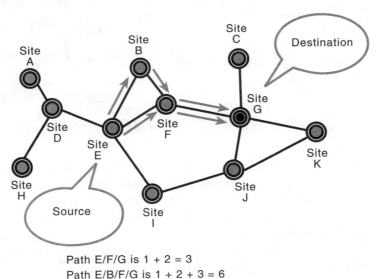

Path E/F/G is 1 + 2 = 3
Path E/B/F/G is 1 + 2 + 3 = 6

FIGURE 4.24 **Distance Vector Algorithm**

A **link state algorithm** creates a database of links and costs. It assigns a sequence number to synchronize databases with neighboring routers. In Figure 4.25, the path is from A to B, the link is 1, the cost is 1, and the sequence number is 2. Looking at the path from A to D, the link is now 3, the cost is 1 and the sequence number is 2. A link state router computes the least cost path from one source to all of its adjacent neighbor routers. It sends a **Link State Announcement (LSA)** to its neighbor routers whenever there is an update to the network. These router neighbors copy the information without changing it and send it to their router neighbors.

Looking again at Figure 4.25, all paths are listed from A to B, A to D, B to A, B to C, B to E, and so on. Depending on which path is selected, the link designator is different based on whether it's going from B to A or B to C or B to E. For instance, the link from A to B is 1, but the link from B to C is 2 and the link from B to E is 4.

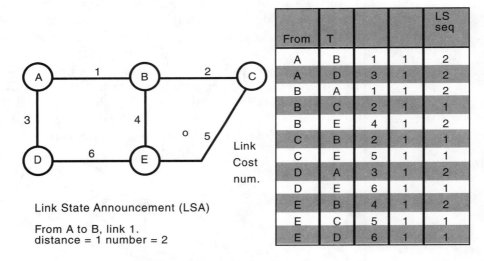

From	T			LS seq
A	B	1	1	2
A	D	3	1	2
B	A	1	1	2
B	C	2	1	1
B	E	4	1	2
C	B	2	1	1
C	E	5	1	1
D	A	3	1	2
D	E	6	1	1
E	B	4	1	2
E	C	5	1	1
E	D	6	1	1

Link State Announcement (LSA)

From A to B, link 1.
distance = 1 number = 2

FIGURE 4.25 **Link State Algorithm Database [Source: Popova, 1]**

A comparison of the characteristics of the two algorithms shows that distance vector algorithms are simpler and less resource intensive. However, they lack the variety of metrics needed for efficient routing and thus can cause slow performance in large networks. Link state algorithms were developed to overcome the disadvantages of distance vector. The advantages of link state are that each router maintains an identical database, each router sends only changes about its adjacent neighbor routers, and it synchronizes as quickly as a database can be updated. [Berkowitz, 277] [Popova, 4]

Routing Protocols

Several routing protocols are available and new ones are currently being developed to handle congestion, compression, audio transmissions, and video transmissions. The various routing protocols and their functions are listed in Table 4.12.

PROTOCOL	FUNCTION
Border Gateway Protocol (BGP)	An Internet protocol used between ISPs. The groups of routers share routing information to establish loop free routes between ISPs.
Enhanced Interior Gateway Routing Protocol (EIGRP)	Used for large-scale internetworks. An EIGRP router stores copies of all its neighbors' routing tables so it can adapt quickly to alternate routes.
IS-IS	An OSI link state routing protocol that dynamically routes packets between routers or intermediate systems. It is primarily used by large ISPs.
Interior Gateway Routing Protocol (IGRP)	A proprietary network protocol developed by Cisco Systems. This distance vector routing protocol uses five criteria to determine the best path: link speed, delay, packet size, loading, and reliability.
Open Shortest Path First (OSPF)	Based on the link state algorithm, it calculates the shortest path to each node based on the network topography. Exchanges only update information about routes to neighboring routers not the entire router table (RIP).
Routing Information Protocol (RIP)	Specifies how routers exchange routing table information. Routers periodically exchange their entire router tables.
Routing Information Protocol 2 (RIP2)	Developed to make RIP more efficient. Allows for better use of assigned IP addresses. Adds authentication for network security and minimizes the effect of network broadcasts by assigning a multicast address to the RIP2 packet.
Routing Information Protocol Next Generation (RIPng for IPv6)	A distance vector protocol intended to allow routers to exchange information for computing routes through an IPv6-based network.

TABLE 4.12 **Routing Protocols [Webopedia, 1] [Malkin & Minnear, 3] [Freesoft, 1]**

Distance Vector Protocols

Routing protocols can be divided by algorithm. The routing protocols that use distance vector algorithms are IRGP, EIGRP, RIP, RIP2, and RIPng for IPv6. The routing protocols that use link state algorithms are BGP, IS-IS, and OSPF.

A direct correlation exists between routing protocols and the performance of IP and TCP protocols within the network. Routing protocols control whether packet delivery is timely or successful. The successful operation of IP depends upon efficient IP routing. If the basic routing service does not work well, slow delivery, lost packets, or duplicate datagrams could result. For example, it was discovered over time that RIPv1 and IGRP did not function well with client/server-based applications in large networks because they were too slow to converge their routing tables. [Source: DiMarzio, 1]

EIGRP and Convergence

Convergence is a dynamic routing process used when a routing table is updated. It describes the state of agreement of router tables between all routers in the network. When a link fails or the network topology changes, updates are sent across the network to other routers to describe the changes. As each router receives the update, they recalculate routes and build new routing tables. After all of the routers in the network have updated their routing tables, convergence is complete.

EIGRP is used today for IP, AppleTalk, and Novell Netware Networks. It supports partial updates, fast convergence, and multiple network layer protocols. Partial updates are sent only when the metric for a route changes. When a router uses EIGRP, it keeps a copy of its neighbor's routing tables. If the router can't find a route, it queries the neighbors to discover an alternate route. The router's neighbors also query until an alternate route is found. Each router is kept aware of the state of its neighbors. [Webopedia, 1]

EIGRP uses a neighbor discovery/recovery mechanism to dynamically learn about other routers on its directly attached networks. A periodic "hello" packet is sent to its neighbors. If a "hello" packet has not been received from a neighbor within a certain period of time, that router is assumed to be unreachable. EIGRP uses **Reliable Transport Protocol (RTP)** to guarantee ordered delivery of all packets to its neighbors. RTP uses a multicast method to send hello packets reliably to all neighbors. Update packets have an indicator included in the packet to request receipt acknowledgement. [Pepelnjak, 1]

EIGRP uses the **Diffusing-Update Algorithm (DUAL)** to determine the least-cost route to a destination. EIGRP consults a DUAL finite-state machine for route computations that have been advertised by its neighbors. The DUAL algorithm considers distance and whether a destination path is loop-free to determine the least-cost route. EIGRP is more efficient than standard distance vector routing protocols because it imposes much less overhead on routers during typical operation. [Sportack, 1]

Link State Routing Protocols

Today, the most frequently used link state routing protocols are OSPF, BGP, and IS-IS. All respond quickly to changes in network topology. These protocols are considered to be superior to RIP for large networks. The primary advantages of these protocols are as follows:

- Autonomous systems can be used to reduce the amount of routing information required on the network.
- Cost metrics support path preferences for a given type of traffic.
- Convergence is faster.
- Classless Inter-Domain Routing (CIDR) addresses are supported.
- Secure encrypted information can be exchanged between routers.

Link state routing protocols use an **autonomous system,** which is a collection of networks under common administration that share a universal routing strategy. Autonomous systems are separated into areas. An **area** is a group of routers within logically defined network segments. When areas are connected with routers, a single autonomous system is established. [Downes, 727]

Routing domains are sets of routers that use the same routing code, administrative rules, and values for metrics. One or more areas can exist inside a routing domain. If multiple areas exist, an association in the form of a hierarchical relationship is created between the areas. Each area is uniquely identified by an area address. For example, if internal network addresses are hidden in a private **network address translation (NAT)** is used to represent all the internal addresses as a single IP address to the Internet. Routers within an autonomous system can send link information to one another. They build a link state database based on the link information it acquires. [Berkowitz, 659]

OSPF

Open Shortest Path First routing is used within larger autonomous system networks. This interior gateway routing protocol is used to send and receive routes from other autonomous systems. It is known as shortest path routing because it calculates the shortest path to each node through the Internet. A change to the network is recognized immediately because the routers send small updates frequently. Each router only sends the specific portion of the router table that describes the status of its own links. Routers within the autonomous system send link information to one another. They build a link state database that contains link path information only for the network defined within their area.

OSPF supports a costing method for paths that allows some paths to be assigned a preference based on type of service (TOS). TOS specifies how to make routing decisions based on throughput, delay, reliability, and cost. OSPF also provides secure encrypted information exchange between routers. Finally, it supports **Classless Inter-Domain Routing (CIDR)** for more efficient addressing over the Internet. [Sheldon, 947, 1259]

OSPF and CIDR

CIDR allows routers to group routes together to reduce the quantity of routing information that is carried by the core routers. This new IP addressing scheme allows a single IP address to designate several unique IP addresses. The purpose of CIDR is to reduce the size of routing tables and offer more IP addresses within an organization. CIDR also enables route aggregation, which is used to summarize routes so there are fewer routes to advertise across the Internet. For example, in 1995 there were 65,000 routes. The number of routes now has been reduced to 35,000 after CIDR aggregation has been implemented. [Sheldon, 205, 1070]

CIDR has restructured IP address assignments by adding a network **prefix**. A special mask indicates how many bits in the address represent the network prefix. The syntax of an IP prefix is a slash followed by a number at the end of an IP address. Prefixes can have a value ranging from 13 to 27 bits. For example, in the CIDR address *206.200.18.48/25*, "/25" indicates the first 25 bits are used to identify the unique private network. The remaining bits identify a specific host on that network. [Webopedia, 1] [Pacific Bell, 2]

Although the introduction of CIDR has helped increase the number of Internet addresses, there is still a limited supply. CIDR has become the routing system of choice for virtually all gateway hosts on the Internet's backbone. This backbone is made up of many routing domains formed by local, regional, and backbone service providers. Each of these domains is an autonomous system. Each autonomous system is managed independently and manages its own internal routing within the perimeters of its domain. Interior routing protocols are called **intradomain routing** because they provide routing within a domain. Routing between autonomous systems is called **interdomain, or exterior routing**. [Sheldon, 946]

Intermediate System-to-Intermediate System

IS-IS is one of the most commonly used routing protocols. An intermediate system is defined as an OSI link state hierarchical routing protocol designed to operate in OSI **Connectionless Network Service (CLNP)**. This protocol provides connectionless datagram services such as IP, but it is only used over OSI networks. IS-IS is an interior (intradomain) routing protocol, which offers significant scalability with fast convergence for service providers. Large routing domains use a two-level hierarchy in which groups of routers can be assigned to a domain. Level 1 routers function within a domain and Level 2 routers function in-between domains. [Sheldon, 694] [Cisco, 1] [Webopedia, 1]

IS-IS is similar to OSPF in that it stores information about the state of the links and uses that information to select paths to the destination. IS-IS sends out the link state information from time to time so that each router has a current image of the network topology. IS-IS achieves convergence rapidly over much larger internetworks and is less prone to routing loops. Service providers (ISPs and telcos) use SONET (Synchronous Optical Network) rings to establish high-performance WANs and require IS-IS as their routing protocol. [Berkowitz, 277, 424]

BGP

Interdomain routing uses external connections through gateways to the outside world. These connections are established with a *border router*. A **border router** provides information about all of its internal routes to other border routers belonging to the other autonomous systems. The primary exterior routing protocol used today for autonomous systems is **Border Gateway Protocol (BGP)**. Service providers use BGP to exchange information about routes between domains. In fact, today, ISPs manage 100,000 BGP routes in the Internet core backbone routers. [Sheldon, 118]

BGP actually uses a combination of both distance vector and link state routing algorithms. Distance vector is used when a new BGP router is added to the network. The entire routing information table is exchanged to the new BGP router. However, after the initial router table is loaded, BGP uses the link state algorithm to send updates on a periodic basis. [Sheldon, 120]

The primary function of the BGP routing protocol is to exchange network-access information. Each BGP router maintains a routing table that lists all possible paths to a specific network. BGP uses only one routing metric to determine the best path to a known network. Each link has an assigned value established for stability, speed, or cost. The BGP routing tables include the network address and an AS path value to other autonomous systems. A BGP administrator can use a metric to assign a preference for one path over another. Criteria can be assigned to the bandwidth of a path or the specific autonomous systems it passes through. [Downes, 502]

Routing Policies and Software Architecture

As the amount of traffic increases on the Internet, router administrators need to be able to control traffic through routing policies. **Routing policies** allocate network resources such as: bandwidth, Quality of service (QoS), and firewalls according to defined business policies. The software architecture of the router provides the intelligence to analyze protocols, determine packet forwarding, and enforce policies. Figure 4.26 shows all of the operations within a router. The central processing unit (CPU) inside the router must balance and shift to manage multiple functions.

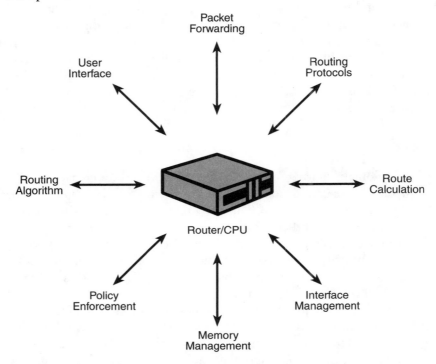

FIGURE 4.26 **Routing Software Architecture [Source: Juniper Networks, 1]**

When routing policies are implemented, the complexity of the process increases. Policies are designed to accept and distribute routing information. Policies for acceptance of data are called **import policies**. **Export policies** are those rules that are distributed across the network to other routers. Policies ask "if/ then" questions about specific conditions. A condition can be a user, a group, a type of application, or a network address. When a policy is initiated, filtering rules are defined that route packets based on "If condition, then action" statements. [Juniper Networks, 1]

Figure 4.27 shows the use of policies to route information between ISPs. In this scenario, there are two ISPs. The large ISP provides ISP services to the smaller ISP. The small ISP has many peers labeled Peer A-F and the large ISP has peers labeled Peer 1-6. The large ISP configures policy rules so that it accepts only the routes it has agreed to from the smaller ISP. The Service Level Agreement (SLA) between the small and large ISP requires notification of changes. If the smaller ISP adds a customer, it informs the large ISP that it will be forwarding new prefixes. The large ISP updates the list of routes by modifying its routing filtering rules to accept the new prefix from the small ISP.

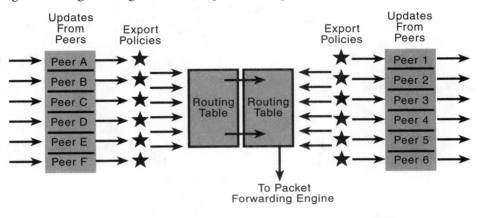

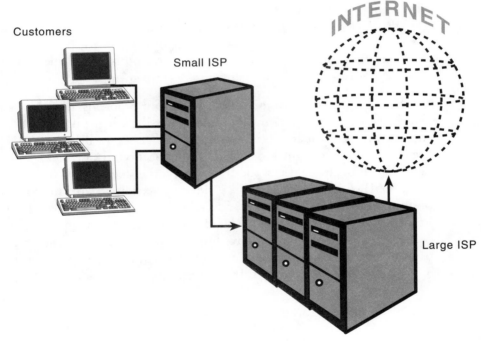

FIGURE 4.27 **Router Policy Filtering [Source: Juniper Networks, 1]**

Based on the router algorithm, either distance vector or link state, routers use different methods to communicate to other routers. Most routers today use link state protocols because they are dynamic and can respond quickly to changes in network topology. Large organizations require policies in routers to accept and distribute routing information. ISPs use policies to route Internet traffic.

Currently, 450 million users are connected to the Internet worldwide. When the current addressing method (**IPv4**) was initially developed, it never anticipated that every person worldwide would have access to a computer and the Internet. There has been a shortage of IP addresses for several years. The IETF developed IPv6 to create a new addressing scheme so there will be plenty of addresses in the future.

IPv4 versus IPv6

A new version of IP was conceived as a solution to support addressing for large global internetworks. This version, **IPv6 or IPng (IP next generation)** provides significant improvements over its predecessor, IPv4, such as:

- IP addresses lengthened from 32 bits to 128 bits
- Header fields reduced from IPv4's 13 fields to 7 fields
- A priority field added for real-time traffic
- Rules defined for three types of addressing
- Unicast—one host to one other host—implemented
- Anycast—one host to the nearest multiple hosts—implemented
- Multicast—one host to many hosts—implemented

The IETF created IPv6 to alleviate two major problems: the address shortage and the lack of security. With IPv6, the addressing scheme uses a 128-bit address, which provides 340 undecillion IP addresses. [Kalyanaraman ,1] Security has been designed to provide authentication, data integrity, and confidentiality through the use of the IPSec encryption method.

In the IPv6 frame in Figure 4.28, only the version number has the same position and meaning as in IPv4. Several fields have been removed such as header length, fragmentation fields (identification, flags, fragment offset), and header checksum. Some fields have been replaced, such as: datagram length by payload length, protocol type by next header, Time to live by hop limit, and (4) Type of service by "class" octet. [Kalyanaraman, 1]

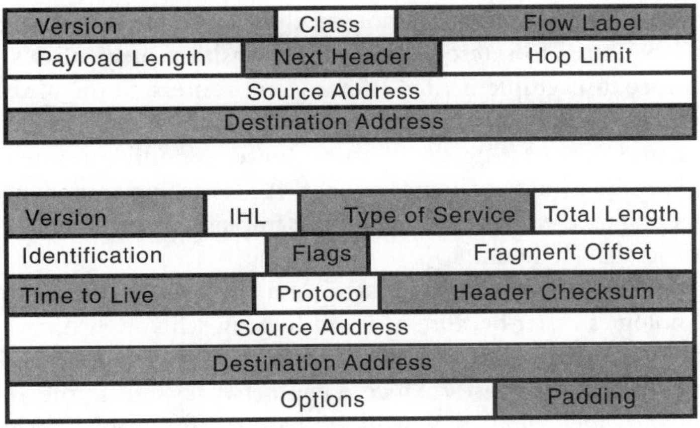

Version		Class		Flow Label	
Payload Length		Next Header		Hop Limit	
Source Address					
Destination Address					

Version	IHL	Type of Service		Total Length	
Identification		Flags		Fragment Offset	
Time to Live		Protocol		Header Checksum	
Source Address					
Destination Address					
Options				Padding	

FIGURE 4.28 **Field Comparison IPv4 to IPv6 [Source: Kalyanaraman, 1]**

In addition, **extension headers** have replaced the optional fields defined in IPv4. In Figure 4.29, the extension headers have been added in between the data and the base header. The use of extension headers allows for authentication, hop-by-hop, and destination options. Most IPv6 extension headers are not examined by any router along the path until the packet arrives at its final destination. In IPv4, the router had to take the time to examine all of the options. The changes in the IP header options for IPv6 offer more efficient forwarding and greater flexibility for new options to be added in the future. [Kalyanaraman, 1]

Base Header	Extension Header 1		Extension Header *n*	Data

FIGURE 4.29 **Extension Headers in IPv6 [Source: Kalyanaraman, 1]**

IPv6 offers several new features as part of the protocol. These features are significant because they implement QoS, authentication, and privacy capabilities. For QoS, packets are labeled to designate specific traffic flows. A 20-bit flow identifier is used to provide bandwidth reservations, flow identification, and traffic prioritization across routers. This significantly improves the flow of traffic across the Internet between service providers. IPv6 also includes extensions for authentication, data integrity, and confidentiality. Security is provided by the use of IPSec encryption, which is built into the protocol for all implementations. [Sheldon, 675]

Because there is a significant difference in the addressing methods of IPv4 and IPv6, designers had to figure how to exchange data between a 32-bit packet and a 128-bit packet. Transition mechanisms had to be developed to allow IPv6 and IPv4 hosts to interoperate. These transition mechanisms are a set of protocol procedures implemented in hosts and routers. Some of the features of these mechanisms are: incremental upgrade deployment, easy addresses, low start-up costs, and dual routing capabilities. Router vendors can integrate IPv6 into their product lines at their own pace. All hosts and routers upgraded to IPv6 are "dual" capable which means they can implement complete IPv4 and IPv6 protocol stacks. [Hinden, 15]

IPv6 has a more flexible design than IPv4, and can accommodate emerging technologies easier because of its addressing scheme. It has significantly improved routing, traffic management, and security. IPv6 is designed to perform well on high performance ATM networks, but at the same time allow for low bandwidth wireless networking required for mobile devices such as PDAs and mobile phones. It also can improve the speed of transmissions for peak congestion periods on the Internet. Both users and service providers can upgrade to IPv6 independently without having to coordinate with each other. [Hinden, 16] [TechTarget, 1]

TOPIC review **Routing Algorithms and Protocols**

1. What one feature is shared between several routing protocols?
2. Why are distance vector algorithms simpler and less resource-intensive than link state algorithms?
3. How do routing protocols affect packet delivery?
4. What do router administrators use to control network traffic?
5. Does IPv6 offer any features for data encryption within a protocol?

CHAPTER SUMMARY

Today, employees can use the Internet to access information resources beyond what their organizations could provide on their own. Every day employees send e-mail messages to other company offices. They often request a Web page for information they need to solve a business problem. Sending mail and retrieving Web pages involve the use of packets, frames, headers, trailers, and protocols to control the communication process.

TCP/IP is the fundamental technology used for communication at the root of the Internet. TCP/IP is used to establish the connection, transmit the data, and close the connection. E-mail is carried across the Internet in a TCP/IP packet.

The most basic element within TCP/IP is the IP datagram. The IP datagram uses IP to transport the data to the Internet. IP has no obligation to guarantee the data will reach its destination, it simply routes the data across the network.

TCP segments are added to the IP datagram to ensure the delivery of the data. TCP segments guarantee delivery through the use of acknowledgements between sender and receiver. The communication process requires that each packet must be acknowledged before another can be sent.

Finally, IP datagrams are sent from the user's desktop to the Internet through routers. The address information and application data are found inside the IP datagram. Routers assume that addresses have been assigned to packets to facilitate data delivery. If an e-mail message is sent to a user in London, the message travels halfway across the world through several routers to arrive at its destination. The router reads the destination address and uses an algorithm to calculate the best path to the destination. A routing protocol is defined to the router to tell it which algorithm to use to find the best path.

Routing protocols determine how routers communicate to other routers. Based on either a distance vector or link state routing algorithm, routers communicate to other routers. Most routers today use link state algorithms—OSPF, BGP, and IS-IS—because these dynamic routing protocols all respond quickly to changes in network topology. Neighbor routers provide path information to each other through updates. The update process tells them the status of the communication links so that they all know which links are available for sending data.

Every computer on the Internet must have an identifying number called an IP address to communicate with other computers. These IP addresses are embedded in IP datagrams and are used to send messages to the destination computer. Currently, these are represented as 32-bit addresses. Network addresses are divided into Classes A, B and C, and D and E, which are used to organize, and are distinguished by the number of networks and hosts in an organization.

The addressing method currently used today, when initially developed, never accounted for the possibility that virtually every person in the world one day would have access to a computer and the Internet. As a result, for a number of years, there has been a shortage of IP addresses. The development of the new IPv6 has been slow. It has taken many years to determine how to create a new addressing scheme that would prevent the Internet community from running out of addresses in the future. IPv6 has been designed to work concurrently with IPv4 through transition mechanisms to protect significant investments by organizations in TCP/IP.

The potential of IPv6 as a replacement for IPv4 is attractive, but widespread immediate deployment is not reasonable given the number of computers and servers that need to be upgraded. It will eventually begin to be adopted; however, it might be a long time before it becomes a standard.

CHAPTER REVIEW QUESTIONS

(This quiz can also be printed out from the Encore! CD that accompanies this textbook. File name—Chap04review.)
Circle a letter (a-d) for each question. Choose only one answer for each.

1. Routers use _____ to determine how to calculate paths and forward packets.
   a. address
   b. interfaces
   c. algorithms
   d. protocols

2. The values collected by routers to calculate routing paths are called
   a. metrics
   b. tables
   c. formulas
   d. protocols

3. A dynamic routing process used during the router table update process is called
   a. recalculation
   b. algorithm
   c. formulation
   d. convergence

4. An autonomous system is defined as
   a. a group of network addresses
   b. a collection of networks under common administration
   c. a geographic area
   d. a routing domain

5. The primary advantage of Classless Inter-Domain Routing is that it
   a. disables route aggregation
   b. increases the size of router tables
   c. reduces the quantity of routing information carried by core routers
   d. decreases the number of IP addresses

6. Interdomain routing uses _____ _____ to travel through gateways to the outside world.
   a. intermediate connections
   b. internal connections
   c. external connections
   d. direct connections

7. A protocol used to convert an IP address into a physical address (MAC or Ethernet) is called
   a. ACK
   b. ARP
   c. DNS
   d. RIP

8. Which is the most significant difference between IPv4 and IPv6
   a. 32- versus 128-bit addressing
   b. 32- versus 64-bit addressing
   c. 32- versus 132-bit addressing
   d. 32- versus 256-bit addressing

9. With IPv6, what has replaced the optional fields?
   a. flow labels
   b. octets
   c. extension headers
   d. identifiers

10. Which routing protocol is used to share routing information among a group of routers to establish loop-free routes between ISPs?
    a. IRGP
    b. EIGRP
    c. RIP2
    d. BGP

Circle the correct letter (A-E) that corresponds to the descriptions below. Choose only one answer for each.
   A. Frame
   B. Payload
   C. Protocol Suite
   D. FCS
   E. Header

11. A B C D E   Contains all of the fields to be used to perform the function of a specific protocol.

12. A B C D E   A set of network protocol layers that work together.

13. A B C D E   The body or data of the packet.

14. A B C D E   Information is formatted as a contiguous series of bits grouped together as a unit of data.

15. A B C D E   Provides error checking for data integrity of the frame.

A. Network
B. Data Link
C. Presentation
D. Transport
E. Session

16. A B C D E   Responsible for end-to-end recovery and flow control.

17. A B C D E   Sets up dialogues between applications at each end.

18. A B C D E   Concerned with moving data to specific locations.

19. A B C D E   Bits are organized into data packets and frames.

20. A B C D E   Formats and encrypts data to be sent across the network.

INTERNET EXERCISES

1. Logon to the Internet and key the following URLs:

   www.faqs.org/rfcs/rfc58.html
   www.telusplanet.net/public/sparkman/netcalc.htm

   Scroll down until you reach IP address converter. Enter the dotted decimal TCP/IP address as follows: 192.171.18.10. Choose the Calculate button; the result displays four octets in binary format. Record the binary number next to each octet.
   A. First Octet:
   B. Second Octet:
   C. Third Octet:
   D. Fourth Octet:

2. Key the following URL:

   www.cs-ipv6.lancs.ac.uk/ipv6/documents/papers/BayNetworks/

   Read the article, and then answer the following questions:
   A. What is the driving force behind IPv6?
   B. Can extensions to IPv4 replicate IPv6 functions?
   C. Will ATM cell switching negate the need for IPv6?
   D. What are IPv6 design goals?

CONCEPT EXERCISES

Concept Narrative
(This narrative exercise can also be printed out from the Encore! CD that accompanies this textbook. File name—Chap04connar.)

Read the following description and fill in the blanks with the correct answers.

Observe Sarah as she requests a Web page from www.protocols.com. She types in the _____ in her Web browser and waits for a response. Look behind the scenes and see how TCP segments are used to set up the connection. It requires _____ segments to open the connection. The first SYN bit is set to _____ and sent to the Web server to request a connection. Next, the second segment SYN is sent to open a connection and it acknowledges the first SYN message. Finally, a _____ message is returned from the Web server to acknowledge receipt of the TCP segment.

Sarah's PC sends the HTTP request. The HTTP request is in the data field of the packet. A header is added to _____ the HTTP request within a TCP segment. After the Web server receives the HTTP request, it sends back an ACK TCP segment to acknowledge receipt. Next, the transport layer process on the Web server passes the HTTP request to the Web server _____ program. The Web server application creates an HTTP Response message to deliver to Sarah's PC. When it is received at Sarah's PC, an acknowledgement is sent to verify receipt of the HTTP Response, which is the Web page for protocols.com.

Sarah views the Web page for some time and she finally downloads the last file. She then decides to leave the site and close her browser. It takes _____ TCP segments to close the connection. The closing process is initiated by the _____ after the last file has been downloaded. The browser sets the _____ bit to 1 to inform the Web server that the connection is going to close. The Web server sends back a _____ response saying it acknowledges the request to close the connection. Next, the browser sends a second FIN to close the connection. The Web server responds with an acknowledgment and closes the connection.

Concept Table
(This table exercise can also be printed out from the Encore! CD that accompanies this textbook. File name—Chap04contab.)

Read each statement carefully and choose the category of protocol being described. Use only one "X" per statement.

STATEMENT	CATEGORIES OF PROTOCOLS			
	LAN	WAN	INTERNET	ROUTING
1. A set of network protocols developed by IBM to communicate with its mainframes.				
2. This protocol is used to connect a computer to the Internet over a dial-up link.				
3. A distance vector protocol that uses five criteria to determine best path: link speed, delay, packet size, loading, and reliability.				
4. A connectionless protocol used in a direct way to send and receive datagrams over an IP network.				
5. The data link protocol used over LAPD ISDN's D channel.				
6. Transfers files between hosts in an internetwork.				
7. Based on the link state algorithm, it calculates the shortest path to each node based on the network topology.				
8. A protocol suite that provides for file sharing between Macintosh computers.				
9. Protocol used to define the reference points between the telco switch and the end system.				
10. A protocol that provides for system-level information for troubleshooting problems on networks.				

Concept Picture

(This picture exercise can also be printed out from the Encore! CD that accompanies this textbook. File name—Chap04conpic.)

Each of the following statements describes a protocol in the TCP/IP suite of protocols shown in the following figure. Examine the figure and in the blank space provided next to each statement, write the protocol it describes.

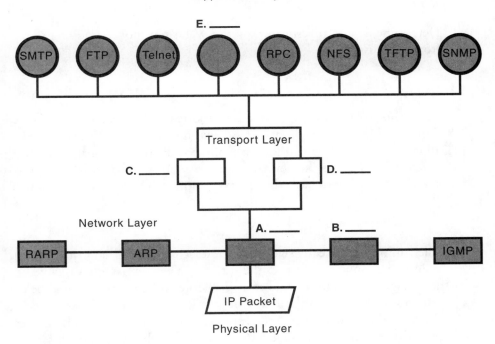

1. _____ A distributed database system used to perform address/name resolution on behalf of client applications.

2. _____ A packet-switched network layer implementation that performs addressing and route selection.

3. _____ Used to notify IP and upper layer protocols about network level errors and flow control problems.

4. _____ Accepts and transports datagrams.

5. _____ Connection-oriented and provides message fragmentation, reassembly and sequence numbering.

CASE STUDY

J & J SHOE COMPANY

Read the following case study about J & J Shoe Company. Think about the challenge presented to the company, and the information solution provided. Then, either by yourself or in a group, answer the case study questions.

Objective:

Determine how to investigate why the Web site is not responding to requests from our customers.

Company Profile:

J & J Shoe Company is a competitive sports and fitness company located in Portland, Maine. The company has been in business for 30 years and has approximately 22,000 employees. It also has distribution agreements with several retail stores across the United States. Its premier product is a line of basketball shoes; many pro basketball players in the NBA wear J & J basketball shoes.

Current Situation:

The company does extensive market research and has found that its customers want a direct buy option over the Internet. The company has weighed the advantages and disadvantages of a Web store and decided it would be cost effective to allow its customers to buy online. Recently, the Company set up a Web site for online ordering over the Internet. However, customers have been calling recently to complain that they can't reach the Web site. The Web server is located in a co-location facility in a suburb just outside of Portland.

Business Information Requirements:

J & J has set up a Web site for general customers to buy direct using its online Web store. The company established a special association with basketball teams in the NBA and has a special link from its Web site for players to order online. Since the Web site went live three months ago, J & J has sold 15,000 pairs of basketball shoes. The Web site has been a great success and customers have come to rely upon the online access system being available 7 days a week, 24 hours a day.

Communication System Requirements:

Because the Web server is located at a co-location facility, it can be constantly monitored 24 hours a day, including weekends. The monitoring staff at the co-location facility ping the server every 30 minutes to check its ability to respond to TCP/IP requests. J & J did not contract for monitoring of applications because it has its own IS staff to check on the Web application. Currently, the Web server is responding to TCP/IP requests, but the Web application is not responding to customers.

Information System Solution:

1. From the packet capture shown in Figure 4.30 (page 224), J & J was able to determine that packets were reaching the router.
2. Further investigation revealed that there were 40 bytes of data still to come to the router for processing.
3. J & J's network engineer contacted the co-location center to ask them to look at the Web server to determine whether the application was still running.
4. The Network Operation Center's engineer checked and the server was up but the application was not responding. He rebooted the server and called the network engineer at J & J.
5. After the reboot, the J & J engineer was able to access Web pages from the server.

```
Frame   Time     Src MAC Addr    Dst MAC Addr    Protocol   Description
13      2.537    2400            Prox            ICMP       Echo,
From 10.00.00.60 To  10.00.00.10
+ FRAME: Base frame properties
+ ETHERNET: ETYPE = 0x0800 : Protocol = IP:  DOD Internet Protocol
 IP: ID = 0x5538; Proto = ICMP; Len: 68
    IP: Version = 4 (0x4)
    IP: Header Length = 28 (0x1C)
  + IP: Service Type = 0 (0x0)
    IP: Total Length = 68 (0x44)
    IP: Identification = 21816 (0x5538)
    IP: Flags Summary = 0 (0x0)
       IP: .......0 = Last fragment in datagram
       IP: ......0. = May fragment datagram if necessary
    IP: Fragment Offset = 0 (0x0) bytes
    IP: Time to Live = 32 (0x20)
    IP: Protocol = ICMP - Internet Control Message
    IP: Checksum = 0x662A
    IP: Source Address = 10.0.0.60
    IP: Destination Address = 10.0.0.10
    IP: Option Fields = 137 (0x89)
       IP: Strict Source Routing Option = 137 (0x89)
          IP: Option Length = 7 (0x7)
          IP: Routing Pointer = 4 (0x4)
          IP: Route Traveled = 10 (0xA)
          IP: Route To Go = 10 (0xA)
             IP: Gateway = 10.0.0.60
       IP: End of Options = 0 (0x0)
    IP: Data: Number of data bytes remaining = 40 (0x0028)
+ ICMP: Echo,    From 10.00.00.60 To  10.00.00.10

+ FRAME: Base frame properties
+ ETHERNET: ETYPE = 0x0800 : Protocol = IP:  DOD Internet Protocol
 IP: ID = 0x5538; Proto = ICMP; Len: 68
    IP: Version = 4 (0x4)
    IP: Header Length = 28 (0x1C)
  + IP: Service Type = 0 (0x0)
    IP: Total Length = 68 (0x44)
    IP: Identification = 21816 (0x5538)
    IP: Flags Summary = 0 (0x0)
       IP: .......0 = Last fragment in datagram
       IP: ......0. = May fragment datagram if necessary

Network Monitor trace  Sun 08/01/99 19:26:43  D:\bookcaps\strict source rt.txt
    IP: Fragment Offset = 0 (0x0) bytes
    IP: Time to Live = 31 (0x1F)
    IP: Protocol = ICMP - Internet Control Message
    IP: Checksum = 0x94F8
    IP: Source Address = 10.0.0.60
    IP: Destination Address = 10.0.0.60
    IP: Option Fields = 137 (0x89)
       IP: Strict Source Routing Option = 137 (0x89)
          IP: Option Length = 7 (0x7)
          IP: Routing Pointer = 8 (0x8)
        + IP: Route Traveled = 10 (0xA)
          IP: Route To Go = 0 (0x0)
       IP: End of Options = 0 (0x0)
    IP: Data: Number of data bytes remaining = 40 (0x0028)
+ ICMP: Echo,    From 10.00.00.60 To  10.00.00.60
```

FIGURE 4.30 **Packet Capture [Source: Wilson, 1]**

J & J engineers were happy with the protocol analyzer they bought earlier this year. It allowed them to capture real-time data instantly. They were able to analyze the transmission frame by frame to determine the cause of the problem. From the packet capture, they determined the packets were reaching the router so then they were able to focus their attention on the server.

Customers were pleased to be able to access the Web page again. They had become dependent on the online Web site. They liked the convenience of being able to access it from anywhere, anytime.

CASE STUDY QUESTIONS:

1. What type of packets did this capture session gather?
2. What is the protocol?
3. What is the source IP address? Is this address public or private?
4. What is the destination IP address? Is this address public or private?
5. What is the IP Route to Go? What is the IP Gateway Address? Is this the address of the router?
6. What is the total number of bytes remaining? Does this mean there are more packets coming?

GROUP TERM PROJECT

In this section, you are asked to clearly define the problem to be solved and define the scope of the project. Convert the requirements (from the Chapter 3 requirements model) into objectives. Assess the needs of the customer in terms of network, types, and number of personnel required as well as any outside services. From this information, develop system and infrastructure objectives. The system objectives should include software applications and implementation goals. Objectives for the infrastructure should include server, router, and other internetworking equipment required and links to interconnect sites. The scope for the project should contain a paragraph that describes the "what, when, where, and why" of the project. Use the *ProjectPlan* file on the Encore! CD that accompanies this book to fill out the information called for in the following form.

WAN PROJECT PLAN

PREPARED BY:	DATE:

I.	Objectives

A.	System Objectives

B.	Infrastructure Objectives

II.	Project Scope

CHAPTER TERMS

CHAPTER BIBLIOGRAPHY

Book, Magazine, Presentation Citations

Berkowitz, Howard. *Designing Routing and Switching Architectures for Enterprise Networks.* Indianapolis: Macmillan Technical Publishing, 1999: 277, 424, 659.

Black, Uyless. *Emerging Communications Technologies*. Upper Saddle River: Prentice Hall, 1997: 63.

Dean, Tamara. *Network+ Guide to Networks*. Canada: Course Technology, 2002: 72, 193, 194, 195, 196, 197.

Downes, Kevin & Ford Merilee. *Internetworking Technologies Handbook*. Indianapolis: Macmillan Technical Publishing, 1998: 502, 727.

Marney-Petix. *LANs! LANs! LANs!* Fremont: Numidia Press, 1996: 9-13.

Novell. *Networking Technologies*. Provo: Novell, Inc., 1995: 6-1 to 12-7, 13, 18, 19.

Novell. *Netware TCP/IP Transport*. Provo: Novell, Inc., 1995: 1-15, 6-3.

Pepelnjak, Ivan. *EIGRP Network Design Solutions*. Indianapolis: Cisco Press, 2000: 1.

Sheldon, Tom. *Encyclopedia of Networking & Telecommunications*. New York: Osborne/McGraw-Hill, 2001: 65, 74, 118, 134, 420, 560, 609, 652, 675, 694, 728, 947, 1259.

Sportack, Mark A. *IP Routing Fundamentals*. Indianapolis: Cisco Press, 1999: 1.

Sybex. *Networking Complete*. San Francisco: Sybex, Network Press: 2000: 110-115.

Wilson, Ed. *Network Monitoring and Analysis: A Protocol Approach to Troubleshooting*. Upper Saddle River: Prentice Hall PTR, 2000: CD ROM (Packet Captures).

Web Citations

Brain, Marshall, "Question of the Day," How Stuff Works, <www.howstuffworks.com/question525.htm> (2002).

Cisco, "Internet Protocols," Cisco Systems, <www.cisco.com/univercd/cc/td/doc/cisintwk/ito_doc/ip.htm> (20 February 2002).

Cisco, "Introduction to Intermediate System-to-Intermediate System Protocol," <cisco.com/warp/public/cc/pd/iosw/prodlit/insys_wp.htm> (25 January 2002).

Cisco, "Open Shortest Path First," Cisco Systems, <www.cisco.com/univercd/cc/td/doc/cisintwk/ito_doc/osp.htm> (20 February 2002).

Cisco, "Introduction to WAN Technologies " Cisco Systems, <www.cisco.com/univercd/cc/td/doc/cisintwk/ito_doc/introwan.htm> (20 February 2002).

Cisco, "Introduction to Wide Area Network Protocols," Cisco Systems, <www.cisco.com/networkers/nw00/pres/2303.pdf> (2000).

DiMarzio, Jerome, "Routing 101: Routing Algorithms," InformIT, <http://www.informit.com/topics/index.asp?st={F1D6A674-A7D5-4C34-BD6C-A972F4BDB638}&session_id={EF1B6058-A9CF-4F89-B7E5-034A5B106E38}> (21 June 2002).

Freesoft, "Q.931 Protocol Overview," An Internet Encyclopedia, <sparky.freesoft.org/CIE/Topics/126.htm> (2002).

Freesoft, "I.430 Protocol Overview," An Internet Encyclopedia, <sparky.freesoft.org/CIE/Topics/124.htm> (2002).

Freesoft, "Q.921 Protocol Overview," An Internet Encyclopedia, <sparky.freesoft.org/CIE/Topics/125.htm> (2002).

Freesoft, "G.711 Protocol Overview," An Internet Encyclopedia, <sparky.freesoft.org/CIE/Topics/127.htm> (2002).

Freesoft, "Protocol Independent Multicast MIB for IPv4," An Internet Encyclopedia, <sparky.freesoft.org/CIE/RFC/bynum.cgi?2934> (2002).

Halley, Maureen, "SBE Expands Telecommunications Product Offerings— LAPD link layer protocol capability added to the HW200," SBE, Inc., <www.sbei.net/archive/prs/2000/022400.htm> (24 February 2000).

Hinden, Robert, "IP Next Generation Overview," Sun, <playground.sun.com/pub/ipng/html/INET-IPng-Paper.html> (1995).

Juniper Networks, "Optimizing Routing Software for Reliable Internet Growth," Juniper Networks, <www.juniper.net/techcenter/techpapers/200003-01.html> (03 July 2002).

Kalyanaraman, Shivkumar, "IP Next Generation (IPv6)," Rensselaer Polytechnic Institute, <www.ecse.rpi.edu/Homepages/shivkuma/teaching/sp2000/i17_ip6/tsld010.htm - 2k> (2002).

Lex-Con, "Protocol Stacks in Relationship to the OSI Model," Lexicon Consulting, <www.lex-con.com/osimodel.htm> (2002).

Lex-Con, "TCP/IP Protocol Suite," Lexicon Consulting, <www.lex-con.com/protocols/ip.htm> (2002).

Malkin, Gary & Minnear, Robert, "RIPng for IPv6," RFC2080, <www.cis.ohio-state.edu/cgi-bin/rfc/rfc2080.html> (January 1997).

Molta, David J., "Living in a Multiprotocol World," Syracuse University, <Web.syr.edu/~djmolta/ist452/PankoChapter2/sld076.htm> (2002).

Nike, "Company Overview," Nike, <www.nikebiz.com> (2002).

Norton, Michael, "Understanding Routing Protocols," O'Reilly Network, <www. Oreillynet.com/pub/a/network/2001/05/22/net_2nd_lang.html> (5 May 2001).

Pacific Bell, "Classless Inter-Domain Routing (CIDR) Overview," Pacific Bell Internet, <http://public.pacbell.net/dedicated/cidr.html>(1999).

Popova, Iskra, "Link State Protocols," CEENet Workshop, <www.ceenet.org/workshops/ppt/ospf97new.ppt> (1997).

QuanMongMo, "Teach Yourself TCP/IP in 14 Days," QuanMongMo, <www.quanmongmo.net/computer/tcpip> (2002).

Spandler, Paul, "Ethernet Tutorial: Ethernet Frames and Packets," University of Brighton, <burks.brighton.ac.uk/burks/pcinfo/hardware/ethernet/framepac.htm> (2002).

Teare, Diane, "Introduction to LAN Protocols," Cisco Systems, <www.cisco.com/univercd/cc/td/doc/cisintwk/ito_doc/introlan.htm> (July 1999).

Tech Target, "IPv6," What is, <http://www.whatis.com> (2002).

Thoresen, Tom, "Demystifying TCP/IP," Sirius User Group, <www.sirius-software.com/sug98/tcpip.html> (1998).

Vonkeman, Al & Tejada, Vicki, "Welcome to Sparkman's World" <www.telusplanet.net/public/sparkman/netcalc.htm> (1 March 2000).

Wack, John, "Introduction to the Internet and Internet Security," John Wack, <csrc.ncs1.nist.gov/nistpubs/800-10/node11.html#SECTION004000000000000000000> (9 February 1995).

Webopedia, "Protocols," <www.webopedia.com> (2002).

Webopedia, "OSI," <www.webopedia.com> (2002).

Webopedia, "SNMP," <www.webopedia.com> (2002).

Webopedia, "CLNP," <www.webopedia.com> (2002).

PART TWO
Telephony, Transmission, and Switching

CHAPTER 5
TRANSMISSION METHODS

C H A P T E R   O B J E C T I V E S

By the end of this chapter, you should understand these concepts:
- The flow of information from sender to receiver
- The process of managing bits and characters
- Why character codes are used to transmit data
- The difference between analog and digital signals
- The different types of modulation
- The use of serial and parallel methods to transmit data between devices
- How timing signals are used to ensure accurate transmission of data
- When asynchronous or synchronous transmission are used
- The modes of transmission: simplex, half duplex, and full duplex
- The differences between baseband, broadband, narrowband, and wideband channels for transmission
- The ways digital broadband are used today for streaming media
- The four basic multiplexing techniques: frequency division, time division, statistical division, and wave division

BASIC COMMUNICATIONS

Communications is the transfer of information from one location to another. The flow of information originates from the sender to the receiver. Information is passed over a transmission link or channel. The transmission channel is the physical path over which the information flows. [Cannon and Luecke, 1-3]

Bits, Signals, Frames, and Codes

Information needs to be translated into a physical pattern that has a common meaning to both sender and receiver. This is generally transmitted as sound, light, or texture. Data communications transfer information using **codes** that are transmitted as **signals**. All communications systems use some form of coding and decoding in sending information. An **encoder** is used to convert the information transmitted by the sender. On the other end, the **decoder** converts the information back to its original form for the receiver (see Figure 5.1). [Cannon and Luecke, 1-5]

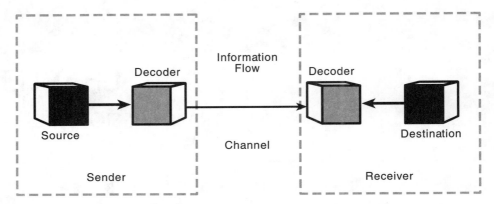

FIGURE 5.1 **Coding and Decoding Information [Source: Cannon and Luecke, 1-5]**

In a telephone conversation, all of the words spoken are made up of sounds that can be translated into sound codes. The transmitter uses voice signals that are sent over the airwaves to the receiver. For computer "conversations," computers store information in series of binary digits called **bits**, meaning the information is encoded into patterns of 0s and 1s. At the physical level, information in the form of bits is converted into signals. When computers are used to send information, **data codes** are transmitted as electric signals over cabling or a wireless connection (Figure 5.2). [Parnell, 24]

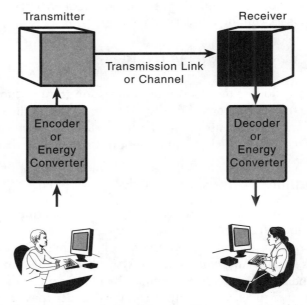

FIGURE 5.2 **Data Transmission [Source: Cannon and Luecke, 1-5]**

The process of managing the flow of information from sender to receiver consists of the following elements:

- Bits
- Characters
- Synchronization and clocks
- Asynchronous and synchronous protocols

Each time a user strikes a particular key on the keyboard, it is translated into a series of bits or, 0s and 1s. The bits used to encode the letters or characters are standardized so that both sender and receiver will understand them.

Character Coding and Translation

Code standards establish universal meanings between signaling elements and characters. The encoding of characters is called **character coding**; a collection of bit combinations is called a character set. The most common character sets are Morse, Baudot, EBCDIC, and ASCII. These standard codes are used in data communications and each code set is built into the computer on a chip. [Time Life, 32] [Infotron, 2.5]

When use of standardized binary codes began, information could be encoded and decoded by mechanical or electrical means through different electronic devices. Using the **Morse code** system, telegraph operators converted characters into dots and dashes by tapping keys on telegraph machines. The codes for these characters were made up of different combinations of dots and dashes. An effort was made to automate this process for the operators, but failed because it was found impossible to account for the varying duration of the dots and dashes used in the Morse code. [Held, 7]

NOT TRUE

Emile Baudot developed a successful method for machine encoding and decoding in 1870. Rather than representing characters as dots and dashes, the **Baudot code** uses 1s and 0s. Baudot's invention addressed the shortcomings of the Morse code by assigning 5 bits of information to each character. It was used for many years on telex equipment, and some Teletype machines still use this code today. [Beyda, 34]

However, there were problems in timing the electromechanical devices, the result being the number of signaling elements had to be limited to five. The 5 information bits used in Baudot code yield only 32 possible combinations of 0s and 1s, and thus only 32 characters, letters, and figures can be represented. Therefore, a 5-bit code could not be sufficient for all 26 characters of the alphabet, the decimal digits 1-10, and punctuation marks. The Baudot code was used as the backbone of communications for almost half a century. [Held, 9] [Beyda, 34-35]

During the 1960s, new codes for data transmission were developed. **Extended-Binary-Coded-Decimal Interchange Code** (**EBCDIC**) was developed by IBM to be used for synchronous communication in systems attached to large mainframe computers. This code uses 8 bits, which can represent 256 characters. IBM's purpose in designing it was to provide a standard code for use with its own products. [Held, 11-12]

The **ASCII** code was developed by the American Standard Code for Information Interchange. It uses numbers to represent English characters. Each letter is assigned a number from 0 to 127. Most character codes currently in use today contain ASCII; it is still the safest character set in use for data transfer. ASCII has been used so widely that the word *ASCII* is often used interchangeably with the words "text" or "plain text." Most word processing applications and text editors can store information in ASCII (or text) format. [Webopedia, 1]

The standard ASCII character set uses 7 bits for each character along with a single parity bit. The 8 bits form a pattern called a **byte**. Bits 1-7 represent the character, and bit 8 is used for parity to provide error checking. ASCII represents all of the letters of the alphabet and the numbers 0-9. It also represents punctuation marks and the control functions of a computer keyboard. It has 128 different possible combinations of 1s and 0s. Several companies have proposed changes to create an extended character set, using an extra bit that provides 128 additional characters. These extra characters are used to represent foreign languages, graphic symbols, and mathematical symbols. [Webopedia, 1]

Each character code has different bit lengths and bit positions. Usually the lower-numbered bit is transmitted first and the other bits follow. Figure 5.3 compares bit position differences between Baudot, EBCDIC, and ASCII.

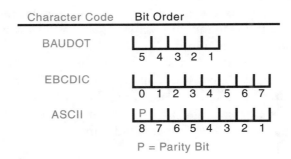

FIGURE 5.3 **Code Bit Order** [Source: Beyda, 40]

Notice the numbering systems used in ASCII and EBCDIC are opposite; a 1 in EBCDIC is a 7 in ASCII.

Table 5.1 lists the number of data bits and **parity bits** required for each character code: Baudot, ASCII, and EBCDIC. A parity bit is an extra bit used in error detection and is appended to a character to achieve the required number of bits for transmission. For example, because ASCII is a 7-bit code, a parity bit must be added to make the total bits equal 8.

CHARACTER CODE	DATA BITS	PARITY BITS	TOTAL BITS
Baudot	5	0	5
ASCII	7	1	8
Extended ASCII	8	0	8
EBCDIC	8	0	8

TABLE 5.1 **Data and Parity Bits Needed for Each Code [Source: Beyda, 40]**

Character translation or code conversion is required to connect devices that use dissimilar character codes. Application software is used on gateways to translate between character code sets. For instance, with a 3270 gateway on a LAN to a mainframe, the character code is converted from ASCII (LAN) to EBCDIC (Mainframe).

TOPIC
review
Basic Communications

1. How does a computer store information?
2. What is the purpose of frames?
3. Explain the four basic elements required to manage the flow of information.
4. Why is character coding necessary?
5. What is the purpose of character translation?

ANALOG VERSUS DIGITAL

Electronic communication uses electrical energy or signals to transmit information rapidly over long distances. In data communications, there are two types of electrical signals: **analog** and **digital**. Analog signals are used to transmit information over telephone lines. An analog signal is a form of propagated energy, such as that of sound waves, that vibrates the medium as it travels through. Digital signals, on the other hand, are used with computers to send electrical pulses in which each pulse is a signal element represented by a binary digit. [Sheldon, 1140]

Many devices today use both analog and digital signals to operate. When someone listens to a CD, the music is in an analog form. When a CD is recorded over the Web, the sounds are translated into a digital form that is encoded on the CD. When the CD is played, the CD player reads the digital data, translates it back into its original form (analog) and sends it to the amplifier and speakers.

Today, many kinds of communications systems use both digital and analog techniques. Most corporations must include analog dial up in their networks for traveling and telecommuting staff. They also support ISDN (Integrated Services Digital Network) and DSL (Digital Subscriber Line), which are strictly digital services for higher-speed connections. Currently, a shift in favor of digital transmission is occurring. The economic benefits of integrated circuits are being applied more often to digital circuitry while the world of communications itself is shifting more and more toward digital transmission. [McWhorter and Luecke, 5-22]

Analog Signal Characteristics

When you use a telephone, current flows through the complete circuit. The power supply is plugged into a wall outlet and supports AC input at 120v and a DC outlet at 11.2v. The current continues to flow through the mouthpiece and earpiece and then back to the power supply (AC/DC converter) through ground connections. The microphone in the mouthpiece acts as a variable resistor, which means it allows more current to pass when it is vibrated by changes in air pressure. The microphone creates waves of electricity called sound waves in its output wire (see Figure 5.4).

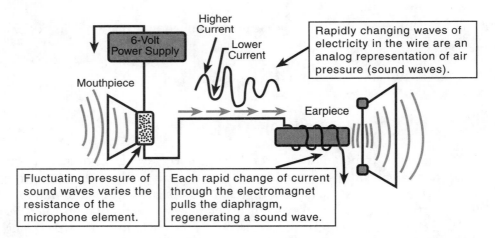

FIGURE 5.4 **Sound Traveling through a Telephone [McWhorter and Luecke, 5-4]**

At the earpiece, the current passes through the coil of a fixed electromagnet, which creates changes in magnetic force in response to the changes in current. This magnetic force attracts a metal diaphragm with each surge, matching the fluctuations of the current waves. By rapidly pushing and pulling air between it and the diaphragm, the electromagnet duplicates the original sound waves. Your eardrums detect the varying air pressure and you recognize it as sound.

Information can be sent electronically in patterns of amplitude and frequency. In analog transmission, signals propagate through the medium as continuously varying electromagnetic waves called **sine waves**. A sine wave is the basic shape of an electrical signal used in communications. Sine waves have these properties: frequency, wavelength, and amplitude. A sine wave signal is often the carrier in analog modulation. However, most analog signals are complex; they can have a number of waveforms and each one can be generated by a different frequency. [Cannon and Luecke, 2-15] [Sheldon, 38]

The basic parameters of an electrical signal are voltage, current, power, amplitude, and frequency. Any series of pulses, sounds, or voltages can be translated into a series of sine waves. These sine waves can have varying frequencies and amplitudes. Frequency and amplitude are different in that frequency is represented as a sound's unique tone or pitch, while amplitude translates as the intensity or volume of that sound. The number of vibrations the sound causes per second is known as its **frequency** while the **amplitude** of the wave indicates its strength. Although the amplitude of a particular signal can change, its frequency always remains the same. [Beyda, 71-73]

The frequency of an electric signal refers to the rate at which the voltages change. Sound frequency is measured by the number of waves or vibrations in a given period. The frequency is measured in cycles per second or **Hertz**. 1 Hertz is equal to 1 cycle per second. The distance between the beginning and end of a cycle is its **wavelength**. Wavelength is measured in meters. The general rule to apply here is the higher the frequency, the shorter the wavelength.

Because of the amounts of data being transmitted today, higher speeds are required to send data quickly. When measuring speed, frequency is usually described in kilohertz (KHz) or one thousand cycles per second. Other times you might hear it associated with megahertz (MHz) (one million cycles per second).

Another property of a sine wave is its **phase**. Phase is used when one wave is compared to another at the same frequency. A sine wave has a cycle, which is measured in degrees; a complete cycle for a sine wave is 360 degrees. Theoretically, if the waves were visible, the phase is the amount by which one leads or lags behind the other.

Modulation Techniques

Frequency, amplitude, and phase are properties of a sine wave that can be varied to achieve modulation. Modems use these properties to modulate the carrier before information is transmitted across the line. A modem is used to modulate and demodulate data pulses. The modem changes digital signals (bits) into analog (tones) to be transmitted over standard telephone lines (see Figure 5.5). All modems use amplitude, frequency, or phase modulation.

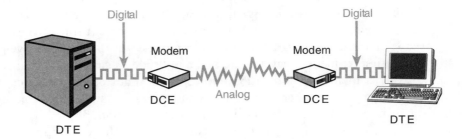

FIGURE 5.5 **Converting Signals with a Modem [Source: Infotron, 4.4]**

Three modulation techniques are used in modems:
- Frequency modulation (FM)
- Amplitude modulation (AM)
- Phase modulation (PM)

In **frequency modulation**, the frequency of a signal changes depending on the binary input. FM uses one frequency to represent a 0 and another frequency to represent a 1 (see Figure 5.6). FM is used to transmit digital signals. This is called **frequency shift keying (FSK)** because only two frequencies are transmitted, as in the Shift key on a typewriter, which can only toggle between lowercase and uppercase. Lower-speed modems usually use FM. [Sheldon, 803]

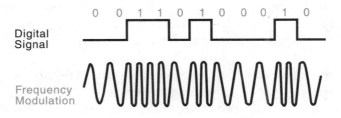

FIGURE 5.6 **Frequency Modulation [Source: Infotron, 4.7]**

In **amplitude modulation**, two different voltage levels of a tone are used to indicate the 0 and 1 states. The height or amplitude of the wave then is changed between the two levels matching the digital data input (see Figure 5.7). This technique is also used with lower-speed modems because it has too many limitations for high-speed data transmissions. [Sheldon, 803]

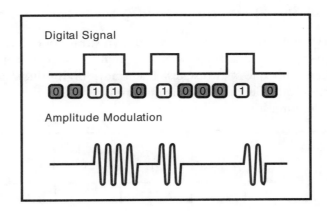

FIGURE 5.7 **Amplitude Modulation [Source: Infotron, 4.6]**

Higher-speed modems use **phase modulation**. In PM, a set frequency or carrier shifts its phase in response to the data being transmitted (see Figure 5.8). If, for example, the phase shift is 0 degrees, it might represent a "0", but if the phase shift is 180 degrees it might represent a "1".

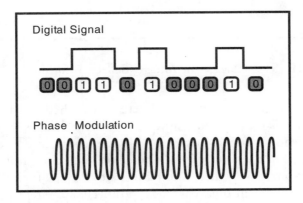

FIGURE 5.8 **Phase Modulation [Source: Infotron, 4.8]**

This phase shift technique is known as **phase shift keying (PSK)**. The phase of the carrier signal is shifted to represent digital data. The period of the wave is shifted at intervals of one-fourth, one-half, or three-quarters of the period of the carrier signal. This shift occurs in relation to the preceding wave period. The shift in the waves can represent some binary value to the receiver. PSK can encode 2 bits (dibit) or 3 bits (tribit) at a time. The highest-speed modems use a combination of PM and AM. When PM and AM are combined, it is called **quadrature amplitude modulation (QAM)** and is capable of encoding 4 bits at a time. [Sheldon, 803]

Digital Signaling and Encoding Schemes

With digital transmission, data is sent as a stream of electrical pulses. This is a one-to-one correspondence wherein a single pulse represents 1 bit. A bit can represent only one of two states. The **binary digit** 0 indicates "off," whereas a 1 indicates "on." Pure digital transmission is represented by changes in voltage on the communications media (Figure 5.9).

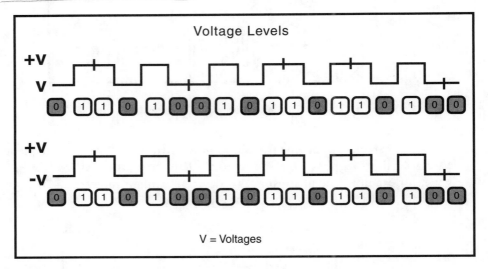

FIGURE 5.9 Changes in Voltage [Source: Infotron, 2.9]

The **voltage** level of the signal determines whether a 1 or 0 is being sent. When data is transmitted, the voltage polarity changes from positive to negative, depending on whether 1 or 0 bits are sent from the computer. At the receiver's end, the voltage is monitored for transitions from positive to negative values. From these values, 1 and 0 bits are derived. Typically, a negative voltage is used to represent binary 0, and a positive voltage represents binary 1. [Gelber, 90-91]

Several signaling and encoding schemes are used with digital transmission. The basic signaling encoding schemes are
- Unipolar
- Bipolar
- RZ (Return to zero)
- NRZ1 (Non-return to zero)
- Manchester

Unipolar

This is the waveform of binary signals used in computers and terminals. There is no special encoding; 1s are represented by the existence of voltage, and 0 represents no voltage present. [Sheldon, 1141]

Bipolar

Bipolar digital transmission reduces power requirements for equipment and lowers the attenuation of high voltage levels. It uses positive and negative voltages to represent digital information. Positive voltage is represented as a 1 and negative voltage is represented as a 0. [Sheldon, 1141]

RZ (Return to 0)

A self-clocking mechanism is used with **RZ** digital transmission. In this scheme, the voltage state returns to zero after a signal state. Zero (0) bits begin at a zero reference; it changes by half a bit and goes negative during the signal period. Then the signal changes to positive and finally becomes zero by the end of the transmission. [Gelber, 91]

NRZ (Non-return to 0)

With NRZ, the voltage level whether high or low does not represent a binary 1 or 0. Rather, a change in voltage indicates a binary 1. When the first 1 bit comes across, it causes the signal to go positive. This signal remains positive until the next 1 bit causes the signal to go negative and remain there. Again, when the next 1 bit is encountered, the signal goes positive. Transitions in the signal represent bit values, not the value (positive or negative) of the signal itself. NRZ is also known as differential encoding. [Gelber, 92]

Manchester

Manchester encoding is usually used in LANs. With this encoding scheme, a signal change occurs in the middle of a bit. This provides the receiver a clocking signal with which to synchronize. A transition to high represents binary 1, and a transition to low represents binary 0. [Sheldon, 1142]

With digital transmission, newer, lower voltage systems are highly susceptible to spurious signals/voltages on the line. This requires line filtering/suppression circuitry and specialized digital circuitry at a minimum acceptable power level for the digital signal to function. Circuitry can be fabricated into integrated circuit chips. Digital circuits can handle information faster than analog methods.

Day-to-day information, however, is currently analog in nature, that is, sound and radio waves. This means that a digital system must also be able to take in and put out analog information. To accomplish this it has to convert the analog input to digital form and then convert it back to analog again at the receiver end. This process is called **analog to digital (AD)** conversion. [McWhorter and Luecke, 5-15]

SERIAL COMMUNICATIONS

The purpose of communications is to transmit information (or data) from one computer to another. Data is transferred when changes occur in the current or voltage on a wire or channel. Character code translation is effective in defining series of bits as characters, but it does not determine how the bits are to be sent. Bits are sent using two basic methods of data transmission: **serial** and **parallel**. As shown in Figure 5.10, with serial communications, only 1 bit is sent at a time.

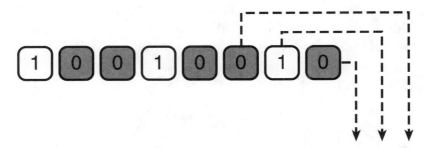

FIGURE 5.10 Serial Communications

Purpose of Serial Communications

Serial communications is used for point-to-point links. Bits are sent one after another in a serial stream over one wire. Serial communications are used when transmitting over long distances. When an external modem is connected to the

COM1 port on a PC, or when a user dials up to the Internet using PPP (point to point), serial communications is being used. The link between the computer and the modem is known as a serial link. The bit stream from the computer is sent across the serial link to the modem. The modem modulates the signal from serial to analog and then transmits it across the telephone line. [Sheldon, 1125]

With serial communications, only two states are on the wire. A positive voltage (+5v) represents a binary 1, and a negative voltage (-5v) represents a binary 0. To read the bits correctly, serial transmission requires synchronization and a clocking scheme.

Modems, mice, and printers can use serial communications. Likewise, all PCs have four serial ports (com1, com2, com3, and com4), for use with serial communications. Today, many serial interfaces are used to transmit data, for example: RS-232, Universal Serial Bus (USB), FireWire, Serial Storage Architecture (SSA), and High Speed Serial Interface (HSS).

Nearly all data communications used today are serial. New higher-speed signaling technologies such as USB and FireWire have recently entered the market and pushed serial communications capabilities into the megabit and gigabit speed range. [Gallo and Hancock, 46]

Usage of Parallel Communications

Parallel communication employs a device that is capable of receiving several bits at a time. In parallel transmission (see Figure 5.11), each bit of a character travels on its own wire or channel. All 8 bits are sent at once; so eight wires are required for transmission.

For computers and printers located near one another, usually parallel transmission is used because it is faster. For instance, Apple SCSI devices use parallel transmission to speed up data transfer time. Another use of parallel transmission is when a printer is directly connected to the parallel (LPT1 or LPT2) port of your computer. There is a 10-foot distance limitation between the computer and printer. When printers are 25-50 feet away from the computer, serial communications is required.

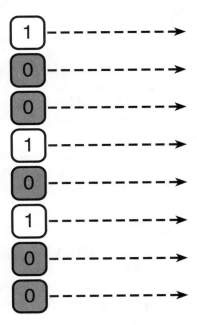

FIGURE 5.11 **Parallel Transmission**

Serial Communications

1. Why is serial communications used when transmitting over long distances?
2. Which is a faster method of data communications, serial or parallel?
3. Which binary digit is used to identify a positive voltage?
4. The number of bits sent at one time for serial communication is _____. The number of bits sent at one time for parallel communication is _____.
5. When dialing up to the Internet using PPP, which communications method is used: serial or parallel?

SYNCHRONIZATION

For communication of data to be successful between the sender and receiver, they must be synchronized at the bit, byte, and frame levels. Standard timing signals called clocks are used to determine when data transmission will occur. **Clocks** must synchronize with the state of a signal characteristic and the transmitting and receiving clocks must be properly aligned. The sender's clock governs the timing of the bits being transmitted. The receiver determines the points at which a block of bits begins and ends by taking a sample measurement of the signal characteristic. Next, the receiver interprets the signal and determines the duration of each bit. It then waits for the right moment to sample the line using the proper timing in reading each bit. As a result, the receiver must know when to measure and decode the signal and extract the data bits. The process of aligning these timing clocks is called **bit synchronization**. [Novell, 6-37]

Bit timing is critical to the accurate transmission and reception of data. Although both the sender and receiver use the same nominal clock rate, the receiver needs to maintain more precise clocking for the decoding of data.

Transmit and Receive Clocking

To establish bit boundaries, data bits are assigned clocks. The receiver retimes its clock on the negative edge of the transition from 1 to 0 of the start bit. It then uses the new timing to find the middle of the start bit within each bit cycle (see Figure 5.12).

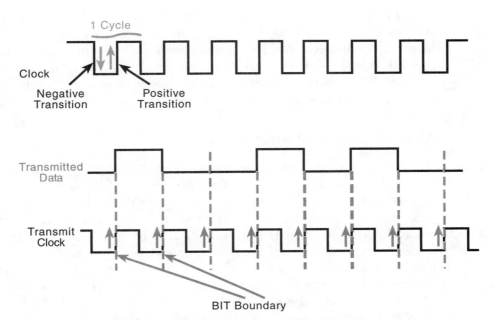

FIGURE 5.12 **Transmit Clocking [Source: Infotron, 2.13]**

At the transmitting end, the clock signal is used to define the data bits. Each bit's length is determined by the bit boundary. At each tick of the clock, 1 bit of data is moved onto the transmission line (see Figure 5.13).

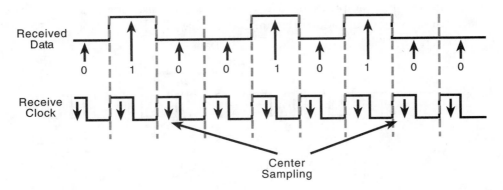

FIGURE 5.13 **Receive Clocking [Source: Infotron, 2.14]**

At the receiving end, the data bits are sampled during one of the clock transitions. This transition occurs in the center of the bit-time enabling the sampling process to begin.

If, for example, a stream of data bits is to be transmitted at 56,000 bps, 1 bit is transmitted every 1/56,000 = 0.178 milliseconds or, rounding it off, 2 milliseconds. The receiver then attempts to sample the medium at the center of each bit cycle. There is an interval between samples of 1 bit cycle or, once every 0.178 milliseconds. The sender and receiver clocks must stay precisely synchronized with this sampling time for successful transmission. [Stallings, 134]

Asynchronous Transmission

Two types of bit synchronization are used in serial communications: asynchronous and synchronous. When you transmit data asynchronously, bits are divided into small groups (bytes) and each is sent individually. Both devices must be set to the same speed or data rate for transmitting and receiving data. This data rate is alternatively referred to as **baud**. Baud is the signaling rate at which data is sent through a channel. If, for example, a user wants to transfer files from his location to a friend's PC, the first step is to set the sending and receiving clocks to 56 Kbps baud. The data rate (or baud) is measured in bits per second (bps). Therefore, the speed of this connection would be 56,000 bps. [Strangio, 3]

With **asynchronous** transmission, the receiver does not necessarily know data is being sent until it gets there. By the time the receiver can detect it and react, the first bit has already come and gone. To alert the receiver that data is coming, an asynchronous device sends two extra bits to signify when a character being transmitted begins and ends. The bit at the beginning of a character is called the **start bit** and is always a 0. The bit at the end of the character is called the **stop bit** and is always a 1. This technique is often referred to as start/stop or simply async. The transmission consists of a total of 10 bits when these two bits are added (Figure 5.14). [Shay, 137]

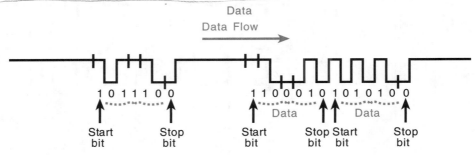

A total of 10 bits are sent: 8 bits are data bits, 1 is a start bit and 1 is a stop bit.

FIGURE 5.14 **Asynchronous Transmission [Source: Infotron, 2.16]**

With asynchronous transmission, the transmitter and receiver work independently of each other. Asynchronous communications uses signal sampling and clock regeneration to specify the signal pattern of the bit transmission. Signal sampling measures the voltage in the channel at a frequency that allows it to determine the width of a bit period at the start of the transmission. Clock regeneration is required during the first period of each transmission frame to inform the receiver that new data is coming. Characters are separated by an arbitrary amount of time and data is transmitted 1 byte at a time. [Jordan, 54]

At the beginning, the transmission line is in a binary 1 condition, meaning it is in an idle state. As each character is transmitted, it is preceded by a binary 0 (start bit) that indicates to the receiving device that a character is being sent. The receiving device looks for this start bit plus the data bits that compose each character. The transmission of start and stop bits allows the receiving device to synchronize itself with the transmitter on a character-by-character basis. At the end of the character transmission, a stop bit tells the line to return to an idle condition. The line is now ready for the transmission of the next character. This process is repeated character by character until the entire message has been sent. [Weissberger, 26]

Synchronous Transmission

With **synchronous** transmission, bits are grouped together and sent as a data frame. This allows for larger bit groups of characters to be sent together. Synchronous transmission is faster because it eliminates the start and stop bits required for each character when using asynchronous transmission.

Synchronous communications can be bit oriented or character oriented. Bit-oriented (bit synchronization) communication is used for the transmission of binary data. Bit-oriented communications are not tied to any one character set and the frame contents don't need to include multiples of 8 bits. It uses a unique 8-bit pattern (01111110) as a flag to start the frame. Bit synchronization is achieved through a received clock signal that is tuned to the received serial data stream. This technique is often referred to as self-clocking. It overcomes the effect of propagation delay and the tendency of electronic circuits to drift. [Sheldon, 1207] [Weissberger, 52]

When character-oriented (**character synchronization**) communication is used, the sender and receiver must be synchronized with one another before data is sent. A special sync character is sent to alert the receiver that a frame is arriving. The sync character synchronizes a block of information and identifies the boundaries of characters. This character synchronization is used to identify a group of bits that represent a character (see Figure 5.15). [Weissberger, 26]

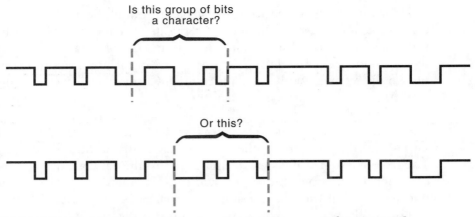

FIGURE 5.15 **Character Synchronization [Source: Infotron, 2.15]**

As shown in Figure 5.16, synchronous transmission uses an internal clocking source within the modem to align the transmitter and receiver. It does not require any start or stop bits to alert the receiver. With synchronous transmission, characters arrive in a continuous stream of bits called data frames. Synchronous transmission is used when you want to send blocks of characters such as those found in ASCII files.

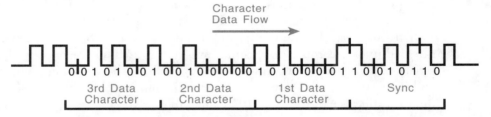

FIGURE 5.16 **Synchronous Transmission [Source: Infotron, 2.17]**

When the receiver finds the sync character, it detects all the other characters as quickly as they arrive. The incoming stream of data bits is interpreted by the receive clock in the receiver's modem. The receiving device accepts data from the modem until it detects the special ending character that indicates the message is complete. [Weissberger, 26]

To maintain clock synchronization over long periods of time, bipolar encoding is used. **Bipolar encoding** is a special bit-transition pattern that is embedded in the digital signal. In this process, the message block is composed of one or two synchronization characters, a number of data and control characters, a terminating character, and one or two error control characters. Synchronous devices must then establish a common interval for bit signals (**bit time**). They must maintain this common bit time throughout the transmission of the frame.

With the use of bipolar encoding, precision timing between sender and receiver is maintained for successful communication. [Sheldon, 1206-1207] [Jordan, 54]

For large blocks of data, synchronous transmission is more efficient than asynchronous transmission. Synchronous communications is used in almost all digital and network communications. Dial-up transmission can use either asynchronous or synchronous modems. Asynchronous modems are used to connect to other PCs or LANs. Synchronous modems are used to transmit data to mainframes over digital lines. [Microsoft, 540-543]

TOPIC review · Synchronization

1. The process of aligning timing clocks is called _____.
2. How are bit boundaries established?
3. Does the receiver know when data is being sent using asynchronous transmission?
4. Is synchronous communication bit oriented, character oriented, or both?
5. What transmission method is most effective for asynchronous communication?

DUPLEXITY

The purpose of a channel is to carry information from one location to another. The electrical and physical characteristics of the path over which it is sent affect the performance and design of the communications system. The information might be transmitted over a single wire, a group of wires, coax cable, or fiber cable. A channel is defined as a path for electrical transmission between two or more stations.

Three basic types of channels are used for wired, cabled, or radio frequency communications: simplex, half-duplex, and full-duplex. Each type of channel controls the direction of the transmission. Duplexity is the relative ability of the channel to transmit along the path in any or all directions, and is also referred to as a mode of transmission.

Simplex Communication

As Figure 5.17 shows, a **simplex** channel supports the flow of data in one direction only.

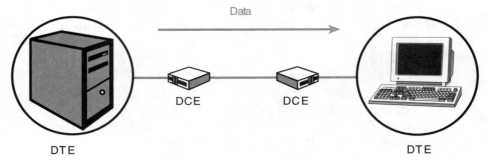

FIGURE 5.17 Simplex Communication [Source: Infotron, 3.6]

In simplex data communications, 1s and 0s can be transmitted in one direction only. Thus, the sender cannot receive and the receiver cannot send. Some common examples of this type of traffic flow are a one-way street, an escalator in a department store, and a badge reader that allows employees to enter a building or room. [Gelber, 73] An example of simplex data communications is a radio. You cannot respond to the radio because it is not interactive. It has a one-way communication path.

Half-Duplex Communication

Half-duplex channels allow data to pass from both directions but only one at a time. Both devices can send and receive, but they cannot do so simultaneously. Half-duplex transmission uses two wires for communication (see Figure 5.18). Early data communications equipment was unable to transmit and receive over one pair of wires at the same time. Therefore, the capacity of the half-duplex channel is similarly limited. [Gelber, 73]

Two-wire twisted pair (see Figure 5.19) is used for simplex transmissions, half-duplex transmissions, and full-duplex transmission at low data rates. The simplest, most common example of half-duplex operation is a two-way radio. Only one person can talk at a time. The first person speaks while the other listens and then the opposite occurs when the second person talks while the first person listens.

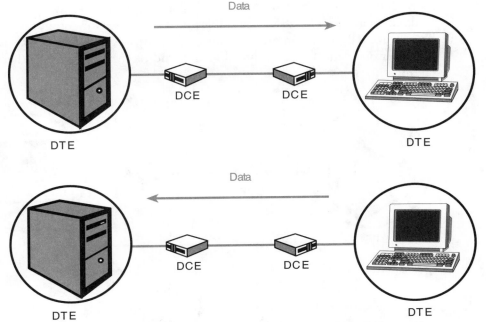

FIGURE 5.18 **Half-Duplex Communication** [Source: Infotron, 3.7]

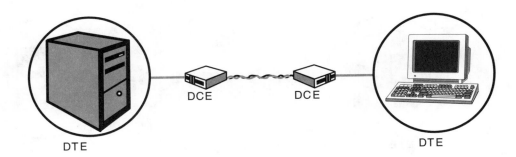

FIGURE 5.19 **Two-Wire Half Duplex** [Source: Infotron, 3.10]

Today, most LANs use half-duplex network interface cards (NICs) to transmit information onto the wire. The connection from the wall jack requires two wires: one for transmitting and one for receiving. With most PCs, only half-duplex network cards are needed because usually both the send and receive functions do not need to be performed simultaneously.

Full-Duplex Communication

As shown in Figure 5.20, **full-duplex** channels support bi-directional data flow.

Both devices can send and receive simultaneously. A two-way path allows for bi-directional flow of traffic. Full-duplex uses four wires for communication, because initially, data communications equipment was designed to transmit data over one pair of wires in one direction and receive data on the other pair. [Beyda, 50]

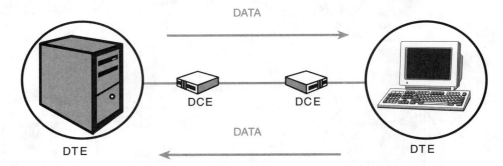

FIGURE 5.20 **Full-Duplex Communication [Source: Infotron, 3.8]**

Four-wire twisted pair circuits are required for full-duplex operation at high data rates (see Figure 5.21). However, full-duplex communication at low data rates is now possible over a single pair of wires.

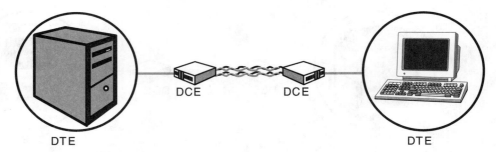

FIGURE 5.21 **Four-Wire Full-Duplex Operation [Source: Infotron, 3.11]**

Full-duplex channels allow incoming and outgoing data to flow in the same way that a two-lane highway allows cars to go forward in both directions (bi-directional) at the same time. The traffic flow on one side of the street is not impeded by traffic coming from the other side of the street; the same is true for data traveling on a full-duplex channel. [Beyda, 49]

On a LAN, if performance of the server is slow, a full-duplex NIC is often installed in the server. The full-duplex NIC allows traffic to flow bi-directionally so data information can be received and sent at the same time. For the NIC to function in full-duplex mode, the port on the hub or Ethernet switch is set to full-duplex mode. To really speed up traffic flow, two full-duplex NICs can be installed in the server using two ports on the Ethernet switch. In this way, network traffic could be split between the two full-duplex cards. The advantage gained here is the ability to load balance the traffic flow improving performance.

TOPIC
review — **Duplexity**

1. What are the three basic types of channels used for wired, cabled, or radio frequency communications?
2. How many twisted pair wires are used for half-duplex communication? For full duplex?
3. When traveling on a two-lane highway, where cars go forward in both directions the traffic flow is similar to that in _____ communications.
4. Are most NICs half duplex or full duplex?
5. What type of channel is used in which the sender cannot receive and the receiver cannot send?

FREQUENCY BANDS AND DIGITAL BROADBAND

Several types of bands are used to transmit voice and data. Bandwidth is the information-carrying capacity of a communications channel. This channel can be analog or digital. Analog transmissions are measured in cycles per second (Hertz or Hz), whereas digital transmissions are measured in bits per second (bps).

Frequency Bands

A **band** is a specific range of frequencies in the radio frequency (RF) spectrum. Each band has an upper and lower frequency limit. There are four types of frequency bands:

- **Baseband**. Information is carried in digital form on a single signal channel. Direct current pulses are applied directly on the cable for transmitting digital signals. Baseband is a digital-only technology. Ethernet LANs use baseband, transmitting one signal at a time over a single channel. [Sheldon, 113]
- **Broadband**. Broadband implies an abundance of bandwidth and operates over a wide band of frequencies. This type of network connection supports a very high bit rate. Broadband media requires the ability to transmit large amounts of information quickly. Because broadband can support a wide range of frequencies, it is the technology of choice for multimedia services to homes and businesses. [Nokia, 1]

- **Narrowband**. This band carries voice information in a specific frequency range. The sender and receiver tune into a fixed frequency band. Narrowband supports only low bit rates, and is used for radio broadcasts. Although the signal can be spread over a wide area and can penetrate through walls, radio reflections, or "ghosting," can cause problems for narrowband transmission. [Sheldon, 1375]
- **Wideband**. This band supports a channel having a wider bandwidth than a single *voice channel*. Service providers offer wideband services as large capacity analog or digital circuits. For analog wideband services, the speed ranges from 19,200 to 256,000 bps. Telephone companies refer to wideband services as a master group or a bundle of 12 voice grade circuits. When they offer 60 voice-grade channels, it is known as a super group. Currently, service providers are only offering dedicated digital wideband services in large metropolitan areas. [Case and Smith, 50-52]

Broadband Media Services

Digital broadband paves the way for use of streaming media services, which are delivered via digitized broadband networks. These services are called streaming media because they are received by the users in continuous real-time streams. The foundation for broadband media services is granted through high speed IP access using a DSL.

An eager market exists for broadband media services that originate from the telephone company's large base of residential voice customers. Broadband media services offer many advantages:
- Telecom providers can use their existing networks.
- Broadband media services do not involve significant civil- and building-code regulations.
- New opportunities are available for telephone companies to increase their revenue by offering broadband services to their customers.
- Telecom providers now have a way to compete with cable (CATV) operators by offering package deals of voice and CATV services.
- A higher level of security is possible with IP networks.
- An individual can create her own content and distribute it electronically around the world.
- Bundled services are no longer predefined; users can decide on the media they want, and determine when they want to use it. [Nokia, 5]

Next Generation IP Network

The next generation network will be broadband IP, which will allow all access to the network to occur according to IP standards. Table 5.2 lists the primary devices used in a broadband IP access network.

CENTRAL OFFICE (CO)	CUSTOMER
1) DSLAM – High speed DSL access multiplexer.	1) DSL modem in home or office with Ethernet interface.
2) Broadband access servers at broadcast facility.	2) Secure access through ISP.
3) Loop management devices to manage DSL services.	3) Virus protection required for e-mail and file transfers.
4) Video servers act as content repositories for video streaming.	4) Firewall required to allow filtering of standard ports to prevent hacking.
5) Video encoders used for MPEG content and support of IP multicast.	5) Cable modem users require set-top box to receive broadband signals.
6) IP network security and authentication for user identification.	6) Home LANs require hub, gateway router, or wireless hub to connect multiple PCs into DSL connection.

TABLE 5.2 **Broadband Access Devices [Nokia, 7]**

Service providers deliver two-way interactive services for TV using digital broadband telco networks. Users are offered broadband services based on asynchronous transfer mode (ATM) technology. User connections are made through modems or media terminals. In 2000, telecom providers spent more than $370 million on broadband equipment. With its rapid expansion, growth is expected to reach $2 billion by 2004. [Hellerstein, 13]

Video servers are used to act as content repositories for the images and information being streamed. They are responsible for streaming out video and audio using the preferred format and network protocol. **Video encoders** are used to create the MPEG content and support IP multicast at varying bit rates. A set-top box is required to interface the TV with the broadband network so consumers can have access to interactive multimedia services and video on demand. [Nokia, 9] Figure 5.22 illustrates a broadband network incorporating multimedia.

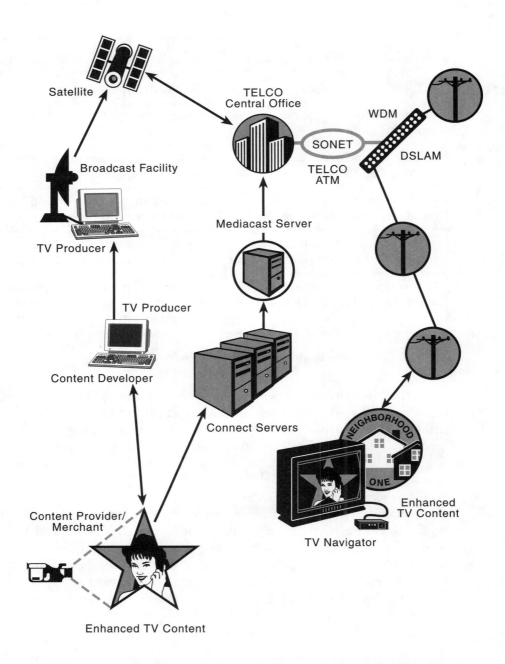

FIGURE 5.22 **Broadband IP Network [Source: Liberate Technologies, 1]**

Frequency Bands and Digital Broadband

1. How are analog signals measured? Digital signals?
2. What are the four types of frequency bands?
3. Which type of frequency band is used for multimedia services to homes and businesses?
4. What type of frequency band is used in Ethernet LANs?
5. The next generation network will use which type of frequency band with what protocol?

MULTIPLEXING

Telephone companies have been multiplexing calls for years. The use of multiplexing affords a greater number of connections over a limited number of lines. **Multiplexing** is a technique that allows a single line to support multiple voice conversations simultaneously, offering greater economy of line use.

Advantages of Line Sharing

When each location uses a point-to-point link, it quickly becomes expensive because the customer is charged separately for each line. Companies are billed 7 days a week, 24 hours a day whether lines are in use or not. In addition, not all locations need to transmit data at the same time, and again lines are left idle. If companies want to take full advantage of their service for data communications, line sharing is a more cost-effective approach. The monthly cost for telephone and data circuits is reduced.

Line sharing requires the multiplexing of signals over one line. With digital multiplexing, many networking devices are connected to the multiplexer for use on one communications circuit. Several file and application servers can share access through the multiplexer to a T1 (1.54 Mbps) or T3 (45 Mbps) dedicated digital line. This allows all devices connected to share the high-speed bandwidth required to connect to remote locations.

The many advantages to multiplexing include:

- Efficient line use
- Lower line costs
- Improved reliability
- Lower DCE costs

When you use a digital line for the communications circuit, a digital multiplexer is required. The digital multiplexer will both **multiplex** (**MUX**) and **demultiplex** (**DEMUX**) channel data across the line. Several types of multiplexers offer error correction, traffic statistics, and diagnostics (see Figure 5.23).

However, there are some problems with multiplexing. On occasion, problems experienced on one line will go on to affect many other channels. Sometimes, the end-to-end delay time becomes excessive.

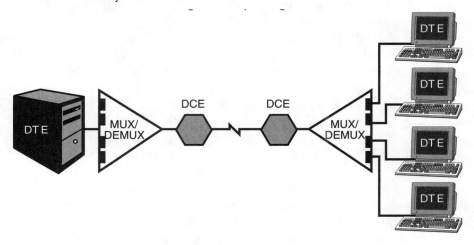

FIGURE 5.23 **Digital Multiplexing [Source: Infotron, 6.4]**

Elements of Multiplexing

Multiplexers are normally installed in pairs with one at each end of the circuit. A **CSU/DSU** provides ports for the physical connection of the equipment. One end connects the local loop to the CO and the other end is attached to the multiplexer. Channel interface units are available for synchronous or asynchronous data using several types of interfaces or connectors.

After the connection has been made, the multiplexer takes over to process the information through to the destination network or server. Four basic elements are required for multiplexing:
- CSU/DSU
- Buffer
- Frame Builder/Multiplexer
- Line Interface

Figure 5.24 shows the inside of a multiplexer. Usually, enough memory is contained within the multiplexer to temporarily store information. This memory is used to **buffer** incoming data and provide data bit storage. This buffer provides for the reading and writing of data between the channels and the line.

The **frame builder** multiplexes the information coming in from the channel interface units into an aggregate stream ready for transmission over the line. It then demultiplexes the data received into separate channels and delivers the information to the correct device to complete the transmission.

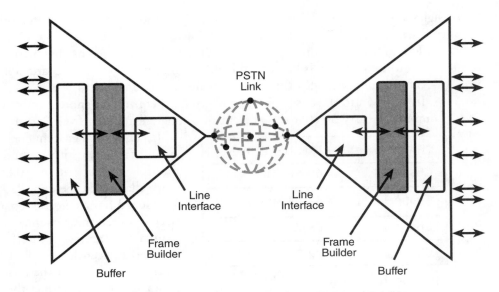

FIGURE 5.24 **Inside a Multiplexer**

The primary function of the line interface is to convert the aggregate stream of data from the frame builder to a format suitable for line transmission. It provides for the conversion and encoding of signals from **unipolar** to bipolar. The line interface also controls the transmit and receive functions on the line and controls the framing. It provides for sufficient ones density, meaning it requires that each group of 8 bits have a least one bit that is a 1. Without that 1 bit, the group is considered in error because it does not match any 01 combination in the ASCII character code set.

Multiplexing Techniques

Currently, four basic multiplexing techniques are used for voice and data communications:
- Frequency Division
- Time Division
- Statistical Division
- Wave Division

Frequency division multiplexing (FDM) divides one channel into several channels or frequency bands. Each band carries a different signal frequency. Digital signals are combined on the multiplexer and each is assigned its own carrier frequency. All signals are sent through the multiplexer at the same time. At the receiving end of the link, another multiplexer is used to demultiplex the signal coming in. Each frequency is then filtered to separate it from the others and sent to its final destination.

The FDM operation developed by AT&T uses 12 different channels. This basic group of channels has a total bandwidth of 48 KHz. Each channel has a 4-KHz frequency range of its own as demonstrated in Table 5.3.

In addition to the basic 12-channel group, there are five more groups, which combine to carry 60 channels at frequency ranges extending from 312 to 552 KHz. These higher frequencies add more channels, which expand the multiplexing capacity to 10,800 voice channels. [Sheldon, 829]

Guard bands ensure separations between these channels are maintained to prevent interference between adjacent channels. The receiving multiplexer then uses bandpass filters to extract the individual modulated signals. Finally, the multiplexer demodulates the signals and the original signal is passed on to its destination. [Shay, 155]

FDM is a method still used today for voice transmission. A variation of FDM is also currently being employed today in Wave Division Multiplexing (WDM) over fiber-optic cable.

The next type of multiplexing is called **time division multiplexing** (TDM). This is a baseband technology in which individual channels of data or voice are interwoven into a single stream of framed bits and transmitted across the communications channel. TDMs use dedicated data grade lines at a constant frequency. A time slot is assigned to each channel. TDM also splits a circuit into time slots and assigns a channel to a repeating set of slots. In Figure 5.25, four channels are identified A-D. The multiplexer passes data on each channel (A-D) but only during its assigned time slot. When no data is being passed during those time slots, channels are left idle and bandwidth is wasted.

CHANNEL	FREQUENCY RANGE
Channel 1	60-64 KHz
Channel 2	64-68 KHz
Channel 3	68-72 KHz
Channel 4	72-76 KHz
Channel 5	76-80 KHz
Channel 6	80-84 KHz
Channel 7	84-88 KHz
Channel 8	88-92 KHz
Channel 9	92-96 KHz
Channel 10	96-100 KHz
Channel 11	100-104 KHz
Channel 12	104-108 KHz

TABLE 5.3 **Frequency Divisions**

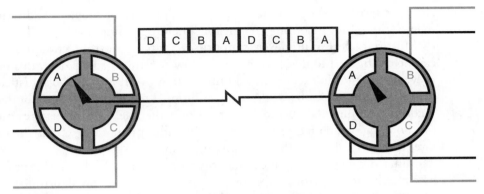

FIGURE 5.25 **Time Division Multiplexing [Source: Infotron, 6.7]**

TDM is also referred to as **bandsplitting** because it divides the line and bandwidth into smaller data rates (see Figure 5.26). Channels are each assigned a separate portion of a data rate that is divided equally among them.

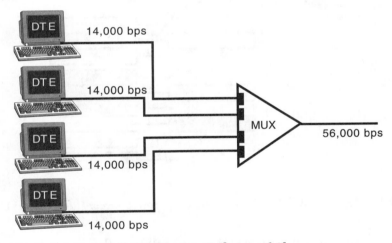

FIGURE 5.26 **Bandsplitting [Source: Infotron, 6.8]**

Bandsplitting handles several signals at once by removing 1 byte (8 bits) of data at a time from each signal. The signals are rotated, the bytes are combined to form one stream of data, and then that stream is transmitted through the line. When this data stream arrives at its destination, a multiplexer separates the bytes and re-combines the original signals for transmission to the designated user or workstation.

Statistical multiplexers use microprocessor technology to greatly increase the efficiency of line sharing. These multiplexers allocate time slots through a microprocessor that monitors the incoming channel data allowing only active channels to pass data onto the line. The microprocessor provides additional memory to buffer incoming channel data before sending it over the line.

Most statistical multiplexers support several flow control techniques. They can be configured to detect or generate flow control. If so enabled, this device prevents the multiplexer's internal buffers from overflowing. The statistical multiplexer's microprocessor works using additional memory to act as a buffer for incoming channel data before sending it over the line. This sometimes causes overbooking, which happens when the total input data rate exceeds the line rate, which is known as the overbooking ratio.

Buffered data is sent via the line in numbered frames. Each frame is protected by a checksum for error correction. The multiplexer uses an algorithm called **automatic retransmission queue (ARQ)** to handle data errors. If a block is received with an error, it is retransmitted (see Figure 5.27). [Infotron, 6.9]

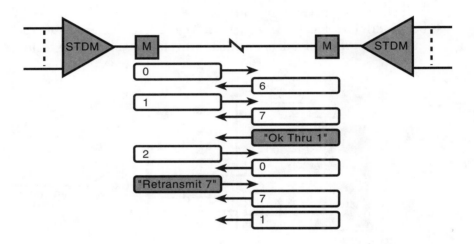

FIGURE 5.27 **Retransmission on Error [Source: Infotron, 6.11]**

Statistical multiplexers (see Figure 5.28) use flow control to regulate the flow of data through routers ensuring that no network segment becomes overloaded with transmissions. Flow control methods are employed to stop and resume data flow. These methods include character (XON, XOFF) and control signal flow control. Flow control is also used to manage the packet flow so that a sender does not transmit more packets than a receiver can process. This is similar to traffic management on city streets and highways.

Application of flow control helps sender and receiver each to synchronize their respective rates to prevent dropped packets. When packets are dropped, they must be retransmitted, which wastes network bandwidth.

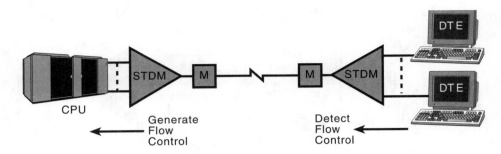

FIGURE 5.28 **Buffer Overflow Protection [Source: Infotron, 6.13]**

Statistical Time Division Multiplexers (STDM) have overtaken the FDM market. STDM constantly changes the allocation of time slots to accommodate the requests from attached devices. STDM offers several advantages over its competitor in improving data transmission:

- Microprocessor that offers buffering capability
- Instructions that can be down-line loaded
- System statistics
- Line and channel diagnostics
- Event reporting
- Dual line sharing
- Load balancing between lines
- Data switching

Figure 5.29 shows a comparison of FDM, TDM, and STDM and how signals for voice and data can be multiplexed using each. With FDM, the input signals use different frequency bandwidths. Each one is assigned a channel (1, 2, or 3) to transmit to the receiving multiplexer. With TDM, each channel has instead an assigned time slot (A, B, C, or D) used for transmission. The data streams each have a single frame from each slot. Thus, the first stream reads as A1, B1, C1, and D1 and the second A2, B2, C2, and D2 stream follows suit. In contrast to these two methods, STDM allows frames to be transmitted out of sequence and reassembled at the receiving multiplexer.

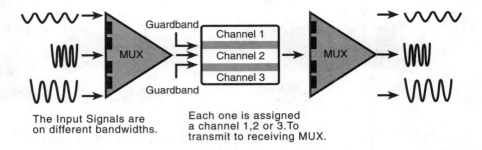

Frequency Division Multiplexing

Guardband

Channel 1
Channel 2
Channel 3

Guardband

The Input Signals are on different bandwidths.

Each one is assigned a channel 1,2 or 3. To transmit to receiving MUX.

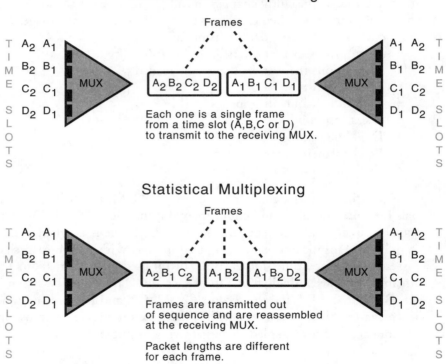

Time Division Multiplexing

Frames

TIME SLOTS

A₂ A₁
B₂ B₁
C₂ C₁
D₂ D₁

$A_2\ B_2\ C_2\ D_2$ $A_1\ B_1\ C_1\ D_1$

A₁ A₂
B₁ B₂
C₁ C₂
D₁ D₂

TIME SLOTS

Each one is a single frame from a time slot (A,B,C or D) to transmit to the receiving MUX.

Statistical Multiplexing

Frames

TIME SLOTS

A₂ A₁
B₂ B₁
C₂ C₁
D₂ D₁

$A_2\ B_1\ C_2$ $A_1\ B_2$ $A_1\ B_2\ D_2$

A₁ A₂
B₁ B₂
C₁ C₂
D₁ D₂

TIME SLOTS

Frames are transmitted out of sequence and are reassembled at the receiving MUX.

Packet lengths are different for each frame.

FIGURE 5.29 **Frequency Division, Time Division, and Statistical Multiplexing [Source: Shay, 156-158]**

With the growth of the Internet, more bandwidth is being required to meet consumer demand. Service providers have installed additional optical fiber across the world to take advantage of optical technology. New multiplexing methods have been developed for the same reason. **Wave Division**

Multiplexing (WDM) is an FDM technique for use with fiber-optic cable. It divides the light traveling through a single strand of fiber into wavelengths or lambdas. (Lambda is the Greek letter used to represent wavelength.) The optical signal channels are referred to as lambda circuits. Multiple channels can be transmitted over a single fiber because each is sent at a different wavelength. Each wavelength is, in fact, a different color of light in the infrared range capable of carrying data.

A fiber-optic cable transports the light from end to end. The light signal is inserted in one end of the fiber cable by a semiconductor laser or light emitting diode (LED). The laser produces light in a range called a window. These "windows" use the near infrared range at wavelengths of 850, 1,320, 1,400, 1,550, and 1,620 nanometers (nm). WDM currently supports 24 channels. Through WDM, the wavelengths can each carry independent signals. One wavelength can carry ATM OC-3 for voice, another ATM OC-12 for data, while analog video can be carried on another wavelength.

Jitter and Wander Issues in WDM

When you use WDM services, the timing needs to be precise and synchronized with the network. This requires a stable reference clock. A digital signal has short- and long-term variations. It continually changes its position in time, moving backward and forward as it compares itself to the reference clock.

Figure 5.30 illustrates the occurrence of a jittered clock. Jitter and wander are the distortions on a data signal caused by a phase modulation of the clock signal used to generate the data. **Jitter** is defined as a phase variation with frequency components greater than or equal to 10 Hz. **Wander** is described as a phase variation at a rate of less than 10 Hz.

Jitter is composed of a broad range of frequencies at different amplitudes. It is usually calculated as the maximum phase amplitude within one or more measurement bandwidths. When you compare signals against the reference clock, jitter refers to the difference between one timed signal and another or, in other words, a phase variation between the two signals.

Causes of jitter or wander include the following:

- Changes in cable delay due to temperature changes
- Drift due to DC offsets in the phase-locked loops of the synchronization clock
- Random phase transients as the synchronization distribution chain are reconfigured
- Frequency differences due to loss of synchronization at a node within the network

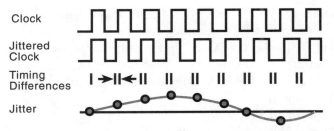

FIGURE 5.30 **Phase Variation between Two Signals [Source: Lum and Wolaver, 3]**

The concern that service providers have about phase jitter is that video carried in the payload might suffer degradation. Jitter is a unique phenomenon within a SDH/PDH ATM network. The SDH data stream is regenerated by either optical or radio link repeaters. This process introduces jitter and tends to build up as more regenerator sections are added. This process is called SDH line jitter. The dangers associated with SSH (European equivalent) line jitter are avoided by using scrambling. Scrambling creates a new data stream pattern for every regenerated section.

Good synchronization is the foundation of successful use of integrated voice, video, and data services. This integration is called convergence. In fact, without proper management of timing, convergence simply cannot happen. In response to the need for integrated services, new equipment and network timing and synchronization standards have been developed to address.

Recently, WDM has evolved into *Dense Wave Division Multiplexing,* enabling service providers to better address ever-increasing consumer demand for bandwidth. **Dense Wave Division Multiplexing (DWDM)** is a fiber-optic transmission technique that employs wavelengths of light transmitting data either parallel by bit or serial by character. [Lucent, 1]

Originally, WDM supported two to four wavelengths per fiber. With DWDM, its capacity has increased to support eight or more wavelengths per channel. Through the use of DWDM, service providers are able to offer greater capacity for handling e-mail, video, and multimedia traffic. Data and video traffic are carried as IP data over ATM devices, whereas voice is carried over the SONET/SDH framework.

DWDM combines multiple optical signals so they can be grouped and transported over a single fiber to increase its capacity (see Figure 5.31). With DWDM, incoming optical signals are assigned to specific frequencies within a designated frequency band and the resulting signals are multiplexed out onto one fiber. Because the incoming signals are never terminated in the optical layer, the interface can be bit-rate or format independent. Optical amplifiers operate with existing fiber allowing it to boost the light wave signals without having to convert them back to electrical form.

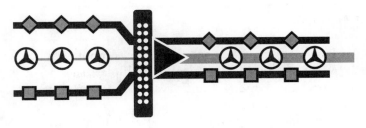

Bit Rates and Formats Are Independent

FIGURE 5.31 **Wave Division Multiplexing [Source: Lucent, 1]**

DWDM also can reduce costs and can work around potential WAN traffic bottlenecks (see Figure 5.32). It connects different types of ATM and IP traffic to an optical-based network. The development of high-speed interfaces to routers and switches will enable data and voice traffic to be multiplexed by SONET before going over DWDM. In addition, IP and ATM data can be connected directly to the DWDM without going through SONET TDM by using add/drop multiplexers.

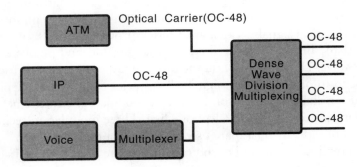

FIGURE 5.32 **Dense Wave Division Multiplexing [Source: Fitzgerald, 1]**

Because the optical layer carries signals without any additional multiplexing, service providers can quickly deliver ATM or IP services at specific places within their networks. Optical networking offers almost limitless bandwidth capacity. Service providers can offer different levels of bandwidth to customers by making individual wavelengths available. They also can offer the option to lease wavelengths, which might enable the development of new applications requiring mass quantities of bandwidth.

CHAPTER SUMMARY

Basic communication involves the passing of information from sender to receiver over a physical path. Information is transmitted using codes (ASCII, EBCDIC), which are sent as signals. Sometimes, the character coding needs to be translated so that it has a common meaning to both sender and receiver. Gateways use software to provide code conversion between character codes.

Two types of signals (analog, digital) are used to transmit information. Analog signals are used to transmit information over telephone lines. Analog uses electrical signals, which are a series of pulses, sounds, or voltages that are translated into sine waves. Frequency, amplitude, and phase are properties of a sine wave. Digital signals, on the other hand, are the signals used by computers to send information over digital (fiber-optic) lines. When telephone lines are used for dial-up connections, modems modulate the carrier before information is transmitted across the telephone line. Three modulation techniques (frequency, amplitude, or phase) are used to send data to the receiver.

Several signaling and encoding schemes are used with digital transmissions (unipolar, bipolar, return to zero, non-return to zero, and Manchester). Manchester encoding provides the receiver with a clocking signal to synchronize transmission. Digital circuits can transmit information faster than with analog methods. The use of integrated circuits is moving more telecommunications services toward digital transmission.

The data transmission (serial and parallel) methods are used to transmit bits across the line. Serial communication sends 1 bit at a time. Parallel communications sends 8 bits at a time. The speed of transmission has been improved to megabit and gigabit for serial communications with the introduction of USB and FireWire.

Bit timing is critical for accurate transmission and reception of data. Clocks are used that synchronize with the state of the signal characteristic to govern the timing of the bits. Bit synchronization methods (asynchronous or synchronous) are used to transmit data. Synchronous transmission is more efficient for large blocks of data. Asynchronous modems are used in PCs to dial up and connect to the home office or the Internet. Modes of transmission (simplex, half duplex, full duplex) control the direction of the transmission.

Several frequency bands (baseband, broadband, narrowband, and wideband) are used to transmit voice and data. Digital broadband provides for streaming media services for video and audio traffic. Video traffic occurs in real time and must be continuous. The delivery of innovative video solutions for the WAN is offered by digital broadband services. Broadband access provides pipes to carry the traffic. The next generation network will provide broadband IP services to deliver interactive multimedia services and video on demand.

Multiplexing provides for sharing expensive digital lines. Several networking devices can be connected to the multiplexer to allow a dedicated digital line to be shared. Four basic multiplexing techniques (frequency, time, statistical, and wave division) are used for voice and data communications. WDM uses light, which travels through a single strand of fiber, to transmit data over different wavelengths. Sometimes jitter and wander cause distortions of the data. Good synchronization provides for successful integrated services of voice, data, and video.

Many corporations are implementing distributed business applications, e-commerce and extensive use of multimedia applications. As the Internet continues to expand, consumers will increasingly demand greater bandwidth and faster connection speeds. With optical layer services, telecom providers will be able to offer different wavelengths to deliver bandwidth on demand for their customers.

CHAPTER REVIEW QUESTIONS

(This quiz can also be printed out from the Encore! CD that accompanies this textbook. File name—Chap05review.)
Circle a letter (a-d) for each question. Choose only one answer for each.

1. When application software is used on gateways to convert between different character code sets, this is known as:
   a. Character synchronization
   b. Character parity
   c. Character translation
   d. Character positions

2. Sine waves have three basic properties:
   a. Frequency, phase, and modulation
   b. Phase, amplitude, and modulation
   c. Frequency, waves, and air pressure
   d. Frequency, wavelength, and amplitude

3. For digital transmission, the _____ level of the signal determines whether a 1 or 0 is being sent.
   a. bit
   b. voltage
   c. clock
   d. tick

4. When computers and printers are located near one another, _____ transmission is used because it is faster.
   a. parallel
   b. serial
   c. asynchronous
   d. synchronous

5. To establish bit boundaries, data bits are assigned _____.
   a. cycles
   b. ticks
   c. clocks
   d. bit-time

6. This type of multiplexing divides one channel into several frequency bands:
   a. Time division
   b. Frequency division
   c. Statistical division
   d. Wave division

7. DWDM supports how many wavelengths per fiber?
   a. 5
   b. 8
   c. 25
   d. 30

8. These devices are used with fiber to boost the light wave signals without having to convert them back to electrical form.
   a. Optical amplifiers
   b. Frequency amplifiers
   c. Wave amplifiers
   d. Digital amplifiers

9. What is the foundation for the successful use of integrated voice, video, and data services?
   a. Bandsplitting
   b. Flow control
   c. Proper management
   d. Synchronization

10. Statistical multiplexers use _____ _____ to regulate the flow of data through routers ensuring that no network segment becomes over-loaded with transmissions.
    a. line sharing
    b. flow control
    c. guard bands
    d. frame builder

Circle the correct letter (A-E) that corresponds to the descriptions below. Choose only one answer for each.
    A. Encoder
    B. Codes
    C. Decoder
    D. Character Translation
    E. Character Synchronization

11. A B C D E   Used to synchronize a block of information and identify the boundaries of the characters.

12. A B C D E   Used to convert the information transmitted by the sender.

13. A B C D E   Information needs to be translated into a physical pattern that has a common meaning to both sender and receiver.

14. A B C D E   Also known as code conversion. It is required when character codes do not match between sender and receiver.

15. A B C D E   Converts information back to its original form for the receiver.

    A. Sine Waves
    B. Jitter
    C. Bit Time
    D. Video Encoders
    E. Voltage

16. A B C D E   Used to create the MPEG content in streaming video.

17. A B C D E   Level of the polarity of a signal that can be positive or negative.

18. A B C D E   Critical to the accurate transmission and reception of data.

19. A B C D E   Continuously varying electromagnetic waves.

20. A B C D E   A phase variation with frequency components greater than or equal to 10Hz.

INTERNET EXERCISES

1. Log on to the Internet and key the following URL:

   www.faqs.org/rfcs/rfc58.html.

   A. What was his fundamental argument?
   B. Why were they considering using bit count or data type to precede the
      logical message?
   C. Which technique was found to be much safer than the others and why?
   D. Did he suggest a solution to the problem or merely offer it up for discussion?

2. Key the following URL:

   **www.cisco.com/warp/public/779/servpro/solutions/optical/docs/
   whatiswdm.html**

   A. What speed can each optical signal or wavelength operate at?
   B. What type of standard interface is used for DWDM?
   C. What has been the result of the introduction of optical amplifiers?
   D. A DWDM channel is much the same as _____ _____.

CONCEPT EXERCISES

Concept Narrative
*(This narrative exercise can also be printed out from the Encore! CD that accompanies
this textbook. File name—Chap05connar.)*

Read the following description and fill in the blanks with the correct answers.

The purpose of a _____ is to carry information from one location
to another. The information can be transmitted over a single wire, a
group of wires, coax cable, or fiber cable. A channel is defined as a _____
for electrical transmission between two or more stations. _____ is
also referred to as a mode of transmission. Each type of channel controls
the _____ of the transmission.

In simplex data communications, 1s and 0s can be transmitted in _____
direction only. Thus, the sender cannot receive and the receiver cannot
send. Some common examples of traffic flow like that used in simplex
mode are a one-way street, an escalator in a department store, or a badge
reader that allows employees to enter a building or room. You cannot
respond to the radio because it is not interactive. It has a one-way
_____ path.

_____ channels allow for data to pass from _____ directions, but only one at a time. Both devices can send and receive, but cannot do so simultaneously. Half-duplex transmission uses two wires for communication. Early data communications equipment was unable to transmit and receive over one pair of wires at the same time. Therefore, the capacity of the half-duplex channel is similarly limited.

_____ channels support bi-directional data flow. Both devices can send and receive _____. A two-way path allows for bi-directional flow of traffic. Full-duplex uses four wires for communication because initially, DCE was designed to transmit data over one pair of wires in one direction and receive data on the other pair.

Concept Table
(This table exercise can also be printed out from the Encore! CD that accompanies this textbook. File name—Chap05contab.)

Read each statement carefully and choose the category of multiplexing technique being described. Use only one "X" per statement.

STATEMENT	CATEGORIES OF MULTIPLEXING			
	FDM	TDM	STDM	WDM
1. A time slot is assigned to each channel.				
2. Each band carries a different signal frequency.				
3. Uses flow control to regulate the flow of data through routers.				
4. Uses microprocessor technology to increase the efficiency of line sharing.				
5. Guard bands ensure separation between channels.				
6. Uses dedicated data grade lines at a constant frequency.				
7. Divides light traveling through a single strand of fiber into wavelengths.				

STATEMENT	CATEGORIES OF MULTIPLEXING			
	FDM	TDM	STDM	WDM
8. Each frequency is filtered to separate it from the others, and sent to its final destination.				
9. Allows frames to be transmitted out of sequence and reassembled at the receiving multiplexer.				
10. Jitter and wander can cause distortion of data with this technique.				

Concept Picture
(This picture exercise can also be printed out from the Encore! CD that accompanies this textbook. File name—Chap05conpic.)

Each of the following statements describes the inside of a multiplexer shown in the following figure. Examine the figure and in the blank space provided next to each statement (A, B, or C), please write the part or function described.

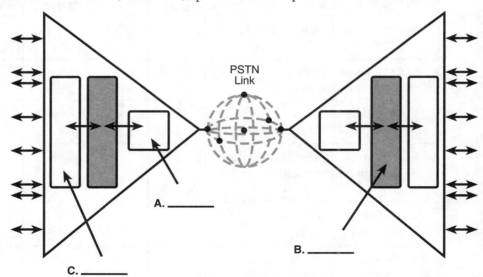

_____ A. Multiplexes the information from the CSU/DSU into an aggregate stream for transmission over the line.
_____ B. Memory used to hold incoming data and provide data bit storage.
_____ C. Converts the aggregate stream of data to a format suitable for line transmission.

CASE STUDY

FPC, INC

Read the following case study about FPC, Inc. Think about the challenge presented to the company, and the information solution provided. Then, either by yourself or in a group, answer the case study questions.

Objective:

Analyze the company's data communications requirements and design a solution using multiplexers to connect to the remote office.

Company Profile:

FPC is a full-service brokerage company that is expanding its services and establishing a remote office in Atlanta, Georgia. The corporate headquarters are in Chicago, Illinois. FPC offers clients a full range of investment products and financial planning services. The company is quickly penetrating the market and becoming a leader in the securities industry. Its core services include sales, research, and trading for individuals, corporations, and government entities.

Current Situation:

The remote office in Atlanta, Georgia operates autonomously and manages its IT infrastructure. There are major inconsistencies, however, in the way the information is processed and delivered to corporate headquarters. The database it is using for individual financial planning is not compatible with the corporate system. The remote office must extract files from the database as text files, import them into Excel, and then recalculate the formulas. A spreadsheet is sent to corporate by overnight courier nightly.

Business Information Requirements:

Auditors want to implement an easy-to-use system that provides the corporate headquarters with accurate numerical data. They want financial planning transactions to be input directly into the corporate financial planning database. This solution requires a database flexible enough to meet the constantly evolving requirements of the financial industry.

Communication System Requirements:

The MIS department wants the remote office to have easy access to the network connection at corporate headquarters. The goal is to incorporate an application into a centrally located database that could eventually be used for a number of future remote offices. The objective is to provide an effective, fault-tolerant system that will be easy to maintain and troubleshoot.

Information System Solution:

1. Representatives from corporate headquarters and the Atlanta office formed an evaluation committee to study the problem and find a solution. The committee reviewed a number of financial planning applications and selected a client-server based application database. This was installed on a server centrally located at the corporate headquarters in Chicago, Illinois.
2. A T1 dedicated line was installed between the Chicago and Atlanta office.
3. Two T1 digital multiplexers were installed, one at each end of the T1 line.
4. The multiplexer was connected to several servers to access file sharing services with corporate users. It was also connected to the Etherswitch allowing Atlanta users to access the new client-server application database for financial planning.
5. At the Atlanta office, the multiplexer was used to connect the 50 user workstations so they could share the T1 line to corporate headquarters.

The system they installed is shown in Figure 5.33.

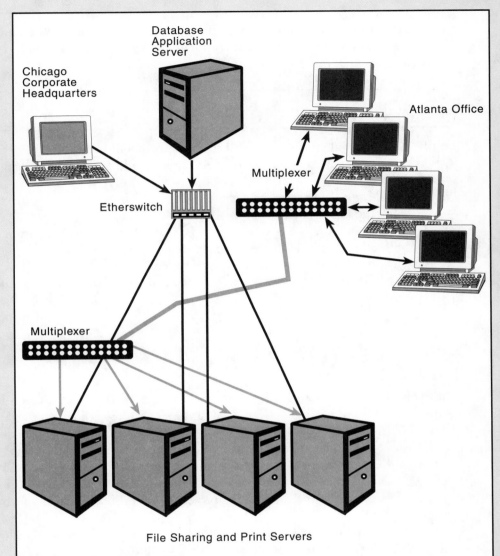

Database
Application
Server

Chicago
Corporate
Headquarters

Atlanta Office

Multiplexer

Etherswitch

Multiplexer

File Sharing and Print Servers

FIGURE 5.33 **FPC Incorporated**

The new system has been in place now for a month. Users are not experiencing any delay in accessing the financial planning database at corporate headquarters. They feel the speed of the link is sufficient. The new financial planning database is easy to use and supports many pull-down boxes for menu selection.

The MIS department is happy with the new implementation, as they have been able to reduce their budget allocation by using line sharing of the T1 line. They also have found the new financial planning database application easy to manage and upgrade. Users at Corporate are pleased because they can now share files from the corporate file servers with users in Atlanta.

CASE STUDY QUESTIONS:

1. Do you think analog or digital transmission should have been used to connect the Atlanta office to the corporate headquarters in Chicago, Illinois?
2. Would it be more cost effective to use line sharing or multiplexing to share the digital line?
3. Do you think it makes sense to have one database server application for both corporate headquarters and Atlanta users?
4. How do you provide a fault-tolerant system?
5. What happens if you connect each server to both the Etherswitch and the multiplexer?

GROUP TERM PROJECT

Identify the personnel and skill sets needed for your WAN Services Consulting project, and fill out Sections III and IV of the WAN Project Plan you printed out in Chapter 4.

In the staffing plan section, list the titles of the personnel required and describe their role in the project. Determine how many customers you will need at each location to test the final project solution. List the titles of the customers required and describe their role in the project in the customer staffing plan section.

Assumptions are used to clarify responsibilities such as ordering, installing, and paying for equipment. Some of these tasks will be done by the organization. The contractor or consulting company will be responsible for other tasks. Select the most critical assumptions and list them in the assumptions section of the Project Plan. Project risks are used to define perceived events that might cause the project to be delayed. Identify the risks for this project and list them in the project risk section of the Project Plan.

III. Organization	
A.	**Staffing Plan**
B.	**Customer Staffing Plan**

IV. Project Approach	
A.	**Project Assumptions**
B.	**Project Risks**

CHAPTER TERMS

CHAPTER BIBLIOGRAPHY

Book, Magazine, Presentation Citations

Beyda, William. *Data Communications from Basics to Broadband*. New Jersey: Prentice Hall, 1996: 34-40, 49-50, 71-73.

Cannon, Don and Gerald Luecke. *Understanding Communications Systems*. Texas: Texas Instruments, 1980: 1-3, 1-5, 2-15.

Case, Thomas and Larry Smith. *Managing Local Area Networks*. New York: McGraw-Hill, 1995: 50-52.

Gallo, Michael and William Hancock. *Computer Communications and Networking Technologies*. California: Brooks/Cole, 2002: 46.

Gelber, Stan. *Data Communications Today*. New Jersey: Prentice Hall, 1997: 73, 91-92.

Held, Gilbert. *Understanding Data Communications*. California: Sams, 1991: 7, 11-12.

Infotron Systems. *How does your network grow?* New Jersey: Infotron Systems Incorporated, 1984: (2.1-2.17) (3.7-3.11) (6.4-6.13).

Jordan, Larry. *System Integration for the IBM PS/2 and PC*. New York: Brady, 1990: 54.

McWhorter, Gene and Gerald Luecke. *Understanding Digital Electronics*. Texas: Texas Instruments, 1978: 5-4, 5-15, 5-22.

Microsoft. *Networking Essentials*. Washington: Microsoft Press, 1998: 540-543.

Nirenberg, Isabel, Uta Merzbach, and Richard Murray. *Computer Basics*. Illinois: Time Life Books, 1985: 32-35.

Novell. *Networking Technologies*. Utah: Novell, Inc., 1989: 6, 37.

Parnell, Tere. *LAN TIMES Guide to Wide Area Networks*. Berkeley: Osborne/McGraw-Hill, 2001: 24.

Shay, William. *Understanding Data Communications and Networks*. Massachusetts: PWS Publishing Company: 1995: 137, 156-158.

Sheldon, Tom. *Encyclopedia of Networking & Telecommunications*. New York: Osborne/McGraw-Hill, 2001: 38, 223, 803, 829, 1125, 1140-42, 1375.

Stallings, William. *Data and Computer Communications*. New York: MacMillan Publishing Company, 1991: 134.

Time Life. *Communications (Understanding Computers)*. New York: Time Life Books, 1990: 32.

Weissberger, Alan. *Data Communications Handbook*. California: Signetics Corporation, 1978: 26, 52.

Web Citations

Fitzgerald, Paul, "Network Operators Deploy Multichannel DWDM Testing," Lightwave, <www.lightwave.com> (February 2001).

Hellerstein & Associates, "The Evolution of Broadband," Web ProForum Tutorials, <http://www.iec.org> (06 March 2002).

Liberate Technologies, "Digital Broadband Telco," Liberate, <www.liberate.com> (2001).

Lucent Technologies, "Dense Wavelength Division Multiplexing (DWDM) Tutorial," Lucent Technologies, <www.iec.org/tutorials> (3 August 2000).

Lum, Mark and Dan Wolaver, "Performance Assessment of Timing and Synchronization in Broadband Networks," Tektronix, <www.tektronix.com> (1999).

Nokia, "Broadband Media Services," Web ProForum Tutorials, <www.iec.org> (06 March 2002).

Strangio, Christopher, "A Brief Introduction to Digital Data Transfer," CAMI Research Inc., <www.camiresearch.com> (1993-1997).

Webopedia, "ASCII," <www.pcwebopedia.com/TERM/A/ASCII.html> (10 October 2001).

CHAPTER 6

BRANCH OFFICE REMOTE ACCESS TECHNOLOGIES

CHAPTER OBJECTIVES

By the end of this chapter, you should understand these concepts:
- The factors to consider when designing a remote access strategy for branch offices
- The difference between multidrop and multipoint leased-line connections
- T1 and E1 carrier services and how they use time-division multiplexing for channels
- ISDN PRI's capability to consolidate several BRIs from several remote branch offices
- Uses for communications servers and the space-saving implications of consolidating services in one box
- Satellite technology, GEOs, LEOs, and MEOs as solutions for branch offices
- The use of optical submarine networks for voice, data, and Internet communication

Corporate offices today span the globe. Branch offices can exist anywhere in the United States as well as in Europe, the Pacific Rim, or in South America. As locations vary, so does the size of and number of users at each office. They all have a need, however, to transmit data back to corporate headquarters. Remote access must be easy for the users, yet secure and manageable for the administrators.

Designers must consider many factors when designing **remote access** solutions. The designer needs to examine the following issues:
- Number of users per location
- Number of users to be connected simultaneously
- Number of hours per day users will be connected
- Type of access required, such as e-mail, file transfer, data entry to corporate databases
- Whether the access required is continuous or intermittent

Most organizations need to use multiple technologies to achieve each branch office connection. The type of usage, the speed of the link, and the amount of **bandwidth** required will vary per location. Because of rising costs, it is important wherever possible to consolidate technologies into fewer pieces of equipment. For security purposes, it is important to minimize the number of entry points into the corporate network.

Another factor in planning for branch offices is the cost and availability of these technologies in different locations. Sometimes the right of way to a remote office must be wireless because cabling or leased-line services are unavailable. Of course, large metropolitan cities usually are better able to provide the type of connection required. However, many times the office location is 20 miles outside the city. The most important factor in determining the type of connection used is what is available over the last few miles.

This chapter explores the technologies used to connect the branch office to the corporate network, such as leased lines, ISDN BRI and PRI, communication servers, electromagnetic waves, and satellite.

LEASED LINES

A **leased line** is a permanent telephone connection between two points set up for an organization by a telco. The organization "owns" the leased line and does not share the connection with anyone else. Because no one else can be on the line, the quality of the line and access to it is assured. [Hurricane, 1]

As shown in Figure 6.1, a point-to-point connection has two pieces of **Data Terminal Equipment (DTE)**, one at each end. In between, two pieces of **Data Communications Equipment (DCE)** are used to send the data or message over the wire. The point-to-point connection is called a dedicated circuit or leased line. The dedicated circuit can be supported via modems (DCE) and an analog voice-grade circuit, or via a digital circuit using a T-1 service. [Sheldon, 986]

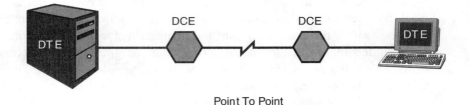

Point To Point

FIGURE 6.1 **Dedicated Point-to-Point Connection**

Typically, leased lines are used to connect geographically distant offices. Today, many companies use leased lines to connect to the Internet. If the Internet is used heavily, faster data rates warrant the cost. As shown in Figure 6.2, a leased line gives an organization a direct connection from its network to the long-distance carrier's POP (point of presence). Costs are based on the distance between end points and the speed of the circuit. The fee for the connection is a fixed monthly rate.

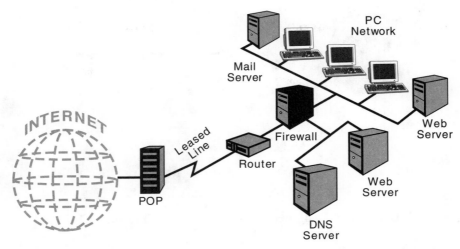

FIGURE 6.2 **Leased Line Connection to the Internet [Source: Onyx, 1]**

Because the Internet has become an essential communication, collaboration, and marketing tool, users rely on its availability 7 days a week, 24 hours a day. In addition, on the corporate side, security is a concern. A leased line, because it is a permanent dedicated connection, provides tighter security than other types of public links. However, the growing threat of Internet misuse has prompted most companies to add **firewalls** to even private leased lines to filter traffic coming into their networks. [Onyx, 1]

The firewall filters different types of traffic based on rules. It can block several types of attacks, and provides comprehensive monitoring of network traffic. However, the firewall cannot protect against virus attacks.

Leased Line Connections

Many times, organizations have a number of sites to connect to and they want to leverage the dedicated line to those locations. Splitting usage of a single dedicated line is called a **multidrop connection** (see Figure 6.3). This connection allows many DTEs to share one line with only two DTEs conversing at a time. Each location requires a DCE device, a CSU/DSU (Channel Service Unit/Data Service Unit) with a multiplexer or a router. [Infotron, 3.16]

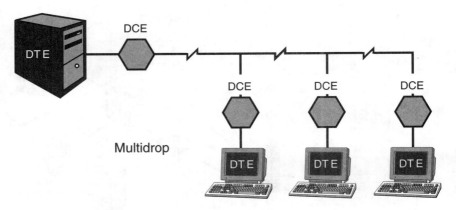

Multidrop

FIGURE 6.3 **Dedicated Multidrop** [**Source: Infotron, 3.16**]

Without multidrop, the organization would need three separate dedicated lines: one for each location. The monthly telephone bill would triple because of the additional point-to-point connections. However, this extra cost might be required if sustained usage is needed for 8 hours a day for 50 or more people per location.

For large companies, a combination of multidrop and multipoint are used to make the connection to multiple sites. A **multipoint connection** (see Figure 6.4) has many point-to-point connections and multidrop connections integrated into one large network. [Infotron, 3.17]

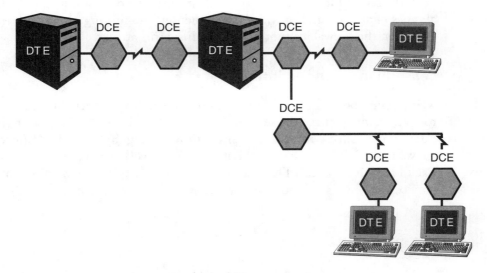

FIGURE 6.4 **Dedicated Multipoint** [**Source: Infotron, 3.17**]

The annual cost of a leased line depends on the leased line's capacity, length, and required bandwidth. The cost of the private circuit depends on the distance from the site to the POP. Bandwidth connections can vary per location. Some locations need more bandwidth based on the type of traffic, such as multimedia with high graphic content, or data entry into a corporate database. Another factor is the number of users or PCs per location and the number of hours per day they will be logged on simultaneously.

Leased Line Speeds

Leased lines of various speeds are available, ranging from 64 Kbps to 45 Mbps. Among the most commonly leased lines are **T1** lines (1.54 Mbps), which provide high bandwidth connections. T1 leased lines can carry high volumes of voice, data, and multimedia traffic. The T1 connection can be divided into different channels used for data and voice communications through multiplexing. There are 24 channels in a T1 line. Each channel provides 64 Kbps, so the total bandwidth is 24×64 Kbps = 1.536 Mbps, which is rounded off to 1.54 Mbps.

The most commonly leased lines in Europe are **E1** lines. An E1 line supports 30 channels plus 2 channels for control and synchronization. Each channel provides 64 Kbps, so the total bandwidth is 32×64 Kbps = 2.048 Mbps. [Sheldon, 1209]

T1 Devices

The 24 channels in a T1 line are managed by a **Time Division Multiplexer (TDM)**, which divides the channels into time slots. Each time slot can be used to carry a different phone call or data circuit. Each phone call or data circuit is allocated 64 Kbps. Time slots can be allocated in a variety of ways. For instance, there might be 12 time slots for voice, 6 time slots for data, and another 6 time slots for video conferencing.

At the end of every T1 line is a **Channel Service Unit (CSU)**. The CSU is the demarcation point from the telco to the customer. This device provides termination for the digital signal. The CSU converts customer data and voice signals into the format needed by the telco for transmission.

The telco uses the CSU to run a diagnostic loop back to test how the service is functioning. The CSU keeps the line connected if other communication equipment attached to it fails. A CSU can stand alone or it can be built into the front end of a router or into the multiplexing equipment. [Sheldon, 282]

Also required at the end of each T1 line is a **Data Service Unit (DSU)**. This unit converts customer data signals from other devices. The T1 line connects to the DSU via an RJ interface and the bridge/router connects via a V.35 device. The DSU converts data signals to the format required as input into the CSU.

In other words, the DSU converts signals from bridges, routers, and multiplexers to bipolar digital signals used by the T1 digital lines. [Sheldon, 282]

For voice-only applications, the CSU is used exclusively. Figure 6.5 shows how voice calls are carried between PBXs (private branch exchanges) at two locations in the same company. Using a T1 line saves long-distance charges if the volume of traffic between the locations is significant. [Joffe, 10]

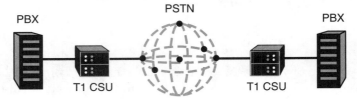

FIGURE 6.5 **T1 Voice Only [Source: Joffe, 10]**

In Figure 6.6, LAN data, rather than voice, is carried between the locations. The T1 lines are connected directly to the T1 CSU/DSUs. The DSU is needed to convert data coming from the router. The router supports a connection to the LANs. Today many CSU/DSUs are built into other devices, such as multiplexers or routers. Others are built into line cards installed on the PBX.

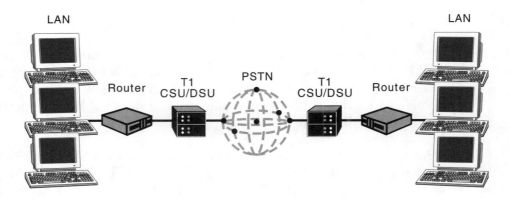

FIGURE 6.6 **T1 Data Internetworking [Source: Joffe, 10]**

For those companies that cannot afford the cost of a full T1 service, a **fractional T1 service** is available that allows sharing bandwidth with another company. The ½ T1 circuit or (768 Kbps) is shared between the PBXs and a quarter of a T1 (or 384 Kbps) is used for video. [Source, Joffe: 11]

Fractional T1 lines are used to save costs. The amount of bandwidth and number of channels provided per fraction are listed in Table 6.1.

TI TYPE	NUMBER OF CHANNELS	BANDWIDTH
Full T1	24	1.54 Mbps
1/2 T1	12	768 Kbps
1/4 T1	6	384 Kbps
1/8 T1	4	256 Kbps
1/16 T1	2	128 Kbps

TABLE 6.1 **Types of T1, Channels, and Bandwidth [Source: Joffe, 15]**

T1 costs also include distance, because the telco charges per mile. The mileage rate the telco charges is based on the bandwidth selected.

Although many applications require a lot of bandwidth, the bandwidth might only need to be used sporadically. In this case, switched bandwidth might the solution. This is a combination of switched (dial on demand) and dedicated bandwidth, which can be multiplexed and carried on the same T1 line. In the example shown in Figure 6.7, the organization needs a fractional 1/2 T1 for the long-haul circuit and 1/4 T1 for video conferencing. The video conferencing is sporadic, so it uses dial on demand when it is required. The LAN is connected through an Etherswitch to the multiplexer so users on the LAN can use the fractional T1 line. The multiplexer enables several devices to share the fractional T1 line.

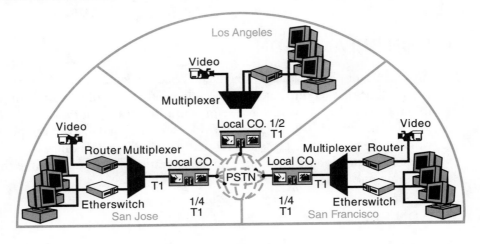

FIGURE 6.7 **T1 Switched Data [Source: Joffe, 13]**

T1 lines provide high bandwidth Internet connections for businesses and schools. They can access the Internet, send and receive e-mail, or transfer large amounts of data between locations. Many companies that provide e-commerce sites use T1 lines for heavy traffic Web hosting. Other uses for T1 lines include streaming audio, video, and video conferencing.

Leased-line purchases are still increasing by $1 million a year within the United States and will see sustained use for the next few years. [Horak, 1-6] Although leased lines are routinely used in the United States for direct connections, in Europe and Asia the high price of leased lines has hampered the spread of the Internet. Competition in the leased-line market has been slow to develop. The telecommunications infrastructure has concentrated on building high-capacity routers between big cities, as the cost of short-distance local leased lines is too expensive for most companies. [Europa, 1-4]

TOPIC *review* **Leased Lines**

1. What are the three ways an organization can support a point-to-point dedicated circuit?
2. Do permanent dedicated connections have better security than public links?
3. Why would an organization use a firewall on a permanent dedicated link?
4. How can an organization save money on its phone bills with a dedicated link?
5. What does the annual cost of a leased line depend on?

ISDN BRI AND ISDN PRI

An organization uses ISDN (Integrated Services Digital Network) when it has applications that require bandwidth on demand and flexible digital connections to public-switched networks. Many organizations use it for switched LAN to WAN connections. Today, ISDN provides for sending data over the phone network in digital format. The same twisted-pair copper telephone wire used for years now can support three separate "conversations" at the same time through the same line.

ISDN BRI

The basic ISDN-to-user connection is called *Basic Rate Interface (BRI)*. As shown in Figure 6.8, **Basic Rate Interface** (**BRI**) supports two channels (B channels) to carry user "conversations" from a telephone, computer, fax, or any other device. The **B channel** is known as the "Bearer" channel. On the third channel (**D channel**), call setup information and signaling is carried for the network, but it also can carry user data transmissions. The bearer channels carry 64 Kbps each and the D channel carries 16 Kbps.

B Channel = 64 Kbps
B Channel = 64 Kbps
+ D Channel = 16 Kbps

2B + D = 144 Kbps

FIGURE 6.8 **ISDN Basic Rate Interface (BRI) [Source: Angell, 32]**

Because ISDN delivers two separate channels (see Figure 6.9), it is possible to conduct a phone conversation on one channel and connect the other channel to a PC or fax machine. Using inverse multiplexing, two channels can be combined to offer one device (128 Kbps) for transmission. [Angell, 32]

ISDN is used for telecommuting, video conferencing, teleradiology, teleteaching, interactive publishing, remote broadcasting, and sound transfer. Implementing ISDN has required all the local telco's COs (central offices) to upgrade to digital switches so they can offer ISDN services. ISDN requires special equipment (see Figure 6.10) to interface with the phone, computer, and fax machine.

This equipment can be purchased or leased from the local phone company. A device called a **network termination device (NT1)** serves as the network interface for the BRI connection. The NT1 includes the physical and electrical termination functions of the ISDN service coming from the local CO. Because the ISDN line does not have any power, an NT1 requires a power supply. The power supply can plug into a standard wall outlet. The NT1 has a series of LEDs on the front and hosts one **U-interface port**, which is used to connect to the **RJ-11** cable for the telephone. The back of the unit supports two S/T **RJ-45 interface ports**, which are connected into the ISDN devices. [Angell, 71]

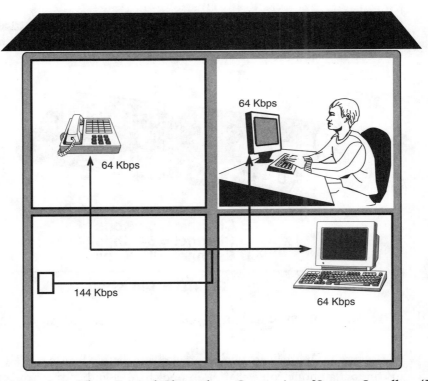

FIGURE 6.9 Three Logical Channels to Connections [Source: Spradley, 4]

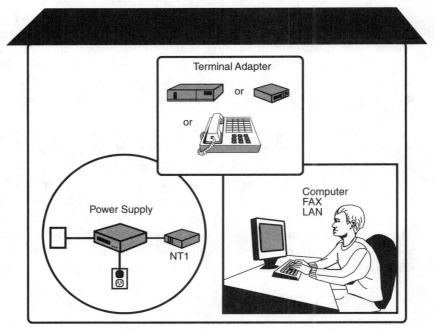

FIGURE 6.10 ISDN Special Equipment for Home Connection [Source: Spradley, 5]

A **terminal adapter** (**TA**) can be used to provide ISDN access for PCs. The TA is a protocol converter that adapts equipment not designed for ISDN. TAs are usually cards that plug into a PC. However, there are external terminal boxes used to connect analog telephones, faxes, and modems to an ISDN line. ISDN telephones incorporate a TA inside and use an advanced LCD screen for messaging and feature control. [Angell, 73]

ISDN devices that support the ISDN line directly are referred to as **Terminal Equipment** (**TE1**). Digital phones, digital faxes, and integrated voice/data terminal devices are considered TE1 devices. [Black, 68]

At the CO, call routing is used to connect to local and long-distance services. As part of the Telecommunications Act of 1996, all carriers—AT&T, Sprint, MCI, and Qwest—are granted points of presence (POPs) to provide long-distance services (see Figure 6.11). The link can remain an ISDN line to any location through the digital switch, and the customer can choose the long-distance carrier to complete the connection. [Spradley, 6]

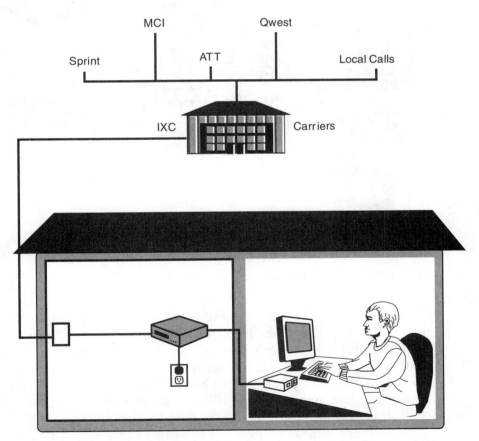

FIGURE 6.11 **Interexchange (IXC) Carrier Access (CO)** [**Source: Spradley, 6**]

ISDN PRI

At the corporate office, multiple BRIs are combined into an *ISDN PRI* device. The ISDN **Primary Rate Interface (PRI)** is made up of dedicated trunks used to connect corporate locations to the telco CO. PRI is designed to support multiple individual BRIs for both internal and external voice and data communications. A remote user from home or a branch office LAN can connect to the PRI line at corporate to access the LAN. ISDN PRI provides multiple channels to consolidate several BRIs into one unit. As shown in Figure 6.12, the ISDN PRI is connected to the corporate backbone to provide access to corporate servers on the LAN.

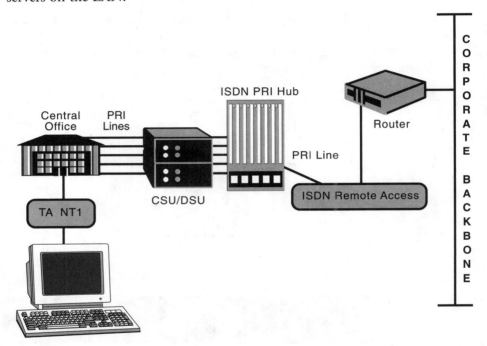

FIGURE 6.12 **ISDN PRI to Corporate Backbone**

Because PRI supports so many channels, it can be connected to PBXs, mainframes, LANs, WANs, multiplexers, ISDN controllers, and video conferencing units. [Sheldon, 692] ISDN PRI provides a total bandwidth of 1.544 Mbps through a standard T1 trunk. In the United States, PRI consists of 23 (64 Kbps) Bearer (B) channels and 1 (64 Kbps) Data (D) channel. The B channels are used for data and the D channel is used for signaling, timing, and diagnostics. [Sheldon, 692]

In the Pacific Rim and Europe, PRI provides 2.048 Mbps E1 channels. The E1 channel is supplied by 31 B channels (each 64 Kbps) and 1 D channel (64

Kbps). ISDN implementations overseas vary from nation to nation. However, because of international standards (see Chapter 2), many systems can be interconnected across the world. [Quigley, 9] Figure 6.13 shows PRI channels for T1 and E1 lines.

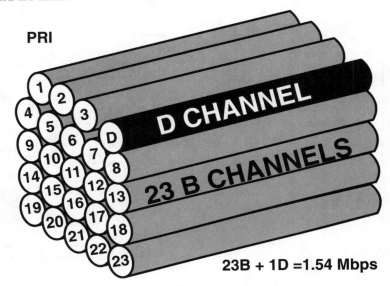

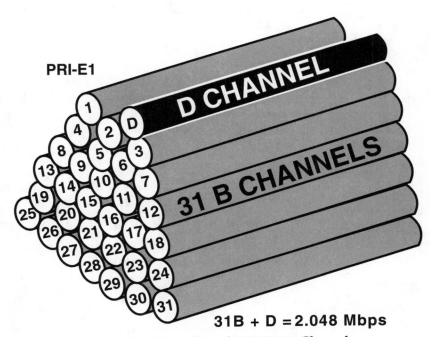

FIGURE 6.13 PRI 24 Channels and PRI-E1 32 Channels

As shown in Figure 6.14, ISDN BRI provides the connection for a small branch office LAN (usually 10 or fewer devices) to the corporate headquarters or to the Internet through a router. Multiple users can share the ISDN line and make connections to different networks at the same time. ISDN is used as a background conduit for connecting client and server computers to support data entry into application databases.

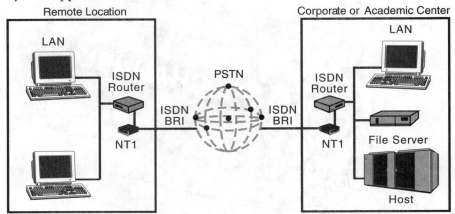

FIGURE 6.14 **Remote LAN to Host LAN [Source: Spradley, 9]**

The remote LAN does not require local file or mail services. The ISDN call is set up automatically and is made by the bridge or router only when data needs to be sent across LANs. Otherwise the ISDN line remains idle.

ISDN Terminal Equipment

ISDN terminal equipment consists of TE1 and TE2 devices, which are responsible for user communications, and network termination devices, such as NT1 and NT2, which are responsible for network communications. Table 6.2 describes each of these devices.

TE1	An end-user ISDN terminal type 1 device that connects to the ISDN line through a twisted pair four-wire digital link.
TE2	An ISDN terminal type 2 device that is used to connect to a terminal adapter.
NT1	Network termination device that connects the four-wire subscriber wiring to the conventional two-wire local loop.
NT2	A device typically found in a digital PBX, which is capable of performing concentration services.

TABLE 6.2 **ISDN Terminal Equipment [Black, 69]**

ISDN uses reference points, also called interfaces, to define the communications between different terminal devices. These interfaces define the operating limits for the functional devices. Four interfaces are defined for ISDN: R, S, T, and U interfaces. Table 6.3 lists and explains the function of each interface.

R Interface	Defines the relationship between the terminal equipment (**TE2**) device and a non-ISDN-ready device. It is a proprietary specification; the manufacturer determines how a TE2 device and the TA device will communicate with each other.
S/T Interface	S-interface is between ISDN user equipment (TE1 or TE2) and the NT1 device. T-interface is between the local switching device (**NT2**) and the PBXs. An S/T interface cannot be plugged directly into the ISDN line without an NT1 device.
U Interface	Also called the U-loop because it represents the loop between the user's premises and the local telco CO. A U-interface device can plug into S/T-interface and analog devices.

TABLE 6.3 **ISDN Interfaces [Source: Black 68]**

Most ISDN equipment vendors sell equipment that supports either the U interface or S/T interface. As shown in Figure 6.15, ISDN equipment that supports the U interface has the NT1 device built in. ISDN equipment that supports the S/T interface requires that the NT1 function be connected to the ISDN line. A single ISDN line can have multiple S/T interface devices.

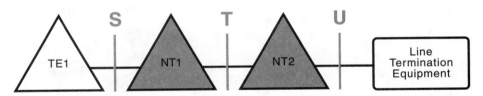

FIGURE 6.15 **ISDN Terminal Equipment Interfaces [Source: Black, 68]**

In Figure 6.16, the TA allows a non-ISDN-ready device to work over the ISDN connection. The most common use of the terminal adapter is to allow a PC to communicate over the ISDN line. An ISDN PRI/BRI hub is used to concentrate multiple incoming ISDN BRI remote data calls into a PRI line at the host. The PRI/BRI hub also can be directly connected to the router to provide users access to the Internet. [Angell, 39]

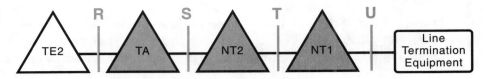

FIGURE 6.16 **ISDN Interfaces [Source: Black, 68]**

Instead of terminal adapters, some companies use digital modems to access the ISDN line. The digital modem is used as a terminal adapter and is connected to an NT1 as shown in Figure 6.17. The digital modem allows the user to access other ISDN services on the other end of the ISDN connection, such as fax machines and analog modems. The user also can connect to the PRI hub, which provides a connection to the Internet.

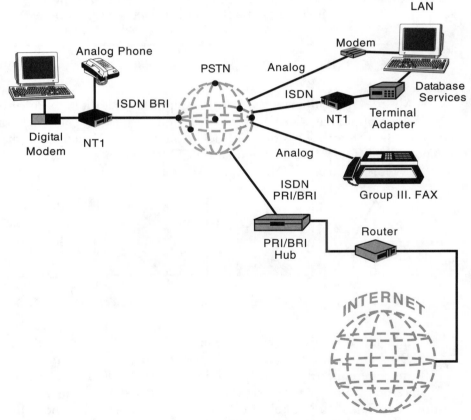

FIGURE 6.17 **Digital Modem ISDN Access [Source: Spradley, 10]**

ISDN and Desktop Video

One of the most rapidly growing areas of ISDN is desktop video. ISDN allows for better sound and image quality for electronic meetings that use **video conferencing** equipment. Video conferencing can take place through a PC because of ISDN lines. A dial-up session is established between the two locations using video conferencing equipment at each end. This requires two video adapter cards, one for each desktop. Each adapter card is attached to the S/T interface of the NT1. [Spradley, 11] With desktop video systems, users can share documents, photographs, PowerPoint presentations, and spreadsheets.

Figure 6.18 shows how ISDN PRI/BRI is used to provide desktop video conferencing.

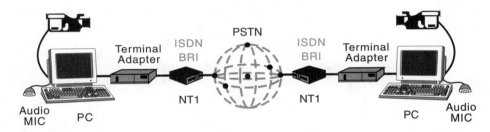

FIGURE 6.18 **Desktop Video**

ISDN PRI can support a number of video conferencing meetings per day between varying locations. The user's speech can be captured through high-quality microphones with full quality digital sound. The connection is free of static, line noise, or other distortions, and good quality video is possible through as little as 112 Kbps transmission. ISDN managers choose the most cost-effective speed for each type of video meeting and allocate the right amount of ISDN channels accordingly. [Angell, 239]

Benefits of ISDN PRI

ISDN PRI supplies many benefits, including the following:
- Reduced call setup time
- Reduced costs
- High-speed switched access to low-volume remote locations
- Uses both local and interexchange carrier services
- Provides bandwidth on demand

ISDN PRI, when compared with T1 leased-line services, is more cost effective. Call setup time is much faster, less than 300 milliseconds. Channels can be allocated for different activities or for different times of day. The channel is not allocated if the destination number is busy, which results in 25% more efficient use of channels. Table 6.4 compares PRI and T1 connections in more detail.

COMPARISON FEATURE	PRI	T1
Speed	64 Kbps on each channel 24 channels 24th channel used for signaling Call setup time: 300 ms	64 Kbps on each channel 24 channels Uses 16 Kbps for in-band signaling Call setup time: 3-5 seconds
Flexibility	On a call-by-call basis, any channel can be used for inward calls, outward calls, WATs calls, or 800 calls.	Channels are pre-assigned for the type of call. Some channels can sit idle while other channels ring busy.
	ISDN PRI uses look ahead routing and does not allocate a channel if the destination number is busy.	Channel is allocated for the call while it determines whether the destination line is busy. Need more channels to ensure a free line.
	Channels can be allocated by time of day. High-speed data transfer can occur at night while more voice calls are used during the day.	Voice and data channel assignments are fixed and can't borrow from each other.
Cost	ISDN PRI is less expensive than T1(HiCap) service.	

TABLE 6.4 **Comparison of PRI and T1 [Source: Spradley, 17]**

ISDN PRI is an economical solution for connecting several branch offices to headquarters because it provides the required bandwidth and has enough channels to support both voice and data communications.

COMMUNICATIONS SERVERS

Organizations often find they have too many communication devices to manage to support their branch office connections. *Communications servers* offer a way to combine several remote access methods into one server.

Communications servers are universal, managed, PC platforms for network services. They combine the flexibility of a terminal server for connecting individual computers with the capability to run client-server applications between a dial-in remote device and a LAN. Communications servers can combine fax, bulletin board, e-mail, Lotus Notes, telephony, and database services. [Cubix, 1]

Communications Server Components

Communications servers are made up of communication processors and software. Most communications servers have plug-in computer boards, called **processor cards**, which have a central processing unit (CPU), memory, and a serial RS-232 port. SNMP (Simple Network Management Protocol) is built into the circuitry to provide remote management for mission-critical applications. [Cubix, 1] The CPU board combines a number of integrated components onto a single board. Controllers that are integrated include video, hard drive (SCSI or EIDE), and dual Ethernet controllers. Serial connections include Com1, Com2, and USB. The CPU is a Pentium III processor. Without processor cards and a chassis, each remote control session would require a separate PC. [Cubix, 1]

Multiservers

Inside a communications server is a collection of independent servers. An entire network of services can be configured as a centralized IT solution using this multiserver structure. As Figure 6.19 shows, with independent processor cards, the communications server can run different Intel-based operating systems on each card. Windows NT can work alongside Linux and Free BSD UNIX. [Cubix, 1]

All the processor cards are hot swappable and can be added without interrupting the other operating systems in the chassis.

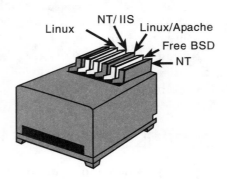

FIGURE 6.19 **Multiple Operating Systems [Source: Cubix, 1]**

The multiserver platform is ideal for building multiple Internet server systems, such as the one shown in Figure 6.20. The multiserver chassis takes up less space; is SNMP managed, and costs significantly less than the several stand-alone servers that would be required. SQL databases, Web IIS servers, FTP access, and firewall and proxy servers can be hosted side by side. The Web site can grow exponentially by simply adding more single processor cards. Remote administrators can manage the entire site from one SNMP console and have the ability to reset power off/on for each server processor card. [Cubix, 1]

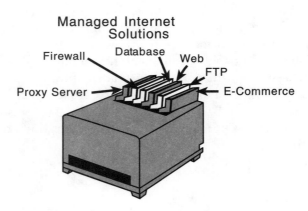

FIGURE 6.20 **Managed Internet Services [Source: Cubix, 1]**

Users can choose from analog or digital access lines to connect to the communications server. With analog access, a modem is necessary to convert the digital information from a dial-in device into analog waveforms for transmission across the network. Analog access is sufficient for casual use in transferring small files and access to e-mail and client-server databases. Analog access is provided through a **digiboard**, which is a serial card with multiple RS-232 ports. The RS-232 ports are connected to a pool of modems.

Analog lines are not sufficient for supporting more traffic-intensive applications. Accordingly, the communications server has been designed to support digital lines also, in order to provide clear, high-speed connections between the remote user and the LAN.

As Figure 6.21 shows, multiple cards can be installed in the communications server to offer different levels of service for users as required. If users need higher speed for traffic-intensive applications, a T1 card can be added into the communications server to provide dedicated T1 access. For slower speed dedicated access, the communications server can be connected to dedicated leased lines at 56 Kbps, 64 Kbps, 128 Kbps, and 256 Kbps. If ISDN is required, a single ISDN interface card can be added into the communications server to connect to an ISDN line.

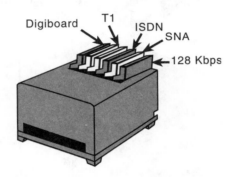

FIGURE 6.21 **Communications Services [Source: Cubix, 1]**

Multiservers and Multiple Remote Users

Many organizations are looking for alternatives to the high cost of providing software applications on individual desktops. In response to this trend, Microsoft has developed Windows 2000 **terminal services (TSE)**, which allows Microsoft software applications to run from a server. Remote users can run the software through their browsers, so they do not need to install the software applications on a client computer. Windows 2000 allows up to two client sessions per CPU using TSE. [Cubix, 1] A more powerful configuration is available through Citrix called *Metaframe*. **Metaframe** allows multiple client sessions to be supported through one processor card. It time slices the CPU's processing power so that multiple sessions can run concurrently. [Cubix, 1]

Dual processor cards can be deployed in the communication server to provide for thin client-server farms. Each dual processor card can support as many as 200 (average) TSE/Metaframe users. The thin client-server environment allows for access 7 days a week, 24 hours a day. The multiserver platform supports this environment by providing redundant power supplies and other safeguards to provide reliable terminal services.

A number of multiserver platforms can be mounted in a single rack to provide for server consolidation. The rack can accommodate at least eight Celeron-based Web servers or it can support 24 Pentium III-based applications servers. If clustering is used, eight Dual SMP Pentium III-based clustered data resource servers can be supported in one standard 19" rack, as shown in Figure 6.22.

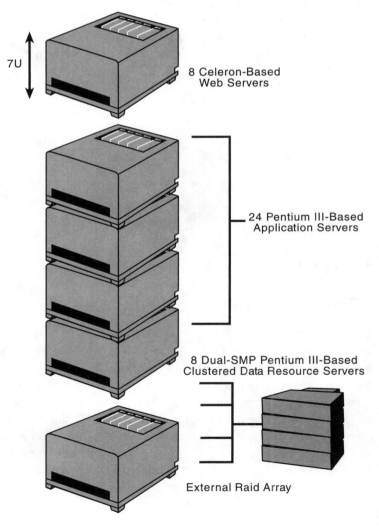

FIGURE 6.22 **Racking Communications Servers [Source: Cubix, 1]**

Chapter 6 • Branch Office Remote Access Technologies

After organizations understand the space-saving implications of consolidating services into one box, they often choose to implement them in strategic locations across the country. One or more communications servers are placed at regional centers. Nearby states then access the communications servers in their region.

TOPIC
review

Communications Servers

1. What types of services do communications servers support?
2. What is the purpose of a processor card?
3. What are Windows Terminal Services used for?
4. What does the digiboard connect to?
5. How do redundant power supplies provide a more reliable communication device?

ELECTROMAGNETIC WAVES

Signals are most often carried over LANs and WANs by physical cables; however, data is also passed over electromagnetic waves. The term used to describe these electromagnet wave transmission methods is **"unguided media."** [Sheldon, 157]

Data communication carriers find it advantageous to use unguided media because they don't have to dig up stretches of ground to lay cables. Unguided media transmission can be divided into three categories:

- Broadcast
- Line of sight
- Spread Spectrum Technology

Broadcast Transmission

Radio **broadcasting** is **omni-directional**, which means the signals are broadcast in all directions at once to guarantee wide coverage. Cellular phones use omni-directional two-way radio to communicate through a cell's base station. The base station is linked into the telephone network as if it were a local exchange. As the user moves out of one range, the adjacent cell's base station picks up the transmission to maintain the communication. Although broadcast transmission provides flexibility, it is not a secure method for data communications because outsiders can easily tap into it. [Black, 298]

Line of Sight Transmission

Line of sight transmits information from one point to another in a straight line and is more frequently used for data transmission than for voice. The three types of line of sight transmission methods are

- Microwave
- Infrared
- Laser

Microwave Transmission

Microwave transmission is considered a form of radio and uses a high-frequency range. Microwave is not considered a reliable method to transmit data because it is susceptible to interference, jamming, and eavesdropping. Also, because it is a type of radio transmission a license might be required to use it. [Sheldon, 782]

No !

Yes ! /

Microwave technology is used to move large amounts of data over very long distances. Microwave dishes are set up to transmit signals dish to dish. The dishes must be lined up so they face one another. When locations are very far apart, a series of dishes must be set up back to back to establish a route for the data to travel. As the signal reaches the next dish, it is automatically relayed to the next satellite station. The curvature of the earth imposes a limit on the distance allowed between dishes.

A **dish antenna** is commonly used in microwave systems for satellite communication and broadcast reception, space communications, radio astronomy, and radar. **Horn antennas** are also used for transmission of microwave signals. The antenna resembles an acoustic horn. Horn antennas are used as the active element in a dish antenna. The electromagnetic feed line or wave guide connects the antenna to the receiver, transmitter, or transceiver. The feed line transfers radio-frequency (RF) energy from a transmitter to an antenna. [TechTarget, 1]

Waveguides transmit radio waves through a rectangular or cylindrical metal tube or pipe. The electromagnetic field propagates lengthwise through the tube. Waveguides transmit waves of very high frequency and provide for very high data transfer rates. However, the construction of the tubes is expensive and the tubes cannot be sharply bent. The technology is sound, fast, and reliable, but it is not as flexible as optical fiber. [TechTarget, 1]

Infrared and Laser

Power Levels Are Relative

Infrared and **laser** are light-based technologies that operate on low power levels. They are primarily used in LANs because they can only carry signals over a limited distance. [Sheldon, 619] Infrared and laser use high frequencies, large bandwidth, and do not require licenses. As these are primarily LAN-based technologies, they are only mentioned briefly in this book.

Spread Spectrum Technology (SST)

Another type of unbounded transmission used in LANs is **Spread Spectrum Technology (SST)**. With SST, signals are spread out over a very high frequency range, over 200 times the bandwidth of the original signal. SST is not a line of sight transmission method because it does not pass data from point to point in a straight line. The signal is transmitted at a very low power level and therefore is relatively secure and safe from interference. SST is used for wireless mobile communications and wireless LANs. [Sheldon, 1175]

    Table 6.5 summarizes and compares the various kinds of unguided transmission methods.

BROADCAST	MICROWAVE	SST	INFRARED/LASER
Can penetrate walls	Can penetrate walls	Cannot penetrate walls	Cannot penetrate walls
Omni-directional method	Line of sight method	None	Line of sight method
Subject to interference	Insecure	Somewhat secure	Somewhat secure
License if necessary	May need a license	No license required	No license required
Used in cellular radio	Used in LANs & WANs	Used in LANs only	Used in LANs only
High power level	Can use either low or high power level	Low power level	Low power level

TABLE 6.5 **Characteristics of Unguided Transmission Methods [Source: Black, 75]**

TOPIC *review* Electromagnetic Waves

1. Is broadcast radio a secure method for data communications?
2. How are waveguides used?
3. Can microwave be used to transmit video signals?
4. What types of antennas are used with microwave technology?
5. What imposes a distance limitation between microwave dishes?

SATELLITE LINKS

Data can be transmitted via microwave over great distances via satellites. Satellites are used for weather forecasting, television broadcast, Internet communications, and Global Positions Systems (GPS).

Geostationary Satellites

In satellite technology, a **geostationary satellite** is used to transmit data and TV signals across the Atlantic and Pacific oceans. Geostationary satellite means it is stationary in relation to a specific location on earth. Geostationary satellites orbit 22,238 miles from the earth and can transmit at a speed up to 155 Mbps. They experience a very short delay of about 0.25 to .50 seconds. [Gareiss, 3] Today, more than 100 communications satellites orbit the Earth. Figure 6.23 shows an Echostar3 communications satellite.

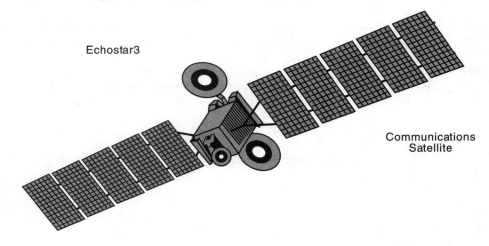

Echostar3

Communications
Satellite

FIGURE 6.23 **Communications Satellite [Source: San Jose Tech Museum, 1]**

Chapter 6 • Branch Office Remote Access Technologies

Even though the satellite is in orbit, it appears from the Earth to be always in the same place. Because the satellite is out in space, the curvature of the Earth is less involved in the transmission of data, and therefore, the distance limitation for data transmission is resolved. Satellites are most often used for transmitting TV programs. The station on Earth relays a signal to the satellite in space, which then sends the signal to a receiver station somewhere else on earth.

Figure 6.24 shows the elements of a satellite, which include antennas, cameras, radar, and electronics. A communications satellite supports large antennas to transmit TV or telephone signals to Earth. The sun provides power to satellites orbiting the Earth. Solar arrays are used to make electricity from sunlight. There are batteries on the satellite that store the electricity produced. Distribution units are used to send power to the satellite's instruments. [San Jose Tech Museum, 1]

A thermal blanket covers the entire satellite with a thin foil material. This foil keeps the satellite warm in the cold and cool in the extreme heat. Satellites are exposed to temperatures that range from (-120 to +180 degrees). [San Jose Tech Museum, 1]

The flight computer is the brain of the satellite that controls the antenna, transmitter/receiver, digital camera, and image sensors. The image sensors process the pictures captured by the digital camera and turn them into electronic signals. The transmitter sends large amounts of data between the satellite and the Earth. [San Jose Tech Museum, 1]

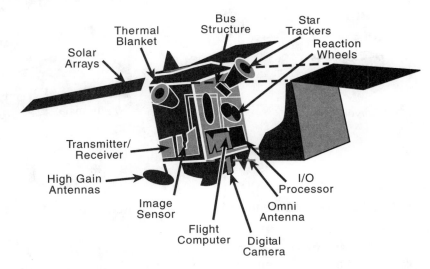

FIGURE 6.24 **Satellite Anatomy [Source: San Jose Tech Museum, 1]**

When engineers send a command to the satellite, the transmitter/receiver picks up the signal and converts it into a message the satellite's computer can understand. Satellites for television use one-way transmission, and satellites used for data communications use two-way transmission.

On the ground, special terminals called **Very Small Aperture Terminals (VSATs)** are used to transmit data signals to and from geostationary satellites. The opening for the microwave beam is very narrow. Satellite station uses different frequencies for transmitting and receiving data.

Shell Oil Products in Houston (shown in Figure 6.25) has recently installed VSATs at 5,000 gas stations across the country for point-of-sale and credit card processing. Before installing the satellite connection, Shell had to send a technician to each station to upgrade the software, which took two-four hours per station to complete. Now Shell upgrades the software at all of its gas stations using a single broadcast transmission via satellite. Station terminals load and store the new version of the software until the end of day reports are completed. Then the terminal automatically switches to the upgrade. [Gareiss, 4]

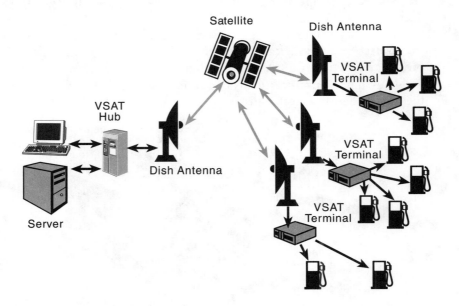

FIGURE 6.25 **Shell Oil VSAT Network [Source: Gareiss, 4]**

As the data is relayed from the satellite station to the receiving VSAT on Earth, the change of frequencies between transmitting and receiving prevents interference and makes data transmission more reliable.

LEO and MEO Satellites

In addition to geostationary, two other types of satellites are used for communications. Low Earth Orbit (LEO) and Middle Earth Orbit (MEO) satellites are used for low- and high-speed data and voice. [TechTarget, 1]

LEO satellites are in orbit at a constant altitude a few hundred miles from the Earth. Because LEOs are so close to the earth, they must travel very fast so that gravity won't pull them back into the atmosphere. LEOs are in orbit from approximately 400 to 1,000 miles from the Earth and can transmit from 2.4 to 9.5 Kbps. A LEO travels at 17,000 miles per hour and can circle the earth in approximately 90 minutes. LEOs are used for mobile voice, low-speed data, and high-speed data. Their transmission delay is only .05 seconds. LEOs make it possible for anyone to access the Internet via mobile phones, PDAs, and automobile communications systems.

MEOs, on the other hand, are used for global wireless communication coverage. MEO satellites are closer to the Earth than geostationary, but farther away than LEOs. MEOs are in orbit 8,000 miles from the Earth and they can orbit in about 2-12 hours. They can transmit from 9.6 Kbps to 38.4 Kbps. Because MEOs are closer to the Earth than geostationary satellites, they can be accessed by relatively low power transmitters and modest-sized antennas. MEOs experience very short transmission delays of only 0.10 second.

Satellites provide a wide geographic reach; they can go where cable cannot. A number of industries use satellites, such as maritime, transportation, and oil industries. When an organization has more than 1,000 geographically dispersed sites, satellite is a good transmission method. It is especially useful when a corporation needs to run the same technology to every site regardless of location.

In 2001, Futron Corporation launched 16 commercial geosynchronous (GEO) satellites and 19 non-GEO satellites. The satellite industry is experiencing a slowdown in launches, however, due to changes in U.S. export laws. The world market share for U.S. satellite manufacturers has declined significantly from 75% to 45% in the last year. [Satnews, 1]

TOPIC review — Satellite Links

1. What types of communication can be used over a satellite link?
2. What prevents interference when data is relayed from the satellite station on earth?
3. How are LEO satellites used?
4. How are MEO satellites used?
5. What types of industries use satellite communications?

SUBMARINE NETWORKING

Unguided media are not the only options for transmitting data and voice over large areas. Connecting people across continents also can be accomplished by using submarine networking. Over 70% of our planet is covered with oceans. As early as 1858, the first transatlantic cable was installed between the United States and Europe. Submarine coaxial cable had been used for years to transmit information over bodies of water to replace or augment high-frequency radio schemes.

Today, optical submarine networks are used for voice, data, and Internet communications WDM (Using Wave Division Multiplexing), submarine network transmission capacity has risen to 8.4 terabits (Tb) per fiber pair. WDM is a frequency division multiplexing technique for fiber-optic cable in which multiple optical signal channels are carried across a single strand of fiber at different wavelengths of light. Each wavelength is a different color of light in the infrared range that can carry data. [Sheldon, 1337]

Submarine cable is designed to perform without repair for 20 years. It is cost effective, provides security, and does not have a long signal propagation delay.

Metallic submarine cables are gradually being replaced with optical fiber. The optical fibers are encased with many steel wires to protect them from external and mechanical stress. Optically amplified repeaters are used to strengthen the signal as it travels across the depths of the ocean. [Alcatel, 1] Occasionally, fishing boats damage the submarine cable. However, recent installations of optical fiber cable are done under seabed's to minimize the hazards caused by fishing trawlers and ships. [Alcatel, 1]

Submarine cable connections to Pacific Rim and Europe are an affordable alternative for most organizations. Over 116,000 miles of undersea submarine cable were recently laid to Europe. [Plunkett, 18] This new cabling system is called Apollo and is being built as a joint venture of Cable & Wireless and Alcatel. Apollo is the world's most advanced IP trans-Atlantic cable, which links Long Island, N.Y. to Cornwall, England and connects to Brittany, France. The cable will transmit data at 3.2 Tbps. Alcatel's cable protection design makes it less vulnerable to damage from fishing trawlers. [Burt, 39]

TOPIC
review **Submarine Networking**

1. When was the first transatlantic cable installed?
2. Which type of submarine cable has been used for years to transmit over bodies of water?
3. Which type of multiplexing is used with optical submarine network?
4. Are companies in the United States still installing submarine cable to Europe and Pacific Rim?
5. What is being used to replace metallic submarine cables?

CHAPTER SUMMARY

Some organizations have moved into the Internet marketplace for business services and software applications. Organizations are also exploring the option to move voice, video, and data between their office locations across the WAN. Most organizations require multiple technologies to set up these Internet and branch office connections.

Designing remote access solutions for branch offices requires the analysis of the number of users per location, number of users to be connected simultaneously, number of hours per day users will be connected, type of access required, and whether it will be continuous or intermittent. Cost and availability of telecom services also influences the selection of remote access solutions.

Leased lines are widely used to connect offices together. T1 leased lines carry high volumes of voice, data, video, and multimedia traffic. Channels are multiplexed and can be divided between data, voice, and video. Fractional T1 services allow organizations to save costs by sharing the bandwidth with another organization.

Small remote offices and telecommuters often use ISDN BRI to connect to the organization's headquarters. ISDN BRI provides for sending data over the telephone network in digital format. At headquarters, ISDB PRI is used to support multiple ISDN BRIs connections from several locations. Terminal adapters are used to connect analog phones, faxes, and modems to the ISDN line. Using video conferencing over ISDN lines provides static free connections at speeds that are cost effective for organizations.

Multiserver platforms called communication servers are often used by organizations to consolidate several services such as e-mail, telephony, Web services, and database services into one box. Processor cards installed in the communication server enable a collection of independent servers to run side by side simultaneously.

As organizations face global competition, they are always seeking better ways to establish quality connections at a low cost. Organizations with offices spread across the globe are finding satellite services a good method for providing access to headquarters. New satellite systems are being built and launched to provide more organizations with affordable access to different parts of the world. Many organizations are using satellite for broadband access through digital TV and broadcast applications.

Submarine coaxial cable had been used for many years to transmit information over bodies of water to replace or augment high-frequency radio schemes. Today, optical submarine networks are used for voice, data, and Internet communications to connect to locations worldwide.

CHAPTER REVIEW QUESTIONS

(This quiz can also be printed out from the Encore! CD that accompanies this textbook. File name—Chap06review.)
Circle the correct answer (A-D) for each question. Choose only one answer for each.

1. A satellite dish is used to transmit data across the Pacific Ocean. The satellite is moving because it is in orbit. This satellite is called:
   a. A stationary satellite
   b. A television satellite
   c. A geostationary satellite
   d. A graphical satellite

2. A satellite dish uses a powerful _____ to transmit data over long distances.
   a. spread spectrum
   b. radio
   c. laser
   d. microwave

3. What is the most important advantage gained by using a communications server for remote access to/from a LAN?
   a. Cost savings due to reduced number of modems
   b. Cost savings due to reduced number of phone lines
   c. Control over the remote access to the LAN and its attached resources
   d. Cost savings due to reduced number of software licenses

4. A factor to consider in designing remote access solutions is:
   a. Number of square feet in the building
   b. Number of floors in the building
   c. Number of users per floor
   d. Number of users to be connected simultaneously

5. Which statement best describes a leased line?
   a. A leased line gives the customer a direct connection from his network to the long-distance carrier's POP.
   b. Leased-line costs are not based on distance.
   c. You share the leased line with other companies.
   d. A leased line is not used to connect to the Internet.

6. A DSU is used to:
   a. Provide termination for the digital signal.
   b. Convert signals from bridges, routers, and multiplexers to bipolar digital signals used by the T1 digital line.
   c. Keep the line connected if other communication equipment is attached to it.
   d. Convert customer data and voice signals into the format needed by the telephone company for transmission.

7. Which statement best describes ISDN PRI?
   a. Provides multiple channels to consolidate several BRIs into one unit.
   b. The multiple bearer (B) channels used with PRI are used for signaling, timing, and diagnostics.
   c. In Europe, PRI provides 23 B channels and 1 D channel.
   d. Remote users from home or branch offices cannot connect to the PRI line at corporate.

8. Communications servers are made up of:
   a. Bulletin board services for advertising
   b. Software used for database services
   c. Communications processors, enclosures, and software
   d. Serial RS-232 communication boards

9. Microwave technology is used to:
   a. Move large amounts of data over very long distances
   b. Move small amounts of data over very short distances
   c. Move data to routers
   d. Move radio-frequency energy to the ground

10. This type of cable is used under seabeds in the ocean to minimize the hazards caused by fishing trawlers and ships.
    a. CAT V Twisted Pair
    b. 10 Base 2 Coaxial cable
    c. Optical fiber
    d. CAT 3 Twisted Pair

Choose only one answer for each description. Circle the correct letter (A-E) for each description.
   A. Omni-directional
   B. LEO
   C. Multiplexer
   D. Light
   E. Waveguide

11. A B C D E   Transmits radio waves through a tube.

12. A B C D E   Signals are broadcast in all directions.

13. A B C D E   Used in optical fiber, a form of electromagnetic energy.

14. A B C D E   Shares the channel to support multiple devices to be connected to the WAN.

15. A B C D E   These satellites orbit very close to the earth.

   A. Multidrop
   B. POP
   C. TDM
   D. ISP
   E. PRI

16. A B C D E   Data is transmitted in time slots with guaranteed bandwidth.

17. A B C D E   Provides 23 B channels and one 64 Kbps D channel.

18. A B C D E   A place where long-distance service providers connect into regional or local telephone system.

19. A B C D E   Connects company to the Internet.

20. A B C D E   Dedicated line has split usage to three locations.

INTERNET EXERCISES

1. Logon to the Internet and key in the following URL:

   www.thetech.org/exhibits/online/satellite/2/2.html

   What are the two elements that are common to all satellites? Define each element and explain how it is used.

2. Key the following URL:

   www.usc.edu/dept/engineering/eleceng/Adv_Network_Tech /Html/telco/sld030.htm

   List the names and descriptions of each undersea fiber optic project.

CONCEPT EXERCISES

Concept Narrative

(This narrative exercise can also be printed out from the Encore! CD that accompanies this textbook. File name—Chap06connar.)

Read the following description and fill in the blanks with the correct answers.

Today satellites are used to _____ signals and data over very long distances. Satellites are used for weather forecasting, television broadcast, Internet communications, and GPS. Even though the satellite is in _____, it appears from the Earth to be always in the same place. The satellite on Earth _____ a signal to the satellite in space, which then sends the _____ to a receiver station somewhere else on Earth.

Elements of a satellite include antennas, cameras, radar, and electronics. The sun provides _____ to satellites orbiting the Earth. _____ _____ are used to make electricity from sunlight. There are batteries on the satellite that store the electricity produced. Distribution units are used to send _____ to the satellite's instruments. A _____ blanket covers the entire satellite with a thin foil material. This foil keeps the satellite warm in the cold and cool in the extreme heat. Satellites are exposed to temperatures that range from -120 to +180 degrees.

The flight computer is the _____ of the satellite. It controls the antenna, transmitter/receiver, digital camera, and image sensors. The _____ _____ processes the pictures captured by the digital camera and turns them into electronic signals. The _____ sends large amounts of data between the satellite and the Earth.

When engineers send a command to the satellite, the _____ _____ picks up the signal and converts it into a message that the satellite's computer can understand. Satellites for television use _____ _____ transmission. However, satellites used for data communications use _____ _____ transmission.

On the ground, special terminals called _____ (VSAT) are used to transmit data signals to and from the satellites. The opening for the _____ beam is very narrow. Satellite stations use different frequencies for _____ and _____ data.

Concept Table

(This table exercise can also be printed out from the Encore! CD that accompanies this textbook. File name—Chap06contab.)

Read each statement carefully and choose the type of satellite being described. Use only one "X" per statement.

STATEMENT	TYPES OF COMMUNICATIONS SATELLITES		
	LEO	MEO	GEO
1. This satellite is used to transmit and receive signals to/from phones, PDAs, and automobile communications systems.			
2. This satellite is in orbit 8,000 miles from Earth.			
3. This satellite is used for broadcast VSAT point-to-point connections.			
4. This satellite can circle the Earth in approximately 90 minutes.			
5. This satellite is 22,238 miles from Earth.			
6. These satellites travel very fast so gravity won't pull them back into the atmosphere.			
7. This satellite is used for global wireless communication coverage.			
8. This satellite can orbit the Earth in about 2-12 hours.			
9. This satellite is used to transmit data and TV signals.			
10. This satellite is in orbit 400 to 1,000 miles from Earth.			

Concept Picture

(This picture exercise can also be printed out from the Encore! CD that accompanies this textbook. File name—Chap06conpic.)

Elements of a satellite include antennas, cameras, radar, and electronics. In this exercise, look at the picture of the satellite and label the missing elements.

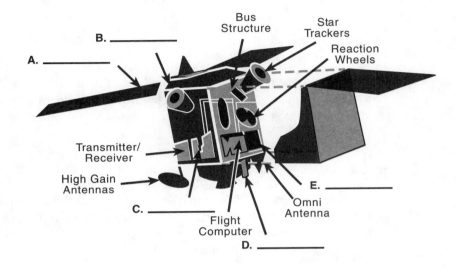

1. _____ These panels are used to make electricity from sunlight.

2. _____ This device captures pictures.

3. _____ This device runs the flight computer.

4. _____ This is a thin foil material that covers the entire satellite.

5. _____ Pictures captured by the digital camera are turned into electronic signals by this device.

CASE STUDY

UVW INSURANCE COMPANY

Read the following case study about the UVW Insurance Company. Think about the challenge presented to the company, and the information solution provided. Then, either by yourself or in a group, answer the case study questions.

Objective:

Determine the communications links required for each remote office. Provide for a centralized database application managed from the corporate headquarters. Use a communications server to consolidate remote control services for the branch offices.

Company Profile:

UVW Insurance Company is a property and casualty insurance company based in Wisconsin. It is licensed to underwrite insurance policies in 30 states. UVW has five remote independent insurance agencies that send information to its headquarters in Sheboygan, Wisconsin.

Current Situation:

Each of the five independent insurance offices uses its own insurance agency application. At the corporate headquarters, the MIS department must process data from four different insurance agency applications. None of the programs is compatible with the others. Four of the five independent insurance offices have 100 people who are continuously connected to corporate headquarters eight hours per day. The fifth office is a new facility with only 25 people, which is expected to grow to 100 over the next two years. These 25 people are connected continuously eight hours per day.

Business Information Requirements:

Each independent office has two servers, one SQL database server and a Windows 2000 server for file and printer sharing. The SQL database server is running the insurance agency application program. The company wants to provide a system that is centralized and provides remote access for information queries to the corporate headquarters. UVW also wants to have connectivity so that it can share information with agents in the other independent insurance offices.

Communication System Requirements:

The MIS department wants a new system that is cost effective and easy to maintain. The company needs to integrate all remote offices into a centralized database platform. One software package is needed to provide insurance agency management for all offices. MIS wants to continue to support and maintain the Windows 2000 file and print-sharing servers at each office.

Information Systems Solution:

1. Two offices are located close to each other in neighboring states. A dedicated ¼ T1 (384 Kbps) communication line was purchased for each office.
2. The new office is located near the mountains and, as no cable right of way existed, a Satellite (128 Kbps) connection was established.
3. The other three offices are geographically dispersed and two of the sites have ISDN service available in their area. The speed of the ISDN links is 128 Kbps. The last two offices were doing twice the transactions of all the other offices so they received a point-to-point fractional ¼ T1 at 384 Kbps.
4. A communications server was located at Corporate and connected via two statistical multiplexers.
5. Remote control access was provided to the agency management application. Citrix Metaframe provided the software.
6. The communications server at Corporate had five processor boards installed. The configuration of the processor cards is shown in Table 6.6.

Card 1	SQL Database
Card 2	FTP
Card 3	Firewall
Card 4	Agency Application
Card 5	Internal Web Site
2 - 100 Mbps Ethernet cards	
1 - Digiboard for dial-up remote access	

TABLE 6.6 **Processor Cards Configuration**

The agency application and the SQL database are used to support agency management for the remote offices. Processor cards one and four use Citrix Metaframe to provide multiple remote control connections to the agency application.

FTP services provide for large file uploads to the database. A firewall provides traffic filtering and security for the agency application. An internal Web site is used for company news and information and is being maintained by Corporate.

In addition, the communications server has two 100 Mbps Ethernet cards added to connect the communications server to the corporate backbone.

An ISDN PRI/BRI hub has been installed at Corporate to handle the ISDN links from the branch offices. The T1 line is connected to a statistical multiplexer to provide for the fractional T1 connection. A satellite dish receives the transmission from the new branch office located near the mountains.

The new system has been in place now for about eight months. All five remote offices received training on the new software and came up to speed quickly with the new insurance agency program. Employees at these offices appreciate that everything is centralized now and their response time is adequate.

As for the MIS side, employees there like the centralized solution much better. They are better able to maintain the communications server with SMNP. They are even considering setting up a second server with Citrix Metaframe and Windows 2000 terminal services to support other applications in the future.

Look at Figure 6.26 and answer the case study questions that follow.

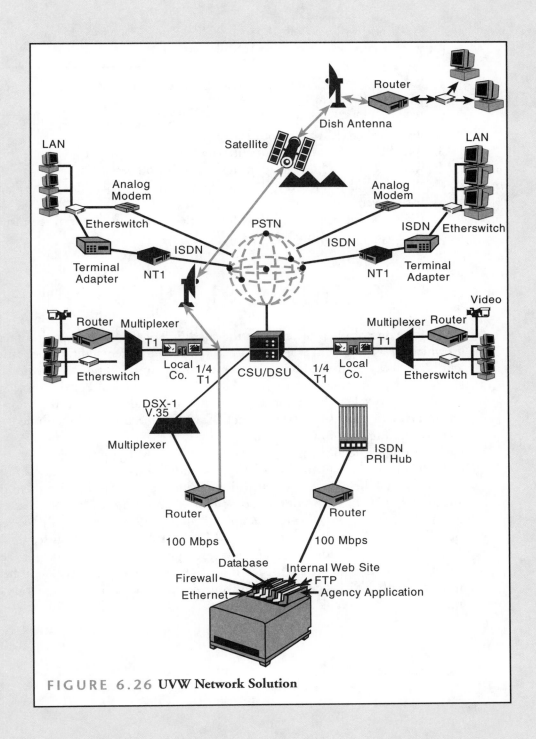

FIGURE 6.26 **UVW Network Solution**

CASE STUDY QUESTIONS:

1. What type of remote access was used to handle users who are connected continuously eight hours a day?
2. What type of communications link was used to link the independent insurance offices to each other?
3. As a MIS professional, what criteria would you evaluate to find one software package to manage all insurance agency offices?
4. What would you recommend for monitoring the availability of the database server?
5. Do you think the employees will adjust easily to a new centralized insurance agency program?

GROUP TERM PROJECT

For this section of the project, assess the condition of the physical environment in which new equipment will reside in each location. Often additional electrical outlets or racks are needed or the movement of existing equipment is required. These costs need to be estimated and included in the project. For this project, assume you have had the opportunity to inspect each location. List the equipment, racks, or outlets required for each location in Section V of the Project Plan you printed out in Chapter 4.

Most projects lend themselves to being accomplished in phases. At this point, come up with a concept of how these project phases can be distinguished, name the phases (1-6), provide a title for each phase, and list them in the Phases of Work sub-section of Section VI of your Project Plan. Next, assign a time frame for each phase; for example, Phase I – WAN Design (July 8 - Sept. 30). List this time frame in the Estimated Phase Start and End Dates section. In the Time Line Schedule section, draw a straight line and tick marks for each month in the time frame. Label each month and the phase to be accomplished in that month. This schedule provides you with a quick visual representation of the entire time line for the project.

WAN PROJECT PLAN

PREPARED BY: **DATE:**

V.	Facility Requirements

VI.	Schedule

A.	Phases of Work

B.	Estimated Phase Start and End Dates
C.	Time Line Schedule

CHAPTER TERMS

CHAPTER BIBLIOGRAPHY

Book, Magazine, Presentation Citations

Angell, David. *ISDN for Dummies.* Foster City: IDG Books Worldwide, 1996: 1-123.

Black, Uyless. *Emerging Communications Technologies.* Upper Saddle River: Prentice Hall, 1997: 36-81.

Infotron Systems Corporation. *How does your network grow?* Cherry Hill: Infotron Systems Corporation, 1984: 1-110.

Internetworking Technology. "Integrated Services Digital Network (ISDN) Overview," (1999): 1-5.

Joffe, Daniel M. *The Inside Guide to T1 and Fractional T1 Services.* Bridgewater: Integrated Network Corporation, 1994: 3-22.

Parnell, Tere. *LAN TIMES Guide to Wide Area Networks.* Berkeley: Osborne/McGraw-Hill, 2001: 203-227.

Plunkett, Jack W. *Plunkett's InfoTech Industry Almanac 2001-2002.* Houston: Plunkett Research, Ltd.: 7-33.

Quigley, Phil. *A User's Guide to Services, Applications & Resources in California.* Connecticut: The Corporate Forum for Pacific Bell, 1994: 1-54.

Sheldon, Tom. *Encyclopedia of Networking & Telecommunications.* New York: Osborne/McGraw-Hill, 2001: 1-1447.

Spradley, Ella. "Simple ISDN Overview." California: Pacific Bell, 1995: 1-22.

Web Citations

2Wire Learning Center, "High-speed Satellite Internet Service," <www.2wire.com/lcenter/sat.html> (20 June 2001).

Alcatel, "Hot Technologies: Submarine Networking," <www.cid.alcatel.com> (17 October 2001).

Burt, Jeffrey, "Cable to link U.S., Europe," <www.Eweek.com> (15 January 2002).

Commission Online, "Leased lines: Commission acts to bring down cost of communications in Europe," <www.europa.eu.int> (19 October 2001).

Cubix Corporation, "Multiple Services Managed as One Enterprise," <cubix.com/corporate/solutions/consol.htm> (19 October 2001).

Cubix Corporation, "If You Are Deploying Windows TSE/MetaFrame," <www.cubix.com/corporate/solutions/thinmenu.htm> (19 October 2001).

Cubix Corporation, "Internet and ISP Server Platforms," <www.cubix.com/corporate/internet/internet.htm> (19 October 2001).

Cubix Corporation, "Case Study: Ascend Communications Interoperability," <cubix.com> (19 October 2001).

Europa, "Leased lines: Commission acts to bring down cost of communications in Europe," Europa, <http://europa.eu.int/rapid/start/cgi/guesten.ksh?p_action.gettxt=gt&doc=IP/99/873|0|RAPID&lg=EN> (24 November 1999).

Gareiss, Robin, "Satellite Services: Down to Earth and Ready for Business,"<www.data.com/roundups/earth.html> (17 January 1998).

Horak, Ray, "T-Carrier Basics," The Context Corporation, <www.commweb.com/article/COM20010807S0013> (9 October 2001).

Hurricane Electric Internet Services, "Leased Lines,"<www.he.com/leased.html> (19 October 2001).

INTUG, "International Leased Lines national versus international costs," <www.intug.net/surveys/ill/explanation.html> (19 October 2001).

Missouri Research & Education Network, "eMINTS WAN: Point to Point Example,"<www.more.net/consulting/eMINTS-g.html> (17 April 2001).

Onyx Connections, "Onyx Connections Leased Line," <www.onyx-connections.net/leaseline> (19 October 2001).

Puetz, John, "Comparative Approaches in Implementing Wide Area Satellite Networks," ViaSat Inc, <www,viasat.com> (27 January 2002).

San Jose Tech Museum, "Satellites/Communications," <www.thetech.org/exhibits_events/online/satellite> (10 May 2001).

Satnews, "Prospects for the Satellite Industry in 2002," <www.satnews.com/feature/feature-2002-prospect.html> (28 January 2002).

StarBand Communications, "EchoStar/GM/Hughes Announcement," <www.dishnetwork.com/content/promotions/starband/index.shtml> (29 October 2001).

Tag's Broadcasting Services, "TSE-Glossary," <www.tbs-satellite.com/tse/online/thema_glossary.html> (30 October 2001).

TechTarget, "What is," <whatis.techtarget.com/definition> (30 October 2001).

CHAPTER 7

CLIENT REMOTE ACCESS TECHNOLOGIES

By the end of this chapter, you should understand these concepts:
- The evolution of remote access methods used from 1970-2002.
- The client-based remote access services: dial up, DSL, cable modems, consumer satellite service, and Fiber to the Home (FTTH).
- The difference between remote node and remote control.
- Various DSL services and the differences among them.
- The basic elements of cable modem service.
- One-way and two-way consumer satellite services.
- How Fiber to the Home works and where it is being deployed.

There has been explosive growth in the size and scope of corporate networks. Organizations have expanded their business activities within the United States and overseas. The corporate focus on decreasing cost and increasing efficiency has spurred growth in telecommuting and mobile use. The challenge facing organizations today is to provide remote users and branch offices, dispersed by geography, with access to the corporate network.

Remote access is divided into two distinct categories: remote user access (telecommuters and mobile users) and remote branch office users. Remote access users (such as sales representatives and corporate management) use dial-up access from laptops and Personal Digital Assistants (PDAs) to access the corporate network. Most recently, a number of organizations have been supporting telecommuting workers who need to connect from home.

Branch office access involves connecting LAN-to-LAN between a remote office and the corporate network. The branch office is connected with a router or a remote bridge over a dedicated link or a switched connection. Corporate headquarters is at the center with several remote connections coming in from every direction from anywhere, all using different methods to connect. More equipment must be purchased at the corporate headquarters to accommodate all of the types of remote access connections used.

The products and methods used to provide remote access have changed dramatically over the past 30 years. As each remote access solution had its capacity challenged by changes in telecommunication, the resulting limitations led to a new generation of remote access methods and products.

EVOLUTION OF REMOTE ACCESS TECHNOLOGY

In the 1970s, efforts were focused on delivering access to the organization's mainframe computer to provide connections to applications and share remote printers. On the client side, terminals or PCs and a modem connected to the mainframe. To access the network, users "dialed up" using their own computers, modems, and telephone lines. The computers required **terminal emulation** software that allowed the PC to act as if it was a mainframe terminal. [Deng, 1]

At the corporate end, modem pools attached to a terminal server (see Figure 7.1) allowed multiple users to connect and have access to their applications. Data rates were limited by the speed of the modems from 300 bps (bits per second) to 2,400 bps. [Deng, 2]

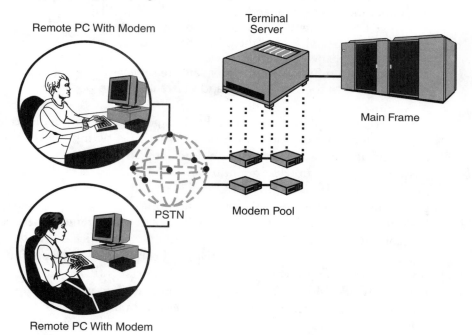

FIGURE 7.1 Remote Access Architecture in the 1970s [Source: Deng, 2]

In the 1980s, the growth of **client-server** LAN technology required more people to connect to corporate headquarters. This resulted in the need to supply many simultaneous connections to LAN applications. New technology emerged that integrated the modem, terminal server, and LAN access into one card called a **line/modem** card. Line/modem cards were placed in data communication equipment (DCE). Organizations moved to **digital circuits** between offices and began to use digital modems. As digital technology became more prevalent, the capability increased substantially to support data rates of 56 Kbps to 1.54 Mbps. [Deng, 2]

In the 1990s, the rise of the Internet created WANs with many powerful servers, all interconnected to control the flow of information. Once connected via dial-up lines, DSL (Digital Subscriber Lines), or cable modem, e-mail messages could be passed quickly around the Internet. Users could connect to an **ISP** (Internet Service Provider) to access servers at corporate headquarters.

Servers on the Internet were connected to routers to support PPP (Point to Point Protocol) and IP (Internet Protocol) access (see Figure 7.2). **Access concentrators** provided a central point for the connection of communication devices and routed IP traffic to local Ethernet ports. During this time, security became a concern and organizations started to use RADIUS servers. These servers provided a database for verifying the identity of a system entity, also known as **authentication**, and tracking resources for billing purposes, also known as **accounting**. As a result of these technological changes, data rates increased to 384 Kbps for home users and 45 Mbps for branch office connections. [Deng, 3-4]

In 2000 and beyond, voice, video, and data merged into a "one-for-all" network. Soon, information and media of all types will be completely integrated. ISPs and carrier service providers will be challenged to maintain more permanent connections to the Internet for more users. When users go online, they expect to be able to transmit pictures, sounds, or movies to their friends and colleagues without delay.

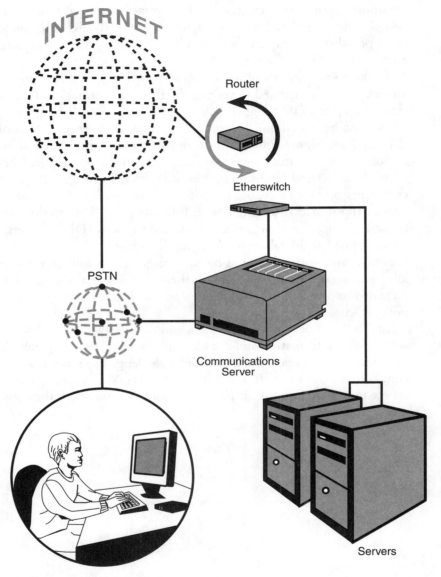

FIGURE 7.2 **Remote Access Architecture in the 1990s [Source: Deng, 3]**

Table 7.1 summarizes the history of remote access technologies.

1970	1980	1990	2000
Access to mainframe.	LAN-based client-server.	Internet explosion.	ISPs and telcos.
Used serial links.	Simultaneous connections were required to support multiple user access.	Carrier class switches.	Racks of access switches need to support 5,000 to 10,000 calls per rack.
Terminal server attached to hosts.	Integrated modem, terminal server, and LAN access into one card.	Dial up to ISP.	Support dial up and broadband DSL on the same platform.
Modem pools supported terminal server.	Began use of digital modems.	Servers connected to routers to support PPP and IP access.	Develop Quality of service (QoS) to manage the same throughput regardless of traffic load.
Clients used either terminals or PCs with modems.	Initiated use of line/modem and router cards.	Access concentrators routed IP traffic to local Ethernet ports.	Address packet and cell data with integrated native buses.
Used terminal emulation and telnet to access applications.	Organizations moved to digital circuits between offices.	Use of RADIUS servers for authentication and accounting.	Organizations are outsourcing remote access. Wholesaling of ISP access.
Data rates - 300 to 2,400 bps.	Data rates - 56 Kbps to 1.54 Mbps.	Data rates - 384 Kbps to 45 Mbps.	Data rates - 45 Mbps to gigabytes.

TABLE 7.1 **Evolution of Remote Access [Deng, 1-4]**

At ISP and telco facilities, many racks of programmable digital systems (called **access switches**) handle Internet traffic. In the future, as access to the World Wide Web grows, the performance of these access switches must increase by 5,000 to 10,000 calls per rack and be able to support both dial-up and broadband DSL on the same platform. [Deng, 4]

The industry needs to develop new products to address how local integrated buses handle both packet and cell data. The products must provide for the same throughput regardless of traffic load. If the products are to improve (QoS), they need to address performance for different types of traffic. [Deng, 4]

Evolution of Remote Access Technology

1. Why did organizations use terminal emulation software in the 1970s?
2. What types of modems were used in the 1980s?
3. What was used in the 1990s to authenticate remote access users?
4. What does "one for all" mean?
5. What created the need for a new generation of products and remote access methods?

REMOTE ACCESS METHODS

User demand for mobile access to information resources continues to increase. Users are faced with many alternatives, some of which are shown in Figure 7.3.

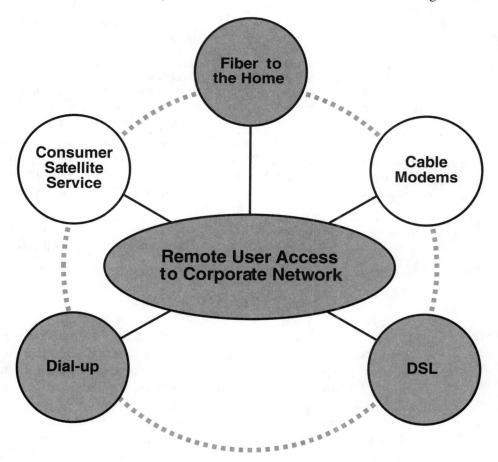

FIGURE 7.3 **Methods of Remote Access to the Corporate Network**

The following sections summarize these alternatives, some of which will be discussed in more detail later.

Dial Up

Remote users dial up over the POTS (plain old telephone service) to connect to corporate applications. A modem establishes the remote session. Many organizations provide phone numbers for users to dial in to that provide access to specific servers. Other companies allow access to corporate networks through an ISP or a subscription service such as AOL or MSN. For most connections, a method called **remote node** is used to connect the remote computer to the organization's headquarters as if it were a node on the LAN. If remote users need to perform data entry for a database application on the LAN, remote control (see the upcoming "Remote Control" section) can be used. This allows the remote user to "take over the keyboard" of a computer on the LAN.

Digital Subscriber Lines (DSL)

Digital Subscriber Lines (DSL) use an existing telephone line to provide "always-on" Internet access. DSL uses two-wire copper wiring to deliver high-speed data services to homes and businesses. DSL can deliver streaming audio/video, online games, application programs, **video conferencing**, and standard telephone calls. The distance between the customer and the service provider's CO (central office) determines the maximum DSL speed. A DSL link can deliver speeds from 144 Kbps to 6 Mbps.

Cable Modems

Cable modems operate over ordinary cable TV, providing high-speed (typically between 3 to 50 Mbps) access to the Internet. The cable modem is connected to the user's computer via a 10 Mbps Ethernet port. Using cable modems, cable companies can provide high-speed service to thousands of customers in a neighborhood. They can combine data channels with video, pay-per-view TV, audio, and local advertiser programming.

Consumer Satellite Services

In some areas of the country, the local CO has not yet upgraded its equipment to digital technology and cannot provide DSL services. In these cases, remote users tend to use satellite technology to access corporate applications. **Consumer satellite service** uses a single satellite dish antenna for receiving and sending information. It can bring the Internet and hundreds of channels of television all through a single dish antenna into the home. Consumer satellite service features "always on" Internet access, which means a high-speed link is available as long as the user's computer is on. Satellite download speed can reach up to 500 Kbps and current upload speeds range from 40-60 Kbps.

Fiber to the Home (FTTH)

Fiber-optic cable can now be strung all the way from the service provider's CO to the remote user's home. Usually, the local utility company deploys the fiber and many homes in a neighborhood are wired at the same time. A service provider can then supply telephone, video, and Internet services to the homes. The Internet link provides speeds of 4.5 Mbps upload and 7 Mbps download. This option, often called **Fiber to the Home (FTTH)**, is just beginning to penetrate the market. With FTTH, users will soon be able to have interactive television, distance learning, motion picture video conferencing, and video-phones for their homes.

TOPIC
review — **Remote Access Methods**

1. How is a remote session established with dial-up access?
2. Which remote access method uses two-wire copper for high-speed data services?
3. How is a cable modem connected to the user's computer?
4. Which is faster, the upload or download speed for a consumer satellite?
5. What type of services will be available to consumers who purchase FTTH?

DIAL-UP ACCESS

Approximately 70% of remote access is supported through dial-up access. Users such as traveling staff need remote access when they are away from work. In such a case, they will usually carry a laptop and access their e-mail from a restaurant, airport, or hotel room.

Dial-up remote access uses clients, servers, modems, and phone lines to connect remote users to the corporate LAN. Establishing connectivity for remote users is usually achieved by implementing one of the following methods: terminal emulation, remote node, or remote control.

Terminal Emulation

The most common method for remote dial-up access is *terminal emulation*. The terminal emulation software, which is installed on a microcomputer, allows the PC to act like an IBM or VAX terminal. The remote user can then connect across a WAN to the mainframe as though they were directly attached to it. Terminal emulation works well for host-based asynchronous applications. Most terminal emulation products support several protocols, such as TCP/IP, DEC LAT, TN 3270, and Xremote over wide area protocols such as PPP, SLIP, and X.25. Terminal emulation cannot support client-server environments because the terminal emulators are limited to the functions of a terminal device. [Wu, 2]

Remote Node

The new client-server environment provides a central database of information that needs to be shared among multiple locations. Each client must be able to access the database remotely to add and update information for its location. Two remote access methods are usually offered to the client: remote node and remote control.

Remote node connectivity can be provided using an access server over standard telephone lines and public-switched data networks. An access server is usually a hybrid of router and modem technology, which transmits packets of data between systems as if they were directly connected to the LAN. Because these servers are directly connected to the corporate network, remote node connections are treated as peers to other network devices (see Figure 7.4). [Wu, 3]

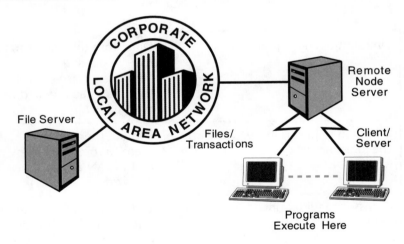

FIGURE 7.4 **Remote Node Access to the Corporate Network [Source: CommVision, 1]**

A remote node PC treats the modem as if it were a LAN. The processing occurs at the remote user's computer. Network data packets are transmitted between the LAN and the remote user. The remote user's PC or laptop must have sufficient processor, memory, and hard disk space to run the client application. [Network Computing, 1]

The remote node method attaches the remote PC, Macintosh, or UNIX workstation to the LAN over a dial-up connection. Once connected, the remote user has access to e-mail, documents, printers, and file servers.

The remote node connection uses PPP, which communicates using a serial port, modem, and switched dial-up link. Many remote users describe remote node as "just like being there" because it makes their remote computer function as if it were connected to their office. The major difference for the remote user is that the remote PC is 10 times slower than when directly connected to the network. In fact, most organizations suggest remote node computers are too slow to run applications. Rather, they recommend using them for data entry into a database, updating documents, and transferring files. [Network Computing, 1]

Remote node technology connects the remote computer to the LAN just as if it were direct-wired to the LAN. All of the traffic destined for a LAN-based computer goes to the remote computer. Table 7.2 lists the advantages and disadvantages of using remote node access.

ADVANTAGES OF REMOTE NODE	DISADVANTAGES OF REMOTE NODE
Only requires purchase of multiport serial board, modems, and a host PC.	Performance is slow because remote node uses the phone line to pass packets.
Limited training is required.	Data from the LAN is transported to the remote site via file transfer. Sensitive information is not protected to the degree it would be if it stayed on the LAN.
Users log in just as if they were on the local network.	Remote user can revise files and save them to the server. New files updated by the LAN administrator might be overwritten.
Access is required only during the file-transfer operation.	The number of software licenses and software upgrades required makes it more expensive because they are required for each individual remote user.
	Installation time is more extensive because each PC, laptop, or notebook must be sent in for the upgrade.

TABLE 7.2 **Advantages and Disadvantages of Remote Node [Source: CommVision, 1]**

Remote Control

First developed in the 1980s, **remote control** software enabled a remote user to take control of a dedicated PC residing on the corporate network. With remote control, the calling PC sends keystrokes and mouse cursor movements across the remote connection to a host PC on the LAN. The LAN provides access to the application running on the file server and sends back screen images of the application to the remote PC. The application's programs run on the host PC and the data files stay on the LAN (see Figure 7.5). [Wu, 3]

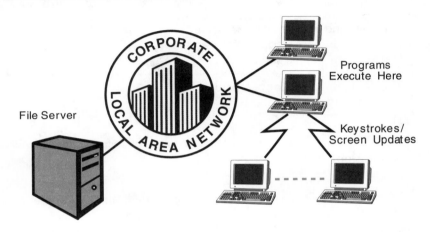

FIGURE 7.5 **Remote Control Access to the Corporate Network [Source: CommVision, 1]**

Remote control works by placing the corporate server in host mode, which means it is running and waiting to answer a call. On the remote side, the client is set up in remote mode, which allows it to remotely control the host server or PC. When the call is established, the remote PC connects. The user then sees the screen of the host PC and begins a remote control session. During the session, the remote PC sends keyboard strokes and mouse movements that cause the host PC to react. The remote PC receives screen changes back from the host PC. Remote control uses compression and caching techniques to enhance performance. Graphics that have been loaded once are stored in a temporary hard disk buffer called a cache. The images are called to the remote screen as needed, but they do not need to be transferred again across the WAN link. [Network Computing, 1]

Remote control software allows the user to remotely connect to a host computer and take control of the mouse and keyboard at that computer. The user can see on his monitor what is running on the host computer. Once connected, the user can run programs at the host computer or transfer files back and forth. Table 7.3 lists the advantages and disadvantages of using remote control access.

ADVANTAGES OF REMOTE CONTROL	DISADVANTAGES OF REMOTE CONTROL
Performance is fast because only video, keyboard, and mouse signals move across the remote connection.	The initial cost of dedicated processors required to provide access to application hosts.
Files never leave the LAN.	Connection to the LAN must be maintained throughout the remote session.
LAN administrator maintains control over the database files.	Users must learn how to use the new remote control software.
Software and license costs are lower because LAN-based applications are loaded from the file server.	
The LAN administrator can control revisions and upgrades.	

TABLE 7.3 **Advantages and Disadvantages of Remote Control Access [Source: CommVision, 1]**

Remote-node and remote control access methods are complementary technologies and many organizations use both methods to provide remote dial-up access to their LANs. Table 7.4 shows the difference among the methods in the traffic on the LAN and the communications line. Some applications are better suited for remote node and others are better for remote control.

ACCESS TYPE	EXECUTION LOCATION	APPLICATION SUITABILITY	TRAFFIC ON LAN	TRAFFIC ON COMM LINE
Terminal Emulation	Local	Customized for company	Programs	Keystrokes
Remote Control	Local	File-intensive applications	Program/files	Keystrokes/ screen updates
Remote Node	Remote client	Personal productivity	Files/ transactions	Files/ transactions
Gateway	N/A	Link to host and other LANs	Files/data	Files/data
Outbound	Remote host	Remote services	Keystrokes/ screen updates/data	Keystrokes/ screen updates/data

TABLE 7.4 **Remote Access Methods [Source: CommVision, 4]**

1. When is remote control recommended over remote node as a remote access method?
2. What is the most common method for remote dial-up access?
3. Which is more secure, remote node or remote control?
4. Which is faster, remote node or remote control?
5. When using remote node, what type of traffic is on the communication line?

DIGITAL SUBSCRIBER LINES (DSL)

Because so many users have purchased equipment to access the Internet, their need for more **bandwidth** has driven the development of even faster digital services. DSL brings an even faster digital network to the individual user's desktop.

DSL is a digital transport service that moves PC data traffic from one user to a data network at very high speeds. DSL technology delivers broadband services to homes and small businesses. DSL can support high-bandwidth applications such as Internet access, telecommuting, and streaming multimedia. DSL uses the existing phone line, yet gives "always on" Internet access. DSL takes existing voice lines and connects them to the local telco's CO. It then establishes a high-speed digital link. [Black Box Network Services, 1]

The DSL user has a dedicated, LAN-like connection from the home to the CO where it is multiplexed and sent to an ISP. DSL offers a choice of speeds from 144 Kbps to 1.5 Mbps. Compared to a 56 Kbps modem, DSL is up to 25 times faster. With DSL access, there are no more busy signals or dropped connections. [Verizon, 1] Applications that can be used with DSL include computer-aided design (CAD) software such as CAD/CAM, file transfer, distance learning, video, e-mail, and conferencing. DSL is designed to service telecommuters who work from home or branch offices that need to be interconnected. DSL offers two types of service, Internet and Remote LAN, as shown in Table 7.5. Both use the same DSL equipment, but their patterns of usage differ. The Remote LAN is primarily used for connecting a small number of users from a remote branch office. The Internet service is used solely to connect an individual or small business to the Internet. [Verizon, 1]

TYPE OF SERVICE	WHERE CONNECTED	USE
Internet	DSL equipment installation Internet service	Used by the hobbyist, those who work from home offices, or for small businesses.
Remote LAN	DSL equipment installation at host connection	Used by people who work from home or remote branch offices.

TABLE 7.5 **Type of Service for DSL Connection**

DSL Interfaces

At the host connection or local telco CO, the DSL multiplexer provides the modulation scheme, concentration, and cell conversion. DSL services the local loop, often called the "last mile," and is provided by the Local Exchange Carrier (LEC). The distance between the user's home or office and the local CO determines the maximum DSL speed. The DSL interface equipment for the home appears in Figure 7.6. [Verizon, 1]

At the user connection, users can use either an internal or external ADSL (Asymmetric DSL) modem. ADSL is asymmetric, which means it allows more bandwidth **downstream** than **upstream**. The external modems can be connected to the user's computer via USB, 10 Base T Ethernet, or DSL router. An ADSL circuit connects an ADSL modem from the home user to another ADSL modem at the CO. The speed of transmission upstream is 1.54 Mbps. However, the downstream transmission is much faster, between 1.5 to 8 Mbps. Figure 7.7 shows that DSL has a distance limitation of 12,000-18,000 feet from the CO. [Sheldon, 406]

At the DSL customer site, a DSL router or modem connects to an individual computer or even a small LAN. Once installed, it provides a continuous connection to the Internet and the user is able to use her telephone at the same time. The basic telephone service is split off from the digital modem by filters called **splitters**, which guarantee uninterrupted basic phone service.

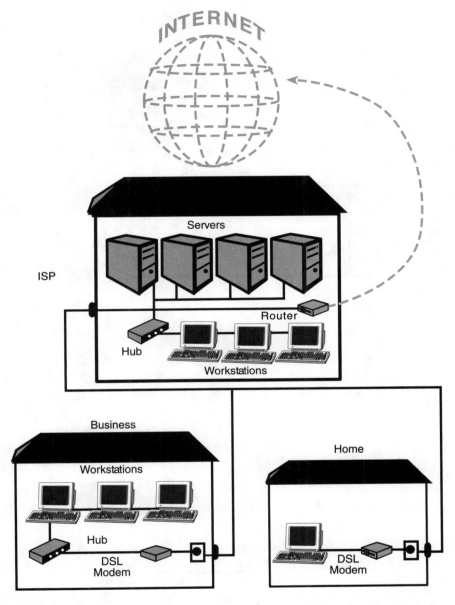

FIGURE 7.6 **DSL Interface Equipment for the Home [Source: Verizon, 1]**

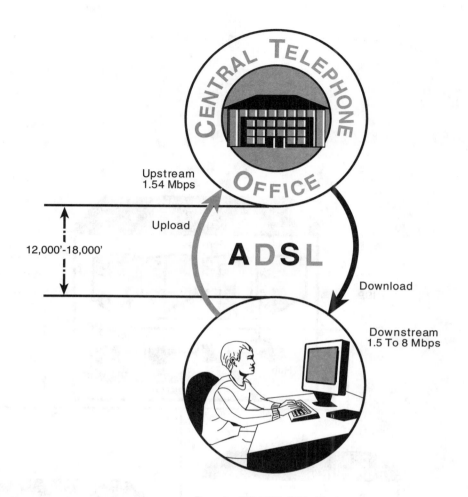

Upstream
1.54 Mbps

Upload

12,000'-18,000'

ADSL

Download

Downstream
1.5 To 8 Mbps

Remote PC With DSL Modem

FIGURE 7.7 **Operation of Asymmetric Digital Service Line (ADSL)**

DSL technology allows service providers to offer bundled services, which include voice, Internet, and LAN services over existing phone lines. Many home or other subscribers can be supported via ADSL. ADSL modems divide the bandwidth of a telephone line by using either **Frequency Division Multiplexing (FDM)** or **echo cancellation**. FDM assigns one band to upload data and another band to download data. Next, **Time Division Multiplexing (TDM)** divides the downstream path into one or more high- or low-speed channels. The frequencies below 4 KHz are used for voice, and those above 4 KHz are reserved for data. [Cisco, 15-4]

If echo cancellation is used, the **upstream band** is assigned to overlap the downstream and then separate the two using a technique called *local echo can-*

cellation. **Local echo cancellation** has been used for years in V.32 and V.34 modems. Telcos use active devices that suppress singing echo, or feedback, on the phone network. The signal goes into an **endless loop** bouncing back and forth between the transmitter and the receiver. Modems deactivate these devices by sending the 2,100 Hz answer tone with 180 phase reversals every 450 ms at the beginning of the connection. [Internetworking Technology, 15-4]

The longer the distance of the transmission, the more **echoes** can distort the signal. By controlling the length of the copper line, its wire gauge, and the distance to the customer's location, along with the aid of **bridge taps**—which join into an existing unused local loop left behind by a former customer—the phone company prevents **distortions** or echoes. [Internetworking Technology, 15-2]

The phone company uses other techniques and devices to manage DSL transmissions and provide reliable service. **ADSL** uses advanced digital signal processing. This new technique has required changes to transformers, analog filters, and analog/digital (A/D) converters. Advanced digital signal processing provides transmission rates of 1.5 Mbps to 9 Mbps downstream and from 16 Kbps to 800 Kbps upstream.

Table 7.6 provides a comparison of download speeds between regular dial-up access at 56 Kbps, ISDN at 128 Kbps, and DSL at 384 Kbps. Downloading via DSL modems is much faster than downloading via analog modems at 56 Kbps or using digital ISDN services at 128 Kbps. DSL voice calls are connected to the telco PBX (private branch exchange) and the consumer's ISP provides the Internet service.

ACTIVITY	FILE SIZE	MODEM – 56 KBPS	ISDN – 128 KBPS	DSL – 384 KBPS
Browsing the Net (25 Web pages)	2.5 MB	6 minutes	2 1/2 minutes	52 seconds
Video clip (20 seconds)	8 MB	18 minutes	8 1/2 minutes	2 minutes
Software download	25 MB	60 minutes	26 minutes	8 minutes

TABLE 7.6 **Comparisons of Download Speeds [Verizon, 1]**

ADSL service providers vary depending on the location. At some Local-Access and Transport Areas (LATAs), DSL service is not yet available. The DSL build out required by service providers is often accomplished incrementally with small levels of investment. Nevertheless, nearly every major telecommunications provider in the United States, Europe, Canada, and Asia Pacific has implemented DSL in large metropolitan areas. [Alcatel, 1]

Types of DSL

There are currently eight types of DSL, as shown in Table 7.7. When referring to xDSL, the "x" is replaced by the name of the type.

TYPE OF XDSL	SPEED	DISTANCE
ADSL	1.5 - 8 Mbps downstream; 1.54 Mbps upstream	12,000 - 18,000 feet
SDSL	1.54 Mbps either way	15,000 feet
SHDSL	192 Kbps - 2.3 Mbps either way	8,000 - 15,000 feet
HDSL	1.54 Mbps either way	10,000 feet
HDSL-2	1.54 Mbps either way	12,000 feet
IDSL	144 Kbps either way	15,000 - 36,000 feet
VDSL	51 - 55 Mbps. either way	1,000 feet
G. Lite	1.5 Mbps downstream; 384 Kbps upstream	18,000 feet

TABLE 7.7 Types of DSL [Source: Alcatel, 1][Webopedia, 1]

Symmetrical High-Speed DSL (SHDSL) is a symmetrical high-speed version of DSL that allows for a maximum data rate of 2.3 Mbps in both directions—upstream and downstream (see Figure 7.8). **Symmetrical** means it provides equal bandwidth for data going upstream or downstream. SHDSL can provide private line, digital voice transmission, IP, or Frame Relay services. It was specifically designed for small- and medium-size businesses. [Alcatel, 1]

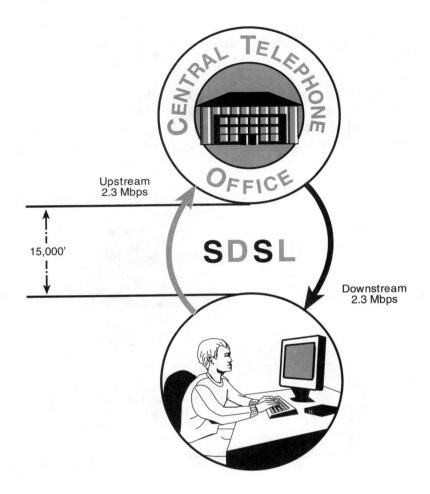

Upstream
2.3 Mbps

15,000'

SDSL

Downstream
2.3 Mbps

Remote PC With DSL Modem

FIGURE 7.8 **Symmetrical High-Speed DSL**

SHDSL was designed to improve upon HDSL and SDSL. As defined, SHDSL delivers high-speed symmetric DSL over a single copper pair. The data rate is equal both upstream and downstream. SHDSL addresses rate/range adaptability, multiple voice-line delivery, and **impairment tolerance**, which refers to the amount of errors, distortions, or echoes that are allowed. It accommodates data rate speeds of 2.3 Mbps upstream and downstream. SHDSL offers the benefits of T1/E1 with higher speed for less cost. [Alcatel, 1]

ISDN Digital Subscriber Line (**IDSL**) is a combined technology that allows the use of existing ISDN (Integrated Services Digital Network) card technology for data only. It is designed for homes and businesses located too far from the local CO. IDSL transmits faster than standard ISDN. Speeds can reach 144 Kbps on existing telephone lines. The telco uses a special router that bypasses the CO's voice network. IDSL differs from ISDN in that it is a dedicated service and does not require call setup or per-call fees. [Alcatel, 1]

High Bit Rate Subscriber Line–2 (HDSL-2) is a new version of DSL technology that supports voice, data, and video using ATM, T1, and Frame Relay services (see Figure 7.9). HDSL-2 is symmetrical, so it sends and receives at data rates of up to 1.5 Mbps. Data is sent over a single pair of copper wires. Its distance limitation between the CO and the user is 12,000 feet. [Alcatel, 1]

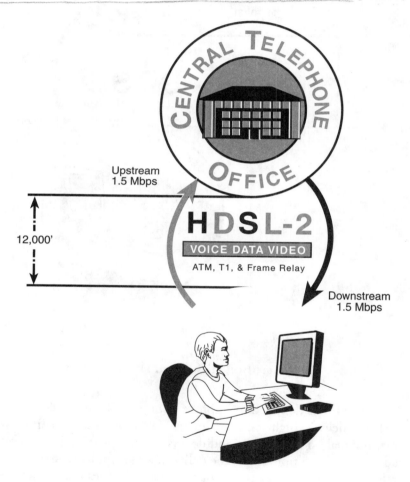

FIGURE 7.9 HDSL-2 Supports Voice, Data, and Video

Very High Bit-Rate Digital Subscriber Line (VDSL) (see Figure 7.10) technology transmits high-speed data over existing telephone lines to provide for interactive TV, video on demand, and high definition TV. VDSL offers downstream transfer speeds from 51 Mbps to 55 Mbps. Its upstream channel supports transfer speeds of 1.6 Mbps to 2.3 Mbps. [Alcatel, 1]

VDSL is designed to carry high bandwidth signals over a short distance. It has a range of 1,000 to 6,000 feet from the CO. Of course, the shorter the distance, the faster the connection rate will be. VDSL connects to neighborhood optical network units (ONUs). The **ONU** is directly connected to the local CO main fiber network backbone. The silicon microchips for VDSL adapters are very expensive. In fact, there currently is not a specification for mass-producing VDSL silicon. [Alcatel, 1]

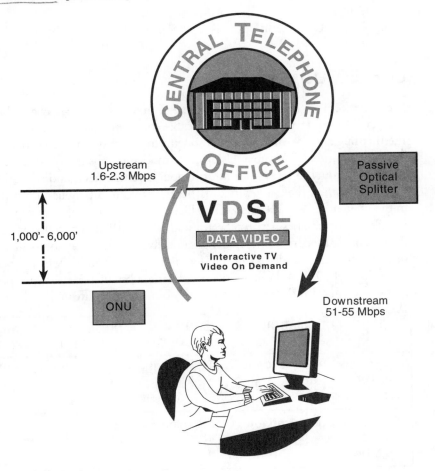

FIGURE 7.10 **Very High Bit-Rate Digital Subscriber Line (VDSL)**

The latest DSL technology to emerge is **G.Lite,** which is also known as DSL Lite or Universal ADSL. It offers lower speeds than ADSL, but does not require the POTS splitter for voice at the user's location. Data transmit speed is limited to 1.5 Mbps downstream and 384 Kbps upstream. G.Lite offers a lower cost for installation. [Alcatel, 1]

TOPIC review **DSL**

1. Why is DSL service described as "always on"?
2. How many twisted pair wires are used to provide the DSL connection?
3. Is DSL faster on the upstream than dial up?
4. Can a user still talk on the phone while his computer is connected to a DSL line?
5. Which DSL technology uses silicon microchips?

CABLE MODEMS

Everyone seems to be subscribing to cable TV today to increase channel selections and get access to favorite shows. Most cable companies have been bitten by the Internet bug and are offering cable modems to consumers to access data over the Internet using their TV cable. Using cable modems, consumers can access the Internet instantly to browse for information, entertainment, and education.

The growth of the market in 2001 has increased to 5.5 million cable modems sold in the United States and Canada. The U.S. National Cable Network spans hundreds of miles to major cities between Seattle and Miami. [Plunkett, 32] Compared with a typical analog modem, cable modems can deliver information approximately 500 times faster. Cable modems can transfer information at 30-40 Mbps in one 6 MHz cable channel. DSL and cable modems provide substantial increases in speed over current dial-up and ISDN services. Table 7.8 compares the different kinds of modems.

ACTIVITY	DIAL UP (56 KBPS)	ISDN (128 KBPS)	XDSL (1.5 MBPS)	CABLE (4 MBPS) MODEM
Image file transfer Size: 2 Mbps	60 seconds	17 seconds	1.3 seconds	0.05 second
Complex image transfer Size: 16 Mbps	4.1 minutes	2.4 minutes	10.7 seconds	4 seconds
Short video	23 minutes	10 minutes	48 seconds	18 seconds

TABLE 7.8 **Time Comparisons for Image and Video Transfer [Source: Spradley, 2]**

A consumer can continue to receive cable programs while simultaneously receiving data on the cable modem. A consumer can simply connect the cable modem to the TV outlet for cable. The cable operator then connects to a *Cable Modem Termination System (CMTS)* at their *Head-End center*. A **CMTS** is a data-switching system specifically designed to route data from many cable modem users simultaneously. In fact, one CMTS can support approximately 2,000 cable modem users simultaneously on a single TV channel. [Cadant, 5] The **Head-End center** is the head office of a cable network in which multiple CMTSs and connections are provided to the Internet (see Figure 7.11).

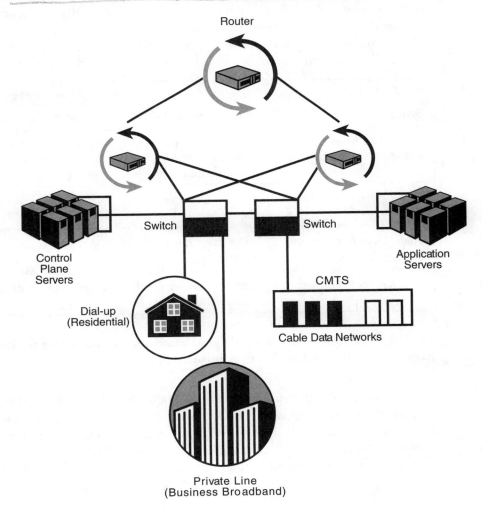

FIGURE 7.11 **Basic Distribution Hub [Source: Cadant, 5]**

Most cable companies use **Hybrid Fiber-Coax (HFC)** networks. The signals are transmitted over fiber-optic cables from the Head-End center to locations near the consumer. As the signal gets closer to the consumer's location, it is converted to coaxial cable. [Cadant, 5] Upstream demodulators filter data from consumers for further processing by a CMTS.

A CMTS provides an extended Ethernet network over a WAN with a geographic reach of up to 100 miles. Regional centers connect a few cable Head-End centers via fiber links. A typical Head-End center is equipped with satellite receivers and upstream radio frequency (RF) receivers for pay-per-view and other data services. A regional center is connected to other regional centers by a national backbone network. [Cadant, 2]

Cable modems are compared to ISDN and XDSL in Table 7.9 to show the distinct differences in bandwidth, speed, power, wiring, and voice features.

ISDN	XDSL	CABLE MODEMS
Switched bandwidth	Dedicated bandwidth	Shared bandwidth
Up to 128 Kbps upstream and downstream	Up to 1.5 Mbps downstream; 384 Kbps upstream	Up to 1.5 Mbps downstream; 384 Kbps upstream
ISDN voice features	POTS with custom calling features	No telephone; retains TV
Voice service requires electrical power	Voice does not require electrical power	TV reliant on electrical
Copper - conditioned	Copper - non-loaded; under 18,000 feet	Coax - conditioned

TABLE 7.9 Differences in Bandwidth, Speed, Power, and Wiring for ISDN, XDSL, and Cable Modems [Source: Spradley, 3]z

The consumer's cable modem can only talk to the cable network. If two cable modem consumers want to talk to each other, they must connect to the CMTS at the cable network, which then relays the messages. Through multiple network connections, a cable data network is capable of connecting users between neighborhoods and to the Internet (see Figure 7.12). [Cadant, 3]

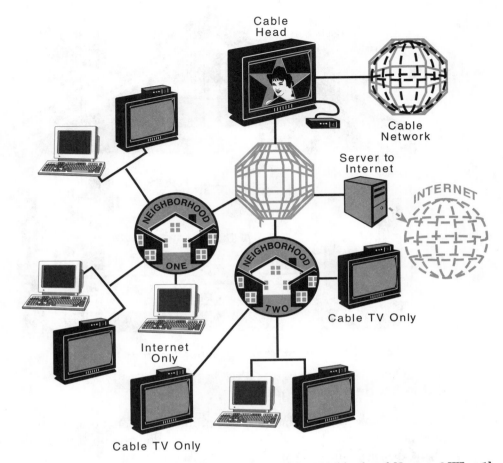

FIGURE 7.12 **Cable Modem Connection to the Neighborhood [Source: 2 Wire, 1]**

Installing a Cable Modem

A power splitter and a new cable are usually necessary when installing a cable modem. The splitter divides the signal between the new segment that connects to the cable modem and the other for the TV (see Figure 7.13). The cable modem attaches to the PC through an interface cable, which can be either USB or Ethernet. [Ostergaard, 1]

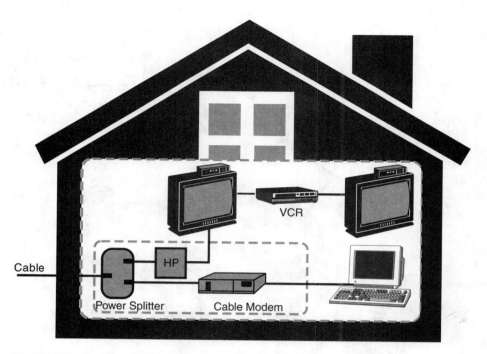

FIGURE 7.13 **Cable Modem Installation [Source: Ostergaard, 1]**

Cable Modem Components

Inside the cable modem, there are four primary components and an interface to Ethernet. The four components are: tuner, demodulator, burst modulator, and Media Access Control (MAC) device (see Figure 7.14).

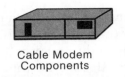

Cable Modem
Components

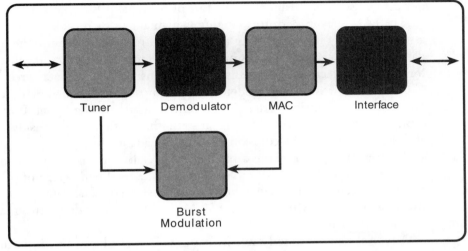

FIGURE 7.14 **Primary Components Inside a Cable Modem [Source: Ostergaard, 1]**

The **tuner** connects directly to the cable outlet. The tuner receives digitally modulated **Quadrature Amplitude Modulation (QAM)** signals. A **diplexer** is used to provide for both upstream and downstream signals to be transmitted through the same tuner. [Ostergaard, 1]

The **demodulator** is the receiver of the RF signal. The demodulator has an analog to digital converter (AD), a QAM-64/256 receiver demodulator, **MPEG** frame synchronization, and error correction. The demodulator component is also required in the digital set-top box used to connect to the TV. [Ostergaard, 1]

The **burst modulator** is unique to the cable modem. When it transmits, it feeds the tuner. The integrity of the data is assured by the burst modulator, which uses **Reed Solomon** encoding of each burst. It modulates using the QPSK/QAM-16 transmitters on the selected lower frequency. Finally, the burst modulator performs a digital to analog conversion. Unknown cable loss is controlled by the output signal, which is fed through a driver that allows the signal to be adjusted to a variable output level. [Ostergaard, 1]

The signal transmitted by the cable modem is called the upstream. Upstream is always in bursts. Each cable modem sends bursts in time slots using TDM. Data is sent in MPEG frames. A **media access control (MAC)** device is used to extract data from the MPEG frames. [Ostergaard, 1]

Many cable modems can transmit on the same frequency. MAC is used to filter data from other cable modems. It is responsible for the protocol and it times the transmission of the upstream bursts. The frequency for the upstream burst is between 5-65 MHz and the bandwidth is approximately 2 MHz. MAC devices can send upstream at a data rate of 3 Mbps. [Ostergaard, 1]

The MAC device performs ranging, which allows each cable modem to assess time delay in transmitting to the Head-End center. Because the upstream data channel is shared for transmission to the Head-End center, it must provide for collision detection and retransmission to ensure that the data is received. Consequently, if two cable modems transmit upstream at the same time, but one sends a weaker signal, the CMTS only hears the strong signal. If the two cable modems send at the same signal strength, the signal becomes distorted and the CMTS knows a collision occurred. [Cadant, 9]

The signal received by the cable modem is called downstream. The downstream data is received by all cable modems. The total bandwidth of 6 MHz is shared between all active cable modems on the system. The data is sent downstream at a frequency between 65-850 MHz. Data is sent downstream at a data rate of 27-56 Mbps. [Cadant, 8]

A typical neighborhood cable network looks like a big LAN. After the user is connected via the PC, the user can click on Network Neighborhood and see the desktops of all the connected neighbors in the user's virtual neighborhood. [2 Wire, 1]

There is also some concern about the performance, security, and reliability of cable modems. Privacy of user data is achieved by encrypting the data between cable modems and the CMTS. The data encryption standard used is **DES** (see Chapter 8 *WAN Security*), which is typically used for most corporate data. The encryption is integrated directly within the MAC hardware and software interface. [Cadant, 10]

TOPIC *review* **Cable Modems**

1. Can a consumer download data to a PC and receive cable programs at the same time?
2. What is the basic purpose of a cable modem?
3. If two cable modem users want to talk to each other, how do they make the connection?
4. What is the power splitter used for?
5. When using a cable modem, can users see desktops of their connected neighbors in their neighborhood?

CONSUMER SATELLITE SERVICES

Various satellite solutions have emerged to address the need for greater speed and higher capacity access to the Internet for consumers. Satellite is a good solution when no cable right of way exists or where DSL or cable modem service is unavailable.

Satellites can interconnect widely dispersed servers to the Internet infrastructure located thousands of miles away. Several service providers have installed dedicated point-to-point **single channel per carrier (SCPC)** links to connect local POP (point of presence) servers to Internet gateways. These satellite links establish data conduits between the ISP and the Internet gateway site (see Figure 7.15). [Puetz, 5]

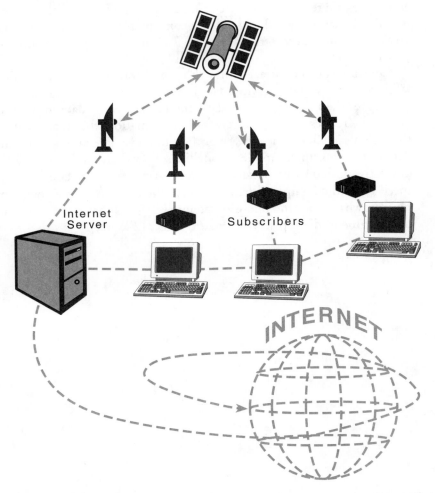

FIGURE 7.15 **SCPC Network for Consumer Satellite Services [Source: Puetz, 2]**

Consumers are connected via their connection to the LAN or by dial-up phone lines through the PSTN (Public Switched Telephone Network). The connection is provided by a port server, which connects to the WAN. Users establish a PPP, SLIP, or TCP/IP connection to the Internet gateway. [Puetz, 2]

Consumer satellite service is wireless and ideal for areas where cable and DSL services are not available. Consumers can request files, home pages, or video clips through the **Satellite Network Service (SNS)**. The link from the gateway to consumer is used to transport the requested data. [Plunkett, 21]

Signals are delivered to and from the ISP through the satellite service. Designated satellites in the Earth's orbit send the signals to the consumer's satellite dish. Satellite service is always on. Users can access the Internet and use the telephone at the same time. Because it works like satellite television service, no extra wires are required for the connection. In the United States, satellite service is available nationwide. However, for consumers to receive consumer satellite service at their location, they must have a "clear view" of the southern sky. [StarBand, 1]

Consumers can contract to use either one-way or two-way satellite service. With one-way satellite service, data is sent to the ISP through a dial-up connection. After the ISP receives the data, the ISP sends the data to the Internet. When the requested server receives the information, that server sends the data through a satellite to the consumer dish antenna. The antenna transmits the data to the consumer's modem. Satellite services can send data at 500 Kbps downstream. However, because one-way service travels over an analog line, the speed to send data upstream is limited to the capacity of the analog modem. One drawback to using one-way satellite service is that the user is also required to subscribe to dial-up service (Figure 7.16). [2 Wire, 1]

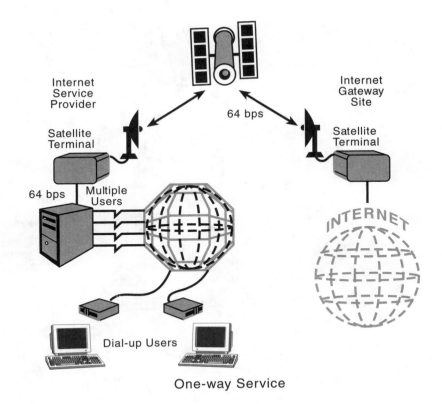

FIGURE 7.16 **One-Way Satellite Service [Source: 2 Wire, 1]**

Two-way satellite service allows consumers to send and receive data through their satellite modems. No additional dial-up connection is required. The two-way satellite can carry data upstream at 150 Kbps because the data is sent directly to the satellite (Figure 7.17).

Like cable modem service, satellite service requires users to share bandwidth with their neighbors. This means the number of neighbors using the service at the same time affects service. Access speeds vary based on the type of usage of other satellite users in the area.

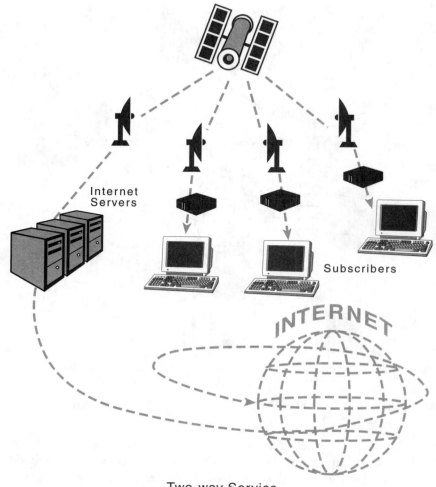

Internet
Servers

Subscribers

INTERNET

Two-way Service

FIGURE 7.17 **Two-Way Satellite Service [Source: 2 Wire, 1]**

TOPIC
review **Consumer Satellite Services**

1. When is consumer satellite a good solution for establishing a connection to the Internet?
2. Is consumer satellite an "always on" service?
3. If using consumer satellite service, can users use the telephone at the same time they connect to the Internet through their computers?
4. Which satellite service requires an analog line?
5. Is a dial-up connection required with two-way satellite service?

FIBER TO THE HOME (FTTH)

Service providers are starting to deliver broadband access over fiber lines directly connected to consumer homes. Fiber to the Home (FTTH) enables service providers to offer basic telephone service, broadcast cable, and **direct broadcast satellite (DBS)** television all over a single optical fiber to the home. [Marconi, 1]

At the service provider's CO, optical switching equipment provided by Marconi is used to transmit and amplify signals to distribute them to consumers. Figure 7.18 (page 364) shows the FTTH equipment required at the CO. The right side of the figure shows a connection between the Video Distribution unit and a Marconi Splitter WDM Frame (SWFX). The SWFX is used to multiplex the 1310 nanometer (NM) telephony traffic with the 1550 (NM) RF signals for distribution over the **Passive Optical Network (PON)**. The SWFX is connected to a Marconi DISC*SMX unit. The DISC*SMX unit uses a 1310 (NM) optical network to transport telephony traffic to the ONU at the home. Also, at the Head-End center or CO, the broadband RF (video and data) is placed onto the video transport layer. The RF is transmitted over 1550 (NM) optical transmitters and fiber amplifiers. RF signals are distributed by splitter optical cross-connects (SWXs) that deliver the RF signal in optical format to each ONU. Telephone signals are rendered as digital service (DS-0) telephony signals to 24 twisted-pair punch-down locations within the ONU. RF signals are transported to and from customer location via coaxial cable. [Marconi, 1]

From the service provider's location, a single strand of fiber-optic cable is run to a Passive Optical Splitter (POS). In Figure 7.19 (page 365), the POS accommodates both the telephony 1310 (NM) traffic and the RF 1550 (NM) video and data traffic. The POS is a small device, which divides the optical signal into four identical optical signals. The POS is located near the consumer's location. Each of the four signals runs into the residence. The POS is located about 30,000 feet from the CO. The split ratio ranges from 2 to 32 users. This splitting is done without using any active components in the network. The signal is delivered over the last 3,000 feet over a single optical fiber. [City of Palo Alto, 1]

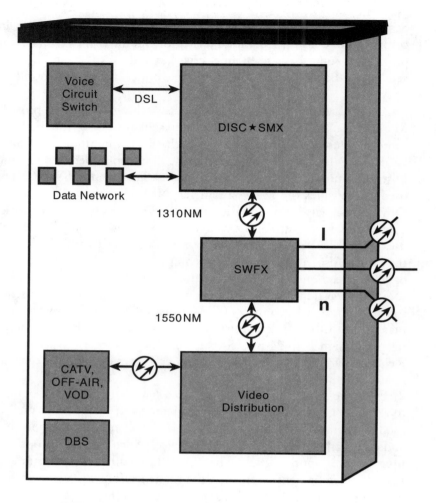

FIGURE 7.18 **View of FTTH Equipment at the CO**

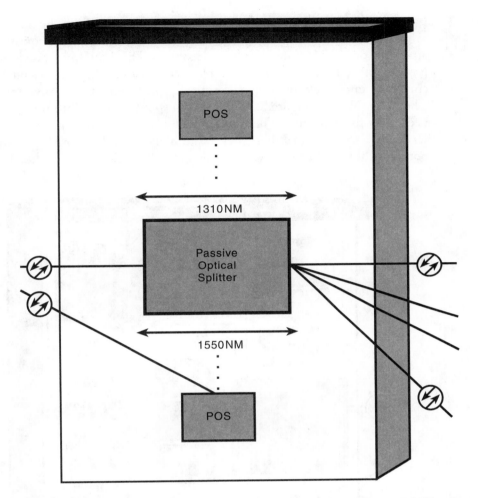

FIGURE 7.19 Use of Passive Optical Splitter for Connection to CO [Source: City of Palo Alto, 1]

Currently, two methods are being tested for FTTH. One method uses ATM over a PON. Network services are transported in ATM cells. The key feature of this method is the capability to offer QoS guarantees for voice, video, and data traffic. The other alternative is based on Wavelength Division Multiplexing (WDM). All of the signals are consolidated onto a single fiber using WDM techniques and transmitted to the consumer via a POS. [City of Palo Alto, 1]

On the service provider side, the equipment at the Head-End center or CO is interfaced to the PSTN using digital service and is connected to ATM or Ethernet interfaces. Video services are captured from the cable Head-End center or from a satellite feed. [Marconi, 1]

At the consumer's home, the fiber-optic cable coming into the home is terminated into a **Home Networking Unit (HNU)** box where the consumer can attach his or her TV, computer, and telephone. This HNU box provides WDM for the optical transmission and electrical conversion. The optical signal is converted into an electrical signal using an **optical electrical converter (OEC)**. The three OECs in Figure 7.20 are used to split the signal into the services needed by the consumer. The OEC provides standard RJ-11 jacks for telephone service, RJ-45 jacks for Ethernet access to high-speed data, and 75-ohm coax ports for cable and DBS service (see Figure 7.20). [City of Palo Alto, 1]

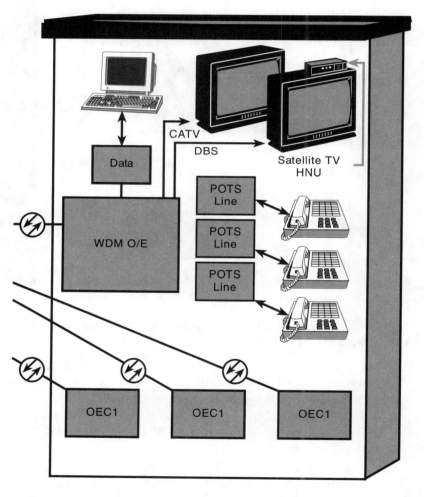

FIGURE 7.20 Residential Connection for Telephone, DSL, cable, or DBS [Source: City of Palo Alto, 1]

Three RJ-11 phone jacks are mounted on the OEC for POTS. Each RJ-11 interface is provisioned individually and each line has a unique phone number. The OEC is also equipped with two "F" connectors for delivery of cable and DBS video. POTS is delivered to the PSTN as TDM, data as Ethernet, and video as broadcast RF. [City of Palo Alto, 1]

FTTH is a passive network, so there are no active components from the CO to the consumer. FTTH does not need DC power; it supports local battery backup and low-power consumption. Service providers claim that FTTH is reliable, scalable, and secure. [City of Palo Alto, 1]

Other service providers are beginning to install FTTH in various parts of the country. Bell South has provided fiber for up to 400 homes in Dunwoody, Georgia as a permanent installation. In Dunwoody, Bell South is laying fiber parallel to existing copper wires at homes. A Canadian phone company called Future Way Communications is stringing fiber to homes in Toronto. By the year 2005, 100 Mbps connections are expected to be available for FTTH. [Hecht, 1]

TOPIC *review* **Fiber to the Home**

1. How does FTTH work?
2. Does FTTH require DC power?
3. How many signals are run into the home?
4. What is the purpose of the optical electrical converter (OEC)?
5. Does FTTH support RJ-11 jacks for telephone service?

CHAPTER SUMMARY

Remote access has changed drastically since the 1970s when dial-up access was used to access the mainframe. The line/modem cards used in the 1980s were replaced by DSL, cable modems, and consumer satellite in the 1990s. Traveling users still use dial-up service, because it is the only service available to them. Organizations often require traveling users to check their e-mail while on the road. They can use either remote node or remote control to reach their organization's servers and the Internet.

The Internet has brought about a major change in the way a client accesses the corporate network from remote locations. Clients have demanded more bandwidth to take advantage of all of the multimedia content available to them. They expect to be able to download images, movie clips, and sound files and send them to their friends and associates. This demand has prompted service providers to develop new services for home use.

The nature of the home and office has changed to suit the consumer demand for special services. Consumers purchase new Internet devices to achieve complete integration of information and media of all types. There has been a significant increase in the use of broadband services for entertainment, data, voice, and video over fiber-optic, consumer satellite, and cable modems.

DSL uses the consumer's existing phone line to provide support for high-bandwidth applications and provides for "always on" Internet access. Several types of DSL (ADSL, SDSL, SHDSL, HDSL, HDSL-2, IDSL, VDSL, and G.Lite) are available, and they vary in speed and distance from the CO. Asymmetric DSL (ADSL) allows more bandwidth downstream than upstream. Symmetric DSL (SDSL) allows the same speed of transmission for upstream and downstream.

Cable companies have built hybrid Fiber to Coax networks to provide cable modem services for consumers. Signals are transmitted over fiber until they reach the consumer's neighborhood where they are then sent across coaxial cable. A data switching system (CMTS) receives and routes cable-modem traffic. Cable modem users must connect to the CMTS to communicate with each other. A national backbone network connects all the regional CMTS centers together to offer additional pay-for-view and other data services.

When cable modem or DSL services are not available, consumer satellite offers a good solution to address the need for higher-bandwidth capacity and speed. Consumers use consumer satellite services to request files, home pages, or video clips through the SNS. The satellite service provides a link to and from the ISP through the satellite network. Satellite services offer one-way or two-way transmission services. Two-way satellite service allows consumers to send and receive data through their satellite modem. Satellite requires consumers to share bandwidth with their neighbors.

Recently, service providers have begun to install fiber lines directly to consumer's homes. A new service, FTTH, enables service providers to offer basic telephone service, broadcast cable, and direct broadcast satellite television all over a single optical fiber to the home. FTTH uses optical technology for transmission and uses an OEC to provide services into the box at the consumer's home. Service providers have begun to install FTTH in certain areas of the country to determine its usage and viability for the future.

CHAPTER REVIEW QUESTIONS

(This quiz can also be printed out from the Encore! CD that accompanies this textbook. File name—Chap07review.)
Circle the correct answer (a-d) for each question. Choose only one answer for each.

1. As part of the Telecommunications Act of 1996, all carriers are granted points of presence (POP) to offer:
   a. cable modem services.
   b. dial-up access services.
   c. long-distance services.
   d. equipment services.

2. When did the use of digital modems and dedicated digital circuits begin?
   a. 1970s
   b. 1980s
   c. 1990s
   d. 2000s

3. Remote users dial up over POTS to connect to corporate applications. What does POTS mean?
   a. Plain Old Telephone Service
   b. Public Old Telephone Service
   c. Private Old Telephone Service
   d. Primary Old Telephone Service

4. Which remote access method uses two-wire twisted copper wiring to deliver high-speed data services to homes and businesses?
   a. Dial up
   b. Cable modem
   c. DSL
   d. Fiber to the Home

5. What is the PC software that allows the PC to act as if it were a main-frame terminal?
   a. Modem emulation
   b. Link emulation
   c. Terminal emulation
   d. Protocol emulation

6. Because they are directly connected to the corporate network, remote node connections are treated as:
   a. primary connections to other network devices.
   b. superior to other network devices.
   c. temporary connections to other network devices.
   d. peers to other network devices.

7. When the call is established, the remote PC connects and the user sees the screen of the _____ PC or server and begins a remote control session.
   a. peer
   b. host
   c. remote
   d. graphic

8. One-way consumer satellite transmission requires:
   a. a broadband line.
   b. a digital line.
   c. an analog line.
   d. a leased line.

9. The local loop provided between the user's site and the LEC is often referred to as:
   a. the "loop mile."
   b. the "local mile."
   c. the "last mile."
   d. the "LEC mile."

10. What is the data-switching system specifically designed to route data from many cable modem users simultaneously?
    a. HFC
    b. CMTS
    c. RFTS
    d. QAM-64/256 receiver

Circle the correct letter (A-E) for each description. Choose only one answer for each.
   A. SCPC
   B. Splitters
   C. SNS
   D. Local echo cancellation
   E. HFC

11. A B C D E   The basic telephone service for DSL is split off from the digital modem by filters called _____.

12. A B C D E   Has been used for years in V.32 and V.34 modems.

13. A B C D E   Most cable companies use this kind of network.

14. A B C D E   Several service providers have installed these dedicated point-to-point single channel links to connect local POP servers to Internet gateways.

15. A B C D E   Consumers can request files, home pages, or video clips through this satellite-based service.

A. POS
B. DES
C. FTTH
D. OEC
E. Head-End center

16. A B C D E   Service providers can offer basic telephone service, broadcast cable, and direct broadcast satellite television all over a single optical fiber to the home.

17. A B C D E   At the consumer's home, the optical signal is converted into an electrical signal using this device.

18. A B C D E   A small device that divides the optical signal into four identical optical signals.

19. A B C D E   A data encryption standard.

20. A B C D E   The signals are transmitted over fiber-optic cables from this point to locations near the consumer.

INTERNET EXERCISES

1. Log on to the Internet and key the following URL:

   www.cable-modem.net/tt/primer.html

   Read the Cable Modem Primer, find the information requested, and answer the following questions:

   A. What is the Data Over Cable Service Interface Specification?
   B. Why was it developed?
   C. What acronym does it use?

2. Key the following URL:

   www.cpau.com/fth/index.html

   Answer the following questions:

   A. Will any FTTH installations be in public buildings?
   B. How many phone connections can the Marconi network provide?
   C. What are the upload and download speeds of the Internet link?
   D. What are the goals of the FTTH Trial Project?

CONCEPT EXERCISES

Concept Narrative

(This narrative exercise can also be printed out from the Encore! CD that accompanies this textbook. File name—Chap07connar.)

Fill in the blanks of the following description with the correct answers.

Inside the cable modem are four primary components and an interface to Ethernet. The four components are tuner, demodulator, burst modulator, and MAC device. The _____ connects directly to the cable outlet. The tuner receives digitally modulated QAM signals. A diplexer is used to provide for both upstream and downstream signals to be transmitted through the same tuner. The _____ is the receiver of the _____ signal.

The demodulator has an analog to digital converter (AD), a QAM-64/256 receiver demodulator, _____ frame synchronization and error correction. The demodulator component is also required in the digital set-top box used to connect to the TV.

The _____ _____ is unique to the cable modem. When it transmits, it feeds the tuner. The integrity of the data is assured by the burst modulator, which uses Reed Solomon encoding of each burst. It modulates using the QPSK/QAM-16 transmitters on the selected lower frequency. Finally, it performs a digital to analog conversion. Unknown cable loss is controlled by the _____ signal. It is fed through a driver, which allows the signal to be adjusted to a variable output level.

The signal transmitted by the cable modem is called the upstream. Upstream is always in bursts. Each cable modem sends bursts in time slots using TDM. Data is sent in MPEG frames. A MAC device is used to extract data from the MPEG frames.

Many cable modems can transmit on the same frequency. _____ is used to filter data from other cable modems. It is responsible for the protocol and it times the transmission of the upstream bursts. The frequency for the upstream burst is between 5-65 MHz and the bandwidth is approximately 2 MHz. It can send upstream at a data rate of 3 Mbps.

The MAC device performs ranging, which allows each cable modem to assess time delay in transmitting to the Head-End center. Because the upstream data channel is shared for transmission to the Head-End center, it must provide for collision detection and retransmission to ensure the data is received. Consequently, if two cable modems transmit upstream at the same time, but one sends a weaker signal, the _____ only hears the strong signal. If the two cable modems send at the same signal strength, the signal becomes distorted and the CMTS knows a _____ occurred.

Concept Table

(This table exercise can also be printed out from the Encore! CD that accompanies this textbook. File name—Chap07contab.)

Read each statement carefully and choose the type of remote access service being described. Use only one "X" per statement.

STATEMENT	DSL	CABLE MODEM	CONSUMER SATELLITE	FTTH
1. This user has a dedicated LAN-like connection from the home to the CO where it is multiplexed and sent to an ISP.				
2. This consumer service is wireless and ideal for areas where cable and DSL services are not available.				
3. At the consumer's home, the optical signal is converted into an electrical signal using an OEC.				
4. The signals are transmitted over fiber-optic cables from the Head-End center to locations near the consumer.				
5. Several service providers have installed dedicated point-to-point SCPC links to connect local POP servers to Internet gateways.				
6. It uses the existing phone line yet gives "always on" Internet access.				
7. It is a passive network and therefore there are no active components from the CO to the consumer.				

8. If two consumers want to talk to each other, they must connect to the CMTS, which then relays the messages.				
9. Consumers can request files, home pages, or video clips through the SNS.				
10. Privacy of user data is achieved by encrypting the data between the modems and the CMTS.				

Concept Picture

*(This picture exercise can also be printed out from the Encore! CD that accompanies this textbook. File name—*Chap07conpic.*)*

In this exercise, look at the picture of a cable modem installation and label the missing elements.

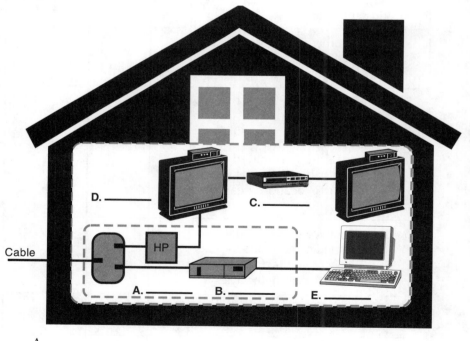

A. _____

B. _____

C. _____

D. _____

E. _____

CASE STUDY

MLE WINERY

Objective:

Determine which client access method is appropriate for each location to connect to corporate headquarters.

Company Profile:

MLE Winery in Napa Valley, California produces, markets, and sells more than 40 well-known brands of wine. The company is a leader in the production and marketing of wine brands in North America and the United Kingdom. MLE has distribution sales offices in six cities within the United States (Morgan Hill, California; Palo Alto, California; New York City; Denver; Atlanta; Miami; and Boston) and three cities in the United Kingdom (London, York, and Leeds).

Current Situation:

Recently, MLE Winery has developed a Web site to provide its customers with useful information about brands, wines, vineyards, and interesting facts about the winemaker. Customers are also able to order shipments of wine over the Web.

MLE's sales representatives are often on the road marketing the wines to various restaurants. The company has determined that the overhead of office space and utilities to support separate sales offices is no longer cost effective. Consequently, the company has decided to close all of its nine sales offices in North America and the United Kingdom. The sales representatives will now telecommute from home.

Each day, MLE relies on dial-up communications to gather information from each of the sales representatives about daily wine sales to customers. The client dial-up connections are at standard modem speeds of 56 Kbps. The winery has decided to host a client-server SQL GUI-based application to collect daily sales information over the Internet. It takes 15 minutes to load the application over a 56 Kbps modem connection. Recently, the sales representatives have become frustrated with the time it takes to do data entry and they have stopped using the system.

Business Information Requirements:

MLE wants to provide a cost-effective, highly dependable communication system between headquarters and sales representatives. The client-server system should provide tools for service planning, forecasting, operations control, business analysis, computer training, and system administration. MLE also hopes to provide faster access to the heavily GUI-based application for remote users.

Communication System Requirements:

At MLE headquarters, the heart of the communications system will require new hardware to support high-speed data access. MLE wants to reduce the amount of time it takes to load the application for the client to under 3 minutes.

Information System Solution:

1. The modem pool was retained to support analog dial up for sales representatives, who need to access the winery application while on the road from a restaurant or hotel.
2. At MLE headquarters in Napa Valley, a Cisco VPN (Virtual Private Network) concentrator was purchased to support high-speed access for telecommuters who use DSL or cable modems.
3. An ISDN router was implemented at the Napa Valley location to receive ISDN remote-access connections.

For U.S. sites, the telecommuters used the following:

LOCATION	TYPE OF SERVICE
Morgan Hill, CA	Consumer Satellite
Palo Alto, CA	FTTH
New York City	DSL
Denver	ISDN
Atlanta	Cable Modem
Miami	Cable Modem

For the U.K. sites, the telecommuters used the following:

LOCATION	TYPE OF SERVICE
London	DSL
York	ISDN
Leeds	Cable Modem

For DSL and cable modem users, the client used remote control and the application loaded in less than 2 minutes.

MLE provided dial-up access over IPLink from CompuServe. This allowed the sales representatives to dial a local number near their homes and ride over the WorldCom IP backbone to headquarters. The IP link also provided Internet access from remote locations. Costs were controlled because the contract has a fixed monthly rate.

Telephone bills for telecommuters were reduced 20% by establishing flat rate services for ISDN, cable modems, DSL, and IPLink for dial-up users.

Study Figure 7.21 and then answer the Study Questions that follow.

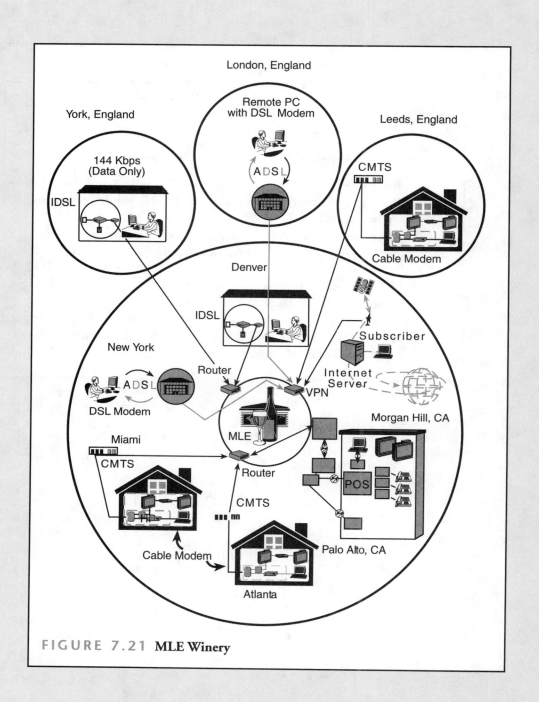

FIGURE 7.21 **MLE Winery**

CASE STUDY QUESTIONS:

1. Will analog dial-up access still be required in the new system?
2. What devices are needed at MLE headquarters to accommodate access from ISDN, cable modems, and DSL?
3. How did they shorten the time required to load the application at the client?
4. Will the new system require remote node or remote control access for users?
5. Are there are any opportunities to reduce telephone bills?

GROUP TERM PROJECT

This part of the project is considered as the Business/Technical Design stage and requires you to determine the equipment, plans, and processes needed to meet the customer's requirements. Print out the Summary Schedule and Implementation Plan from the Encore! CD that accompanies this book (file names *SummarySched* and *ImplementPlan*).

Research your solution for all requirements and determine the equipment and services required for each phase of your project. As you gather this information, try to assess timelines for each phase of the project. List the project phases, projected start and end dates, and a status (either pending or completed) in the Summary Schedule worksheet. This schedule is to be used to communicate project status to the customer. It should be sent to the customer each week so the customer knows how the project is proceeding and whether there are any delays.

After the Summary Schedule of activities is completed, it is important to meet with members of the project team to determine roles and responsibilities for all providers of services. The activities need to be divided into tasks with an estimate of the number of days needed to accomplish each task. Fill in the Implementation Plan assigning tasks and estimated days to different members of your group. At any point in the project, you can look at this implementation plan and determine whether delays will impact the final end date of the project.

WAN PROJECT PLAN

SUMMARY SCHEDULE

DESCRIPTION:

PROJECT SCHEDULE:

Activity	Start Date	Completion Date	Status

WAN PROJECT
IMPLEMENTATION PLAN

I. Implementation Plan Overview/Strategy

II. Implementation Plan Task List

Task #	Implementation Plan Task Description	Resource Required Days	Responsible Person	Start Date mm/dd/yy	End Date mm/dd/yy

CHAPTER TERMS

CHAPTER BIBLIOGRAPHY

Book, Magazine, Presentation Citations

Plunkett, Jack W. *Plunkett's InfoTech Industry Almanac 2001-2002*. Houston: Plunkett Research, Ltd., 2002: 21, 32.

Sheldon, Tom. *Encyclopedia of Networking & Telecommunications*. New York: Osborne/McGraw-Hill, 2001: 406.

Spradley, Ella. "Digital Subscriber Line (DSL) Description." California: Pacific Bell, 1995: 1-10.

Wu, Cheng. "Remote Access Technology Connectivity Beyond the Network Edge." Littleton: XYPLEX, 1994: 1-14.

Web Citations

2 Wire Learning Center, "What is ADSL?," High-Speed Digital Subscriber Line Internet Service, <www.2wire.com> (16 October 2001).

2 Wire Learning Center, "What is cable modem service?," High-Speed Cable Internet Service, <www.2wire.com> (15 October 2001).

Alcatel, "Types of DSL," <www.cid.alcatel.com/doctypes/techpaper/dsl/dsl_types.jhtml> (4 February 2002).

Alcatel, "What are you waiting for?," <www.cid.alcatel.com/doctypes/techp.../dsl_technology.jhml> (2 February 2002).

Alcatel, "What is ADSL?," <www.cid.alcatel.com/doctypes/techprime.../adsl_index.jhtml> (15 October 2001).

Black Box Network Services, "DSL," Black Box Network Services, <www.blackbox.com/tech_docs/tech_overviews/dsl.html> (8 October 2001).

Cadant, "Cable Modems," Web ProForum Tutorials, <www.iec.org> (6 March 2002).

Cisco, "Digital Subscriber Line," Internetworking Technology Overview, <www.cisco.com> (15 February 2002).

City of Palo Alto, "FTTH (Fiber to the Home Trial)," <www.cpau.com/fth> (1 March 2002).

CommVision, "Market Trends – Decade of Information Distribution," <www.commvision.com> (14 March 2002).

Deng, Shuang, "Remote Access Market and Product Evolution," Nortel Networks, <www.nortelnetworks.com> (24 October 2001).

Hecht, Jeff, "Fiber Optics to the Home," <www.technologyreview.com/magazine/mar00/hecht.asp> (17 October 2001).

Helmig, J., "ADSL," <www.wown.com/j_helmig/adslinfo.htm> (10 October 2001).

Internetworking Technology Overview "Digital Subscriber Line," June 1999, <http://www.cisco.com> (15 February 2002)

Marconi, "Fiber to the Home Tutorial," The International Engineering Consortium, <www.iec.org/tutorials/fiber_home/index.html> (5 March 2002).

Network Computing, "Combining Remote Node and Remote Control," <www.networkcomputing.com/shared/printArticle?article=n.../remacc4.html&pub=nw> (19 October 2001).

Ostergaard, Rolf V., "Typical Cable Modem Installation," Cable-Modems Org, <www.cable-modems.org/tutorial/05.htm> (17 October 2001).

Puetz, John, "Comparative Approaches in Implementing Wide Area Satellite Networks," ViaSat, <www.viasat.com/pdfs/compare_WAN.pdf> (2002).

StarBand Communications, "EchoStar/GM/Hughes Announcement," <www.dishnetwork.com/content/promotions/starband/index.shtml> (29 October 2001).

StarBand, "What is Starband?," <www.starband.com/whatis/index.htm> (5 November 2001).

Verizon, "What is DSL?," Everything DSL, <www.everythingdsl.com> (16 October 2001).

Web Management, "ISDN," <searchwebmanagement.techtarget.com/sDefinition/0,,sid27_gci212399,00.html> (2 October 2001).

Webopedia, 10 October 2001, <www.pcwebopedia.com/TERM/G/G_lite.html> (25 February 2002).

CHAPTER 8
WAN SECURITY

By the end of this chapter, you should understand these concepts:
- The activities that govern the foundation of security.
- Types of security breaches or threats that organizations face in an Internet economy.
- The difference between e-mail viruses, worms, and Trojan Horses.
- Several types of Denial of Service (DoS) attacks against Web servers.
- Security within the enterprise and how a security policy protects the company's physical and information technology assets.
- Programs designed specifically for providing security for online transactions using electronic payments.
- Importance of a layered defense strategy.
- The five factors of security.
- The application of tunneling protocols and encryption to provide security for Virtual Private Networks (VPNs).
- Use of firewalls to enforce security policies.

AN INTRODUCTION TO WAN SECURITY

In recent years, organizations the world over have Internet-enabled their operations and moved into the global economy. Mergers and acquisitions have resulted in the expansion of many business services to different parts of the world. Along with this expansion, organizations have embraced the primary values of electronic commerce (e-commerce): cost savings, revenue growth, streamlined operations, and improved customer satisfaction. Because of this, organizations have been challenged to provide security for high-volume transactions and to protect the privacy of data. [Ingrian, 2]

The Internet economy is expected to generate $2 billion in e-commerce transactions by 2003. WANs help enable the growth of the Internet economy. Using a mix of optical and Ethernet technologies, WANs provide organizations with an international presence. In the Internet economy, data has to flow to all locations within an organization, wherever they are. Figure 8.1 shows WAN links spreading out to telecommuters, branch offices, and overseas locations.

Customers and business partners desire to be connected for transacting business electronically. The challenge now is to protect this data from flowing outside the boundaries and borders of the organization. Organizations are naturally concerned about the security, integrity, and privacy of company data that is accessible over the Internet. They seek solutions that will provide protection of data from end to end. To achieve an end-to-end solution, security techniques must be applied to transmission, use, and storage of data. [Ingrian, 2]

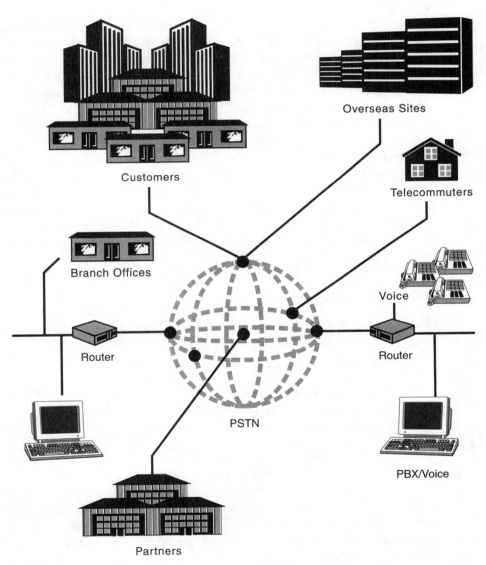

FIGURE 8.1 **Internet Economy Wan Links [Source: Cisco, 1]**

Security techniques are used to ensure that data stored on computers and servers cannot be read or compromised in any way. For the WAN, deciding on a security solution involves choices between cost, access, and protection. With worldwide operations, it is natural to consider the economic benefits of using the Internet to route traffic between several locations. However, if the organization chooses to send traffic over the Internet, it must then rely on the security provided at each router hop through all the Internet Service Providers (ISPs) involved.

Figure 8.2 shows the two primary types of WAN connections. Business partners, overseas sites, home workers, and remote workers are connected over the Internet. These connections are defined as **public connections**. Meanwhile, regional, branch, and corporate headquarters locations use **private connections** of T1 lines. In terms of security, the private network of T1s is better than the public access provided through the Internet. Although it might seem plausible to build WANs that are secure simply by constructing private networks, most organizations cannot afford the high cost of providing private connections to all locations. The only option is to use the public connection provided by the Internet and apply rigid security techniques to protect the integrity of the data.

An organization can suffer significant financial loss and a damaged reputation in the wake of a security breach. Those who transact business with an organization over the Internet need to feel they can trust that personal information (including credit card numbers, financial data, and medical records) is transmitted securely and safely. [Ingrian, 2]

Security Threats

Many security threats exist on the Internet; they are grouped into five types of risks:

- Data exposure in transit and storage
- Application-level attacks
- Mismanagement of encryption techniques
- Inattention to access and identity risks
- Misconfigurations by security administrators

Data flows across the Internet, passes through a number of network routers, and finally lands at the destination router. After the data reaches the destination router, any security **encryption** (translation of data into a secret code) it had is removed and the data is left in a plain-text format to be delivered over a LAN to the intended user. Unfortunately, this data can be read easily both in transit and in storage. In fact, plain-text format is so vulnerable that theft or compromise can occur inside or outside the network by anyone who can gain access to the Web servers or the database. [Ingrian, 1]

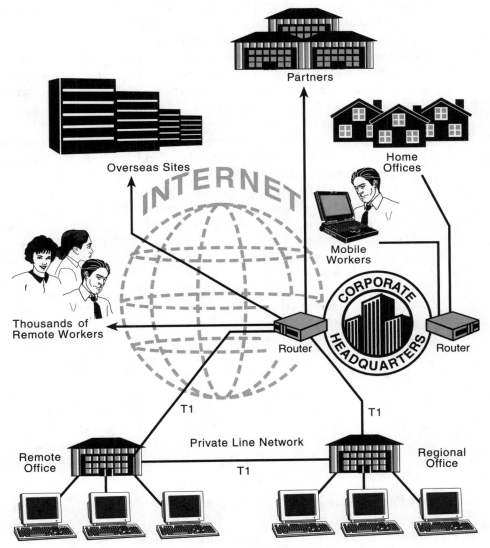

FIGURE 8.2 **Remote WAN Connections** [Source: Cisco, 1]

Customers, employees, and business partners use browsers to access applications over the Internet. With so many people trying to access the application server at once, administrators must find ways to correctly identify authorized and unauthorized users. Additionally, after users are connected, the same managers must control their access to servers and data. They must also protect against **intrusion** from *hackers*. A **hacker** is someone who tries to break into computer systems. Usually hackers are expert programmers whose aim is to gain unauthorized access to either steal or corrupt data.

Security risks also can be attributed to improper configuration of security parameters on a server. Although these errors are usually occasional and unintentional, a simple typo or omission in the security parameter can cause a serious security breach. Securing the infrastructure of the organization is the key to protecting its information assets.

Many attacks against an organization are in the form of *viruses*. Viruses show a security administrator how unknowingly vulnerable an organization can be. In the past few years, for example, several viruses have gone undetected, causing major organizations such as Microsoft, Yahoo, and the U.S. government to shut down their e-mail services. [Ingrian, 1]

A **virus** is a small piece of software that attaches itself to a program. Each time the program runs, the virus also runs, and then reproduces by attaching itself to other programs. Viruses are security threats because they either corrupt or erase organization data. Many forms of virus infections exist; the three main ones are as follows:

- **E-mail Virus**. An e-mail virus attaches itself to e-mail messages and replicates by automatically mailing itself to everyone in the user's e-mail address book.
- **Worm**. A worm is a small piece of software that uses computer networks and security holes to replicate itself. A copy of the worm scans the network for a PC with a security hole, copies itself using the security hole, and begins replicating again.
- **Trojan Horse**. A Trojan Horse disguises itself and appears to the user as a normal computer program such as a game program. After the user downloads it and runs it on a PC, the program is executed and usually erases the hard disk. Fortunately, Trojan Horses do not have a way to replicate automatically. [Brain, 1]

Numerous examples exist of the damage viruses can do to an organization. For instance, the U.S. Information Agency (USAI) once had a Web site that published statements on American policy or texts of official speeches. On January 21, 1999, the Web site was broken into. Internet vandals had left a Trojan Horse on the server that caused basic hardware damage as well as the destruction of the Web site. [Paller, 1]

Most of the more recent virus attacks have been worms. On July 19, 2001, a worm called **Code Red** replicated itself 250,000 times over a period of about nine hours. The worm scanned the Internet for Windows NT or Windows 2000 servers that did not have the Microsoft security patch installed. When it found an unsecured server, it copied itself to that server. The worm continued to scan for other unsecured servers and passed very quickly through a network of servers.

The Code Red worm was designed to replicate itself for the first 20 days of each month, replace Web pages on infected servers with a page that read "Hacked by Chinese," and launch an attack on the White House Web server in an attempt to overwhelm it. At 8:00 EST, the worm caused an infected server to connect to the *whitehouse* domain. The attack infected several systems simultaneously by sending 100 connections to port 80 of www.whitehouse.gov/. The U.S. government was forced to change its IP address to circumvent the attack. [Brain, 1]

Web Security

As shown from these examples, security risks affect Web sites, **Web servers**, and Web browsers. When a Web server is installed, a window is opened into the LAN that the entire Internet can peer through. [Stein, 1]

Providing Web security presents a bit of a paradox. On the one hand, the purpose of network security is to provide protection that keeps strangers out. On the other hand, security that is too tight defeats the purpose of a Web site, which is to provide the world with access to the organization and its network. Web security requires a strategy for protecting the Web servers while serving the needs of Web clients.

Web servers typically are standard PC or UNIX servers that support a Web site or Web application. If the Web server hosts an application, the server must recognize and authenticate several groups of users (customers, business partners, and employees). **Authentication** is a process of validating the identity of the user through the use of a password. This is often followed by a second level of security provided by **authorization** that specifies the level of access permitted to applications and data on the network. (IBM, 1)

Many organizations feel secure enough in supporting browsing of their Web sites by the public that they do not believe authentication is necessary. Additionally, Web browsing feels safe and anonymous to the end user. However, neither side is really safe. Browsing leaves an electronic record of the user's surfing history. This provides hackers with a way to create a profile of the user's tastes and habits. On the Web server's side, Web browsing can introduce a pathway for viruses or other malicious software to enter the LAN. Also, the integrity of the Web site can be compromised by *IP spoofing*. **IP spoofing** is a method used by hackers to re-direct customers to a fake Web site, where they collect and process orders. With spoofing, a system attempts to illicitly impersonate another system by using its IP address. [Laudon, 245] [Stein, 1]

Recently, several security vulnerabilities have been discovered in Microsoft's IIS (Internet Information Server) and Linux Apache Web server software. The operating systems that support these complex programs unfortunately contain security flaws. These flaws are attributed to the way a Web server passes uploaded data, and can cause the software to misinterpret the size of large pieces of incoming data. This means a hacker could gain complete control over a weak system simply by sending a malicious request to the server. [Evers, 1]

Security flaws introduce more opportunities for hackers to penetrate the network. Other types of security attacks also can occur; the most common is **Denial of Service (DoS)** attacks. A DoS attack is designed to render a computer or network incapable of providing normal services. Hackers use bandwidth attacks to flood the network with such a high volume of traffic that all network resources are consumed. Legitimate user requests cannot get through because of the high volume of connection requests. Table 8.1 lists different types of DoS attacks. [Stein, 1]

DDoS	Distributed Denial of Service. Many computers launch a coordinated DoS attack against one or more servers. Using client-server technology, a master program can launch an attack through agent programs installed on several servers. Within seconds, the master can initiate an attack to hundreds or thousands of agent programs. [Stein, 1]
Smurf Attack	A type of DDoS attack that takes advantage of ICMP (Internet Control Message Protocol). A Smurf Attack uses the ping program (sends an echo request to determine whether a server is up) with a forged source address to continuously ping one or more servers on a network. The forged source address is overwhelmed by response traffic generated by the pings. [Stein, 1]
Trinoo	A complex DDoS program that uses "master" programs to automate the control of several agent programs. The agent programs then attack one or more servers by flooding the network with UDP (User Datagram Protocol) packets. [Stein, 1]
TFN	Tribal Flood Network. Launches a DoS attack that can generate packets with spoofed source IP addresses. The attacker accesses the master program and sends either a UDP, TCP SYN, ICMP echo request flood, or an ICMP directed broadcast to all agent programs on several networked servers. [Stein, 1]
TFN2K	Tribal Flood Network 2K. A more advanced version of TFN that sends corrupt packets to cause a system to crash or become unstable. It can defeat router filters by spoofing IP source addresses to make packets appear to come from a neighboring router on the LAN. [Stein, 1]
Stacheldraht	A German word that translates in English as "barbed wire." Launches a DoS attack using encrypted communication between the attacker and the master program. It also updates the agents automatically using the rcp (remote copy) UNIX command. [Stein, 1]

TABLE 8.1 **DoS Attacks**

In 2001, the **Security Administration, Networking, and Security (SANS) Institute** published a list of the top 20 security flaws it had discovered. This *SANS/FBI Top Twenty List* informs more than 156,000 security professionals, auditors, and system and network administrators of the solutions they can find for security attacks. SANS publishes news digests, research summaries, security alerts, and white papers on security. These publications are free to download from the SANS Web site (www.sans.org/). [SANS Institute, 1]

To summarize, several types of viruses and DoS attacks target Web servers and can cause severe damage. Yet, neither attacks nor software flaws have deterred organizations from conducting business transactions over the Internet.

Commerce on the Internet

Organizations conduct business over the Internet as a way to increase revenue and decrease costs. Customers can easily order products and services, and make payments online through a Web site. Financial institutions provide Web sites for banking services such as checking the status of accounts and transferring funds between accounts. The information organizations publish online is referred to as content, and e-commerce requires that this content be secured so that the privacy of customer information is protected. [Ingrian, 1]

A "trusted" e-commerce site gives customers the confidence to continue ordering and conducting business over the Internet. Organizations need to protect the information they publish and gather through online forms. Privacy of the data is critical. A **privacy policy** must be clearly communicated to those who use the Web site. The policy should specifically state the penalties for intrusion. In addition, several technological strategies (discussed later in this chapter) can be deployed to protect the data. [IBM, 1] Programs are designed specifically to provide security for online transactions using electronic payments. These systems have specifications and protocols that have been developed to provide secure methods for electronic payments.

Electronic Payment Systems

Electronic payment systems are available worldwide over the Internet. With a global economy, these payment systems at the least need to perform currency exchange. In addition, an electronic payment system should support incremental purchases, purchase reversal, and purchase cancellation for transaction processing. In some cases, a Web site might require a link to financial institutions to process electronic checks or cash purchases. [CEPS, 1].

Standard protocols and specifications have been developed to support interoperability for such e-commerce transactions. Two primary standard protocols are listed in Table 8.2.

Common Electronic Purse Specifications (CEPS)	Defines the requirements for all components to implement a global electronic purse program. Provides a method for establishing accountability and auditability. The issuer has access to transaction detail. The organization CEPSCO was officially created in October of 1999 to manage the on-going development and administration of this standard. [CEPS, 1].
Micro Payment Transfer Protocol (MPTP)	Defined for the transfer of payments through the services of a common broker. The broker is referred to as a financial intermediary (an ISP or telephone company) capable of billing significant numbers of customers at a small cost. Designed for small payment amounts and for use in interactive applications. An asynchronous protocol that allows most of the processing to occur offline. [Hallam-Baker, 1]

TABLE 8.2 **Protocols for Electronic Transactions**

Without the use of specifications and protocols, the only effective way to protect data is encryption. Encryption allows data to be converted into *ciphertext*. **Ciphertext** is text that cannot be easily understood by unauthorized users. To read an encrypted file, users must have access to a secret key or password enabling them to *decrypt*. When users **decrypt** data, they convert the data back to plain text so it can be read. [Webopedia, 1]

Security Solutions and Policies

Solutions for security require a strong foundation built around tools and procedures. A good security solution has an organization security policy at the center. This policy is a document that states in writing how a company plans to protect the company's physical and information technology assets. Security within an enterprise is a problem both of people and processes. Trust is a major principle when defining security policies. Most organizations apply different **trust models** to different parts of an organization. Different levels of trust are defined for employees, customers, and business partners. The culture of the organization plays a major role in determining the amount of security control that is appropriate.

The security policy should aim to be flexible enough to balance the level of productivity and openness against the level of security control. If this balance is not achieved, policies become too restrictive and people either find ways to circumvent controls or don't participate in the business activity. [Guel, 9-10]

The basis of a security policy should be a document that defines acceptable use. The document should specify the following:

- How the organization plans to educate its employees about protecting their assets
- How security measurements will be carried out and enforced
- A procedure for evaluating the effectiveness of the security policy to ensure that corrections will be made [Webopedia, 1]

Organizations vary as to the minimum number of policies they will publish, however, all organizations should have some key policies, including the following:

- Acceptable Use
- Remote Access
- Information Protection
- Perimeter Security
- Host/Device Security
- User Account/Password Policy

Each of these separate policies needs to include certain basic elements. Figure 8.3 shows that the basic elements of security include instructions on how to secure, manage, test, and monitor an organization's data. They define the amount of network exposure that is acceptable and the amount of control of the network perimeter that is necessary to minimize security risks. Another important part of the security policy is documenting the dates of intrusion and types of intruders detected. Finally, organizations need to publish a privacy policy that clearly states who has access to data and under what circumstances. [IBM, 1]

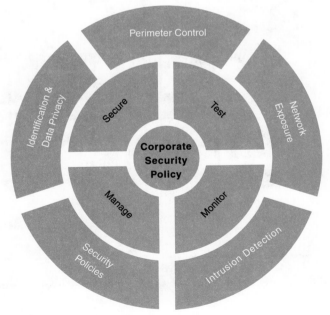

FIGURE 8.3 **Elements of Security**

The bottom line on security is that without a written policy, management has nothing to reference to punish an employee/guest who is in violation of acceptable, safe computing practices. Likewise, for the FBI to prosecute an intruder, all servers must display a message that states this server supports restricted access and is limited to authorized users only. Without this message, the FBI cannot prosecute because there is no notification to intruders that they are breaking into a restricted site.

Defining Security and Access

Security safeguards should be defined for transmission of data both inside and outside the organization. Figure 8.4 shows a clear separation between the two. A technique called **Network address translation (NAT)** is used to protect IP addresses inside the organization's network. Inside the network, private IP addresses are used and they are not published to the Internet. Instead, either through a router or firewall, these private IP addresses are mapped to public IP addresses that are published to the Internet.

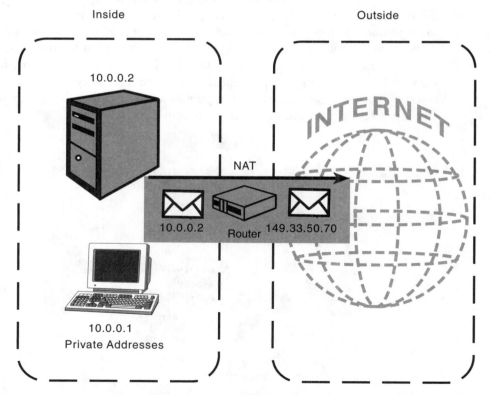

FIGURE 8.4 **Inside/Outside the Corporate Network [Source: Cisco, 1]**

The mapping for NAT is defined in the router or firewall table. For example, in Figure 8.5, the local IP address 10.0.0.1 is mapped to a global IP address 149.33.50.70 and the second local device 10.0.0.2 is mapped to 149.33.50.71. People on the Internet only see the global IP addresses and cannot see internal local IP addresses.

Inside Local IP Address	Inside Global IP Address
10.0.0.1	149.33.50.70
10.0.0.2	149.33.50.71

FIGURE 8.5 **Network Address Translation (NAT) [Source: Cisco, 1]**

Firewalls and DMZs

Most organizations build layers of defense against security violations. In many organizations, defense begins at the edge of the LAN called the perimeter. Perimeters exist at points where the private LAN meets the interface to the public Internet. **Perimeter security** is traditionally provided by a firewall. Firewalls inspect packets and determine whether a packet should be transmitted or dropped. The firewall has become the central point of entry for both incoming and outgoing traffic into an organization's network. [Paul, 1] [Cisco, 1]

Although firewalls are capable of enforcing security policies, organizations might choose to add another layer of defense by creating a *demilitarized zone (DMZ)*. A **DMZ** is an area behind the firewall that is accessible from the Internet. It is an isolated network segment. The servers placed in the DMZ require different levels of access than other network servers. Usually, the external DNS (Domain Name System), FTP (File Transfer Protocol), Web server, and/or a mail relay server are placed in the DMZ. Figure 8.6 shows an example of a layered approach to perimeter security. Both a firewall and a DMZ protect access into the network. In addition, servers and other devices are used for authentication, intrusion detection, application gateways, and VPN end points. The internal network is in the manufacturing area, which is isolated from the DMZ by a firewall. The firewall has highly restrictive rules for traffic into the internal network. Less restrictive rules are specified in the DMZ to make access available to the general public. [Cole, 1] [Taylor, 1]

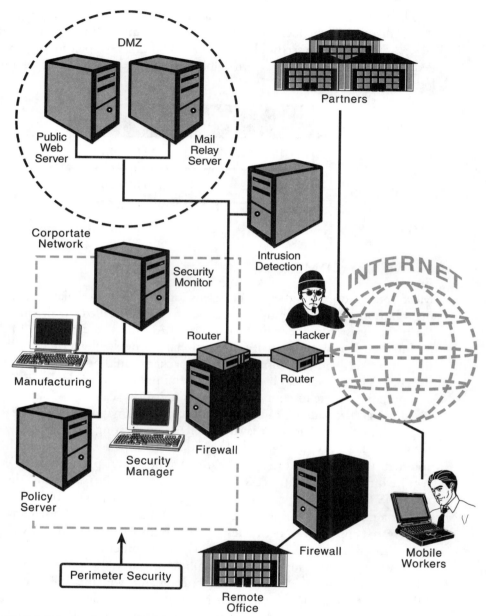

DMZ

Public
Web
Server

Mail
Relay
Server

Partners

Intrusion
Detection

Corporate
Network

Security
Monitor

Hacker

Router

Manufacturing

Router

Security
Manager

Firewall

Policy
Server

Firewall

Mobile
Workers

Perimeter Security

Remote
Office

FIGURE 8.6 **Perimeter Security**

Some organizations build a DMZ configuration with intrusion detection, as shown in Figure 8.7, to add another layer to the security on the perimeter. An intrusion is defined as an instance of someone trying to break into or misuse a computer system. An **intrusion-detection system** attempts to determine whether an intruder is breaking into the system or a legitimate user is misusing the organization's computers. The intrusion-detection systems in Figure 8.7 perform system monitoring for activities by users and number of attempted logins. The statistics gathered are continually updated and correlated to determine whether a series of actions constitutes a potential intrusion.

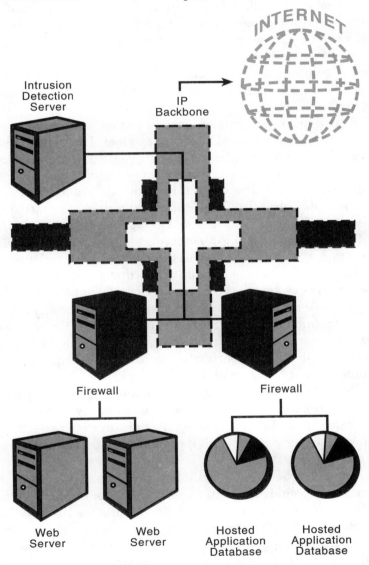

FIGURE 8.7 **Intrusion Detection [Source: Qwest, 1]**

Intrusion-detection systems scan traffic for protocol anomalies and monitors protocol states for violations of standard protocol behavior. The system also uses statistical rate counters to watch for packet floods and packet reassembly monitoring to thwart fragmented packet attacks. Basically, the product consists of an engine that performs sensing and correlation analysis. [Conry-Murray, 58]

Several servers called **sensors** are used to watch all traffic. The sensors scan network traffic and pass any suspicious events to a correlation engine. All sensors communicate to each other to determine whether they are reporting related events. If a relationship between events is identified, the sensor captures the type of event, source IP address, destination IP address, and the time of the event. The engine then alerts an administrator to potential trouble. [Conry-Murray, 62-63]

A good intrusion-detection system must resist subversion, observe deviations from normal behavior, and be difficult to fool. The system must monitor itself to ensure that it has not been used or comprised. It must also be able to run continually without human supervision or intervention. [Price, 1]

When security is monitored throughout an organization, suspicious activities can be readily identified. This level of security monitoring requires a great deal of vigilance as servers and security devices must be monitored 24 hours a day, 365 days a year. Some organizations opt to hire a security organization to perform their system monitoring. Figure 8.8 shows that the system monitoring is dedicated to the internal network supporting manufacturing. **Security monitoring** goes beyond the capabilities of firewalls and intrusion-detection systems. It provides a staff of security experts who monitor security alerts generated by an organization's network. Security experts examine the audit log files from all devices (routers, firewalls, intrusion-detection systems, and servers) to verify whether an attack is real or a false alarm. Then, they quickly contact the organization with corrective actions.

Depending on organization budgets, some organizations find that the cost and level of experience required to manage security for their networks is overwhelming. To address this, many ISPs and telcos offer co-location services, as shown in Figure 8.9, in which they monitor and manage an organization's Web-hosting servers. These service providers invest heavily in security monitoring, intrusion detection, and firewalls to build a strong perimeter for the organization. For a monthly fee, they provide floor space for the servers, network connections to the Internet, and a full-time, round-the-clock staff to monitor the systems. All security alerts are forwarded to the appropriate network engineers within the organization. Most network managers feel the level of expert monitoring provided for their Web-hosting environment is well worth the monthly cost.

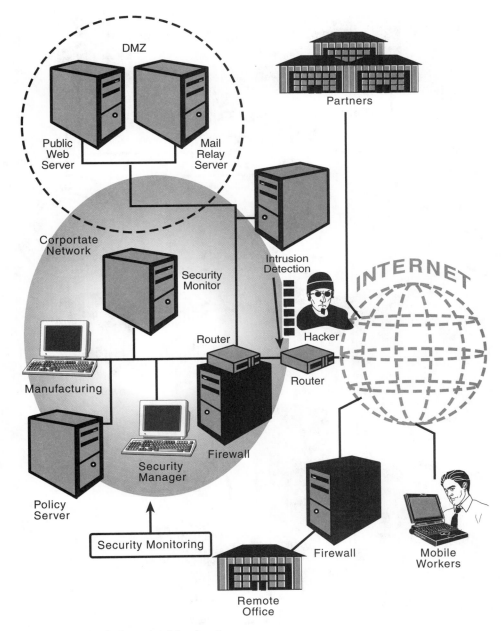

FIGURE 8.8 **Security Monitoring**

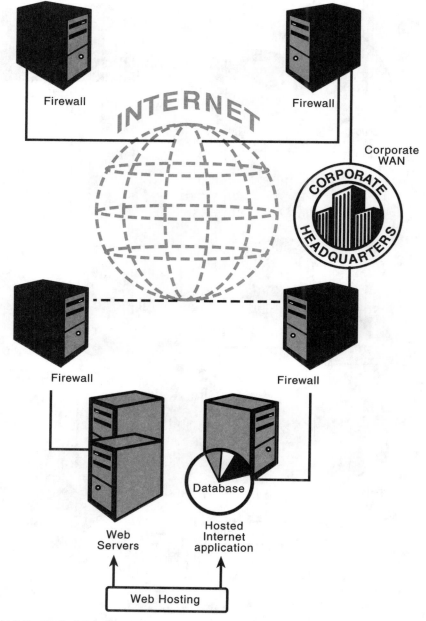

FIGURE 8.9 **Web Hosting Security** [Source: Qwest, 1]

Internet Security

Information security is provided over the Internet using a variety of methods. Recently, a new method sponsored by the World Wide Web Consortium (W3C), called **Platform for Privacy Preferences Project (P3P)** has begun to control the amount of personal information users share with Web sites. P3P is often called a "privacy on the Internet assistant." When users use a P3P application, they can enter personal information once rather than having to enter it repeatedly at each different Web site. [Web Management, 1]

A new standard called **Open Profiling Standard (OPS)** allows users to control how much personal information they want to share with a Web site. The OPS's basic framework provides privacy and profiling on the Web. This framework is called the **Resource Definition Framework** and it uses a vocabulary and a standard data format for expressing personal information. The **personal profile** it creates contains:

- A unique identifier for the profile itself
- A unique identifier for each Web site visited
- Demographic data (country, ZIP code, age, and gender)
- Contact information (name, address, ZIP or postal code, telephone number, and e-mail address)
- Credit card information
- Personal preferences (hobbies, favorite magazines, favorite books, and activities) [Web Management, 1]

This personal profile gives users much finer control over the use of their personal information. Users are able to define what information a specific site may or may not be provided. Although P3P is a step in the right direction toward protecting privacy over the Internet, encryption is still necessary to achieve true data security. The capability to store and transfer sensitive information using encryption has become a significant issue for e-commerce.

Internal Security

Most people think the largest threat to their security is from outside the organization. However, FBI studies have revealed that 80% of intrusions and attacks come from inside the organization. After all, an insider already knows the layout of the system and where valuable data is located on the servers. This individual might also know what security measures are in place within the organization. [Price, 1]

Security within an organization is an on-going process, not a product. As discussed earlier in this chapter, building layers is one effective way to manage security. However, an organization can be of further help in preventing attacks from within by having strong security policies for authentication, authorization, accounting, and auditing. Enforcing these policies is key to a successful security program.

Network engineers and security administrators must use these centralized management tools to enforce a security policy across an organization. A good authentication and authorization system should correctly identify remote users and verify their access privileges against a central directory service or database. Authentication also can be strengthened by a strong user/account policy that defines how long passwords must be, which characters and numbers they should contain, and how often they must be changed. The accounting system should record all user activity and support detailed reports of these activities. Audit logs are priceless for diagnosing system failures or intrusions. A good auditing system logs failed performance data, unusual system usage, and error conditions. [Feghhi, 221]

With proper attention given to security and proactive management by network engineers and security administrators, an organization can provide a trusted e-commerce solution for its customers. A few other security techniques are worth mentioning, however, that offer even more protection. Taking these measures might not prevent all attacks, but it will greatly reduce the number of attacks. An organization can apply the following security measures to its LANs and WANs:

- Check for virus alerts daily on a virus-checker Web site.
- Review the SANS list of security breaches and attacks.
- Apply security software patches recommended by the operating system developer on standard servers and Web hosting servers.
- Use encryption techniques on browsers.
- Enable virus checkers for network servers to detect viruses on all incoming data.
- Make sure the e-mail server has a special virus checker just for checking mail.
- Provide a virus checker for every desktop.

In addition, the organization might want to apply these personnel security measures:

- Install personal firewalls for remote users with high-speed connections (such as DSL [Digital Subscriber Lines] and cable modems)
- Create a strong password policy that requires changing passwords periodically at scheduled intervals.
- Create a very restrictive policy regarding termination of accounts when people leave the organization.

In summary, security for an organization requires policies, technical controls, staff cooperation, and, most importantly, management commitment to the level of control required. A good security program should be updated annually to reflect changes within the organization.

1. What are the three activities that comprise the foundation of security?
2. What does an organization suffer as the result of a security breach?
3. What is the difference between a worm virus and a Trojan Horse virus?
4. What is a security flaw within an operating system?
5. Where can information be found about security flaws?

ENCRYPTION

Encryption is based on the science of *cryptography*. Computers use **cryptography** to scramble ordinary text (plain text) into ciphertext (encryption). [Web Management, 1] Cryptography is designed to protect the following:

- **Confidentiality**. Only the intended receiver can read the information.
- **Integrity**. The information cannot be altered in storage or transit between sender and intended receiver.
- **Non-repudiation**. The senders of information cannot, at a later stage, deny their intentions in the creation nor deny transmission of the information.
- **Authentication**. The sender and receiver can confirm each other's identity and the origin/destination of the information. [Search Security, 1]

Encryption Ciphers and Keys

Cryptography is the foundation used for encryption. Encryption standards use mathematical algorithms to create *ciphers* as a method to encrypt the text. **Ciphers** are codes that substitute symbols or other letters for letters, such as representing an A with an F. After text has been encrypted using the cipher, it becomes ciphertext.

Most ciphers used today use a *key* to encrypt and decrypt text. The **key** is a variable that is combined with an algorithm. An algorithm, in this instance, is a formula used to scramble the unencrypted text. The length of the key determines how difficult the text will be to decrypt. Two basic ciphers, *block ciphers* and *stream ciphers*, are used. With a **block cipher**, the cryptographic key and algorithm are applied to a block of data, usually 64 bits at once, rather than to one bit at a time. An initialization vector is derived from a random number generator and is applied with the text in the first block and key. This prevents identical messages encrypted on the same day from producing identical ciphertext. With a **stream cipher**, the cryptographic key and algorithm are applied to each binary digit in a data stream, one bit at a time. The block cipher has become the preferred method, so the stream cipher is rarely used today. [Search Security, 1]

Encryption using keys ensures that only the person with the key can decode the encrypted text. Computer encryption systems today use one of three categories of keys: *symmetric key encryption, private key encryption,* or *public key encryption.*

Symmetric Key Encryption

With **symmetric key encryption** (also known as secret-key cryptography), the sender and receiver of a message share a single key to encrypt and decrypt the message. This key must be exchanged in a secure way and the key must be installed on each of the two computers that will be exchanging data. Symmetric keys are simpler and faster than other encryption keys. Data Encryption Standard (DES) uses a symmetric key system. [Webopedia, 1]

Figure 8.10 shows the use of a symmetric key. Each of the computers must know the key to decode the message. Symmetric key uses a letter substitution algorithm. Each letter is shifted a certain number of positions. For example, a two-position shift would replace every "a" with a "c." In this example, the letter "a" becomes a "c," whereas the letter "t" becomes a "v." The key allows the authorized receiver to decode the original message. The message reads as gibberish to anyone else.

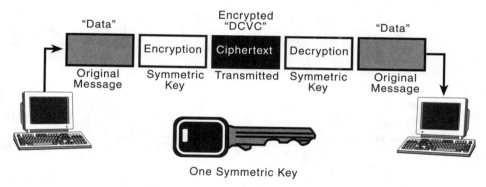

FIGURE 8.10 Symmetric Key Encryption

Private Key Encryption

Private key encryption uses a private key, which is a single secret key that is known only to the two people that exchange messages. The **private key** is used to encrypt and decrypt messages. There is a risk inherent with a private key in that if the key is lost or stolen, the data is essentially lost because it cannot be decrypted. [Search Security, 1]

Figure 8.11 shows a private key. Only the two people that exchange the message know the private key. The key is shared between the two computers so that each can encrypt and decrypt messages. After the data is decrypted, it is converted back to plain text.

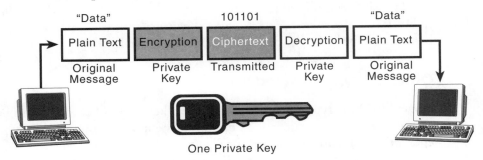

FIGURE 8.11 **Private Key Encryption**

Public Key Encryption

Public key encryption uses a public key to encrypt and another private key to decrypt. A **public key** is a value provided by a designated authority to be applied with a private key to encrypt messages and digital signatures. The private key's value is derived from that of the public key. A digital signature is an electronic signature used to authenticate the identity of the sender of a message or signer of a document. The digital signature ensures that the original content of the message or document has not been modified. [Search Security, 1]

Figure 8.12 shows the use of a public/private key combination. Only the user's computer knows the private key. The user's computer sends the public key to any computer that wants to communicate with it securely. To decode the message, the destination computer must use both the public key and its own private key.

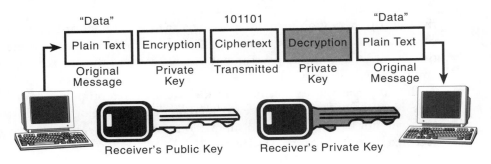

FIGURE 8.12 **Public Key Encryption**

The key in public key encryption uses a **hash algorithm**. A **hash value** is computed from a base input number. Basically, the hash value is a summary of the original value. Public keys use large hash values for encrypting, which is considered to be very secure. When public keys use 128-bit numbers, there are 2^{128} possible combinations to use for the hash values. It is extremely difficult to break this algorithm. A hacker would have to know the original input number and the multiplier to derive the hash value. [Brain, 1]

Other Encryption Standards

Several other encryption standards can use a key or another method to provide secure access to an organization's network. The most commonly used types of encryption standards today are as follows:

- Data Encryption Standard (DES)
- RSA Algorithm
- Public Key Infrastructure (PKI)
- Digital Certificates
- Internet Protocol Security (IPsec)
- Kerberos
- Pretty Good Privacy (PGP)
- Secure Sockets Layer (SSL)
- Secure HyperText Transfer Protocol (S-HTTP)

Data Encryption Standard (DES)

A widely used method of data encryption, **Data Encryption Standard (DES)**, applies a 56-bit private key to each 64-bit block of data. This is considered strong encryption. The DES process can run in several modes and the algorithm is programmed to be executed 16 times. This confuses hackers and prevents them from identifying the original key. Another version of DES called triple DES applies three keys in succession. DES is not widely available. It was the security encryption method selected by the Department of Defense in 1977 because it was judged to be extremely difficult to break. To maintain the effectiveness of DES, the U.S. government decided at that time to restrict its exportation. [Search Security, 1]

Recently, free versions of the software have appeared on public domain Web sites. Now the National Institute of Standards and Technology (NIST) says DES will not be re-certified and submissions for its replacement are being accepted. [Search Security, 1]

RSA Algorithm

Ron Riverst, Adi Shamir, and Leonard Adleman for RSA Security developed the **RSA algorithm** in 1977. The RSA algorithm uses a combination of public and private keys for encrypting data. The RSA algorithm is used by nearly everyone for encryption and authentication. The most popular Web browsers, Microsoft Internet Explorer and Netscape, use RSA security.

The RSA algorithm multiplies two large prime numbers (numbers divisible only by themselves and 1) to derive a set of two numbers that become the public and private keys. After the keys have been derived, the original prime numbers are discarded. The private key is used to decrypt the data that has been encrypted with the public key. When RSA encryption is used, the private key never needs to be sent across the Internet.

Public Key Infrastructure (PKI)

The **Public Key Infrastructure (PKI)** standard uses public key cryptography for encrypting and decrypting messages or data over the Internet. Public and private keys are created simultaneously using the same algorithm. The private key is given to the receiver while the public key is publicly available in a directory that all parties can access. The private key is never shared with anyone or sent across the Internet. PKI provides several components, such as:
- **Digital certificates**. Used to identify an individual or organization.
- **Certificate Authority (CA)**. Issues and verifies the digital certificate.
- **Registration Authority (RA)**. Acts as the verifier for the CA.
- **Directories (Registries)**. Use databases that contain the certificates with their public keys.

All of these components, CA, RA, digital certificates, and directories define a certificate management system.

Certificate Management System

When you use a digital certificate, the CA checks with an RA to verify the information provided by the requestor's digital certificate. After the RA positively identifies the requestor's information, the CA issues a certificate. The **digital certificate** is issued in the form of an electronic "credit card" that establishes your credentials for conducting transactions over the Web. A CA issues these certificates. The following information is contained inside the digital certificate:
- Name
- Serial number
- Expiration date
- Copy of the certificate holder's public key
- Digital signature of the CA

Registries (directories) are available for digital certificates to allow authenticated users to look up other users' public keys.

Internet Protocol Security (IPsec)

Developed by the IETF (Internet Engineering Task Force), **IPsec** is a set of protocols used to support secure exchange of packets at the IP layer of the TCP/IP (Transmission Control Protocol/Internet Protocol) suite. IPsec requires the sending and receiving devices to share a public key. It uses the Internet Security Association and the Key Management Protocol/Oakley (ISAKMP/Oakley) encryption method allows the receiver to obtain a public key and authenticate the sender using digital certificates. Table 8.3 describes the two encryption modes supported by IPsec.

Transport Mode (Authentication Header)	Only the data portion (payload) of each packet is encrypted. The header is left untouched. Supports the Authentication Header (AH) service, which allows authentication of the sender of the data. [Webopedia, 1] [Search Security, 1]
Tunnel Mode (Encapsulating Security Payload)	With this mode, both header and payload are encrypted. Supports the Encapsulating Security Payload (ESP) for both authentication of the sender and encryption of the data. The AH is inserted into the packet after the IP packet header. An IPsec-compliant device decrypts each packet for the receiver. [Webopedia, 1] [Search Security, 1]

TABLE 8.3 **IPsec Encryption Modes**

Kerberos

Kerberos assigns a unique key to enable two parties to exchange private information across an open network. The unique key is referred to as a ticket. The ticket is encrypted and assigned to each user as that user logs on to the network. The ticket is embedded in messages to identify the sender of the message. The user's password does not have to pass through the network. The ticket is time-stamped for a limited period of time—usually eight hours. This means it can be used several times during the eight-hour period without having to be re-authenticated. Currently, Microsoft uses Kerberos authentication with Windows 2000 servers and Active Directory. [Webopedia, 1] [Search Security, 1]

Pretty Good Privacy

Pretty Good Privacy (PGP) is used to encrypt and decrypt e-mail over the Internet. Based on the public key method, this free encryption method is generally regarded by the public as effective and easy-to-use. Using PGP encryption software, a public key is available for the user to send to anyone from whom he or she wants to receive a message. A private key is then used to decrypt the messages you receive.

PGP also can use an encrypted digital signature for authentication and encryption. It uses an efficient algorithm that generates a hash (mathematical summary) derived from the user's name and other signature information. This hash code is then encrypted with the sender's private key. The receiver uses the sender's public key to decrypt the hash code.

Several versions of PGP are available; it is published as two different public key versions: **RSA** and **Diffie-Hellman**. These PGP versions use different algorithms and are not compatible with each other. The RSA version of PGP is not free and requires purchasing a licensing key. The RSA version uses the **International Data Encryption Algorithm (IDEA)** to generate a short key for the entire message and uses RSA to encrypt the short key. IDEA uses block cipher with a 128-bit key and is considered very secure. The Diffie-Hellman version of PGP uses the *CAST algorithm* for the short key to encrypt the message and the Diffie-Hellman algorithm to encrypt the short key. The **CAST algorithm** (Carlisle Adams and Stafford Tavares algorithm) is a symmetric cipher that uses a 128-bit key. [Search Security, 1] [Adams, 1]

The U.S. government originally restricted exportation of PGP technology outside the United States. Today, it can be exchanged with users outside the United States, provided that both ends have installed the correct versions of PGP. The international version is just as secure as the domestic version. [Search Security, 1]

Secure Sockets Layer

Secure Sockets Layer (SSL) is a secure negotiated session between the client browser and the Web server that provides for authentication and confidentiality using digital certificates. SSL establishes a unique symmetric key called a session key, which is only used once for that specific session. [Laudon, 257]

Secure HyperText Transfer Protocol

Secure HyperText Transfer Protocol (S-HTTP) is a secure communications protocol designed to handle HTTP messages and to send individual messages securely. S-HTTP cannot be used to secure non-HTTP messages. [Laudon, 260]

TOPIC review
Encryption

1. What does a personal profile contain that allows users to control how much personal information to share with a Web site?
2. What is cryptography designed to protect?
3. What is the difference between a public and private key?
4. Which public encryption standard uses digital certificates?
5. What is the difference between transport and tunnel mode used with IPsec encryption?

VIRTUAL PRIVATE NETWORKS (VPNS)

A **virtual private network (VPN)** is a private data network that runs through a public telecommunications network or the Internet. VPNs use encryption and other security techniques to protect the privacy of data. Only authorized users can access the private network. Privacy is maintained through the use of a **tunneling protocol**. VPN is a private tunnel, or pathway, through the Internet. There are cost savings when deploying a VPN solution over a shared public infrastructure rather than building a private network with T1 leased lines.

VPN Connections

VPNs are good solutions for mobile workers, telecommuters, business partners, and dial-up users. Connections are established to points of presence (POPs) of their ISPs. In Figure 8.13, two separate connections are made to the POP, one for mobile users and the other for telecommuters. VPN point-to-point tunnels are provided for business partners, remote users, and regional offices directly over the Internet to corporate headquarters. Data is encrypted before it is passed between VPN sites to protect against eavesdropping and tampering with the data by hackers or unauthorized personnel. [Nortel, 2]

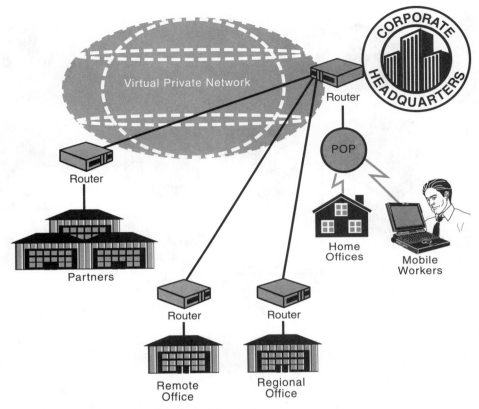

FIGURE 8.13 **Virtual Private Network**

VPN Equipment

VPN technology is complicated, and various approaches are used in the construction of VPNs. Figure 8.14 shows two separate VPNs. One VPN has several devices, such as security gateways, security policy servers, a CA, a router, and a firewall. In the second VPN, all the security and firewall functions are built into a single router. [Nortel, 9]

When designing a VPN, there are trade-offs when choosing to invest in separate pieces of equipment or to integrate all VPN functions into one device. When evaluating equipment options, it is important to consider how many functions should be integrated into a single device. The disadvantage with a single device solution is that the organization has a single point of failure for all remote connections. To compensate for this weakness, the single device should at least have dual power supplies and failover capabilities to ensure reliability. [Nortel, 9]

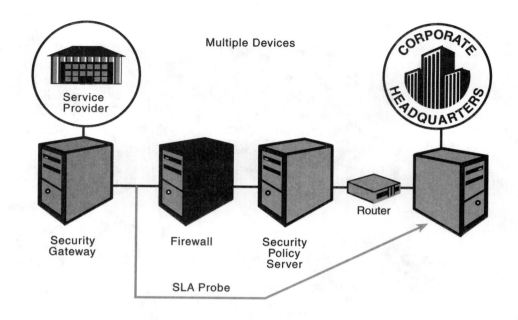

Multiple Devices

Service Provider

Security Gateway

Firewall

Security Policy Server

Router

SLA Probe

CORPORATE HEADQUARTERS

Integrated Services

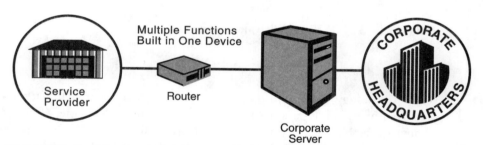

Multiple Functions Built in One Device

Service Provider

Router

Corporate Server

CORPORATE HEADQUARTERS

FIGURE 8.14 **Multiple Versus Integrated Devices**

In each of the VPN solutions shown in Figure 8.14, security gateways are installed between the public and private networks. Their job is to prevent unauthorized intrusions into the private network. They also can be configured to provide encryption and tunneling functions. The router can support encryption tasks, which is a good solution for small networks. The only disadvantage is if the router goes down, so does the VPN. Firewalls also can provide for encryption and tunneling; however, if the firewall must examine a large amount of traffic, it slows down performance. On small networks with low volumes of traffic, combining tunneling, encryption, and firewall services into one device is likely to reduce costs without sacrificing performance. [Nortel, 1]

VPN Protocols

Several protocols are used to provide VPN security over the Internet. Currently, the four protocols commonly used to create VPNs are the following:

- Point-to-Point Tunneling Protocol (PPTP)
- Layer-2 Forwarding (L2F)
- Layer-2 Tunneling Protocol (L2TP)
- IPsec

The PPTP, L2F, and L2TF protocols support dial-up VPN connections. IPsec is used for LAN-to-LAN solutions for remote and regional offices. Table 8.4 describes each of the protocols.

Point-to-Point Tunneling Protocol (PPTP)	Used to ensure messages transmitted from one VPN node to another are secure. It encapsulates PPP packets using a modified version of the generic routing encapsulation (GRE) protocol. The GRE protocol allows PPTP to support other protocols, such as IPX (Internetwork Packet Exchange) and NetBEUI (NetBios Enhanced User Interface) as well as IP. PPTP uses both PAP and CHAP authentication methods. Its disadvantage is that it does not provide strong encryption or allow for key-based methods for authenticating users. [Nortel, 6]
Layer 2 Forwarding Protocol (L2F)	A tunneling protocol developed by Cisco systems. L2F tunneling is not dependent on IP; it can interface with Frame Relay or ATM (Asynchronous Transfer Mode). L2F uses PPP for authentication of a remote user. It allows tunnels to support more than one connection. L2F also supports the following protocols: IP, IPX, and NetBEUI. [Nortel, 6]
Layer 2 Tunneling Protocol (L2TP)	Merges the best features of PPTP and L2F. Requires ISPs to support the protocol. L2TP defines it own tunneling protocol and uses IPsec as its encryption method. It can interface with X.25, Frame-Relay, or ATM. A disadvantage is that it does not include any method to manage cryptographic keys. It uses the same authentication techniques as PPP.
IPsec	Has been widely deployed to implement VPNs. A standard approved by the IETF, it is a security method that operates at the IP layer of the TCP/IP suite. It allows the sender to authenticate or encrypt each IP packet or apply both operations to the packet.

TABLE 8.4 **VPN Protocols**

For LAN-to-LAN connections, IPsec is the preferred method for VPN because it supports several cryptographic methods to provide confidentiality, data integrity, and authentication. The Diffie-Hellman key is used to deliver secret keys between peers on a public network. Public-key cryptography is supported by IPsec to protect the identities of users. IPsec supports bulk encryption algorithms such as DES to encrypt data, and also uses digital certificates for validating public keys and keyed hash algorithms to authenticate packets. [Nortel, 8]

VPNs do not maintain permanent links between the end points of the corporate network. A connection between two sites is created as needed. Similarly, when the connection is no longer needed, it is dismantled to open up the bandwidth for other uses. Clients must have special client software installed on their computers to communicate through the security gateway protecting the destination LAN. [Nortel, 4, 5]

VPNs use carrier protocols to carry information across the LAN-to-LAN connection. VPN packets are formatted to travel through private tunnels through the Internet. Different packet types and tunneling modes are used to send the data.

VPN Packet Format and Modes

The tunneling packet format uses three types of protocols. The IP/UDP protocol is the carrier protocol; L2F is the encapsulation protocol; and PPP is the passenger protocol. The data is contained in the PPP packet. PPP provides authentication and L2F provides encryption for the entire packet.

In a LAN-to-LAN configuration, two modes are used for transporting the packets that are formatted by protocol for transmission over the VPN. In Figure 8.15, transport and tunneling modes are used for the LAN-to-LAN VPN. The tunnel mode is used to establish the private tunnel through the Internet backbone and depends on the Internet to deliver the data to the destination LAN. The transport mode is used between the LAN server and the router to deliver the packets to be transmitted across the Internet.

The private tunnel allows users on either LAN to communicate transparently with each other. Tunneling allows the sender to encapsulate the data in IP packets. The routing and switching infrastructure of the LAN is hidden from the Internet by providing security gateways at each end.

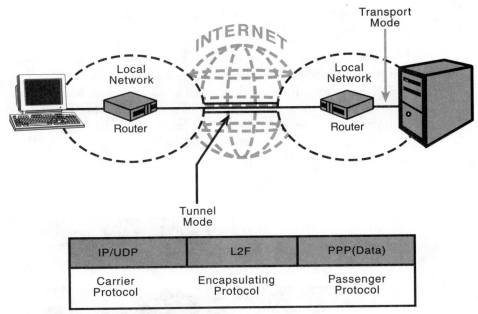

IP/UDP	L2F	PPP(Data)
Carrier Protocol	Encapsulating Protocol	Passenger Protocol

FIGURE 8.15 **VPN Tunnel Mode**

VPN IPsec Packet Format and Modes

Figure 8.16 shows the inside of a packet. At the top layer, the data could be an e-mail message, a Web browser request, or a database transaction. The transport protocol is provided by TCP and UDP. IPsec is at the bottom layer of the packet. IPsec is considered the best VPN solution for IP environments because it provides encryption, authentication, and key management to secure the data.

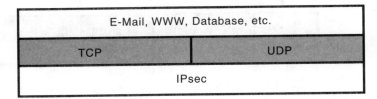

FIGURE 8.16 **IPsec Packet**

Standards developed for network security on IP networks provide for four critical functions:

- **Authentication.** Ensures the identity of the sender of the data.
- **Access Control.** Restricts unauthorized users from gaining access to the LAN.
- **Confidentiality.** Prevents anyone from reading or copying data as it travels across the Internet.

- **Data Integrity**. Guarantees that no one tampers with data as it travels across the Internet.

IPsec uses headers on the packets to provide for these four functions. IPsec has two primary modes of operation: tunneling and transport.

In Figure 8.17, the IPsec headers are placed in different locations with each mode. With tunnel mode, the outer IP header specifies the IPsec processing destination. The inner header is used to specify the destination for the packet. With transport mode, the IPsec header follows directly behind the IP header, but in front of the TCP/UDP packet.

Tunnel Mode

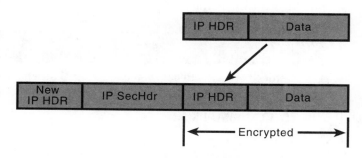

Transport Mode

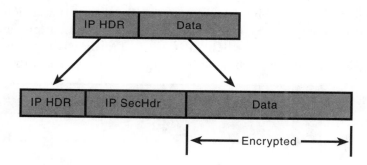

FIGURE 8.17 **Tunnel Mode and Transport Mode [Source: Cisco, 1]**

In summary, the transport mode encrypts only the data portion of each packet. The tunneling protocol is more secure because it encrypts both the header and the data, and also requires a VPN device at the receiver end to decrypt each packet.

VPN Intranets and Extranets

Organizations now use VPN to build intranet and extranet networks for their employees, customers, and business partners.

VPN Intranets

For years, intranets have been built using leased or T1 lines with point-to-point connections between locations. This was once the preferred method to build an intranet because the leased lines were not shared with other companies. That method provided privacy and security for all data passed over the private network. However, these private networks have now become expensive to build and maintain.

Today, organizations are looking instead to VPNs for building their intranets. With the use of IPsec, they finally have the privacy and security provisions they need to feel secure with VPN technology. The deployment of an intranet VPN reduces costs for leased lines and support staff to maintain the network. When using VPN, users can connect to the Internet via ISP POPs. The ISPs and the Internet transport the data to the destination. The ISP purchases and maintains the hardware devices used to support their backbone. The organization then only has to pay the fee required by the ISP to gain access to the Internet. [Search Security, 1]

VPN Extranets

In addition to maintaining intranets, organizations today collaborate more with their primary business partners and customers from outside the organization. The typical intranet resides behind a firewall and is accessible only to employees within the organization. When the organization wants to share information with their partners and customers, it extends the intranet to users outside the organization. This extension of an intranet is called an **extranet**. An extranet should incorporate a firewall, digital certificates, and encryption. Figure 8.18 shows what appears to be an intranet constructed with VPN tunnels between remote offices; however, it also includes business partner and customer locations that are trusted and have shared access of the VPN infrastructure, making it an extranet. [Webopedia, 1]

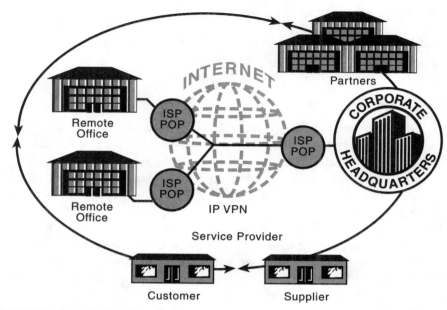

FIGURE 8.18 **VPN Extranet**

Today, extranets are used for several purposes, such as sharing product catalogs exclusively with wholesalers, collaborating with other companies on joint development efforts, and sharing training programs with other companies. VPNs ensure that the proper level of authorized access, encryption, and privacy is provided for a secure extranet. [Search Security, 1]

TOPIC review **Virtual Private Networks (VPNs)**

1. What is the purpose of a security gateway in a VPN?
2. Which protocol is used to provide VPN security for LAN-to-LAN solutions?
3. What is the difference between authentication and access control?
4. How does the deployment of an Internet VPN reduce costs?
5. What are extranets used for and why would an organization want to use one?

FIREWALLS

As you learned in Chapter 6, a firewall is a computer, router, or other communication device that filters access to a protected network. Firewall systems use authentication and filtering policies to build a strong security system. They are an essential component to any WAN security method.

Firewall Systems

Firewalls work closely with network routers to examine each network packet and determine whether or not it should be forwarded to its destination. Many firewall systems used today contain features that control, authenticate, and secure access to the organization's private network. **Filters** are rules that a network engineer specifies in the firewall configuration to either allow or disallow different types of packets, IP addresses, or domain names. When the filters flag an incoming packet of data, the packet is not allowed through. [Carleton, 1] [Search Security, 1] [Brain, 1]

Firewalls control traffic flowing into and out of the network using three methods: *packet filtering*, *proxy service*, and *stateful inspection*.

Packet Filtering

In **packet filtering**, packets are analyzed against a set of filters. If the filters approve a packet, it is sent to the intended receiver. If the packet violates one of the filters, it is discarded. [Brain, 1]

Proxy Service

A **proxy service** makes network requests on behalf of workstation users. A server is set up and configured through software to manage network requests to other servers. The proxy server protects the servers inside the firewall from intrusion. [Search Security, 1]

Stateful Inspection

In **stateful inspection** (also known as dynamic packet filtering), certain key parts of the packet are checked against a database of trusted information. Packets are monitored for specific characteristics. Stateful inspection tracks each connection through each interface of the firewall and makes sure it is valid. It follows administrator-defined rules based on the context that has been established by prior packets that have passed through the firewall. [Webopedia, 1]

Firewall Components and Goals

The primary components of a firewall are listed in Table 8.5.

Network Policy	A policy specific to the firewall that defines the rules used to permit access to the private network. It can permit any service unless it is expressly denied or it can deny any service unless it is expressly permitted.
Advanced Authentication	Some users are granted access from the Internet to selected hosts in a private network. This access is granted based on advanced authentication such as digital certificates with a CA.
Router Packet Filtering	Uses routers and packet filtering rules to grant or deny access. It can either grant or deny access by source address (host) or by port (service).
Application Gateway	Service is provided by processes that maintain complete TCP connection state and sequencing. These processes often re-address traffic so that it appears to have originated from the firewall, rather than the internal host.

TABLE 8.5 **Firewall Components**

Simple methods are preferred for managing the methods and mechanisms used to implement security on a firewall. User identification is vitally important if users are to be allowed to connect through the firewall. The firewall should gather as much information as possible to track security violations. It is easier to compress, consolidate, summarize, and delete log files than it is to capture information on a single event. An effective firewall should do the following:

- Restrict people to enter the network at a carefully controlled point.
- Prevent attackers from getting close to other defenses.
- Restrict people to leave the network at a carefully controlled point.

Types of Firewalls

Several types of firewalls are available that use different methods for filtering or blocking traffic. Some firewalls are combined with application gateways to manage and route application traffic. Four types of firewalls are used today: packet filtering, dual-homed gateway, screened host, and screened subnet firewall.

Packet Filtering Firewalls

A packet filtering firewall uses a packet filtering router installed at the Internet gateway and uses packet filtering rules in the router to block or filter protocols and IP addresses. Workstations within the private network have direct access to the Internet while most access to site systems from the Internet is blocked. Although this is the easiest and most common type of firewall to install, packet-filtering firewalls have several disadvantages, such as:

- Limited logging capability
- Difficulty in testing packet-filtering rules
- Complex filtering rules that can sometimes become unmanageable
- Advanced authentication measures [Wack, 1]

Dual-Homed Gateway Firewall

A **dual-homed gateway** firewall is a complete block to IP traffic between the Internet and the private network. It uses a host system having two network interfaces, and its IP-forwarding capabilities are disabled. Dual-homed gateways creates an inner subnet for specialized servers and modem pools. They must be configured in such a way that no packets can pass unfiltered. The dual-homed gateway provides extensive event logging. However, the second network interface adds to the cost. Another unfortunate disadvantage of a dual-homed gateway firewall is that an attacker might be able to take over the application gateway and, when this happens, the whole security system is lost. Most organizations add a packet filtering router in front of the dual-homed gateway firewall for greater protection. [Bundesamt, 1]

Screened Host Firewall

A **screened host firewall** combines a packet-filtering router with an application gateway. This gateway is located on the protected side of the router, needs only one network interface, and does not require a separate subnet between the application gateway and the router. The router filters or screens dangerous protocols, preventing them from reaching the application gateway. The router operates according to the following rules:

- Application traffic from Internet sites is routed.
- All other traffic from Internet sites is rejected.
- All application traffic from the inside is rejected unless the router can be determined that it came from the application gateway.

Screened Subnet Firewall

A **screened subnet firewall** incorporates an intermediate perimeter network to shield the private network or intranet. On the perimeter network, the host computer is installed, which users can access through two separate routers. One router controls access to the intranet and the second router connects to the Internet. The configuration of the two routers is used to create an inner, screened subnet.

The router that attaches to the Internet operates according to the following rules:

- Application traffic from the application gateway to Internet systems is routed.
- E-mail traffic from the e-mail server is routed.
- FTP and Gopher traffic from Internet sites is routed.
- NFS (Network File System) and NIS (Network Information Service) packets are blocked.

By properly configuring the firewall with the two-router combination, reasonable security can be achieved to protect against Internet intruders.

Firewall Policies

Policies, or rules, are defined as filters. These filters can be customized for each organization, depending upon the strength of security the organization desires. Some of the most common filters used on firewalls are described in Table 8.6.

IP Addresses	The firewall can block all traffic to or from a specific IP address.
Protocols	Filters can be set for IP, TCP, HTTP, FTP, UDP, ICMP, SMTP (Simple Mail Transfer Protocol), SNMP (Simple Network Management Protocol), and Telnet. A special server could be set up for a specific protocol and be restricted from all other servers.
Domain Names	The firewall can block all traffic from specific domain names or allow access only to specific domain names.
Ports	Filters can be set to block certain port access on all servers but one. For example, FTP access uses port 21. Only one server would be allowed to accept data through port 21.

TABLE 8.6 **Firewall Policies**

Specific Words and Phrases	The firewall can be instructed to block certain words or phrases. It has to be a exact match. There is no limit on the number of words or phrases that can be used.

TABLE 8.6 Firewall Policies, continued

Figure 8.19 shows that the firewall is configured to block all Telnet packets from the UNIX host. This is an example of filtering by protocol. Telnet is an application layer service that is part of the TCP/IP suite. It allows a user to remotely log in to another user or server machine that can then execute processes. It makes sense to block this access from servers.

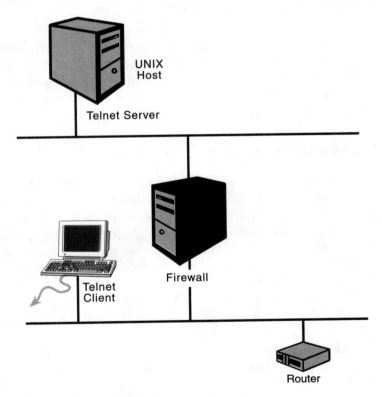

FIGURE 8.19 **Firewall Filters Traffic [Source: Hall, 1]**

Figure 8.20 provides another example of filtering based on protocol. A packet filtering router is used to filter SMTP and Telnet services to specific workstations. These are the only workstations able to receive those services through the firewall.

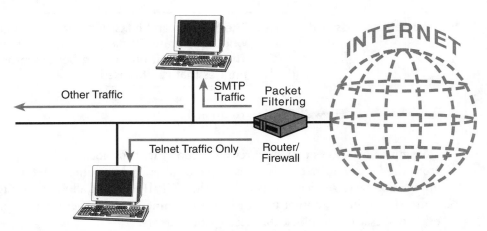

FIGURE 8.20 Packet Filtering Firewall [Source: Hall, 1]

Organizations can use router/firewall combinations to build intranets. Figure 8.21 shows how the router also acts as a firewall to restrict traffic into the intranet. Restricting sections of the intranet to various groups of employees minimizes security concerns. When IPsec is the encryption method, anyone trying to attack the network without proper verifiable credentials will be rejected.

Issues and Problems with Firewalls

Firewalls do a good job of filtering out unwanted traffic but cannot prevent all Internet security problems. Some of the problems with firewalls are the restriction of access to desired services, the potential for infiltration, and the limited protection offered from insider attacks. A strong **security policy** will balance security requirements with user needs. Sometimes a security administrator will open up a protocol or port temporarily for specific projects and then restrict it again when the project is completed.

On some occasions, security administrators will allow a dial-up connection to bypass the firewall. However, when SLIP (Serial Line Internet Protocol) or PPP access is allowed to bypass the firewall, essentially a back door has been created for outsiders as well. Firewalls generally do not provide protection from insider threats. A firewall cannot, for instance, prevent an insider from copying the data to a Zip disk or CDR/W and taking it out of the facility.

A firewall system is less complex than multiple systems. A firewall system concentrates security in one spot as opposed to distributing it to multiple systems. However, firewalls do not provide the level of protection that multiple systems can. They do not protect against viruses transferred through downloads or sent as e-mail attachments.

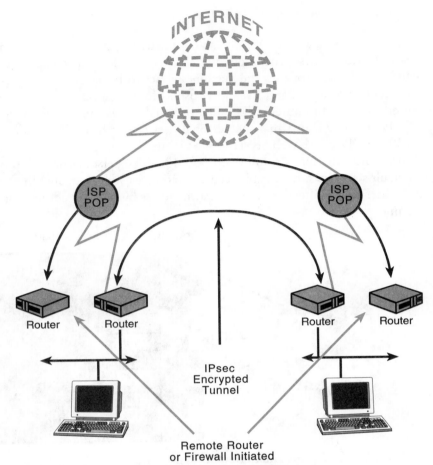

FIGURE 8.21 **Firewall with IPsec Encrypted Tunnel**

The firewall is the predominant protection for a private LAN network. Most organizations have only one firewall. A new software clustering technology called **Reliable Array of Independent Nodes (RAIN)** provides for redundant firewalls. RAIN was originally developed by the California Institute of Technology as a joint development project with NASA's Jet Propulsion Laboratory and the Defense Advanced Research Projects Agency (DARPA). NASA needed a no-downtime system because they couldn't send someone out in space to fix a component that had failed. The software used for RAIN monitors user activity, picks up any failure that might occur, and reroutes the user to the working firewall. [Zipperer, 41]

Personal Firewalls

Many users today have DSL or cable modem access from home to corporate headquarters. These technologies offer always-on high-speed access to the Internet. Because of this, the machines attached to the Internet are vulnerable to security breaches, attacks, and viruses. Most organizations require mobile users and telecommuters to install a personal firewall to protect their machines.

Figure 8.22 shows that the personal firewall can listen in on ports 80 and 139. The Personal Web Server (PWS) is running on port 80 and Windows file and printer sharing is running on port 139. The personal firewall provides for a default setup with reasonable security. However, most personal firewalls allow the user to use filters or rules to restrict access by port, IP address, or domain name.

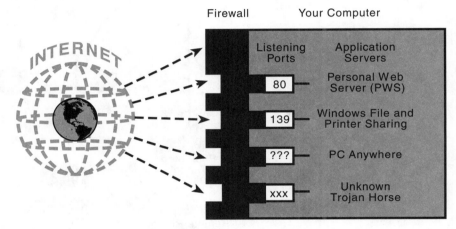

FIGURE 8.22 **Personal Firewall [Source: Boran, 1]**

The increasing complexity of Windows and browser/PC applications has contributed to the continual discovery of security weaknesses. The bottom line is that the longer a user is connected to the Internet, the more likely that user will be attacked. A personal firewall can offer protection from network attacks from hostile networks, prevent an infected e-mail from installing a back door, and help to ensure the user's PC is not used to attack others. At the very least, a personal firewall should alert the user to dangerous attacks, be able to identify the attacker, and defend against known Trojan Horses, viruses, and DoS attacks.

1. What are the three methods used by firewalls to control traffic flow?
2. What is the disadvantage of deploying a dual-homed gateway?
3. What are the most common filters used on firewalls?
4. What are some of the problems associated with firewalls?
5. What type of security threat isn't protected by firewalls?

CHAPTER SUMMARY

The security of an infrastructure is greatly dependent on people and processes. A well-written security policy can protect an organization. The security policy defines who needs access to which services, applications, and data. It also addresses the access points to the network from outside the organization. A detailed analysis specifies what information is being protected and why, and also specifies when access is available during business hours and after business hours. The key to a successful implementation of security is enforcement.

Viruses, worms, Trojan Horses, and other security threats add to an organization's vulnerability to attacks. It is crucial to determine exactly what types of security tools the organization will use to combat these threats. All Internet-accessible systems, including Web servers, e-mail, and DNS servers, should be protected by authentication and authorization. DoS attacks (DDoS, Smurf Attack, Trinoo, TFN, TFN2K, and Stacheldraht) flood the network with a high volume of traffic to render all the computers and servers on the LAN useless.

Encryption protects the privacy, confidentiality, and integrity of information within an organization. Encryption standards (DES, RSA, PKI, digital certificates, IPsec, Kerberos, PGP, SSL, and S-HTTP) help provide secure access to an organization's network. Encryption schemes use algorithms and hash keys to encrypt and decrypt files. These schemes use cryptography to convert plain text data into ciphertext by scrambling it up so that the original information is hidden beneath a level of encryption. Only the person (or machine) doing the scrambling and the recipient of the ciphertext knows how to decrypt (unscramble) it. The problems associated with encrypted keys are they can be lost or stolen.

Today's Internet backbones (ISPs) and VPNs are the future for the corporate network. VPNs save money without sacrificing performance. Several VPN protocols (PPTP, L2F, L2TF, and IPsec) provide for tunneling of data across the Internet. Networks connected by IPsec routers over the Internet are secure because they are encrypted. By using encrypted tunnels, an organization can achieve a security level similar to that offered by a private network created with point-to-point leased lines.

The demand for remote access is growing because users have high-speed access lines (DSL and cable modems) from their homes. Remote users require a secure method to access the primary databases, e-mail, and home directories within their organization. VPNs provide for key signing and digital certificates to authenticate and authorize these users.

With an Internet business infrastructure, all electronic transactions travel over the Internet. Encryption protects the data from being intruded upon while it travels. However, after the data reaches its destination, firewalls are required to filter and block unknown traffic. Firewalls (packet filtering, dual-homed gateway, screen host, and screened subnet) use an examination process that can adequately protect an organization against hackers. Firewalls use policies or filters to block traffic based on IP addresses, protocols, domain names, ports, and specific words or phrases. An organization can change the filters based on its needs and level of security required.

The single point of failure and bottleneck within the network is the firewall. Intrusion-detection systems offer scanning, intrusion testing, and monitoring for password hacking. Therefore, the building of a layered defense strategy, with dual firewalls and an intrusion-detection system is considered the correct approach to provide for a secure network.

CHAPTER REVIEW QUESTIONS

(This quiz can also be printed out from the Encore! CD that accompanies this textbook. File name—Chap08review.)

Circle a letter (a-d) for each question. Choose only one answer for each.

1. Which protocol is used most frequently for remote access to the Internet?
   a. L2F
   b. PPTP
   c. PPP
   d. IPsec

2. Which format is the data in when it is passed over the LAN to the intended user?
   a. Scrambled text
   b. Encrypted text
   c. Plain text
   d. Ciphertext

3. Why are viruses considered security threats?
   a. They target vulnerable systems.
   b. They corrupt or erase organization data.
   c. They attach and replicate throughout an organization.
   d. They disguise themselves and appear as normal programs to a user.

4. Which worm virus launched an attack and replicated itself for the first 20 days of each month?
   a. Code Blue
   b. Code Yellow
   c. Code Orange
   d. Code Red

5. Which client application introduces a pathway for viruses to enter the LAN?
   a. Web browser
   b. LAN client
   c. VPN client
   d. OSI client

6. What is the area behind the firewall that is accessible from the Internet called?
   a. intranet
   b. VPN
   c. DMZ
   d. extranet

7. Which file records failed performance data, unusual system usage, and error conditions?
   a. Audit log
   b. Accounting log
   c. Authentication log
   d. Authorization log

8. What is the variable that is combined with an algorithm to encrypt and decrypt data?
   a. Ciphertext
   b. Cipher
   c. Code
   d. Key

9. What is an electronic "credit card" that establishes your credentials for transactions over the Web called?
   a. Code certificate
   b. Key certificate
   c. Digital certificate
   d. Cipher certificate

10. Which is the preferred encryption protocol for VPNs?
    a. PPP
    b. PPTP
    c. L2F
    d. IPsec

Circle the correct letter (A-E) that corresponds to the descriptions below. Choose only one answer for each.

A. Packet filtering
B. RAIN
C. Advanced authentication
D. Stateful inspection
E. Screened host firewall

11. A B C D E   Compares certain key parts of the packet to a database of trusted information.

12. A B C D E   Packets are analyzed against a set of filters.

13. A B C D E   Some users are granted access from the Internet to selected hosts in a private network.

14. A B C D E   A software clustering technology called Reliable Array of Independent Nodes.

15. A B C D E   Combines a packet-filtering router with an application gateway.

A. L2TP
B. VPN
C. Confidentiality
D. PPTP
E. Data integrity

16. A B C D E   Prevents anyone from reading or copying data as it travels across the Internet.

17. A B C D E   Used to ensure that messages are transmitted from one VPN node to another securely.

18. A B C D E   Tunneling protocol used to interface with X.25, Frame Relay, or ATM.

19. A B C D E   A private data network through a public telecommunications network or the Internet.

20. A B C D E   Guarantees that no one tampers with data as it travels across the Internet.

INTERNET EXERCISES

1. Log on to the Internet, key

   www.sans.org/top20.htm

   and answer the following questions:

   A. _____ References used to identify the top priority vulnerabilities.
   B. _____ The top 20 scanner can be downloaded from this Web site (URL).
   C. _____ Where (URL) can you find the vulnerability indexing service?
   D. _____ Which organization has developed a consensus benchmark for minimum-security configuration of Solaris and Windows 2000, based on the combined experience and knowledge of more than 170 organizations from a dozen countries?

2. Key the following URL:

   www.nist.gov/public_affairs/techbeat/tb9810.htm

   Select the first option, *NIST Sponsors Historic Data Scrambling Battle.* Answer the following questions.

   1. _____ What was the number of the position shift used by Alexander the Great to encode messages to his army commanders?
   2. _____ What encryption standard are they trying to break?
   3. _____ How many countries submitted candidates for the Advanced Encryption Standard?
   4. _____ Who has been asked to attack each of the formulas to discover weaknesses that could crack the codes?

CONCEPT EXERCISES

Concept Narrative
(This narrative exercise can also be printed out from the Encore! CD that accompanies this textbook. File name—Chap08connar.)

Fill in the blanks of the following description with the correct answers.

Computers use _____ to scramble ordinary text (plain text) into _____ (encryption). Cryptography is designed to protect: confidentiality, the information can only be read by the intended receiver;

integrity, the information cannot be altered in storage or transit between sender and intended receiver; non-repudiation, the sender of the information cannot, at a later stage, deny their intentions in the creation nor deny transmission of the information; and authentication, the sender and receiver can confirm each other's identity and the origin/destination of the information.

Encryption standards use mathematical algorithms to create _____ as a method to encrypt the text. Ciphers are codes and can use symbol substitution for letters or manipulate the text by letter substitution, such as representing an A with an F. After text has been encrypted using the cipher, it becomes ciphertext. Most ciphers used today use a key to _____ and _____ text. The _____ is a variable that is combined with an algorithm. An _____, in this instance, is a formula that is used to scramble the unencrypted text. The length of the key determines how difficult the text will be to decrypt.

The cryptographic key and algorithm applied to a block of data usually 64 bits at once as a group rather than to 1 bit at a time is called a _____ _____. An initialization vector is derived from a random-number generator and is applied with the text in the first block and key. This prevents identical messages encrypted on the same day from producing identical ciphertext. When a cryptographic key and algorithm are applied to each binary digit in a data stream, one bit at a time, it is called a _____ _____. As the block cipher has become the preferred method, this method is rarely used today.

Encryption using keys ensures that only the person with the key can decode a message. The sender and receiver of a message share a single, common key called a _____ _____ to encrypt and decrypt the message. This key must be exchanged in a secure way. It is also necessary that the key be installed on each of the two computers that will be exchanging data. On the other hand, _____ _____ encryption is a secret key that is known only to the two people that exchange messages. There is a risk inherent with a secret key in that if the key is lost or stolen, the data is essentially lost because it cannot be decrypted.

When a designated authority is used to apply a private key to encrypt messages and digital signatures to authenticate the identity of the sender, it is called _____ _____ encryption. The digital signature ensures that the original content of the message or document has not been modified.

Concept Table

(This table exercise can also be printed out from the Encore! CD that accompanies this textbook. File name—Chap08contab.)

Following are some statements, some of which describe one type of WAN security. Others describe an attack that might be prevented. Please make an "X" under the type of security that relates to each statement. Use only one "X" per statement.

STATEMENT	TYPES OF WAN SECURITY		
	FIREWALLS	ANTIVIRUS	INTRUSION DETECTION
1. Web pages are replaced on infected servers with a page that reads "Hacked by the Chinese."			
2. A bandwidth attack used to flood the network with a high volume of traffic so that all network resources are consumed.			
3. Compares certain key parts of the packet to a database of trusted information.			
4. Replicates itself by automatically mailing itself to everyone in the user's e-mail address book.			
5. The agent programs attack one or more servers by flooding the network with UDP packets.			
6. Blocks all Telnet packets from the UNIX host.			
7. Disguises itself and appears to the user as a normal computer program, such as a game program.			
8. Performs system monitoring for activities by users and number of attempted logins.			
9. Blocks all traffic to or from a specific IP address.			
10. A small piece of software that uses computer networks and security holes to replicate itself.			

Concept Picture

(This picture exercise can also be printed out from the Encore! CD that accompanies this textbook. File name—Chap08conpic.)

In this exercise, look at the picture of the encryption methods and label the missing elements.

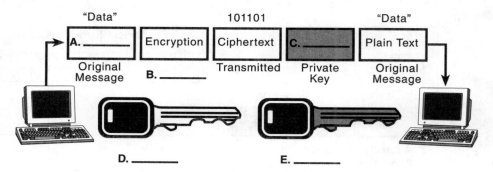

A. _____
B. _____
C. _____
D. _____
E. _____

CASE STUDY

CHILDREN'S HOSPITAL

Objective:

Investigate alternatives for intrusion-detection technology that can be used to protect an organization from various Internet security threats.

Company Profile:

Children's Hospital is a 350-bed facility specializing in pediatric care located in Kennebunkport, Maine. Doctors and nurses depend on the applications provided by the hospital information system to keep track of patient records. Doctors on occasion need to access patient information from their offices or homes when emergencies occur. If the applications at the hospital fail, the doctors and nurses have to use paper forms to record data and enter the information into the system later.

Current Situation:

Recently, the hospital suffered a major outage due to a DoS attack. The firewall was overwhelmed with abnormal network traffic, and access to the hospital network was down for two days. Nurses rely on the patient information database application to keep track of the exact dosages of specific medicines given to patients. During the two-day period in which the application was down, the data regarding the exact time intervals of medicine dispersal was lost. As nurses could not rely on memory to give the correct doses to patients, the loss of the system affected the progress of some patients' scheduled surgeries.

Business Information Requirements:

Since the security threat incident occurred, the doctors and nurses are demanding 99.9% uptime on the patient information database system. The consequences of server downtime have upset the operations of the emergency room, operating rooms, admitting offices, and inpatient care facilities. Doctors feel that having access to patient records quickly is essential to successful treatment of their patients.

Communication System Requirements:

The IT department feels more than just a firewall is required to protect the hospital from unknown security threats or attacks. IT must be able to monitor for suspicious activities and correlate abnormal network behavior quickly. The existing firewall has been configured to block certain known IP addresses and they have restricted the use of common TCP/IP protocols such as HTTP, FTP, and SMTP to specific servers. However, the hospital is still vulnerable to DoS attacks and is ready to investigate and implement an intrusion-detection system.

Information System Solution:

1. The IT department created a DMZ and moved the mail relay and a Web server into it. The Web server provides Web access to the patient database. Password access protects the patient record information.
2. An encrypted IP tunnel was created to allow remote access for doctors from their offices and homes.
3. An intrusion-detection system was installed to observe deviations from normal behavior and report abnormal network traffic to the security administrator.
4. The security administrator started to monitor the logs on the intrusion-detection system in order to audit attack information.
5. The intrusion-detection system began scanning network traffic continuously and compiling relationship correlations when multiple access devices were being targeted.

Children's Hospital has averted several security threats since the installation of the intrusion-detection system shown in Figure 8.23. The new system has been installed for 60 days and they have not experienced any downtime. The security administrator has received about 10 notifications of possible security threats. Only 5 of these required corrective action. The IT department feels the hospital avoided what in the past would have caused substantial downtime.

The IT department is pleased with the installation of the intrusion-detection system and does not know how the hospital lived without it before. The doctors are happy with the Web access to the patient information database. They now have faster access for retrieving patient records and they can retrieve them quickly from home or the office.

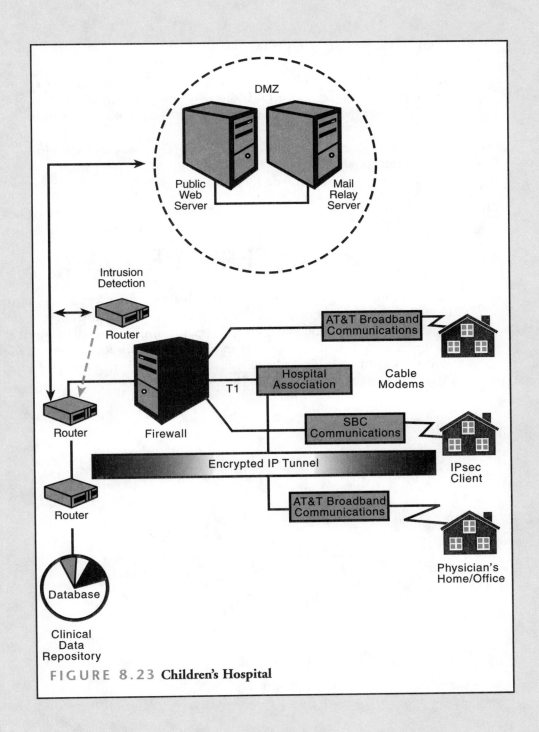

FIGURE 8.23 **Children's Hospital**

CASE STUDY QUESTIONS:

1. Why do you think Children's built out a DMZ for further protection?
2. Will the installation of a DMZ prevent future security attacks?
3. Why can't the firewall protect them against new unknown security threats?
4. What services will be provided by the installation of an intrusion-detection system?
5. What types of activities do they need to monitor to protect the hospital from DoS attacks in the future?

GROUP TERM PROJECT

In this section of the project, you need to define a contingency plan. Print the file *WANCon* from the Encore! CD that comes with this book. Start to think about what could go wrong with the implementation. What could happen that would require de-installation or delay in installing the system into production? Fill in the Contingency Plan, define the tasks, the people responsible, number of days required, and start and end dates.

WAN CONTINGENCY PLAN

DE-INSTALLATION PLAN

I. Contingency De-Installation Plan Overview/Strategy

II. Contingency De-Installation Plan Task List

Task #	Contingency/De-Installation Plan Task Description	Resource Required Days	Responsible Person	Start Date mm/dd/yy	End Date mm/dd/yy

CHAPTER TERMS

CHAPTER BIBLIOGRAPHY

Book, Magazine, Presentation Citations

Conry-Murray, Andrew. "Sony Pictures Casts Intrusion Detection in Starring Role for Network Security," *Network Magazine,* July 2002: 58-63.

Feghhi, Jalal & Jalil Feghhi. *Secure Networking with Windows 2000 and Trust Services.* Boston: Addison-Wesley, 2001: 221.

Laudon, Kenneth & Carol Traver. *E-commerce Business, Technology, Society.* Boston: Addison-Wesley, 2002: 245, 257, 260.

Zipperer, John. *Bayer Stabilizes Its Firewalls.* A Penton Publication: Internet World, July 2002: 40-41.

Web Citations

Adams, Carlisle "The CAST-256 Encryption Algorithm," Entrust, <http://www.entrust.com/resources/pdf/cast-256.pdf> (3 November 1997).

Boran, Sean, "Personal Firewalls/Intrusion Detection Systems, Security Portal, <http://www.securityportal.com/articles/pf_main20001023.html> 26 January 2001).

Brain, Marshall, "How Computer Viruses Work," How Stuff Works, <www.howstuffworks.com/virus.htm> (2002).

Brain, Marshall, "How Encryption Works," How Stuff Works, <www.howstuff works.com/encryption.htm> (2002).

Bundesamt, "Selecting a Suitable Firewall," IT Baseline Protection Manual, <http://www.bsi.bund.de/gshb/english/s/s2073.htm> (July, 1999).

Carleton, L., "Firewalls, What they are and how they work," University of Colorado, <http://www-ece.engr.ucf.edu/~jza/classes/4781/Firewalls/firewall.html> (26 July 1999).

CEPS, "Welcome to the CEPSCO LLC Web Site," CEPSCO, <www.cepsco.com/cgi/home.pl> (2000).

Cisco, "Building a Perimeter Security Solution with the Cisco Secure Integrated Software," Cisco Systems, <www.cisco.com/warp/public/cc/pd/iosw/ioft/iofwft/tech/firew_wp.htm> (2 July 2002).

Cisco, "Extranet VPN Design, Cisco Systems, <www.cisco.com/warp/public/779/largeent/design/extranet_vpn.html> (2000).

Cisco, "Site to Site VPN Design," Cisco Systems, <www.cisco.com/warp/public/779/largeent/design/intranet_vpn.html> (2000).

Cole, Eric, "Securing the corporate jewels with a DMZ," Web Management News & Analysis, <searchWebmanagement.techtarget.com/qna/0,289202,sid27_gci820120,00.html> (29 April 2002).

Evers, Joris, "Study: Web more vulnerable now than ever," IDG News Service, <www.nwfusion.com/news/2002/0702netcraft.html> (2 July 2002).

Guel, Michele, "A Short Primer for Developing Security Policies," SANS Institute, <http://www.sans.org> (2001).

Hall, Eric, "Internet Firewall Essentials," Network Computing, <hechWeb.cmp.com/nc/netdesign/wall2.htm> (28 January 1997).

IBM, "Linking security needs to e-business evolution," IBM e.Business Infrastructure, <www-1.ibm.com/services/security/> (July 2001).

Ingrian, "Content Encryption Service Engine," Ingrian Networks, <www2.ingrian.com/techlib/whitepapers/wp1.htm> (2002).

Nortel, "Virtual Private Networks (VPNs), Web ProForum, <www. iec.org> (2001).

Paller, Alan, "Fighting Back Against Cybercriminals," SANS Institute, <www.sans.org/newlook/resources/FBACC/sld001.htm> (4 May 2000).

Paul, Brooke, "Building an In-Depth Defense," Network Computing, <www.networkcomputing.com/1214/1214ws1.html> (9 July 2001).

Price, Katherine, "Intrusion Detection Pages," Coast, <www.cerias.purdue.edu/coast/intrusion-detection/welcome.html> (17 February 2002).

Qwest, "Hosting and Access Services," Qwest Communications, <www.qwest.com/> (2002).

SANS Institute, "The Twenty Most Critical Internet Security Vulnerabilities," SANS Institute, <www.sans.org/top20.htm> (2 May 2002).

Search Security, "Cipher," Tech Target, <searchsecurity.techtarget.com/sDefinition/0,,sid14_gci213593,00.html> (2002).

Search Security, " Block Cipher," Tech Target, <searchsecurity.techtarget.com/sDefinition/0,,sid14_gci213594,00.html> (2002).

Search Security, "Stream Cipher," Tech Target, <searchsecurity.techtarget.com/sDefinition/0,,sid14_gci213595,00.html> (2002).

Search Security, "Digital Certificate," Tech Target, <searchsecurity.techtarget.com/sDefinition/0,,sid14_gci211947,00.html> (2002).

Search Security, "PKI," Tech Target,
<searchsecurity.techtarget.com/sDefinition/0,,sid14_gci214299,00.html>
(2002).

Search Security, "International Data Encryption Algorithm," Tech Target,
<searchsecurity.techtarget.com/sDefinition/0,,sid14_gci213675,00.html>
(2002).

Search Security, "Pretty Good Privacy," Tech Target,
<searchsecurity.techtarget.com/sDefinition/0,,sid14_gci214292,00.html>
(2002).

Search Security, "Kerberos," Tech Target,
<searchsecurity.techtarget.com/sDefinition/0,,sid14_gci212437,00.html>
(2002).

Search Security, "IPsec," Tech Target,
<searchsecurity.techtarget.com/sDefinition/0,,sid14_gci214037,00.html>
(2002).

Search Security, "RSA," Tech Target,
<searchsecurity.techtarget.com/sDefinition/0,,sid14_gci214273,00.html>
(2002).

Search Security, "Data Encryption Standard," Tech Target,
<searchsecurity.techtarget.com/sDefinition/0,,sid14_gci213893,00.html>
(2002).

Search Security, "Digital Signature," Tech Target,
<searchsecurity.techtarget.com/sDefinition/0,,sid14_gci211953,00.html>
(2002).

Search Security, "Registration Authority," Tech Target,
<searchsecurity.techtarget.com/sDefinition/0,,sid14_gci214245,00.html>
(2002).

Search Security, "Certificate Authority," Tech Target,
<searchsecurity.techtarget.com/sDefinition/0,,sid14_gci213831,00.html>
(2002).

Search Web Management, "Open Profiling Standard," Tech Target,
<searchWebmanagement.techtarget.com/sDefinition/
0,,sid27_gci214208,00.html> (2002).

Search Web Management, "Platform for Privacy Preferences Project," Tech
Target, <searchWebmanagement.techtarget.com/sDefinition/
0,,sid27_gci214227,00.html> (2002).

Stein, Lincoln & John Stewart, "The World Wide Web Security FAQ," World
Wide Web Consortium, <www.w3.org/Security/Faq/wwwsf1.html> (28 July
2001).

Taylor, Laura, "DMZs for dummies," Tech Update,
<www.zdnet.com/filters/printerfriendly/0,6061,2717224-92,00.html> (9
May 2001).

Wack, John, "Putting the Pieces Together: Firewall Examples," NIST Publications,
<csrc.ncs1.nist.gov/nistpubs/800-10/node54.html> (9 February 1995).

Webopedia, "Encryption," Webopedia, <www.Webopedia.com> (2002).

Webopedia, "Security Policy," Webopedia, <www.Webopedia.com> (2002).

Webopedia, "Kerberos," Webopedia, <www.Webopedia.com> (2002).

Webopedia, "IPsec," Webopedia, <www.Webopedia.com> (2002).

Webopedia, "Pretty Good Privacy," Webopedia, <www.Webopedia.com> (2002).

PART THREE
WAN Applications and Services

CHAPTER 9
BUSINESS/APPLICATION SERVICE MODELS

By the end of this chapter, you should understand these concepts:
- The issues and business challenges faced by organizations planning to deliver products and services electronically over the Internet.
- The basic elements of e-commerce systems and the architectures used for them.
- Benefits and disadvantages of different application delivery models for e-commerce applications over the WAN.
- The difference between two-tier and three-tier architectures used for client-server and ASP software delivery models.
- Fault-tolerant methods, such as server farms, load balancing, and server clustering, designed to ensure high availability of e-commerce systems.
- The benefits of centralizing critical company information into integrated Enterprise Resource Planning (ERP) databases.
- Data exchange methods used between suppliers and buyers with an eHub private marketplace.
- Factors and guidelines to consider when designing Web server connections to the Internet.
- Security techniques used to protect e-commerce systems from hackers.
- The role ISPs play in enabling buyers and sellers to reach e-commerce systems.

The convenience of using the Internet has transformed industries and how they transact business. Today, ordinary users log on to the Web for personal needs and to purchase products and have them shipped to their homes. A new competitive strategy for serving the needs of these users has emerged. Organizations must now strive to provide traditional business processes over the Internet.

BUSINESS AND THE INTERNET

Figure 9.1 shows several of the business models that challenge organizations today. To provide network access for any of these business models, network designers need to fully understand how each business model works, what it is trying to accomplish, the expected traffic flows, and the number of locations within the organization to be included.

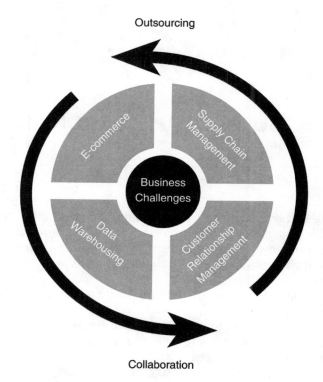

Outsourcing

Supply Chain Management

E-commerce

Business Challenges

Customer Relationship Management

Data Warehousing

Collaboration

FIGURE 9.1 **Business Challenges**

Collaboration

In the past, workers could collaborate in person, by letter, or by telephone. Today, employees within the same organization are often located in different parts of the world. Collaboration methods have evolved to allow these workers to display documents online and discuss the contents via e-mail, teleconferencing, or video conferencing. **Electronic collaboration** enables individuals to connect electronically via the Internet using e-mail. **Teleconferencing**, once limited to telephone use, now allows employees to hold conferences over an Internet connection. **Video conferencing** is essentially teleconferencing with pictures. [Webopedia, 1]

To be effective, visual and audio communications must occur immediately in real time. This has required organizations to develop new methods of communication over the WAN. Presently these electronic collaboration methods include corporate instant messaging, white boarding, live group discussions, and document collaboration. **Instant messaging** allows a person to "chat" with another user who is online at the same time. **White boarding** uses a display screen, so that multiple users can write or draw on the screen and the people on the other end can both see and hear the ideas being presented. White boards use teleconferencing applications to share documents, visual presentations, and engineering drawings. It is expected that the enterprise-collaboration-tools market will increase significantly as companies turn to it to provide new ways for teams to share information without direct personal contact. To respond to consumer demand for these types of applications, design for the WAN needs to encompass both real time and asynchronous products over the Internet. [Webopedia, 1]

E-Commerce

E-commerce involves conducting traditional business operations, such as the selling and purchasing of products over the Internet, as well as electronic collaboration between members and suppliers. An e-commerce application can provide catalogs of items, pricing sheets, rapid order entry, inventory status reports, and shipping notification.

As shown in Figure 9.2, users of e-commerce applications can create purchase requisitions, have them approved, and generate purchase orders all through the Web applications server. They can see pictures of the products they are ordering, review prices and quantities, and submit purchase orders. After the order is submitted, it is stored in the database. Program logic then tells it to send a notification to supplier fulfillment where the product is loaded and shipped. [Kalakota, 234]

As large firms become more comfortable with using e-commerce, they will test the boundaries of their networks' capabilities through the use of various kinds of *applications software*. **Applications software** can include database programs that provide the rules for the business process, logical flow of transactions, electronic catalogs, pricing, and reporting information. However, many organizations cannot afford to purchase their own application software for e-commerce. Instead, they contract with third-party companies called *hosting companies* that provide the **hosting platform**, which is the hardware and application software used to manage their business activities. The **computing architecture** is the design and placement of servers, databases, backup devices, and telecommunications links. Although it varies for each e-commerce application, e-commerce systems are designed for 365-day, 24-hour management and availability. Customers can order at any time day or night and expect their orders to be processed in a timely manner. The network includes the architecture, the platform, and the link to the Internet to support access by customers and business partners. [Giotto, 1]

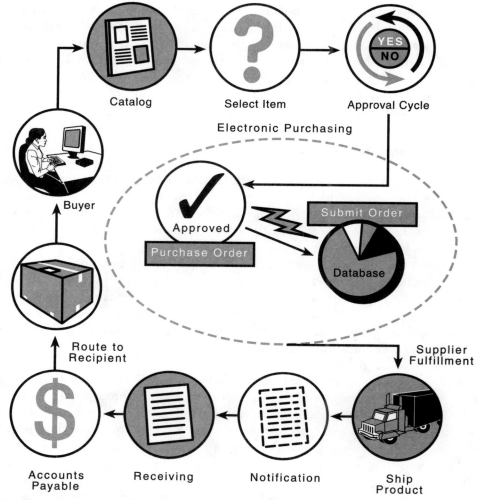

FIGURE 9.2 **E-Commerce [Source: Kalakota, 234]**

Data Warehousing

As companies process more of their orders online, a database called a **data warehouse** becomes necessary to log all of the transactions. This **database** is used for offline analysis on the number and types of orders received. Data warehouses grow very quickly and in some cases terabytes of storage are required to store the data. Basically, a data warehouse provides a centralized storage repository to consolidate customer data and transaction information. [Laudon & Traver, 369-370]

Figure 9.3 shows an example of a retail data warehouse located in the center as the main consolidation point with data coming in from several sources (A-E). From these sources, sales, merchandising, marketing, and financial data are gathered. A Web-based architecture is provided for the customer and business partner interface to the data warehouse. Security is provided by a firewall with access to the data warehouse controlled by login ID and URL access. [Johnson, 1]

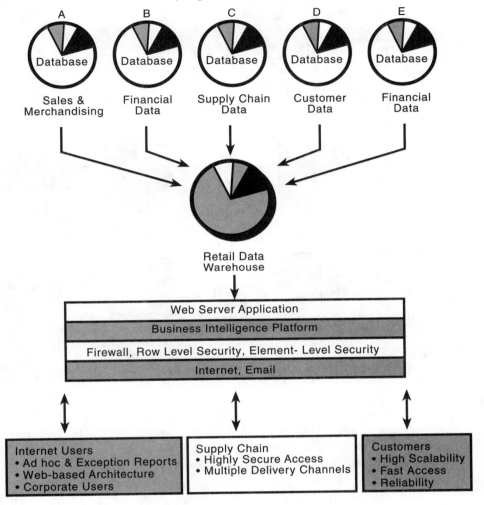

FIGURE 9.3 **Data Warehouse [Source: Johnson, 1]**

Outsourcing

Organizations are rethinking their Internet-based business strategies, and viewing outsourcing as an increasingly important component. Web hosting providers offer managed firewall services along with security monitoring devices. Figure 9.4 shows several Web and database servers managed by the provider. The provider extends services for physical connectivity to the Internet, storage, tape backup, offsite disaster recovery, and telecommunications links to the Internet.

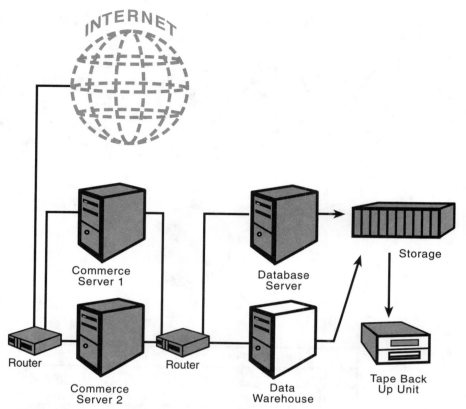

FIGURE 9.4 **Outsourcing E-Commerce Services [Source: Laudon and Traver, 209]**

Information such as price lists and product catalogs are among the documents published on an e-commerce Web site. This information is referred to as Web content. This content, in turn, is classified as an intangible company asset known as **intellectual property**. Many companies contract with other companies to manage their Web content. Unfortunately, by doing this the companies are essentially creating a hole in the security protecting their intellectual property. To address this, **outsourcing** agreements are needed. These agreements provide rigid guidelines regarding the use of Web content by the company providing outsourcing services. They allow client companies to maintain control over the use of their content. The use of outsourcing for Web hosting is growing in popularity and is expected to increase by 39% each year through 2005. [Lake, 1]

Supply Chain Management

Supply chain management involves matching procurement activities between buyers and sellers within an industry. Most suppliers have long-term contracts for products. Likewise, buyers usually have established volume-purchasing agreements. Supply chain management links the buying, selling, and shipping activities into a single e-commerce system to run over the Internet. This development has led to a more cost-effective business model in which companies don't need to stockpile inventory because production can begin when an order is received. [Kalakota, 274]

Supply chain management is considered a business-to-business model (B2B) because it links buyers and suppliers together. In 1999, the volume of B2B transactions exceeded $145 billion and the projection for 2004 is $7 trillion. [Hirsh, 1]

Customer Relationship Management

Customer Relationship Management (CRM) is a database created to store information about a company's relationships with all of its customers. This database keeps track of customer service requirements and summarizes product purchases. CRM applications are currently moving toward browser-based Web sites, replacing previous client-server applications. This approach provides the opportunity to reach large corporate workforces distributed across many locations worldwide.

Figure 9.5 shows that CRM exists between inventory and shipping. Follow-up on purchases and fulfillment tracking is done through the e-commerce system. Organizations are able to configure the system to give out the information they require by requesting customized reports.

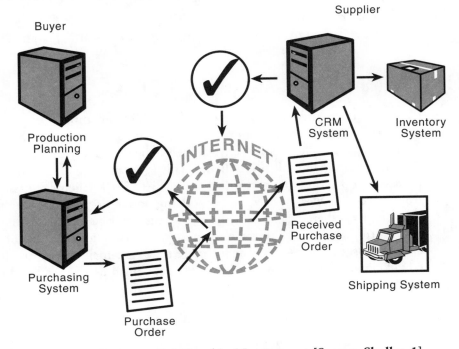

FIGURE 9.5 **Customer Relationship Management [Source: Sholler, 1]**

WAN Service Availability

The efficiency of a WAN is vital to the success of any e-commerce application. If users of the software application suffer disconnections or slow response time, they might become unwilling to adopt or continue to use the system. Unfortunately, the availability of WAN services can vary from location to location. Additionally, company budgets can play a role in determining which services are available at each location. When planning for an e-commerce implementation, a thorough analysis of the current WAN connections from each customer or business partner site is required.

The architecture chosen to support the interaction between the user and the server can significantly affect performance over the WAN. WANs have two common architectures: client-server and application server. Within these architectures, different methods are used to manage the application and the delivery model.

TOPIC *review* **Business and the Internet**

1. How has the demand for real-time applications impacted the WAN?
2. What are several benefits derived from e-commerce?
3. What is the difference between the computing architecture and the network used to support e-commerce?
4. What is supply chain management?
5. Why might WAN services vary in different parts of the country?

CLIENT-SERVER ARCHITECTURE

Client-server architecture is a network in which each computer or process is either a client or a server. **Clients** are PCs or workstations on which users run applications. In a client-server environment, clients that have an application on their workstation are called **fat clients**. This is because the bulk of the data-processing operations are performed at the client itself. Clients request services from servers for files, devices, and processing power. **Servers** are more powerful than clients and are machines dedicated to managing processes, storing data, and controlling network traffic into and out of an application. One of the most common uses of client-server architecture today is e-mail. In this architecture, e-mail client software is installed on a PC enabling a user to send and receive messages through an e-mail server.

Two-Tier Architecture

A client-server architecture is sometimes called a **two-tier architecture**, as shown in Figure 9.6. In a two-tier architecture, the user interface runs on the client and the database is stored on the server. The client is shown making a request over the network to the server. The server then provides a response to the client request. The software application logic can either run on the client or on the server. On the server side, a collection of programs is used called a **database management system (DMBS)**. This enables a client to communicate with the database to store, modify, and extract information. [Webopedia, 1]

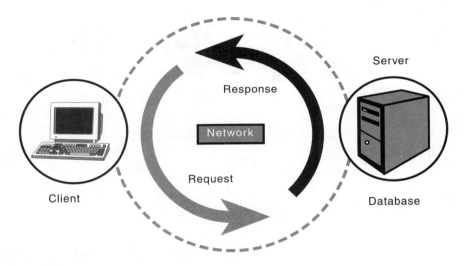

FIGURE 9.6 Two-Tier Architecture

An automatic teller machine at a bank is an example of a database management system. It allows customers to check the database to find out their bank balance, and to transfer and withdraw funds. Banks allow two types of processing with bank accounts: transaction processing and batch processing. **Transaction processing** is a type of computer processing in which the computer responds immediately to user requests. Each request is considered a transaction. **Batch processing** involves a batch of requests that is stored and then executed all at one time. [Whatis, 1]

Computer System Processing

In the past, computer systems used a method called **centralized processing** in which all the programs and software logic were executed in a central computer called a mainframe. The clients used terminals, which lacked any memory or disk storage. Consequently, they could only process commands back to the mainframe, which would then execute processes and programs (see Figure 9.7). [Webopedia, 1]

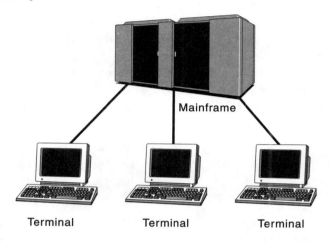

FIGURE 9.7 Centralized Processing

When client-server architecture came along, **distributed processing** began to be used with computer systems. This is a method in which both the client and the server execute part of the process. The business logic is therefore split between the client and server. This was made possible by the development of the PC, which has its own memory, CPU, and disk space. Computing is distributed when the computer programming and data that computers use is spread out over multiple servers (see Figure 9.8). Distributed processing is network-based, whereas centralized processing is one-device processing. [Webopedia, 1]

Most business applications written today use the client-server model. Client-server models use a **distributed computing environment** in which computing and data exchange is distributed over a system of distributed computers. In a large network system, several servers are scattered geographically. Users or clients can access applications and databases at servers remote from their locations. The network expands to accommodate the need for access to information available anywhere within the organization. In between headquarters and remote networks, intermediate applications called *middleware* and devices called *gateways* provide an interface between the applications and databases. [Whatis, 1]

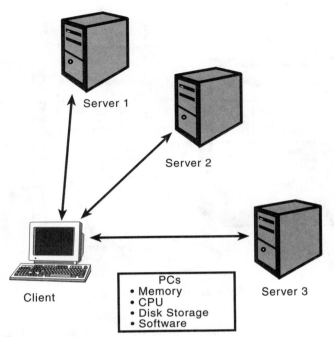

FIGURE 9.8 **Distributed Processing**

Middleware

With client-server platforms, **middleware** is used to connect two otherwise separate applications. Middleware passes data between them using querying and messaging techniques. The user's client makes a request for data and the middleware program passes the request through to the database server. Figure 9.9 shows that middleware provides the structure around which network applications communicate across the network. [Network Computing, 1]

The client interface to the database server is provided by middleware client software. An *application programming interface* is used to communicate to the operating system or to another software application or database. An **application programming interface (API)** is a set of routines, protocols, and tools used for building software applications. The application programmers write an API to make requests and process replies with the operating system or database application. [Webopedia, 1]

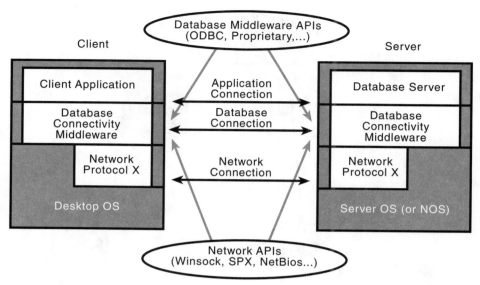

FIGURE 9.9 **Middleware [Network Computing, 1]**

In Figure 9.9, a standard database access method API called **Open Database Connectivity (ODBC)** is used to provide access to all data from any application regardless of which database management system (DBMS) is handling the data. It inserts a middle layer called a *database driver* between an application and the database. The **database driver** translates the application's queries into commands that the database can understand and execute. Middleware provides a link between the database driver and the data access software. ODBC is commonly used with databases such as Microsoft Access, DB2, SAP, and Oracle. ODBC also can be used to interface with Excel spreadsheet files and standard text files. [Microsoft, 1]

Another technique used with databases and ODBC is an interface with **Structured Query Language (SQL)**. SQL is a standard programming language used to get information from and into a database. ODBC handles the SQL request and converts it into a request that the database system understands. SQL uses a command language to select, insert, and update data in a database. ODBC allows programs to use SQL requests to access databases without having to know the proprietary interfaces to the databases. [Microsoft, 1]

Client-server models often use **remote procedure calls (RPC)** to assist in the communication between the database server and the network. RPC is a type of protocol that allows a program on one computer to execute a program on a server computer. With RPC, the client program sends a procedure call to the server to execute a program and the server returns the results of the program executed back to the client. RPC is a synchronous operation that requires the requesting program to be suspended until the results of the remote procedure are returned. [Whatis, 1]

Another middleware technique used for communication between the database server and client is **message queuing**. Messages are exchanged between client and server regarding events, requests, and replies. In the middle is a messaging server, which acts as a message exchange program for client programs. Messaging enables programs to communicate across different programming languages, compilers, and operating systems. [Microsoft, 1]

Client-server models that use middleware are able to provide a bridge between the client and the server allowing them to interact. However, the client still needs a client software application on every desktop and laptop to interface with the application and the middleware.

Gateways

With middleware, client and server do not need to have intimate knowledge of each other to process data requests. Middleware provides its own API for client applications. However, when clients need access to remote databases located in another city or country, sometimes database gateways are used. A **database gateway** is an intermediary device or server that accepts connections from clients using one set of APIs and network protocols to another remote site using a completely different set of APIs and protocols. The database gateway translates the APIs and protocols between the client and server systems. [Network Computing, 1]

In Figure 9.10 (page 460), the protocol on the client side is "X" and the protocol on the server side is "Y." In between the servers are two database gateways, each of which can translate protocol "X" to protocol "Y" and vice versa. The database gateway offloads the overhead of translating the protocol and APIs from the database server.

Client-Server over the WAN

Most client-server applications operate less efficiently over the WAN than over the LAN. Over a LAN, users have the advantage of high-speed access to databases over 100 Mbps connections. Most WAN connections, however, are low bandwidth connections, typically from 56 Kbps to 1.5 Mbps. End users experience slower response times because of increased latency over the WAN. With client-server architectures, request/response exchanges are sent over the WAN continuously between client and server. A single data request from the client can generate hundreds of small packets. Each of these packets is sent individually and requires an acknowledgment before the next packet can be sent. The transmission delay or latency of the WAN controls how quickly the client can ask for more data. [Jessup, 1]

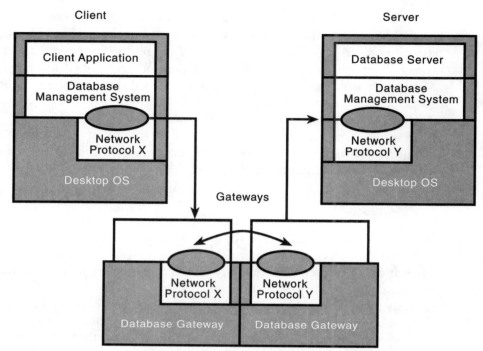

FIGURE 9.10 **Database Gateways [Source: Network Computing, 1]**

Several factors add to the time it takes for a conversation to take place between the client and the server over a WAN. Switches and routers add processing delay when they move packets between ports and queuing delay when they hold packets in buffers.

In addition, the length of a circuit can cause an unavoidable slowdown because of the physics of the transmission. The delay occurs when a circuit cannot support the amount of information being relayed at the speed it is being processed. Propagation delay is measured as the time it takes for a signal to travel from one point to another. Regardless of the amount of bandwidth, a circuit that is 5,000 kilometers in length regularly incurs 60 milliseconds of propagation delay. For this reason, sometimes organizations choose to use leased lines to enhance performance over a WAN. [Jessup, 1] Several solutions are available to address the propagation delay issue:

- Position the database servers closer to the clients.
- Select WAN services that have the lowest latency.
- Shift clients to servers at a central site.
- Monitor traffic generated by routing updates, service advertisements, name queries, and SNMP (Simple Network Management Protocol) alerts.
- Filter unroutable protocols off the WAN.
- Use link state routing protocols such as OSPF (Open Shortest Path First)

and EIGRP (Enhanced Interior Gateway Routing Protocol) over the WAN.

- Have software developers optimize application code to speed up communications. [Jessup, 1]

Client-server architectures operate faster over leased lines because the latency is low and predictable. However, most organizations cannot afford the cost of private leased lines to each location. They do use leased lines between their largest locations with the greatest concentration of people and data. Some WAN services—such as ATM (Asynchronous Transfer Mode) and SMDS (Switch Multimegabit Data Service)—handle switching, processing, and queuing in the hardware so propagation delay is reduced. An organization also might choose to use communications servers in which the PCs function like terminals, with their only job being to send screen update information over the WAN. [Jessup, 1]

Other strategies exist for reducing propagation delay on a WAN. Using link state routing protocols minimizes the traffic created over the WAN because they only send router updates. Software developers can reduce the number of separate tables used in the database to help reduce packet cycles. Read-ahead caching can save repeat requests because it enables the read request to include neighboring information from the server disk. This lessens transmission delay because HTTP (HyperText Transfer Protocol) is very efficient across the circuit [Jessup, 1]

Today, many organizations are moving from a client-server model to a Web-based ASP (Application Service Provider) model of computing in which clients access the database server over the Internet simply by typing in a URL.

TOPIC review — Client–Server Architecture

1. Where does the software application reside in a client-server architecture?
2. What enabled the use of distributed processing?
3. What communication techniques are used by middleware?
4. What is the purpose of a database driver?
5. Why do most client-server applications operate less efficiently over the WAN than the LAN?

APPLICATION SERVER ARCHITECTURE

Driven by the growth of the Internet, new models are emerging for application software delivery. Many organizations need a better, faster, cheaper way to manage software applications. They now look to Web-based application services to achieve integration with customers and business partners. The new **Application Service Providers (ASP)** provide and manage software services over the WAN from a central data center. ASPs can provide applications for a specific need or industry. They also can provide prepackaged application services or deliver high-end business applications to small- and medium-sized businesses.

Applications Used through ASP

ASPs are organizations that provide the hardware architecture to support access to software applications over the Internet. Several types of applications are delivered today to small- and medium-sized businesses. Applications commonly used through ASPs are listed in Table 9.1.

Communications	60%
Financial, Accounting	37%
E-commerce	37%
Education, Training	36%
Customer Relationship Management	30%
Human Resources	22%
Personal Productivity	18%
Supply-Chain Management	14%
Project Management	13%
Sales Force Automation	10%
Enterprise Resource Planning	5%
Based on a survey of 87 businesses that use ASP Service.	

TABLE 9.1 **Types of Applications Used through ASPs [Source: Lake, 1] [ZONA Research, May 2000]**

Companies are interested in ASP services because they offer specialized applications that otherwise would be too expensive to install and maintain. ASP services are attractive to small companies with low budgets for information technology. In fact, the use of ASP services is expected to triple over the next three years.

ASP Model Components

The ASP model operates over the World Wide Web by using HTTP to define how messages are formatted and transmitted. **HTTP** is a set of rules for exchanging files (text, graphic images, sound, video, and multimedia files) on the World Wide Web. It specifies the actions for browser requests and Web responses to various commands. [Webopedia, 1]

Web servers are computers that deliver Web pages to clients. Server software is installed on the computer and it is connected to the Internet. Every computer on the Internet that contains a Web site must have a Web server application program. Web server applications such as Apache (Linux servers) and Microsoft IIS (Windows 2000 servers) are frequently used. The Web server hosts a server program that provides the business logic for an application. [Webopedia, 1]

Figure 9.11 shows how the client uses HTML to format requests to the Web server. **HTML** is an authoring language used to format documents and provide links to graphics, audio, and video files to create Web pages. The use of a scripting language such as Common Gateway Interface (CGI) along with other approaches for data presentation such as Active Server Pages and Java Server Pages, allows a programmer to create Web pages that interact with the user's Web browser. [Whatis, 1]

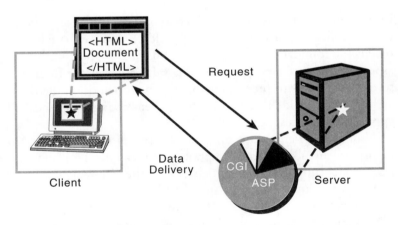

FIGURE 9.11 **ASP Client-Server Interaction [Source: Chambers, 1]**

When a Web browser-based user interface is used, it is often referred to as a *thin client*. The **thin client** is free of application business logic. The client browser is designed to be especially small so that the bulk of the processing occurs on the Web server. Figure 9.12 shows all of the ASP model components. The Web server is connected to the database server over a LAN. The client uses its Web browser to request account information stored in the database over the WAN. The Web browser requests the page from the Web server by specifying a

Uniform Resource Locator (URL); the URL identifies the location of the Web server. The HTTP process on the destination Web server receives the request and provides a response with the requested file (Web page).

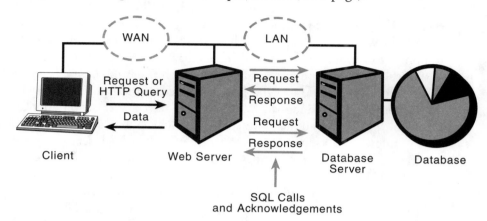

FIGURE 9.12 **ASP Model Components [Source: Jessup, 1]**

Three-Tier Architecture

In a **three-tier architecture**, the tiers typically consist of client presentation (top), application or business logic (middle), and database (bottom). The database is the foundation of the Internet business application because it stores all aspects of the business system. Doing business over the Internet requires strong security measures to protect databases. The top and middle tiers of the ASP architecture provide this security by authenticating users and authorizing the application services.

Using three-tier architecture, an ASP can provide a robust, scalable, and high-performance system to support mission-critical business applications. The ASP model supports software delivery for the following:

- Numerous users with a universal business purpose
- Real-time interaction with customers or business partners
- Complex transactions through Web pages
- Easy-to-use interfaces (browsers) for clients
- Business logic accessed through Web servers [IEC, 1]

The application server handles all application operations between users and an organization's business applications or databases. The **application server model (ASM)** is viewed as a three-tier application architecture as shown in Figure 9.13. The ASM consists of the following:

- Client presentation through a graphical user interface (GUI) (Web browser)
- Application or business logic
- Data and resources provided by a database [Microsoft, 5]

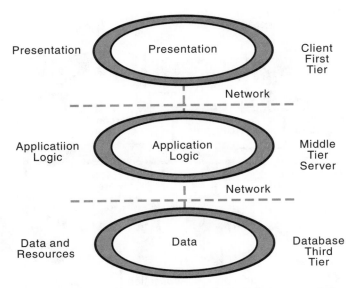

FIGURE 9.13 **Three-Tier Application Architecture [Source: Microsoft, 5]**

The three-tier application architecture is supported by a specific hardware infrastructure. This hardware architecture has three tiers:

- **Tier 1**. PCs as the user interface.
- **Tier 2**. Web or application servers.
- **Tier 3**. Database and transaction servers.

In Figure 9.14, the user interface is the first tier provided by a PC. At the second tier, the application servers provide the business logic and rules for processing requests to the database. The third (bottom) tier is the database and transaction servers, which can exist on a mainframe or a large UNIX server. These servers are often referred to as **back-end systems**. As shown in Figure 9.14 (page 466), an organization needs to invest a substantial amount of money in hardware to support the ASM. Many organizations decide instead to have an outsourcing company provide the ASM. [Whatis, 1]

ASP Versus Client-Server Delivery Model

The ASP model evolved from the client-server delivery model. Organizations turned away from the client-server delivery model because of the following:

- They had to purchase or lease all their equipment.
- Application upgrades required replacement of client applications on every desktop and laptop.
- The processing split between client and server over low bandwidth circuits resulted in slow response time and latency over the WAN. [Jessup, 1]

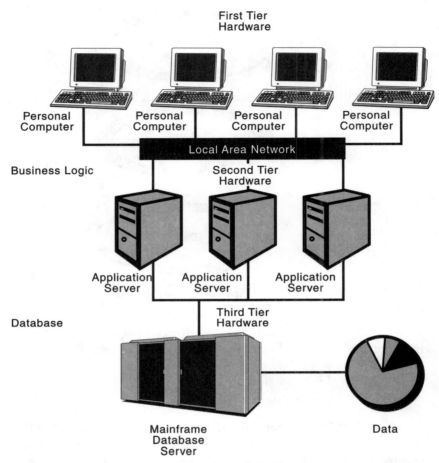

First Tier
Hardware

Personal
Computer

Personal
Computer

Personal
Computer

Personal
Computer

Local Area Network

Business Logic

Second Tier
Hardware

Application
Server

Application
Server

Application
Server

Database

Third Tier
Hardware

Mainframe
Database
Server

Data

FIGURE 9.14 **Three-Tier ASP Hardware Architecture [Source: IEC, 3]**

The key advantage of ASP models is that they can offer access to applications at a lower cost than companies can deliver internally. ASPs aggregate computer resources and provide multiple companies with access to their network backbone. They offer the built-in redundancy of equipment required to support reliable uptime for business applications. ASPs can provide a single point of management and administration for several organizations at once. Many provide network storage devices to store data and provide for disaster recovery. ASPs use both firewalls and intrusion detection to strengthen security for Web and database servers. The ASP model trusts that the provider will provide the performance levels that ensure reliable service. Service Level Agreements (SLAs) clearly define performance levels and restitution if these levels are not met.

ASP Model over the WAN

With the ASP model, the speed of the WAN link that connects users to the ASP server is a critical factor affecting performance levels. For many organizations, private circuits are required to provide enough bandwidth to run the application over the WAN, depending on the ASP application used. Common bandwidth speed requirements are from 256 Kbps to 512 Kbps. Most ISP (Internet Service Provider) data centers encourage the Web provider to purchase a private T1 connection directly from their location to the data center. Once connected to the data center, the Web provider can take advantage of the ISP's backbone for its customers. Usually ISPs have several dedicated links across the country with high-speed access of 48-768 Mbps. [Hannington, 1]

When organizations use ASPs for software delivery over the WAN, they face issues such as network availability, acceptable packet loss, latency service delivery timetables, and WAN management. When contracting for services, an organization becomes completely dependent on the ASP to provide their software 7 days a week, 24 hours a day. The SLA should clearly define acceptable service levels. In addition, the ISP should be held accountable for maintaining reliable service. [Hannington, 1]

Companies such as Microsoft and Adobe have introduced ASP models to deliver their software over the WAN. However, the economies of scale for ASP software delivery on a large scale are not practical because it would require huge data centers, very high-speed WAN links, and a reasonable cost to millions of users. These larger companies are still evaluating whether they can deliver their software through the ASP model and still make a profit. At least for now, the use of ASP is generally limited to centers that serve thousands, rather than millions, of customers and have a single data center location with several high-end servers and plenty of data storage. [ASP Article, 1]

TOPIC *review* **Application Server Architecture**

1. Why are companies interested in ASP models?
2. How are requests to a Web server formatted?
3. What are the three tiers of an application architecture?
4. How are the databases protected in an ASP architecture?
5. Why have organizations switched from the client-server delivery model to the ASP model?

E-COMMERCE ARCHITECTURE

Buying and selling goods and services over the Internet is defined as **e-commerce** or e-business. E-commerce hosting is a business in which a company supplies whatever network support is necessary for another company to sell its products and services over the World Wide Web. Services provided by e-commerce hosts include a Web server to serve the company's pages, Web site design, and online catalog setup. The Web software application is designed to accept, process, and confirm sales orders, as well as provide tools for tracking and managing inventory. E-commerce hosting companies manage all of the technical aspects of creating and maintaining a commercial Web site.

Elements of E-Commerce

Several e-commerce elements are required to conduct transactions:
- Products
- Web site to display the products for sale
- A way to accept orders and payments (by credit card)
- A fulfillment facility to ship products to customers
- Warranty claims, returns, and customer service [Brain, 1]

When B2B e-commerce is used, the procurement process between buyers and sellers is automated through the use of online forms. These forms are then integrated into company databases. An e-commerce system is the central **hub** between the buyers and the sellers. Buyers purchase a good or service and sellers or suppliers offer goods and services to buyers. [Brain, 1]

The e-commerce system enables buyers and suppliers to submit purchase orders online rather than by phone or fax. Most often, companies have existing buying arrangements and pricing defined by their suppliers. A catalog is built listing all of the suppliers' products and price lists. Thumbnail images of each item are created so that the buyer can see the products. The online procurement system allows for quick catalog searching and some systems allow for a customized list of the top 10 most frequently ordered items.

E-Commerce Business Models

Today, four types of B2B e-commerce business models exist:
- Online catalogs
- Auctions
- Exchanges
- Community

Online catalogs take paper-based catalogs of multiple vendors (suppliers), and digitize the product information to provide buyers with access to order over the Internet. **Auctions** provide for the purchase and sale of surplus inventory, used capital equipment, discontinued goods, and perishable items. The auction allows for competitive bidding over the Internet. **Exchanges** provide a market for commodities with high price volatility such as the purchase and sale of natural gas, electricity, and telecommunications bandwidth. **Community sites**

are Web sites designed to feature industry-specific content and community information. [Merrill Lynch, 1]

Current e-commerce models can be enterprise focused, partner focused, or direct focused. Figure 9.15 shows an example of each. The **enterprise focus model** has the supply chain that flows from supplier to manufacturer to retailer. The retailer has a storefront where customers can pick up products. In the next model, **partner focus** involves an online collaborative system, called a Web store, which integrates the supplier, manufacturer, and retailer into a private marketplace. Participating suppliers and buyers are specified by the market maker, with buying/selling activities limited to those participating in the marketplace. Finally, the **direct focus** e-business model consists of only supplier and manufacturer. An online catalog features products and services, and buyers can order directly over the Internet. After an order is placed, it is billed and shipped directly to the consumer. [Kalakota, 203]

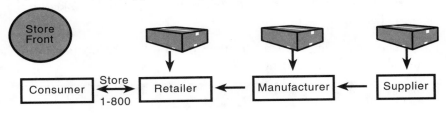

Enterprise Supply Chain

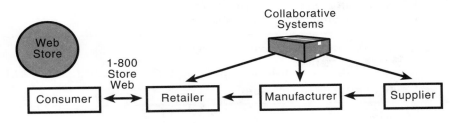

Business Partner Supply Chain

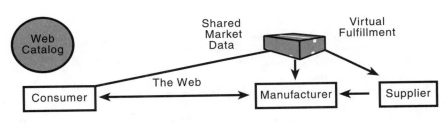

Direct Supply Chain

FIGURE 9.15 **Focus of E-Commerce Systems [Source: Kalakota, 203]**

Computing Elements of an E-Commerce System

Business models drive the e-commerce architecture. The elements of an e-commerce system are different for storefront retailing than they are for *electronic hubs*. An **electronic hub (eHub)** uses a spoke and wheel concept in which the hub is typically a large company at the center and the **spokes** are its suppliers.

The e-commerce architecture is built around the ASP model using application and Web servers at the middle tier. This Web-based model is designed for information exchange and transaction processing between buyers and sellers. Typically the architecture requires the ability to support:

- Faster bandwidth to Web servers
- Higher data storage capabilities for online catalogs
- Transactions and information exchanged in real time on the Web
- Supply chains that require sellers and buyers to be linked to the Internet [Broadview, 1]

The computing elements for the storefront and eHub architecture are listed in Table 9.2. [Merrill Lynch, 17]

ELEMENT	STOREFRONT	eHUB
Operating system and Web server software	X	X
Web creation tool (HTML or Java)	X	X
Database commerce server (catalog/order entry/workflow/inventory/shopping cart)	X	X
Transaction commerce server (transaction server for payments)	X	X
Server management software	X	X
Archiving	X	X
Custom or packaged shared applications (information tracking and sharing)		X
Groupware features (collaboration for e-mail, discussion groups, chat video conferencing, scheduling)	X	X
Security (password, encryption, directory authentication)		X

TABLE 9.2 **Computing Elements of an E-Commerce System [Source: Brain, 1]**

Fault Tolerance for E-Commerce Architecture

When building e-commerce architectures, designing for *fault tolerance* is a primary concern. **Fault tolerance** is defined as the capability of a system to respond quickly to an unexpected hardware or software failure. Fault tolerance is often achieved through redundancy. Redundancy provides backup to primary resources in case they fail. The backup component can immediately take its place without any loss of service. Redundancy is used to provide fault tolerance for components inside the servers, equipment for connecting to the Internet, servers used for server farms (see the upcoming "Server Farms" section), and mirroring or clustering of servers and hard drives.

Installing redundant fans, power supplies, network interface cards (NICs), and hard drives inside servers is generally considered wise. Redundant servers are used to provide *failover*. **Failover** supplies software that provides a means for user requests to be redirected immediately to a secondary (backup) system that duplicates the operations of the primary system. This backup operation automatically switches to a standby database, server, or network if the primary system fails. Failover is critical to e-commerce architectures, which must have around-the-clock availability. The capacity for automatic failover assures that normal functions can be maintained in spite of interruptions caused by problems with equipment or software. [Webopedia, 1]

The following strategies are generally used to build fault-tolerant e-commerce architectures:

- Mirroring
- Server farms
- Load balancing
- Clustering

Mirroring

Many organizations that provide Web servers for e-commerce businesses use a technique called *mirroring* to provide redundancy for the data located on the hard drives. **Mirroring** requires that two hard drives be configured to have data written to them simultaneously. If one drive fails, the other drive has all of the same data on it and takes over immediately.

Server Farms

In an e-commerce network, a **server farm** is a group of computers housed together in a single location. Server farms provide for fault tolerance as well as a way to handle the massive amount of tasks and services required by e-commerce businesses. A Web server farm is used to provide Web site hosting on multiple servers. In some cases, as few as two servers are sufficient to provide the server farm. In larger Web sites, such as Amazon.com, multiple servers are used to provide faster access and failover. [Whatis, 1]

As illustrated in Figure 9.16, several computers are grouped together into a server farm. Any one of these servers can provide access to the e-commerce application and database located on the other side of the high-speed switch. The high-speed switch provides for multiple channels to connect the servers together for parallel processing. **Parallel processing** provides for simultaneous use of more than one processor (CPU) to execute a program. With parallel processing on a network, CPUs can be used from different servers to execute programs. Parallel processing requires distributed processing software to manage the execution of several programs at once. This software detects CPUs that are idle and parcels out programs to use them. [Webopedia, 1]

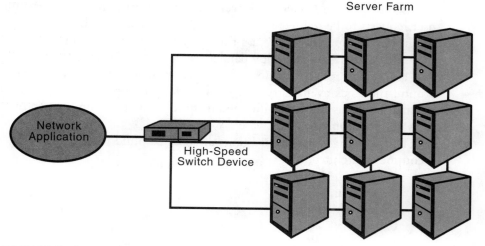

FIGURE 9.16 Server Farm [Source: Network Computing, 1]

On some e-commerce sites that have server farms, the processing is divided between distributed databases. **Distributed databases** are often used for crucial company information such as inventory, customer orders, and accounting. When a distributed database is used, the databases are stored across two or more computer systems. The database system keeps track of which server the data is located on and the users are not aware that the database has been distributed. To keep the best level of integrity between the databases, replication is used between the databases. **Replication** is the process of making a replica (copy) of the database on another database server. The replicas are synchronized so that changes made to one replica are made to the other. Database users share the same level of information because the databases are always refreshing through the replication process. [Whatis, 1]

A vital issue facing designers of e-commerce sites is whether or not to replicate databases over the WAN. This action requires high-speed WAN links with plenty of bandwidth to allow the replication process to occur frequently. Only with high-speed links can replication occur every 10-15 minutes. If the WAN link is slow, replication will most often occur at night when fewer users are on the system. If replication occurs in the evening, the database integrity might be comprised because the updating process occurs every 8-10 hours. This means each database might contain different data than the others.

Load Balancing

A server farm also can be used to streamline services by distributing the workload between the individual components of the farm, which expedites computing processes by harnessing the power of multiple servers. The server farm uses a technique called *load balancing* to manage the processing power from multiple servers. Load balancing differs from parallel processing in that it just distributes tasks to idle CPUs. [Network Computing, 1]

Busy Web sites usually have two or more Web servers installed and use load balancing to distribute the processing. **Load balancing** distributes processing and communications actions evenly across a computer network. The goal of load balancing is to make sure no single device is overwhelmed. If one server becomes inundated with requests for service, requests are forwarded to a server with more capacity. Load balancing is particularly vital for networks in which it is difficult to predict the number of requests that will be issued to a particular server. [Network Computing, 1]

Load balancing also can be used for communication channels. In Figure 9.17, two WAN load-balancing devices provide for multiple connections to the Internet. If one communication channel fails, the site is still connected to the Internet via the other channel.

Notice that in Figure 9.17, the load balancing devices are located between the Internet and the server farm to provide maximum benefit for performance and scalability. There are two load-balancing devices for each channel. These load-balancing devices can be used to manage traffic to the Web servers. They automatically detect changes in server status and route requests accordingly. They also can determine which server in the network is the least loaded and route requests to that server. Load balancers optimize the distribution of requests based on capacity, availability, response time, current load, and historical performance. They provide for efficient resource use of all the servers in the server farm. [Coyote Point, 1]

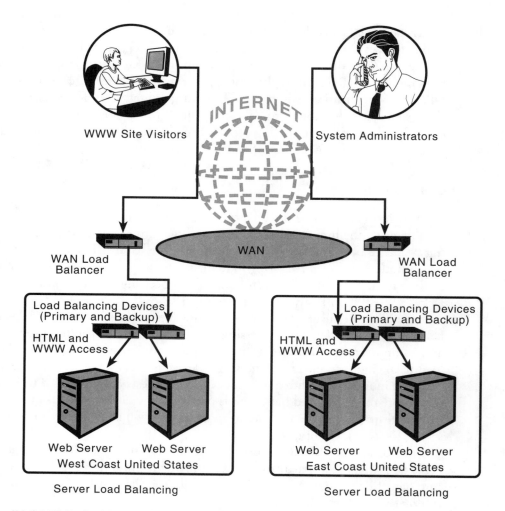

FIGURE 9.17 **Load Balancing [Source: IEC, 2]**

With load balancers, servers can be added or removed at any time without bringing down the site. Load balancers are ideal for large Web sites with a significant number of users. They can handle up to 15,000,000 users per hour. Some load balancers can handle 64 clusters of 8 servers each. For extreme demands of heavily loaded Web sites, the load balancer can handle over 130,000 HTTP requests per minute. Load balancers also can balance e-mail, news, and FTP traffic. [Coyote Point, 1]

Server Clustering

Server clustering is a server-use strategy used to provide for parallel processing, load balancing, and fault tolerance. **Clustering** allows two or more computers to use multiple storage devices and redundant interconnections to form a single system. The servers are linked physically together via cable. The result is that the cluster provides for managing the applications programmatically. The clustering approach is used to provide reliable, high-availability Web sites for e-commerce applications. A server cluster is designed to maintain data integrity and provide failover support. The server cluster appears as a single system. Clusters can be formed in one of two ways: server clustering, and clustering of Web presentation and business components of the Web site. [Network Computing, 1]

With server clustering, data is written to both servers simultaneously. This means that the data on one server exactly matches that of the other. If one server fails, the other takes over. Clusters use an algorithm to detect a failure and then consult failover policies to determine how to control the work of the failed server. A failover process automatically shifts the failed server's workload to another server to provide continuous service. Server clustering is an ideal strategy to use to protect back-end database servers. [Microsoft, 1]

When Web presentation and business components are clustered, two servers are linked together allowing all data and transactions to be shared between both. Communication is coordinated between the two servers so that they can effectively perform common tasks. **Component load balancing** is used to distribute components within the application across servers. It assures that Web pages being requested are available continuously and delivered in real time. [Microsoft, 1]

Microsoft Windows 2000 clustering technology also can be configured to support load balancing, which can be used for spreading incoming requests across several servers. Based upon application policies, clusters can be set up to route processing chores to another CPU based on availability. Network load balancing also can provide for distributing IP (Internet Protocol) traffic to multiple copies of a TCP/IP (Transmission Control Protocol/Internet Protocol) service running on a Web server farm. The load balancer can transparently partition the client requests among the servers allowing clients to access the cluster by using "virtual IP addresses."

Figure 9.18 shows a cluster of four servers connected to a high-speed switch. The cluster service provided by Microsoft allows for a two-server failover cluster with Windows 2000 Advanced server and a four-node cluster in Windows 2000 Datacenter server. The cluster service is provided by the operating system. Windows clustering can be used to provide network load balancing on a front-end Web server farm and on the back end to cluster business applications on databases. In this way, an organization can minimize the number of points of failure in the system. Clustering enables the system to quickly scale to meet new user demands and assures that the system is online all the time. [Microsoft, 1]

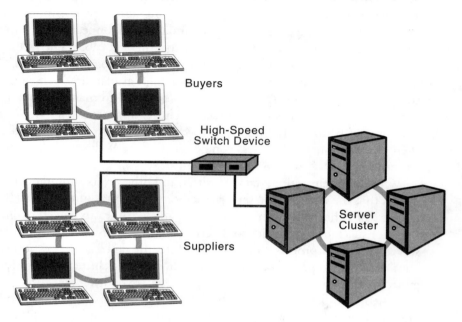

FIGURE 9.18 Server Clusters [Source: Network Computing, 1]

Geographical Load Balancing

Load-balancing products and server clusters helps to create high availability within a single location. However, many organizations establish a worldwide Internet presence by deploying Web servers in many locations. Fortunately, load balancing can be used to spread traffic across the WAN to several regional server clusters to share the workload. Each regional cluster is composed of servers that provide a common service. The afternoon "rush hour" of e-commerce traffic can be directed to any regional server cluster. Quicker response time is achieved by directing clients to the closest server cluster. WAN costs can be reduced for transmitting over costly trans-Atlantic or trans-Pacific hops. [Coyote Point, 1]

Geographic load balancing enables disaster recovery on a global scale, bypassing regional interruptions of service automatically. If one regional server cluster suffers failure due to an earthquake, flood, or other natural disaster, server clusters in other regions of the country or the world are available to take over the processing. Similarly, if a server cluster suffers a telecommunications failure, traffic can be redirected to another regional server cluster. The load balancer routes each client request to another Web server with similar content.

A Web-based configuration tool is provided to manage the load balancer. A load balancer can be configured to support several load-balancing methods:

- **Adaptive**. Considers all factors when selecting a regional site.
- **Round Trip**. Notes client proximity.
- **Load**. Evaluates the measurement of overall server use.
- **Site Weight**. Assigns a static weight to each primary and backup site.

Figure 9.19 shows load balancers located in U.S. East, U.S. West, and Europe. Geographic probes called agents are set up at each regional site. The geographic probe contains information about the client and the requested URL. When a client browser sends an HTTP request for the URL, each agent checks for availability of local resources and responds if the requested URL is unavailable. Each available URL responds after the agent tests the link for latency using the TCP/IP ping utility. Each then returns a response to the probe that initiated the request; all responses from all probes are evaluated and the "best" regional site available to receive the client request is determined. [Coyote Point Systems, 1]

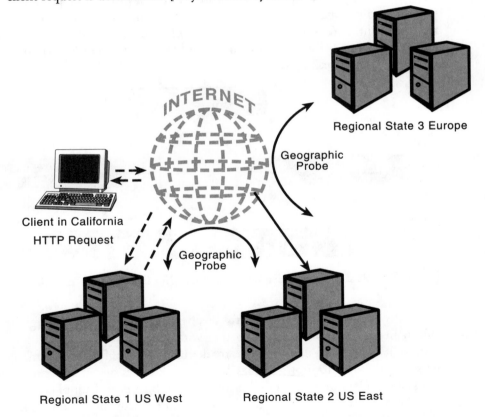

FIGURE 9.19 **Regional Probes for Geographic Load Balancing [Source: Coyote Point Systems]**

Distributed load balancing provides the benefits of regional server installations to deliver high availability while preserving transparency to the client. Organizations with several suppliers in their eHub marketplace can integrate with their back-end database system. Integrating the back-end database system allows the eHub to communicate order requests, information, and acknowledgements to the back-end system to improve inventory management.

ERP Integration

Over the last several years, an increasing number of companies have centralized critical company information about forecasting, inventory, purchasing, accounting, and finance into an integrated **Enterprise Resource Planning (ERP)** database. Figure 9.20 shows basic business processes that are often integrated into an ERP database system. ERP systems facilitate the exchange of data among corporate divisions and unify key business processes within the organization. ERP unites major business processes, such as order processing, general ledger, payroll, and production. All transactions coming into and out of the organization must interface with the ERP system to link up with the business flow of the organization. All transactions then are filtered into the ERP database system, which operates as a data warehouse. [Kalakota, 166]

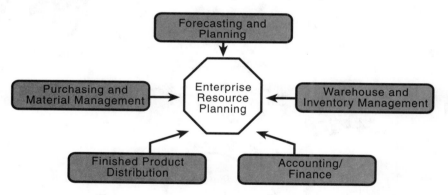

FIGURE 9.20 **Enterprise Resource Planning (ERP) [Source: Kalakota, 94]**

ERP systems manage and control business processes within an organization. When an organization needs to partner with suppliers and buyers in an online system, it requires an eHub private marketplace. The eHub private marketplace preserves the organization's privacy by only linking its buyers and suppliers into the system. Data exchange takes place between buyers and suppliers through the eHub. However, if the eHub is not integrated with the organization's ERP system, data might have to be entered into the ERP system manually. Ideally, the eHub marketplace should be integrated with all of the ERP systems of each supplier and buyer who participates in the eHub marketplace.

Figure 9.21 shows how data exchange between suppliers and buyers is routed through the eHub. Each supplier or buyer ERP system is integrated into the eHub marketplace database. This allows for order and shipping notifications to be sent from the eHub into the appropriate ERP system so that inventory and accounting processes can occur within each organization. [Sand Hill Systems, 2-1]

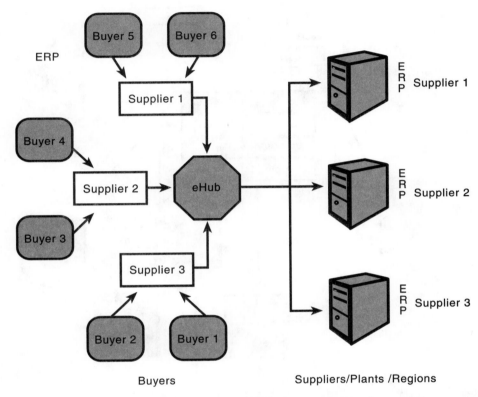

FIGURE 9.21 Integration of eHub Marketplace with Supplier and Buyer ERP Systems [Sand Hill Systems, 1]

The eHub software facilitates the mapping of pairs of buyers and suppliers. Suppliers often negotiate different pricing levels with each buyer. These customer-specific price lists are loaded into the online eHub system. Each custom price list is directly mapped to the appropriate buyer. This mapping process sets up the view that a customer or buyer will have when logging into the marketplace. The customer or buyer only sees the price list allowed by the supplier. [Sand Hill Systems, 2-1]

Business process rules are defined to the eHub to match each supplier's business process. In Figure 9.22, a buyer issues a purchase order. The order is transformed within the eHub according to the business rules determined by the supplier and sent to the supplier's ERP system. The supplier's ERP system sends a purchase order acknowledgement to the eHub. When the supplier ships the material, an order status message is sent to the eHub for tracking purposes. [Sand Hill Systems, 3-7]

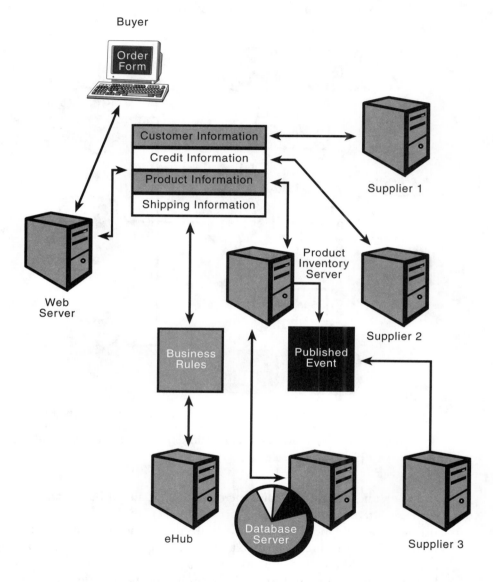

FIGURE 9.22 Order Flow between the eHub and the Supplier's ERP System [Source: Microsoft, 12]

Computing elements of integration requires different formats for message exchange between the eHub and each ERP system. Automated systems can exchange business documents in many ways. Some of the document standards commonly used for integration include:

- Electronic Data Interchange (EDI)
- Open Application Group (OAG)
- Rosettanet
- XML (Extensible Markup Language)
- CSV

Each document standard specifies exactly how each message must be formatted for data exchange with other systems. Messages are transformed between systems according to agreed-upon rules between the suppliers and buyers. Each ERP system has a unique method of receiving and sending information. Most of the business process flows involved in eHub integration work in a "batch" mode. This can introduce delay time into the business process. [Sand Hill Systems, 3-5]

Often middleware is used to transform message formats between systems. For instance, Microsoft BizTalk server can handle several different message formats, such as EDI, XML, and CSV. In Figure 9.23, a BizTalk server is placed in the center between the buyers and the eHub. The server can process several incoming transactions from ERP systems with EDI, XML, and flat file formats. It transforms each message into a format the eHub understands and the eHub then processes the request to the database. A response to the ERP system is sent back through the BizTalk server where it is translated to the appropriate format (EDI, XML, or flat file) as required by the ERP system. [Sand Hill Systems, 4-3]

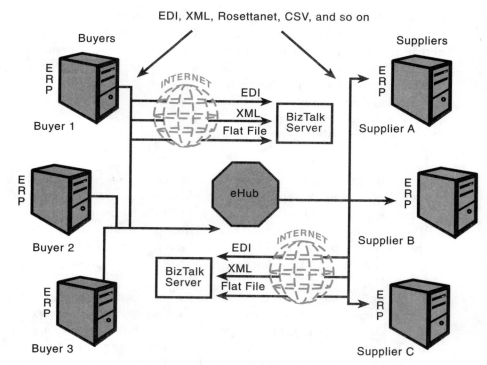

FIGURE 9.23 Incoming and Outgoing Transactions Using Middleware to ERP Systems [Source: Sand Hill Systems]

TOPIC *review* **E-Commerce Architecture**

1. Which elements are required to conduct transactions for e-commerce over the Internet?
2. What are the four types of e-commerce business models?
3. What is the spoke-and-wheel concept used for eHub e-commerce systems?
4. What is the advantage gained from automatic failover?
5. What impact does replicating distributed databases have on the WAN?

WEB SERVER PERFORMANCE MANAGEMENT AND SECURITY

E-commerce over the Internet will continue to grow at a rapid pace. As buyers and suppliers reach for e-commerce solutions, they are readily adopting high-speed Internet connections to support access for their customers and business partners.

Designing for High Availability Performance

Reliable integration of e-commerce systems accommodates large volumes of transactions without delays in processing. Planning for the system architecture often requires distributing connections to protect services that should remain private from ending up out on the Internet.

Several factors should be considered when designing Web server connections for headquarters and remote offices to the Internet. The following list of guidelines for designers describes real-world techniques that guarantee high-availability:

- Maintain connectivity to more than one ISP to increase the reliability of the Internet connection.
- Deploy server farms, clusters, and load balancers.
- Secure back-end services from the Internet.
- Eliminate single points of failure.
- Eliminate bottlenecks to scaling—allow new servers to be dynamically added as user demand increases.
- Allow for hardware and operating system independence.
- Make sure fault tolerance or failover occurs transparently.
- Find an easy-to-use single software system to manage and monitor servers and operating systems. [BEA, 1]

Figure 9.24 (page 484) shows that the connection to the Internet is separated from the back-end system. The Internet connection and the private WAN remain independent through the use of separated dedicated lines.

Separation of Internet and WAN Access

Keeping traffic physically separate is a good technique for ensuring each application and server has enough bandwidth. This solution is expensive and even though it offers better quality of service, some organizations might not be able to afford it. Shared T1 access is one of several cost-effective alternatives.

Shared T1 Access to the Internet

In Figure 9.25 (page 485), T1 (1.54 Mbps) access is shared from the customer to the ISP. Notice the single T1 connection efficiently provides access for up to 14 customers. T1 lines are idle some of the time, so customers can share access across these digital leased lines. For faster connection to the Internet, a dedicated T3 (45 Mbps) line is provided between the ISP and the Internet. For high availability, the ISP has contracted for redundant T3s to minimize downtime. Leased line costs decrease the closer the customer is to the provider's POP (point of presence). [Network Computing, 1]

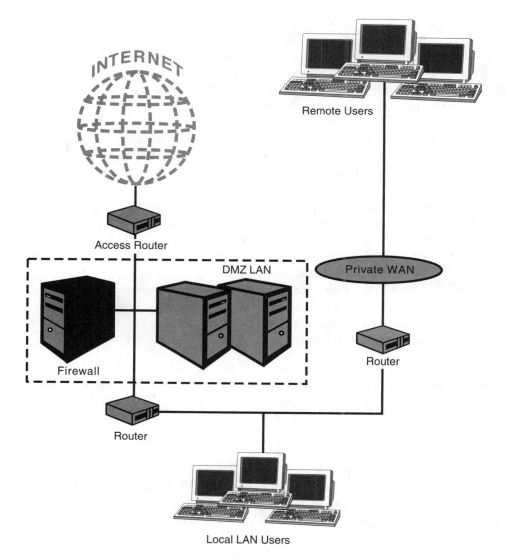

FIGURE 9.24 Separation of Internet and WAN Access [Source: Jessup, 1]

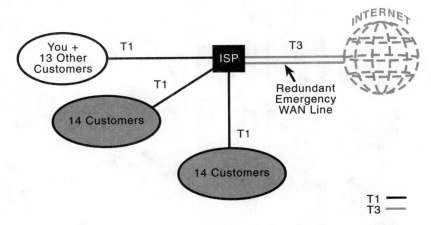

**FIGURE 9.25 Shared T1 Access with a T3 Connection to the Internet
[Source: Network Computing, 1]**

Multiple ISP Strategy

Another strategy for achieving reliable e-commerce operations is to maintain connectivity to more than one ISP for the Internet connection. In Figure 9.26 (page 486), two different ISPs offer access to the Internet. This design strategy provides an emergency backup in case an ISP fails to provide service. Likewise, if one ISP experiences downtime, the second ISP connection can be used to reroute traffic to the Internet. The design offers redundancy and higher availability. However, the costs are greater because an additional router and a second T1 line are required, as well as a service fee for the second connection. [Network Computing, 1]

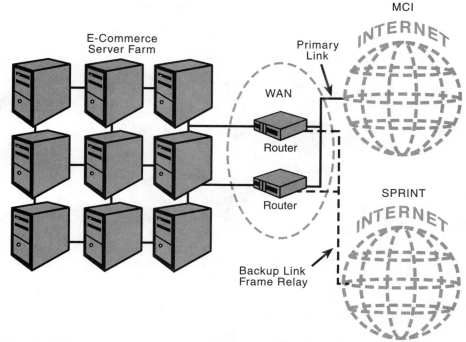

FIGURE 9.26 Emergency Backup Plan [Network Computing, 1]

Highly Fault-Tolerant Architecture

The ultimate design for support of an e-commerce system is illustrated in Figure 9.27. This design approach assumes a generous budget. The design has a Web server farm in the middle that is connected to two switches. Each switch is connected to a router and both routers are connected to each ISP. This is an example of a fully redundant network structure that offers complete redundancy for all equipment, which guarantees more uptime for network availability. [Gourlay, 1]

Web Server Security

When companies connect their operations to the Internet, they soon realize the need to protect the security, integrity, and privacy of their e-commerce Web sites. A security breach can cause substantial financial losses as well as damage to company reputations. To continue to provide services over the Internet, e-commerce system design needs to ensure the protection, safe transmission, and storage of data.

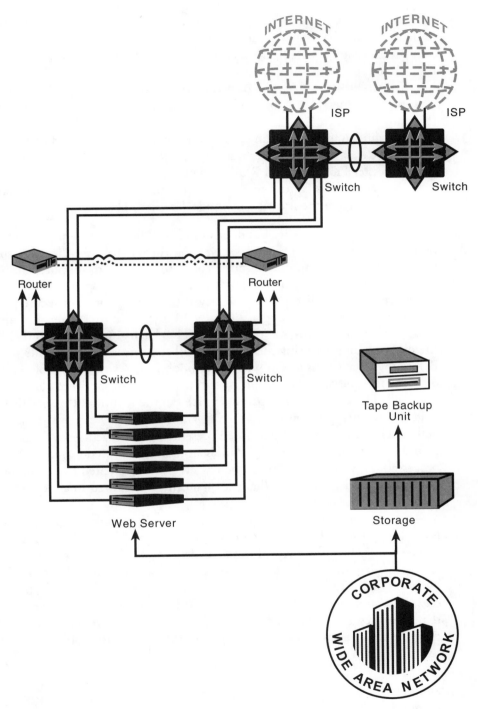

FIGURE 9.27 **E-Commerce Fault-Tolerant Architecture [Source: Gourlay, 1]**

End-to-end data security requires protection not only for the transportation of data, but also for the content within that data. To protect content in transit over the Internet, Secure Sockets Layer (SSL) encrypts data as it leaves the user's browser and decrypts the data as it reaches the Web site. On the Web site's internal network, however, the data is transmitted as clear (or plain) text. This clear text is vulnerable to attack if someone hacks into the internal network. [Ingrian, 1]

Some guidelines for building a secure e-commerce system include:

- Have a secure Web server that supports SSL, S-HTTP (Secure HyperText Transfer Protocol), and RSA encryption.
- Manage access control to the back-end database and transaction servers.
- Use strong authentication methods. [Ingrian, 1]

End-to-end data security has disadvantages. Often the techniques used to protect the data between the Web server and the database slow server response times. Significant computing resources are also required to support SSL because the encryption algorithm is computationally intensive. [Ingrian, 1]

Secure content delivery can be achieved through application-secure private keys and certificates. Looking at Figure 9.28, the client user enters his credit card number into a form on a Web page. The data is transmitted to the Web site over the Internet using the SSL protocol to protect the data while in transit. Before the data arrives at the Web server pool, it passes through a platform device where the SSL connection is terminated and the clear text data is obtained. The **content encryption service engine** identifies the sensitive data field and re-encrypts it using a 3DES (Data Encryption Standard) or RSA public key. The re-encrypted data is then presented to the Web server, which passes it to the back-end database. The data is stored in encrypted format until it is processed. However, the data can be retrieved and decrypted by a content encryption service engine so that the data can be presented intact to an authorized user. [Ingrian, 1]

The content encryption service engine scans all incoming requests and looks for fields containing a predefined tag. When a tagged field is located, the engine applies a cryptographic algorithm to the data in that field and passes the encrypted data to the server. Back-end services can be secured from the Internet by protecting user passwords, protecting secret encryption keys, and protecting *cookies*. A **cookie** is a message given to a Web client browser by a Web server that identifies a user. The client browser stores this message in a text file. Each time the client browser requests a page from the server, the cookie is sent to the server. [Ingrian, 1]

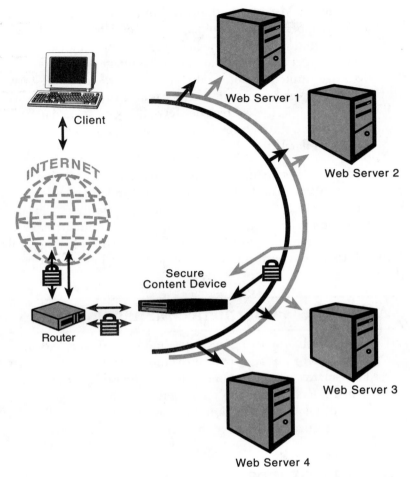

FIGURE 9.28 Web Server Security [Source: Ingrian, 1]

Security techniques are employed to protect the following elements of an e-commerce system:

- **User Passwords.** For security purposes, the original password is replaced with a keyed hash of the password. The authentication process compares the keyed hash of the password originally entered by the user with the stored one in the Web site's database. Access is only granted if the two hashes match.
- **Secret Encryption Keys.** When any server initiates an HTTP request to encrypt or decrypt required fields of data, a device applies the appropriate cryptographic key and generates an HTTP request. This allows all of the servers within the internal network to communicate using standard Web protocols and eliminates the need for a special dedicated key server for encryption.

- **Cookies.** A **Message Authentication Code**, a programming encryption code, is appended to a cookie. If the cookie has been altered, the Message Authentication Code immediately rejects the cookie as soon as the unauthorized user attempts to log in. If the integrity of the cookie is good, the Message Authentication Code is removed, the cookie is forwarded to the back-end Web server, and the user is able to log in to the Web site. [Ingrian, 1] Secure content delivery allows sensitive data to enter the Web site and pass through the internal network in an encrypted form to the back-end database.

An e-commerce system that employs credit card processing should deploy the standard **Secure Electronic Transaction (SET)**, which is the standard used by MasterCard and Visa. SET was designed specifically to allow for secure credit card transactions over the Internet. It protects both merchants and customers by protecting payment information confidentiality, providing cardholder authentication, and ensuring the transmitted data integrity of payments. [Ingrian, 1]

TOPIC *review* | **Web Server Performance Management and Security**

1. How can the Internet connection and the private WAN access be separated to provide each application and server with enough bandwidth?
2. How many customers can share access to a single T1 line?
3. When is a cookie sent to the server?
4. How can emergency backup be provided in case an ISP fails?
5. How can back-end services be secured from the Internet?

THE ROLE OF ISPS

For e-commerce operations, the role of an ISP is to provide a direct connection from the company's network to the Internet. An ISP has the telecommunications equipment and link access required for a POP on the Internet backbone for the geographic area served. POPs are strategically located across the United States by major telecommunications companies. Most ISPs have more than one POP on the Internet.

Network Access Points (NAPs)

ISPs are connected to one another over the Internet backbone through *Network Access Points*. **Network Access Points (NAPs)** determine how traffic is routed over the Internet backbone. They also provide switching facilities that select the path for sending data to its next destination, which might be another NAP. [Whatis, 1]

Several NAPs are located across the United States. Figure 9.29 shows the Internet backbone with POPs and NAPs available in major cities such as New York, Washington, Chicago, and San Francisco. Some NAPs are privately owned by a particular ISP. The **private NAPs** in this map are owned by SAVVIS, an Internet solutions company that has built a global intelligent IP network that bypasses the public Internet POPs. With a private NAP architecture, SAVVIS can guarantee direct routes or paths over its network. [SAVVIS, 1]

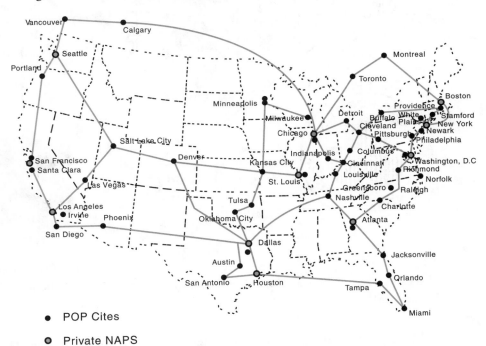

● POP Cites

◎ Private NAPS

FIGURE 9.29 **Network Access Points (NAPs) [Source: SAVVIS, 1]**

Metropolitan Area Exchange (MAE)

ISPs also can connect with each other through a *Metropolitan Area Exchange*. A **Metropolitan Area Exchange (MAE)** is a major center in the United States where traffic is switched between ISPs. As shown in Figure 9.30, two major MAEs are located in the United States. MAE-East is located in Washington, D.C. and MAE-West is located in San Jose, California. Five regional "Tier-2" MAEs (not shown in Figure 9.30) are also located in Chicago, Dallas, Houston, Los Angeles, and New York City. [Whatis, 1]

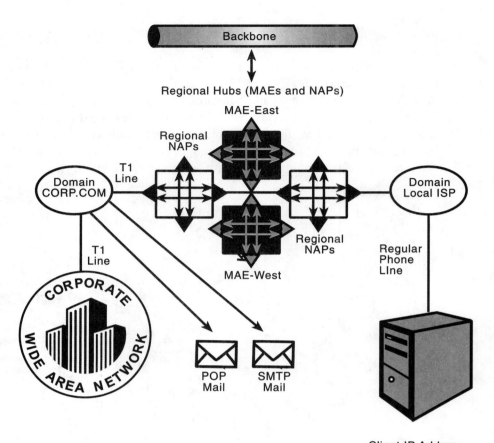

FIGURE 9.30 **Metropolitan Area Exchange (MAE) [Source: Laudon and Traver, 126]**

MAEs are basically giant routing switches used to manage Internet traffic. Routers at MAE-East and MAE-West have large routing tables to encompass all of the paths required by ISPs. The only ISP device that can interconnect to a MAE switch is a router or a computer host acting as a router. ISPs are responsible for managing their own routers that connect to MAEs or NAPs to reach the Internet backbone. [Webopedia, 1]

Peering Agreements for Traffic Exchange

Often, larger ISPs that have their own backbones agree to allow traffic from other large ISPs in exchange for traffic on their backbones. **Peering agreements** provide rules for traffic exchange between ISPs. The peering agreement describes the terms and conditions under which it will peer with other networks for various types of traffic. Peering charges can include transit charges or line access charges to the larger ISP backbone. [Webopedia, 1]

The explosive growth of Internet traffic has prompted several providers to examine their ISP architecture to determine how they can continue to deliver service with high reliability. The most crucial area of the network is at the IP edge. Large IP edge routers are used to rapidly recover from hardware and software faults and thus maintain continuity of service. These large edge routers support hundreds of thousands of subscribers. Most ISPs experience at least one system failure (hardware or software) per year. In Figure 9.31, IP edge routers create serious single point-of-failure risks at the service edge. If they are not fully redundant, they cannot provide the needed resiliency to avoid service downtime. [Nokia, 1]

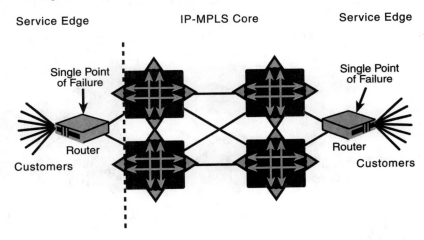

FIGURE 9.31 **Edge Router (Single Point of Failure) [Source: Nokia, 1]**

Hot Standby Controllers

Many ISPs have addressed this inefficiency through the use of **"hot standby" controllers**, which are secondary cards installed in the large edge router to provide for restoration of service in case of a network fault. However, the recovery time for each failure with a "hot standby" controller is 7 to 10 minutes. Time is lost because the standby routing card has to reboot the router operating system and reconverge the routing protocols to recover service. The edge router failure causes adjacent routers to report loss of communication with the failed router. The failed router's neighbors also report that the failed router is no longer available. All of these failure messages are then propagated across the thousands of networks and routers that comprise the Internet backbone. The entire notification process starts all over again when the router recovers. [Nokia, 1]

Aggregation Service Routers

To minimize the impact of a large edge router failure, new devices called *aggregation service routers* have been developed to increase fault tolerance at the IP network's edge.

Aggregation service routers (ASRs) are more reliable because they deliver a hot standby processor, line card, and port-by-port protection. Figure 9.32 shows new ASR edge routers at each end of the IP network. These ASR routers support a fault-tolerant operating system and full route-state redundancy for several routing protocols. ASRs also can be used to transport non-IP traffic over IP or Multiprotocol Label Switching (MPLS) networks. [Nokia, 1]

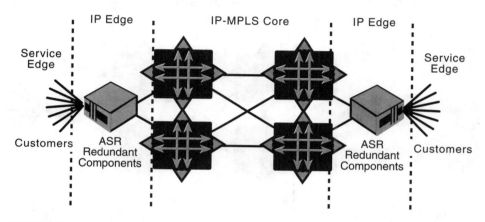

FIGURE 9.32 **Aggregation Service Routers [Source: Nokia, 1]**

ASRs provide several benefits that simplify capacity planning and traffic management:

- Improved network performance
- Improved reliability through redundant components
- Improved customer satisfaction and retention

In addition, ASRs incorporate QoS (Quality of service) features, IP flow classification, traffic policy, and rate limiting. These features allow service agreements to become more flexible in order to offer a better QoS. [Nokia, 1]

Network Availability

The redundant components in the ASR routers ensure reliability for the mission-critical services required by e-commerce operations. **Reliability** of an ISP is measured as a percentage of uptime and network availability. These two factors describe the amount of time a network is available or unavailable. Measuring these factors is a key element in predicting an ISP network's performance. Reliability is measured by the number of times the number nine appears in the reliability rating. Network availability is measured in days, hours, or minutes of downtime (unavailability) per year. When it is 99.999% reliable, it means the network is unavailable for five minutes per year. When an ISP is less reliable, the number of nines will decrease while the number of hours or days of downtime increase. The level of availability from the ISP requires at least "**five-nines**" reliability for e-commerce operations.

Today, ISPs need to achieve the same 99.999% level of availability that is supported with the traditional PSTN (Public Switched Telephone Network) infrastructure. To achieve high availability, ISPs seek to eliminate single points of failure from their networks. They deploy redundant core switches and routers and use automatic protection switching to gain fault tolerance in their core networks. [Nokia, 1]

TOPIC *review* — The Role of ISPs

1. What is the purpose of NAPs?
2. How many major MAEs are available in the United States?
3. How are "hot standby" controllers inefficient for ISPs?
4. What benefits are provided by ASRs?
5. How do ISPs measure the reliability of their networks?

CHAPTER SUMMARY

Organizations today want to use the Internet to improve business. They consider the adoption of B2B models to automate strategic activities. Even in an e-commerce Internet business, people want to do business with people they know and like. The procurement process in many companies is still manual and paper-intensive. E-commerce increases efficiency in ordering, scheduling, and tracking delivery of orders.

Several business challenges/models (collaboration, e-commerce, data warehousing, outsourcing, supply chain management, and customer relationship management) require computing architectures to support the e-business over the Internet. The use of the Internet brings organizations to edges of the WAN. Depending on the architecture used, performance can be significantly different between the LAN and WAN. Today's LANs operate at 100 Mbps to the desktop and therefore users are accustomed to quick response time. WAN services vary in speed and cost. Most high-speed services over 100 Mbps are prohibitively expensive. Consequently, organizations have learned to accept that response time over the WAN will be slower.

The design of the architecture, however, using an ASP model with a "thin client" rather than a client-server model with a "fat client" can significantly enhance response time for the user. Analysis of request/response exchanges over the WAN between client and Web server leads to design solutions that will improve performance. Some of the solutions involve the following:

- Selecting WAN services that have the lowest latency
- Using dedicated leased lines from the Web provider's location to the ISP
- Securing a high-speed connection to the Internet
- Selecting an ISP with a high-speed backbone inside and outside the country

ASP models offer various cost-saving advantages that often lead to outsourcing the management and administration of the Web services, equipment, and IT staff. Organizations find that the database is the foundation of their Internet business application. Doing business over the Internet requires strong security measures to protect the databases and the Web content, which are the organization's intellectual property.

E-commerce provides a central electronic hub between buyers and sellers. E-business models and the focus of their architectures vary depending on the flow of information between an organization's buyers and sellers. Direct supply chain marketplaces provide for a simple architecture to connect supplier to manufacturer and then directly to the consumer. Some organizations need more sophisticated architectures to provide for collaborative systems and a Web store to satisfy the supply chain of supplier, manufacturer, and retailer to consumer.

E-commerce is a transaction-oriented, Web-based model designed for information exchange and processing transactions between buyer and sellers. This model requires an architecture that can support the following:

- Faster bandwidth to Web servers
- Higher data storage capabilities for online catalogs
- Real-time transactions and information
- Supply chains that link sellers and buyers to the Internet.

E-commerce needs to be available 7 days a week, 24 hours a day, and 365 days a year. For e-commerce Web providers to offer reliable services, they must rely on their ISPs. SLAs need to specify the level of fault tolerance required to provide continuous uptime. Redundancy is the key to reliability. Techniques used are failover, mirroring, server farms, distributed databases, replication, load balancing, server clustering, and geographic load balancing. Each of these techniques requires different software and hardware to support either server component failure or connection failures that require redirection. The goal is to deliver high availability while preserving transparency for the client.

CHAPTER REVIEW QUESTIONS

(This quiz can also be printed out from the Encore! CD that accompanies this textbook. File name—Chap09review.)

Circle a letter (a-d) for each question. Choose only one answer for each.

1. Which of the following is not an example of real-time collaboration?
   a. Faxing
   b. White boarding
   c. Video conferencing
   d. Instant messaging

2. The four basic elements of e-commerce systems are:
   a. Application software, business process, hosting platform, network
   b. Application software, collaboration, hosting platform, network
   c. Application software, computing architecture, hosting platform, network
   d. Application software, data warehouse, hosting platform, network

3. A system that enables a client to communicate with a database to store, modify, and extract information is a:
   a. Transaction processing system
   b. Distributed processing system
   c. Data warehouse
   d. Database Management System (DBMS)

4. Organizations that provide the hardware architecture to support access over the Internet to software applications are called:
   a. PAS
   b. ASP
   c. AST
   d. SAP

5. The three-tiered application architecture of the ASP model includes:
   a. Software application, client presentation, data, and resources
   b. Client presentation, application logic, data, and resources
   c. Software delivery, application logic, data, and resources
   d. User interface, software application, application logic

6. When more than one processor (CPU) is used to execute a program, it is called:
   a. Batch processing
   b. Transaction processing
   c. Parallel processing
   d. Distributed processing

7. Traffic that is spread across the WAN to several regional clusters to share the workload is referred to as:
   a. Adaptive load balancing
   b. Geographic load balancing
   c. Disaster recovery
   d. Component load balancing

8. Secure Electronic Transaction (SET) is designed to allow:
   a. Secure method for authenticating users
   b. Secure access to Web pages
   c. Encryption of communications across the Internet
   d. Secure credit card transactions over the Internet

9. Downtime caused by edge routers can affect:
   a. The service provider's own network
   b. The entire Internet
   c. Other operator networks
   d. All of the above

10. Five-nines reliability is described as:
    a. Up to 9 hours of network downtime per year
    b. Up to 12 minutes of network downtime per year
    c. Up to 36 hours of network downtime per year
    d. Up to 5 minutes of network downtime per year

Circle the correct letter (A-E) that corresponds to the descriptions below. Choose only one answer for each.
   A. White boarding
   B. Intellectual property
   C. Real time
   D. Middleware
   E. CRM

11. A B C D E   A database is created to store information about a company's relationships with all of its customers.

12. A B C D E   Used to connect two otherwise separate applications together.

13. A B C D E   Multiple users can write or draw on a display screen and the people on the other end can see and hear the ideas being presented.

14. A B C D E   Information is classified as an intangible company asset.

15. A B C D E   Communication activities occur immediately.

A. Server farm
B. Load balancing
C. Failover
D. Server clustering
E. Fault tolerance

16. A B C D E   Distributes the processing and communication actions evenly across a computer network.

17. A B C D E   The capability of a system to respond quickly to an unexpected hardware or software failure.

18. A B C D E   Data is written to both servers simultaneously; the data on one server matches exactly with that of the other.

19. A B C D E   A group of computers housed together in a single location.

20. A B C D E   The system redirects user requests immediately to a secondary backup system that duplicates the operations of the primary system.

INTERNET EXERCISES

1. Log on to the Internet and key the following URL:

   saforum.org/downloads/white_paper.pdf

   Find the formula for availability on page 6 and answer which of the following statements is correct.

   A. Availability is MTBF divided by MTTR
   B. Availability is MTBF divided by MTBF+MTTR
   C. Availability is MTTR divided by MTBF
   D. Availability is MTTR divided by MTBF+MTTR

2. Key the following URL:

   www.system4hire.com/new_rules.html

   Look at Rule #1. What is the path to the new economy for B2B and B2C businesses?
   A. Profit forecasts three to four years into the future.
   B. Build a brand over a couple of years.

C. Path to Profitability—target profitability one year after an initial public offering.

D. The median age of an IPO company is 4.1 years.

CONCEPT EXERCISES

Concept Narrative

(This narrative exercise can also be printed out from the Encore! CD that accompanies this textbook. File name—Chap09connar.)

Fill in the blanks of the following description with the correct answers.

The client user enters a credit card number into a form on a Web page. The data is transmitted to the Web site over the Internet using the _____ protocol to protect the data while in transit. Before the data arrives at the Web site server pool, it passes through a platform device where the SSL connection is terminated and the _____ text data is obtained. The content encryption service engine identifies the sensitive data fields and re-encrypts them using a 3DES or RSA public key. The re-encrypted data is then presented to the Web server, which then passes it to the back-end database. The data is stored in _____ format until it is processed. However, it can be retrieved and _____ by the Ingrian content encryption service engine so that the data can be presented intact to an authorized user.

The content encryption service engine scans all _____ requests and looks for fields containing a predefined tag. When it locates a _____ field, it applies a cryptographic _____ to the data in that field and passes the encrypted data to the server. Back-end services can be secured from the Internet by protecting user passwords, protecting secret encryption keys, and protecting cookies. Cookies are used to identify users. A _____ is a message given to a Web client browser by a Web server. The client browser stores the message in a _____ file. Each time the client _____ a page from the server, a cookie is sent to the server.

Concept Table

(This table exercise can also be printed out from the Encore! CD that accompanies this textbook. File name—Chap09contab.)

Read each statement carefully and choose the tier of the ASP application architecture being described. Use only one "X" per statement.

	TIER OF ASP APPLICATION ARCHITECTURE		
STATEMENT	CLIENT PRESENTATION	APPLICATION LOGIC	DATA AND RESOURCES
1. A client uses its Web browser to request account information.			
2. Handles all application operations between users and the organization's business applications.			
3. Referred to as a back-end system.			
4. Provides rules for processing requests to the database.			
5. The PC that provides the user interface to the Web server.			
6. The foundation of the Internet business application is the database.			
7. A server program that provides the business logic for an application.			
8. Uses HTTP to interact with the Web server.			
9. Web server receives HTTP request and provides response with the requested file (Web page).			
10. Database and transaction servers are located on a mainframe or large UNIX server.			

Concept Picture

(This picture exercise can also be printed out from the Encore! CD that accompanies this textbook. File name—Chap09conpic.)

In this exercise, look at the picture of the ASP architecture and label the missing elements.

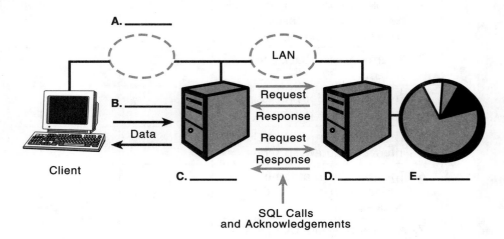

A. _____
B. _____
C. _____
D. _____
E. _____

CASE STUDY

G&J COMPUTER EQUIPMENT COMPANY

Objective:

Learn how an e-commerce system is designed for a mail-order company selling computer equipment over the Internet.

Company Profile:

G&J Computer Equipment Company has been in business for 14 years as a mail-order company that supplies pre-assembled computer equipment and peripherals to companies all over the world. The company has two warehouses, one in Austin, Texas and another in Atlanta, Georgia. The corporate headquarters is located in Las Vegas, Nevada. All orders received are processed through the Las Vegas headquarters.

Current Situation:

Recently the company has been evaluating whether to expand operations or establish a Web site for Internet marketing. The company has decided to form a separate company to handle Internet sales and marketing. The company expects a gross margin on Internet sales of approximately 50%. The company expects the Web site will open new operating channels for pre-assembled computer equipment, and there will be substantial cost savings on packaging, warehousing, shipping, and handling of equipment when using the e-commerce system.

Business Information Requirements:

G&J Computer Equipment Company is a global computer equipment provider with sites in Europe and South America. The company requires the ability to service several time zones and multi-currency payment processing. The company needs to open appropriate banking facilities in the companies overseas to arrange for online credit card processing directly authorized through the bank. The company also needs to complete the application process to secure a registered domain name for the Web site.

Communication System Requirements:

G&J is concerned about providing redundancy in its ASP architecture. G&J requires co-location of the Web site at the ISP's server in London for the

European operation and another one in Buenos Aires for the operation in South America. The company needs three dedicated leased lines to the Internet from all three sites: Las Vegas, London, and Buenos Aires. Currently, the company is investigating the costs of providing geographic load balancing to provide fault-tolerance worldwide.

Information System Solution:

1. A Web site was designed and the mail order catalog items were loaded into the e-commerce database located at corporate headquarters in Las Vegas.
2. Forms were created for ordering and a shopping cart was added for online credit card processing.
3. Web site forms delivered from the Web servers are programmed to calculate multi-currency information for the overseas locations.
4. Dedicated T1 lines have been established to the ISP in Las Vegas, London, and Buenos Aires to provide stronger security.
5. Dedicated T1 lines were also installed at the two warehouses in Austin and Atlanta for faster response time in processing orders.
6. The company investigated geographic load balancing but felt it was too expensive at this time. After the Web site has been "live" for three-to-six months and revenue figures are available, the company will reassess it.
7. An ISDN connection was established in Buenos Aires to the bank for credit card processing. ISDN services were available and economical. Because transaction files were small, ISDN provided enough bandwidth.

G&J Computer Equipment Company installed its new e-commerce site approximately 45 days ago. The biggest challenge has been training everyone at the headquarters, warehouses, and overseas on how to use the system. For the past 15 days, orders have been flowing through the system regularly. Shipments from the warehouse are arriving more quickly now because they can check inventory immediately and print the shipping label from the e-commerce application. The site in Buenos Aires took 30 days longer for installation than expected. The banks have been connected with ISDN lines because they remain idle until a transaction needs to be sent over the ISDN line. ISDN is usage based, so the company is not billed for idle time.

The company has already seen a slight increase in profit after the Web site went "live." The net margin so far is 4.5%. G&J Computer Equipment Company invested approximately $40,000 for the entire project. The company is pleased with the success of the deployment of the e-commerce site and is anticipating future benefits and substantial cost savings within the next 90 days.

Study Figure 9.33, and then answer the Study Questions that follow.

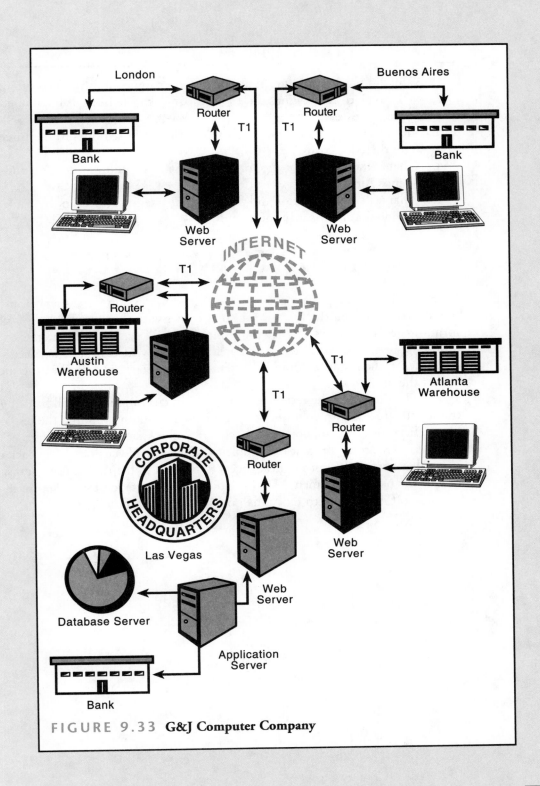

FIGURE 9.33 **G&J Computer Company**

CASE STUDY QUESTIONS:

1. Why did G&J Computer Equipment Company establish a Web site?
2. What type of cost savings did the company achieve from its e-commerce system?
3. Should the company have purchased dedicated leased lines to the Internet at all three locations?
4. What is the purpose of the co-location of its Web sites in London and Buenos Aires?
5. What type of connection did the company use to connect to the bank to provide for credit card processing?

GROUP TERM PROJECT

In this section of the project plan, you are asked to develop a test plan. Print the file *TestPlan* from the Encore! CD that comes with this text. In the test plan form, list test conditions and the procedures you will use to verify the test conditions. As each test condition is executed, record any successful or unsuccessful outcomes in the results column. This phase of the project is critical to the success of the project.

Usually after all of the tests have been passed, customers who will be using the system are asked to volunteer to participate in running through the test plan. They test each function completely on a pilot system to determine whether there are any glitches or problems. They provide customer feedback on issues that need to be put in cheat sheets to be used to help other users transition to the new environment. After the pilot is complete, customer approval and sign off is obtained to move the new system into production.

WAN PROJECT

TEST PLAN

		UAT	Unit
Type of Testing:			
PROJECT NAME:		**TEST CYCLE NO:**	
PROGRAM NAME:			
PREPARED BY:		**DATE:**	
TESTED BY:		**DATE:**	

Test Case #	Test Conditions	Test Procedures	Results	Date Tested mm/dd	Pass/ Fail P/F

CHAPTER TERMS

CHAPTER BIBLIOGRAPHY

Book, Magazine, Presentation Citations

Broadview. *eBusiness Perspective*. New York: Broadview, 2000: 1.

Kalakota, Dr. Ravi & Marcia Robinson. *e-Business Roadmap for Success*. Reading: Addison Wesley Longman, Inc., 1999: 94, 166, 203, 234.

Laudon, Kenneth & Carol Traver. *E-commerce business, technology, society*. Boston: Addison Wesley, 2001: 126, 209, 369-370.

Merrill Lynch. *The B2B Market Maker Book*. New York: Merrill Lynch, 2000: 1-2, 17, 19-20.

Sand Hill Systems, Larry Riss; Pushpathan Johnson; and Carol Trivedi. *eHub ERP Integration Guide*. San Jose: Sand Hill Systems, 2002: 2-1, 3-5, 3-7, 4-3.

Web Citations

ASP Article, "ASP. An Industry in Decline," ASPscope, <www.aspscope.com/articles/1137.htm> (7 August 2002).

BEA, "Achieving Scalability and High Availability for E-commerce and Other Web Applications, <www.beasys.com/> (June 1999).

BPMI, "BPMI Specification," Business Process Management Initiative, <www.bpmi.org/> (2002).

Brain, Marshall, "How E-commerce Works," How Stuff Works, <www.howstuffworks.com/ecommerce.htm> (2002).

Chambers, Mike, "An overview of client/server interaction using Macromedia Flash and databases," Macromedia, <http://www.macromedia.com/desdev/articles/flash_databases.html> (2002).

Coyote Point, "Establishing Geographically-Distributed, High-Availability Internet Presence with Coyote Point Envoy," Coyote Point Systems, Inc., <www.coyotepoint.com/equalizer.htm> (2000).

Giotto, "How ASPs Deliver Value: Next Generation Portals for Business Applications," TRG International, <http://www.trginternational.com/HTML/giotto.htm> (3 May 1999).

Gourlay, Douglas, "Designing E-Commerce Networks," Cisco Systems, <www.cisco.com/> (2001).

Hannington, Steve, "On the horns of an ASP dilemma," Network News, <www.vnunet.com/Features/1105543/> (07 April 2000).

Hirsh, Lou, "How Big is E-Commerce," E-Commerce Times, <www.ecommercetimes.com/perl/printer/18403/> (27 June 2002).

IEC, "Intranet Business Applications," International Engineering Consortium, <www.iec.org/online/tutorials/int_bus/topic01.html?Next.x=27&Next.y=12> (2002).

IEC, "IN-IP World Forum Web Hosting," Web ProForum, <www.iec.org/online/tutorials/Web_host/> (2002).

Ingrian, "Content Encryption Service Engine," Ingrian Networks, <www2.ingrain.com/techlib/whitepapers/wpl.htm> (2002).

Jessup, Toby, "WAN Design With Client-server in Mind," Data Communications, <www.data.com/> (August 1996).

Jessup, Toby, "Merging Old and New Worlds," Network Magazine, <www.data.com/> (August, 2001).

Johnson, Erik & Megan Lordeon, "Meeting Industry-Specific Challenges with Business Intelligence Solutions, <www.dmreview.com/> (January 2002).

Lake, David, "US top 11 types of software applications/tools accessed through application service providers (ASPs) based on percent of May 2000 survey responses," RDS Tablebase, <rdsWeb1.rdsinc.com/texis/rds/suite/> (6 November 2000).

Microsoft, "Introducing Windows 2000 Clustering Technologies," Microsoft Corporation, <www.microsoft.com/windows2000/techinfo/howitworks/cluster/introcluster.asp> (29 December 2000).

Microsoft, "Solution Spotlight: Keep Applications Responsive with Network Load Balancing," Microsoft Corporation, <www.microsoft.com/windows2000/advancedserver/evaluation/business/nlb.asp>, (03 October 2000).

Microsoft, "Solution Spotlight: Keep Critical Applications Available with Cluster Service," Microsoft Corporation, <www.microsoft.com/windows2000/advancedserver/evaluation/business/cluster.asp> (15 September 2000).

Microsoft, "Windows Clustering Technologies – An Overview," Microsoft Corporation, <www.Microsoft.com/windows2000/techinfo/planning/clustering.asp> (22 November 2001).

Network Computing, "Building E-Commerce," Network Computing, <www.networkcomputing.com/shared/printArticle?article=nc/netdesign/ecom2.html&pub=nwc> (15 December 1998).

Network Computing, "What is Middleware," Network Computing, <www.networkcomputing.com/shared/printArticle?article=nc/netdesign/cdmwdef.htm&pub=nwc> (15 November 1995).

Nokia, "Five-Nines Availability: An IP Network Requirement," International Engineering Consortium, <www.iec.org/online/tutorials/five-nines/topic01.html?Next.x=38&Nest=14> (2002).

SAVVIS, "SAVVIS, Built for Wall Street, Priced for Main Street," SAVVIS, <www.savis.com/> (2002).

Service Availability Forum, "What is the Service Availability Solution," Service Availability Forum, <www.saforum.org/downloads/white_paper.pdf> (2002).

Sholler, Daniel, "Business-to-Business Integration for the New Network Economy," Active Software, (2000).

Webopedia, "Whiteboards," Webopedia, (2002).

Webopedia, "Video Conferencing," Webopedia, (2002).

Webopedia, "Database Management System," Webopedia, (2002).

Webopedia, "API," Webopedia, (2002).

Webopedia, "HTTP," Webopedia, (2002).

Webopedia, "Web Server," Webopedia, (2002).

Webopedia, "Failover," Webopedia, (2002).

Webopedia, "Parallel Processing," Webopedia, (2002).

Webopedia, "MAE," Webopedia, (2002).

Webopedia, "Centralized Processing," Webopedia, (2002).

Webopedia, "Distributed Processing," Webopedia, (2002).

Whatis, "Batch Processing," Tech Target, (2002).

Whatis, "Transaction Processing," Tech Target, (2002).

Whatis, "HTML," Tech Target, (2002).

Whatis, "Gateway," Tech Target, (2002).

Whatis, "Replication," Tech Target, (2002).

Whatis, "MAE," Tech Target, (2002).

ZONA Research, "Application Service Providers and the Evolution of the Internet Integrated Enterprise," ASP Street, http://www.aspstreet.com/resources/publications/d.taf/pid,8 (May, 2000).

CHAPTER 10
DIRECTORY SERVICES

DIRECTORY SERVICES

Directories help people find the things they need by describing and organizing information. Every day, people search for one another in local telephone directories. This process involves simply turning pages until the correct name, address, and phone number is found. In the corporate world, mergers and acquisitions have produced large organizations that span the globe. Attempting to find a particular person in such an organization can be discouraging because they often lack a single source of information or a comprehensive directory listing.

The Internet, however, has provided a solution. Internet access has enabled the creation of online, electronic directories of people in an organization. These specialized databases also are used to keep track of other information distributed on a network. They contain user names, passwords, e-mail addresses, computers, printers, and servers. Directories are used for look-up operations, allowing users to easily search or browse for information or people within an organization. [Cohen, 1]

A **directory service** is a network service that identifies all resources on a network and makes them accessible to users and applications. This collection of software, hardware, processes, and policies works together to provide a service to the network's users. A directory service is software that can be installed on a server or on multiple servers. The servers require an operating system and a network infrastructure to connect to clients. Users can access the server and browse the directory database to retrieve information. [Howe, Smith, and Good, 1]

As shown in Figure 10.1, a directory service provides information about network applications, files, documents, and printers. It lists information about employees in different countries, branch offices, and manufacturing plants within an organization. Each of these items becomes part of the directory database. [Reed, 10-11]

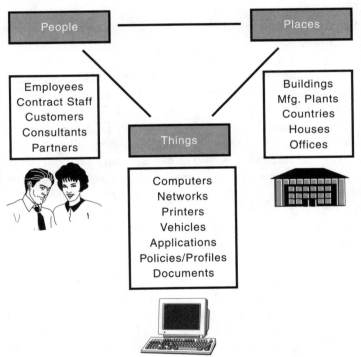

FIGURE 10.1 **Foundation of Directory Services [Source: Reed, 10]**

Foundation of Directory Services X.500 and LDAP

Directory services widely used in WANs today are based on the *X.500* directory standard. **X.500** is a global directory service framework defined by a set of international standards published jointly by the International Standards Organization (ISO) and the International Telecommunication Union (ITU). X.500 is equipped with tools that enable it to join and organize information from various database sources and directories. It provides a cataloging service by which pieces of information can be arranged systematically across sites within a global network. [Reed, 1] [Shuh, 1]

In its original form, X.500 was criticized for being too complex and difficult to implement. To address these complaints, a simplified version, called **Lightweight Directory Access Protocol (LDAP)**, was developed by the University of Michigan in 1996. It provides an open standard for directory services. LDAP is actually a set of protocols for accessing information directories. It operates over TCP, which enables it to provide services over the Internet. LDAP has simpler functions than X.500 and it streamlines coding/decoding of directory requests. LDAP's queries are 1.5 to 14 times smaller than those of X.500, which leads to quicker response times and lower network traffic over the WAN. [Benett, 1]

LDAP also has some shortcomings, including limited security control, character set limited to ASCII, and no method for replicating data between multiple sites (original version). These limitations are a problem for e-commerce. LDAP version 3 addresses this by providing for authentication, encryption, integrity, and replication (discussed later in this chapter), which are the features most needed by e-commerce organizations. LDAP has the potential to improve Web productivity and navigability; for example, LDAP has improved browsing by adding the "ldap://" resource to the URL syntax. These enhancements to LDAP have renewed interest in X.500 global directories in general. [Benett, 1]

As directory services have matured, they have become more sophisticated. In the past few years, new directory services have emerged that have been built using the LDAP model as a foundation. These directories offer bandwidth management policies, profiles, e-commerce information, and QoS (Quality of Service).

Three Levels of Directory Services

The Aberdeen Research Group, a leading IT (information technology) market analysis firm, helps IT vendors establish leadership in emerging markets. The group aids clients in identifying new market opportunities, entering those markets successfully, and accelerating the adoption of new technologies. This group has studied directory services for several years and has organized them into three levels as shown in Figure 10.2. Level 1 represents application-specific directories such as e-mail or ERP (Enterprise Resource Planning). These directories have their own security services to provide authentication and authorization services for a single application. At level 2, metadirectory services bring application-specific directories together into one global view of the organization. Finally, at level 3, is the full-service directory, which can support all of the needs of an organization. This chapter examines levels 2 and 3 in detail. [Aberdeen Group, 1]

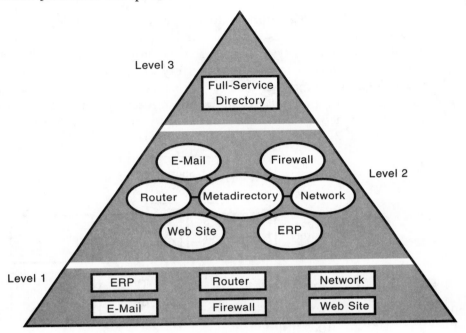

FIGURE 10.2 **Levels of Directory Services [Source: Reed, 81]**

Metadirectories

Organizations use different directory services based on the organization's goals, business objectives, and strategic direction. When organizations have several application-specific directories and databases throughout an organization, integrating and managing identity information can be difficult. A metadirectory solution integrates and manages identity information for an entire organization. Often described as a directory of directories, a **metadirectory** is a centralized service that stores and integrates identity information from multiple application-specific directories in an organization. **Identity information** is the summary of information about people, applications, and resources that is contained in incompatible directories and databases. [Microsoft, 1]

A metadirectory collects information from different data sources and combines all of the information into an integrated, unified view. A metadirectory is used to:

- Combine all of the information about each person or resource into a single entry in the metadirectory.

- Remove redundant or conflicting information between data sources.
- Present a unified view of a person's or resource's identity to an organization. [Microsoft, 1]

In Figure 10.3, an enterprise solution metadirectory links e-mail systems, network operating systems, databases, and directories together into one unified global metadirectory service. It integrates the disparate directories together and defines exactly how changes in one directory will cause changes in other directories. A set of enterprise-defined rules specifies which system will be the authority for any given piece of information. After a piece of information is added to the metadirectory, it is propagated to the other directories. [Fischer International, 2]

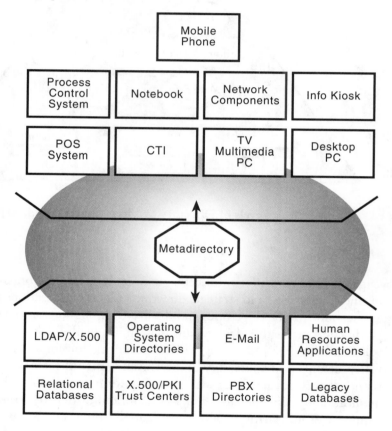

FIGURE 10.3 **Metadirectory [Source: Fischer International, 2]**

Different directories can contain conflicting identity information about a person or resource. The enterprise-defined rules determine the specific identity information to import from each directory for each metadirectory entry. A metadirectory can detect changes in identity information and then propagate those changes to the other directories.

Full-Service Directories

A **full-service directory** is an LDAP-enabled, directory-based identity management system that is used to centralize the management of user identities, access privileges, and other network resources. It enables the use of directory-enabled applications to create secure, customized relationships between an organization's network and the networks implemented by its customers and partners. A full-service directory lays the foundation for capturing, storing, organizing, and leveraging important identity information.

An example of a full-service directory is a product called **eDirectory** developed by Novell. The eDirectory, as shown in Figure 10.4, focuses on four major tasks: *discovery*, *security*, *storage*, and *relationship*.

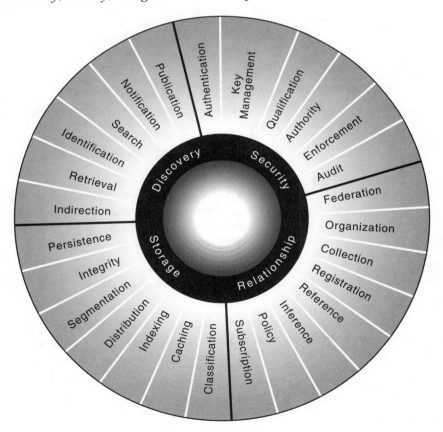

FIGURE 10.4 **eDirectory [Source: Novell, 1]**

Each of the eDirectory tasks has several functions. **Discovery** enables a user or application to browse the contents of the directory. Applications search the directory to find preferences, policies, and available services. Discovery is responsible for assigning characteristics to people and resources, establishing relationships, updating changes, and optimizing searches within the directory. Table 10.1 describes each of the functions within the discovery process.

FUNCTIONS	DESCRIPTION
Publication	Adds or updates information about people and resources in the directory data. Provides data storage for the directory allowing global access.
Notification	Provides a method to alert an external system about an event that has occurred in the directory. Ensures that data in the directory is current and reliable.
Search	Offers ad-hoc retrieval of multiple data types. Enables optimized searches against data not typically indexed by the directory.
Identification	Provides each object with a globally unique name. Uses a highly reliable reference/resolve mechanism to remain accurate.
Retrieval	Retrieves directory data in any form that is required by a user or an application.
Indirection	Enables the directory to establish a relationship between a user and physical assignments on the network. Objects that use indirection include groups, organization roles, file mappings, and application objects.

TABLE 10.1 **eDirectory Discovery Functions [Reed, 83-84]**

Security controls access to information in the directory. It allows rules to be established and the rights to be granted to users for various types of information within the directory. Table 10.2 describes each of the functions within the security process.

FUNCTIONS	DESCRIPTION
Authentication	Verifies a user's identity to the network and supplies the proper credentials to the system to provide access to the data in the directory.
Key Management	Delivers key-based credentials for inter- and intra-company communications. Provides the keys and certificates for strong information security inside or outside the boundaries of the local organization.
Qualification	Provides multiple levels of access to directory information. Determines the extent of information that each person can access in the directory.
Authority	Empowers the user to grant or deny access to others in the directory. Recognizes the rights of a user with authority to permit or deny access to objects and services represented in the directory.
Enforcement	Powerful control mechanisms mandate the security policies established by the network administrator.
Audit	Tracks changes or transactions that occur in the directory.

TABLE 10.2 eDirectory Security Functions [Reed, 85-86]

Storage is the database structure of the directory. It also enables the user to automatically control the type of data stored by applying classifications to the data structures. Table 10.3 describes each of the functions within the storage process.

FUNCTIONS	DESCRIPTION
Persistence	Stores data securely by protecting it against corruption or hardware failure.
Integrity	A resilient method for synchronizing changes that occur between copies of the data. The schema validates the data when entered into the directory.
Segmentation	Provides the ability to partition the directory database into smaller components that can be distributed across a network.
Distribution	Multiple copies of the directory database are stored on separate servers to provide fault tolerance for directory data.

TABLE 10.3 eDirectory Storage Functions [Reed, 87]

FUNCTIONS	DESCRIPTION
Indexing	Directory data can be sorted by any object or attribute in the directory.
Caching	Stores directory information in the server's memory for optimal performance.
Classification	Directory information can be categorized into different object types, such as users, printers, servers, or applications.

TABLE 10.3 eDirectory Storage Functions continued

Relationship is responsible for building associations between people, network devices, network applications, and information on the network. Table 10.4 describes each of the functions within the relationship process.

FUNCTIONS	DESCRIPTION
Federation	Establishes a governing authority over separate directory databases. Can recognize two companies in a supply-chain structure so they can share information easily to conduct business.
Organization	Provides the hierarchical structure to the directory in the form of a tree. Permits objects to be containers that hold other objects, such as users, printers, servers, and applications.
Collection	People or resources can be grouped according to similar roles, interests, or behaviors.
Registration	Applies a set of rules that enables objects to be unique in the database.
Reference	Maintains a link between the object and a membership list or from a membership list back to an object.
Inference	Applies access privileges and policies based on the location of an object in the directory tree.
Policy	Grants users and resources special consideration for task-specific requirements, such as desktop preferences, bandwidth, and configuration settings.
Subscription	Enables a user or application to enroll for a particular service. Users can receive specific alerts when an event happens; for example, an alert when a subscriber's stock hits a new high.

TABLE 10.4 eDirectory Relationship Functions [Reed, 89]

The full-service directory can be used to create secure relationships between an organization's network and networks owned by its customers or partners. Business partners can directly communicate with and update each other's directories. The full-service directory allows organizations to lay an e-commerce foundation within directory services. Now customer demographics, product interest, and buying patterns can be part of the directory. The full-service directory enables organizations to extend network support to customers and partners who use the Web as their primary channel for conducting business. [Novell, 1]

TOPIC
review

Directory Services

1. What has enabled organizations to create electronic directories of people?
2. What has generated renewed interest in X.500 global directories?
3. What are application-specific directories?
4. How do metadirectories control the flow of identity information between directories?
5. What is the difference between a metadirectory and a full-service directory?

STRUCTURE AND OPERATION OF DIRECTORY SERVICES

The X.500 model functions within a client-server architecture, where the client queries and receives responses from one or more servers within the directory service. This architecture follows a standard information structure called the *Global Directory Information Tree*. The **Global Directory Information Tree (DIT)** is a hierarchical naming model used to represent countries, organizations, and localities. Processing elements in the DIT provide access and maintain the tree. The X.500 model has three primary processing elements, which are described in Table 10.5.

Directory Information Base (DIB)	The collection of information managed by the directory.
Directory System Agents (DSA)	A database in which the directory information is stored. Can represent one organization or a group of organizations. Provides fast, efficient search and retrieval of information from the database.
Directory User Agents (DUA)	A client user interface program that is used to access the information in the directory. Supports user activities such as searching, browsing, and retrieving information from the directory databases.

TABLE 10.5 **Processing Elements of X.500 [Shuh, 1]**

Table 10.6 shows the three primary protocols within the X.500 model.

Directory Access Protocol (DAP)	The primary protocol used to control communication between the client and server. Manages communication between a DUA and a DSA.
Directory System Protocol (DSP)	A protocol used to control the interaction between DSAs.
Directory Information Shadowing Protocol (DISP)	Protocol used to replicate data between servers.

TABLE 10.6 **Primary Protocols of X.500 [Reed, 603-604]**

Figure 10.5 shows how a user might access the X.500 directory service. The user has a DUA client application on her workstation. The DUA issues inquiries and updates to the directory using the DAP. Three DSAs are also in the figure. A directory can be composed of several DSAs. These DSAs resolve inquires and updates to the directory. When a query is made, a response can come from the nearest DSA or it can be referred to a remote DSA. The DSP handles the process of interaction between the DSAs.

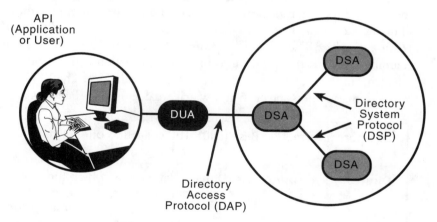

FIGURE 10.5 **Directory Protocols [Source: Blum and Litwack, 296]**

DSAs hold directory information and use any physical database within the global directory that will allow them to deliver the information required.

Directory Information Trees (DIT)

The simplified version of X.500, LDAP, enables the formation of a DIT that reflects the geographic and organizational boundaries of an organization. Each entry in the tree is known as an **object**. The tree structure consists of several objects related to one another. Figure 10.6 shows an example of a directory tree structure that is distributed to multiple locations. Here, again, are DSAs (labeled A-D), with each DSA taking responsibility for a portion of the directory tree. The naming structure is divided into country, organization, organizational unit, and locality categories.

At the top of the hierarchical naming tree structure is the **root**. The first level of names below the root consists of the names of countries (*C*). The country name level is defined as a code, called the country code. The appropriate country codes for every country in the world are specified in a standard published as **ISO 3166**.

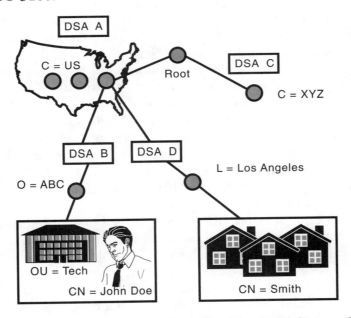

FIGURE 10.6 **Global Directory Information Tree (DIT) [Source: Blum and Litwack, 298]**

In Figure 10.6, *C=US* and *C=XYZ* translate to Country = United States and Country = XYZ. At the organization (O) level, there is one entry: *O=ABC*. The organization (O) level is used for names of organizations, corporations, or government institutions. The organization level can contain additional subordinate levels called **organizational units (OUs)**. These OUs can be states, cities, divisions, or departments within an organization. As shown in the figure, *OU=tech*. Tech is an OU, which exists within the organization called ABC.

Locality (L) is used to represent a state or province. In Figure 10.6, *L=Los Angeles*, which means the locality is the city of Los Angeles. At the bottom of the naming tree is the user, who is represented by a common name (CN). In this example, *CN=John Doe* and *CN=Smith,* which means the common name for the user can be John Doe or Smith. Each user has a unique common name in the directory information tree.

Of the DSAs shown in Figure 10.6, DSA *A* and *C* are managing country level objects. DSAs *B* and *D* are responsible for organization and locality objects within the tree. A DSA can control an entire organization or it can distribute administrative authority to subordinate DSAs. In Figure 10.6, DSA B alone manages the entire organization called ABC.

X.500 Naming Model

The X.500 naming model has a standard structure for naming objects within the DIT. This DIT is a data structure containing objects that are attached to one or more objects directly beneath it. The objects are grouped according to **classes**, which are used to organize levels or layers of the DIT. Each organization can implement a directory in its own way as long as it adheres to the basic schema. The **schema** is the organization or structure of the database. The schema for a relational database (directory service) defines the tables, fields in each table, and the relationships between fields and tables of the database. The schema rules dictate the naming and relationship of the objects and properties that can exist in the directory. The object class is used for creating individual objects and determining an object's set of characters. Each object consists of a naming attribute and its value. The naming attribute determines how the object will be used in the DIT.

As shown in Figure 10.7, objects are used to store and retrieve information about people, organizations, or network components. The upper layer objects are called **container objects** because they hold other objects. Container objects are situated at the "branches" of the tree. Examples of container objects are organization (O), organizational unit (OU) and locality (L). At the bottom of the tree are **leaf objects**. Leaf objects cannot contain other objects. Users, servers, and printers are examples of leaf objects.

Leaf objects are real-world objects and are described by a common name (CN). At each level of the DIT, an object can have certain attributes or properties of information that further describe the object.

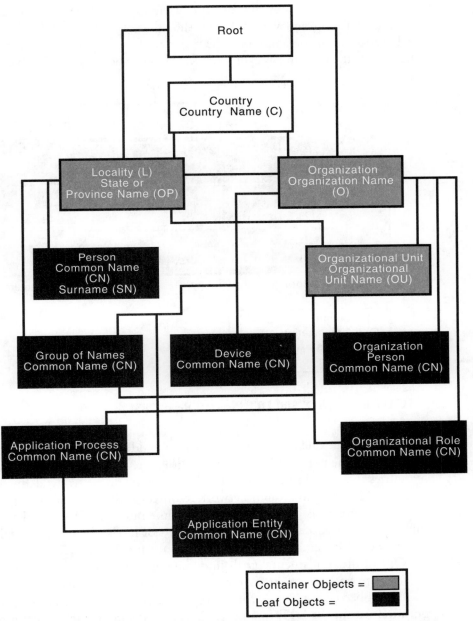

FIGURE 10.7 Organizational Hierarchy of Directory Service Using X.500 Model [Source: Reed, 628]

The X.500 directory structure shown in Figure 10.8 follows the hierarchy of country, organization, and OU. An X.500 directory structure should resemble a pyramid shape in which the bottom layers are derived from the top layers. A very flat and wide tree design is not as efficient as a tree designed in the shape of a pyramid. The bottom layers of the tree should ideally offer flexibility for moves and changes in the organization. The majority of the leaf objects are contained in the OUs at the bottom layers of the tree. [Hughes and Thomas, 26-27]

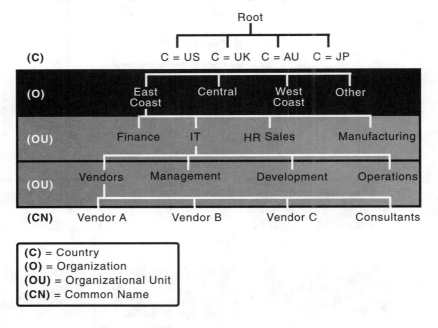

FIGURE 10.8 X.500 DIT [Source: Reed, 283]

The bottom, OU level of the structure should define the LAN and WAN locations of the network infrastructure. In Figure 10.8, the top level represents countries included in the WAN. The bottom level of the tree is defined by the LAN and is designed around network resources such as divisions, departments, or workgroups. It is important to consider the number of levels or layers being built into the tree structure. The more layers or levels, the harder it will be for users to find one another in the tree. [Hughes and Thomas, 23-24]

One of the fundamental goals in designing a directory structure is to simplify access to network resources for the users. When navigating through the DIT, each level becomes a part of the context. The context defines its position or location within the DIT. In an organizational hierarchy, each object is given a distinguished name during its creation. The naming of the object determines the location or position of the object in the tree. The distinguished name defines all of the containers that form a path from the top of the tree to an object. The deeper the number of levels of hierarchy in the DIT, the harder it is for users to find other users or resources in it. [Hughes and Thomas, 163-166]

LDAP Naming Model

The LDAP directory structure is simpler than X.500 because it doesn't use as many levels in the tree structure. Notice in Figure 10.9 that the top layer of the tree is divided into domain components (DCs). The bottom layers are OUs, which are people, places, groups, and applications.

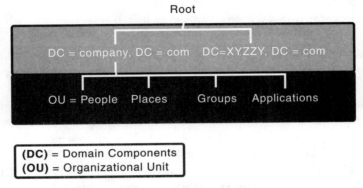

FIGURE 10.9 **LDAP DIT [Source: Reed, 283]**

TOPIC *review* **Structure and Operation of Directory Services**

1. What are the three primary protocols used within the X.500 model?
2. What is always at the top of the hierarchical naming tree structure?
3. If each organization can implement a directory in its own way, how can they be integrated so they can exchange directory information?
4. What are the building blocks of a directory?
5. What determines the location or position of an object in the tree?

THE DOMAIN NAME SYSTEM

Directories can be described as repositories for network names. Within the Internet, *domains* are defined by their IP (Internet Protocol) addresses. A **domain** is a group of computers and devices on a network that are administered as one unit with common rules and procedures. All devices sharing a common part of its IP address are said to be the domain. In TCP/IP (Transmission Control Protocol/Internet Protocol) networks, the DNS (Domain Name System) is the global directory system used to match domain names to specific network IP addresses. DNS divides the larger networks into domains. DNS is a database of domain names. The domains exist at different levels connected together in a hierarchy. The entire DNS domain structure is called the *DNS namespace*. The **DNS namespace** identifies the structure of the

527

domains that are used to form a complete domain. The name assigned to a domain or computer relates to its position in the namespace.

DNS Namespace

A DNS namespace plays a key role in a directory service because it allows reference and retrieval of related information. A hierarchical namespace is characteristic of most global systems, and allows information and authority to be distributed through the namespace. For example, the DNS hierarchy consists of the root-level domain at the top, followed by top-level domains, second-level domains, and subdomains. The top-level domain (TLD) is a system of 13 file servers distributed around the globe. These file servers contain authoritative databases that form a master list of all TLD names. Every name in the TLD must be unique with a central server that replicates changes to the other 12 servers on the root server system. Every domain name has a suffix indicating to which TLD it belongs. (A list of the TLDs appears in Chapter 4.)

Domain names are placed within URLs to identify a particular Web page. Every Web server requires a DNS server to translate domain names into IP addresses. For example, the domain name for Yahoo is Yahoo.com. When users browse for this domain name, a DNS server on the Internet is contacted that translates the domain name Yahoo.com to the IP address of 66.218.71.89.

DNS forms one of the largest distributed databases in the world. When users use the Web or send an e-mail message, they use a domain name to execute the request. The Internet's DNS translates the domain name to the matching IP address. If one DNS server is unable to translate a domain name, it asks another server to translate the name, and continues searching through DNS servers until the correct IP address is found. Actually the name server starts its search for an IP address by contacting one of the root name servers. The root servers know the IP address of all name servers for the TLDs. The name server contacts the first root server in the list, and if that doesn't work, it contacts the next one on the list. [Brain, 2-3]

Billions of IP addresses and requests are made to DNSs every day. Any person on the Internet can easily generate more than a hundred requests per day. In addition, DNSs are updated daily with new domain names and IP addresses. A central authority, Network Solutions, registers domain names in the **whois database**, which is a central database that contains information about the owner and name servers for each domain. After a name server resolves a request, it caches all of the IP addresses it receives. Caching stores the IP addresses in memory on the DNS server. A function called **Time to Live (TTL)** controls how long a server will cache the IP address or other information. If another client requests the same IP address while it is cached, the address can be retrieved quickly from memory rather than from disk. [Brain, 6]

DNS also can be used to do reverse mapping to e-mail service locations for a domain name. A **mail exchange record (MX)** provides a mapping from a domain name to the name of one or more hosts performing mail service for that domain. When MX is compared to directory services, a **directory exchange (DX)** record is used to point to a host performing the directory service for a domain instead of an e-mail service. A DX record specifies a protocol for retrieving directory information as well as the host name. [Howe and Smith, 4-5]

DNS and LDAP

Figure 10.10 shows the typical two-step process for interaction between a client and the LDAP and DNS servers. The client inquires for the domain from the DNS server and asks for DX address records. If no DX records are found, the client assumes an LDAP service is running on the standard port at the given address. If one or more DX records are found, the client chooses based on priority and protocol. It contacts the LDAP server and retrieves the information. The client receives the LDAP directory name, which is returned as an URL pointing to the directory. The client can then search the directory to find the site or e-mail address at which to establish communication for the exchange of information. [Howe and Smith, 5-6]

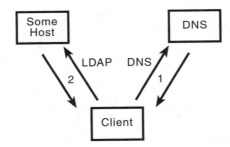

FIGURE 10.10 LDAP and DNS Interaction [Source: Howe and Smith, 6]

LDAP performs several operations using *daemons* on UNIX servers to process the requests. A **daemon** is a process that runs in the background on a UNIX server and performs the specified operation at predefined times or in response to certain events. Typical daemon processes include print spoolers, e-mail handlers, and other programs that perform administrative tasks for an operating system. LDAP uses a daemon called **slapd** to handle connection management, access control, and protocol interpretation. Another daemon called **slurpd** provides replication services to update slave databases (discussed later in the chapter under "Replication") on other servers. Changes to be submitted to the LDAP server are written to the replication log. This replication log provides a timestamp, the domain name of the entry being modified, and a series of lines that specify the changes to make. [Umich, 1]

Figure 10.11 shows an LDAP query for a modify operation.

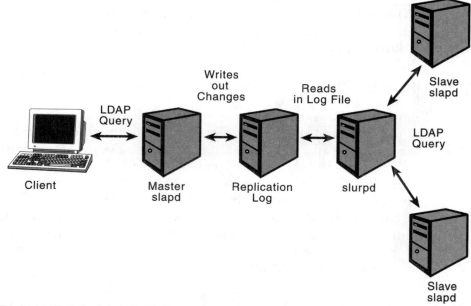

FIGURE 10.11 **LDAP Query Using slapd and slurpd [Source: Marshall, 9]**

The steps in an LDAP query are as follows:
1. The LDAP client submits an LDAP modify request to the slave slapd.
2. The slave slapd returns a referral to the LDAP client referring the client to the master slapd.
3. The LDAP client submits the LDAP modify request to the master slapd.
4. The master slapd performs the modify operation, writes out the change to its replication log file, and returns a success code to the client.
5. The slurpd process notices that a new entry has been added to the replication log file. It reads the replication log entry and sends the change to the slave slapd via LDAP.
6. The slave slapd performs the modify operation and returns a success code to the slurpd process. [OpenLDAP, 1]

Reference and retrieval functions are important to DNS operation. DNS provides the resource database for users to find Web sites or send e-mail messages anywhere in the world. A client can request and receive information from LDAP and DNS servers. Log files keep track of the process, report modifications, and the time when a process was successful or unsuccessful. The entire Internet relies on the DNS process to find users and Web servers across the globe.

The Domain Name System

1. How does the DNS namespace play a key role in a directory service?
2. In the DNS hierarchy, what does the TLD provide?
3. How are domains defined within the Internet?
4. What does the function TTL control?
5. Describe the two-step process for interaction between a client and the LDAP and DNS servers.

DIRECTORY SERVICE PRODUCTS

LDAP provides a global framework for incorporating existing local directory services impartially by using the existing DNS namespace. Other directory services use the DNS namespace and LDAP to integrate their directories, enabling global directory services to be formed between customers and business partners.

Electronic directory services come in many forms. They are mainly used to manage information about persons, organizations, computer applications, and network components within an organization. Directory standards and specifications provide an information structure as well as the protocols necessary for communicating information. [Anderson, 1]

The adoption of directory services by organizations has increased dramatically over the past few years. The most commonly used directories are Netscape Directory Services, Microsoft Active Directory, and Novell Directory Services (NDS). Each product offers different features for the structure of the DIT, principles for security, and replication. Administrative ease is one of the most compelling reasons organizations move to directory services. Administrative tasks can be delegated or distributed to remote offices. At the same time, each product has several useful tools and functions that can be used to manage the network and its resources from a single database. Applications, patches, and updates can be easily pushed to all clients' desktops with the assistance of directory services. [Boyle, 1]

Netscape Directory Services and LDAP

Netscape Directory Services are based on LDAP. The Netscape Directory Server centralizes management of people, their profiles, and their preferences. It supports presence awareness that enables a network to detect a user online. The foundation for security is built upon strong certificate-based authentication, which is used in conjunction with a public key certificate solution. This provides for more than 50 million user entries on a single system. The directory server can handle more than 5,000 queries per second.

Netscape Security

The Netscape Directory Server includes the directory itself and any software used to implement LDAP. A graphical user interface (GUI) allows end users to search and change entries in the directory. Netscape also offers a secure e-commerce server that simplifies administration and deployment of e-commerce applications. The directory enables customer self-service and uses SSL (Secure Sockets Layer) for secure communication. It supports PKI (Public Key Infrastructure) certificate based authentication (see Chapter 8). The directory server can be used to manage extranet user authentication, create access control, set up user preference, and centralize user management. Multiple clients can bind to the server at the same time over the same network because the directory server is a **multi-threaded application**. A thread is a semi-process, which has its own stack and executes a given piece of code. Multi-threaded means several operations can be carried out in parallel, and events can be handled immediately as they arrive. Threads can be divided between handling a user interface and handling database queries. Directory servers can be placed in strategic locations around the network to support distributed directory services.

Directory data is stored in Netscape's database. This database offers storage, performance, replication, and indexing. It also supports importing, exporting, backing up, restoring, and indexing of database records. The directory server uses a single database to contain the DIT. Entries are stored in a hierarchical structure in the DIT. Netscape has a metadirectory product that can support a single user ID and password. It provides flexibility to organizations by providing a standard method through LDAP for access to previously established database systems. The Netscape Directory Server can be designated as the central authoritative source of account information for all other applications.

Netscape's Metadirectory

As shown in Figure 10.12, Netscape uses LDAP connectors to interface the metadirectory with HR (Human Resources), network operating system (NOS), and messaging directories. The LDAP connectors translate directories' entries into an LDAP format for acceptance by the metadirectory. The metadirectory accepts SQL (Structured Query Language) directly from SQL databases while also supporting LDAP-enabled directories.

The directory server provides mission-critical reliability through the use of a transactional data store that maintains data integrity during power outages and hardware failures. It also has the capability to modify server parameters, update the schema, and perform backups while the server is online and operational. Replication through distributed databases helps eliminate single points of failure while transaction logging enables failure recovery.

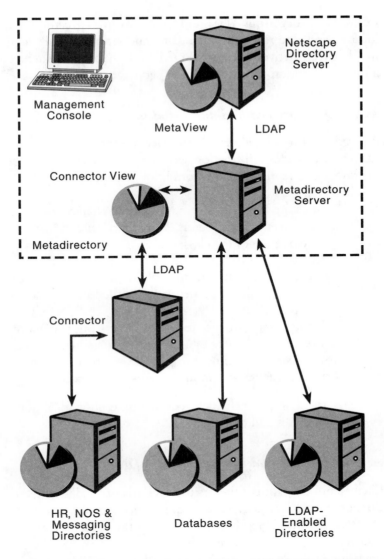

FIGURE 10.12 **Netscape Metadirectory Using LDAP [Source: Netscape, 1]**

Microsoft Active Directory

Microsoft's Active Directory product provides an information repository and services to manage information for users and applications. Like Netscape's Directory Services, Active Directory uses LDAP to send queries to servers. The use of LDAP enables interoperability with other directory service products. Active Directory uses an Active Directory Services Interface (ADSI) as a connector to support an application-programming interface (API) for LDAP. Other directory service applications can be easily modified to access information in

Active Directory using ADSI and LDAP. Active Directory also uses DNS as a locator service to resolve domain, site, and services names to an IP address. The link between Active Directory, LDAP, and DNS establishes Active Directory as a major contributor to the directory services market.

Active Directory Features and Benefits

Active Directory is the directory service used for Windows 2000 Server. Active Directory provides information security, policy-based administration, flexibility querying, and replication of information. Active Directory offers these features and benefits:

- A data store holding information about shared resources, such as servers, files, printers, network users, and computer accounts.
- Its schema defines the classes of objects and attributes contained in the directory.
- A global catalog contains information about every object in the directory.
- Objects and their properties are published through a query and index mechanism.
- Directory data is distributed across a network using a replication service. All domain controllers in a domain participate in replication.
- Provides a security model to provide secure logon, and access control on both data queries and modifications. [Microsoft, 1]

An Active Directory client is required on each workstation to access directory service features and benefits.

Active Directory and Integration with DNS

Clients and domain controllers use *SRV records* to determine the IP addresses of domain controllers. **SRV records** are service location resource records as defined in **RFC 2052**. SRV resource records map the name of a service to the name of a server offering that service. With Active Directory, SRV records are used to determine the IP addresses of domain controllers. The domain controller is automatically registered with the DNS server when it is started. Resource records of the domain controller are created in a file called Netlogon.dns that contains all of the records needed to register the resource records with the domain controller.

When you log on to an Active Directory domain, an Active Directory client queries the DNS server for the IP address of the LDAP service running on a domain controller for a specified domain. The response from the DNS server contains the DNS names of the domain controllers in the domain and their IP addresses. The first domain controller to respond will be the one used for the logon process.

Active Directory Domains and Trusts

Domains are defined in Active Directory as security boundaries. The directory can span multiple physical locations and include one or more domains. Every domain has its own security policies and trust relationships with other domains. Each domain stores only the information about the objects located in that specific domain. Domains are combined into hierarchical structures called **domain trees**. Multiple domains form a **forest**. With Windows 2000, domains in a tree are joined together through two-way transitive trust relationships. These trust relationships allow a single logon process to authenticate a user on all domains within the domain tree or forest.

When a domain trust is established between two domains, a domain controller in one domain can authenticate users in another domain. Figure 10.13 shows two domains in a trust relationship: the *trusting domain* (resource) and the *trusted domain* (account). The **trusting domain** contains all of the servers, printers and workstations. The **trusted domain** contains all of the user accounts and their privileges. In Windows 2000, all trusts are transitive and two-way, meaning that trust occurs automatically between both domains.

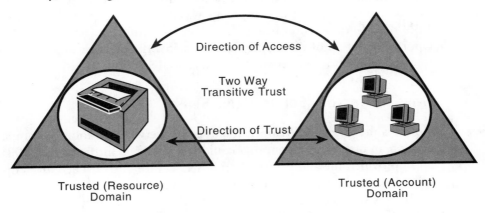

Trusted (Resource) Domain

Direction of Access

Two Way Transitive Trust

Direction of Trust

Trusted (Account) Domain

FIGURE 10.13 Domain Trusts [Source: Microsoft, 1]

All Windows 2000 domains in all of the domain trees in a forest share transitive trust relationships between the domains and transitive trust relationships between domain trees. Domains map the logical structure of an organization. There is not necessarily a correlation between a network's physical structure and its domain structure. Active Directory uses sites to distinguish the physical layout of the network. [Microsoft, 1]

Active Directory Sites and Services

Computers are assigned to sites based on their location within a subnet or a set of well-connected subnets. Subnets report physical information about network connectivity to the directory. Sites map the physical structure of the network. All computers within a site must have low latency and high-speed connections to be described as a well-connected subnet. Sites are used to facilitate authentication, replication, and services. Directory information is replicated both within and among sites. Within a site, replication between domain controllers is automatic. Between sites, replication occurs according to customized schedules. [Microsoft, 1]

An outstanding example of an implementation of Active Directory is ABN AMRO located in the Netherlands. ABN AMRO provides electronic financial services that include everything from consumer banking Web sites to electronic transactions between wholesale institutions. This project involves more than 25,000 users and 30,000 workstations distributed across more than 1,000 locations. The architecture of ABN AMRO includes a central data center with a mainframe system and several branch offices connected in a hub-and-spoke topology.

Microsoft used its Metadirectory Services (MMS) product to integrate with its large-scale implementation of Active Directory. Careful planning and design led to a robust security and authentication infrastructure implemented with Microsoft PKI. The network topology was designed for redundancy with the ABN AMRO data center being located at two facilities to provide for failover. Upon completion of the installation, the network operations staff has been able to manage most of the network from a central location.

Novell Directory Services (NDS)

Novell is the original developer of a directory service and the first company to develop an operating system that could create LANs. Introduced in 1983, the NOS provided file and printer sharing services for LANs. The Novell operating system was so popular that it became an industry standard for LANs. Novell developers stunned the industry with the first ever directory service product in 1993. Novell has a 10-year proven track record of providing directory services and an installed base of 70 million users. It provides features that operate across a wide array of platforms, such as SunOS, LINUX, and Windows 2000 servers. Novell supports several file protocols, including AppleTalk Filing Protocol for Macintosh (AFP), Network File System (NFS), and Common Internet File System (CIFS). Novell's operating system, Netware 6, supports communication over TCP/IP and native applications run over the network. Netware 6 eliminates the need for Novell client-software on each workstation. It offers users Web-based access to files, information, and printers. Users need only a standard Web browser to log into the network.

Netware 6, in addition to supporting directory services and the management of files, printers, directories, e-mail, and databases, offers several new tools:

- Clustering and multiprocessing technologies to maintain non-stop service
- Global, browser-based access to network files and printers
- Directory-based security and support for open Internet standards
- Reduced network-maintenance costs
- Uninterrupted access to network resources
- Secure, browser-based management tools for administration of the directory

Novell iFolder and iPrint

A unique new feature of Netware 6 is the *iFolder*. **iFolder** enables the user to access personal files from anywhere at any time. Users always have access to the most recent version of their files, so they can work online, offline, at home, or in the office. Anything users save in iFolder on one machine will be synchronized in iFolder on all other machines.

Netware 6 also provides a new printing solution that provides global access to all network printers through a standard Web browser called **iPrint**. It gives reliable secure printing capabilities using SSL encryption. iPrint is based on **Internet Printing Protocol (IPP),** which is a new standard that provides for easy network setup for printers and lets the user print using IP over the Internet. IPP helps reduce network-maintenance costs by offering a single point to manage all of the networked printers.

Additional Features of Novell's eDirectory

In addition to iFolder and iPrint, Novell also offers a LDAP-enabled, directory-based identity management system called eDirectory, discussed briefly in the beginning of this chapter. eDirectory supports an extensible schema and hierarchical tree structure that allows it to manage nearly any type of object. eDirectory centralizes the management of user identities, access rights, platforms, and network resources. It has the capability to manage large numbers of customers and partners over the Internet. The directory can scale to more than one billion objects in the directory tree. [Novell, 1]

eDirectory uses DNS federation, which means an eDirectory tree can be established using the DNS naming convention. This eliminates the barrier between Internet, intranet, and extranet resources, and can extend the reach of the network infrastructure to customers and business partners. If a business also installs a DNS-based eDirectory tree, it is possible to manage users in the trees of its business partners. [Novell, 1]

Using eDirectory enables an organization to lay a foundation for e-commerce. eDirectory supports **Directory-Enabled Applications (DEN).** DEN integrates policy and directory services into an authoritative, distributed, intelligent repository of information. Policy rules in a directory can define the type of QoS and traffic routing assigned to a specific person, group, service, or resource. Devices check with the centralized directory for update information or policy changes. The directory works with network equipment such as switches and routers. It allows administrators to assign bandwidth to applications and users. [Sheldon, 365-366]

Figure 10.14 shows an example of directory enabling applications for supply chain management. A supplier (Company A) and a manufacturer (Company B) have installed eDirectory to improve communication between their businesses. They have established a notification system in which Company B (manufacturer) automatically alerts Company A (supplier) when it needs another shipment. Company B has granted Company A access to its materials inventory database so the supplier will know when supplies are low and how much the manufacturer requires. The security protocols within eDirectory prevent the supplier from getting access to more information than it needs. [Novell, 3]

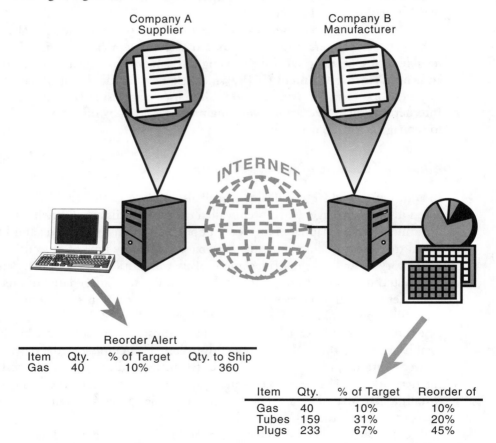

FIGURE 10.14 Supplier to Manufacturer Notification System [Source: Novell, 3]

The eDirectory also can expedite complex business processes. Using directory-enabled software, eDirectory can automatically update directories on other companies' networks. For example, the Australian Tourism Commission and Novell have recently launched a world-class portal site for Australia.com. International tourism in Australia had reached a record 4.9 million in 2000. The challenge for Novell has been to manage more than 10,000 pages of text with content translated into nine languages. Novell also needed to display more than 2,200 digital images on the Web site. Other requirements included a media-servicing component, major opportunities for partner promotions, a brochure builder, currency converter, and travel club registration. This truly global Web site caters to country level requirements. Visitors to the site find it simple to use with content relevant to their country. All information is presented in a suitable style for that country and in their language. The site services customers across five regions: the Americas, Europe, Asia, Japan, and New Zealand. [Novell, 1]

Directory services products by Novell, Netscape, and Microsoft all provide similar services for organizing users, authentication, and managing permissions to information. Each product has its own proprietary database management system. They differ in maturity, management, and replication methods. Organizations should always evaluate their requirements with each product's features. Implementation of any directory service product requires in-depth training and support from the vendor.

TOPIC review **Directory Service Products**

1. What is one of the most compelling reasons to move to directory services?
2. What type of connectors does Netscape Metadirectory use to interface with HR, NOS, and messaging directories?
3. What are SRV records used with in Microsoft Active Directory?
4. How are domains defined in Microsoft Active Directory?
5. How does Novell Netware 6 provide for access to personal files from anywhere at anytime?

REPLICATION

Directory replication is used to provide redundant copies of a directory. It can distribute directory data geographically to multiple servers to eliminate single points of failure. Directory replication often uses an import/export replication scheme. The master server is designated as an export server while other servers become import servers. The export server replicates data to one or more import servers. Any changes made to files stored on the export server are automatically replicated to import servers. Import servers are located on the LAN, or they can cross WAN links.

Replication Benefits

The benefits associated with directory replication are listed in Table 10.7.

Fault Tolerance/Failover	If a hardware, software, or network problem prevents the client from accessing a specific directory server, multiservers that support replication can refer clients to another directory for read and write operations.
Load Balancing	When someone replicates directory data across servers, it helps reduce the access load on each server.
Reduced Response Times	Directory response times can be improved by replicating entries to a location close to users.
Local Data Management	Replication allows data to be managed locally while still being shared among other directory servers across the enterprise.

TABLE 10.7 **Benefits of Replication [Netscape, 96]**

The smallest unit of replication is a database. A database that participates in replication is defined as a **replica**. There are two types of replicas: *read-write* and *read-only*. The **read-write replicas** can be written to and they contain master copies of the directory information. **Read-only replications** cannot be written to, but can be read. Any update operations they receive are referred to read-write replicas. When designing a replication strategy, the designer must decide:

- What directory information will be replicated
- Which server (or servers) will hold the master copy or (read-write replica) of the directory information
- Which server (or servers) will hold the read-only copy (read-only replica) of the directory information
- How should a read-only replica refer an update request and which server should it refer the request to [Netscape, 96]

Several replication models are available to an organization for managing the update flow from server to server. The design rules are important for organizing the placement of replicas for the network. At each organization, people need to understand how the replication topology works before deciding on the best model for their network.

Elements of the Replication Architecture

The replication architecture is based on the LDAP recommendations from the IETF (Internet Engineering Task Force). The architecture includes all elements of managing directory services. Developers of directory service products have adopted different techniques to provide for replication. These techniques are referred to as replication models and they exist within the replication architecture. Today, replication models for each directory service product use proprietary replication schemes based on keeping a log of changes or reporting on the state of objects. However, the IETF is working on standardizing the architecture used for replication. The LDAP Replication Architecture consists of replication agreements, consistency models, replication topologies, management of deleted objects and their states, and administration and management. The primary elements of the replication architecture model are listed in Table 10.8.

Replication Relationship	Established between two or more replicas. These replicas are hosted on servers that cooperate to service a common area of the DIT.
Replication Agreements	Defined between two servers in a replication relationship. The agreement defines the properties of replication. The properties are the Update Transfer Protocol and the replication schedule to be used.
Replication Session	An LDAP session occurs between the two servers specified in the replication agreement.
Consistency Models	Supports a loose consistency model between replicas. Contents of each replica can be different, but over time, they will be converged to the same state. The consistency of each replication model is based on the series of read and write operations. Replicas can be synchronized immediately or updates can be scheduled for a particular time of day, or day of the week.
Change Sequence Number (CSN)	Used to determine the order in which sequence updates are applied to all replicas. Every LDAP update operation is assigned at least one CSN. Each modify operation must be assigned one CSN per

TABLE 10.8 **Elements of Replication Architecture [Netscape, 97-99]**

	modification. When applying CSNs to modifications, four components define the operation: time, change count, replica identifier, and a modification number. These components assure that each CSN is unique. When evaluating changes to an object between replicas, each component is compared in sequence: first the time, then the change count, then the replica identifier, and finally the modification number.
Change Log	A record is kept of modifications that occur on a replica. Every supplier server maintains a change log. When an entry or object is modified, a change record is written to the change that describes the LDAP operation that was performed.

TABLE 10.8 Elements of Replication Architecture, continued

Replication models define names for each server in the replication session. The initiator of a replication session is the initiating server. Servers that respond to the replication initiation requests are called responder servers. A server that holds a replica that is copied to a replica on a different server is called a supplier for that replica. A server that holds a replica that is copied from a different server is called a *consumer* for that replica. The way the supplier and the consumer interact is critical to the replication process. Each has designated responsibilities for its part of the replication process.

The supplier server must:
- Respond to read requests and update requests from directory clients
- Maintain state information and a change log for the replica
- Initiate replication to consumer servers

The consumer server must:
- Respond to read requests
- Refer update requests to a supplier server for the replica

Replication Topology

The placement of the supplier and consumer servers in the network is known as the **replication topology**. Replication models are designed to fit a replication topology. In a replication topology, a supplier is often referred to as a master and a consumer is called a slave. The replication topology can use any of the four primary models used for replication: master-slave (or single master), multi-master, cascading, or mixed environment.

Determining the right strategy for replication requires significant knowledge of the layout of the network and the speed of the connection links between locations. Initially, it is important to decide the level of service desired for locations that are remote from the central headquarters.

Single-Master Replication

In single-master replication, there is one master directory and one or more slave directories. The slaves contain read-only replicas of the directory data. Any directory modifications occur on the read-write replica on the supplier server. In Figure 10.15, Server A is the supplier server that holds the read-write replica and the change log. Servers B and C are consumer servers that hold read-only replicas of directory information. Server A can replicate (copy) all modifications of the read-write replica to consumer servers B and C. Because servers B and C are read-only replicas (slaves), they can only be written to by the master, which is supplier server A. The interaction and replication process between supplier and consumers generates network traffic, which is referred to as **replication traffic**.

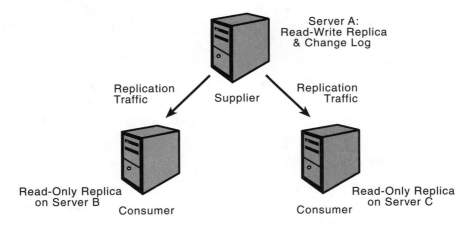

FIGURE 10.15 **Single-Master Replication [Source: Netscape, 101]**

Multi-Master Replication

In a multi-master replication model, replicas exist on multiple servers. This allows changes to be made to any replica without having to first notify the other replicas. Data can be updated simultaneously in two different locations. Servers are treated as peers, meaning that each server plays the roles of both supplier and consumer. Master copies of the directory information are the same on all servers. The changes that occur on each server are replicated simultaneously on the other server. The number of masters or suppliers is limited to two. In Figure 10.16, the supplier servers are Server A and Server B and they hold a read-write replica of the same data. Both masters can update consumer information (Servers C and D). The supplier (master) servers ensure that the changes do not collide. A conflict resolution procedure determines which change will be kept when both servers modify the same data. The most recent change is the valid one. Replicas in multi-master replication are described as "loosely consistent" because there can be differences in the data stored on each master.

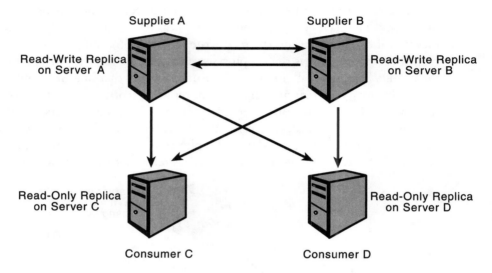

FIGURE 10.16 **Multi-Master Replication [Source: Netscape, 103]**

Cascading Replication

With cascading replication, a **hub supplier** receives updates from a supplier server. The hub supplier is considered a hybrid because it holds a read-only replica (consumer server) and a change log (supplier server). In Figure 10.17, Server A is the supplier and holds the read-write replica. Hub suppliers (Server B) do not keep copies of the master data, but merely pass it on as they receive it from the original supplier (master). Consequently, Server B holds only a read-only replica and a change log. If the hub supplier receives an update request from a directory client, it refers the client to the supplier (master) server. On Server C, the consumer holds a read-only replica of the directory information. Replica information is sent over an acceptable WAN link between Server A (supplier) and Server B (hub supplier) and then it passes it along over the slower WAN link to Server C. Cascading replication is useful for replicating directory information over slow WAN links.

Mixed-Environment Replication

A mixed environment can be any combination of the three previously discussed replication models. Mixed environment takes into account the bandwidth requirements of each site and allows for more than one model to be used at different locations. This model provides a higher-speed WAN connection between servers in the multi-master configuration and uses the cascading model for slower WAN connections. Figure 10.18 shows three layers of replication. Servers A and B are in a multi-master configuration with read-write replicas and change logs on both servers. At the data link layer of the OSI (Open System Interconnection) model (layer 2), Servers C and D each function as both the consumer and supplier. They hold read-only replicas, are designated as hub suppliers, and send updates to Consumer Servers E, F, G, and H. Many large organizations use the mixed model because it supports several different remote connections at variable bandwidth rates over the WAN.

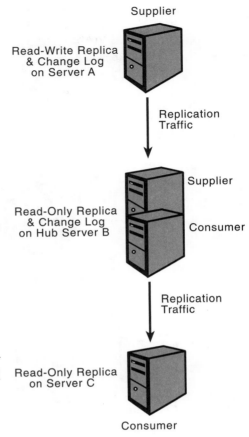

FIGURE 10.17 Cascading Replication [Source: Netscape, 104]

Factors affecting replication success within a mixed environment are:
- The amount and quality of the bandwidth for the WAN connections between building and remote locations
- The number of users, types of activities they perform, and their physical location
- The number of applications that must access the directory, as well as the percentage of read/search/compare operations to write operations
- The number and size of entries (objects) in the directory

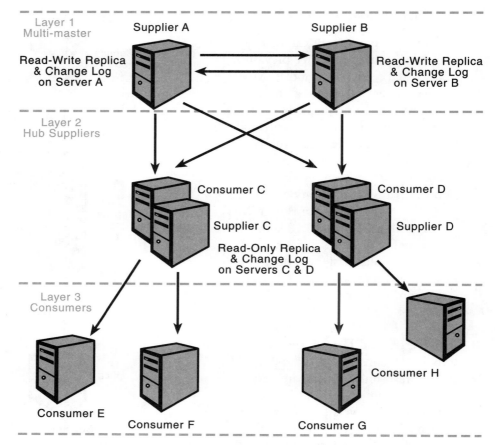

FIGURE 10.18 **Mixed Replication Model [Source: Netscape, 106]**

Directory Services over the WAN

Balancing the workload on the network requires network connections with speed and reliability. When directory entries are replicated, it is important to move data to servers that can be accessed quickly. Directory entries (objects) are around 1 KB. Every directory lookup adds about 1 KB to the network load. If the WAN is heavily loaded, slow, or unreliable, performance of directory lookups will be affected. A better strategy is to place the replica on a local server to speed up directory lookups and authentication.

In the example shown in Figure 10.19, the directory has 1,000,000 user objects clustered in 4 time zones. The peak usage across time zones is 12 hours long. Directory lookups average 10 per user. As a result, the directory supports 10,000,000 reads per day. In addition, a messaging server handles 25,000,000 mail messages a day. The messaging server performs 5 directory lookups for every mail message. This results in 125,000,000 reads per day. When combining normal directory lookups with e-mail lookups, the total number of directory lookups is 135,000,000 in a 12-hour day.

Directory Lookups		
1,000,000 Users	10 Lookups Per User	10,000,000 Reads/Day
25,000,000 Messages	5 Lookups Per Message	125,000,000 Reads/Day
	Total Reads/Day =	135,000,000 Reads/Day
Assumes a 12 - Hour Day	Total Reads/Second = 3,125	43,200 Seconds

FIGURE 10.19 **Directory Lookups [Source: Netscape, 1]**

Calculating the total potential directory lookups helps to determine how many directory servers are required to support directory services for the organization. On the average, a directory server allows 500 reads per second. In this example, after dividing 135,000,000/500, it is determined that at least 7 directory servers will be needed. [Netscape, 1]

Replication costs are based on the speed of the bandwidth and the amount of directory information being replicated. In addition, the cost includes analysis of the current traffic requirements for other applications using the WAN links. Sites that are multi-master replicas need to be high speed with low latency. Other sites with slower WAN links can tolerate a loosely consistent replication strategy.

In Figure 10.20, five locations and the headquarters are located in New York. Each of the five locations will participate in the replication model. To build a replication model, designers must first identify the WAN connection speeds between the locations and each WAN connection and the speed, latency, and cost assigned to each WAN link. London and New York are larger sites with 500-800 users respectively. The other sites are local sales offices and have less than 15 people in each site. Cost is determined by latency, current traffic patterns, and speed of the link.

Replication across Time Zones

There are 25 standard time zones around the world. People living at the same longitude usually have the same local time. Universal Time Coordination (UTC) is used as the base for calculating time. Each time zone is an integer offset of hours to UTC time. The offset can be the UTC time + x hours or − x hours depending on the location. If the UTC time is 12:00 (noon/pm) and the offset is +5 hours, the local time is 5:00 p.m. (in military time, 17:00 hours). [World Clock, 1]

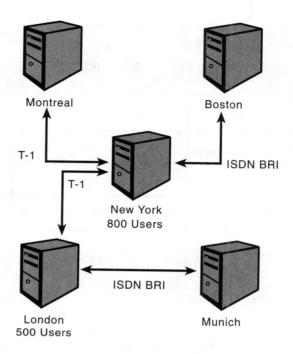

Montreal

Boston

T-1

ISDN BRI

T-1

New York
800 Users

ISDN BRI

London
500 Users

Munich

FIGURE 10.20 **WAN Site Connections and Costs**

When planning a replication model for all of the sites in an organization, the designer must know the correct time zone for each site where there will be a server with a replica. Usually the server at the corporate headquarters site is designated as the source of time and the replication schedule is defined on this server. Frequently, the time provider server is connected to an atomic clock. This clock provides time for the United States and is provided by National Institute of Standards and Technology (NIST) and the U.S. Naval Observatory (USNO). The time maintained by both agencies is never more than 0.000.0001 seconds from UTC. [U.S. Naval Observatory, 1]

A software utility must be installed on the server at the corporate headquarters to automatically check the time once a day or more often if required.

Looking at Figure 10.21, the corporate headquarters is located in New York and is connected to the atomic clock to keep accurate time. The time schedule for replication is set on the New York server.

The replication model for Figure 10.21 is a multi-master. A read-write replica exists on the New York and London servers. The London office has 500 people, so putting a read-write replica there gives them local authentication. The WAN link between New York and London is a high-speed T1 connection, so directory updates should be timely. The replication schedule is set to replicate every two hours.

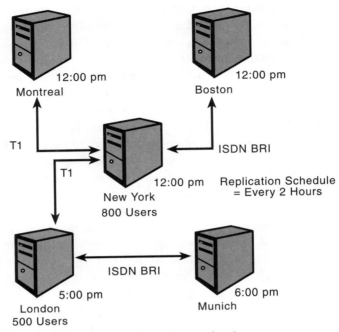

FIGURE 10.21 Replication Schedules [Microsoft, 7]

The interval of time determines how often replications occur within the scheduled window. Replication intervals of about one to three hours increase WAN traffic, and therefore the cost. Larger intervals of more than three hours do not increase WAN traffic but increase the latency of updates, which affects the integrity of the directory service database. In addition, clock differences between servers can cause problems with database integrity.

If timestamps are not accurate and a server produces timestamps that are older than the other servers, its updates will not be recorded. This means the contents of the replicated databases do not exactly match at a given point in time. Consistency with time between servers is critical to maintaining the integrity of the directory service database. [Reed, 10]

Replication with Current Directory Service Products

All directory service products use replication models to keep their directory databases consistent. With Microsoft Active Directory, the domain controllers contain a read-write copy of the database and are domain peers in the hierarchy. Active Directory changes are replicated between the domain controllers within the domain tree. The whole object is replicated rather than individual fields. Active Directory employs **Update Sequence Numbers (USNs),** which are numbers assigned to each object. Using a time-based formula, Active Directory recognizes when an object has been created or modified and then compares this new information with that of other domain controllers in the domain tree. If one USN is higher than another, Active Directory replicates the changed object on the domain controller. [Boyle, 1]

Active Directory uses the **Global Catalog (GC)** server to service requests without having to traverse the WAN to a domain controller to get directory information. The GC server contains a full replica of all objects in the directory for its host domain. It also contains a partial replica of all objects contained in the directory of every other domain in the forest. The GC contains a limited set of the most common properties for querying objects in a domain. It is designed to respond to user queries about objects anywhere in the forest efficiently. This reduces WAN traffic and speeds up access to Active Directory objects. Site-links are also used to reduce traffic propagated around the WAN. Site-links allow the administrator to specify which servers will talk to whom, when, and by what protocol. GCs should be placed over fast WAN links to maintain directory database integrity. [Microsoft, 1]

Novell's Netware 6 Directory Services (NDS) and eDirectory use a replication model that differs slightly from that of Netscape and Active Directory. This model uses a concept called *partitioning*. **Partitioning** cuts the NDS database into smaller pieces. A partition is stored on a server at each location. The partition is set at the location so local users are not authenticating across WAN links. The replica ring maintains the integrity of the NDS database. The replica ring is formed on designated servers strategically placed within an organization. Four types of replicas exist in a replica ring: master replica, read-write, read-only, and subordinate. The master replica controls all operations such as additions, deletions, and modifications of objects that occur in the replica ring. The read-write replica also performs the same tasks, however, the master server synchronizes the information between replicas in the replica ring. [Boyle, 1]

Database integrity for NDS is maintained by using the timestamp. Timestamps are associated with each object change within the partition to avoid replication errors. All servers in an NDS tree must be in proper time synchronization to avoid replication problems. Novell uses reference, primary, and secondary timeservers to manage time synchronization. The reference server uses the Network Time Protocol (NTP) to receive time from the atomic clock to maintain the most accurate time for the replica ring. NDS now uses TCP/IP as the protocol for replication and time synchronization between servers. [Boyle, 1]

Replication

1. What is the advantage of distributing data geographically to multiple servers?
2. What is a replica?
3. What are CSNs used for in the replication process?
4. How are servers treated in a multi-master replication model?
5. What are the factors affecting replication success between directory servers?

CHAPTER SUMMARY

Many large companies are looking to directory services to integrate multiple systems and applications. The need for electronic directory services is escalating. Users have become accustomed to the Web and enjoy how seamlessly it joins information together. Users desire their directory information to be easy to access as well. They are looking for an enterprise database that can provide information about people, places, and things within their organization. Directory services simplify the process of finding other employees in different countries, branch offices, and manufacturing. A directory service is useful for lookup operations, allowing a user to easily search or browse for names, departments, phone numbers, or locations of employees within an organization.

Considering the predicted growth of e-commerce activities over the next five years, meta- and full directories have the potential to provide strategic benefits to companies. Each is capable of bringing application-specific directories such as HR, e-mail systems, and various other databases into one unified global enterprise directory. Full-service directories create secure directory relationships with customers and business partners, who can directly communicate and even update each other's directories.

The creation of standards for directories has helped pave the way for proprietary directories to interface with LDAP directories. Proprietary directories now follow the X.500 and LDAP directory standards for the DIT, protocols, naming schemes, and security. Every directory has schema rules that dictate the naming and relationship of objects and properties that can exist in the directory. The simplified design of LDAP permits it to be easily embedded into e-mail, browser, or groupware applications. In addition, LDAP operations are less complicated and more cost effective than X.500 directories.

Within the Internet, DNS forms the largest distributed databases in the world. LDAP integrates well with DNS. LDAP incorporates existing local directory services by using the existing DNS namespace. DNS resolves IP addresses to domain names. The database schema for DNS simply does not offer the range of functions provided in a LDAP directory service. When used in conjunction, they can provide everything required for supporting directory services.

The directory landscape today is comprised of Netscape Directory Services, Microsoft Active Directory, and Novell Directory Services (NDS). All of these directory services have been successful in managing and replicating directory information. Successfully implementing directory services relies on appropriate planning for gathering all of the information required to populate the directory service. An efficient tree design is critical for easy access for users. The more levels in the tree, the longer it takes users to find each other within it.

Replication is the key to designing a fault-tolerant directory service. The placement of replicas within the WAN structure is important for providing quick access for users to perform authentication and directory lookups. The replication architecture and method of providing updates predicts the level of consistency and the integrity of the directory database. Most organizations today use multi-master replication models to provide for failover and load balancing. Change logs are important for providing records of modifications that have occurred on a replica. Determining the right strategy for replication requires an in-depth understanding of the layout of the network and the speed of the connect links over the WAN. The trade-off is whether to reduce WAN costs and replicate less often, or maintain a high level of integrity in the directory database and replicate more frequently, thereby increasing WAN costs.

The future of directory services, meta- and full directories, appears promising. The development of new standards for replication models and interoperability between directories will empower the implementation of directory services with e-commerce and ERP systems in the future. Going forward with directory services, users will be able to log on to any machine and have their applications, personal profiles, and systems configurations follow them dynamically. Organizations are likely to use the type of directory service that is most compatible with their existing applications. They will use directory services to conduct electronic business and collaborate with their customers and business partners.

CHAPTER REVIEW QUESTIONS

(This quiz can also be printed out from the Encore! CD that accompanies this textbook. File name—Chap10review.)

Circle a letter (a-d) for each question. Choose only one answer for each.

1. X.500 can be described as:
   a. A directory that allows replication of data between sites.
   b. A directory with simpler functions than LDAP.
   c. A directory that provides a cataloging service by which pieces of information can be arranged systematically across sites within a global network.
   d. A directory that provides encryption and authentication.

2. Which of the following statements is true about a metadirectory?
   a. It offers bandwidth management, policies, profiles, e-commerce information, and QoS.
   b. It is a set of enterprise rules that specifies which system will be the authority for any given piece of information.
   c. It is a set of protocols for accessing information directories.
   d. It is a global directory service framework defined by the ISO.

3. The full-service directory that can be used to create secure relationships between an organization's network and networks owned by its customers or partners is called:
   a. Metadirectory
   b. X.500 Directory
   c. LDAP Directory
   d. eDirectory

4. This is the primary protocol used to control communication between the client and the server in an X.500 directory.
   a. DAP
   b. DSP
   c. DISP
   d. DUP

5. What object designation is used for directory tree objects such as divisions or departments?
   a. Organization (O)
   b. Country (C)
   c. Organizational unit (OU)
   d. Locality (L)

6. What types of objects are located at the bottom of the directory tree?
   a. Resource objects
   b. Container objects
   c. Organizational objects
   d. Leaf objects

7. How many servers comprise the TLD of the DNS hierarchy?
   a. 5
   b. 20
   c. 13
   d. 7

8. The smallest unit of replication is a:
   a. file
   b. database
   c. document
   d. thread

9. A server that holds a replica that is copied to a replica on a different server is called a:
   a. slave
   b. consumer
   c. supplier
   d. peer

10. What is the size of a directory object?
    a. 2 KB
    b. 5 KB
    c. 8 KB
    d. 1 KB

Circle the correct letter (A-E) that corresponds to the descriptions below. Choose only one answer for each.
   A. schema
   B. leaf object
   C. forest
   D. replica
   E. global catalog

11. A B C D E Provides for redundant copies of a directory database.

12. A B C D E Formed by creating multiple domains in a tree.

13. A B C D E The organization or structure of the database.

14. A B C D E A server that contains a full replica of all objects in the directory for its host domain.

15. A B C D E An end object such as a user, server, or printer, which cannot contain other objects.

   A. slapd
   B. SRV records
   C. partitioning
   D. DEN
   E. daemon

16. A B C D E A process that runs in the background of a UNIX server.

17. A B C D E   Cuts an NDS database into smaller pieces.

18. A B C D E   They map the name of a service to the name of a server offering that service.

19. A B C D E   Used by LDAP to handle connection management, access control, and protocol interpretation.

20. A B C D E   Integrates policy and directory services into an authoritative, distributed, intelligent repository of information.

INTERNET EXERCISES

1. Log on to the Internet and key the following URL:

   http://developer.novell.com/edirectory/gettoknowldap.html

   On a separate sheet of paper, list the five benefits of LDAP directories.

2. Key the following URL:

   gort.metaparadigm.com/ldap/Practical-LDAP-and-Linux.pdf.

   On a separate sheet of paper, answer the following questions:
   1. What is OpenLDAP?
   2. Can Linux integrate with LDAP servers running Microsoft Active Directory or Novell's eDirectory?

CONCEPT EXERCISES

Concept Narrative
(This narrative exercise can also be printed out from the Encore! CD that accompanies this textbook. File name—Chap10connar.)

Fill in the blanks of the following description with the correct answers.

Domains are defined in Active Directory as _____ boundaries. The directory can span multiple physical locations and include one or more domains. Every domain has its own security policies and _____ relationships with other domains. Each domain stores only the information about the _____ located in that specific domain. Domains are combined into hierarchical structures called _____ _____. Multiple domains form a _____. With Windows 2000, domains in a tree are joined together through two-way transitive trust relationships. These trust relationships allow a single logon process to authenticate a user on all domains within the domain tree or forest.

When a domain trust is established between two domains, a domain controller in one domain can authenticate users in another domain. The _____ _____ contains all of the servers, printers, and workstations. The _____ _____ contains all user accounts and their privileges. In Windows 2000, all trusts are transitive and two-way, meaning that trust occurs automatically between both domains.

Concept Table

(This table exercise can also be printed out from the Encore! CD that accompanies this textbook. File name—Chap10contab.)

Read each statement carefully and choose the type of directory service being described. Use only one "X" per statement.

STATEMENT	TYPES OF DIRECTORY SERVICE		
	APPLICATION-SPECIFIC DIRECTORY	METADIRECTORY	FULL-SERVICE DIRECTORY
1. A centralized service that stores and integrates identity information from multiple directories.			
2. Provides authentication and authorization services for a single application.			
3. An LDAP-enabled directory-based identity management system.			
4. Removes redundant or conflicting information between data sources.			
5. Has its own security services for each application.			
6. Creates secure, customized relationships between an organization and its customers' or partners' networks.			

7. Presents a unified view of a person's or resource's identity to an organization.			
8. Delivers key-based credentials for inter- and intra-company communications.			
9. Links e-mail, NOSs, databases, and directories together into one global service.			
10. Capability to partition the directory database into smaller components that can be distributed across a network.			

Concept Picture

(This picture exercise can also be printed out from the Encore! CD that accompanies this textbook. File name—Chap10conpic.)

In this exercise, look at the picture of the directory tree and label the missing elements.

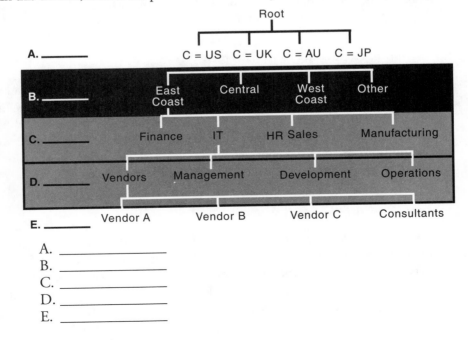

A. _____
B. _____
C. _____
D. _____
E. _____

Objective:

Design a replication scheme for a directory service network.

Company Profile:

Lopez and Fuller is a law firm that represents small- to mid-size technology companies in the United States. The firm has three large offices located in San Diego, California; Phoenix, Arizona; and Redmond, Washington. Its 600 employees handle cases for several software development companies and hardware chip manufacturers in Silicon Valley.

Current Situation:

The company's infrastructure network is a TCP/IP LAN. Offices are connected together with high-speed T1 lines. There are 300 employees in San Diego; Phoenix and Redmond have 150 employees each. Recently, Lopez and Fuller has been working on some joint cases that require the employees to access several servers in Phoenix and Redmond. Currently, each server requires a separate login and users are always calling the help desk for password resets.

Business Information Requirements:

Representing high technology companies requires Lopez and Fuller to keep abreast of all of the latest information on technology law, investments, and government demographics. However, users do not have easy access to servers in the other locations to exchange meeting schedules and copies of published articles. In addition, several legal contracts, briefs, and documents are worked on together by attorneys in the Phoenix and Redmond offices.

Communication System Requirements:

Lopez and Fuller wants to take advantage of directory services to better organize its users and organization. It wants its attorneys to have a single login to the network. Often new attorneys are hired at the Phoenix or Redmond offices and attorneys in San Diego need to be able to find them quickly so they can work together on contracts and briefs.

Information System Solution:

1. The 10 servers split between the 3 locations were upgraded from the Microsoft NT 4.0 to the Windows 2000 operating system.
2. Active Directory was designed and implemented to provide single sign-on and to ease querying for user names, locations, and so on.
3. One GC server was set up at each location. This provided easy navigation between sites because the GC server had user information from all locations.
4. Lopez and Fuller decided to implement one tree and its namespace became LF-AD.com because LF.com is its public namespace.
5. Because the locations were well connected with high-speed T1 connections, Lopez and Fuller decided to divide its site topology into three sites: Site 1 – San Diego, Site 2 – Phoenix, and Site 3 – Redmond.
6. One protocol—IP—was used for all sites.
7. Intra-site replication between domain controllers is automatic. In Phoenix, replication occurs between AZ DC1-DC4. For Redmond, WA DC5-DC7 replicate between each other. In San Diego, CA DC8-DC10 replicate within that site. Inter-site domain replication was established across the T1 lines to each location.

Figure 10.22 illustrates the network solution Lopez and Fuller implemented. Study the figure, and then answer the Case Study Questions that follow.

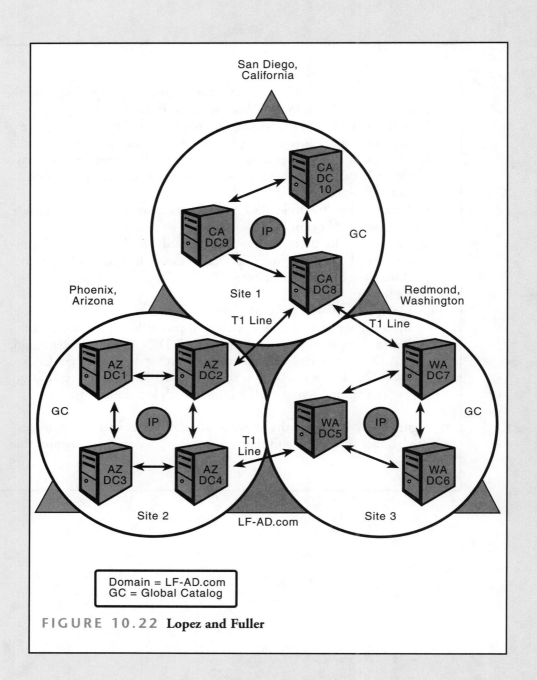

FIGURE 10.22 Lopez and Fuller

CASE STUDY QUESTIONS:

1. How did Lopez and Fuller eliminate separate logins for each server at each location?
2. Why do you think Lopez and Fuller decided to install a GC server at each location?
3. Do you think Lopez and Fuller should have created a forest instead of a single directory tree?
4. Why did Lopez and Fuller set up inter-site replication between all three sites?
5. Why are well-connected high-speed links required for replication?

GROUP TERM PROJECT

In this section of the group project, it is important to assess whether the requirements for the project have been met. Print the file *Require* from the Encore! CD that accompanies this text. In the first column, list all of the "musts" from the requirements model that you created in Chapter 3. In the second column, write a description of what must occur to demonstrate that the requirement has been met. This might be a description of a hardware device or software that was selected to solve the requirement. Each requirement must have a validation statement. In this way, a project's success is guaranteed because each requirement has been mapped to a specific solution.

WAN PROJECT

REQUIREMENTS SCOPE

A. High-Level Requirements

Reqmt No.	Requirement Statement [Statement must be clearly defined, complete, and verifiable.]	Validation Method [Description of what must occur to demonstrate that the requirement has been met.]
1		
2		
3		
4		
5		
6		
7		
8		
9		
10		
11		
12		
13		
14		
15		
16		
17		
18		
19		
20		

CHAPTER TERMS

CHAPTER BIBLIOGRAPHY

Book, Magazine, Presentation Citations

Blum, Daniel and David Litwack. *The E-Mail Frontier Emerging Markets and Evolving Technologies*. Reading: Addison Wesley, 1995.

Howe, Tim; Mark Smith; and Gordon Good. *Understanding and Deploying LDAP Directory Services*. New York: Macmillan Network Architecture and Development Series, 1998: 1, 4-5.

Hughes, Jeffrey and Blair Thomas. *Four Principles of NDS Design*. San Jose: Novell Press, 1996: 23, 24, 26, 27, 163-166.

Reed, Archie. *Implementing Directory Services*. New York: McGraw-Hill, 2000: 10-11.

Reed, James. "X.500: Truly Global directory services," *Unix Review*, 1995: 1.

Sheldon, Tom. *Encyclopedia of Networking and Telecommunications*. New York: Osborne/McGraw-Hill, 2001: 365-366.

Web Citations

Aberdeen Group, <www.aberdeen.com/ab_company/about/about.htm> ( ).

Anderson, Erik, "X.500 Directory Technology," ISSS, <www.cenorm.be/isss/Workshop/dir/details/dirtech.htm> (4 April 2001).

Benett, Gordon, "LDAP: A Next Generation Directory Protocol," Intranet Journal, <www.intranetjournal.com/foundation/ldap.shtml> (June 1996).

Boyle, Padraic, "The War of the directory services," ExtremeTech, <www.extremetech.com/print_article/0,3998,a=1559,00.asp> (8 June 2001).

Brain, Marshall, "How Domain Name Servers Work," How Stuff Works, <www.howstuffworks.com/dns.htm> (2002).

Cohen, Beth, "LDAP 101: Glue Your Network's Pieces Together," EarthWeb Networking and Communications, <networking.earthWeb.com/netsp/article/0,,12090_1444871,00.html> (12 August).

Fischer International, "Prio! Enterprise Meta Directory," Fischer International <http://www.fisc.com/products/priodocs/prio-meta-dir-tech-wp.pdf> (2001).

Marshall, Brad, "Introduction to LDAP," PI Software, <staff/pisoftware.com/bmarshal/publications/ldap_tut.html> (5 August 2002).

Microsoft, "Active Directory Overview," Microsoft Corporation, <www.Microsoft.com/windows2000/en/server/help/sag_adintro.htm?id=249> (28 February 2000).

Microsoft, " Implementing Active Directory for a Large Scale, Branch Office Configuration," Microsoft Corporation, <www.microsoft.com/windows2000/> (2002).

Netscape, "Directory Server Frequently Asked Questions," Netscape, <wp.netscape.com/directory/v4.0/faq.html> (2002).

Netscape, "Directory Server," AOL: Strategic Business Solutions, <enterprise.netscape.com/products/identsvcs/directory.html> (2002).

Novell, "Novell eDirectory 8.6.1: Detailed View," Novell, <www.novell.com/source/printer_friendly/dt14360_en.html> (2002).

Novell, "Novell Helps Take Australia to the World in Nine Languages," Novell, <www.novell.com/news/leadstories/2002/aug6/> (6 August 2002).

Novell, "Netware 6.0," Novell, <www.novell.com/> (2002).

OpenLDAP, "Replication with slurpd," OpenLDAP 2.1 Administrators Guide, <www.openldap.org/doc/admin/replication.html> (2002).

Reed, Ed, "LDAP Replication Architecture," Oracle, Inc., <www.ietf.org/internet-drafts/draft-ietf-ldup-model-07.txt> (March 2002).

Shuh, Barbara, "Directories and X.500: An Introduction," National Library of Canada, <www.nlc-bnc.ca/9/1/pl-244-e.html> (14 March 1997).

Umich, "Appendix A: Writing a slapd Backend," University of Michigan, <umich.edu/~dirsvcs/ldap/doc/guides/slapd/12.html> (2002).

U.S. Naval Observatory, "World Time Zone Map," U.S. Naval Observatory, <aa.usno.navy.mil/faq/docs/world_tzones.html> (April 2001).

World Clock, "About the World Clock," Time and Date.com, <www.timeanddate.com/worldclock/about.html> (2002).

PART FOUR
WAN Architecture, Resources, and Management

CHAPTER 11

PACKET-SWITCHING NETWORKS

CHAPTER OBJECTIVES

By the end of this chapter, you should understand these concepts:
- The difference between virtual circuit and datagram packet switching
- X.25 networks and how they are used to integrate an organization's locations
- The use of the LAPB protocol on X.25 networks to provide flow and error control
- Packet Switching Exchanges (PSEs) and how they perform packet-handling functions
- The use of X.25 for both switched and permanent virtual circuits
- The Frame Relay packet-switching service reduces the amount of processing for error recovery
- Data Link Connection Identifiers (DLCI) and how they are used to distinguish separate virtual circuits
- How Frame Relay places the responsibility of ensuring data delivery on the end point devices
- How Frame Relay charges are based on port charges, burst rates, and each permanent virtual circuit (PVC)
- Frame Relay Service Level Agreements (SLAs)
- How VoIP (Voice Over Internet Protocol) uses digitized voice over IP networks
- How computer telephony applies the power of the computer and the functions of the telephone to IP networks
- The importance of QoS (Quality of service) and prioritization in managing delay and dropped packets

PACKET-SWITCHING TECHNOLOGY

The diversity and complexity of today's networks demand higher speeds and greater transmission capacity for data. Packet-switching technology has paved the way for efficient transmission of packets of data across the Internet. Recent developments in digital signaling and fiber cabling have enabled the creation of enterprise technology systems for both data and voice.

Chapter 2 explored the use and difference between circuit-switching and packet-switching technologies. This chapter covers the use of X.25, Frame Relay, and IP Telephony. There are two primary methods for packet switching: virtual-circuit packet switching and datagram switching.

Virtual Circuit Packet Switching

Virtual circuit packet-switching networks operate like standard circuit-switched networks in that they dedicate a particular path for the duration of the connection. Virtual-circuit packet switching requires that a route be set up between the source and destination networks. An entry setup in the router table indicates a path for the virtual circuit. Each packet has a short header, which defines the virtual circuit identifier that will be used for transmission. As packets travel across the virtual circuit in sequence, they arrive at the destination in correct sequence. X.25 and Frame Relay, which are discussed in greater detail later, are examples of virtual circuit packet-switching methods used with public data networks. [Ohana and Parush, 1]

Virtual circuits can be multiplexed onto a single physical circuit. Figure 11.1 shows four virtual circuits identified between the source and destination. These virtual circuits are actually pathways defined through a switch. Each pathway or virtual circuit is defined in the switch for an organization. The telco providing the switch defines the virtual circuit and provides a **virtual circuit identifier (VCI)** number for input into the organization's router table. [Cisco, 17-3]

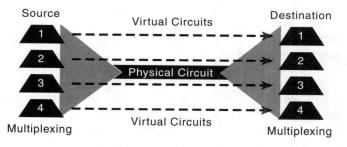

FIGURE 11.1 **Virtual Circuits [Source: Cisco, 17-3]**

Datagram Packet Switching

When datagram packet switching is used, the packets do not follow a pre-established route. Each packet can follow a different route to its destination. In this method, routers examine the header of a packet and find the shortest way possible to pass it to the destination. If a link is congested, an alternate route is found. In a datagram network, delivery is not guaranteed, because there is no prior knowledge of the routes to be used. [Ohana and Parush, 1]

Figure 11.2 shows that packet switching is simply a matrix of channels or pathways through a switch. Source A uses virtual-circuit packet switching and a defined pathway (labeled as 2) through the switch. Source B, on the other hand, uses datagram packet switching in which each packet can travel over a different pathway through the switch. Each packet is routed individually as an independent entity. The process is dynamic and does not need to set up and tear down the path. Overload conditions do not delay transmissions in datagram packet switching. [Ohana and Parush, 1]

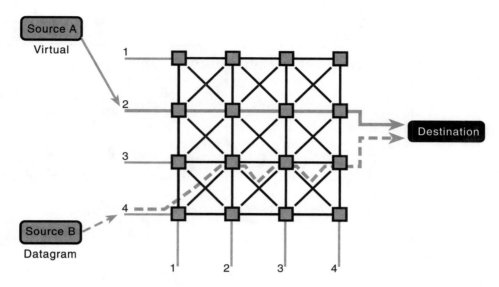

FIGURE 11.2 **Packet Switch Is a Matrix [Source: Ohana and Parush, 1]**

The primary differences between virtual-circuit packet switching and datagram packet switching are listed in Table 11.1.

Switching Techniques	Datagram Packet Switching	Virtual-Circuit Packet Switching
Conversation Establishment	Route established for each packet	Route established for entire conversation
Setup/Transmission Delay	Packet transmission delay	Delay on call setup; packet transmission delay
Delivery Notification	Sender notified if packet not delivered	Sender notified of connection denial
Overload Condition	Overload increases packet delay	Overload blocks call setup; increases packet delay

TABLE 11.1 **Differences between Virtual-Circuit and Datagram Packet Switching**

The benefits provided by datagram packet switching have greatly improved the transmission of information across WANs. Dividing information into smaller packets and only allocating the transmission path for a short period of time allows for fairer sharing of network resources across WAN links.

TOPIC *review* **Packet–Switching Technology**

1. How do virtual-circuit packet-switching networks operate like standard circuit-switched networks?
2. Why don't packets follow a pre-established route to the destination when using datagram packet switching?
3. How does datagram packet switching handle overload conditions?
4. Does datagram packet switching require setting up and tearing down the path?
5. How has datagram packet switching improved the transmission of information across WANs?

X.25 PROTOCOL FOR PACKET SWITCHING

Since the early 1970s, X.25 packet-switched networks have provided worldwide communications for mission-critical business applications. The X.25 standard was approved by the ITU in 1976. X.25 is a WAN protocol that uses packet-switching technologies. The X.25 protocol allows computers on different public networks to communicate through an intermediary device to a Packet-Switched Public Data Network (PSDN). A PSDN supports a network in which small packets are routed through a network based on the destination address contained within each packet. The same data path can be shared among several users in the network. The X.25 protocol defines an interface into the PSDN. Several network devices as shown in Figure 11.3, such as terminals, routers, gateways, servers, PBX (private branch exchange), front-end processors, and multiplexers, can all connect to the PSDN using X.25. [Webopedia, 1]

Benefits of X.25

X.25 has gained wide popularity because of its global availability. Golden Telecom Inc. (GTI), for instance, has deployed an X.25 network in more than 90 locations in Russia. X.25 offers secure, cost-effective, long-distance service for bursty data communication over low-quality circuits. Built-in functions for error detection and correction ensure safe data transfer. X.25 use of packet-switching technology makes more efficient use of available capacity because the total available bandwidth can be shared among several users. Some benefits of X.25 are:

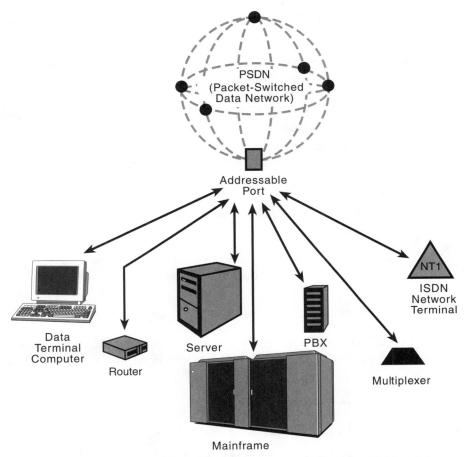

FIGURE 11.3 Packet-Switched Public Data Network (PSDN) [Source: Ericsson, 1]

- Data can be sent to more than one receiver at the same time.
- Communication is enabled between terminals with different interfaces and transfer rates.
- An error-free environment for transmission of all types of business data.
- Fast throughput and excellent response times.
- Dial-up and dedicated port options.
- Up to 1,024 simultaneous logical channels per link.
- Reliable connection over copper lines.
- A speed range of 9.6 Kbps to 2 Mbps. [Golden Telecom, 1]

X.25 Applications

Traditionally, X.25 has been used in place of dial-up or leased-line circuits as a way to set up links to remote branch offices or remote users. Its most effective usage is for connecting terminals to a mainframe. X.25 networks serve numerous locations worldwide and offer applications ranging from retail point of sale and electronic funds transfers to airline reservations. Several other applications used over X.25 networks include:

- Remote order entry
- Information retrieval in national and international databases
- File transfer
- E-mail
- Automatic teller machines and card-operated gasoline pumps [Golden Telecom, 1]

X.25 networks offer easy access from anywhere at any time and provide economical solutions for data communications.

X.25 Protocol Suite

The X.25 protocol maps to the three lower layers of the OSI (Open System Interconnection) reference model shown in Figure 11.4. Table 11.2 describes how X.25 supports the functions of each of these layers.

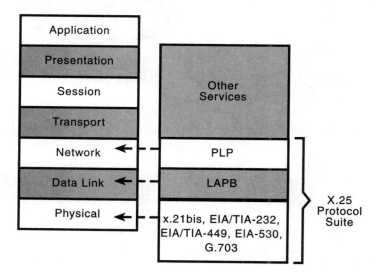

FIGURE 11.4 **X.25 Protocol Suite [Source: Cisco, 17-4]**

Physical Layer (Layer 1)	Physical Layer supports electrical and signaling functions. For X.25, it supports V.35, RS232, and X.21. The **X.21 bis** is a physical-layer protocol used to define the electrical and mechanical procedures for using the physical medium. It supports point-to-point connections, synchronous full-duplex transmission at 19.2 Kbps over four-wire media.
Data Link Layer (Layer 2)	Data Link Layer provides an error-free link between two connected devices. It uses Link Access Procedures-Balanced (LAPB) (see below) to manage communication and packet framing between DTE (data terminal equipment) and DCE (data communications equipment) devices.
Network Layer (Layer 3)	Network Layer provides communications between devices connected to a common network. At this layer, X.25 uses the Packet Layer Protocol (PLP) for managing packet exchange between DTE devices across virtual circuits. PLP handles segmentation, reassembly, bit padding, and error and flow control. It is primarily used for network routing functions and multiplexing of simultaneous logical connections over a single physical connection. PLP uses the **X.121 addressing scheme** to set up the virtual circuit. X.121 is an ITU specification-addressing scheme used in X.25 networks.

TABLE 11.2 **X.25 and the Bottom Three Layers of the OSI Model [Sangoma, 1]**

Operation of X.25

In an X.25 network, a packet is moved toward its destination along a route determined by various network conditions. Variations of *High-Level Data Link Control (HDLC)* are used in X.25 networks. **HDLC** organizes data into a frame and manages the flow where data is sent. It uses peer-to-peer communication with both ends able to initiate communication on full-duplex links. This mode of HDLC is known as *Link Access Procedures-Balanced*. **Link Access Procedures-Balanced (LAPB)** is a data link layer protocol based on *Synchronous Data Link Control*. **Synchronous Data Link Control (SDLC)** is a protocol used to connect remote devices to mainframes at central locations in either point-to-point or point-to-multipoint connections. [Sheldon, 1391] [Webopedia, 1]

LAPB provides flow and error control for transmissions that take place over physical point-to-point links. LAPB is monitored bit by bit. In addition, it can send and receive commands/responses over separate channels to improve throughput. LAPB manages packets on shared-line packet-switched networks. X.25 sessions are established to request communication with destination devices that then can either accept or refuse the connection. If either the source or destination DTE device terminates the connection, a new session is established to resume communication.

Structure of the LAPB Frame

The basic frame used in X.25 is LAPB. An LAPB frame includes a header, a trailer, and encapsulated data. Figure 11.5 shows the structure of a LAPB frame, while Table 11.3 describes the fields within the LAPB frame structure.

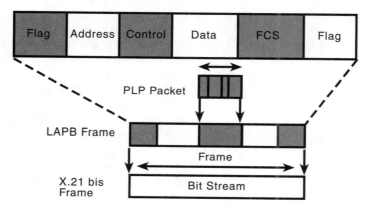

FIGURE 11.5 X.25 LAPB Frame Structure [Source: Cisco, 17-7]

Flag	Indicates the start and end of the frame
Address	Contains the address of the DTE/DCE which is used to identify the destination DTE
Control	Contains sequence numbers, commands, and responses for controlling the data flow between the DTE and DCE
Data	Contains upper-layer data in an encapsulated PLP (packet layer procedures) packet
FCS (Frame Check Sequence)	Uses checksum to indicate the presence of errors in transmission; a variation of CRC (Cyclic Redundancy Check)

TABLE 11.3 X.25 LAPB Frame Structure Fields [Cisco, 17-7]

The flow controls in LAPB use sliding windows to provide reliable services. LAPB supports an extended window size in which the number of possible outstanding frames for acknowledgement is increased from 8 to 128. This extended window size is used for satellite transmission in which the acknowledgement delays are significantly greater than the frame transmission times.

Functions of an X.25 Network

An X.25 network uses DTE, DCE, and a *packet-switching exchange*. **Packet-switching exchanges (PSEs)** are switches located throughout a carrier's network. They transfer data from one DTE device to another and perform packet-handling functions. Usually, PSEs use computers with special software and input/output devices to provide subscriber and line connections. [Glinoyer and Nir, 1]

Figure 11.6 follows a packet through a packet-switched network. First, all data to be transmitted is assembled into packets. Each packet is passed from the source DTE to a local PSE. The PSE receives the packet and looks inside for its destination address. Next, it consults its routing directory to determine which outgoing link to use for the destination network address. The packet is forwarded on the appropriate link at the maximum available bit rate. At each intermediate PSE, error and flow control checks are made before sending the packet along the route to its destination. The packet is interspersed with other packets destined for the same network address. Finally, it arrives at the receiving PSE, where the packet is passed to the destination DTE. [Ohana and Parush, 1] [Cisco, 17-2]

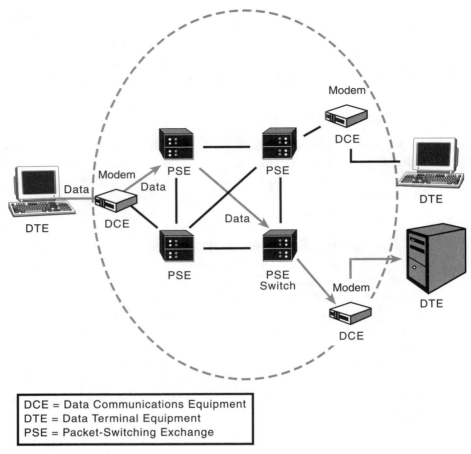

FIGURE 11.6 **Packet-Switching Exchanges (PSEs) in X.25 Network [Source: Cisco, 17-2]**

Figure 11.7 shows the intermediary device used in an X.25 network called a *packet assembler/disassembler.* A **packet assembler/disassembler (PAD)** device performs three primary functions: buffering, packet assembly, and packet disassembly. When data packets are sent to the PAD, it buffers (or holds) the data until the PAD device can process it. A PAD accepts synchronous characters and places them into packets of the proper length. It also assembles outgoing data into packets and forwards them to a modem, multiplexer, or CSU/DSU (Channel Service Unit/Data Service Unit) device. When a packet reaches its destination, the PAD disassembles and translates the packet to the proper characters. [Cisco, 17-2]

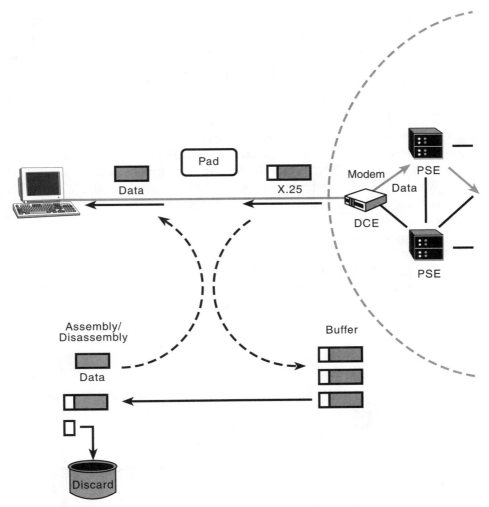

FIGURE 11.7 **Packet Assembly/Disassembly (PAD) [Source: Cisco, 17-2]**

When a DTE is connected to an X.25 network, a number of logical channels are allocated to it. These channels are divided into 16 groups with each group containing up to 256 channels, for a total of 4,096 channels. When data is transferred over virtual circuits, precise channel numbers and channel group numbers are assigned for use by all packets included in that data transfer. The destination for each packet is identified by means of a **logical channel identifier (LCI)** or **logical channel number (LCN)**. The LCI establishes the routers for each packet to the destination address. [Sangoma, 1]

X.25 uses two types of virtual circuits: switched and permanent. A **switched virtual circuit (SVC)** is a temporary virtual circuit established and maintained only for the duration of a data transfer session. With switched virtual circuits, a shared pool of logical circuits is used to support connections for multiple users as needed. A connection is established, data is transferred, and then the connection is released. This is the same operation that is performed over circuit-switched networks that provide telephone service. [Sangoma, 1]

When a connection is established on an SVC, the calling (source) DTE sends a **call request packet**, which includes the address of the destination DTE. The destination DTE must decide whether or not to accept the call request packet. When a call is accepted by the destination DTE, it issues a **call-accepted packet**. At the origination point, the source DTE receives the call-accepted packet. The virtual circuit is then established and data transfer begins. When either the sending or receiving DTE wants to terminate the call, a **clear request packet** is sent to the remote DTE. This remote DTE responds with a **clear confirmation packet**. [Sangoma, 1]

A **permanent virtual circuit (PVC)**, as shown in Figure 11.8, is a continuously dedicated virtual circuit. PVCs are used for frequent and regular data transfers. The logical connection is established permanently, like that of a leased line, and is always present. In contrast to SVCs, PVCs do not require that sessions be established and terminated. The session is always active. [Sangoma, 1]

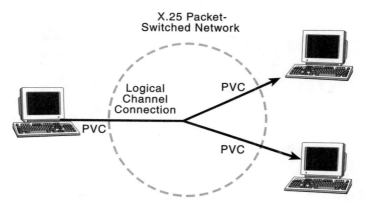

Logical Channel Connections = Virtual Circuits

FIGURE 11.8 **Logical Channel Connections [Source: JBM, 1]**

For some time now, the use of X.25 as a backbone network has been declining. Although X.25 networks are stable and virtually error free, there is an inherent delay caused by the store-and-forward mechanism used by them.

Each PSE first stores the packet and then sends it forward. Additional delays are caused by the amount of buffering required at each PSE for error checking. Packets are error checked at each and every router hop across the X.25 network. To prevent unpredictably long delays, X.25 networks allow a maximum length for each packet. Although packet sizes vary from 64 bytes to 4,096 bytes, most X.25 networks have a default size of 128 bytes. [SANGOMA, 1]

X.25 provides tremendous cost savings, especially when multiple subscribers share the same infrastructure. Organizations pay for X.25 by way of a monthly connect fee plus packet charges. Most carrier service providers offer X.25 services with a price/performance agreement based on fees for applications, locations, and traffic volume.

Network Management

The original structure of X.25 networks consisted of physical circuits that interconnected domestic transit and international exchanges. **Datapak Network**, a PSDN in the Nordic countries, provides operational control and monitoring of the X.25 network backbone. There is also a single network control center serving the entire United States. Datapak Network provides maintenance of network components, customer circuits, and PSEs. In addition, it provides customer service for handling problems and eliminating equipment failures. [Golden Telecom, 1]

Aging X.25 networking equipment used for X.25 dial-up services is causing reliability problems, particularly in poorer countries. Some regions often experience problems caused by intermittent dial tone availability or failure of X.25 dial-up nodes to answer or connect. Although the X.25 backbone networks continue to be reliable and perform without error, many organizations that want to adopt Internet access in these countries are looking instead to Frame Relay and ATM (Asynchronous Transfer Mode) networks to carry their traffic.

TOPIC *review* X.25 Protocol for Packet Switching

1. What has been the most effective usage of X.25?
2. Which layers of the OSI model does X.25 map to?
3. What is the protocol SDLC used for?
4. What is the maximum number of logical channels available on a X.25 network?
5. What is happening with X.25 in underdeveloped countries?

FRAME RELAY

Frame Relay was designed to offer higher speed data transmission for long distance networks at a reasonable cost. As was mentioned in Chapter 1, the first Frame Relay service was offered by several major telcos in the early 1990s. Telecommunication companies placed Frame Relay equipment throughout major cities in the United States and provided access to this equipment at the

POP (point of presence) with a local access line. Frame Relay offered organizations a new high-speed service that based costs on an organization's usage.

Frame Relay was originally designed as a fast packet service targeted to replace X.25. A **fast packet** is a packet transmitted without any error checking at points along the route. Frame Relay has a low incidence of error or data loss because it uses fiber-optic media. It leaves any necessary error correction or retransmission of data up to the end points or devices. The receiver is responsible for ensuring that the packet has arrived without error. [Webopedia, 1]

Benefits of Frame Relay

Frame Relay was originally devised as a service to connect LANs to major backbones and public WAN services. Frame Relay is provided on fractional T1 or full T-carrier systems and offers speeds ranging from 56 Kbps to 1.544 Mbps. Frame Relay is well suited to client-server computing because it can support the sporadic, random, high-volume traffic patterns produced by client-server applications. Frame Relay is popular because it is fast and economical, providing bandwidth-on-demand service, in which customers pay only for what they use. [Black Box, 1004]

After using X.25 services, companies began looking for a "better way" to internetwork geographically dispersed locations. In response to this demand, digital fiber data circuits that offered high speed and low error rates became more widely available. Intelligent CPE (customer premise equipment) was developed that supported higher-layer communication protocols that could perform error detection; it also provided Frame Relay with an entry point into the market.

Frame Relay services can be provided by routers or by a *Frame Relay assembler/disassembler*. A **Frame Relay assembler/disassembler (FRAD)**, as shown in Figure 11.9, is a communications device that breaks a data stream into frames for transmission by encapsulating outgoing data packets and decapsulating incoming packets. [Webopedia, 1]

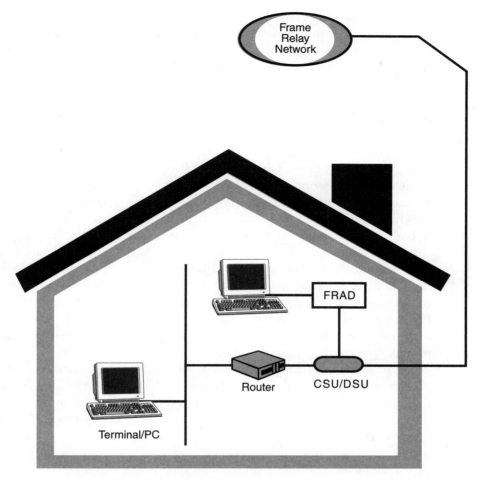

FIGURE 11.9 **Frame Relay Hardware Devices [Source: Black Box, 1004]**

Frame Relay is a simplified form of packet switching. It offers higher throughput while still retaining the bandwidth and equipment efficiencies that come from having multiple virtual circuits share a single port and transmission facility. Frame Relay provides a common transport for multiple protocols and is optimized for network traffic over WANs. Benefits of Frame Relay include the following:

- Cost effectiveness
- Reduces the cost of transmission facilities and equipment
- Offers high speed connectivity and reduced transmission delays
- Provides increased performance, reliability, and application response time
- Greater efficiency for distributed networks
- Supports high bandwidth applications
- Increases interoperability through well-defined international standards [Spohn, 288]

With Frame Relay, equipment costs are lowered because fewer port connections are required to access other networks. Frame Relay provides multiple logical connections through a single physical connection, thus reducing access costs. Because of these advantages, major telecommunications carriers have simplified the service and further reduced pricing for Frame Relay services. This makes Frame Relay easier to buy and implement and more cost effective than many other WAN services.

Frame Relay reduces the complexity of the physical network without disrupting higher-level network functions. Frame Relay functions using only the bottom two layers of the OSI model, and requires less processing overhead because it operates only in the physical and data link layers.

Frame Relay reduces the amount of processing required for error recovery. It uses high-speed digital transmission lines and can improve performance and response times for most applications. Frame Relay's simplified link layer protocol can be implemented over existing technology. Access devices often require only software changes or simple hardware modifications to support the interface standard. Existing packet-switching equipment and T1/E1 multiplexers often can be upgraded to support Frame Relay over existing backbone networks. Frame Relay service is preferred when high-speed connectivity between remote locations is required, legacy networks need replacing, and support of a multiple protocol transport is required. [Spohn, 288]

Frame Relay is an accepted interface standard that both vendors and service providers are implementing and adhering to. The simplicity of the Frame Relay packet-switching protocol accommodates quick and easy interoperability testing procedures between devices from different vendors. There is exceptionally good interoperability between the various implementations.

For example, LANs that once merely connected an assortment of intelligent PCs, now include PC applications, with their quick response times and capability to handle large quantities of data. These applications generally assume that LAN bandwidth (typically running at 4, 10, 16, and 100 Mbps) is available and that there are no reoccurring costs for use of bandwidth. As a result, the applications for the LAN are typically designed to take advantage of the wide-ranging free bandwidth. Because Frame Relay uses fiber connections between sites, as shown in Figure 11.10, the WAN is able to support higher speed transmission between remote locations. [PacBell, 1]

When designing a WAN to support PC applications, the question is which of the available WAN protocols will best accommodate the bursty nature of these applications. In the continuing effort to meet user demand for similar performance over WANs, Frame Relay appears to be an excellent alternative to leased lines and X.25. Unlike X.25, Frame Relay does not provide error recovery for corrupted frames. The advent of highly reliable transmission links has paved the way for Frame Relay to solve the problem of high-speed data networking across packet-switching networks. [Spohn, 354]

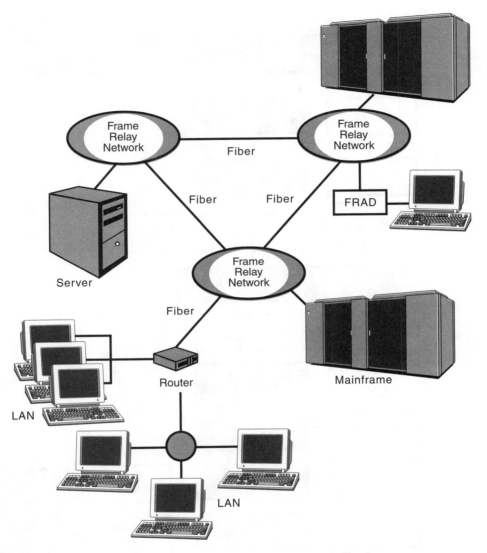

FIGURE 11.10 **Frame Relay Network [Source: PacBell, 1]**

Figure 11.11 shows a flow chart comparing X.25 and Frame Relay procedures. Frame Relay has eliminated all of the error recovery procedures. When X.25 was designed, lower quality lines were used and more error checking procedures were required to ensure the integrity of the data. Error checking occurred at each router hop. This added significant delay to X.25 transmissions. Frame Relay has been able to speed up transmissions significantly by eliminating error checking at each router hop. Frame Relay relies on the network and transport protocols to perform retransmission and error recovery.

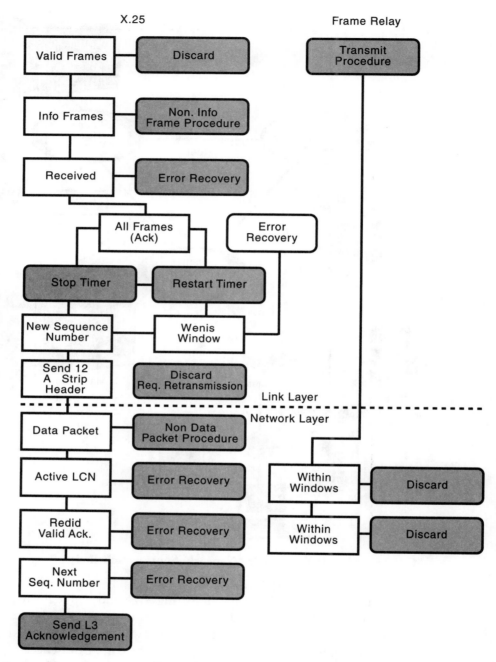

FIGURE 11.11 **X.25 versus Frame Relay Procedures [Source: Spohn, 262]**

Less processing is required within a Frame Relay provider's network nodes. Consequently, there is less delay when transmitting data across a network, which allows higher traffic volumes and greater channel speeds without necessarily increasing equipment cost or complexity.

Frame Relay allows data traffic to move rapidly within network nodes on a data "highway," passing through telephone company switches with a minimum of processing, and can achieve speeds of up to 2.048 Mbps. When compared with the equivalent service provided by dedicated, leased PPP (Point to Point Protocol) lines, Frame Relay services save money in the following areas:

- Logical connections
- Port connections
- Equipment costs
- Circuit costs
- Mileage charges

Due to its "mesh" design, a Frame Relay network requires fewer ports and local loops than a private line network, as shown in Figure 11.12. In the private line network, three access lines and three ports are required from each CPE. With Frame Relay, only one access line and port are required. [Spohn, 363]

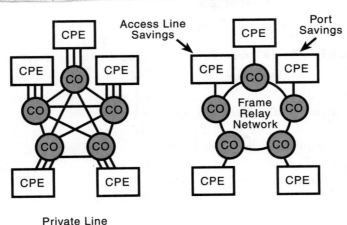

FIGURE 11.12 Frame Relay versus Private Line Port Connections [Source: Spohn, 313]

Functions of Frame Relay

Frame Relay is a permanent, connection-oriented protocol using PVCs (see Figure 11.13), set up through a telco. Each PVC is a software-defined logical end-to-end connection between two sites. After the connection is established, it cannot be torn down and is independent of the physical network topology. Several PVCs can be used to establish end-to-end connections that always exist.

No dialing or connection establishment is required. The network is permanently available until the network itself shuts down. A PVC ensures that packets always arrive in the right order so they can be reassembled successfully. [Webopedia, 1]

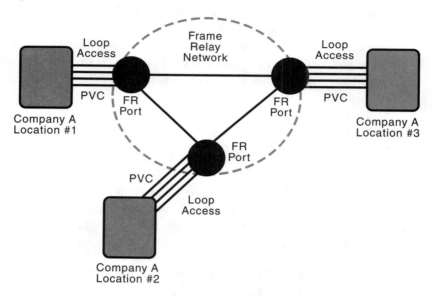

FIGURE 11.13 Frame Relay PVC Loop Access [Source: Spohn, 313]

After the PVC is configured, a LAN router or FRAD device is configured with the proper *data link connection identifier* to use for communication. The **data link connection identifier (DLCI)** is a number of a private or switched virtual circuit that tells Frame Relay how to route the data. The DLCI field in a packet (see Figure 11.14) identifies which logical circuit the data travels over. DLCI numbers are provided by a telco and represent the Frame Relay CPU LAN addresses. This path is available immediately for communication between the routers.

The area within the Frame Relay packet structure that contains the information necessary for communication with other routers is sometimes referred as the address field. DLCI is the address used to distinguish separate virtual circuits across each access connection. As Figure 11.14 illustrates, DLCIs are defined to servers at each location: New York, Baltimore, and Boston. Two PVCs provide access to Server 1, DLCI 139 from Baltimore and DLCI 176 from Boston. At corporate headquarters in New York, different DLCIs (122, 130) are used for each direction of the PVC. [Spohn, 349]

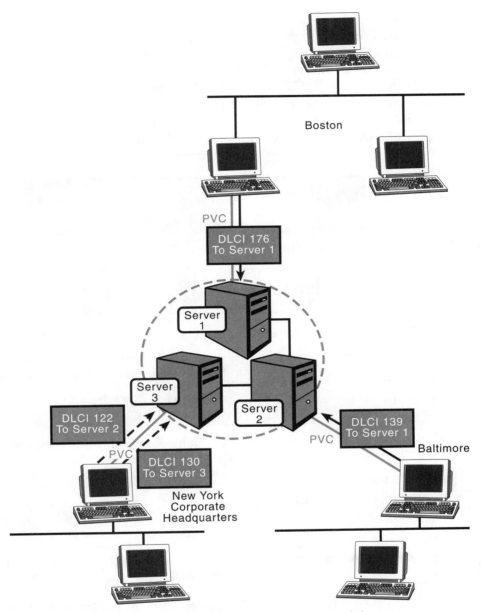

FIGURE 11.14 **Frame Relay DLCI [Source: Spohn, 349]**

Structure of a Frame Relay Packet Format

Like other bit-synchronous protocols, Frame Relay uses a frame or packet structure as the basis for transmission. The frame format used by Frame Relay is based on Link Access Protocol for ISDN-D channels (LAPD), which defines the functions for the OSI data link layer. The frame structure for Frame Relay is derived from the high-level data link control (HDLC) procedure.

Frame Relay was originally defined as a network service within the framework of ISDN (Integrated Services Digital Network). Because hardware already provides support of ISDN, using the derivative of the LAPD cuts down on protocol implementation and the need to change hardware. In Figure 11.15, the Frame Relay header provides 10 bits to accompany each transmission. The purpose of each of the 10 bits in the header is described in Table 11.4.

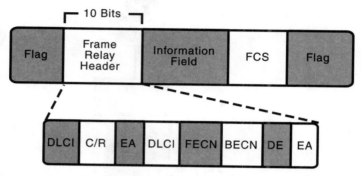

FIGURE 11.15 Frame Relay Packet Format [Source: Cisco, 10-7]

Flag Fields	Indicates where the data begins and ends.
Frame Relay Header	Contains the DLCI, FECN, and BECN bits, and other information.
DLCI Fields	In the Frame Relay address header, contain the data link connection identifier. These fields can store two octets containing a 10-bit DLCI.
Command/Response (C/R) Field	Relates to congestion information stored if the network is experiencing congestion or several sources contend for the same bandwidth.
Extended Address (EA)	Makes it possible to extend the header field to support DLCI addresses of more than 10 bits.
Forward Explicit Congestion Notification (FECN)	Can be used to notify the user that congestion was experienced in the direction of the frame carrying the FECN indication.
Backward Explicit Congestion Notification (BECN)	Can be used to notify the user that congestion was experienced in the opposite direction of the frame carrying the FECN indication.

TABLE 11.4 Bits in a Frame Relay Header [Cisco, 10-7]

Discard Eligibility (DE)	Allows the network to determine which frames can be discarded under congestion situations.
Information Field	Holds the actual data being transmitted (the "payload"). Can hold from 262 to 1,600 or more octets equivalent to a byte. For router traffic, this includes the RFC 1490 protocol header and the actual data packet.
Frame Check Sequence (FCS)	An error-checking field. Frame Relay uses a CRC. If Frame Relay detects an error, it drops the frame. The network or transport protocol must then request a retransmission.

TABLE 11.4 **Bits in a Frame Relay Header, continued**

Frame Relay Operation

Multiple protocols can be multiplexed over a DLCI, which identifies a pre-established path (the PVC) through the Frame Relay network to the correct destination. DLCI is used to identify the logical channel between the router and the network. This allows data coming into a Frame Relay network node to be sent across the interface by specifying the DLCI rather than a destination address. The DLCI denotes which destination is to receive the frame. For a DLCI, the RFC 1490 header denotes which network-layer protocol is to receive that frame. [Spohn, 345]

Frame Relay places the responsibility of ensuring data delivery on the end point devices that are operating with multi-level protocols. End points can be devices such as networks, workstations, and hosts. To ensure that all packets have been received, the transport layer places a sequence number on the frames that are sent.

Special management frames, with unique DLCI addresses, can be passed between the network and the access device. These frames monitor the status of the link and indicate whether it is active or inactive. They also can pass information regarding the status of the PVC and DLCI changes. **Local Management Interface (LMI)** features handle information exchanges between the network and the router (or other network device). LMI provides the router with status and configuration information on the PVCs that are active at that time. Originally, the Frame Relay specification did not provide for this kind of status. A method for LMI has since been incorporated into the ANSI (American National Standards Institute) and ITU (International Telecommunication Union) standards. [Spohn, 299]

Frame Relay Network Management

Frame Relay network management is implemented within the network by the Frame Relay **Management Information Base (MIB)** to support the Simple Network Management Protocol (SNMP). MIB describes a set of network objects that can be managed using SNMP. Managed objects are organized into two tables accessible via an SNMP manager, which are listed in Table 11.5. [Whatis, 1]

Frame Relay Data-Link Connection Management Interface Table	Contains data-link connection management interface parameters of a Frame-Relay interface attachment.
Frame Relay Circuit Table	The virtual circuit is identified by an interface index and the corresponding DLCI. Virtual circuits associated with the same Frame Relay interface attachment are contained in one table. [Spohn, 370]

TABLE 11.5 **Managed Object Tables**

Frame Relay Capacity and Costs

With leased lines, users buy capacity and availability, making it easy to compare prices because every carrier offering can be reduced to these two services. With Frame Relay, carriers don't sell the service based on any structured standards. Some carriers base their service on the attributes listed in Table 11.6.

Committed information rate (CIR)	A minimum sustained rate at which a Frame Relay provider agrees to transfer data.
Committed burst size (Be)	A minimum sustained rate at which the Frame Relay provider agrees to transfer data. Also the maximum size of a single traffic burst.
Burst excess	The maximum number of bits that the network agrees to transfer during any time interval.

TABLE 11.6 **Capacity Attributes of Frame Relay**

The CIR is a specified amount of guaranteed bandwidth on a Frame Relay service expressed in bits per second. The CIR is defined in software, which means traffic bandwidths can be redefined in a relatively short amount of time. The Frame Relay service provider guarantees that frames not exceeding the CIR will be delivered. Traffic above the CIR might also be delivered, but is not guaranteed. CIR represents the maximum bandwidth a user can burst and still be guaranteed delivery of all data. [Spohn, 365]

This can make it difficult for a user to decide which configuration to use. For instance, a user could have one CIR at 56 Kbps and a committed burst rate of 10,000 bits, and another with the same CIR and a committed burst rate of 1,000 bits. The first one gives the user the ability to send data continually for nearly two-tenths of a second, compared to the second which allows data throughput at two one-hundredths of a second. [Novell, 1]

Telecommunications providers offer "Management Tools" as an added service. These tools can determine use on the WAN. Methods can be used for measuring traffic prior to going out onto the WAN. It is important for a user subscribing to a Frame Relay service to set up a SLA with the telco of choice. This agreement should define: CIR, Be, burst excess, delay, and discard rate. [Novell, 1]

One method to measure traffic transmission in Frame Relay is time interval calculation, which measures the transfer of data across a Frame Relay link. The time interval over which the rate is measured is proportional to the burst size by using the following formula:

$$T = Be/CIR$$

For example, consider a network with a committed burst size of 256 Kbps and a CIR rate of 64 Kbps, which would be calculated as T=256 Kbps/64 Kb=4 seconds. The network makes its best effort to deliver 256 Kb of data over any 4-second period, or supports an average user rate of 64 Kbps averaged over a 4-second period. [Novell, 1]

Frame Relay charges do not include the mileage fees that come with leased lines. This can add significant costs savings especially if locations are several thousand miles apart. Leased lines are charged at a rate of a few cents per mile; the more miles between locations the higher the monthly cost.

Currently, Frame Relay implementations offer only PVCs. A Frame Relay provider supplies the PVC management protocol that its network uses. In the future, Frame Relay support with SVCs might become available.

Problems with Frame Relay

Although Frame Relay has many advantages, two areas within Frame Relay can promote potential problems: congestion and the discarding of frames.

Managing Congestion

As with most WAN services, without careful design, a Frame Relay network can quickly become congested. The CIR is only a guideline for the access device to follow. It is still possible for an access device to burst beyond the CIR. When frames are sent beyond the agreed CIR, frames might be discarded due to the congestion. [Spohn, 338]

When a problem is experienced with a single frame, Frame Relay simply ignores the problem and discards the frame. If a large number of problems occur, significant numbers of frames are discarded that the end user system then must recover. These errors cause retransmissions and place additional bandwidth demands on the network.

ANSI applied specifications for congestion notification mechanisms to allow Frame Relay devices to indicate the existence of congestion in the network. In the Frame Relay packet header, two bits are used for FECN. A FECN bit is sent in the same direction in which the frame was traveling toward its destination. This notification requests that the destination slow down its requests for data. BECN is a header bit that notifies the source to send data more slowly. A BECN bit is sent in the opposite direction in which the frame is traveling toward its transmission source. [Spohn, 339]

In the case of Figure 11.16, traffic is going in one direction from Texas to Michigan. Frame Relay standards prohibit the network from generating any frames with the DLCI of a particular virtual circuit causing the traffic. Therefore, the congestion notification must wait for traffic in the reverse direction to pass.

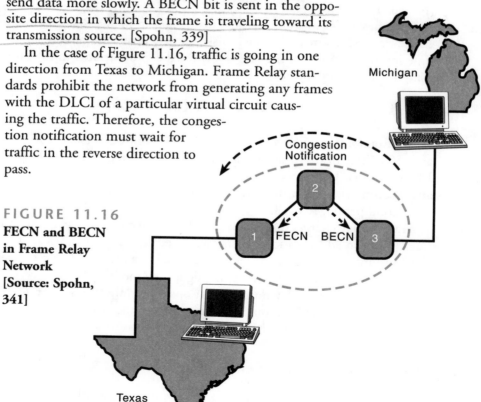

FIGURE 11.16
FECN and BECN in Frame Relay Network
[Source: Spohn, 341]

When a node on the network approaches a congestion condition caused by a temporary peak in traffic, the node detects the onset of congestion and signals all downstream nodes. All attached devices are notified that congestion is occurring until the network traffic subsides. The root cause of this congestion is a lack of available bandwidth during the time in which FECN or BECN bits are generated. Outdated hardware, heavy network traffic, high levels of line noise, or device failure can affect bandwidth availability. [Spohn, 339]

ANSI has defined another mechanism called **Consolidated Link Layer Management (CLLM)**, which reserves DLCI number 1023 on a Frame Relay interface for sending messages back to the source. The fact that the burden rests on the protocols to take advantage of using the FECN and BECN bits is one of the attractive features of Frame Relay.

However, the Frame Relay standards simply provide congestion notification mechanisms to allow flow control; they do not guarantee that they will be implemented. These vendor-specific issues can result in product performance differences, but they do not usually interfere with basic Frame Relay operation. The protocols IPX/SPX (Internetwork Packet Exchange/Secure Packet Exchange), TCP/IP (Transmission Control Protocol/Internet Protocol), AppleTalk, and SNA have no design in the OSI model to address notification from the FECN and BECN bits.

Frame Relay's congestion control mechanism works well in large, public-switch environments because congestion can be controlled between the Frame Relay switches. CPEs must be designed to handle congestion notification between the CPE and the Frame Relay switch. Until this happens, network traffic between these devices can continue to generate traffic until it is no longer manageable.

A major reason for the high level of interest in Frame Relay is that the technology has been developed in response to a clear market need. With the proliferation of powerful end point devices operating with intelligent protocols (such as TCP/IP and SNA [Systems Network Architecture]), users are seeking WAN communication methods that offer higher throughput and more cost-effective use of digital lines. Routers can be equipped with a special SNA card to support SNA protocol access to the mainframe. With that need in mind, Frame Relay has been developed and standardized to have precisely the combination of characteristics needed by today's corporate networks.

1. How can Frame Relay provide for low incidences of error or data loss when it leaves error correction and retransmission up to the receiver?
2. How can a Frame Relay network require fewer ports and local loops than a private line network?
3. Is dialing or connection establishment required with Frame Relay?
4. How does Frame Relay ensure that all packets are received and delivered to the destination in the same order that they were sent?
5. Why does Frame Relay require both FECN and BECN?

VOICE OVER IP

With the convergence of voice and data information flow over digital networks, significant progress has been made by carriers to move voice services to IP-based, packet-switched networks. **Voice over Internet Protocol (VoIP)** sends voice information in digital form as separate packets rather than over the traditional PSTN (Public Switched Telephone Network). A set of facilities is used for IP telephony to manage the delivery of voice information using IP. As shown in Figure 11.17, gateway servers enable users to communicate using standard telephones, allowing for telephone calls to be transmitted via the Internet. The clear advantage of VoIP and Internet telephony over PSTN is that it avoids the tolls charged by ordinary telephone service. [Webopedia, 1]

The PSTN actually furnishes much of the Internet's long distance infrastructure. Internet Service Providers (ISPs) pay the long-distance providers for access to their infrastructure. The circuits then are shared among many users through packet-switching technology. Internet users only pay the ISP subscription fee, not the long-distance charges.

Telcos offload voice calls to VoIP networks because it is cheaper to carry voice traffic over them. Compared with circuit-switched networks, IP telephony makes better use of available bandwidth. Digitized voice is highly compressed and carried in packets over IP networks. This compression method allows a VoIP network to carry many times the number of voice calls than can be supported by the circuit-based PSTN.

IP telephony services can be provided by both hardware and software, as shown in Figure 11.18. Several major equipment vendors including Cisco, VocalTec, 3Com, and Netspeak are behind a major effort to send voice and video using IP on the public Internet. They supported the draft of the *H.323* standard, currently the standard of choice for VoIP. **H.323** is defined as an interoperability standard for voice and multimedia applications over the Internet. Its focus is directed toward end point negotiation and information format. VoIP vendor equipment incompatibility is addressed with the help of gateways and gatekeepers. The standard does not address encoding, prioritization, or security. [Search Networking, 1]

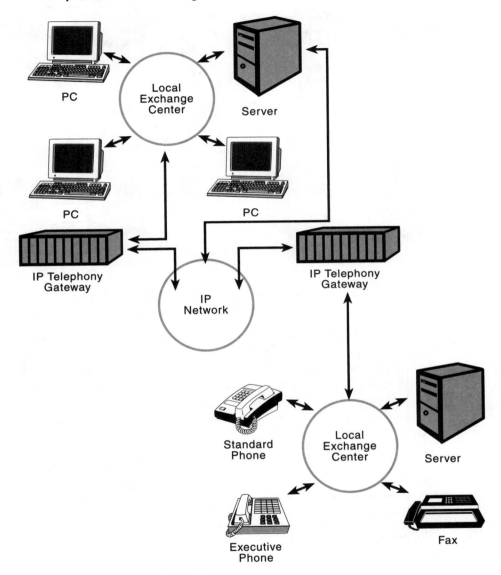

FIGURE 11.17 **IP Telephony [Source: IEC, 2]**

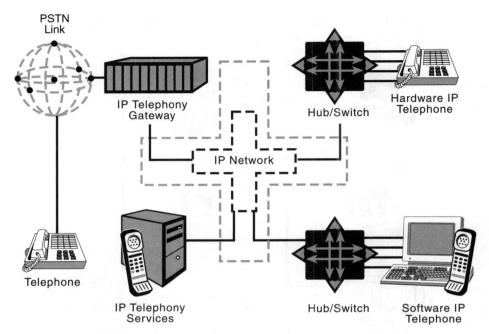

FIGURE 11.18 VoIP Connections to PSTN [Source: Carden, 1]

The characteristics and requirements of voice and data transmission over the Internet are significantly different. Voice transmission is "real time" and very sensitive to interference and delays. Data is more tolerable of reasonable delays because it can be sent anytime. Table 11.7 lists the basic differences between voice and data:

VOICE	DATA
Higher tolerance for errors	Low error rate
Short delay	Reasonable delay
Constant delay	Variable delay
No loss	Packet loss
No retransmission	Retransmission
Direct pass through	Uses protocols

TABLE 11.7 Differing Characteristics of Voice and Data Transmission over the Internet

SS7 Signaling in Switched-Circuit Networks

Switched-circuit networks are used to transmit voice traffic to provide telephone service. On the PSTN, **Signaling System 7 (SS7)** is used to put the information required to set up and manage telephone calls in a separate network than the one the telephone call is made on. SS7 is defined as a telecommunications protocol used to offload PSTN data traffic congestion onto a wireless or wireline digital broadband network. SS7 uses out-of-band signaling; it does not take place over the same path as the conversation or telephone call. Instead, a separate digital channel is created called a signaling link. This link exchanges messages between network elements at 56 to 64 Kbps. [Carden, 1]

With SS7, telephone calls can be set up more efficiently and with greater security. The SS7 architecture is set up so that any node can exchange signaling with any other SS7-capable node. SS7 uses signaling points (SSP [Service Switching Point], STP [Signal Transfer Point], and SCP [Service Control Point]), as shown in Figure 11.19 and Table 11.8. Each one is uniquely identified by a numeric point code. These point codes are carried in messages to identify the source and destination of each message. At each signaling point, a routing table is consulted and the appropriate signaling path for each message is selected.

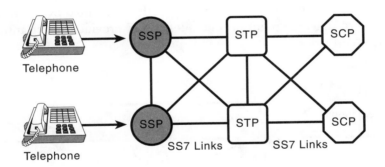

FIGURE 11.19 **SS7 Architecture [Source: PT, 1]**

Service Switching Point (SSP)	Sends signaling messages to other SSPs to set up, manage, and release voice circuits required to complete a call.
Signal Transfer Point (STP)	A packet switch is used to route network traffic between signaling points. Each incoming message is routed to an outgoing signaling link based on routing information defined in the SS7 message.
Service Control Point (SCP)	A centralized database used to determine how a call will be routed. An SCP sends a response to the originating SSP containing the routing number associated with the dialed number. [PT, 1]

TABLE 11.8 **SS7 Signaling Points**

The SS7 network is an essential element of call processing. To ensure network-wide service, SCPs and STPs are implemented in matched pair configurations and in separate physical locations in case of equipment failures. Links between signaling points are also provisioned in pairs, as shown in Figure 11.20. If one link fails, the signaling traffic is rerouted over another link. In the event of signaling point or link failures, SS7 provides for retransmission and error correction.

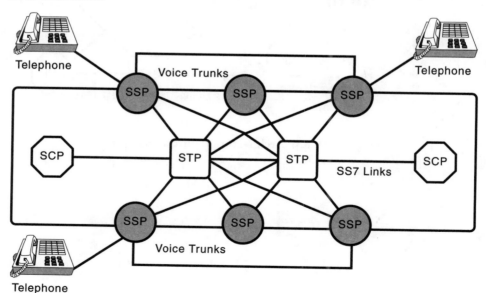

FIGURE 11.20 **SS7 Signaling End Points [Source: PT, 1]**

Signaling messages called **ISUP (ISDN User Part)** are used to set up, manage, and release trunk circuits that carry voice calls between central office (CO) switches. Calls that originate and terminate at the same switch do not use ISUP signaling. In Figure 11.21, ISUP messages carry caller ID information and are used for both ISDN and non-ISDN calls between CO switches. [PT, 1]

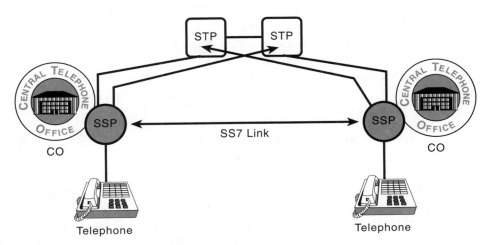

FIGURE 11.21 **ISUP Signaling [Source: PT, 1]**

Sigtran Protocols for SS7 over IP

The Internet Engineering Task Force (IETF) has defined a set of protocols called the **sigtran protocols**, which specify a method for carrying SS7 over IP in VoIP networks. The sigtran protocols provide the following to SS7 signaling over IP networks:

- Flow control
- In-sequence delivery of signaling messages within a single control stream
- Identification of the originating and terminating signaling points
- Identification of voice circuits
- Error detection, retransmission, and other error-correcting procedures
- Recovery from outages of components in the transit path
- Controls to avoid congestion on the Internet
- Detection of status of in-service or out-of-service units
- Support for security to protect the integrity of the signaling information [PT, 2]

Stream Control Transmission Protocol (SCTP)

SS7 messages are transported over IP networks using the *Stream Control Transmission Protocol*. The **Stream Control Transmission Protocol (SCTP)** allows the reliable transfer of signaling messages between signaling end points in an IP network. SCTP end points establish an association with each other; one end point provides the other with a list of IP addresses in combination with an SCTP. These IP transport addresses identify the addresses that will send and receive SCTP packets. [PT, 2] SCTP provides support for:

- Error-free, non-duplicated transfer of signaling information
- In-sequence delivery of messages within multiple streams
- Optional bundling of multiple messages into a single SCTP packet
- Data fragmentation
- Multi-homing at either or both ends of an association
- Congestion avoidance and resistance to flooding (Denial of Service [DoS]) and IP spoofing attacks [PT, 2]

Many signaling end points are used in IP signaling traffic. The traffic is composed of many independent message sequences. SCTP allows signaling messages to be independently ordered within multiple streams. This ensures in-sequence delivery between associated end points. When independent message sequences are transferred in separate SCTP streams, *head-of-line blocking* is avoided. **Head-of-line blocking** is the piling up of packets behind the first packet while it waits for access to a resource that is busy. Packets also can become blocked by lost messages. The IETF recommends that SCTP be used for SS7 messages rather than TCP/IP because TCP/IP does not enforce head-of-line blocking. In addition, VoIP uses the real-time protocol (RTP) to help ensure that packets are delivered in a timely manner.

Signaling Information Exchange in VoIP Networks

In IP telephony networks, three functional elements are used to exchange signaling information. Media and signaling gateways as shown in Figure 11.22 are used to compress voice signals into packets to transmit over the IP network. A description of each type of gateway and controller is found in Table 11.9.

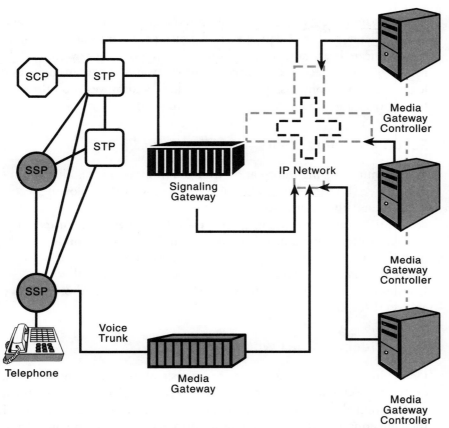

FIGURE 11.22 **Media and Signaling Gateways [Source: PT, 2]**

Media Gateway	Used to terminate voice calls on inter-switch trunks from the PSTN. Compresses the voice signals, separates them into packets, and then delivers compressed voice packets to the IP network.
Media Gateway Controller	Used to handle the registration and management of controller resources at the media gateways. Often called a soft switch because vendors use off-the-shelf computer platforms. A media gateway controller exchanges ISUP messages with CO switches using a signaling gateway.
Signaling Gateway	Used to interwork the signaling between switched-circuit and IP networks. Terminates SS7 signaling, and also translates and relays messages over an IP network to a media gateway controller or another signaling gateway.

TABLE 11.9 **Gateways Used in IP Telephony [PT, 2]**

Gateways are now emerging as an interface between the Internet and the PSTN. Gateway servers equipped with voice-processing cards enable users to communicate over standard telephones. When a call goes over the PSTN, it is routed to the nearest gateway server. The gateway server then digitizes the analog voice signal, compresses it into IP packets, and moves it on the Internet for transport to another gateway at the receiving end.

Security Requirements for SS7 over IP

To transmit signaling information over the Internet, the IETF recommends using IPsec (Internet Protocol Security). The use of the following security measures is mandatory: authentication, integrity, confidentiality, and availability. It is critical to ensure information is sent to/from a known and trusted partner (authentication), guaranteeing that the signaling information has not been modified in-transit (integrity). The transported information must be encrypted to avoid illegal use or violation of privacy laws (confidentiality). Communicating end points must remain in service for authorized use (availability). [PT, 2]

Voice Quality Issues with VoIP

Unlike most data applications, voice is sensitive to delay. Long and variable delays between packets result in unnatural speech and interfere with conversation. Dropped packets result in clipped speech and poor voice quality. Fax transmissions are even less tolerant of dropped packets than voice. Packet-switching networks are less efficient than circuit-switching networks in managing voice. Transmissions can be delayed because of network congestion. Voice traffic can be caught behind a long data transmission. The best solution to avoid delays and dropped packets is to set priorities for the different types of traffic.

Internet telephony aims to achieve the same reliable high quality of service provided by the PSTN. On the Internet, however, reliability and sound quality are marginal because of the heavy use of the Internet's limited bandwidth. Delays can be caused in packet transmission, which often results in lost packets. The various speech-coding algorithms used in media gateways produce varying levels of fidelity in sound transmitted over the Internet. When an IP PBX (private branch exchange) is used, as shown in Figure 11.23, existing telephones can be used to connect VoIP to the PSTN. [Carden, 1]

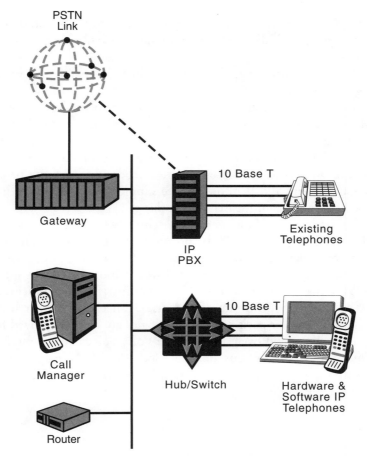

FIGURE 11.23 **IP Software or Hardware Telephones [Source: Carden, 1]**

With circuit-switched PSTN, a call is routed over a single path. However, when voice travels over a packet-switched network, each voice signal travels over a separate network path and requires reassembly in the proper sequence at the destination. This method increases the chances of packet loss.

Managing Voice Signals

An analog voice signal is received and the signal is converted to a **Pulse Code Modulation (PCM)** digital stream. PCM is a digital scheme for transmitting analog signals. Next the PCM stream is analyzed and it performs three steps: removes the echo, uses voice activity detector (VAD) to remove silence, and detects tone. The PCM stream is fed into the codec and voice frames are created. A **coder/decoder (codec)** device performs analog-to-digital conversion and digital-to-analog conversion functions within a single chip. Each frame is 10 ms long (G.729a) and contains 10 bytes of speech. PCM can digitize all forms of analog data, including full-motion video, voices, music, telemetry, and virtual reality. [Carden, 1]

VAD is a software application used in VoIP that allows a data network carrying voice traffic over the Internet to detect the absence of audio. It conserves bandwidth by preventing the transmission of silent packets over the network. Most voice conversations include about 50% silence. **Silence suppression** is used to monitor signals for voice activity so that when silence is detected for a specified amount of time, the application informs the Packet Voice Protocol. Silence suppression also prevents the encoder output from being transported across the network. Without silence suppression, the listener might think the line had gone dead. [Search Networking, 1]

In modern telephone networks, echoes between devices are controlled as illustrated in Figure 11.24, by positioning echo cancellers in the digital circuit. Echo cancellation removes from 80 to 90% of the echo across the network. Today, echo cancellers are designed with standard **digital signal processors (DSPs)** that share process time in a circuit within a channel or across channels. DSPs provide a maximum of 128 ms of cancellation. [Search Networking, 1]

Three popular packet/cell technologies are being deployed for improving voice transmission over IP. These are VoIP, Voice over Frame Relay (VoFR) and Voice over Asynchronous Transfer Mode (VoATM). Each technology uses several techniques to improve voice traffic flow, which are described and compared in Table 11.10.

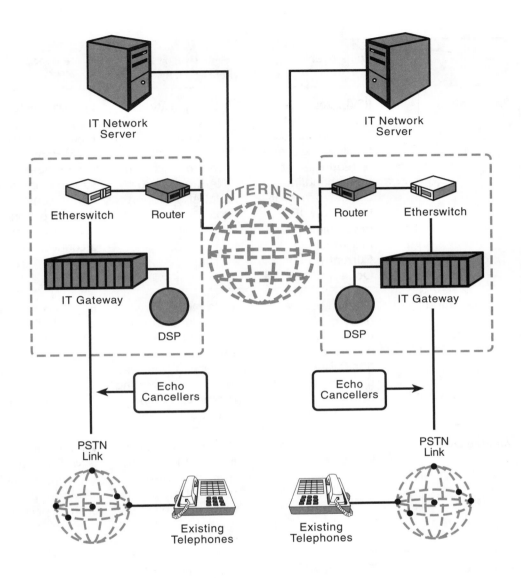

DSP = Digital Signal Processor

FIGURE 11.24 **Phone-to-Phone Connection through Internet [Source: IEC, 4]**

	Voice over IP (VoIP)	Voice over Frame Relay (VoFR)	Voice over ATM (VoATM)
Prioritization	RSVP (Resource Reservation Setup Protocol) was used to allow the sender to request a set of traffic-handling characteristics for traffic flow. IETF is developing a simpler model. Currently, no viable QoS for IP services.	Tags applications according to sensitivity to delay. Higher priority is given to voice and SNA time-sensitive data. Also supports QoS.	QoS parameters are supported. Circuit Emulation Service (CES) transmits a continuous bit stream of information. A constant amount of bandwidth is allocated to a connection for the duration of transmission.
Fragmentation	Used to reduce delay of voice traffic. Adds a lot of overhead to IP transmissions due to the large size of IP headers.	Data packets are divided into small fragments. Higher priority voice packets receive right-of-way without waiting for the end of long data transmissions.	Built into ATM with its small, fixed-size, 53-byte cells.
Variable Delay	Similar to Frame Relay.	Detains each packet in a jitter buffer. This gives subsequent packets time to arrive and still fit in natural voice flow.	Variable Bit Rate service. Using the structure of AAL2 allows for packing of short packets into mini-cells in one or more ATM cells.
Voice Compression	Traffic travels over low-speed links. Standard for voice compression (ITU G.723.1) over IP ensures toll-quality voice.	Voice compression algorithms are built-in to Frame Relay access devices. Offers reduced network congestion, bandwidth savings, and high-quality voice transmissions.	Not necessary in pure-ATM networks. However, ATM must be equipped to support voice compression in order to work with VoFR equipment at the remote site.

TABLE 11.10 Voice Enhancement Technologies for IP [Biran, 3-9]

	Voice over IP (VoIP)	Voice over Frame Relay (VoFR)	Voice over ATM (VoATM)
Silence Suppression	Similar to Frame Relay.	Frees 60% of bandwidth on the full-duplex link for other voice or data transmissions.	
Echo Cancellation	Similar to Frame Relay.	Eliminates the echo between VFRAD and the telephones.	

TABLE 11.10 **Voice Enhancement Technologies for IP, continued**

Future of VoIP Telephony

The most promising areas for future VoIP deployment are corporate intranets and commercial extranets. VoIP gateways will evolve into robust embedded systems able to handle hundreds of simultaneous calls. Organizations will be able to deploy significant numbers of VoIP gateways to reduce expenses for high-volume voice, fax, and video conferencing traffic.

In large corporate networks, Frame Relay is used to support connections to several branch offices. The corporate headquarters also might need ATM service to support larger amounts of traffic. When Frame Relay and ATM are part of the network, there must be internetworking between VoFR and VoATM. Due to the lack of interoperability standards for voice communications over Frame Relay, IP, and ATM, vendors at this time are developing proprietary internetworking solutions. Significant investment is required to increase the backbone bandwidth and access speeds. The implementation of more IP, ATM, and SONET (Synchronous Optical Network) technologies will better support ISDN, cable modem, and DSL (Digital Subscriber Line) access in the future. [Biran, 9-11] [Sampson, 1]

Carrier service providers will deploy next-generation switches, as shown in Figure 11.25 to support converged data, voice, and video traffic. These switches will be deployed in a distributed architecture in which media gateways, signaling, call control, and applications elements will be divided into separate logical network components. This distributed model will be capable of supporting hundreds of thousands of subscriber ports per node. [Biran, 9-11]

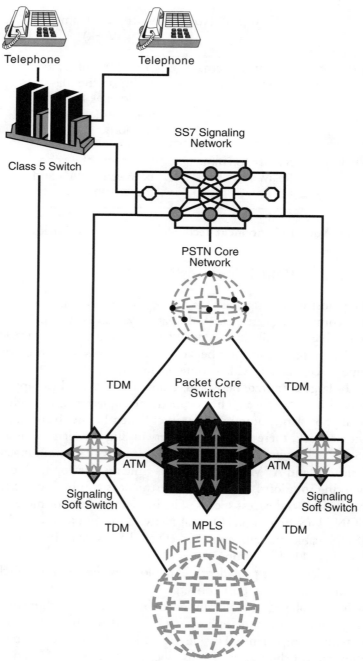

FIGURE 11.25 **Next-Generation Switching Platform [Source: Telica, 2]**

Although VoATM is used today by large carrier service providers to support VoIP, the long-term future for VoIP will most likely be MPLS-based (Multiprotocol Label Switching) QoS. The full migration to packet-based transmission will happen when all Class 5 switches in the PSTN become packet-based and differentiated Class-5 services become available. The installation of numerous media gateways will be required to migrate voice traffic onto a packetized network. [Telica, 2]

TOPIC *review*

Voice Over IP

1. What enables VoIP network to carry many times more than the number of voice calls supported by the circuit based PSTN?
2. How is SS7 used for transmitting voice traffic for telephone service?
3. What is the purpose of media and signaling gateways?
4. Why is VAD software needed in VoIP networks?
5. What type of architecture will be used to deploy next-generation switches to support voice, data, and video in the future?

CHAPTER SUMMARY

The packet approach to WANs has simplified the delivery of information. Packet-switching protocols X.25 and Frame Relay have provided high-speed connections at a lower cost. Organizations today use both virtual-circuit and datagram packet-switching technologies. Virtual-circuit packet switching provides a predetermined pathway from source to destination. Packets travel and arrive together. Datagram packet switching allows packets to travel different routes to the destination. If a link is congested, it offers an alternate route for the packet to reach the destination. Using computer telephony, voice communications are packetized and sent over the Internet.

Packet-switched networks have provided worldwide communications of business applications since the 1970s. The first generation of packet switching, X.25 provided global availability for secure, cost-effective, long-distance transmission for data over low-quality circuits. It supported a high level of data integrity because of its aggressive approach to error detection and correction. X.25 uses the LAPB protocol to manage packets on shared-line packet-switched networks. PSE switches are located in various locations across the telecommunications carrier's network. They route packets through the network to the correct destination address. X.25 uses PAD devices to assemble, disassemble, and translate the packets. Although the X.25 backbone network is reliable, organizations have directed their communications traffic to faster packet-switching techniques such as Frame Relay and ATM.

Frame Relay was developed to solve communication problems and better manage bandwidth efficiency. It was designed to reduce the amount of overhead processing required by X.25, operating only at the physical and data link layers of the OSI model. Internetworking costs with Frame Relay are lower because several logical connections can be sent over a single physical connection. Fewer port connections are required to access other networks. Frame Relay packet switching is well suited to unpredictable and bursty traffic volumes. Frame Relay also reduces the amount of processing required for error recovery because it relies on the network and transport protocols to perform retransmission and error recovery. Outgoing data is formatted by FRADs or routers into the format required by a Frame Relay network. Frame Relay provides high-speed connectivity between remote locations. Each location is assigned a DLCI field that identifies the logical circuit the data travels over.

When computer telephony is used, the power of the computer is applied to the functions of the telephone by integrating calling and messaging tasks into one system. The use of the data network for voice communications has resulted in significant cost savings on long-distance charges. VoIP sends voice information in digital form as separate packets rather than over the traditional PSTN. ISPs pay the long-distance providers for access to their infrastructure. SS7 is used for setup and management of telephone calls in a separate network than the one the telephone call is made on. The SS7 network is critical to call processing. ISUP signaling is used to set up, manage, and release trunk circuits that carry voice calls between CO switches.

Media and signaling gateways are used for signaling information exchange in VoIP networks. Gateways act as an interface between the Internet and the PSTN. The analog voice signal is compressed into IP packets and moves onto the Internet for transport. Sigtran protocols approved by the IETF specify the method for carrying SS7 over IP in VoIP networks. VoIP uses the RTP to help ensure that packets are delivered in a timely fashion. Voice traffic is sensitive to delay, because speech can become unnatural or clipped as a result of dropped packets. Management of voice over packet-switching networks is less efficient than circuit-switching networks. QoS and prioritization are the keys to managing delay and dropped packets in VoIP networks. In the near future, using QoS techniques and next-generation switches, data, voice, and video traffic will be converged and routed across the Internet.

CHAPTER REVIEW QUESTIONS

(This quiz also can be printed from the Encore! CD that accompanies this book. File name—Chap11review.)

Circle a letter (a-d) for each question. Choose only one answer for each.

1. When you purchase a virtual circuit, what organization provides you with the VCI number?
   a. switch vendor
   b. equipment manufacturer
   c. telco
   d. ISP

2. What is X.25?
   a. an interface
   b. a protocol
   c. a dial-up service
   d. a logical channel

3. Which protocol provides flow and error control for X.25 transmissions over point-to-point links?
   a. LAPD
   b. SDLC
   c. HDLC
   d. LAPB

4. Frame Relay has eliminated what type of procedures to speed up transmission?
   a. error recovery
   b. retransmission
   c. reassembly
   d. disassembly

5. Frame Relay places the responsibility of ensuring data delivery on:
   a. frame format
   b. multi-level protocols
   c. end point devices
   d. interfaces

6. How many bits are present in a frame relay header?
   a. 8
   b. 6
   c. 7
   d. 10

7. The SS7 network is an essential element of :
   a. signaling
   b. call processing
   c. message exchange
   d. shared circuits

8. How are echoes between devices controlled in modern telephone networks?
   a. VAD
   b. Silence suppression
   c. Pulse code modulation
   d. Echo cancellers

9. In the future, how will organizations reduce expenses for high-volume voice, fax, and videoconferencing traffic?
   a. Position more echo cancellers in the digital circuit
   b. Deploy significant numbers of VoIP gateways
   c. Set priorities for different types of traffic
   d. Conserve bandwidth by preventing the transmission of silent packets

10. How do large carrier service providers support VoIP today?
    a. VoISDN
    b. VoFR
    c. VoATM
    d. VoDSL

Circle the correct letter (A-E) that corresponds to the descriptions below. Choose only one answer for each.
   A. SVC
   B. SDLC
   C. FRAD
   D. HDLC
   E. DLCI

11. A B C D E   A communications device that breaks a datastream into frames for transmission.

12. A B C D E   Organizes data into a frame and manages the flow where data is sent.

13. A B C D E   Used to identify the logical circuit the data travels over.

14. A B C D E   Protocol used to connect remote devices to mainframes at central locations.

15. A B C D E   Temporary virtual circuit established and maintained only for the duration of a data transfer session.

    A. CIR
    B. FECN
    C. SS7
    D. STP
    E. VAD

16. A B C D E   Software application used in VoIP that allows a data network carrying voice traffic over the Internet to detect the absence of audio.

17. A B C D E   Represents the maximum bandwidth a user can burst and still be guaranteed delivery of all data.

18. A B C D E   A telecommunications protocol used to offload PSTN data traffic congestion onto a wireless or wireline broadband network.

19. A B C D E   Indicates the existence of congestion in the network.

20. A B C D E   Each incoming message is routed to an outgoing signaling link based on routing information defined in the SS7 message.

INTERNET EXERCISES

1. Log on to the Internet and key the following URL:

   www.networkcomputing.com/netdesign/frame1.html

   List the five major advantages for selection of Frame Relay.

2. Key the following URL:

   www.networkmagazine.com/article/NMG20021104S0016

   List the issues discussed regarding the value proposition for VoIP.

CONCEPT EXERCISES

Concept Narrative
(This narrative exercise also can be printed from the Encore! CD that accompanies this book. File name—Chap11connar.)

Fill in the blanks of the following narrative.

Frame Relay is a permanent, connection-oriented protocol using a
_____ _____ _____ set up through a telco. Each PVC
is a software-defined logical end-to-end connection between two sites.
After the connection is established, it cannot be torn down. It is independent of the physical network topology. Several PVCs can be used to
establish end-to-end connections that always exist. No dialing or
_____ establishment is required. The network is permanently available until the network itself shuts down. A PVC ensures that packets
always arrive in the right order so they can be _____ successfully.

After the PVC is configured, a LAN router or FRAD device is configured
with the proper DLCI to use for communication. The _____ _____
_____ _____ is a number of a PVC or SVC that tells
Frame Relay how to route the data. The DLCI field in a packet identifies
which _____ circuit the data travels over. DLCI numbers are provided
by a telco and represent the Frame Relay CPU LAN addresses. This path
is available immediately for communication between the routers.

Concept Table
(This table exercise also can be printed from the Encore! CD that accompanies this book. File name—Chap11contab.)

Read each statement carefully and choose the type of Voice Packet/Cell
Technology being described. Use only one "X" per statement.

	VOICE PACKET/CELL TECHNOLOGIES		
STATEMENT	VoIP	VoFR	VoATM
1. Higher priority voice packets receive right-of-way without waiting for long data transmissions.			
2. Eliminates the echo between VFRAD and the telephones.			
3. Traffic travels over low-speed links.			
4. Voice compression algorithms are built-in.			
5. Uses fixed size, 53-byte cells.			
6. Fragmentation is used to reduce delay of voice traffic.			
7. Tags applications by their sensitivity to delay.			
8. Uses CES to transmit a continuous stream of information.			
9. Adds a lot of overhead to IP transmissions due to the large size of IP headers.			
10. Each packet is detained in a jitter buffer.			

Concept Picture
(This picture exercise also can be printed from the Encore! CD that accompanies this book. File name—Chap11conpic.)

Look at the picture of the Next-Generation Switching Platform and label the missing elements.

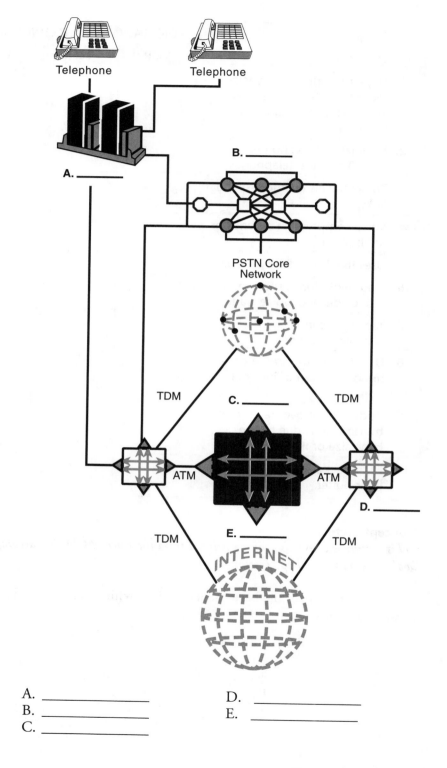

Telephone **Telephone**

A. _____

B. _____

PSTN Core
Network

TDM   **C.** _____   TDM

ATM   ATM

D. _____

TDM   **E.** _____   TDM

INTERNET

A. _____   D. _____
B. _____   E. _____
C. _____

CASE STUDY

FOSTER CARE FAMILY AGENCY

Objective:

Examine how a Frame Relay network can provide for faster and less costly data communications for a foster care agency. Determine whether or not the agency should deploy VoIP to save money on long-distance calling between offices.

Company Profile:

The Foster Care Family Agency is a statewide, long-term foster care provider headquartered in Topeka, Kansas. The agency provides services for the developmentally disabled and medically fragile as well as psychiatric care, aftercare, and independent living skills instruction. Recently, the agency expanded their program to include a special family program for family counseling, a shelter for battered women, and child advocacy services.

Current Situation:

Presently, the agency has 25 sites located throughout the state of Kansas. These sites are connected through a network of dedicated 56 Kbps data lines. The disaster recovery center is in Wichita, Kansas. The agency has no backup link for its circuits because the agency could not afford a fully meshed leased-line network.

Business Information Requirements:

The agency hopes to reduce its telecommunications costs by 25%. The agency also wants to purchase redundant links to Wichita for disaster recovery. Currently, the agency is incurring $5,000 a month in long-distance calling charges between the 25 locations. The agency is considering VoIP technology to reduce long-distance calling charges within Kansas.

Communication System Requirements:

A Frame Relay network should replace the existing dedicated 56 Kbps data lines. In addition, a redundant link needs to be built from Wichita to the agency's headquarters in Topeka. The current WAN traffic has been limited to standard e-mail communication. With the new solution, the agency wants an online database accessible to all 25 offices. Often the agency needs to transfer birth records, social security records, and other assessment information between offices. Today, employees either fax or courier this information to the other offices. They want a quicker way to transfer the documents. They are looking to scan the images and attach them to an e-mail or FTP them to other offices.

Information System Solution:

1. The 24 sites were linked using 128 Kbps Frame Relay PVCs.
2. The link between Wichita and Topeka required more bandwidth for backup data. The agency purchased a 256 Kbps Frame Relay link and a backup 128 Kbps ISDN line for disaster recovery.
3. Monthly charges for data lines decreased from $20,000 to $12,000.
4. At the headquarters in Topeka, the agency purchased a H.323 Media Gateway for VoIP services and opted for VoFR service. Each branch office now has a VFRAD router.
5. After four months of operation, the VoIP service has reduced the agency's long-distance charges from $5,000 to $2,500 a month.

Overall, the agency and its employees are pleased with the speed of the connection to the headquarters in Topeka. The disaster recovery site in Wichita is receiving backup information daily. Employees at the agency were a little concerned about the voice quality of VoIP, but were pleasantly surprised to find out it provided the same quality as they had before. The application development department is working on developing new software for the agency database, which should be ready in 60 days.

In Figure 11.26, a partial network diagram shows 4 of the 25 locations in Kansas. Study the diagram and then answer the Study Questions that follow.

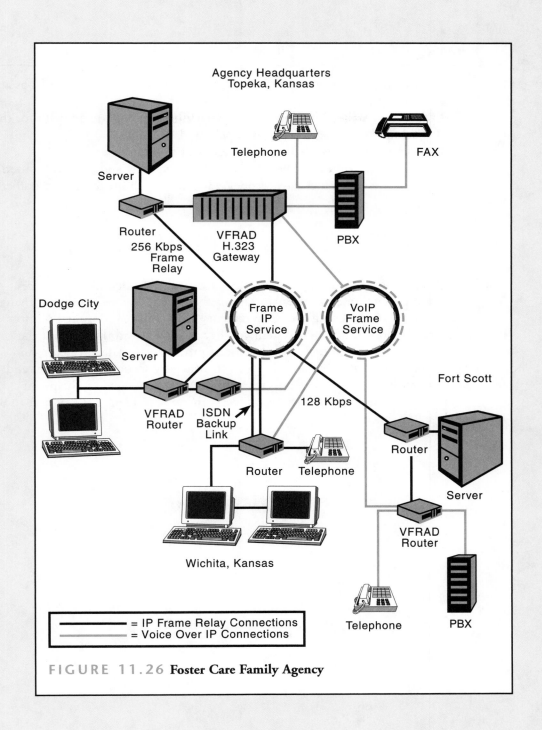

FIGURE 11.26 **Foster Care Family Agency**

CASE STUDY QUESTIONS:

1. How is the agency able to increase the bandwidth speed to 128 Kbps and still save money?
2. Do you think a 256 Kbps Frame Relay link is enough bandwidth for the backup data transfer between Topeka and Wichita?
3. Why did they need a VFRAD gateway at headquarters?
4. What is the difference between a VFRAD gateway and VFRAD router?
5. Why does the agency have secondary routers at each site for IP data traffic?

GROUP TERM PROJECT

In this section of the group term project, the goal is to identify the services, operations, departments, or organizations that might be affected by the change to the new system. Using the Requirements Scope form you printed out for chapter 10, look at the new system you have designed and think about the impact it will have on each area: functions/processes, user departments, and subsystems. Identify each area, list it in the category section of the form, and then describe how it will be affected. This exercise is designed to help you determine if there are any "show-stoppers" that would require the project to be delayed or cancelled.

B. Affected/Unaffected Products, Services, Operations, and Organizations

Category	A/U *	Description (If Affected [A])
Functions/Processes:		
User Departments:		
Subsystems:		

*A/U: Enter **A** for Affected and **U** for Unaffected.

CHAPTER TERMS

CHAPTER BIBLIOGRAPHY

Book, Magazine, Presentation Citations

Black Box. *Network Services*. Lawrence: Black Box Corporation, 2000: 1,004.
Sheldon, Tom. *Encyclopedia of Networking and Telecommunications*. New York: Osborne/McGraw-Hill, 2001: 1391.
Spohn, Darren. *Data Network Design*. New York: McGraw-Hill, Inc., 1993: 262, 288, 299, 313, 338-341, 345, 349, 354, 363, 365-367, 370.

Web Citations

Biran, Gil, "Voice over Frame Relay, IP and ATM," RAD Data Communications, <www.protocols.com/papers/voe.htm> (2002).

Carden, Phillip, "Building Voice over IP," Network Computing, <www.networkcomputing.com/netdesign/1109voipfull.html> (8 May 2000).

Cisco, "X.25 Devices and Protocol Operation," Internetworking Technology Overview, <www.cisco.com/univercd/cc/td/doc/cisintwk/ito_doc/preface.htm> (1999).

Cisco, "Frame Relay," Internetworking Technology Overview, <www.cisco.com/univercd/cc/td/doc/cisintwk/ito_doc/preface.htm> (1999).

Ericsson, "Understanding Telecommunications," Ericsson, <www.ericsson.com/about/telecom/part-fl/fl-1-1.shtml> (2002).

Glinoyer, Shmolikand and Eli Nir, "Introduction to Packet Switching and X.25 in Public Data Networks," RAD Data Communications, <www.rad.com/networks/1994/packet/packet.htm> (1994).

Golden Telecom, "Packet Switched Data Services X.25," Golden Telecom, <goldentelecom.ru/eng/services/x25.htm> (1999).

IEC, "Internet Telephony," International Engineering Consortium, <www.iec.org/> (2002).

JBM, "X.25 Packet Switching Protocol Support," JBM Electronics, <www.jbmelectronics.com/x25.htm> (2002).

Novell, "How Frame Relay Works," Novell, <www.novell.com/documentation/lg/nw5/docui/index.html#../uscomm/rtcf_enu/data/hcqwtyci.html> (2002).

Ohana, Gilbert and Ohad Parush, "Packet Switching Simulation," RAD, <www.rad.com/networks/1998/packet/ps.htm> (1998).

PacBell, "FasTrak Frame Relay" SBC Pacific Bell, <www.pacbell.com/> (2002).

PT, "SS7 Tutorial," Performance Technologies, <www.pt.com/tutorials/ss7/> (7 May 2001).

PT, "IP Telephony," Performance Technologies, <www.pt.com/tutorials/iptelephony/> (27 August 2001).

Sampson, Michael, "Computer Telephony for the Enterprise," Network Computing, <www.networkcomputing.com/shared/printArticle.jhtml?article=/netdesign/cti1.htmlandpub=nwc> (2000).

Sangoma, "X.25 Packet Switching," Sangoma Technologies, <www.sangoma.com/x25.htm> (2002).

Search Networking, "VAD," Search Networking, <www.whatis.com/> (2002).

Search Networking, "Echo Cancellers," Search Networking, <www.whatis.com/> (2002).

Search Networking, "X.25," Search Networking, <www.whatis.com/> (2002).

Search Networking, "Frame Relay," Search Networking, <www.whatis.com/> (2002).

Search Networking, "VoIP," Search Networking, <www.whatis.com/> (2002).

Telica, "Accelerating the Deployment of Voice over IP (VoIP) and Voice over ATM (VoATM) Tutorial," IEC, <www.iec.org/tutorials/voip_voatm/topic01.html> (12 February 2001).

Webopedia, "X.25," Webopedia, <www.webopedia.com/> (2002).

Webopedia, " LAPB," Webopedia, <www.webopedia.com/> (2002).

Webopedia, " PVC," Webopedia, <www.webopedia.com/> (2002).

Webopedia, "Frame Relay," Webopedia, <www.webopedia.com/> (2002).

Webopedia, "VoIP," Webopedia, <www.webopedia.com/> (2002).

CHAPTER 12

RING-BASED NETWORKS

CHAPTER OBJECTIVES

By the end of this chapter, you should understand these concepts:

- The topology and operation of a Fiber Distributed Data Interface (FDDI) network
- Optical bypass switches and dual homing techniques
- A high-speed packet switching service called Switched Megabit Digital Service (SMDS)
- A dual ring architecture called Dual Queue Dual Bus (DQDB)
- The basic operation of the reservation process used for traffic flow in SMDS networks
- SMDS Interface Protocol (SIP) connectionless service
- SMDS addressing and network components
- Synchronized Optical Network (SONET) high-speed international fiber-optical network
- Levels of Optical Carrier (OC) transmission rates used in SONET networks
- Add/drop multiplexing techniques used to provide bandwidth on demand for SONET networks
- SONET Ring Automatic Protection Switching (APS) used for fault tolerance
- New developments in semiconductor technology
- Advances in transmission/amplification for empowered Optical Networks

Ring-based networks provide reliable backbones for LANs (Local Area Networks), WANs (Wide Area Networks), and MANs (Metropolitan Area Networks). The most common ring-based networks are FDDI (LAN), SMDS (MAN), and SONET (WAN). All three ring-based networks support independent rings that deploy failover methods if service is disrupted, a station or node fails, or a cable breaks. Another common element between all three ring-based networks is the use of fiber-optic cabling. Fiber-optic cabling provides the speed, resiliency, and immunity to interference required for backbone networks.

FIBER DISTRIBUTED DATA INTERFACE (FDDI)

Fiber Distributed Data Interface (**FDDI**) is a high-speed backbone technology. Its dual-ring topology uses fiber-optic cable to transmit light pulses to convey information between stations. The optical fiber channel operates at a rate of 100 Mbps and is frequently used in LANs to connect buildings together within an organization. The ring circumference can extend to 200 kilometers and the distance between nodes can be up to 200 kilometers (124.28 miles) apart. An FDDI network can host up to 1,000 nodes on 1 optical fiber. [Sheldon, 494-495]

FDDI Topology

The topology of a FDDI network consists of two independent rings. As Figure 12.1 shows, there is a primary ring (A) and a secondary ring (B). The primary ring transmits data and the secondary ring provides an alternate data path. The secondary ring remains idle unless the primary ring fails. Notice also in Figure 12.1, the traffic flows in opposite directions on each ring. Optical fiber rings are **counter-rotating**, with two signal paths provided, one in each direction. A station is a computer, workstation, or node connected to the FDDI network. A station must be connected to both rings to use the secondary ring as an alternate data path. [UNH, 1]

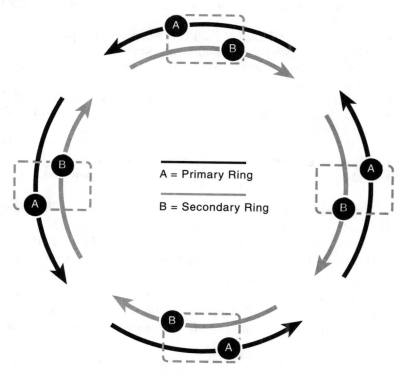

FIGURE 12.1 FDDI Architecture [Source: UNH, 1]

Token Passing Scheme

FDDI uses a token passing protocol to move data around the ring, and another protocol based on timers. Timing is critical to the token passing scheme because the scheme is designed for delay-sensitive, synchronous data. FDDI allows for high data rates, in which each ring interface has its own clock. All outgoing data is transmitted using this clock. [Frenkel & Abarbanel]

The timing sequence within the Token Ring executes as follows:
1. A node gets packets within a specified amount of time.
2. As the packet circles the ring with the token behind, each station retimes and regenerates the packets.
3. When the station seizes the token, the ring is made idle for a brief period of time while the packet is being set up. This allows for more time between the DTE (data terminal equipment) and ring interface unit to structure and move the packet across the interface. [UNH, 1]

Synchronous transmission requires sending data in order of sequence. Timers ensure guaranteed delays for synchronous transmissions. FDDI also supports bursty traffic for asynchronous traffic. Asynchronous transmission can be out of order and must be re-sequenced at the destination. An eight-level priority scheme is used to manage asynchronous traffic. Each station is assigned an asynchronous priority level. The priority scheme can lock out stations that cannot use synchronous bandwidth and have an asynchronous priority level that is too low. [Alves, 1] [Humboldt, 1]

Timed Token Approach

FDDI allows multiple frames to occupy the media at the same time, which means that multiple tokens can circulate the ring at any time. FDDI uses "early release" of the token, which means it releases the token as soon as FDDI has finished transmitting the frame. This can cause frame fragments to occur because stations release the token before having received the beginning of the frame they are sending. This increases the probability that frame fragments will be propagated on the ring. These fragments are eliminated when the recipient of the token discards all data received while transmitting its own frame. Early token release is required because of the high speed and extensive distance provided by FDDI. [Humboldt, 1]

FDDI uses time to ensure equal access to the ring. It measures rotation time by calculating the distance of the segments, the processing time, and the number of stations. **Rotation time** refers to how long it takes a signal to propagate around the ring. A clock called a **Token Rotation Timer (TRT)** times the period between the receipt of tokens. Rotation time is used to control the priority operation of the FDDI ring. The operation of the MAC (Media Access

Control) layer is governed by a MAC receiver and is calculated by the **Target Token Rotation Timer** (**TTRT**). TTRT values vary depending on whether or not the ring is operational. [UNH, 1]

The timers in FDDI are used to measure token arrivals and departures. Before transmission, a **Pre-Negotiated Target Time** (**PTT**) is coordinated for the arrival of the transmission. The transmission occurs as follows:

1. Each node measures the time it takes for the token to return to it (TRT).
2. The node then compares the time to a PTT for its arrival. The node is allowed to transmit as long as its full transmission stream does not exceed the PTT.
3. If the token comes back sooner than the threshold in the PTT, it is deemed as a light load on the network.
4. If the token comes back later than the PTT, it indicates a heavy traffic load. Low priority traffic must then be deferred until the load on the network becomes lighter. [Spohn, 182]

All hosts (defined in Chapter 4) agree upon a common TTRT and strive to have the token rotate around the network at least once per TTRT. Each host maintains a TRT to indicate when the token is next expected to arrive. If the token arrives before TRT expires, then it is early. However, if the token arrives after TRT expires, it is late. The primary rule for FDDI is as follows: A host can only transmit if it receives the token early.

A **Token Holding Timer** (**THT**) is used to calculate the maximum length of time a station can hold the token to initiate asynchronous transmissions. It calculates the difference between the arrival of the token and the TTRT and keeps track of the amount of time a host can transmit. The formula for calculating THT is:

$$THT = TTRT - TRT$$

The rule governing THT says, if the THT < 0, stations (defined earlier in this chapter) can only transmit synchronous traffic. However, if the THT > 0, stations can transmit both synchronous traffic and any asynchronous traffic during the THT. When the THT reaches 0, the host cannot start a new packet. If many stations on the ring are inactive, time is wasted forwarding the token. If at all possible, the token holding time should increase as the number of active stations decreases. [NWU, 1] [McKeown, 1]

FDDI Devices

Three main devices are used within an FDDI network: *Single-Attachment Stations (SAS)*, *Dual-Attachment Stations (DAS)*, and an *FDDI concentrator*. Stations are attached to an **FDDI concentrator**, which is the device used to integrate FDDI stations into an FDDI network. An FDDI concentrator connects to both the primary and secondary rings and ensures that a station failure does not bring down the ring. The concentrator supports multiple ports and can be configured as 6, 8, 10, or 12 ports. [UNH, 1]

In Figure 12.2, ports A and B provide the connection to both rings. Also, 10 **Master ports** known as "**M**" ports are used to connect stations or additional concentrators into an FDDI network. There are two ways to connect nodes or stations to the FDDI concentrator. A **Single Attachment Station (SAS)** or node uses one cable to connect to the concentrator and represents a single attachment to the FDDI network. A SAS node is connected only to the primary ring. SAS stations are classified as Class B stations and are considered lower priority devices. [UNH, 1]

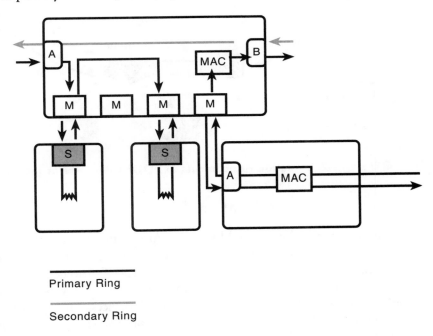

Primary Ring

Secondary Ring

FIGURE 12.2 **FDDI Concentrator [Source: UNH, 1]**

To take advantage of the fault tolerance offered by dual rings, a **Dual Attachment Station (DAS)** is required. It is referred to as dual attachment because it is capable of connecting to both rings, as shown in Figure 12.3. DAS configurations vary, and can consist of a node-to-node connection, a connection between one node and one concentrator, or between one node and two concentrators.

Each DAS has two ports, designated as port A and B. In Figure 12.3, each port provides a connection for both the primary and secondary ring. DAS stations are classified as Class A stations and have higher channel speeds and priority than SAS stations.

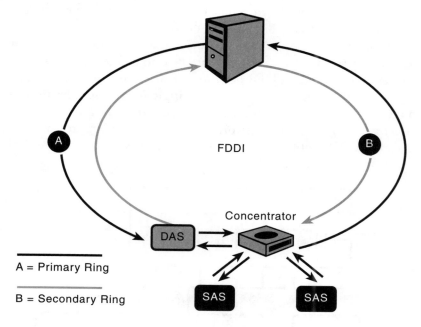

FIGURE 12.3 **Station Attachments to FDDI Concentrator [Source: Alves, 6]**

FDDI Standard Specifications

The FDDI standard published by ANSI (American National Standards Institute) defines four specifications for managing FDDI transmissions. Each specification has a specific function. The four specifications provide connectivity between upper OSI (Open Systems Interconnection) layers of common protocols and the media used to connect network devices. The upper layer protocols are usually TCP/IP (Transmission Control Protocol/Internet Protocol) and IPX (Internetwork Packet Exchange). The media is usually fiber optic but can also be copper.

The four standard specifications for FDDI are listed and described in Table 12.1.

Media Access Control (MAC)	Defines how the medium is accessed. Includes frame format, token handling, addressing, and error-recovery mechanisms. Also provides the algorithm for calculating the cyclic redundancy check (CRC) value.
Physical Layer Protocol (PHY)	Defines the data encoding/decoding procedures, clocking requirements, and framing.
Physical Layer Medium (PMD)	Defines the characteristics of the transmission medium. Includes the fiber-optic link, power levels, bit error rates, optical components, and connectors.
Station Management (SMT)	Defines the FDDI station and ring configurations, initialization, scheduling, collection of statistics, fault isolation, and recovery. Also specifies ring control features such as station insertion and removal.

TABLE 12.1 **FDDI Standard Specifications [Cisco, 8-3]**

Figure 12.4 shows how the specifications are mapped to the Logical Link Control (LLC) portion of the data link layer (layer 2) in the OSI model. These specifications are used to provide station management as defined by the FDDI standards.

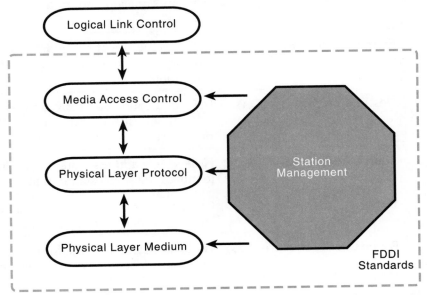

FIGURE 12.4 **FDDI Specifications Mapped to OSI Model [Source: Alves, 6]**

FDDI Frame Format

The FDDI frame format has been specifically designed to enable data to be transmitted at 100 Mbps. It uses a token passing access method such as Token Ring, however, the FDDI frame is as large as 4,500 bytes, whereas Token Ring is 4,096 bytes. The function of each part of the FDDI data frame and token fields is illustrated in Figure 12.5 and described in Table 12.2. Table 12.2 shows the arrangement of fields within the packet, correlating to the fields shown in the figure.

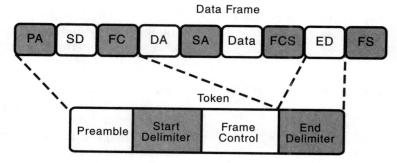

FIGURE 12.5 **FDDI Data Frame and Token Fields [Source: Cisco, 8-9]**

Preamble (PA)	Provides a unique sequence that prepares each station for an upcoming frame.
Start Delimiter (SD)	Indicates the beginning of a frame by using a different signaling pattern than the rest of the frame.
Frame Control (FC)	Indicates the size of the address fields and whether the frame contains asynchronous or synchronous data.
Destination Address (DA)	FDDI destination address is 6 bytes long. They contain unicast (singular), multicast (group), or broadcast (every station) address.
Source Address (SA)	FDDI source addresses are 6 bytes long. Identifies the single station that sent the frame.
Data	Contains information destined for an upper-layer protocol or control information.
Frame Check Sequence (FCS)	The source station fills the field with a calculated CRC value dependent on the frame contents.

TABLE 12.2 **FDDI Data Frame [Cisco, 8-9]**

End Delimiter (ED)	Contains unique symbols that indicate the end of the frame.
Frame Status (FS)	Allows the source station to determine whether an error occurred. Also identifies where the frame was recognized and copied by a receiving station.

TABLE 12.2 **FDDI Data Frame, continued**

Encoding

FDDI encodes all data prior to transmission and uses a 4 or 5 group code method. For each 4 bits of data, the encoder generates a corresponding 5-bit word or symbol. Therefore, from every 4 bits transmitted from a station, FDDI creates 5 bits. These 5 bits provide clocking for the signal itself. As discussed in Chapter 5, a bit can have only one of two values, either 0 or 1. In FDDI, the status of the bit reflects a change of state of the light on the other side. As shown in Figure 12.6, a station takes a sample of light from the other machine approximately every 8 nanoseconds (ns). The light is either on or off. If the light has changed since the last sample, the bit is translated to 1. If the light has not changed since the last sample, the bit is 0. [UNH, 1] Consequently, each time a transition in light occurs (from off to on or on to off), it is translated as a one. If there is not a transition, then it is translated to a 0.

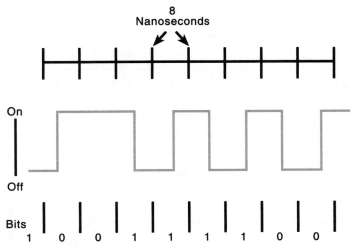

FIGURE 12.6 **Encoding 4 out of 5 Group Method [Source: UNH, 1]**

SYMBOL	BIT STREAM
0	11110
1	01001
2	10100
3	10101
4	01010
5	01011
6	01110
7	01111
8	10010
9	10011
A	10110
B	10111
C	11010
D	11011
E	11100
F	11101
Q	00000
H	00100
I	11111
J	11000
K	10001
T	01101
R	00111
S	11001

TABLE 12.3 **Symbol Codes and Their Corresponding Bit Streams**

Information is communicated in FDDI by using symbols. Symbols are comprised of 5-bit sequences. When taken with another symbol, the bits form 1 byte. There are 16 data symbols (0–F), 8 control symbols (Q, H, I, J, K, T, R, S), and 8 violation symbols (V). The coding of the symbols prevents the occurrence of four consecutive 0 bits in a row. This is necessary to ensure that each station's clock is in sync with the others. [UNH, 1]

The coding of the symbols and their bit streams is listed in Table 12.3.

The arrangement and contents of each field of the token are shown in Figure 12.7 and Table 12.4.

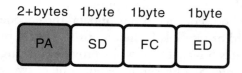

Token Format

FIGURE 12.7 **Token Field Format [Source: UNH, 1]**

Preamble (PA)	Starts field with four or more symbols of idle.
Start Delimiter (SD)	Field begins with symbols "J" and "K".
Frame Control (FC)	The type of token is described by 2 symbols.
Ending Delimiter (ED)	Ends the field with two "T" symbols.

TABLE 12.4 **Token Field Contents**

Fault Tolerance

The primary fault-tolerant feature of FDDI is the dual ring. FDDI uses a ring wrap technique to manage failures. If a station fails or a cable is damaged, the dual ring is automatically wrapped. The two adjacent ports connecting to the broken link will be removed from the ring and both stations enter the *wrap state*. The FDDI concentrator switches to the **wrap** state, and the ring is doubled back onto itself, as shown in Figure 12.8. In the figure, the ring wraps back to a single ring. Data continues to be transmitted on the FDDI single ring. Performance is not impacted negatively during the wrap condition. [UNH, 1]

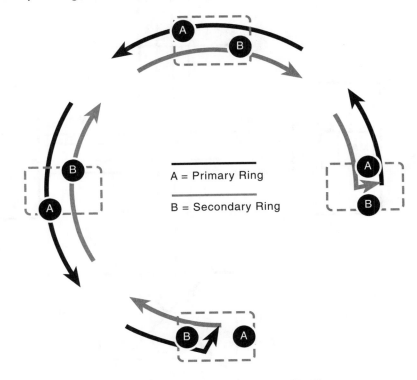

A = Primary Ring

B = Secondary Ring

FIGURE 12.8 **FDDI Wrapped Ring [Source: UNH, 1]**

Figure 12.9 shows an example of a station failure and its effect on the FDDI network. When Station 3 fails, the dual ring is automatically wrapped to Stations 2 and 4. This forms a single ring that allows the FDDI network to continue to function for the remaining stations. Station 3 is bypassed if it malfunctions or loses power. Signals are diverted away from the failing device.

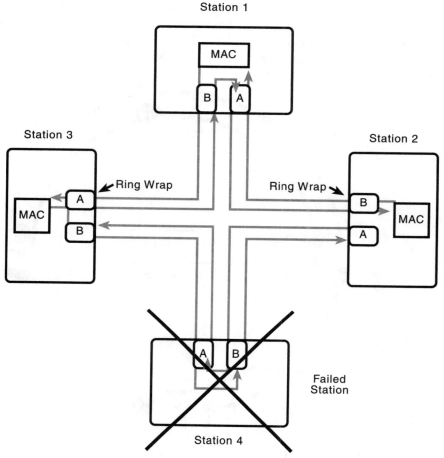

FIGURE 12.9 **FDDI Station Failure [Source: Cisco, 8-6]**

In the case of a cable failure as shown in Figure 12.10, Stations 3 and 4 wrap the ring within themselves when the wiring fails between them. The FDDI network continues to operate for all stations. FDDI is designed to manage a single failure (either station or wiring) only.

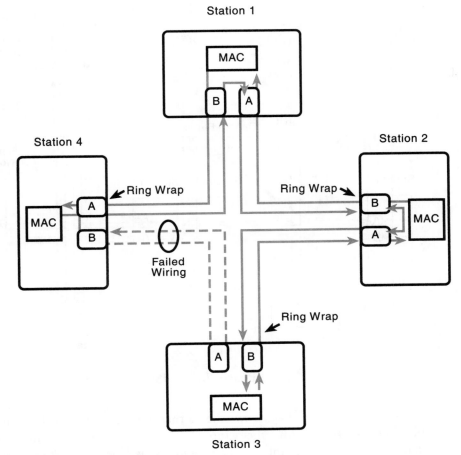

FIGURE 12.10 **Cable Failure Recovery [Source: Cisco, 8-7]**

When two or more failures occur, the rings are segmented back into two independent rings that are incapable of communicating with each other. Any additional failures can cause further ring segmentation. **Optical bypass switches** can eliminate failed stations from the ring to prevent ring segmentation. The optical bypass switch has optical mirrors that pass light from the ring directly to the DAS during normal operation. If a DAS experiences a power loss, the optical bypass switch passes the light through itself by using internal mirrors to maintain the ring's integrity.

In the example shown in Figure 12.11, Station 1 has lost power. However, the ring does not enter a wrapped condition as a result of the failure. The optical bypass switch provides continuous dual-ring operation by eliminating the failed station from the ring.

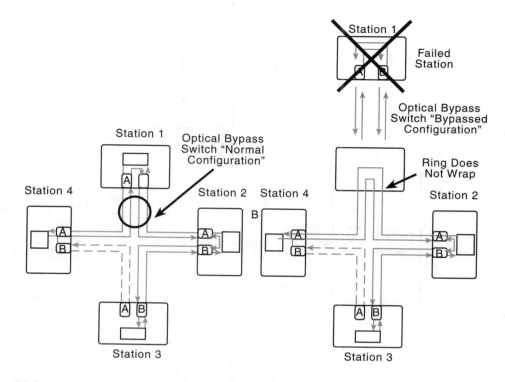

FIGURE 12.11 **Optical Bypass Switch** **[Source: Cisco, 8-8]**

One problem with bypass switches is that they attenuate the light in the fiber. This means that the fiber cannot sustain too many losses without loss of data. The maximum number of failures in a row depends on the bypass loss and the structure of the cable plant. When the bypass switch is used to join two fiber links, the number of connectors between the optical transmitter and receiver usually increases. This results in multiple potential points of failure. [Cisco, 8-8]

Another fault-tolerance technique used with FDDI is *dual homing*. **Dual homing** is used for critical devices such as routers or mainframe hosts and provides additional redundancy for maintaining operation of the FDDI network. With dual homing, a router or DAS is connected to two concentrator ports on the FDDI concentrator as exhibited in Figure 12.12.

On the FDDI concentrator, one port provides a connection to the active fiber link while the other port is in hot-standby (passive) mode. The hot standby is constantly tested and will take over if the primary link fails. In a typical DAS configuration, the B port is designated as the active port and the A port is configured as the hot standby. When the primary link fails, the passive link automatically activates and the hot standby becomes operational.

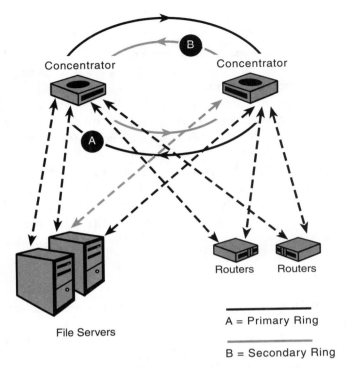

Concentrator   Concentrator

Routers   Routers

File Servers

A = Primary Ring

B = Secondary Ring

FIGURE 12.12 **FDDI Dual Homing [Source: Cisco, 8-9]**

FDDI has been extensively used as a network backbone topology to connect LANs together into a WAN. Because FDDI uses fiber-optic cabling, it is immune to electrical noise and interference. FDDI technology and components offer fault-tolerant features for continuous operation even if a cable breaks, a station malfunctions, or a concentrator fails. Today FDDI networks are often linked to SONETs (Synchronous Optical Networks—discussed later in this chapter) for high-speed transmission overseas.

TOPIC *review* — **Fiber Distributed Data Interface (FDDI)**

1. How is information conveyed between stations on a FDDI LAN?
2. Which protocol is used to move data around the ring?
3. What does FDDI use to ensure equal access to the ring?
4. What is the primary rule of transmission on a FDDI network?
5. When would an optical bypass switch be used in a FDDI network?

SMDS

Switched Multimegabit Data Services (SMDS) provide a high-speed packet-switch service for data exchange. SMDS is a WAN service designed for LAN interconnection through the PSTN (Public Switched Telephone Network). This connectionless service was developed by Bellcore and is based on the IEEE 802.6 standard used for MANs. It supports moderate bandwidth connections of between 1 to 45 Mbps. SMDS is well suited for "**bursty**" LAN traffic that consumes high bandwidth for short time periods. [Sheldon, 1152]

SMDS is designed to provide a transport service for organizations that have four or more locations within a city. For example, city governments often use SMDS to connect a city hall, courthouse, police station, and library together for inter-government networking. SMDS offers LAN-like performance for users who need to extend their data communications over a wider geographical area.

Dual Queue Dual Bus (DQDB)

SMDS supports connectionless and connection-oriented service for voice, data, and video. It uses a dual ring architecture called *Dual Queue Dual Bus (DQDB)*. **DQDB** is a data link communication protocol compatible with LANs and FDDI. DQDB specifies a topology composed of two unconnected fiber-optic buses. The bus design is based on a broadcast topology in which all nodes are directly connected to the same communications channel. In SMDS, each bus operates independently of the other. A reservation process is used to manage data transmission. [Cisco, 14-2] The structure of DQDB provides for the following:

- Each bus is unidirectional (transmits traffic in one direction only).
- Each bus is independent of the other in the transfer of traffic.
- Both buses run at the same speed.
- A queue is maintained for each bus.

A distributed queuing algorithm called a **Queued-Packet Distributed Switch (QPSX)** manages access to each bus. The distributed queue allows nodes or users to place data traffic in a queue for later transmission onto a bus. The bus is partitioned into time slots. These slots are used to transmit data. Prior to sending data, a node must first reserve a time slot on one bus to be used on the second bus. The process of reserving time slots enables nodes to notify their neighbors that they have data to transmit. The speed of the bus determines the number of time slots on a network. For example, eight time slots are available per frame when the speed of the bus is 34 Mbps. [Sheldon, 1152]

Connections in SMDS are set up with access to a distributed queue at each node, which is connected to both buses at the same time. The buses have a constant number of time slots circulating on them. Time slots for both data and voice are sampled at a rate of 8,000 slots per second. In Figure 12.13, two fiber-optic buses are labeled Bus A and Bus B. The arrows indicate that traffic on one bus flows in the opposite direction from the other. The traffic flows from the head end of each bus to the terminator. Each head end acts as a time-slot generator for its bus. The direction of traffic from the head end to the terminator determines whether one node is considered either upstream or downstream from another. [Source: Gallo & Hancock, 445]

Looking at the flow of traffic on Bus A (see Figure 12.13), Nodes 2, 3, and 4 are upstream in relation to Node 1. At Bus B, Nodes 3, 2, and 1 are downstream from Node 4. A node is downstream from any station through which the token has already passed.

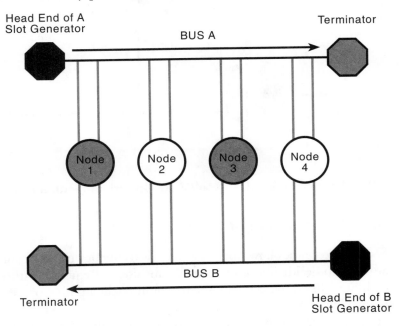

FIGURE 12.13 SMDS Traffic Flow [Source: Gallo & Hancock, 445]

An SMDS router is used to read and write into the DQDB slots. Stations or nodes that are attached read and write traffic from the time slots on the bus. In Figure 12.14, each node has two attachments to each bus. The order of node attachment dictates whether a read or write operation will occur.

The first attachment reads the bus time slots and the next attachment writes in the bus time slot. The read function is always placed in front of the write function on each bus. This allows one node to read time slots only, while another writes into them. To illustrate this process, imagine a customer is planning an airline trip to New York. She first reserves a seat on the plane (read time slot). Next, if a seat is available on the flight, she is able to reserve a seat. When the travel date arrives, she boards the airplane (write to time slot) and travels across the country to New York. [Black, 150]

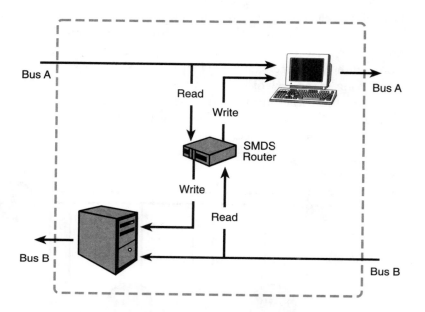

FIGURE 12.14 **SMDS Read/Write Operations [Source: Black, 150]**

Basic Operation of SMDS

SMDS determines how nodes gain access to the bus using a counter. Counters are used to decide if a slot is available for use. A **Request Counter (RQ)** on each bus is used to keep an accurate count of the number of data requests not reserved by downstream nodes. Each node examines and reserves slots on one bus to use the slots on the other bus. A node gains access by putting itself into a queue. A node "counts up" upon reading reserved slots on one bus and "counts down" by reading empty slots on the other bus. Each time a node detects a slot that has a reservation from an upstream node, it increments a counter. As empty time slots pass by on the other bus, the counter is decremented. When this counter equals 0, the node is allowed to use the next free slot and place traffic into the time slot. [Black, 152]

Figure 12.15 illustrates the reservation process. Each slot has a reservation bit (R). The DBDQ operation shown can be broken down into the following steps:

1. When the node is idling, the requests that pass on bus B (request counter) are counted.

2. The upstream nodes ahead of node A have reserved three time slots by setting the R bit equal to 1.
3. Node A determines that three requests are ahead of it by incrementing a counter by 1 for each reserved time slot.
4. The RQ is decremented by 1 with each empty slot on bus A (3 empty slots). Empty slots are designated as B=0.
5. The node keeps a count of the number of downstream requests and balances that against the number of the empty slots.
6. To send, a node puts a request on a slot on bus B and remembers the slot count.
7. By sending the RQ to a countdown counter, a node can determine an empty slot.
8. When the counter equals 0, nodes use the slot and can transmit data.

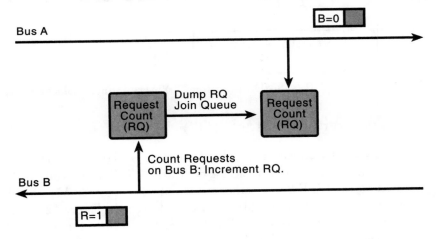

FIGURE 12.15 **SMDS DQDB Queuing Operations [Source: Black, 152]**

The SMDS router reads the source address in the header of the packet and determines whether the station is upstream or downstream on the two buses. In Figure 12.16, station E is the source address. The destination address is station A. The traffic is currently flowing across bus B. The router has determined that for station E to reach station A, it must transmit on bus A. This operation is referred to as **location discovery**. [Black, 155]

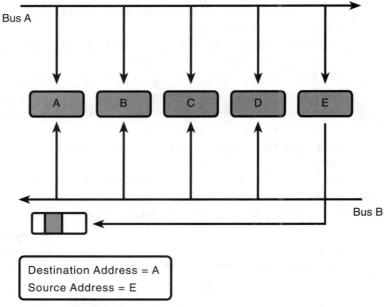

Destination Address = A
Source Address = E

FIGURE 12.16 **SMDS Location Discovery [Source: Black, 155]**

SMDS Interface Protocol (SIP)

The **SMDS Interface Protocol (SIP)** provides a connectionless service that allows the SMDS router to access the carrier's SMDS network. SIP is a protocol based on the IEEE 802.6 standard for cell relay across MANs. SIP is subdivided into three protocol levels: SIP1, SIP2, and SIP3. In Figure 12.17, SIP1 operates at the physical layer of the OSI model. SIP2 and SIP3 function at the MAC sublayer of the data link layer.

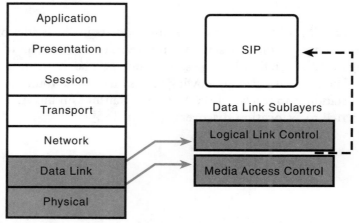

FIGURE 12.17 **SIP Services and the OSI Model [Source: Cisco, 14-3]**

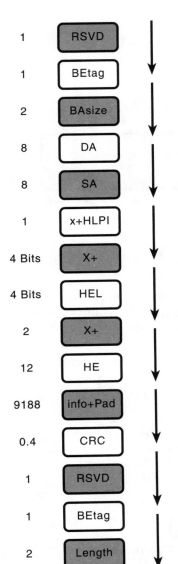

1	RSVD
1	BEtag
2	BAsize
8	DA
8	SA
1	x+HLPI
4 Bits	X+
4 Bits	HEL
2	X+
12	HE
9188	info+Pad
0.4	CRC
1	RSVD
1	BEtag
2	Length

FIGURE 12.18 SIP3 Protocol Data Unit (PDU)[Source: Cisco, 14-5]

User information is passed to SIP3 in the form of SDUs (Service Data Units) encapsulated in a SIP3 header and trailer. As information passes down the protocol layer, it creates a frame called an SIP3 PDU (Protocol Data Unit). The SIP3 PDUs are passed to SIP2. The SIP3 PDU consists of 15 fields (see Figure 12.18). These fields are described in Table 12.5. [Gallo & Hancock, 447]

RSVD (Reserved)	This field consists of 0s.
BEtag (Beginning-end Tag)	Forms an association between first and last segments of a segmented SIP Level 3 PDU.
BAsize (Buffer Allocation Size)	Contains the buffer allocation size.
DA (Destination Address)	The individual or group SMDS address for the destination.
SA (Source Address)	This field contains the individual SMDS address of the source.
HLPI (Higher-layer Protocol Identifier)	Indicates the type of protocol encapsulated in the Information field.
X+ (Carried Across Network Unchanged)	Ensures that the SIP PDU format aligns with the DQDB protocol format.
HEL (Header Extension Length)	Indicates the number of 32-bit words in the Header Extension (HE) field.
HE (Header Extension)	Contains the SMDS version number.
Info+Pad (Information + Padding)	Contains an encapsulated SMDS SDU and padding that ensures the field ends on a 32-bit boundary.
CRC (Cyclic Redundancy Check)	Contains a value used for error checking.

TABLE 12.5 **Fields in an SIP3 PDU**

At SIP2, the PDUs are segmented into fixed-sized cells 53 octets long: 48 bytes for payload and 5 bytes of header information (see Figure 12.19). The SIP2 cell contains packets of information that hold payload (data) and header information.

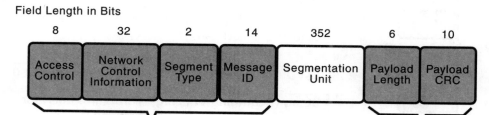

FIGURE 12.19 **SIP2 Cell [Source: Cisco, 14-6]**

The header contains channel and path information to direct the cell to its destination. The fixed-sized cells are passed to SIP1. The header is composed of the fields listed and described in Table 12.6.

Access Control	This field can carry request bits that indicate bids for the cell on the bus going from the switch to the CPE (customer premise equipment) device.
Network Control Information	Indicates whether the PDU contains information.
Segment Type	Indicates whether the cell is the first, last, or middle cell from a segmented Level 3 PDU.
Message ID	This is the same for all of the segments of a given Level 3 PDU.
Segmentation Unit	Contains the data portion of the cell. If the Level 2 cell is empty, this field is populated with 0s.

TABLE 12.6 **SIP2 Cell Header Fields**

The trailer fields in an SIP2 cell are listed in Table 12.7.

Payload Unit	Indicates how many bytes of a Level 3 PDU are actually in the Segmentation Unit field. If the Level 2 cell is empty, this field is populated with 0s.
Payload Cyclic Redundancy Check (CRC)	Contains a CRC value used to detect errors in segment type, message ID, segmentation unit, payload length, and payload CRC.

TABLE 12.7 SIP2 Cell Trailer Fields

SIP1 provides the physical interface to the SMDS network. It has two sublayers: the transmission system and the **Physical Layer Convergence Protocol (PLCP)**. The transmission system is used to specify how cells are placed on the medium. Meanwhile, PLCP formats the 53-byte cells for their actual delivery across the network. [Source: Cisco, 14-6]

As shown in Figure 12.20, SIP provides a connectionless service between the CPE and the equipment provided by the carrier. The interface between the CPE and carrier equipment is called the **Subscriber Network Interface (SNI)**. [Source: Cisco, 14-2]

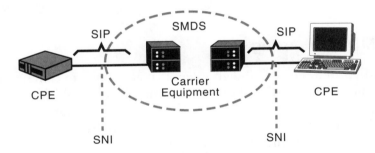

FIGURE 12.20 SIP Interface to Carrier Equipment [Source: Cisco, 14-2]

SMDS Network Components

Several components are required to interface to an SMDS network, including a router that supports the SIP, an SMDS CSU/DSU (Channel Service Unit/Data Service Unit), a circuit, and an SMDS switch. In Figure 12.21, the SMDS router interfaces the LAN to the SMDS DSU. From the SMDS DSU, the circuit is connected to the LEC (Local Exchange Carrier) SMDS switch. Then it travels through the SMDS cloud to the destination network.

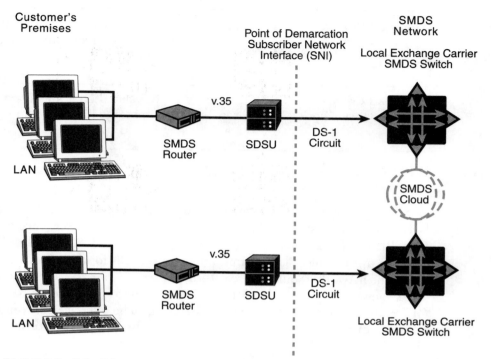

Customer's
Premises

Point of Demarcation
Subscriber Network
Interface (SNI)

SMDS
Network

Local Exchange Carrier
SMDS Switch

v.35

SMDS
Router

SDSU

DS-1
Circuit

LAN

SMDS
Cloud

v.35

SMDS
Router

SDSU

DS-1
Circuit

LAN

Local Exchange Carrier
SMDS Switch

FIGURE 12.21 **SMDS Network Components [Source: Gallo & Hancock, 448]**

SMDS Addressing

SMDS addresses are 10-digit values that are similar to conventional phone numbers. The SMDS address is constructed with two fields: a 4-bit address type and variable length E.164 address. The E.164 address is based on the ISDN (Integrated Services Digital Network) global numbering addressing format specified by the ITU-T (International Telecommunication Union). The address includes a country code, area or city code, and a local number. For example, the country code for Taiwan is 886. Area or city codes are usually no more than four digits long. [Gallo & Hancock, 451]

SMDS offers two different types of addressing. In the address type field of the PDU, it indicates one of two address types: individual or group. Individual addresses are used for unicast transmissions. Group addresses are used for multicast transmissions. SMDS group addresses allow a single address to refer to multiple CPU stations or locations. In Figure 12.22, the SMDS switch is able to address an individual address, Customer C, at location 1 or 2. It also can address a multiple group, Customers A and B (two devices—one at each Location 1) and Customers A and B (two devices—one at each Location 2). The group address is specified in the destination address field of the PDU.

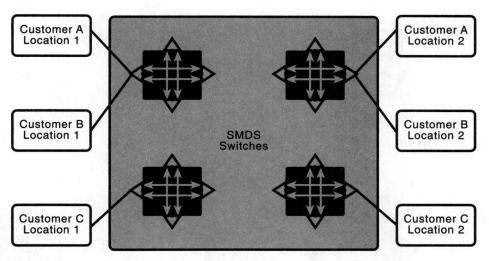

FIGURE 12.22 SMDS Switch Group Addressing [Source: SBC, 1]

SMDS implements two security features: *source address validation* and *address screening*. **Source address validation** verifies that the PDU source address is correctly assigned to the SNI from which it originated. This validation helps prevent address "spoofing," in which illegal traffic assumes the source address of a legitimate device. **Address screening** allows a subscriber to establish a Virtual Private Network (VPN), which enables the user to exclude unwanted traffic. If an address is disallowed, the data unit is not delivered. [Cisco, 14-5]

A Deployment Example of SMDS

In the example shown in Figure 12.23, a university in California has deployed an SMDS network to connect two extension campuses back to the main campus. Extension Campus A has connected a 5-user LAN through an SMDS router and CSU to SMDS. It also has connected a larger 75-user LAN from Extension Campus B. The main campus has a 205-user LAN connected to SMDS. The SMDS network is used for e-mail, file transfer, and student registration.

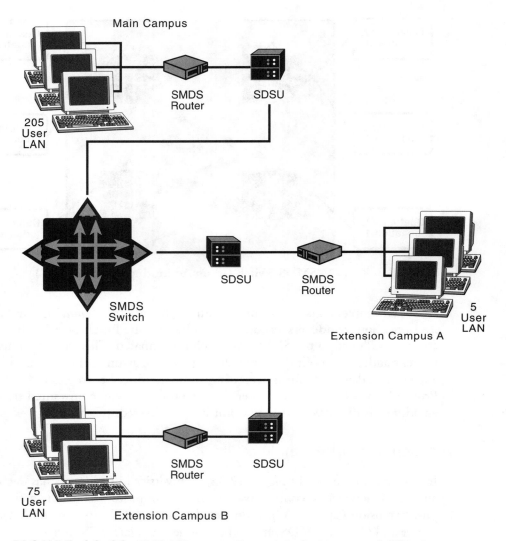

FIGURE 12.23 **SMDS Connects Extension Campuses at California University [Source: SBC, 40]**

SMDS has been more successful in Europe than in the United States. A number of European service providers such as British Telecom, France Telecom, and Deutsche Telecom offer this service. Each has several deployments throughout Europe. SMDS can operate with Frame Relay and ATM (Asynchronous Transfer Mode) for LAN-to-LAN connectivity. In the United States, major support of SMDS has declined and several LECs have discontinued service of SMDS. The market has shifted and now favors lower cost services such as the Internet and VPNs. [Gallo & Hancock, 454]

1. Which standard specified the connectionless service used by SMDS?
2. Are the buses in DQDB unidirectional or bidirectional?
3. Do both buses run at the same speed?
4. How does SMDS determine how nodes gain access to the bus?
5. What provides the physical interface to the SMDS network?

SONET

Synchronized Optical Network (SONET) is a high-speed international fiber-optic network that supports data, voice, and video applications. SONET was developed by Bellcore to provide higher bandwidth and multiplexed transmissions to interface with PTTs, IXCs (Interexchange Carriers), and LECs. SONET uses a multiple payload transport, which provides enough bandwidth for simultaneous delivery of a 3-D image, the entire contents of an encyclopedia, and full-motion video. The international equivalent of SONET is **Synchronous Digital Hierarchy (SDH).** [Sheldon, 1166-1167]

SONET Applications and Services

SONET supports broadband services and applications and offers real-time transmission for video conferencing, distance learning, CAD/CAM collaborations, aerospace flight simulations, and high-resolution imaging. It allows multiple location distribution and real-time shared modification of documents for virtual work groups. SONET is also used in entertainment to provide video on demand, pay per view, high fidelity sound broadcast, and full-motion catalogs. Additionally, medical personnel use it for 3-D medical teleradiology and remote diagnostics for patient assessment and monitoring.

SONET uses fiber optics to support higher bandwidth. A single glass fiber can transmit 85,000 compressed voice circuits and can achieve speeds up to 10 Gbps. Fiber is immune to electrical interference, remaining unaffected by lightning, downed power lines, or radio transmitters. SONET is a true international standard for fiber transport interconnectivity, and the only international standard for digital to fiber optic communications. SONET transmissions are made up of communications channels. SONET channels are merged into higher-level channels using Time Division Multiplexing (TDM). Each channel is allocated a specific time slot in the transmission. [Search Networking, 1]

Despite being called a Synchronized Optical Network, SONET is only a transport interface and method of transmission—not the network itself. SONET uses a transfer mode that defines switching and multiplexing of a digital transmission protocol. SONET can multiplex several data streams, called tributaries, into optical carriers (OCs). It allows direct multiplexing to transport new services and enable interoperability with ATM, Frame Relay, FDDI, and SMDS. [Spohn, 448]

Asynchronous/Synchronous Interconnections

SONET is often used to construct large multi-ring networks in which rings can be different sizes and speeds. To accommodate these interconnections, SONET requires a method to support both asynchronous and synchronous traffic.

Asynchronous traffic often requires **bit stuffing** (the addition of extra bits) to handle individual data streams and to multiplex up to higher rates. With synchronous traffic, clocking is used to keep the bit rate of the data constant. Clocking is also used to indicate where the 1s and 0s are located in the data stream. SONET keeps the average frequency of all clocks nearly identical on all lines. The network is organized in a master/slave relationship, in which higher-level (master) nodes feed timing signals to clocks of the lower-level (slave) nodes. [Tektronix, 4-5]

When asynchronous communication is required, the SONET device performs bit stuffing to achieve the desired bandwidth. Extra bits are inserted into the data stream and then stripped off at the destination SONET device. The major interface options available for SONET are as follows:

- Direct CPE or CO (central office) hardware interface
- Gateway device to convert to OC levels
- Conversion within the SONET switch itself [Spohn, 465]

In SONET, each node is synchronized to a central clock. This makes it possible for a node to access traffic without complex packing and unpacking of various signals. The traffic that flows into a node is exactly equal to that flowing out—there is no peak rate. SONET provides bandwidth as required and does not recognize congestion or priority. To address this lack of recognition, ATM runs on top of SONET to provide Quality of Service (QoS) features for priority and alleviation of congestion. [Nortel Networks, 3]

Levels of Optical Carrier Transmission Rates

SONET line transmission rates for long distances require optical fibers. An **optical carrier (OC)** designation is used to specify the speed of transmission for digital signals on optical fiber. Several levels of signal rates are available ranging from OC-1 at 51.84 Mbps to OC-768 at 40 Gbps. Table 12.8 lists the standard SONET line rates and OC levels.

OC LEVEL	RATE
OC-1/STS-1	51.84 Mbps
OC-3/STS-3	155.52 Mbps
OC-3c/STS-3c	155.52 Mbps
OC-12/STS-12	622.08 Mbps
OC-12/STS-12c	622.08 Mbps
OC-48/STS-48	2,488 Mbps
OC-192	10 Gbps
OC-256	13.271 Gbps
OC-768	40 Gbps

TABLE 12.8 Standard SONET OC Speed [Sheldon, 919]

Add/Drop Multiplexing (ADM)

SONET offers transport services for interconnection of both telephone and data switches by using **Add/Drop Multiplexing (ADM)** to provide interfaces between different network signals and SONET signals. In Figure 12.24, DS1 and DS3 signals are connected to OC-m signals. SONET's multiplexing function allows lower-level signals (DS1 and DS3) to be added or dropped from a high-speed OC channel in a wire center. The wire center is a location where customer loops converge. ADM allows new signals to come into and existing signals to be dropped out of a carrier channel by passing through the add/drop multiplexer. The purpose of ADM is to add and drop signals without disrupting the onward transmission of other signals. The connection is established between an add/drop multiplexer and a central office port at a specific digital speed. [Tektronix, 36]

SONET provides "drop and repeat," a key capability for telephone connections and cable TV (CATV) applications. The drop and repeat function allows a signal to terminate at one node, be repeated, and then be sent to the next and subsequent nodes. Drop and repeat also provides alternate routing for traffic passing through interconnecting rings to deliver to the destination node. [Tektronix, 32]

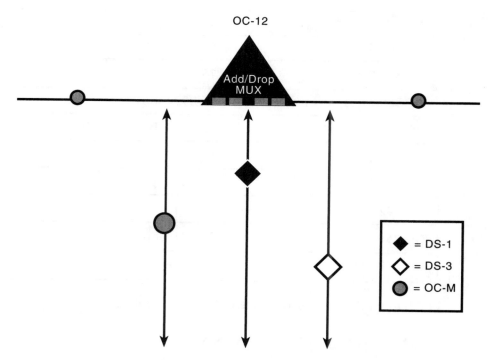

FIGURE 12.24 **SONET Add/Drop Multiplexing (ADM) [Source: SBC, 44]**

In large SONET networks, a signal can be switched to another ring by the ADM. The ADM extracts it and then adds it into the other ring. This process requires performing an optical-to-electrical-to-optical conversion. This allows multiple lower-speed rings to connect into a higher-speed ring. At the point where the ADMs are connected to the rings, a **digital cross connect (DCS)** provides the connection to the lower-speed rings. A DCS is a piece of equipment that provides flexible connections between the termination points of devices used in the network. [Spohn, 468]

SONET Ring Automatic Protection Switching

The top of Figure 12.25 shows the normal operation of standard SONET rings. These standard rings contain two fibers; one transmits signals in one direction while the other waits in standby or protected mode. SONET uses **Automatic Protect Switching (APS)** to enable the protected mode rings to take over in the event of a service disruption. If the fiber is cut, transmissions are looped back onto the secondary fiber on both sides of the break. A new ring is then formed around the break. This is referred to as a **Self-Healing Architecture**. [Sheldon, 1166]

For disaster recovery, a more complicated SONET architecture can be used called **Bi-directional Line Switched Ring (BLSR),** as shown at the bottom of Figure 12.25. A BLSR is a four-fiber, bidirectional line-switched SONET ring. Two fibers are used to carry traffic while the other two fibers are on standby or protect mode. Calls can be rerouted around failure points within 50 milliseconds (ms), should a service disruption occur. [Sheldon, 1166]

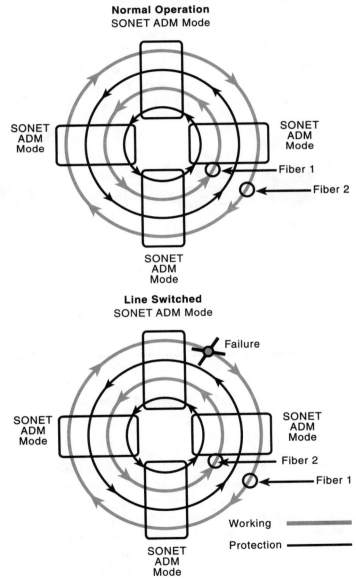

FIGURE 12.25 **SONET Bi-directional Line Switched Ring (BLSR) [Source: SBC, 37]**

Synchronous Transport Signal Level 1

SONET uses a unique framing format in which timing is the most critical element. The basic building block of this format is the **Synchronous Transport Signal Level 1 (STS-1)**. The frame is comprised of overhead and payload. The overhead elements are *section, line,* and *path*. As shown in Figure 12.26, the **section** handles the cable between adjacent network devices, in other words, regenerators. The **line** is the physical path between the SONET hub, switch, or multiplexer in the carrier network. It allows any STS-n, in which "n" is a variable representing any number, signal between any number of STS-n multiplexers. The **path** is part of the payload envelope for STS-1, carrying information end-to-end. The path is terminated at the customer premises. The payload is the actual data to be transported. [Sheldon, 1169-1170]

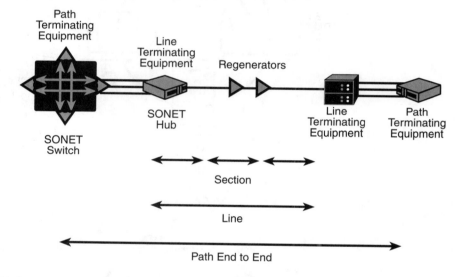

FIGURE 12.26 SONET Overhead Layers [Source: SBC, 34]

SONET Frame Structure

A SONET frame is a specific sequence of 810 bytes or 6,480 bits that carries both data and control information. The control information is referred to as **overhead**. The line overhead provides for reliable transport of payload data through parity checking between elements. Carriers handle section and line overhead and the customer handles the path. As exhibited in Figure 12.27, each frame is composed of 9 rows and 90 columns of 8-bit bytes. The order of byte transmission is left to right, row by row. The first three columns in each row designate section or line overhead often referred to a transport overhead. The path overhead is the first octet of the payload and begins at column 4.

Signals are carried in two different-size containers: a *virtual tributary (VT)* and a *Synchronous Payload Envelope (SPE)*. A **VT** is a structure designed for transporting and switching payloads. It allows slower-speed services to be carried in the payload by putting them into separate VT containers. The VTs are carried in different byte positions within the payload. The **Synchronous Payload Envelope (SPE)** is the actual payload being transported and includes everything but the transport overhead. The section overhead is added to the frame so that the signal and the quality of the transmission are all traceable. [Tektronix, 8]

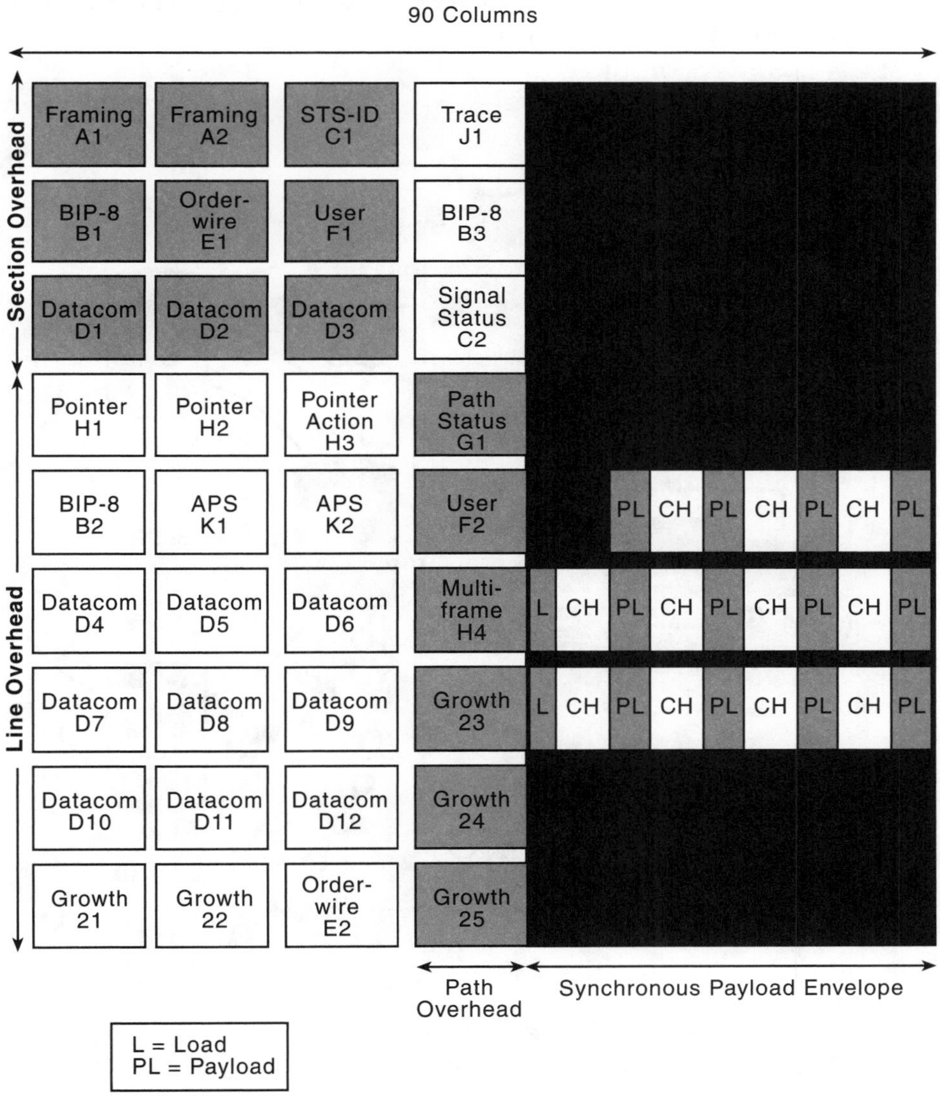

FIGURE 12.27 **SONET Frame [Source: 3COM, 4-6]**

A SONET Network

SONET provides aggregation of low-speed data transport channels into the high-speed backbone trunk transport. Figure 12.28 shows an example of SONET. Bidirectional SONET rings are using OC-48 ADMs. Several lower speed lines (DS1, DS3, and OC3) are coming in and going out of the SONET. The Voice PBX (private branch exchange) is connected over a 1.54 Mbps T-carrier line (DS1). A LAN is connected via a router and a multiplexer over a T-carrier (DS3) 45 Mbps line. In addition, a workstation is connected through an ATM switch over an OC-3 (155 Mbps).

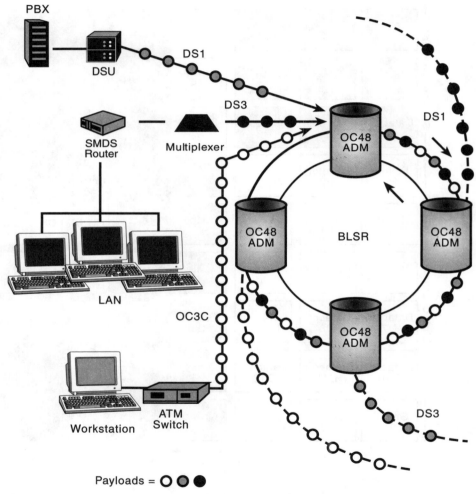

Payloads = ○ ◓ ●

FIGURE 12.28 **SONET Network [Source: SBC, 29]**

SONET provides abundant support for broadband services, lowers transmission costs, adds or drops channels without demultiplexing or remultiplexing, and reduces overall network transport delay. It is an international standard and is supported by vendors and service providers alike.

SONET as a single-wavelength solution is limited. Until now, research scientists have not been able to discover a simple way to aggregate multiple wavelengths within SONET to increase capacity between locations. Also, SONET's hierarchy is not optimized for large data transfers. However, with new technologies emerging such as Dense Wavelength Division Multiplexing (DWDM) and advancement in the optical core, SONET has become more scalable and data optimized.

TOPIC review SONET

1. Can different size and speed rings be connected into a large multi-ring network?
2. How are SONET channels merged into higher-level channels?
3. What is the purpose of an ADM?
4. What is the most critical element for a SONET frame format?
5. How does line overhead provide for reliable transport of payload data?

OPTICAL NETWORKING DEVELOPMENTS

The ITU is working on developing optical technologies for high-volume and high-speed transactions. Currently, the ITU has developed **Optical Transport Network (OTN)** as a standard that will eventually replace SONET. Voice-equipment manufacturers now recommend using OTN, a new high-speed protocol that allows SONET to adapt to the changing times. An OTN interface will support a combination of wavelengths to different channels. The OTN will allow for multiple wavelengths of different carrying capacities. So far, the ITU has defined three throughput rates: 2.5 Gbps, 10 Gbps, and 40 Gbps. Research scientists are working on several other technologies to find better ways to provide and deliver optical networking services. [Greenfield, 5]

Development of Semiconductor Technology

In the networking sector, the most important recent advancement in semiconductors has been the development of an alloy that combines silicon with germanium. Scientists have discovered that transistors made from silicon and germanium are capable of much higher operating speeds than silicon-only transistors. The new advance in semiconductors is the methodology of the micron technology used in constructing the chip that "Stacks" rather than layers the molecules inside the chip connection layers. This significantly reduces heat generation and transfer, thereby allowing the development of much faster chips. Manufacturers now predict they will be able to offer 40 Gbps systems using "big" integrated chips for very high network speeds, including a 40 Gbps Ethernet connection to the desktop. [Bell Labs, 4]

Analog signals are still transported over copper wires in the local loop back to the CO switch. Narrow band radio channels continue to be used over the congested radio spectrum. However, optical, semiconductor, and wireless technologies now provide resources for widening the bottlenecks in analog and narrowband. **Optical Amplification (OA),** which boosts an optical signal without any conversion of the light into an electrical signal, and Wave Division Multiplexing (WDM) minimize the need to convert a wide channel into an electrical format. Someday, customers and service providers might each have their own specific optical wavelengths. A network operator could then assign one wavelength to an ISP and another to a voice service provider. [Bell Labs, 5]

Evolution of Access

The best strategy today for radically boosting network performance is to speed up access over the "last mile." The goal is to eventually provide for a 3-D mix of traffic: video, voice, and data over a single line to the home or small office and deliver this signal at speeds up to 40 Gbps. However, costs for fiber links to homes will need to come down substantially before an all-optical network can be realized. Wireless, fiber, and copper will each require an access method to this all-optical network. [Bell Labs, 5]

Technology Trends and Developments

The technology of tomorrow will include sophisticated hybrid networks that combine electronics and photonics technology. The three technology trends that are leading us forward are:
- **Ultra-dense WDM**. Will greatly increase the number of messages to be transmitted over a fiber connection.
- OA and advances in long-haul transmission. Will eliminate the present need for converting messages into electrons every so often to boost their strength.
- **Optical switching.** Will enable signals to not be bound by Moore's Law. [Bell Labs, 4]

In the future, there will be a shift away from centrally managed traditional circuit-switched systems. Empowered optical networks will be capable of changing dynamically to meet traffic needs. The **next generation mega networks**, as shown in Figure 12.29, will combine semiconductor development with fiber photonics, ultra WDM, and OA to deliver an all-optical network. Consumers will be able to access over the last mile using wireless, fiber, and copper. To provide bandwidth-on-demand, these networks must be self-managing. Intelligence to make these networks self-managing is being built into the software.

Technology Trends and Developments

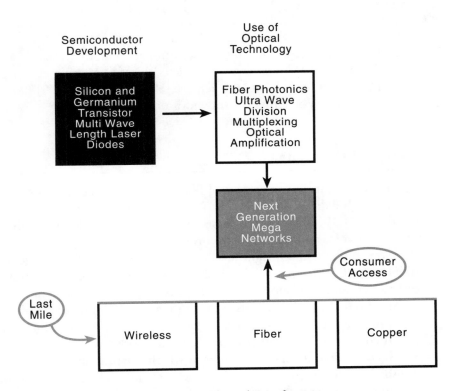

FIGURE 12.29 Technology Trends and Developments

In 2001, research and development scientists at Bell Labs developed an optical switch that set a new world record by transmitting over 1,022 different wavelengths (colors) of light through a single optical fiber, with each wavelength carrying its own stream of information. Each wavelength of this ultradense wavelength division transmitter supports voice, data, or video and occupies only 9.5 GHz. The 1,022-channel transmitter carries information at a rate of 37 Mbps per channel. This results in a total system capacity of more than 37Gb. These scientists designed their system so that it can be scaled up to OC-48 data rates, which would yield a capacity for several terabits per second. [Bell Labs, 4]

Over the years, the advancement in technology has improved transmission rates, performance, and amplification techniques. Research has improved methods for protection and redundancy of the network. Optical networking technology has increased the number of wavelengths available to send information through fiber. At some point, provided there are optimistic economic implications, a bright future is predicted for all-optical networks.

TOPIC review — Optical Networking Developments

1. Why is it predicted that OTNs will replace SONET?
2. Can a channel remain in optical form over long distances?
3. What does OTN use to carry packets across fiber-optic networks?
4. How will OTNs be able to achieve self-management?
5. How do OTNs provide bandwidth-on-demand?

CHAPTER SUMMARY

FDDI uses counter-rotating optical fiber rings to connect LANs together usually between buildings. It uses a token-passing protocol to transmit data around the ring. FDDI uses a protocol based on timers to provide for continuous transmission of voice and video for synchronous traffic. FDDI also supports asynchronous traffic with an eight-level priority scheme used to manage bursty data traffic. Multiple tokens can circulate the ring at any time. FDDI provides for early token release to support its high speed and extensive distance.

An FDDI network supports SAS, DAS, and an FDDI concentrator to make the connection to the FDDI rings. Master ports are used to connect stations or FDDI concentrators together in an FDDI network.

FDDI has two independent rings in which the primary ring is used for data transmission while the secondary ring remains idle. The topology is designed for fault tolerance; if the primary ring fails, the secondary ring takes over and provides an alternate data path. FDDI uses ring wrapping so that the dual ring is automatically wrapped if a failure occurs. Another technique called Optical Bypass Switch provides continuous dual-ring operation by eliminating a failed station from the ring. The most critical network components (routers and mainframe hosts) use dual homing to connect the devices to two ports on the FDDI concentrator.

Another ring-based network, SMDS provides service for voice, data, and video for MANs. It uses two unconnected fiber-optic buses to support connectionless and connection-oriented services. SMDS uses DQDB as a reservation process to manage data transmission. The DQDB technique uses time slots to transmit data. A node reserves a time slot on one bus to be used on the second bus. An SMDS router reads and writes into the DQDB time slots. The SIP provides connectionless service to allow the SMDS router to access the carrier's SMDS network.

The primary components of an SMDS network include an SMDS router, SMDS CSU/DSU, a circuit, and an SMDS switch. LANs are interconnected to the SMDS network through the SMDS router. SMDS supports individual (unicast) and group (multicast) addressing to transmit to several locations. SMDS security provides address screening to exclude unwanted traffic and source address validation to prevent address spoofing.

SONET is used as a high-speed fiber-optic network backbone to connect LEC, IXC, and ISPs (Internet Service Providers) together. SONET supports data, voice, and video applications in real time. It is the only international standard for digital to fiber-optic communications. The most significant features, switching and ADM grant SONET the capability to provide bandwidth on demand. Lower-speed digital services such as DS1 and DS3 can be added or dropped automatically by an OC channel. The ADM allows for a signal to be switched to another ring.

SONET uses dual rings and a self-healing architecture. It offers APS to cause protected mode rings to take over should a service disruption occur. If the fiber is cut, transmissions are looped back onto the secondary fiber on both sides of the break. For extra disaster recovery, a four-fiber, BLSR is used. Timing is the most critical element for the SONET frame. The STS-1 is the building block of the frame. SONET overhead elements are section, line, and path. Section handles the cable and regenerators; line is the physical path between SONET devices; and the path is part of the payload.

SONET uses optical-to-electrical-to-optical transmission. Bandwidth limitations are associated with electrical transmission. As technology develops in the future, the trend will be a move toward an all-optical network. With the use of OA and WDM, scientists will minimize the need for the electrical format. The goal is to provide for a 3-D mix of traffic: video, voice, and data over a single line into the home or office.

CHAPTER REVIEW QUESTIONS

(This quiz also can be printed from the Encore! CD that accompanies this book. File name—Chap12review.)

Circle a letter (a-d) for each question. Choose only one answer for each.

1. What type of scheme does FDDI use to move data around the ring?
    a. collision detection
    b. CSMA
    c. token passing
    d. collision avoidance

2. Each host in an FDDI network maintains this to indicate when the token is next expected to arrive.
   a. PTT
   b. TRT
   c. MAC
   d. THT

3. How does FDDI usually manage ring failures?
   a. ring wrap
   b. dual ring
   c. station management
   d. MAC

4. In an SMDS network, what is the bus partitioned into?
   a. paths
   b. segments
   c. channels
   d. time slots

5. What device is able to read and write into the DQDB slots?
   a. optical bypass switch
   b. SMDS router
   c. FDDI concentrator
   d. SMDS DSU

6. What are source address validation and address screening used for in an SMDS network?
   a. group addressing
   b. overhead
   c. security
   d. channel management

7. In SONET, each node is synchronized to:
   a. a central clock
   b. time rotation timer
   c. an OC
   d. a data stream

8. In large SONETs, a signal can be switched to another ring by:
   a. digital cross connect
   b. router
   c. ADM
   d. optical bypass switch

9. Scientists have discovered that transistors made from silicon and this substance can operate at much higher speeds than silicon-only transistors.
   a. aluminum
   b. germanium
   c. iron
   d. copper

10. The technology of tomorrow will include sophisticated hybrid networks that combine the following:
   a. electronics and radio channels
   b. electronics and photonics
   c. electronics and transistors
   d. electronics and semiconductors

Circle the correct letter (A-E) that corresponds to the descriptions below. Choose only one answer for each.
   A. DQDB
   B. ADM
   C. MAC
   D. OC
   E. RQ

11. A B C D E   Used to provide interconnection of both telephone and data switches.

12. A B C D E   Used to keep an accurate count of the number of data requests not reserved by downstream nodes.

13. A B C D E   A topology composed of two unconnected fiber-optic buses, in which each bus operates independently of the other.

14. A B C D E   Defines how the medium is accessed.

15. A B C D E   Specifies the speed of transmission for digital signals.

   A. VT
   B. PHY
   C. OTN
   D. THT
   E. SAS

16. A B C D E   Defines data encoding/decoding procedures, clocking, and framing requirements for FDDI.

17. A B C D E   A standard being developed by the ITU to eventually replace SONET.

18. A B C D E A station/node that uses one cable to connect to the FDDI concentrator.

19. A B C D E A structure designed for transporting and switching payloads in a SONET frame.

20. A B C D E Used to calculate the maximum length of time a station can hold a token to initiate asynchronous transmissions.

INTERNET EXERCISES

1. Key the following URL:

   www-3.ibm.com/chips/micronews/vol6_no1/ahlgren.html

   Write a brief description about SiGe.

2. Key the following URL:

   www.lightreading.com/document.asp?doc_id=3483.

   Write a brief description about OA.

CONCEPT EXERCISES

Concept Narrative
(This narrative exercise also can be printed from the Encore! CD that accompanies this book. File name—Chap12connar.)

Fill in the blanks of the following narrative.

Three main devices are used within an FDDI network: *Single-Attachment Stations (SAS)*, *Dual-Attachment Stations (DAS)*, and an *FDDI concentrator*. Stations are attached to an _____ _____, which is the device used to integrate FDDI stations into an FDDI network. An FDDI concentrator connects to both the primary and secondary rings to ensure that a station _____ does not bring down the ring. The concentrator supports multiple ports and can be configured as 6, 8, 10, or 12 ports.

There are also ten _____ _____ known as "_____" ports that are used to connect stations or additional concentrators into an FDDI network. There are two ways to connect nodes or stations to the FDDI concentrator. A _____ _____ _____ or node uses one cable to connect to the concentrator. It represents a _____ attachment to the FDDI network. An

SAS node is connected only to the primary ring. SAS stations are classified as Class B stations and are considered lower priority devices.

To take advantage of the fault tolerance offered by dual rings, a _____ _____ _____ is required. It is referred to as dual attachment because it is capable of connecting to both rings. Configurations vary and can consist of a node-to-node connection, a connection between one node and one concentrator, or a connection between one node and two concentrators.

Concept Table
(This table exercise also can be printed from the Encore! CD that accompanies this book. File name—Chap12contab.)

Read each statement carefully and choose the type of Ring-based network being described. Use only one "X" per statement.

STATEMENT	RING–BASED NETWORK		
	FDDI	SMDS	SONET
1. Provides a "drop and repeat" capability for telephone connections and CATV applications.			
2. Addresses are 10-digit values that are similar to conventional phone numbers.			
3. When two or more failures occur, the rings are segmented back into two independent rings.			
4. SIP is used to provide a connectionless service between the CPE and the equipment provided by the carrier.			
5. Uses APS to allow the protected mode rings to take over in the event of a service disruption.			
6. Uses time to ensure equal access to the ring.			
7. Line transmission rates for long distances require optical fiber.			
8. If an address is disallowed, the data unit is not delivered.			
9. The primary fault-tolerant feature is the dual ring.			
10. Its hierarchy is not optimized for large data transfers.			

Concept Picture

(This picture exercise also can be printed from the Encore! CD that accompanies this book. File name—Chap12conpic.)

In this exercise, look at the picture of the SONET overhead layers and label the missing elements.

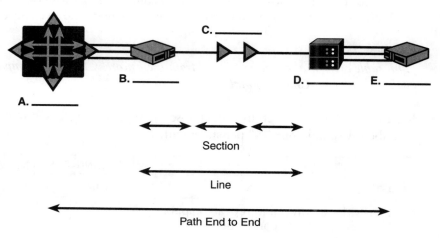

A. _____
B. _____
C. _____
D. _____
E. _____

CASE STUDY

INDEPENDENCE, MISSOURI

Objective:

Research and design an IP-based MAN for six large offices within a city.

Company Profile:

Independence, Missouri, home of the Harry S Truman Library, has a population of 116,000 and covers 78 square miles. Recently, the city has decided to commemorate its 100-year birthday.

Current Situation:

City employees are beginning to prepare for the centennial celebration and as they collect and disseminate information, they realize there is no easy electronic way to transfer information between city offices. Currently they are negotiating a contract to implement a MAN between city offices and the Truman Library.

Business Information Requirements:

The city wants to set up a MAN between the city hall, courthouse, city theater, police headquarters, fire department headquarters, and the Truman Library. Each of the city offices uses a different e-mail system. The agency wants all city offices to standardize on one e-mail program. While they plan the centennial celebration, they will need a way to collaborate on various activities. Therefore, they are also considering building a Web intranet for the city offices to share information.

Communication System Requirements:

The IT department is checking into MAN services from telcos. They are investigating the advantages and disadvantages of running IP services over FDDI, SMDS, and ATM/SONET architectures. IT is also coordinating with e-mail vendors to demonstrate various e-mail systems to the employees to determine the best e-mail solution for the city. As they look into collaboration programs, they are leaning toward a system that has a document management system and offers easy Web-based collaboration.

Information System Solution:

1. After much investigation, the IT department decided to adopt an SMDS MAN. The department also decided to deploy MPLS (Multiprotocol Label Switching) with IP to prioritize traffic. The city leased SMDS services from the local telco and the telco assisted with the installation of equipment and fiber lines required to connect the city offices together.

2. All of the city offices decided to standardize on Microsoft Exchange 2000 as the new e-mail platform. The employees liked the feature set and felt it would be the easiest to implement.

3. For collaboration and document management, the city decided to use Microsoft SharePoint and Team Services. SharePoint offered document management with version control and a check-in/check-out procedure. SharePoint also offered a document flow process for tracking a document through an electronic approval process.

4. Microsoft Team Services offered a quick way to assemble an intranet for information sharing between city offices. Most of the city offices opted to create their own Web sites using Team Services, with each city office having its own home page.

Figure 12.30 illustrates the MAN setup in Independence. Study the figure, and then answer the Study Questions that follow.

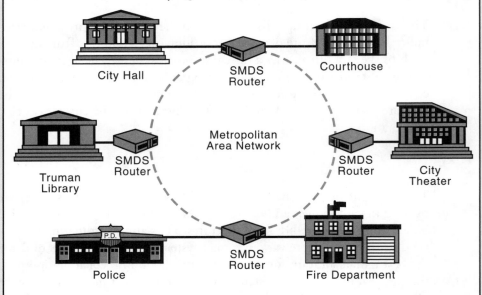

FIGURE 12.30 Independence, Missouri MAN

CASE STUDY QUESTIONS:

1. Why do you think they decided on SMDS rather than FDDI or ATM/SONET for the MAN?
2. What amount of bandwidth will they need for e-mail and collaboration traffic between city offices?
3. What features do you think were important for collaboration and approval routing?
4. Do you think the implementation of the MAN was an expensive solution for their e-mail and collaboration needs?

GROUP TERM PROJECT

In this section of the project, you need to analyze one element, either hardware, software, or telecommunications link, that you are proposing as part of your solution. Open and print the file *Criteria* from the Encore! CD that accompanies this book. List the advantages and disadvantage of each. The purpose is to document the reasons why a particular solution was chosen. If management has a question about the rationale of the solution approach, it is all documented for their review. Use this section to communicate to management how and why you decided on your recommendations.

WAN PROJECT PLAN

SOLUTION CRITERIA

Description:

Advantages:

Disadvantages:

Preliminary Estimate: [of cost and effort required]

CHAPTER TERMS

CHAPTER BIBLIOGRAPHY

Book, Magazine, Presentation Citations

3COM, *ATM Technology Student Guide*. San Jose: 3COM Corporation, 1996: 4-6.

Black, Uyless, *Emerging Communications Technologies*. New York: Prentice Hall PTR, 1997: 150, 152, 155.

Gallo, Michael and William Hancock. *Computer Communications and Networking Technologies*, Pacific Grove: Brooks/Cole, 2002: 445, 448, 451, 454.

SBC Pacific Bell. *Pacific Bell FasTrak Fast Packet Services*. San Jose: SBC Pacific Bell, 1999: 1-54.

SBC Pacific Bell. *SONET*, San Jose: SBC Pacific Bell, 1999: 29, 34, 37, 44.

Sheldon, Tom. *Encyclopedia of Networking & Telecommunications*. New York: Osborne/McGraw-Hill, 2001: 494, 495, 919, 1152, 1166-1167, 1169-1170.

Spohn, Darren. *Data Network Design*. New York: McGraw-Hill, Inc., 1993: 182, 448, 465, 468.

Web Citations

Alves, Don, "Fiber Distributed Data Interface (FDDI)," Bristol Community College, <members.aol.com/ctctutor/fddi_2.htm> (1 May 1998).

Bell Labs, "Technology Predicted to Usher in a Golden Age of Silicon," Lucent Technologies, <www.lucent.com/minds/trends/>, Volume 4 Number 3 (2000).

Bell Labs, "Next-gen Networks Predicted to Advance with the Speed of Light," Lucent Technologies, <www.lucent.com/minds/trends/>, Volume 4 Number 2 (2000).

Bell Labs, "The Last Mile Shall Be First," Lucent Technologies, <www.lucent.com/minds/trends>, Volume 3 Number 1 (1999).

Bell Labs, "An Outlook for Higher Bandwidth, More Data, Greater Speeds, and Lower Costs," <www.lucent.com/minds/trends/>, Volume 4 Number 1 (2000).

Cisco, "Fiber Distributed Data Interface," Cisco Systems, <www.cisco.com/univercd/cc/td/doc/cisintwk/ito_doc/fddi.htm> (1 April 2002).

Cisco, "Switched Multimegabit Data Service (SMDS)," Cisco Systems, <www.cisco.com/univercd/cc/td/doc/cisintwk/ito_doc/smds.htm> (20 February 2002).

Frenkel, Chen and Tanya Abarbanel, "FDDI-Fiber Distributed Data Interface," RAD, <www.rad.com/networks/1995/fddi/fddi.htm> (1995).

Greenfield, David, "Optical Standards: A Blueprint for the Future," <www.networkmagazine.com> (October, 2001)

Humboldt, "FDDI: ANSI X3T9.5," Humboldt State University, <www.Humboldt.edu/~mdh3/network/lect.05.devices/lect.03b.doc> (2002).

McKeown, Nick, "CS244a: An Introduction to Computer Networks," Stanford University, <www.sanford.edu/~nickm/> (2002).

Nortel Networks, "Synchronous Optical Network (SONET) Transmission," International Engineering Consortium, <ww.iec.org/> (2002).

NWU, "ECE 333: Introduction to Communication Networks Fall 2001," Northwestern University, <www.ece.nwu.edu/~rberry/ECE333/Lectures/lec18.pdf> (2001).

Search Networking, "Synchronous Optical Network," TechTarget, <searchnetworking.techtarget.com/sDefinition/0,,sid7_gci214223,00.html> (2002).

Tektronix, "Synchronous Optical Network (SONET)" International Engineering Consortium, <www.iec.org/> (2002).

UNH, "FDDI," University of New Hampshire, <www.iol.unh.edu/training/fddi/htmls/> (28 July 1997).

By the end of this chapter, you should understand these concepts:
- Asynchronous Transfer Mode (ATM) used for broadband transmission networks
- ATM support for both circuit- and packet-switching technologies
- The difference between frame-based and cell-based transmission
- Applications that create the demand for the development of ATM
- The techniques used by ATM to manage different types of traffic
- Using virtual paths and channels to route traffic over an ATM network
- Method used for ATM addressing
- ATM cell switching, routing domains, areas, and multiplexing
- ATM components and functions provided by an ATM backbone switch
- Switching operation implemented by the self-routing switch fabric used in an ATM switch
- Operation of ATM LAN Emulation protocols and devices
- Quality of Service (QoS) parameters used to guarantee the transmission of ATM cells

ASYNCHRONOUS TRANSFER MODE (ATM)

As introduced in Chapter 1, **Asynchronous Transfer Mode (ATM)** is a high-speed, connection-oriented switching and multiplexing technology capable of transmitting voice, video, and data and used to connect LANs to other LANs. An ATM network can connect several services and supports connections to telephones (voice), computers and mainframes (data), and video cameras (video) used for video conferencing. ATM offers the opportunity to combine LAN and WAN technologies into a single network and provides high performance for bursty data traffic coming from the LAN. ATM is also suitable for delay-sensitive voice and video traffic. ATM is asynchronous because information streams can be sent independently without the need of a common clock.

ATM provides bandwidth efficiency because it offers adaptable QoS (Quality of Service). A fiber-based local loop enables the user's data to reach a high-speed broadband switching system at the central ATM location provided by the service provider. The service provider supplies a broadband switching system capable of interconnecting users at their required bandwidth rates. Access speed and other services can be specified over an inter-office network that can support WAN connectivity.

ATM provides the capability to standardize ATM services on one network architecture and platform. ATM provides the switching platform, whereas SONET (Synchronous Optical Network) provides the digital infrastructure and physical transport.

ATM Carrier Backbone Network

AT&T Bell Laboratories developed and used ATM to package voice and/or data traffic and "pipe" it over switched circuits to relieve overcrowded trunks at AT&T. As a result of the success with ATM, AT&T and other carriers realized they could market the service to the business community. ATM provided the telcos with an end-to-end technology with which they could market ATM carrier network access to several types of organizations.

Figure 13.1 shows four market segments of ATM carrier service. In Segment 1, ATM provides a high-speed backbone to connect carriers (telcos) together. Within Segment 2, a PC is equipped with an ATM adapter to connect directly to an ATM backbone. Segment 3 shows a sophisticated ATM switch connecting users in a building/campus backbone to a public ATM network. Finally, users in Segment 4 are connected within a building with ATM switches providing ports to connect each desktop to the ATM network. (3COM, 10-3)

ATM Fast Packet Standards and Services

ATM combines many technologies into an all-in-one service. As shown in Figure 13.2, ATM fits in the middle of the technology spectrum. The technologies range from simple (circuit switching) to complex (packet switching). Because ATM supports both voice and data, it must provide for techniques that can handle both circuit- and packet-switching technologies and it must also accommodate different bit rates. With packet-switching services such as Frame Relay, a variable bit rate is required. On the other hand, circuit switching requires a fixed bit rate to provide a constant speed for voice connections. ATM has the right set of features to move all types of information across the network.

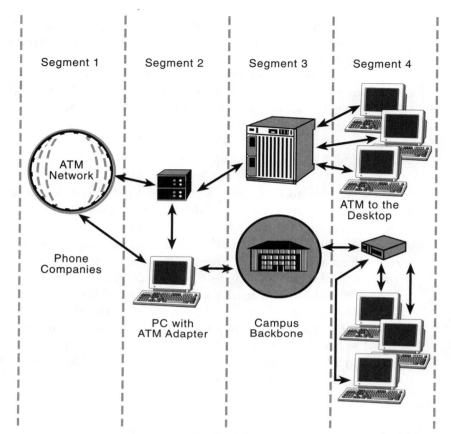

FIGURE 13.1 **Carrier Network Backbone for Telcos** [Source: 3COM, 10-3]

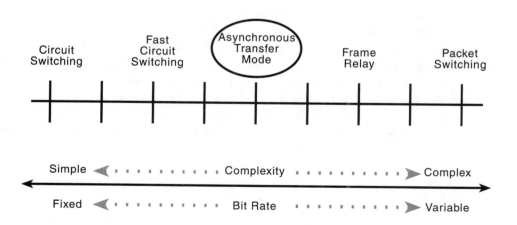

FIGURE 13.2 **ATM Placement in Spectrum of Services [Source: 3COM, 1-4]**

Figure 13.3 shows how ATM fits with other technologies, standards, and services. With fast packet services, a clear distinction exists between Frame Relay and Cell Relay services and the technologies they use. ISDN (Integrated Services Digital Network) and Frame Relay are classified as frame services, whereas ATM and SMDS (Switch Multimegabit Data Service) are categorized as cell services. A primary difference between Frame Relay and Cell Relay services is that Frame Relay uses variable length frames whereas Cell Relay uses a fixed length cell. A **cell** is a formatted packet that uses a fixed length data unit. Using fixed length cells offers predictable performance in the network. Using variable length data units results in unpredictable performance because buffer time cannot be determined. [Black, 17-18]

Frame-based implementations (ISDN and Frame Relay) use LAPD for relaying traffic. ISDN follows the **Q.931 standard**, which specifies control signaling and how connections are set up between the user and the network. Frame Relay adheres to the **Q.922 standard,** which stipulates that protocols must encapsulate their data units within a Q.922 Annex A frame. This frame has to have a field that identifies the protocol being carried within it. [Black, 125]

Both ATM and SMDS use Cell Relay. For both technologies, Cell Relay provides an integrated approach to support the transmission of voice, video, data, and other applications. [Black, 18] **Broadband-Integrated Services Digital Network** (**B-ISDN**) was developed to handle voice, video, and data applications within the same transmission and can provide for on-demand, reserved, or permanent services as stipulated in a contract between the service provider and the organization.

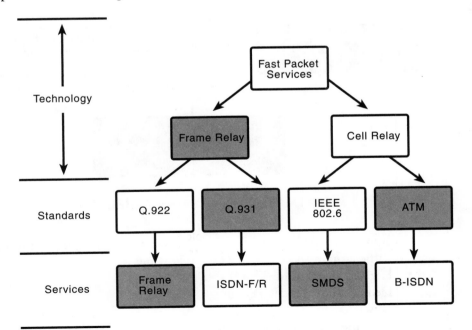

FIGURE 13.3 **Fast Packet Standards and Services [Source: PacBell, 3]**

ATM Applications

ATM is a switching technique for broadband signals that is defined as part of the B-ISDN standard. The network technology provided by ATM makes B-ISDN possible, and is designed to offer high-end multimedia, television, music, and data networking.

Figure 13.4 shows several applications that have driven the development of ATM. The different types of organizations shown in the figure are starting to use multimedia or high-bandwidth image traffic. The medical industry now uses ATM to transmit X-rays between medical facilities and hospitals. Universities use ATM to provide for distance-learning programs. Corporations use ATM for video conferencing across the globe. ATM is also used for around-the-clock collaborative development in international product design and global banking. In the future, ATM will also be used for many home and personal services such as entertainment, video on demand, telecommuting, and home shopping.

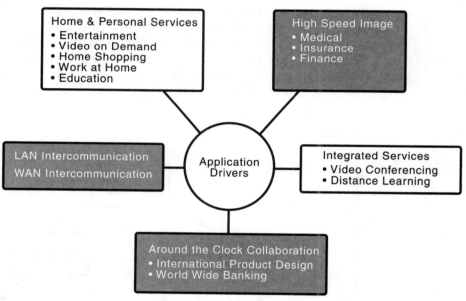

FIGURE 13.4 **ATM Applications [Source: PacBell, 1]**

To summarize, ATM provides several benefits for managing and routing network traffic at high speeds, such as the following:

- High capacity bandwidth
- Dedicated or switched circuits
- Low latency
- Multimedia, data, voice, video, and image transmission

- A uniform packet size that offers predictable traffic flow
- Guaranteed delivery of time-sensitive traffic such as voice and video [Sheldon, 65]

TOPIC *review* **ATM**

1. Why did AT&T Bell Laboratories invent ATM?
2. What is the difference between frame-based and cell-based transmission?
3. What types of signals are switched across an ATM network?
4. Which technology provided ATM with the capability to handle voice, video, and data applications within the same transmission?
5. Why is ATM described as a switching technique for broadband signals?

ATM TRAFFIC ALLOCATION

ATM technology was designed to provide bandwidth on demand. This meant users could request and receive as much bandwidth as they needed dynamically. However, today's applications require even greater throughput and lower delay from communication systems. ATM has been designed to offer the bandwidth required on a connection basis. At the same time, in response to this increased demand, ATM offers a best-effort service by using available bandwidth to establish a connection.

ATM Interfaces and Traffic Types

ATM handles all traffic types through a fast-packet switching technique. This technique reduces the processing of protocols and uses statistical multiplexing. ATM is a connection-oriented technique designed to transport both connection and connectionless services. The operations at the boundary of a network are connection-oriented. The connection exists between the user equipment and the ATM equipment and is called the **user to network interface (UNI)**. Within the network, the operation is connectionless. All traffic travels between ATM devices within the same network via a **network-to-network interface (NNI)** connection. Two other methods are used to establish an interface through an ATM network. An **intercarrier interface (ICI)** is used to send traffic across intermediate networks. When non-ATM equipment is used, a **data exchange interface (DXI)** is used to transmit packets rather than cells to the ATM interface. [Sheldon, 73]

In an effort to better manage various types of traffic, ATM service categories were designed for different types of applications. For example, voice and video applications require a constant, continuous, and precisely timed allocation of bandwidth. However, other applications need to be able to transmit at any time and do not require a fixed timing relationship between the sender and receiver. Service categories allow traffic to be buffered and queued for later transmission. Categories also can permit loose timing and asynchronous operations between sender and receiver. [Black, 43]

Table 13.1 lists and defines the different kinds of ATM service categories. In Figure 13.5, the service categories are illustrated as layers. Service categories are designed to match the type of traffic to its need and provide for higher priority for transmissions that require it.

SERVICE CATEGORY	DESCRIPTION
Constant Bit Rate (CBR)	Specifies a fixed bit rate so that data can be sent in a steady stream. Provides service for voice and video traffic.
Variable Bit Rate (VBR)	Provides a specified throughput capacity; however, unlike CBR, data is not sent in a steady stream. Commonly used for voice and video conferencing.
Unspecified Bit Rate (UBR)	Does not guarantee any throughput levels. Primarily used for file transfers that can tolerate delays.
Available Bit Rate (ABR)	Provides a guaranteed minimum capacity. Also allows data to be bursted at higher capacities when the network is free.
Guaranteed Frame Rate (GFR)	Allows users to send at any rate up to the peak cell rate while the network is only committed to send at the minimum cell rate.

TABLE 13.1 ATM Service Categories for Bandwidth Allocation [Webopedia, 1]

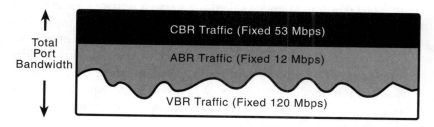

FIGURE 13.5 ATM Service Categories for Bandwidth Allocation [Source: 3COM, 7-11]

ATM Operation

ATM forms a packet (a cell). Each cell has a fixed length of 53 octets (each octet contains 8 bits) and is composed of a 5-octet header and a 48-octet information field. The information field is passed through the network intact. No error checking or correction is performed on the information field. When the cells are sent to the ATM switch, they are placed into a queue. Then, the cells are multiplexed asynchronously with other cells for transmission.

The ATM switch removes idle traffic before transmission and allocates a time slot to channels that have data for transmission. The ATM switch adapts the incoming bit rate to match the transmit channel rate. The switch inserts dummy cells when needed to achieve the aggregate bit stream rate of 155.52 Mbps.

The remote ATM switch separates the good cells from the dummy cells based on the header information, and passes the good cells to the target destination. This method achieves maximum throughput and performance.

ATM Virtual Paths and Channels

As discussed in Chapter 11, virtual circuits are actually pathways defined through a switch. Each pathway or virtual circuit is defined in the switch for an organization. The telco providing the switch defines the virtual circuit and provides a virtual circuit identifier (VCI) for input into the organization's router table.

In ATM networks, a **virtual channel (VC)** is just like a virtual circuit in that it provides a fixed pathway or route between two points. A VC is set up across an ATM network whenever data transfer begins. This is contrasted with the virtual circuit defined to Frame Relay in that it is permanently assigned through the switch. In ATM, VCs are combined to create virtual paths. **Virtual paths (VP)** are a group of VCs used to tell the switch how to forward an ATM cell through the ATM network. (See Figure 13.6.)

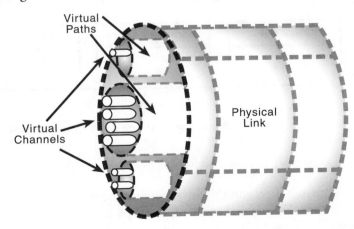

FIGURE 13.6 **ATM Virtual Paths and Channels [Source: 3COM, 2-5]**

In the ATM header, a **virtual path identifier (VPI)** is used to define the route established in the ATM switch. Another identifier included in the ATM header is called a **virtual channel identifier (VCI)**. The VCI identifies a channel within a VP. VCs are combined to create VPs to travel the media or transmission path. The transmission path is the physical media that transports the cells through the VPs and VCs.

The basic operation of an ATM switch is simple. Figure 13.7 shows two ATM switches and two end nodes. The connection from the source end user VCI to the destination user VCI is called a **virtual channel connection (VCC)**. Another connection is identified as the **virtual path connection (VPC)**, and defined as the connection from the source end user VPI to the destination end user VPI. [3COM, 2-6]

The cell is received across a link on a known VCI or VPI value. The switch looks up the connection value in a local translation table, as shown in Figure 13.7, to determine the outgoing port (or ports) of the connection. The new VPI/VCI value of the connection is then assigned on that link. The switch retransmits the cell on that outgoing link with the appropriate connection identifiers. Because all VCIs and VPIs are only significant to the local link, their values are remapped, as necessary, at each switch. Cells are forwarded through each ATM switch until they finally reach the destination ATM switch.

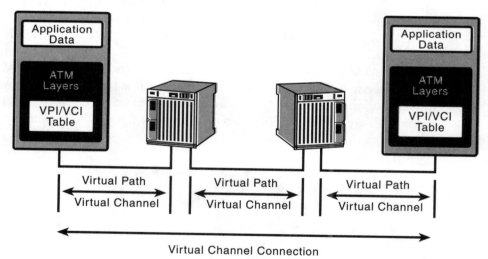

FIGURE 13.7 Virtual Connections between ATM Switches [Source: 3COM, 2-7]

ATM VCI and VPI Swapping

Each ATM switch is responsible for changing the logical ID of one link to a different logical ID on another link as a cell passes through it. This technique is called **logical ID swapping**. The ATM switch changes the cell header VPI/VCI fields to reflect a new VPI and VCI for the outgoing cell. Logical ID swapping is accomplished in one of two ways: the VP is predefined in the switch and the logical IDs from end station to end station use that path identifier in the header of the ATM cell or the VP is set up dynamically with call set-up procedures when the ATM cell reaches the switch. [3COM, 2-9]

The entire forwarding process is dependent on two lookup tables within the ATM switch. The **VP table** maintains a record of the VPs on each link. If the switch in question happens to be an end switch, then it also maintains a pointer to the **VC table**. The VC table maintains the output VP and VC to be used to send the cell.

Figure 13.8 illustrates an example of ATM VCI and VPI swapping. At the top of the figure, the ATM Switching Node shows inbound (Link 1) and outbound (Link 3) paths. The switch examines the header of the cell to identify the correct VPI and VCI. Next, the switch performs a lookup in the translation table. The table for Link 1 shows that VPI 6 can use either VCI 2 or VCI 5 to travel outbound on Link 3. Notice on the outbound table, for VPI 2, the VPI is changed, or "swapped," to 5 and the VCI is changed to 11. Similarly, if the ATM header specifies VCI 5 on the inbound connection, it uses VPI 2 and VCI 21 to travel outbound on Link 3. [3COM, 2-10]

Looking down the table, VPI 9 can use either VC 7 or VC 10 to travel outbound on Link 3. If the VCI is designated as 7, then the VPI is swapped to 5 and the VCI is changed to 31. On the other hand, if the inbound VCI is specified as 10, then the VPI becomes 2 and the VCI is set to 1 to travel outbound on Link 3. [3COM, 2-10]

The path selection is based on the destination address and the result found by lookups in the tables. Each ATM switch uses a procedure called **connection admission control (CAC)** to determine whether it can provide the services required by the connection. After a path is found and the VC is determined, this information is returned to the end station requesting the connection. Transmissions are then directed to the VC that leads to the destination end station. [Sheldon, 75]

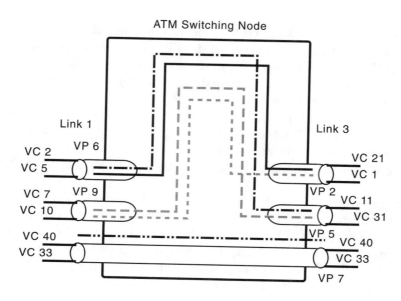

ATM Switching Node

Link 1 ... Link 3

VC 2, VP 6, VC 5 ... VC 21, VC 1
VC 7, VP 9, VC 10 ... VP 2, VC 11, VC 31
VC 40, VC 33 ... VP 5, VC 40, VC 33
VP 7

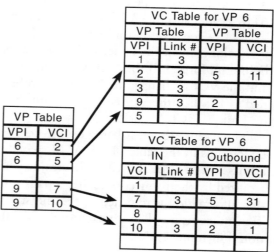

| VC Table for VP 6 | | | |
| VP Table | | VP Table | |
VPI	Link #	VPI	VCI
1	3		
2	3	5	11
3	3		
9	3	2	1
5			

| VP Table | |
VPI	VCI
6	2
6	5
9	7
9	10

| VC Table for VP 6 | | | |
| IN | | Outbound | |
VCI	Link #	VPI	VCI
1			
7	3	5	31
8			
10	3	2	1

FIGURE 13.8 VC and VP Swapping [Source: 3COM, 2-10]

TOPIC review ATM Traffic Allocation

1. What type of multiplexing does ATM use in its networks?
2. What is provided by ATM service categories such as CBR, VBR, UBR, and ABR?
3. Where is the Virtual Path Identifier (VPI) defined in an ATM cell?
4. How does an ATM switch determine the outgoing port of a connection?
5. Why does an ATM switch change the cell header fields for the outgoing cell?

ATM CELL STRUCTURE AND ADDRESSING

ATM uses numerical addressing similar to that used for telephone numbers. It uses E.164 addresses (see Table 13.3) for public ATM (B-ISDN) networks. The ATM Forum has extended ATM addressing to include private networks by using an overlay model in which the ATM layer is responsible for mapping network layer (IP) addresses to ATM addresses. This model provides an alternative to implementing the network layer protocol addresses used by IP (Internet Protocol) and IPX (Internetwork Package Exchange) or routing protocols used by IGRP and RIP. Its address format uses OSI (Open System Interconnection) network service access point (NSAP) addresses. These addresses provide a logical point between the network and transport layers of the OSI model. The location of this point is identified by a network service provider and is called the **NSAP address**.

ATM Cell Structure

As stated previously, ATM transfers information in cells that are a group of data bits that form bytes. Each cell consists of 53 octets (bytes). The basic format of an ATM cell is illustrated in Figure 13.9. The first 5 bytes contain cell-header information, and the remaining 48 bytes contain cell payload (user information).

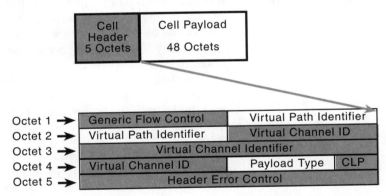

FIGURE 13.9 **ATM Cell Structure [Source: 3COM, 2-11]**

An ATM network is designed as a series of layers. The first layer contains the bulk of the transmission and is known as the adaptation layer. At the adaptation layer, the 48-byte payload divides the data into different types. The ATM layer contains 5 bytes of additional information, referred to as overhead. The overhead is the cell-header information that directs the transmission. Lastly, the physical layer attaches the electrical elements and network interfaces.

As shown in Figure 13.9, 5 octets are used to define the cell header. These octets and their components are defined in Table 13.2.

OCTET NUMBER	OCTET SEGMENT	DESCRIPTION
1	**Generic Flow Control (GFC)**	Provides local functions, such as identifying multiple stations that share a single ATM interface. Used to control congestion on the user interface.
	Virtual Path Identifier (VPI)	Used in combination with the VCI, it identifies the next destination of a cell as it passes through a series of ATM switches on the way to its destination. Used to distinguish VPs between users and in between users and networks.
2	**Virtual Path Identifier (VPI)**	Same as previous.
	Virtual Channel ID	ID associated with the VC.
3	**Virtual Channel Identifier (VCI)**	Along with the VPI, it identifies the next destination of a cell as it passes through a series of ATM switches on the way to its destination. Specifies the VC between users or between users and networks.
4	**Virtual Channel ID**	Same as previous.
	Payload Type (PT)	Indicates the type of payload—either user, network, or management information—in the payload portion of the cell. The first bit indicates whether the cell contains user data or control data. If the cell contains user data, the bit is set to 0. If it contains control data, it is set to 1. The second bit indicates congestion (0 = no congestion, 1 = congestion), and the third bit indicates whether the cell is the last in a series of cells (1 = last cell for the frame).
	Cell Loss Priority (CLP)	Determines whether cells should be dropped if extreme network congestion occurs. If the CLP bit equals 1, the cell should be discarded in preference to cells with the CLP bit equal to 0.
5	**Header Error Control (HEC)**	Used to provide forward error correction. Information is sent in the cell that can be used to fix errors. It first calculates a checksum on the first 4 bytes of the header. If there is a single bit error, HEC can correct it and preserve the cell rather than discard it.

TABLE 13.2 Octet Components [Sheldon, 70]

Currently four address formats are used for ATM networks. These formats, administered by different agencies, are listed in Table 13.3.

ADDRESS FORMAT	DESCRIPTION
Data Country Code (DCC)	Designed to be used with private ATM networks. Administered by ANSI (American National Standards Institute).
International Code Designator (ICD)	Designed for bar codes and library codes. Was not originally intended for network addressing. Administered by the British Standards Institute.
E.164	A public networking scheme similar to telephone numbering. Administered by the ITU (International Telecommunication Union).
E.164 Network Service Access Point (NSAP)	Defined by the ATM Forum, it is another version of E.164. However, the ATM Forum does not administrate it.

TABLE 13.3 **ATM Network Address Formats [Sheldon, 76]**

Figure 13.10 illustrates the ATM address format for specific fields. Notice the fields are divided into two sections, network and user. The fields that have network prefixes include fields needed by the network side of the UNI. The fields in the user section are for the user side of the UNI. Table 13.4 lists and describes the fields that make up the ATM address format.

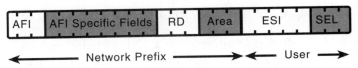

FIGURE 13.10 **ATM Address Format [Source: 3COM, 3-4]**

SECTION	FIELD	DESCRIPTION
Network Prefix	**AFI**	Identifies the type and format of the address based on the authority that provides the address (E.164, ICD, or DCC).
	DCC	Identifies particular countries.
	High-Order Domain-Specific Part (HO-DSP)	Combines the routing domain (RD) and the area identifier (AREA) of the NSAP addresses. Provides a flexible, multilevel addressing hierarchy for prefix-based routing protocols.
User	**End System Identifier (ESI)**	Identifies a unique device within the specified network. Designates the 48-bit MAC (Media Access Control) address, as administered by the Institute of Electrical and Electronics Engineers (IEEE).
	Selector (SEL)	Used for local multiplexing within end stations and has no network significance.
	ICD	Identifies particular international organizations.
	E.164	Indicates the B-ISDN E.164 address.

TABLE 13.4 **Fields of the ATM Address Format [Cisco, 20-10 & 11]**

ATM Routing Domains and Areas

The ATM address is constructed as a 20-byte string that includes fields for a country code, an administrative authority, a routing domain, an area identifier, an end-system identifier, an NSAP, an international code, and an ISDN telephone number.

As shown in Figure 13.11, the ATM address format is mapped field by field to an ATM network. The first byte identifies the format of the 20-byte ATM address. There are three possible values for this AFI field: DCC is hex 39, E.164 is hex 45, and ICD is hex 47. In the AFI-specific fields, the authority that the ATM devices belong to is named in bytes 2-9. [Sheldon, 76]

An ATM network is constructed with *routing domains*. **Routing domains (RD)** are used for traffic management to provide for an effective way to allocate bandwidth capacity. The routing domains are defined in lookup tables in the ATM switch. Figure 13.11 shows three routing domains: RD1, RD2, and RD3. Each routing domain is unique within the ATM network and is specified in bytes 10 and 11.

Also shown in Figure 13.11 are areas 1, 2, and 3. Each identifies a unique area within a routing domain that the ATM device resides in. The area is specified in bytes 12 and 13 of the ATM address.

In bytes 14-19, the **end system identifier (ESI)** identifies an end system (computer or LAN) within the area. The last byte, 20, is the selector field and is not used by an ATM network. [Black, 247]

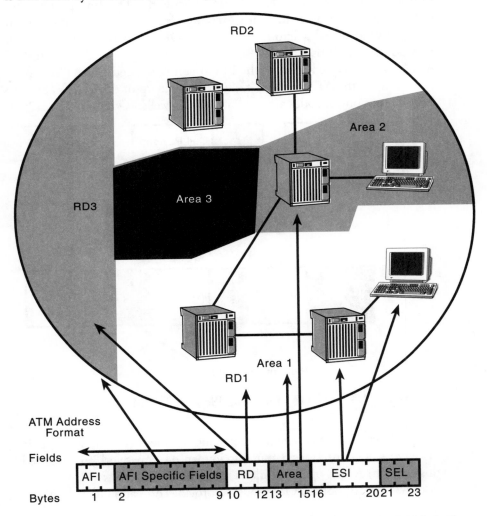

FIGURE 13.11 **ATM Routing Domains and Areas [Source: 3COM, 3-5]**

The purpose of the ATM address format is to identify ATM devices (switches, routers, bridges, or end-user workstations) within an ATM network. Each field identifies the information needed to establish a connection at the user-to-network interface.

ATM Encoding

Often, ATM networks must be interfaced to slower speed network LAN backbones. To make this connection, the cell must be encoded to follow the scheme used by the LAN.

Figure 13.12 illustrates how encoding is used to interface ATM networks with FDDI (Fiber Distributed Data Interface) networks. This transport method is called **transparent asynchronous exchange interface (TAXI)** after the chipset created by Advanced Micro Devices for FDDI networks. For ATM cells to be transported, TAXI uses the FDDI 4B/5B encoding specified for FDDI. The ATM Forum defined some of the FDDI command codes as ATM control codes. For example, the ATM control code *JK* is made up of the FDDI *J* and *K* symbols. These control codes are used to transmit cells. [Goralski, 114, 129-130]

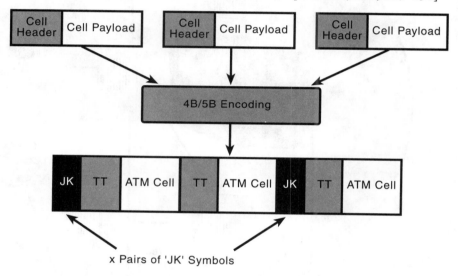

FIGURE 13.12 **ATM Encoding [Source: 3COM, 4-5]**

ATM networks often require interfacing to other LAN and MAN networks. (The types of connections required to join an ATM network are discussed later in this chapter.) ATMs operate under a reference model that is a standard and functions within layers of the OSI model to provide compatibility with other networks.

ATM Layers and the OSI Model

ATM architecture uses a logical reference model to describe its functions. As shown in Figure 13.13, ATM functions correspond to the physical layer and part of the data link layer of the OSI model. The ATM reference model is constructed as three planes, which span all layers:

- **Control**. Generates and manages signaling requests.
- **User.** Manages the transfer of data.
- **Management.** Contains two components: *layer management* and *plane management*. Layer management manages layer-specific functions, such as the detection of failures and protocol problems; *plane management* manages and coordinates functions related to the complete system. [Cisco, 20-6]

The ATM reference model shown in Figure 13.13 is composed of three primary layers: the physical layer, the **ATM layer**, and the **ATM adaptation layer (AAL)**. Table 13.5 provides a description of each layer and function.

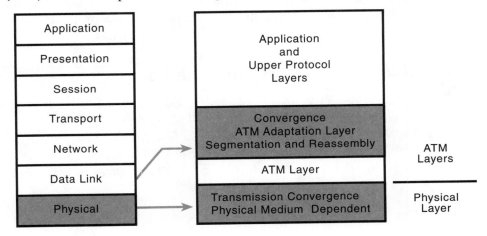

FIGURE 13.13 **ATM and OSI Model [Source: 3COM, 2-12]**

LAYER	DESCRIPTION
Physical	Same as the physical layer of the OSI reference model. The ATM physical layer connects with a physical medium that supports ATM. This includes technologies such as: SONET/SDH, DS-3/E3, Fiber Channel, and FDDI. Responsible for converting outgoing cells into bits and incoming bits into cells. When the physical layer converts cells to bits, it must frame the bits so they have the same frame structure as the other network.
ATM	Combined with the ATM adaptation layer, the ATM layer corresponds approximately to the data link layer of the OSI model. The ATM layer is responsible for establishing, maintaining, and terminating virtual circuits over a physical link. Generally controls passing cells through the ATM network.
ATM adaptation layer (AAL)	Combined with the ATM layer, and also corresponds to the data link layer of the OSI model. Defines a process for converting information from upper layers into ATM cells. The

TABLE 13.5 **ATM Reference Model Layers [Sheldon, 69]**

> adaptation layer prepares user data for conversion into cells,
> and segments the data into 48-byte cell payloads.

TABLE 13.5 **ATM Reference Model Layers, continued**

On its own, ATM has functions that operate at layers 1 and 2 of the OSI model. However, today TCP/IP (Transfer Control Protocol/Internet Protocol) is routed over ATM networks, which means it also can function at layers 3 and 4 of the OSI model. The most important functions occur at the physical layer where bits are converted to cells and packaged for the appropriate frame type for the physical medium to connect to LANs and MANs.

TOPIC *review* ATM Cell Structure and Addressing

1. Why does ATM need to use small fixed-length cells?
2. How many octets are used in an ATM header?
3. Why does an ATM header include a field for Cell Loss Priority (CLP)?
4. What are routing domains used for in an ATM network?
5. How is the ATM layer used by the ATM reference model?

ATM NETWORK FUNCTIONS

ATM moves cells with low delay. Devices at each end translate between the cells and the original traffic. Several devices can be used as customer premise equipment (CPE) to interface to the ATM network. ATM-capable devices may include multiplexers, routers, CSUs (Channel Service Units), or switches. In addition, servers can be moved to the ATM backbone by adding an ATM network adapter card.

The ATM Forum requires that member organizations submit their devices or software implementations for interoperability testing. In this manner, the ATM Forum attempts to ensure that ATM devices will be able to interoperate between various vendors. [Goralski, 294]

ATM Departmental Architecture for LANs

Organizations tend to build ATM networks in phases to accommodate interfacing to other LAN networks. The architecture of an ATM backbone using departmental switches is shown in Figure 13.14. In the computer room, a high-end ATM backbone switch is used to link to ATM workgroup switches on each floor. For large organizations with a lot of multimedia traffic, ATM provides much faster bandwidth than 100 Mbps Ethernet. If the floors are linked together using SONET at the OC-3 level, data transfer between floors occurs at 155 Mbps. Most organizations choose to keep their CAT5 Ethernet cable to the desktop because it is less expensive. However, ATM technology is capable of driving 155 Mbps to the desktop if required.

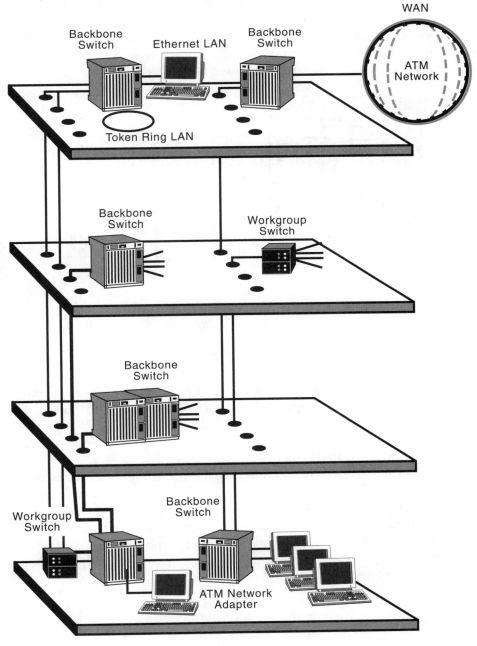

FIGURE 13.14 **ATM Departmental Architecture [Source: 3COM, 10-11]**

ATM Backbone Switch

The core of an ATM network is the backbone switch that centralizes the traffic flow and provides interfaces at various speeds. Many ATM backbone switches use a modular approach to building an ATM network. Several switch cards are available (see Figure 13.15). One switch card or module is called the **switch/control point**. This module implements cell-switching capabilities and can handle an aggregate capacity of 3 Gbps. Threshold levels are provided so that time-critical traffic can be mixed with delay-tolerant traffic.

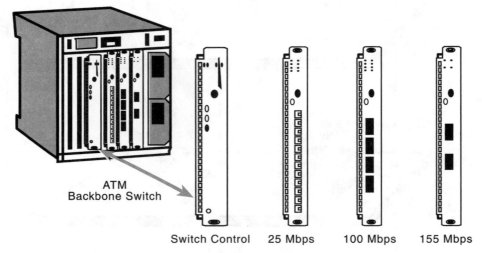

ATM
Backbone Switch

Switch Control   25 Mbps   100 Mbps   155 Mbps

FIGURE 13.15 **ATM Backbone Switch [Source: 3COM, 10-12]**

The other interface cards in the ATM backbone switch can support speeds of 25, 100, or 155 Mbps. Each interface card has four fiber ports at 100 Mbps. The card also can be set up with two fiber and two SONET ports at 155 Mbps. Each port can be configured to support up to 1,024 active VC connections. [3COM, 10-12]

The construction of an ATM switch can affect both performance and reliability. In addition, the structure of the switch table has a significant impact on efficiency. A flat, two-dimensional table is simplest. Another factor to consider is table location and maintenance. Maintaining a table by hand in a consistent manner on a small ATM network can be a monumental task. Most network engineers prefer a switch that can update itself automatically using scripts and signaling protocols.

ATM Routing Switch Fabric

A **routing switch fabric** is used to switch cells within the switch. In Figure
13.16, the switch fabric is self-routing and can manage the flow of ATM cells
through the switch. A binary (0s and 1s) algorithm is used at each element to
determine the output queue. A 3-bit tag is used to send the cell to the appropriate output port. Several output queues are located at each port of the switch.
Buffer management is provided at each output queue to hold traffic temporarily
until the device or network switch is ready to receive it.

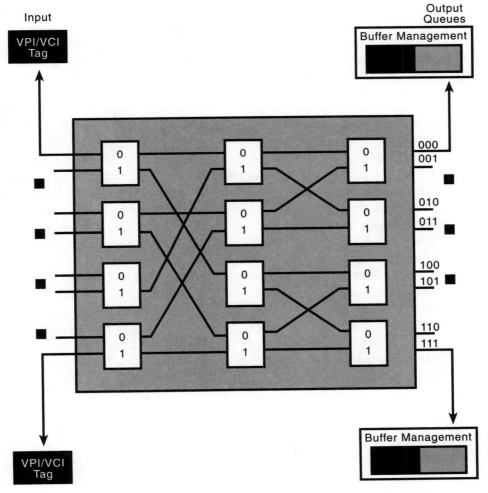

FIGURE 13.16 **ATM Routing Switch Fabric [Source: 3COM, 2-4]**

For the large national ATM networks of ISPs and telcos, optical ATM switches are available that allow cells to be transferred via light waves directly from the input to the output of a SONET link. These switches can handle up to 10,000 user interfaces. Today's optical switches require the light to be converted to electrical current. This requires splitting off the header portion of each cell so that it can be converted to electricity. It then must delay the cell body and use header information to control the optical cell through the switch. After all-optical switches are readily available and affordable, terabit speeds will be supported through the switch fabric.

ATM Cell Switching Transfer Mode

Internally, an ATM switch uses a **translation table** to manage cell transfer through the switch (see Figure 13.17). The translation table includes the incoming port number on the switch, the virtual connection ID, an outgoing port, and the virtual connection ID. The switch interprets the cell headers and consults its table to determine how to forward the cell through the ATM network.

In Figure 13.17, the incoming cells on the left specify the virtual connection ID (c, b, a, z, y, and x). Each of these virtual connection IDs are mapped to specific outgoing ports (g, e, h, m, k, d, and f) in the translation table. *b* is mapped to outgoing port *Om* and will use a virtual connection ID of *d*. The ATM switch inspects each cell and routes it according to the translation table. Lying in between the headers, the payload (PL) is left untouched and is simply passed through the switch.

ATM switches map the topology of the network to determine the best path to use when establishing a connection. The ATM switch provides for connections that can be made "on-the-fly" (without human assistance). Because the switch can route cells so quickly, ATM needs a way to manage traffic between ATM switches. ATM uses an enhanced version of statistical multiplexing to control switch traffic and network capacity. [Sheldon, 74]

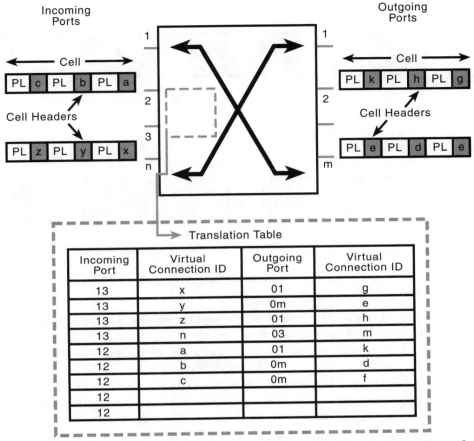

FIGURE 13.17 ATM Cell Switching Transfer Mode [Source: 3COM, 1-11]

ATM Multiplexing

LANs have used Time Division Multiplexing (TDM) techniques (see Chapter 5) for years (see Figure 13.18). Time slots are assigned dynamically to individual users or devices. Transmission is based on priority and need to transmit during the present moment. Using asynchronous TDM, each user or device can transmit only during its own sequential time slot. It cannot borrow from another time slot, even if that time slot is not being used. In the example shown at the top of Figure 13.18, while the user (or device) #1 might be finished transmitting, users (or devices) on time slot #2 and #3 must continue to wait for their assigned time before they can transmit.

ATM uses asynchronous transmission and has its own multiplexing technique called *asynchronous transfer mode multiplexing*. With **ATM multiplexing**, each user or device can use time slots on demand as they become available. In the bottom of Figure 13.18, the user (or device #3) is assigned to every fourth time slot. If user or device #2 requires a lot of bandwidth, the remaining available time slots can be used. [3COM, 1-10]

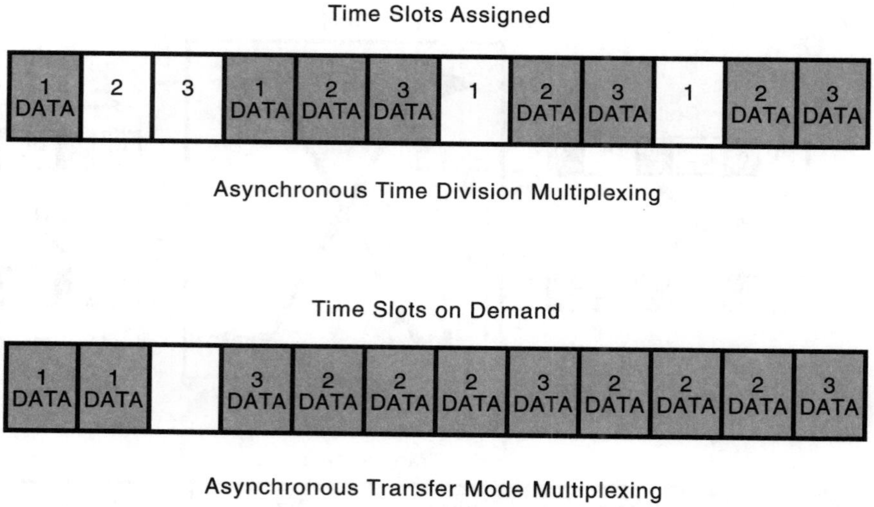

Time Slots Assigned

| 1 DATA | 2 | 3 | 1 DATA | 2 DATA | 3 DATA | 1 | 2 DATA | 3 DATA | 1 | 2 DATA | 3 DATA |

Asynchronous Time Division Multiplexing

Time Slots on Demand

| 1 DATA | 1 DATA | | 3 DATA | 2 DATA | 2 DATA | 2 DATA | 3 DATA | 2 DATA | 2 DATA | 2 DATA | 3 DATA |

Asynchronous Transfer Mode Multiplexing

FIGURE 13.18 **ATM Multiplexing [Source: 3COM, 1-10]**

ATM multiplexers take into account the average and peak bit rate in cells per second for each user or device connection. The port on the multiplexer has to be configured so that the total capacity of the output link will be greater than the average bit rate of all of the inputs. At the same time, the total capacity of the output link should be less than the peak bit rate of all of the inputs. The average and peak cell rate must be specified by the end user or device whenever an ATM network VCC connection is established. If the value is set too close to the sum of the peak cell rates, ATM merely functions the same as a TDM. [Goralski, 281-282]

TOPIC review **ATM Network Functions**

1. What is the difference between a public and private ATM network?
2. Why does the ATM Forum require member organizations to submit ATM devices or software for interoperability testing?
3. What is the core of an ATM network?
4. What does a switch card do in an ATM backbone switch?
5. How does routing switch fabric operate within an ATM switch?

ATM LAN EMULATION

ATM networks were designed to connect LANs together over an ATM backbone. A fundamental difference exists, however, between LANs and ATMs. LANs transmit in bits, whereas ATM routes cells. The ATM Forum developed a standard called **LAN emulation (LANE)** to give stations attached via ATM the same bit-passing capability as is required on an Ethernet or Token Ring LAN. The primary function of the LANE protocol is to emulate a LAN on top of an ATM network. The protocol defines procedures for emulating either an IEEE 802.3 Ethernet or an 802.5 Token Ring LAN. LANE allows existing LAN applications to use an ATM network. [Cisco, 20-14]

ATM LAN Emulation Configuration Servers (LECS) and Servers (LES)

Figure 13.19 shows that to set up an emulated data connection, the ATM switch requires a connection to a **LAN Emulation Server (LES)**, a **LAN Emulation Configuration Server (LECS),** and a **Broadcast Unknown Server (BUS)**. The LES is responsible for registering and resolving Ethernet MAC addresses to ATM addresses. The LECS provides configuration information about each network. The BUS is responsible for handling broadcast, multicast, and initial unicast frames sent from a *LAN emulation client*. A **LAN emulation client** is the end node (workstation or network device) that performs data forwarding and address resolution, as well as several control functions. Each LAN emulation client maintains the LANE software. The LAN emulation software resides between the lower ATM layers and the upper protocol layers and shields the upper layer protocol stack for Ethernet and Token Ring LANs from the ATM network. [3COM, 8-13]

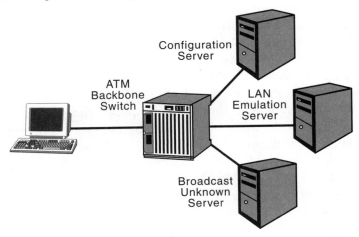

FIGURE 13.19 **LAN Emulation [Source: 3COM, 8-19]**

ATM must provide LANs with a connectionless service for the LANs to operate with it. The ATM network is considered a backbone to existing LANs. LANE provides for several **emulated LANs (ELANs)** that can be logically separated by an ATM network. The LANE protocol defines a service interface for network layer protocols that is identical to that of existing LANs. It defines the operation of a single ELAN; however, LANE does not require any modifications to higher-layer protocols to enable their operation over an ATM network. Data is sent across the ATM network encapsulated in the appropriate LAN MAC packet format. [3COM, 8-10] [Cisco, 20-15]

The LANE system and its components operate the LAN emulation client in stages: performing initialization and configuration, joining and registering with the LES, finding and joining the BUS, and performing data transfer. Figure 13.20 shows that upon initialization, a LAN emulation client finds the LECS to obtain the required configuration information. The LAN emulation client begins this process when it obtains its own ATM address. This usually occurs during address registration. The configuration service provides the LAN emulation client with the type of ELAN supported by either Ethernet or Token Ring. It also provides the maximum frame size allowed.

Next, the LAN emulation client provides its MAC address and ATM address to the configuration server. The LAN emulation client joins the ELAN by creating a bidirectional, control connection to the LES. When LAN emulation client issues a **JOIN REQUEST** to the LES, it provides the LAN emulation client's ATM address, MAC address, type of ELAN, and the maximum frame size. The LES responds with a **JOIN RESPONSE** to the LAN emulation client. At this point, the LAN emulation client is assigned a unique identifier called a **LECID**.

During the registration process, the LAN emulation client joins the ELAN. The LAN emulation client's ATM and MAC addresses are registered with the LES. Next the LAN emulation client requests the ATM address of the BUS. The BUS then adds the LAN emulation client to the point or multipoint connection to the ATM network.

After a connection has been established, the data transfer process begins. The ATM address of the destination LAN emulation client is resolved before the actual data is transferred. If the LAN emulation client knows the target ATM address, it sends the frame over an already established connection. If the LAN emulation client does not know the target ATM address, the LAN emulation client must issue an LE ARP request to the LES to retrieve the ATM address. After the LES responds with the destination ATM address, the source LAN emulation client sets up a direct connection to the target LAN emulation client. Finally, data begins passing over the direct VC. [3COM, 8-19 & 20]

Basically, the function of the LANE protocol is to resolve MAC addresses to ATM addresses. As it progresses through the various stages, the protocol's intent is to resolve the addresses to set up a direct path between end nodes so they can forward the data. Switches within the ATM network negotiate to establish connections with other switches across the network. Although the description of LANE for LAN emulation client, LES, and BUS might seem complicated, it is dedicated to the simple event of establishing a connection and transmitting the data along the path to its destination.

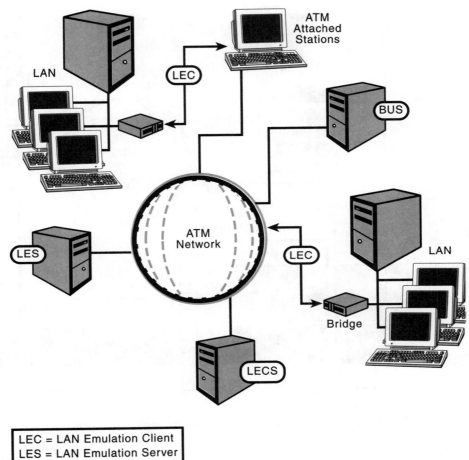

FIGURE 13.20 ATM LANEs using LAN Emulation Clients and LES
[Source: 3COM, 8-13]

ATM LANE through the OSI Model

Data movement through an ATM network is a structured process that involves mapping the ATM network layers to the OSI layers of the LAN. Figure 13.21 illustrates data movement from the source LAN station to the destination LAN station.

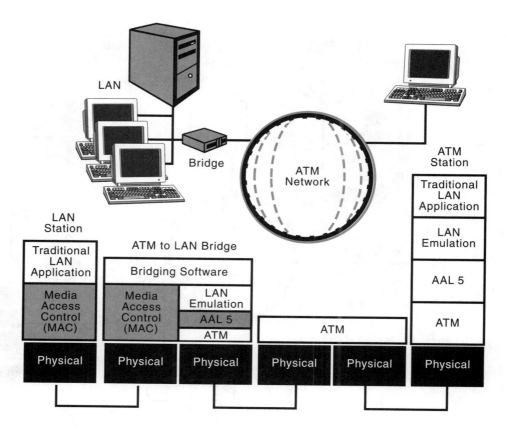

FIGURE 13.21 **ATM LANE Process through OSI Layers [Source: 3COM, 8-12]**

The steps for data movement within LANE are as follows:

1. At the LAN station, a MAC frame is created with the traditional headers, trailers, and data.

2. The ATM to LAN bridge receives the MAC frame and determines that the frame is destined for the ATM port.

3. Bridging software within the ATM to LAN bridge forwards the frame to the LANE software.

4. At the convergence sublayer (AAL 5) of the bridging software, a data unit is created using the information from the LAN Emulation layer.

5. The data unit is moved to ATM layers where it is segmented into a 48-octet cell payload.

6. Each of the cell payload segments are moved to the ATM layer and the correct VPI\VCI is added into the cell header.

7. Each cell is then sent into the network. Each ATM switch in the ATM network handles the switching of the cell using the VPI/VCI defined in the cell header.

8. The ATM cell header is read, the cell headers are stripped off and the payload is forwarded on to the ATM layer.
9. The segmented 48 octet cell payloads are reassembled into the original data unit and forwarded to the convergence sublayer (AAL 5).
10. At the convergence sublayer (AAL 5), the trailer is read and then forwarded to the LAN Emulation layer.
11. The LANE software forwards the frame to the correct LAN port by using the destination's MAC address.
12. The MAC frame is received at the destination ATM station. [3COM, 8-21 to 26]

Within a network, organizations often want to extend the strengths of ATM by blending it with other technologies. Carriers often offer a blend of ATM, IP, and Ethernet options for the WAN. ATM provides universal support for all of these options because it has defined standard procedures for interfacing, translating, and emulating each type of network.

ATM LANE Configurations

LANE provides ATM with the necessary procedures and conversions required to interface several types of LAN configurations. As shown in Figure 13.22, LANE allows for a variety of connections: LAN to LAN, LAN to ATM, and ATM to ATM.

The top of the figure shows that LANs can be connected with emulation bridges to an ATM network. The middle of the figure shows that an ATM station can be connected directly to an ATM network by placing an ATM adapter card directly in the workstation. On the LAN side, an emulation bridge is required to connect to the ATM network. The bottom of the figure shows that a direct ATM-to-ATM connection is possible if workstations at each end have ATM adapters to connect to the ATM network. The use of LANE provides for multiple ELANs to be logically separated by the ATM network.

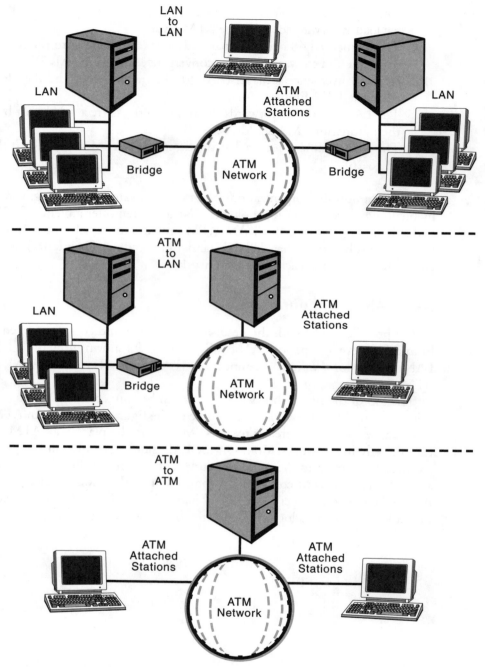

FIGURE 13.22 **ATM LAN Configurations [Source: 3COM, 8-11]**

1. What is the fundamental difference in the transmission method used between a LAN and ATM?
2. What type of service needs to be provided by ATM for it to interface with LANs?
3. When does the LAN emulation client join the ELAN?
4. What is the function of the LANE protocol?
5. What is the purpose of the bridging software used in LANE?

ATM COMMUNICATIONS AND NETWORKS

Internetworking between LANs and ATM networks requires ATM-attached equipment. The LANE protocol is deployed in ATM NICs (network interface cards) and LAN switching equipment. ATM NICs implement the LANE protocol and interface to the ATM network. The current LAN service interfaces to the higher-level protocol drivers within the attached end station. The network layer protocols at the end station continue to communicate just as if they were on a regular LAN. Unlike a LAN, however, the ATM NICs are capable of using the greater bandwidth offered by the ATM network.

ATM-attached LAN switches and routers can be directly attached to ATM hosts equipped with ATM NICs to provide a **virtual LAN (VLAN)** service. The ports on the LAN switches are assigned to particular VLANs independently of the LAN's physical location within a floor or building.

ATM Communication Options

Normally, data passes through at least one router to get from one ELAN to another. Per-hop routing is usually experienced in LAN environments. However, ATM can provide a method to transmit data between ELANs without needing to pass through a router. This is called **Multiprotocol over ATM (MPOA)**, and enables devices in different ELANs to communicate without traveling hop by hop. Instead, only the first few frames between devices pass through routers. The path taken by these frames becomes the default path. After a few frames follow the default path, the MPOA devices discover the NSAP address of the destination device and then build a direct connection for subsequent frames in the flow. [Sheldon, 813]

When MPOA is used, the edge devices that generate the ATM traffic are called **multiprotocol clients (MPC)**. A client can be an ATM-attached workstation or a router. Inter-ELAN routers are called **multiprotocol servers (MPS)** and assist the MPCs in discovering how to build a direct connection to the destination end station. With MPOA, the load on routers is reduced, because they no longer need to sustain a continuous flow between devices. MPOA also can reduce the number of ATM switches needed to support a connection by freeing up virtual circuits and switch resources in the ATM network. [Sheldon, 813]

The ATM Forum supports three primary communication options for ATM: Native ATM, Classical IP, and LANE. In Figure 13.23, both Classical IP's network layer address and LANE's MAC layer address map to an ATM address in Native ATM. Other communications options include network interface drivers such as NDIS and ODI. Several protocols are supported by the ATM standard such as: SNA (Systems Network Architecture), TCP, IPX, and NetBIOS through LANE. Upper layer subprotocols such as IP/ARP, TCP/UDP, and FTP/SNMP (Simple Network Management Protocol) are encapsulated and sent across an ATM network.

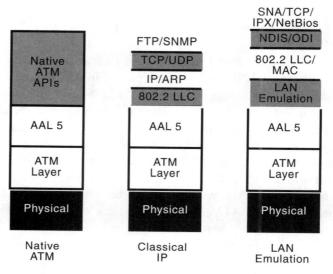

FIGURE 13.23 **ATM Communication Options [Source: 3COM, 8-4]**

When an ATM network uses Native ATM applications, it uses APIs (application programming interfaces) to communicate directly with the ATM layers. When Classical IP is used, IP and ARP are encapsulated and sent over an ATM network. Classical IP also maps the network layer IP address to an ATM address. When LANE is used, the MAC layer address is mapped to an ATM address, which allows traditional LAN applications to operate across an ATM network. [3COM, 8-4]

ATM Network

ATM can successfully use different techniques to communicate with different types of LANs. The ATM network shown in Figure 13.24 illustrates how several devices (servers, hubs, and routers) can be linked together to provide LANs access to an ATM network. Three ATM Cell Relay switches are connected in a point-to-point connection through the service provider's ATM network service. The network at the bottom of the figure provides several devices (mainframe, PBX (private branch exchange), workstation, and video camera) with access to the ATM network. At the top of the figure, several devices (hubs/routers, PBXs, servers, and desktop networks) are connected directly to the private ATM/Cell Relay switch. ATM can provide the connections to route data, voice, video, and image traffic across this network.

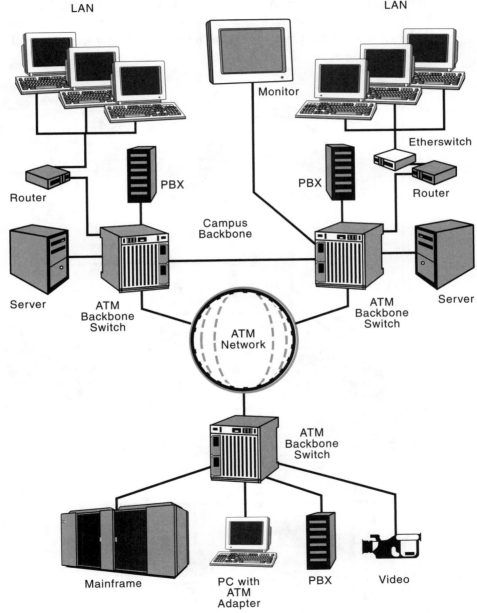

FIGURE 13.24 **ATM Network [Source: PacBell, 1]**

ATM Integration with an FDDI Backbone

Figure 13.25 demonstrates how an ATM solution can keep FDDI and Ethernet segments intact but still offer both a connection to an ATM network. As discussed earlier in the chapter, ATM must be configured to have the same encoding scheme as FDDI to pass data back and forth to an FDDI LAN. The FDDI concentrators are connected directly into the ATM Cell Relay switch. Using LANE, the Ethernet LAN hub/switch also is connected into the ATM switch. Through these connections, the ATM provides a private ATM backbone for both the FDDI and Ethernet LANs.

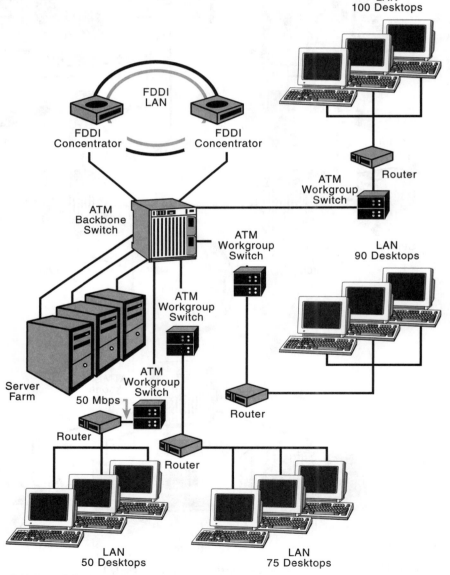

FIGURE 13.25 **ATM Integration with FDDI Backbone [Source: 3COM, 10-20]**

ATM Integration with Frame Relay and SMDS

Fast packet technologies such as Frame Relay and SMDS can also be connected to an ATM network. Frame Relay and SMDS each require different interfaces to an ATM network. In Figure 13.26 (page 712), a Frame Relay switch uses an NNI to connect to the ATM network. The SMDS switch can use either a SMDS ICI or a B-ICI (broadband intercarrier interface) to connect to the ATM network. [PacBell, 1]

Traffic can be submitted to the ATM network as ATM cells, Frame Relay frames, or SMDS PDUs (Protocol Data Units). The Frame Relay and SMDS traffic can both be sent across the B-ICI in an encapsulated format. With Frame Relay, the DLCI (digital link circuit identifier) is sent transparently through the ATM network and is translated at the receiving Frame Relay interface. SMDS PDUs can be either encapsulated or directly mapped into specific VCC or VPC values. [Black, 242-243]

TOPIC
review
ATM Communications and Networks

1. What type of equipment is required to internetwork between LANs and ATM?
2. How does ATM provide a method to transmit data between ELANs without the need to pass through a router?
3. When an ATM network uses Native ATM applications, how does it communicate directly with the ATM layers?
4. What type of encoding scheme must ATM support to pass data to an FDDI LAN?
5. What type of interface is required to connect ATM and SMDS together?

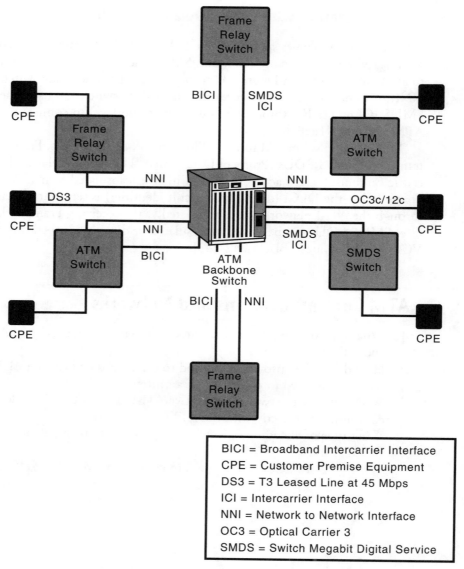

FIGURE 13.26 **ATM Integration with Frame Relay and SMDS [Source: PacBell, 9]**

ATM QoS

ATM has specified QoS parameters for measuring the performance of the network. QoS is concerned with the delivery of the cell to the destination. Under QoS, service classes are defined for different types of traffic. Four service classes have been defined, as shown in Table 13.6.

SERVICE CLASS	CONFIGURATION
A	Circuit Emulation, Constant Bit Rate Video
B	Variable Bit Rate, Audio and Video
C	Connection Oriented, Data Transfer
D	Connectionless, Data Transfer

TABLE 13.6 **Service Classes**

Each class of service provides a different level of support, or guarantee, for the transmission of ATM cells, depending on the traffic type. The QoS parameters are defined at connection setup on a connection-by-connection basis. It is also possible for multiple connections within a specified service class to have different QoS parameters defined. For each class of service, different QoS parameters are specified, as shown in Table 13.7. These QoS parameters can include a bandwidth guarantee, delay variation guarantee, cell loss guarantee, or congestion feedback guarantee.

CLASS OF SERVICE	BANDWIDTH GUARANTEE	DELAY VARIATION GUARANTEE	CELL LOSS GUARANTEE	CONGESTION FEEDBACK GUARANTEE
CBR	X	X	X	
VBR	X	X	X	
UBR				
ABR	X		X	X

TABLE 13.7 **QoS Parameters per Class of Service**

At connection setup, CBR negotiates a maximum data rate called **Peak Cell Rate (PCR)** to be supported without cell loss. It also specifies the greatest amount of jitter allowed, called **Cell Delay Variation (CDV),** and measures the variation in time between cells. At connection setup, VBR negotiates a PCR and CDV. It also includes a **Sustained Cell Rate (SCR)** that is used to specify how long cells can be transmitted at the PCR rate. ABR provides a minimum bandwidth guarantee. The setup parameters used at connection time include PCR and a **Minimum Cell Rate (MCR).** This MCR guarantees a small amount of bandwidth, which is probably just enough to keep an application running. A UBR allows data to be sent through the network without any guarantee and it is described as a best effort service.

Adaptation Layer Classes

AALs are service classes that are selected based on the application type whether it be voice, video, high-priority data, or low-priority data. Each service is illustrated in Figure 13.27 and further described in Table 13.8.

CLASS	SERVICE	DESCRIPTION
A	AAL 1	A connection-oriented service used to handle constant bit rate sources (CBR). Provides for live streaming audio and video applications such as video conferencing. Transports CBR traffic using circuit-emulation services. Circuit-emulation service also offers an attachment for equipment currently using leased lines to an ATM backbone network. AAL-1 requires timing synchronization between the source and the destination. Depends on SONET to support the clocking required for synchronous traffic.
B	AAL 2	This is another connection-oriented service for delivering audio and video. Uses bandwidth more efficiently because it does not emulate a circuit like AAL 1. Bandwidth is only used when there is something to send. Apparently, this AAL has since been eliminated by UNI version 4.
C	AAL 3/4	AAL 3/4 supports both connection-oriented and connectionless data. Designed for non real-time applications and for network service providers to transmit SMDS packets over an ATM network. Also offers a fragmentation and reassembly service for variable length packets in fixed-length cells. Inserts sequence and reassembly information into each cell to be used by the destination. This AAL has also been eliminated by UNI version 4.0.
D	AAL 5	AAL 5 is the primary AAL used for data. Supports both connection-oriented and connectionless data. Used to transfer most non-SMDS data, such as classical IP over ATM and LANE. Fragments frames for delivery in cells but uses a single bit to define the fragmentation and reassembly scheme. Designed to use most of the ATM cell payload for data. One disadvantage is that it can't multiplex transmissions from more than one source across a single circuit.

TABLE 13.8 **Adaptation Layer Classes [Sheldon, 72]**

Adaptation layer classes (A-D) are used to transport various services. As Figure 13.27 shows these services are classified by the timing required between the source and destination, bit rate whether it is constant or variable, and connection type, whether it is connectionless or connection-oriented for each adaptation layer class A, B, C, or D.

	Class A	Class B	Class C	Class D
End to End Timing	Required	Required	Not Required	Not Required
Bit Rate	Constant	Variable	Variable	Variable
Connection Mode	Connection Oriented	Connection Oriented	Connection Oriented	Connectionless
AAL Type	AAL 1	AAL 2	AAL 3	AAL 4
			AAL 5	

AAL 1 = Class A
AAL 2 = Class B
AAL 3 = Class C
AAL 4 = Class D
AAL 5 = Primary Class

FIGURE 13.27 **ATM Adaptation Layer Classes [Source: 3COM, 6-5]**

QoS Parameters

Service providers prepare contracts called Service Level Agreements (SLAs) to finalize the QoS parameters required by an organization. Depending on the type of traffic, some services are specified and others are unspecified. QoS agreements provide for better traffic management and prevent data loss. If a customer attempts to push too much traffic through a connection, the network will drop cells.

QoS parameters are defined in the header of each cell. In Figure 13.28, each VCI has a different cell loss priority (CLP). QoS is either specified or unspecified. The actions of CLP and QoS are considered together. Any cell on a congested VP where the CLP=1 and that meets the QoS service parameter value will be discarded. The QoS action will only encompass the VCIs on a specified path and will not cross path boundaries. [3COM, 7-6]

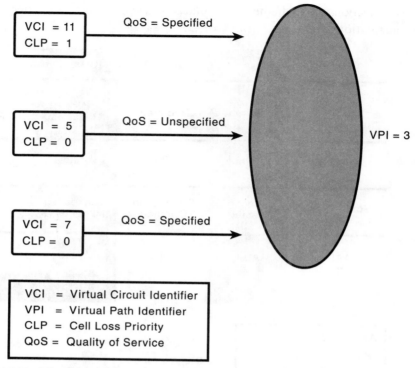

FIGURE 13.28 **ATM Quality of Service [Source: 3COM, 7-6]**

Each VCI can have individual CLP values and QoS parameters. As illustrated in Figure 13.28 and described in Table 13.9, the actions to be taken in case of network congestion are explained for each VCI.

QOS PARAMETERS	ACTION
VCI = 11, QoS is specified, CLP =1	Discard any cell at congestion time.
VCI =5, QoS is unspecified, CLP=0	Do not discard any cell at congestion time.
VCI=7, QoS is specified, CLP=0	Do not discard any cell at congestion time.

TABLE 13.9 **QoS Parameters [3COM, 7-6]**

ATM Congestion Control

ATM traffic management includes ways to control traffic and provide notification to ATM switches when congestion is expected to occur. For congestion control, ATM uses **Explicit Forward Congestion Control Indicator, EFCI**. Figure 13.29 illustrates end-to-end congestion control. ATM uses **Resource**

Management (RM) cells to provide information concerning congestion and send notification when transmission needs to be slowed down. The ATM switches passively forward these RM cells. If congestion is detected, the switch sets the EFCI in the cell header. The source and the end-user or device responds to the notification by either raising or lowering its rate of transmission. [3COM, 7-13]

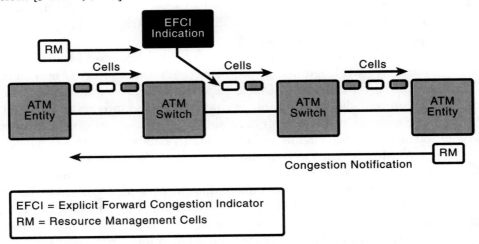

FIGURE 13.29 **ATM Congestion Control [Source: 3COM, 7-13]**

QoS enables better traffic management for core networks used by ISPs and telephone company service providers. ATM has the speed and quality needed for enterprise networking. With the advent of an all-optical network, QoS will soon be offered per wavelength, which might solve many congestion problems.

TOPIC
review **ATM QoS**

1. Describe the use of PCR.
2. Which service class provides for audio and video traffic?
3. How is an adaptation layer selected at connection time?
4. Under what circumstances would you require a specified QoS?
5. What type of cells conveys congestion notification in an ATM network?

CHAPTER SUMMARY

ATM has gained wide acceptance as a WAN technology because it provides high-speed transmission of data, voice, and video within a single system. ATM has been designed to accommodate the differences between data, voice, and video traffic. Using a broadband switching technique, it is able to handle the bursty nature of data traffic and simultaneously provide for continuous streams of voice and video traffic. ATM switching allows adjustment for access speeds appropriate to the type of traffic.

ATM uses cells rather than frames to carry the payload (data, voice, or video). A fixed-length cell is used between sender and receiver over an ATM network. ATM offers predictable performance because it always uses the same cell size and allocates the same amount of time to buffer cells. ATM can provide reserved, permanent, or bandwidth-on-demand services. ATM offers dedicated or switched circuits and high capacity bandwidth with low latency.

ATM is designed to transport both connection (voice and video) and connectionless (data from LANs) services. The user to network interface (UNI) is connection based. The operation within the network is connectionless. The connection between ATM devices within the network is referred to as a network-to-network interface (NNI). When data is sent across intermediate networks, it uses an ICI. Sometimes non-ATM equipment is used and packets are transmitted through a data exchange interface (DXI) to the ATM interface. ATM traffic is allocated by several service categories (CBR, VBR, UBR, and ABR) to match the type of traffic and priority requirements for transmission.

ATM switches are used to transfer cells through a path (virtual channel) from source to destination. In the header of the ATM cell, virtual path identifiers (VPI) and virtual channel identifiers (VCI) are used to pass the information between sender and receiver. An ATM switch uses tables to map inbound virtual paths (VPs) and channels to different outbound VPs and channels through the switch. A routing switch fabric is used to switch cells based on a binary algorithm within the switch. ATM switches map the topology of the network to determine the best path to use to reach the destination. ATM uses cell switching and statistical multiplexing techniques to speed the cells across the ATM network.

LANs can be connected to ATM networks using protocol emulation called LANE. A LANE client uses emulation software to perform data forwarding and address resolution to communicate with an ATM switch. The basic function of LANE is to resolve MAC addresses to ATM addresses so the packets from the LAN can ride over the ATM network.

Quality of Service (QoS) is offered by service and adaptation layer classes within an ATM network. These classes represent the type of traffic (voice, video, or data) required for transmission. QoS parameters are used for bandwidth, delay, cell loss, and congestion guarantees. Adaptation layers involve time, constant, or variable bit rates and type of connection (connection or connectionless) required for transmission. QoS parameters are defined in the header of each cell.

ATM traffic management is used to control traffic and provide notification to ATM switches when congestion is expected to occur. Resource Management (RM) cells provide congestion notification so that transmissions can be slowed down preventing cells from becoming lost in transmission. End-to-end congestion control is provided through Explicit Forward Congestion Control Indicator (EFCI). The source end user or device will raise or lower its rate of transmission based on the type of notification provided.

ATM is a switching technology designed for today's networks. It permits the network to use higher bandwidths and to transmit at access speeds required by the data sent. ATM connections offer dedicated bandwidth through ATM switches that manage several point-to-point virtual connections. ATM manages multimedia, data, voice, and image traffic and has become a universal transport model for backbone WANs.

CHAPTER REVIEW QUESTIONS

(This quiz also can be printed from the Encore! CD that accompanies this book. File name—Chap13review.)

Circle a letter (a-d) for each question. Choose only one answer for each question.

1. Which statement best describes ATM?
   a. Not suitable for delay sensitive voice and video traffic.
   b. Provides a digital infrastructure and physical transport.
   c. A high-speed connection-oriented switching and multiplexing technology capable of transmitting voice, video, and data.
   d. Considered a synchronous technology.

2. ATM has been designed to offer:
   a. greater delay and lower throughput.
   b. bandwidth on demand.
   c. users as much bandwidth as they need.
   d. the bandwidth required on a connection basis.

3. When cells are placed in an ATM switch, they are placed into a
   a. slot.
   b. queue.
   c. path.
   d. channel.

4. These addresses are used to provide a logical point between the network and transport layers of the OSI model.
   a. GFC
   b. PCC
   c. CAC
   d. NSAP

5. An ATM address format is divided into two sections called:
   a. network and user.
   b. network and switch.
   c. network and library codes.
   d. network and prefix.

6. What is the size of an ATM address?
   a. 10-byte string
   b. 15-byte string
   c. 20-byte string
   d. 25-byte string

7. What is the core of an ATM network?
   a. backbone switch
   b. switch control point module
   c. backbone bridge
   d. backbone gateway

8. The fundamental difference between LANs and ATM is:
   a. LANs transmit in cells while ATM routes bits.
   b. LANs transmit in cycles while ATM routes cells.
   c. LANs transmit in bits while ATM routes cells.
   d. LANs transmit in frames while ATM routes cells.

9. What is the standard developed by the ATM Forum to give stations attached via ATM the same bit passing capacity as Ethernet or Token Ring LANs?
   a. LATR
   b. L-BISDN
   c. LATM
   d. LANE

10. Where are QoS parameters defined in the ATM cell?
   a. trailer
   b. header
   c. data
   d. frame

Circle the correct letter (A-E) that corresponds to the descriptions below. Choose only one answer for each.

    A. CLP
    B. ICI
    C. VCI
    D. CBR
    E. UNI

11. A B C D E   The connection that exists between the user equipment and the ATM equipment.

12. A B C D E   Identifies the next destination of a cell as it passes through a series of ATM switches on the way to its destination.

13. A B C D E   Specifies a fixed bit rate so that data can be sent in a steady stream.

14. A B C D E   Determines whether cells should be dropped if extreme network congestion occurs.

15. A B C D E   A method used in establishing an interface through an ATM network where traffic is sent across intermediate networks.

    A. Cell
    B. UBR
    C. DXI
    D. PT
    E. GFR

16. A B C D E   Does not guarantee throughput levels.

17. A B C D E   Allows users to send at any rate up to the PCR while the network is only committed to sending at the MCR.

18. A B C D E   A formatted packet that uses a fixed cell length data unit.

19. A B C D E   A method used when non-ATM equipment is used to transmit packets rather than cells to the ATM interface.

20. A B C D E   Indicates the type of payload (either user, network, or management information) in the payload portion of the cell.

INTERNET EXERCISES

1. Log on to the Internet and key the following URL:

   www.atmforum.com/aboutatm/guide.html

   A. What is ATM best known for?
   B. What percentage of the world's carriers uses ATM in the core of their networks?
   C. Why has it been so widely adopted?
   D. Is distance a problem for high-speed transmission over ATM networks?

2. Key the following URL:

   http://lists.jammed.com/politech/2002/06/0050.html

   A. When will broadband access be available to every American?
   B. What benefits are described for broadband access?

CONCEPT EXERCISES

Concept Narrative
(This narrative exercise also can be printed from the Encore! CD that accompanies this book. File name—Chap13connar.)

Fill in the blanks of the following narrative.

ATM networks were designed to connect LANs together over an ATM backbone. There is a fundamental difference, however, between LANs and ATMs. LANs transmit in _____ while ATM routes _____. The ATM Forum developed a standard called LAN Emulation (LANE) to give stations attached via ATM the same bit passing capability as is required on an Ethernet or Token Ring LAN. The primary function of the _____ protocol is to _____ a LAN on top of an ATM network. It defines procedures for either an IEEE 802.3 Ethernet or an 802.5 Token Ring LAN. LANE allows existing _____ applications to use an ATM network.

The ATM switch requires a connection to a LAN emulation server (_____), a LAN emulation configuration server (_____), and a broadcast unknown server (BUS) to set up an emulated data connection. The _____ is responsible for registering and resolving Ethernet MAC addresses to ATM addresses. The LECS provides configuration information about each network. The _____ is responsible for handling broadcast, multicast, and initial unicast frames sent from a *LAN emulation client*. A LAN emulation client is the end node (workstation or network device). It performs data forwarding and address resolution, as well as several control functions. Each _____ maintains the LAN emulation software. The LAN emulation software resides between the lower ATM layers and the upper protocol layers. It shields the upper layer protocol stack for Ethernet and Token Ring LANs from the ATM network.

Concept Table
(This table exercise also can be printed from the Encore! CD that accompanies this book. File name—Chap13contab.)

Read each statement carefully and choose the layer of the ATM Reference Model being described. Use only one "X" per statement.

STATEMENT	TYPES OF ATM LAYERS		
	PHYSICAL	ATM	AAL
1. Generally controls passing cells through the ATM network.			
2. Responsible for establishing, maintaining, and terminating virtual circuits.			
3. Same as the physical layer of the OSI model.			
4. Responsible for converting outgoing cells into bits and incoming bits into cells.			
5. Corresponds to the data link layer of the OSI model.			
6. Connects with a physical medium that supports ATM.			
7. Defines a process for converting information from upper layers into ATM cells.			
8. When it converts cells to bits, it must frame the bits so they have the same frame structure as the other network.			
9. Segments data into 48-byte cell payloads.			
10. Prepares user data for conversion into cells.			

Concept Picture

(This picture exercise also can be printed from the Encore! CD that accompanies this book. File name—Chap13conpic.)

In this exercise, look at the picture of ATM virtual paths and channels and label the missing elements.

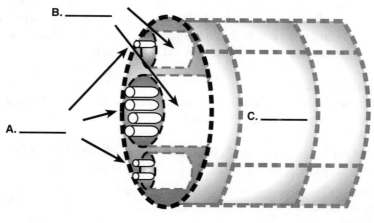

A. _____

B. _____

C. _____

CASE STUDY

LONE STAR OIL EXPLORATION COMPANY

Objective:

Evaluate the performance benefits of the implementation of ATM technology for oil exploration.

Company Profile:

Lone Star Oil Exploration Company is a $25 billion energy company with operations worldwide. The corporate headquarters is in Houston, Texas; two major oil exploration locations are in Saudi Arabia and Brazil. The company also has 400 sites within the United States and 50 sales offices in international locations.

Current Situation:

In the past 10 months, the enterprise network has doubled in size. The oil exploration applications that provide remote access to seismic modeling and simulations for visualizations are not easily supported by the low bandwidth of Lone Star's current network. The current network uses a mesh of T1 links that supports the 400 U.S. sites, and 50 international locations including Saudi Arabia and Brazil. Most of the company's data-processing activities are split between the mainframe and the LAN at the corporate headquarters.

Business Information Requirements:

Lone Star wants to purchase an ATM network to help reduce the enormous costs of oil exploration. The company also wants to enhance the telecommunications network for voice and data applications that they use for business communications worldwide.

Communication System Requirements:

The telecommunications staff has determined that a combination of backbone and workgroup ATM is the only network infrastructure capable of supporting scalable networking for both oil exploration and voice/data applications. Engineering workstations will require ATM to provide the visual simulations of oil exploration. These simulations require real-time transfer of audio and video for overseas collaboration.

Information System Solution:

1. Lone Star decided to use high-end routers with ATM Interface Processor (AIP) cards. A high-end router is located at each of these locations: Houston, Saudi Arabia, and Brazil. They are connected at each end to an ATM switch. A T1 local loop connection was established from each site to the carrier's ATM network.

2. In Houston, a workgroup ATM access was provided by equipping the LAN servers with ATM adapter cards to connect the LAN directly to the ATM switch.

3. Engineers in Brazil had ATM adapter cards installed in their workstations to connect them directly to the ATM switch. This provides the engineering staff an opportunity to share real-life engineering and scientific applications over the ATM network between Saudi Arabia, Brazil, and Houston.

4. Voice communications were routed over the ATM network by attaching the PBX to the router and the ATM switch.

5. In Saudi Arabia, engineers transferred live video feeds of their oil exploration activities to Brazil and Houston. Engineers could then view and discuss strategies to improve how they proceed with oil exploration.

6. The company's telecommunications staff has planned for the coexistence of its leased T1 mesh network for the 400 domestic locations and the 50 other international sites with the ATM service. In the future, the company intends to provide ATM services to all sites worldwide.

Study the illustraion of Lone Star's solution shown in Figure 13.30, and then answer the Study Questions that follow.

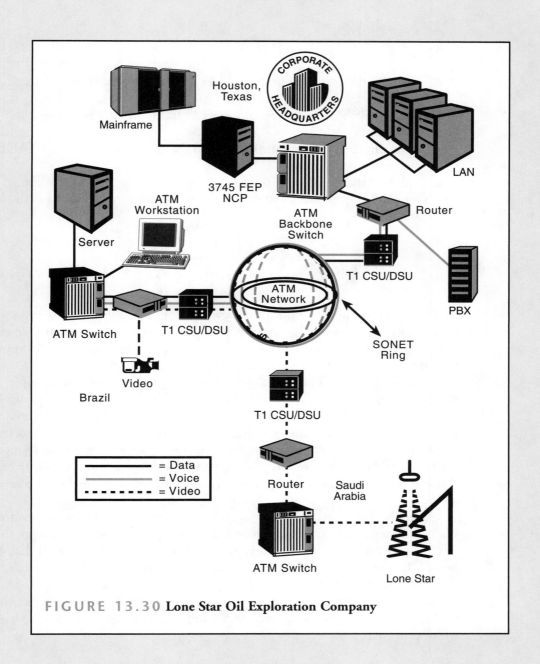

FIGURE 13.30 **Lone Star Oil Exploration Company**

CASE STUDY QUESTIONS:

1. Why did the company need an ATM interface processor card in the router at each location?
2. What happens to the speed of the ATM traffic when it passes over the T1 local loop?
3. Is the direct connection of the LAN to the ATM switch without LANE gateways a good choice?
4. Is the company able to route voice services over the ATM network?
5. Why did the company put ATM adapter cards in the workstation in Brazil?

GROUP TERM PROJECT

In this section of the project, list recommendations for all equipment and software chosen for the solution. Use this section to communicate to management how and why the group decided on this recommendation. Open and print out the form *Recommend* from the Encore! CD that came with this book.

In the Recommendation form, you should also describe your after-implementation support strategy. Communicate how the Help Desk and Technical Support will provide on-going support services required to maintain the system as it was designed. Make sure user recommendations are considered and determine whether they can be implemented. Execute all support strategies to meet the needs when the customer is interfacing with the new system. Describe how you will provide the customer with additional support when the business need arises.

Generally, it is a good idea to include recommendations and provisions for yearly maintenance of the equipment and software. Customers want to be able to anticipate how long it will take to fix failed equipment, such as next day, 4-hour, 8-hour response time from the hardware vendor. On the software side, they want to make sure they don't have to spend again for software upgrades.

Attached to this recommendation, you should present a diagram or drawing of the eight locations showing each WAN link and labeling each with the bandwidth provided.

WAN PROJECT PLAN

RECOMMENDATION

Describe in detail the preferred solution for meeting the customer's requirements including a preliminary estimate for cost, resources, and schedule.

CHAPTER TERMS

AAL   693
ABR   682
AFI   690
ATM   676
ATM layer   693
ATM multiplexing   699
B-ISDN   679
BUS   701
CAC   685
CBR   682
CDV   713
cell   679
CLP   688
DCC   689, 690
DXI   681
E.164   689, 690
E.164 NSAP   689
EFCI   716
ELAN   701
ESI   690, 691
GFC   688
GFR   682
HEC   688
HO-DSP   690
ICD   689, 690
ICI   681
JOIN REQUEST   702
JOIN RESPONSE   702
LANE   701
LAN emulation client   701
LECID   702
LECS   701
LES   701
logical ID swapping   684
MCR   713
MPC   707

MPOA   707
MPS   707
NNI   681
NSAP address   687
PCR   713
PT   688
Q.922 standard   679
Q.931 standard   679
RD   690
RM   717
routing switch fabric   697
SCR   713
SEL   690
switch control point   696
TAXI   692
translation table   698
UBR   682
UNI   681
VBR   682
VC   683
VCI   684, 688
VC table   685
virtual channel connection (VCC)   684
Virtual Channel ID   688
virtual path connection (VPC)   684
VLAN   707
VPI   684
VP table   685

CHAPTER BIBLIOGRAPHY

Book, Magazine, Presentation Citations

3COM. *ATM Technology Student Guide*. California: 3COM Educational
    Services, 1996: 1-4, 1-10, 1-11, 2-4 to 2-11, 3-4, 6-5, 7-6, 7-11, 7-13, 8-4,
    8-10 to 8-12, 8-19 to 8-26, 10-3, 10-12, 10-20.

Black, Uyless. *Emerging Communications Technologies*. New Jersey: Prentice Hall
    PTR, 1997: 17, 18, 43, 125, 247.

Goralski, Walter. *Introduction to ATM Networking*. New York: McGraw-Hill,
    1995: 114, 129-130, 281-282, 294.

PacBell, "ATM Networking" Presentation. San Jose: Pacific Bell, 1998: 1, 3, 9.

Sheldon, Tom. *Encyclopedia of Networking & Telecommunications*. New York:
    Osborne/McGraw-Hill, 2001: 69, 70, 72, 73, 75, 76, 813.

Web Citations

Cisco, "Asynchronous Transfer Mode (ATM) Switching," Internetworking
    Technology Overview,
    <www.cisco.com/univercd/cc/td/doc/cisintwk/ito_doc/atm.htm> (14 March
    2002).

Webopedia, "ATM," <www.webopedia.com/TERM/A/ATM.html> (2002).

CHAPTER 14

WIRELESS AND CELLULAR COMMUNICATIONS

CHAPTER OBJECTIVES

By the end of this chapter, you should understand these concepts:
- Mobile wireless devices and applications
- The difference between cellular and PCS services
- Mobile e-commerce applications
- The use and functions of frequency bands
- The foundation of the Cellular System Architecture
- The Mobile Telephone Switching Office
- Wireless multiplexing methods used to split wireless calls by access method
- The design of the Global Wireless Internet
- The Wireless Solution Model
- Wireless standards and protocols
- The elements of the Wireless Access Protocol (WAP)
- Secure wireless communications
- Satellite versus cellular technology
- Wireless application of satellite phones and portable satellite terminals

WIRELESS DEVICES AND APPLICATIONS

Wireless describes methods of telecommunication that use electromagnetic waves to carry data and voice over the communication path. These electromagnetic waves are produced by the interaction of electric and magnetic fields. Devices used for wireless communication can be divided into the four categories outlined in Table 14.1.

CATEGORY	DESCRIPTION
Fixed Wireless	Devices that are connected to the Internet using special modems (wireless DSL [Digital Subscriber Lines]) in homes and offices.
Mobile Wireless	Devices (mobile phones) that are used from motorized moving vehicles, such as automobiles, buses, trains, and boats.

TABLE 14.1 **Wireless Device Categories**

Portable Wireless	Battery-powered wireless devices, such as cellular phones and PDAs, which travel with the user from office to home to vehicle.
IR Wireless	Devices such as wireless hubs that use infrared radiation (IR) to convey data. Laptops use wireless adapter cards for their network interface to the wireless hub. They are normally used for limited-range communication.

TABLE 14.1 **Wireless Device Categories, continued**

The term **cellular** refers to communications systems that divide a geographic region into sections, called *cells*. The purpose of this division is to make the most use out of a limited number of transmission frequencies. Each connection, or conversation, requires its own dedicated frequency with the total number of available frequencies being limited to about 1,000. To support more than 1,000 simultaneous conversations, cellular systems allocate a set number of frequencies for each cell. Two cells can use the same frequency for different conversations as long as the cells are not adjacent to one another.

Probably the most important contributing factor to the birth of wireless Internet has been the proliferation of digital cell phones in the last few years. The number of mobile-phone users worldwide is expected to reach 500 million by 2003 and 75% of those phones will be Internet-enabled. [Webopedia, 1]

Cellular and PCS Services

Cellular telephones use a short-wave analog or digital transmission. Cell phone technology is actually considered a form of radio. A cell phone has a wireless connection to a nearby transmitter. The transmitter is usually located somewhere along a major highway, so as the cell phone user moves, the telephone can effectively transmit and receive information.

The expanding network of digital cellular devices and **personal communication services (PCS)**, services that offer personal service and extended mobility, has created a solid foundation for wireless Internet services. More than 50 million Web-enabled cell phones are in use today. A definite number of channels are allocated for the operator's (user's) authorized frequency. The frequency plan assigns specific channels to specific cells. A specific reuse pattern is defined for cells as well.

PCS has advanced messaging capabilities (see Figure 14.1) such as messaging, AOL access, and Web browsing. It combines voice and Internet features into one mobile device. PCS has created a solid foundation for wireless Internet services.

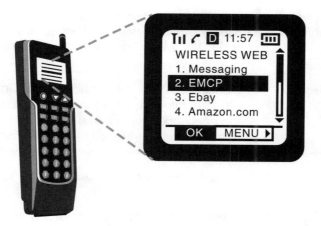

FIGURE 14.1 **Cell Phone with Wireless Internet [Source: Tyson, 1]**

Cell phones can provide an incredible array of functions, and new ones are being added at a breakneck pace. Depending on the model, a cell-phone user can:

- Store contact information
- Create task or to-do lists
- Track appointments and set reminders for meetings
- Use a built-in calculator for simple math
- Send or receive e-mail
- Find the latest news, stock quotes, sports scores, and so on from the Internet
- Integrate with other devices (PDAs [personal data assistants], MP3 players, and GPS [Global Positioning Satellite] receivers)

Wireless access includes data transport and management for dispatching, ordering parts, performing remote diagnostics, and accessing data. As Figure 14.2 shows, cellular phones, modems, controllers, and pagers are devices (machine assets) used to provide connectivity for mobile users (people assets) who need access from anywhere. Mobile access also includes two-way radios used for instant communication for coordinating with people in cars, boats, and trucks. Hosting gateways are used to connect the wireless network to the Internet. Each day, people use wireless devices to better manage inventory, cash reporting, asset management, remote monitoring and diagnostics, dispatch integration, and reporting systems.

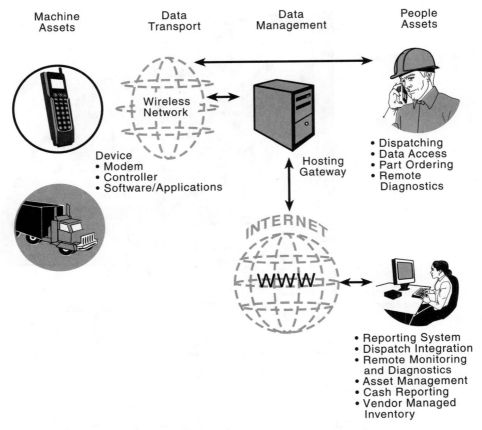

Machine Assets

Device
• Modem
• Controller
• Software/Applications

Data Transport

Wireless Network

Data Management

Hosting Gateway

INTERNET

WWW

People Assets

• Dispatching
• Data Access
• Part Ordering
• Remote Diagnostics

• Reporting System
• Dispatch Integration
• Remote Monitoring and Diagnostics
• Asset Management
• Cash Reporting
• Vendor Managed Inventory

FIGURE 14.2 **Wireless Applications** [Source: Ztango, 11]

Mobile E-Commerce

Mobile e-commerce enables users to communicate, interact, and transact business over the Internet through the use of mobile handheld devices. The mobile carriers provide for an always-on and high-speed connection to the Internet. They provide two-way messaging and data services connected to the Internet. Business travelers require new mobile data services to manage their day-to-day activities. Users can schedule airline flights and receive updates on flight times, schedule overnight stays at hotels, and receive directions to their destinations all through their mobile phones.

Figure 14.3 shows the three levels of mobile communication, which are further described in Table 14.2.

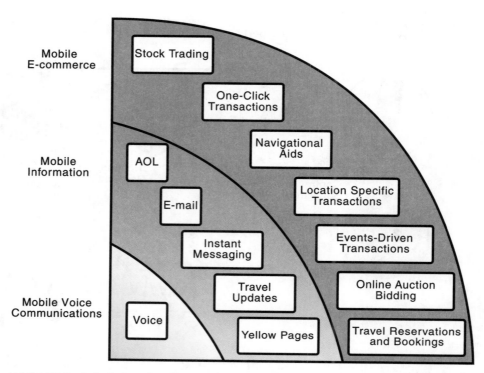

FIGURE 14.3 **Levels of Mobile Communication [Source: Hannigan, Bruton, Roland, Zohar, 12]**

LEVEL	DESCRIPTION
Mobile Voice Communications	Standard voice service is offered with connections established to land lines to communicate with regular phone users.
Mobile Information	Mobile users can contact the office to retrieve priority e-mails. Instant messaging has been extended to provide two-way messaging for mobile phones. Another feature allows access to yellow pages information for phone numbers and street addresses. Mobile carriers have established partnerships with AOL and Yahoo! to provide for content designed for mobile phone users.
Mobile E-Commerce	Features are enhanced at the mobile e-commerce level to include stock trading and online auction access over the Internet. Location-based technology requires location-based content for mobile users. This technology requires commercial position determining equipment to pinpoint a mobile user's wireless location. It is used for dispatch, fleet management, and emergency services. Mobile users are looking for one-click transaction capability to provide for simple transaction notification and ordering.

TABLE 14.2 **Levels of Mobile Communication [Hannigan, Bruton, Roland, Zohar, 12]**

Customization will drive mobile e-commerce applications quickly forward in the future. Mobile subscribers are interested in receiving customized content that is filtered and prioritized for their needs. For example, a subscriber might want to be alerted of special events such as upcoming concerts via mobile phone and then use the phone to purchase tickets immediately. Mobile carriers are upgrading their infrastructure to enhance their data and Internet capacity.

All of these mobile e-commerce applications will require more bandwidth. Carriers are responding to provide the needed wireless data speeds of over 100 Kbps. Several carriers are installing more wireless base stations to provide for these applications. In Europe, they are already using e-commerce applications over mobile phones for banking, stock transactions, and other services.

Mobile Phone Services

Table 14.3 outlines the various mobile telephone systems available.

MOBILE TELEPHONE SYSTEM	DESCRIPTION
Global System for Mobile Communication (GSM)	A digital mobile telephone system that has become the de facto wireless telephone standard in Europe. Digitizes and compresses data to send it down a channel with two other streams of data. Each data stream has its own time slot. GSM operates at either 900 MHz or 1,800 MHz frequency band. [Search Networking, 1]
General Packet Radio Service (GPRS)	A packet-based wireless communication service that provides continuous connection to the Internet for mobile phone and computer users. Can transmit at data rates from 56 Kbps to 114 Kbps. Using a mobile phone, users are able to participate in a video conference and interact with multimedia Web sites. [Search Networking, 1]
Enhanced Data GSM Environment (EDGE)	An enhanced version of the GSM wireless service. Transmits at 384 Kbps and can support delivery of multimedia content to other mobile phone users. [Search Networking, 1]
I-Mode	A packet-based mobile phone service introduced in Japan in 1999. Provides color and video transmission to the mobile phone user. I-Mode supports Web browsing and e-mail, and allows users to execute banking and stock

TABLE 14.3 **Mobile Telephone Systems**

MOBILE TELEPHONE SYSTEM	DESCRIPTION
	transactions from their mobile phones. Already has 5.6 million users worldwide. [Search Networking, 1]
IXRTT	A one-carrier radio transmission technology. A high-capacity voice and data solution that operates at 1.25 MHz and provides a significant increase in speed to 144 Kbps. Offers an increase in RF capacity to enable more connections for simultaneous users. IXRTT is well suited to provide mobile multimedia services for Web browsing over the Internet. The technology is optimized to provide data compression services for better bandwidth management. [AIC, 2]
3G	An ITU (International Telecommunication Union) specification for third-generation mobile communication technology. Designed to work with GSM, TDMA, and CDMA. Bandwidth speeds vary based on whether the mobile device is stationary or moving. When the mobile phone is stationary, it is capable of transmitting at 384 Kbps. However, if the mobile device is in a moving vehicle, the bandwidth speed is lower at 128 Kbps. In the future, broad bandwidth and speeds up to 2 Mbps are expected. Services included with 3G are voice, data, video, and remote control capabilities. The most significant enhancement is its capability to roam throughout Europe, Japan, and North America. [Webopedia, 1]
Universal Mobile Telecommunications System (UMTS)	A worldwide broadband, packet-based service for mobile computer and phone users that supports a roaming service that offers the same set of functions to and from any location. A 3G service designed for high-quality broadband information for e-commerce and entertainment services. Offers low-cost, high-capacity data rates as high as 2 Mbps when the mobile device is stationary. Support for global roaming is also included. This technology is focused toward developing a mass market for highly personalized and user-friendly mobile access. [UMTS, 1]

TABLE 14.3 **Mobile Telephone Systems, continued**

Electromagnetic Radiation Spectrum

Mobile telephone systems use the electromagnetic radiation spectrum to transmit through the airwaves. The electromagnetic spectrum provides different frequencies to manage the transmission of several services through air space.

The **electromagnetic radiation spectrum** is the complete range of wavelengths of electromagnetic radiation. This spectrum represents "from DC to light," beginning with the longest radio waves and extending through visible light. [Whatis, 1]

With wireless communications, the frequency of a signal is related to the wavelength. The mathematical formula states: If f is the frequency of an electromagnetic field in free space as measured in megahertz, and w is the wavelength as measured in meters, then:

$$w = 300/f \quad \text{and conversely} \quad f = 300/w$$

As discussed in Chapter 5, hertz is a unit of frequency. This is represented by a change in state or cycle in a sound wave, an alternating current, or other cyclical waveform of 1 cycle per second. A radio wave is an electromagnetic wave propagated by an antenna. Radio frequency is measured as the number of cycles transmitted or received in 1 second. Each radio wave is produced by a cycle of electric current in a transmitting antenna with the frequency of the current being the same as the wave frequency. The radio frequency spectrum runs from 1 kHz to 300 GHz.

The electromagnetic radiation spectrum includes power, telephone, radio waves, microwaves, infrared, ultraviolet, X-rays, and gamma rays. The frequency ranges from hertz, kilohertz, megahertz, gigahertz, to terahertz. The visible spectrum for light is expressed as photon energy represented as hertz volts (ev).

Signal bandwidth is measured in kilohertz, megahertz, and gigahertz ranges, whereas digital signals are only represented in kilohertz. Kilohertz (kHz) is a unit of alternating current (AC) or electromagnetic (EM) wave frequency equal to one thousand hertz (1,000 Hz). The bandwidth of a digital signal, in kilohertz, is related to the data speed expressed as bits per second (bps). Larger units of frequency are expressed as MHz, which is equal to 1,000,000 Hz or 1,000 kHz. GHz is equal to 1,000,000,000 Hz or 1,000,000 kHz. [Novell, 3-3]

The electromagnetic spectrum is divided into different categories of frequencies. Each category of frequency is described as low, medium, ultra, or very high frequency. You might be more familiar with the more common descriptions such as VHF and UHF used for high frequency TV channels. Just as there are designated frequency ranges for TV and radios, frequency ranges are reserved for cellular and digital PCS mobile phones.

Frequency Range Description and Applications

Table 14.4 explains the radio wave band frequency and provides examples of applications that function at each frequency.

FREQUENCY DESCRIPTION	FREQUENCY RANGE	APPLICATION
Very Low Frequency (VLF)	1 kHz to 10 kHz	Submarines
Low Frequency (LF)	10 kHz to 500 kHz	Marine Navigation
Medium Frequency (MF)	500 kHz to 2 MHz	AM Radio
High Frequency (HF)	2 MHz to 30 MHz	Shortwave Ham Radios
Very High Frequency (VHF)	30 MHz to 300 MHz	FM radio, TV Channels 2-13
Ultra High Frequency (UHF)	300 MHz to 1 GHz	Cell Phones, Pagers, TV Channels 14-69
Super High Frequency (SHF)	1 GHz to 30 GHz	802.11b radios, Satellite, PCS
Extremely High Frequency (EHF)	30 GHz to 300 GHz	Future

TABLE 14.4 **Frequency Bands and Applications [Search Networking, 1]**

Cellular phones use radio waves to transmit and receive signals. Radio frequency (RF) communication implies the transfer of information through the airwaves between sending and receiving radios. The Federal Communications Commission (FCC) tightly controls RF transmission in the United States, allocating some frequency bands for support of radio and others for cellular communications.

Frequency Bands for Cellular and PCS

Figure 14.4 shows a comparison between the frequency bands used for cellular transmissions and PCS transmissions. For cellular, the phone and base stations use frequency A and B bands. The A band transmits at 1 MHz and supports 33 channels of 30 KHz each. The B band transmits at 1.5 MHz and supports 83 channels of 30 KHz each. More bands (A, B, C, D, E, and F) are available for PCS, as the frequency spectrum contains a specific number of channels. Specific channels are assigned to specific cells. PCS, phones, and cell stations use bands A, B, and C, transmit at 15 MHz, and support 449 channels of 30 KHz each. The other bands—D, E, and F—transmit at 5 MHz and support

165 channels each of 30 KHz. Finally, cellular systems operate between 824 MHz and 894 MHz and PCS operates in the 1850 MHz-1990 MHz bands in the United States. [Farley, 1]

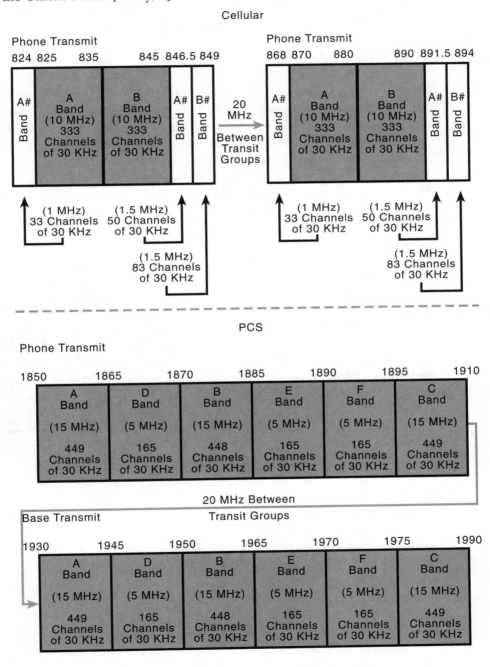

FIGURE 14.4 **Cellular and PCS Frequencies [Source: Farley, 1]**

Cellular System Architecture

In modern cellular telephony, specific provisioning guidelines apply to both rural and urban regions. These regions are divided into areas. Each region includes cells, clusters, frequency reuse, cell splitting, and handovers.

Cells

Cellular radio equipment is located at a base station. This base station can communicate with cellular phones as long as they are within a range. The base station communicates to the cell phone through a channel. The channel provides two frequencies: one is used to transmit to the base station while the other is set to receive from the base station. Cells are base stations transmitting over small geographic areas. The geographic area is represented in the form of a hexagon. The cell size varies according to differences in the terrain and the number of buildings located within the cell.

Clusters

A cluster, as shown in Figure 14.5, is a group of cells or base stations. Clusters do not reuse channels. They provide boundaries for communication. A large number of base stations are located within a city and can support hundreds of cluster towers.

Frequency Reuse

During the development of mobile telephone systems, only a small number of radio channel frequencies were available. Radio channels were reused to provide for more than one conversation at a time. Because only a limited number of frequencies were available, service providers had to reuse frequencies to provide mobile services. **Frequency reuse**

Cluster

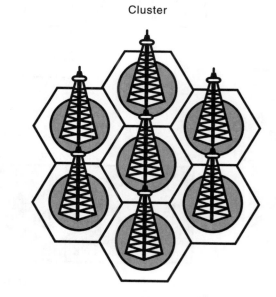

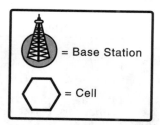

FIGURE 14.5 **Base Stations Cells**
[Source: Brain, 2]

required a group of radio channels to be assigned to each cell within a small geographic area. Each cell was assigned a group of channels that was completely different from neighboring cells. Today, it is a common practice for service providers to employ frequency reuse techniques to keep up with the growing demand from their customers.

The coverage of cells is referred to as the "footprint." A boundary limits the footprint so that the same group of channels can be used in different cells. This allows extensive frequency reuse across a city and allows thousands of people to use their cell phones simultaneously. Cell-phone carriers usually receive about 800 frequencies for use across a city. The carrier divides the city into cells. The size of each cell is about 10 square miles or 26 square kilometers. [IEC, 6]

Cell Splitting

Often a cell-phone carrier's area becomes full of users, the result being that service is compromised. To prevent this, *cell splitting* is used. **Cell splitting** allows a single area to be split into smaller ones. Cities can be split into as many areas as necessary to provide acceptable service levels. [IEC, 6]

Handovers

Handovers were designed to manage communication when a cellular phone user travels from one cell to another during a call. Because adjacent areas do not use the same radio channel, a call needs to be transferred from one radio channel to another when a user crosses the line between adjacent cells. When the cellular phone moves out of the coverage area of a cell, the reception becomes weak. With a **handover,** the system switches the call to a stronger-frequency channel in a new cell. The call is not interrupted and the user does not notice the hand-over. [IEC, 6]

A cellular communications system works with other telephone services to provide mobile service for their subscribers. A cellular system's main mobile switching center, called the **Mobile Telephone Switching Office (MTSO),** is located at the CO (central office). The MTSO includes the mobile switching center (MSC) as well as field monitoring and the relay stations used to switch calls from cell sites to the PSTN (Public Switched Telephone Network). [Brain, 3] [Farley, 1]

Mobile Telephone Switching Office (MTSO)

Each mobile telephone carrier has one MTSO at the CO of a telco in a given city. This office handles all of the phone connections to the normal land-based phone system, and controls all of the base stations in the region. The MTSO communicates with mobile phones using special codes. These codes are used to identify the phone, the phone's owner, and the service provider. All mobile phones have the following codes:

- **Electronic Serial Number (ESN).** A unique 32-bit number programmed into the phone when it is manufactured.
- **Mobile Identification Number (MIN).** A 10-digit number derived from the phone number.
- **System Identification Code (SID).** A unique 5-digit number that is assigned by the FCC to each carrier. [Brain, 3-4]

The ESN code is considered a permanent part of the phone. The MIN and SID codes are programmed into the phone when you purchase a service plan and have the phone activated.

The communication process between the mobile phone and the MTSO occurs in these steps:

1. When the mobile phone is powered on, it listens for an SID on a control channel. The control channel is a special frequency that the phone and base station use to talk to one another. Call set-up and channel changing information is conveyed over the control channel.
2. If the phone cannot find any control channels to listen to, it displays a "no service" message indication that it is out of range of the MTSO.
3. If a signal is found by the MTSO, then it reads the SID. It compares the SID to the one programmed into the phone. If the two SIDs match, the phone knows in what cell it is communicating.
4. The mobile phone along with the SID, transmits a registration request.
5. The MTSO gets the call, and it tries to find you. It looks in its database to see which cell you are in.
6. Next, it selects a frequency pair that your phone will use in that cell to receive the call.
7. The MTSO communicates with the mobile phone over the control channel and tells it the frequencies to use for your phone and the tower switch and connects the call.
8. Base stations in adjacent cells coordinate with each other through the MTSO. When you move to the edge of your cell, your mobile phone will receive a signal over the control channel telling it to change frequencies. This handover switches your phone to a new cell with the appropriate signal strength to continue to handle your call. [Brain, 3-4]

Today, thousands of mobile subscribers make connections to base stations and the MTSO. The MTSO provides centralized management of the phone owner and the service provider. It establishes a connection to the PSTN to carry mobile user's calls to their friends, neighbors, and business associates. As the number of subscribers increases, there will be more demand than the existing wireless provider networks can handle. Scientists are developing different methods to handle frame transmission and multiplexing to offer a more scalable framework for wireless transmissions.

Frame Transmission

Mobility provides today's user with connections to communications services from anywhere at any time. New communications technologies are emerging quickly to simplify the mobile user's experience and to provide even more services. Behind the scenes, researchers are developing different methods to handle frame transmission and multiplexing to offer an even higher level of connectivity.

The key to understanding cellular and PCS systems is that frames, slots, and channels are used to organize digital information. The frame carries the conversation or data along with error detection and correction bits. Slots hold individual call information within a frame. Signaling and control information also accompanies the call in the slot. Each user occupies a radio frequency for a predetermined amount of time. A channel consists of a pair of radio frequencies. One frequency is used for transmittal, while the other is for reception. Channels are used for call processing. A PCS channel is a dedicated time slot within a data or bit stream.

Figure 14.6 shows a generic frame with time slots. Using multiplexing techniques, each user occupies a radio frequency in an assigned time slot. Calls are multiplexed into a digital stream by the base station. The base station combines the bits into the right time slots at the right time. The multiplexing technique puts each time segment into six slots. Slots 1-6 in Figure 14.6 compose one frame. Two of the time slots make up one voice circuit. The other slots are used for data and they support a data rate of 48.6 Kb. [Farley, 3]

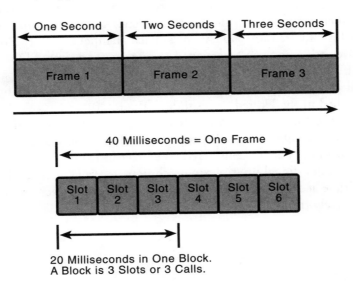

FIGURE 14.6 **Frame Time Slots [Source: Farley, 3]**

A block is three slots or three calls. Each block takes 20 ms to transmit. The entire frame can be transmitted in 40 ms. Multiplexing uses time slots to allow several calls to occupy one channel. Different data channels in a bit stream are sent to a MTSO and then out to the PSTN.

Wireless Multiplexing

Wireless multiplexing provides for the division of wireless calls based on access method. Three different wireless multiplexing techniques are currently in use, each technique with a different function:

- **Frequency Division Multiple Access (FDMA).** Each call is on a separate frequency.
- **Time Division Multiple Access (TDMA).** Assigns each call a certain "slice of time" on a designated frequency.
- **Code Division Multiple Access (CDMA).** A unique code is assigned to each call and spreads it over the available frequencies.

Each of these wireless-multiplexing techniques provides for multiple access, allowing more than one user to use each cell.

FDMA

Frequency Division Multiple Access (FDMA) is used primarily for analog transmission. It separates the spectrum into distinct voice channels. These voice channels are then split into identical sections of bandwidth. The frequency band is allocated into 30 channels. Each channel can carry a different voice conversation and can be assigned to one user at a time. FDMA is widely used with **Advanced Mobile Phone Service (AMPS)**, which is a standard system for analog signal cellular telephone service and is the predominant cellular technology used in the United States today. [Brain, 10]

Figure 14.7 shows that frequency range for FDMA begins at 824.04 MHz and ends at 893.7 MHz. Because the total available bandwidth is only 45 MHz, FDMA is not considered an efficient method for digital transmission.

Another digital multiplexing technique is available that adds time division multiple access to AMPS to gain three channels for each FDMA channel. This effectively triples the number of calls that can be handled on a channel.

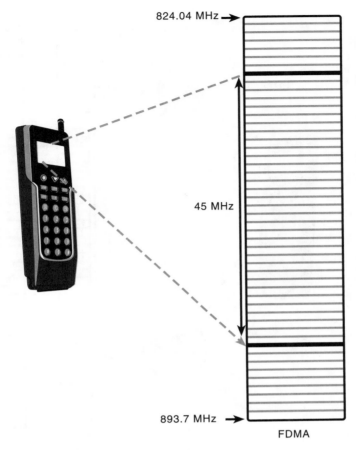

824.04 MHz →

45 MHz

893.7 MHz →

FDMA

FIGURE 14.7 **FDMA [Source: Brain, 9]**

TDMA

Time Division Multiple Access (TDMA) is used with digital cellular telephone communication. It divides each cellular channel into three time slots. Each time slot uses a narrow band of 30 KHz and 6.7 ms long, which is split into the three time slots. Voice data is converted to digital and is compressed. The compression uses less transmission space and increases the amount of data that can be carried.

TDMA uses two primary interim standards that specify the frequency bands available for mobile telephones. Interim standards are intended for trial use and must be reaffirmed every year. The Telecommunications Industry Association (TIA) approved the IS-54 standard at 800 MHz and the IS-136 standard at 1,900 MHz for TDMA. Interim Standard-54 (see Figure 14.8) is a North American wireless standard for second-generation TDMA systems. The Interim Standard I-136 is also referred to as Digital-AMPS, or **D-AMPS**. It divides the frequency bands available into one time slot at regular intervals. [Brain, 12]

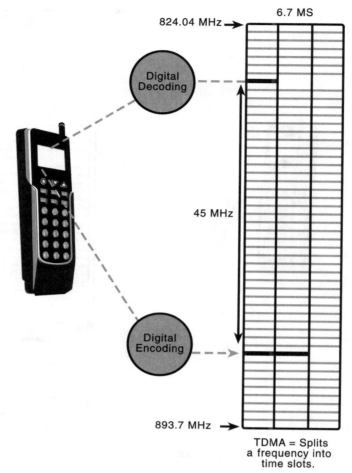

FIGURE 14.8 TDMA [Source: Brain, 13]

These new digital interim standards are currently being used in PCS systems. TDMA is also used as the primary access technology for GSM used in Europe, Australia, Asia, and Africa. TDMA offers the capability for GSM subscribers to use services in multiple countries. GSM stores all of the connection data and identification numbers required to access a specific wireless service provider on a **subscriber identification module (SIM) card**. These cards are small removable disks that can be easily inserted and removed from the GSM phone. When GSM users travel to different countries, they can switch to the SIM card that grants them access to the service provider network. D-AMPS, GSM, and Personal Digital Cellular (PDC) are the mobile phone services that use the TDMA technique. [Brain, 4]

CDMA

Code Division Multiple Access (CDMA) is a radically new concept in wireless communications that uses a form of spread-spectrum technology to provide wider channels for mobile communications. CDMA does not assign a specific frequency to each user. Every channel has the opportunity to use the full available spectrum. Instead, each individual conversation is encoded with a pseudo-random digital sequence.

CDMA is a multiplexing technique used to allow several signals to occupy a single transmission channel. Figure 14.9 shows that by using digital encoding CDMA can achieve speeds from 1,850 MHz to 1,990 MHz. CDMA combines analog-to-digital conversion and spread spectrum technologies. This combination supports many more signals per unit of bandwidth than analog modes do. [Brain, 11]

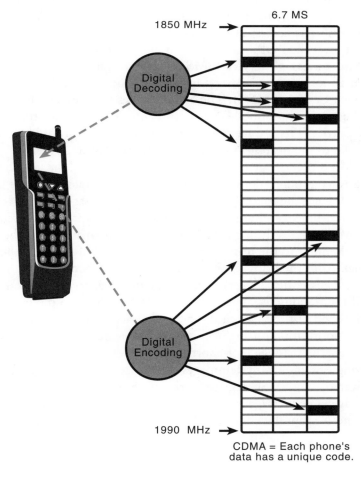

FIGURE 14.9 CDMA [Source: Brain, 11]

Unlike AMPS and D-AMPS, CDMA does not reuse frequency. Mobile phone users can share the same carrier frequency and the same 1.25 MHz band. Signal breakup, which can occur as a mobile phone passes from one cell to another, is minimized through the use of a soft handover on the CDMA network. CDMA requires precise power control to maximize the system's capacity and increase the battery life of the mobile phone. Therefore, some interference issues exist with mobile phones that transmit excessive power.

Global Wireless Internet

For the past 10 years, the ITU has been trying to set a global wireless networking standard. The closest thing to a worldwide standard today is GSM. Figure 14.10 shows an example of a global wireless architecture. **Wireless Access Service Providers (WASPs)** in Asia, Europe, and the United States support a high-speed connection to the Internet. Carrier A in the United States and European Union connects to its nearest POP (point of presence) and is able to transmit and receive signals over the POP's connection to the Internet. [Ztango, 19]

Short message service (SMS) is used to transmit short text messages to and from a mobile phone. After a message is sent, it is received by a **Short Message Service Center (SMSC).** The SMSC passes the message through the network to the destination mobile device. In Figure 14.10, notice that both the U.S. and EU Carrier B have dual connections; one is to the SMSC for SMS, and the other is to the nearest POP for other Internet-related services.

SMS is the next generation of communication and the least expensive mode of wireless communications. It is more or less the mobile version of instant messaging. Messages are routed for a few pennies per message over the Internet. SMS provides real-time communication for short messages for online discussions.

SMS operates through the SMSC in the following way: The SMSC sends a SMS Request to the **home location register (HLR)** to find the roaming customer. After the HLR receives the request, it responds to the SMSC with the subscriber's status. The status might be inactive, active, or roaming.

If the response is "inactive," the SMSC holds onto the message for a specified period of time. When the subscriber accesses the device, the HLR sends a SMS Notification to the SMSC, and the SMSC attempts delivery. The SMSC transfers the message in a Short Message Delivery Point to Point format to the serving system. The system pages the device and, if it responds, the message is delivered. The SMSC receives verification that the end user has received the message. The message is categorized as "sent" and the SMSC will not attempt to send it again. [Webopedia, 1]

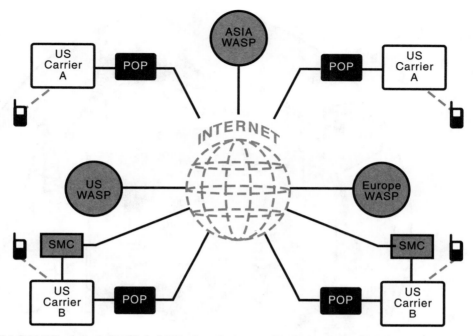

FIGURE 14.10 **Global Wireless Internet** **[Source: Ztango, 19]**

SMS is another catalyst for wireless build outs by WASP. Offering SMS provides carriers with an opportunity to sell new messaging services to their subscriber base. WASP will likely dominate the management of communications technologies over the next decade. This management will require several services designed to maintain reliable networks. Services they provide include remote monitoring for fault diagnostics, dispatching for repairs, database service reporting, and performance data collection.

Wireless Solution Model

WASPs look promising as a solution to offer any type of access required by wireless devices. Figure 14.11 shows that several interconnecting devices are required to establish a complete wireless solution model. The center of the figure shows how the environment gets connected to the Internet backbone and to local POPs. Gateways are provided for WAP (see next section) and SMS. A test environment is available for field-testing of new mobile applications over the network. This model supports multiplexing techniques, such as TDMA and CDMA, to accommodate both analog and digital wireless phones. GSM provides a global solution for messaging and multimedia. Advanced security is provided through co-location of application servers and a WAP gateway.

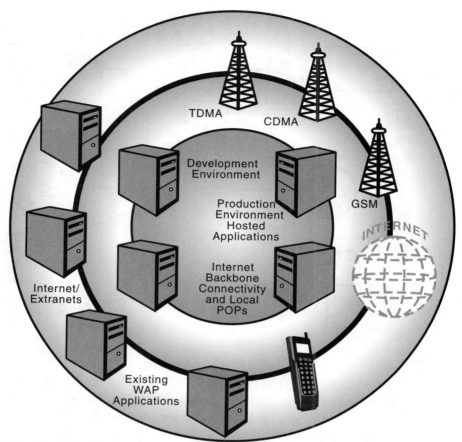

FIGURE 14.11 **Wireless Solutions Using WASPs [Source: Ztango, 15]**

TOPIC
review **Wireless Devices and Applications**

1. What is the purpose of cells?
2. What is the main difference between cellular and PCS technology?
3. What is the de facto wireless telecommunication standard in Europe?
4. What phenomenon makes wireless communication and broadcasting possible?
5. What is the range of frequencies used by cellular phones?

WIRELESS STANDARDS AND PROTOCOLS

In 1997, Nokia, Motorola, Ericsson, and Phone.com came together to create a universal standard to lead to the successful implementation of the wireless

Internet. Since then, more than 350 companies have joined them in the Open Mobile Alliance LTD. This Alliance is continually working on specifications for the wireless standard to ensure that it evolves in a timely and useful manner. The wireless standard they developed called **Wireless Application Protocol (WAP)** is a set of communication protocols that standardizes the ways that wireless devices, such as cellular telephones and radio transceivers, can be used for Internet access. [Tyson, 1] Wireless Internet requires the WAP for three main reasons:

- Transfer speed
- Size and readability
- Navigation

Most cell phones and Web-enabled PDAs have data transfer rates of 14.4 Kbps or less. Because Web pages today are full of graphics that would take an incredibly long time to download at 14.4 Kbps, wireless Internet content is typically text-based. When Web designers need to provide wireless Internet content, they create special text-only or low-graphics versions of the Web site. A Web server sends the data in HTTP format to a WAP gateway. The WAP gateway includes the translators required, which include the WAP encoder, script compiler, and protocol adapters that convert the HTTP information to **Wireless Markup Language (WML)**. The gateway then sends the converted data to the WAP client on the user's wireless device. [Tyson, 1]

The communication process between the gateway and the client relies on features of different parts of the WAP stack. Table 14.5 lists and describes the elements of the WAP stack.

PROTOCOL ELEMENT	DESCRIPTION
WAE	Wireless Application Environment. Holds the tools that wireless Internet content developers use. These include WML and WMLScript, a scripting language used in conjunction with WML. [Tyson, 1]
WSP	The Wireless Session Protocol. Determines whether a session between the device and the network will be connection-oriented or connectionless. In a connection-oriented session, data is passed both ways between the device and the network. Next, WSP sends the packet to the Wireless Transaction Protocol layer. If the session is connectionless, then WSP redirects the packet to the Wireless Datagram Protocol layer. Connectionless is commonly used for information that is broadcast or streamed from the network to the mobile device. [Tyson, 1]

TABLE 14.5 **WAP Elements**

PROTOCOL ELEMENT	DESCRIPTION
WTP	The Wireless Transaction Protocol. Acts like a traffic cop, keeping the data flowing in a logical and smooth manner. Also determines that each transaction request will be classified as: Reliable two-way, Reliable one-way, or Unreliable one-way. The WSP and WTP layers correspond to Hyper-Text Transfer Protocol (HTTP) in the TCP/IP (Transmission Control Protocol/Internet Protocol) suite. [Tyson, 1]
WTLS	Wireless Transport Layer Security. Provides many of the same security features found in the Transport Layer Security (TLS) part of TCP/IP. Checks data integrity, provides encryption, and performs client and server authentication. [Tyson, 1]
WDP	The Wireless Datagram Protocol. Works in conjunction with the network carrier layer. WDP makes it easy to adapt WAP to a variety of network carriers because the only change needed is to the information maintained at this level. [Tyson, 1]
Network carriers	Also called *bearers*. **Bearers** can be any of the existing technologies that wireless providers use, as long as information is provided at the WDP level to interface WAP with the bearer. [Tyson, 1]

TABLE 14.5 **WAP Elements, continued**

WAP enables communication between Web servers and mobile phones. The interaction between the two is described in the following steps:
1. The user turns on the device and opens the minibrowser.
2. The device sends out a radio signal, searching for service.
3. A connection is made with the user's service provider.
4. The user selects the Web site desired.
5. A request is sent to a WAP gateway server.
6. The gateway server retrieves the information via HTTP from the Web site.
7. The gateway server encodes the HTTP data as WML.
8. The WML-encoded data is sent to the user's device.
9. The wireless Internet version of the Web page selected appears on the user's mobile phone. [Tyson, 1]

1. What is the purpose of WAP?
2. How is HTTP information converted to display on mobile phones?
3. Which WAP protocols correspond to HTTP in the TCP/IP protocol suite?
4. What type of security is provided by WTLS?
5. Which WAP protocol works in conjunction with the network carrier layer?

WIRELESS SECURITY

Security is more difficult to provide for mobile devices than it is for LANs because the mobile user moves between locations that are outside the organization and for which the LAN lacks physical control. A wireless network is fundamentally less secure than a wired one. **Wired Equivalent Privacy (WEP)** is a security protocol designed to provide a wireless area network (WLAN) with a level of security and privacy comparable to what is usually expected of a wired LAN. However, WEP does not offer authentication, access control, or data integrity for mobile phones. [Whatis, 1]

Many predict that the next device to be targeted by malicious computer hackers and virus creators is the mobile phone. If a malicious piece of code gets control of a user's phone, it can watch and intercept traffic flows for e-mail, browsing, and file transfers. The hacker will be able to get the user's messages and send them elsewhere. Because mobile phones now can send and retrieve information from the Internet, they are exposed to the same threats and targeted attacks as PCs.

Security Challenges and Limitations

Wireless device security has several challenges and limitations. One challenge involves the security exposure inherent with devices that can travel anywhere. Cellular/PCS devices are vulnerable to interception/detection because the radio link they use is exposed for several miles. Another common limitation is that cell phones have limited processing power, memory, and data storage. Many encryption algorithms used for PCs cannot be used with cell phones because they require too much memory or bandwidth to execute the algorithm. Another challenge is that cell phones are not programmable. Therefore, security encryption keys have to be set up before the cell phone is purchased.

Recently in Japan, malicious e-mail messages were sent to cell phones. The e-mail referenced an Internet link. When the user clicked on the Internet link, it caused phones to repeatedly dial the national emergency number. An apparent bug in the configuration of the phone resulted in the wireless carrier halting all emergency calls until the bug was removed. On the other side of the world in Europe, mobile devices using SMS were randomly sent pieces of binary code that crashed mobile phones. The crash forced the mobile user to detach the battery from the mobile phone and reboot. [ISN, 1]

As yet, no published reports of phone hacking or viruses are currently available. In the future, however, mobile phone owners might have to install personal firewalls on their mobile phones. This might be due in part to flaws within the phones themselves. For example, in 1999, Israeli researchers found a design flaw in the GSM scrambling algorithm. This flaw allowed de-scrambling of the private conversations carried by hundreds of millions of mobile phone users.

Secure Wireless Communications

The key to designing wireless network security is to provide for a method to keep data confidential and private. Most mobile users want to maintain the integrity of their data and prevent unauthorized modification. Likewise, they want to be sure of the authenticity of any messages that they receive. The security must provide protection for communications from the wireless device to the base station.

Some techniques for wireless security include the following:
- WTLS
- SignText
- WIM
- WPKI

WTLS

Wireless Transport Layer Security (WTLS) provides strong security between a WAP client and the gateway. Figure 14.12 shows the elements of a secure transmission from a Web server to a mobile phone. The goal is to keep the customer's data private. Encryption techniques (SSL) extend security all the way to the application server. End-to-end transport security is provided at the WAP gateway and the Web server. WTLS security using RSA algorithms provides encryption of user data. After the data passes through the WAP gateway, it is decrypted from WTLS and then encrypted in SSL to present to the application server. [Ztango, 18]

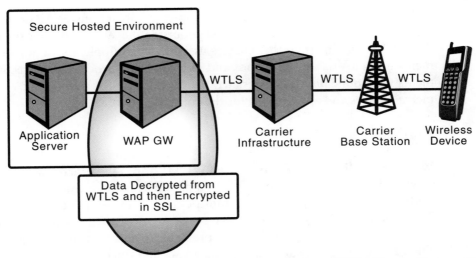

FIGURE 14.12 **Secured Hosted Wireless Access Using WTLS [Source: Ztango, 18]**

SignText

SignText provides a digital signature to WAP applications that require the ability to provide persistent proof that someone has authorized a transaction. This method is ideal for e-commerce transactions. Using WML, the SignText function executes a WML script, which defines the use of a Crypto application programming interface (API) to provide the cryptography. [Certicom, 1]

The WAP browser displays the exact text to be digitally signed and asks the user to confirm it. After the data has been signed, both the signature and the data are sent across the network. When the server receives it, it extracts the digital signature and validates it against a security database. [Certicom, 1]

This method provides authentication security but does not provide confidentiality. It is used mainly to guarantee the integrity of data sent to the server, and also can be used in place of personal identification numbers and passwords used for authentication.

WIM

The **WAP Identity Module (WIM)** is used to store and process information needed for user identification and authentication. Encryption keys are processed and stored within the WIM. This technique is used when performing WTLS and application level security functions. In a cellular phone, WIM is implemented as the **Subscriber Identity Module (SIM)**, which is a unique number that identifies the device. WIM requires the device to be tamper-resistant, which means specific physical hardware is used so that the module cannot be tampered with. [WAP Forum, 1]

WIM is targeted toward mobile e-commerce transactions. WAP devices that use WIM never expose their private keys outside the WIM. For that reason, WIM is a secure method that enables users to, for example, make mobile payments using a Visa card for goods and services. The introduction of secure payments via mobile phone has initiated the development of new mobile e-commerce services and applications for the consumer. [Nokia, 1]

WPKI

Wireless Public Key Infrastructure (WPKI) brings the functions of PKI to wireless devices. WPKI supports the standard PKI components: Certification Authorities (CAs), Registration Authorities (RAs), and end-entities. In addition, WPKI defines a *PKI portal*. The **PKI portal** is essentially a security-protocol converter that translates wireless PKI protocols to and from Internet protocols. The PKI portal is software that uses databases and directories to store and distribute certificates and their status. [Verisign, 1]

A wireless PKI portal enables certificate enrollment for users and devices. It automates the registration functions and allows for transparent authentication of users or devices directly from the authentication source database. [Verisign, 1] WAP devices and gateways contact the PKI portal, which handles RA functions such as user registration, approval/denial of requests for first-time certificates, and renewal of expired certificates. The PKI portal translates the WPKI requests from wireless clients to the appropriate format for the CA. It also processes and converts responses from the CA on behalf of the wireless client. [Certicom, 3-4]

The E-Business Technology Institute provides software solutions for WPKI and has defined a new version of it called **Server-Assisted Wireless Public Key Infrastructure (SAWPKI)**. Mobile devices use SAWPKI to contact a powerful server, which is responsible for the delegation of public key cryptographic processing. The client drives the server to perform the PKI operations. The RSA cryptographic algorithm is reformulated for wireless and the SAWPKI server is driven by the client as a blind calculator to produce the cryptography. The information is sent with encryption and a signature that is masked in a non-decodable format. [ETI, 1] The steps for a SAWPKI operation are as follows:

1. A customer uses the mobile device to establish a secure channel for transacting data and payment instructions.
2. The cryptographic operations are offloaded to a SAWPKI server on the Internet.
3. The customer's mobile device communicates in its normal way just as if it were a full-fledged PKI-enabled computer.
4. E-merchants are able to accept transactions in the same way they do from wired PC users over the Internet. [ETI, 1]

Other Wireless Technologies and Security Methods

Mobile e-commerce brings with it greater concern for strong security for wireless communications. Acceptable use of mobile devices is difficult to control. There is a delicate balance between security and acceptable use. New standards are emerging for wireless LANs and short-range radio technology for mobile devices. These advancements in wireless technology continue to improve secure information-sharing and easy access to the Internet.

Wi-Fi or 802.11b

Wi-Fi stands for wireless fidelity, which describes the degree to which an electronic device accurately reproduces its effect (radio – sound, TV - picture). Wi-Fi is a networking standard for WLANs in homes and offices. It provides broadband Internet access to PCs and laptops within a few hundred feet of a Wi-Fi base station or transmitter and offers easy access to the Internet from conference rooms, airport lounges, or libraries. A special plug-in Wi-Fi circuit card must be installed in each laptop or PC to access the Wi-Fi base station. Wi-Fi operates on an unlicensed airwave spectrum in the 2.4 GHz range and supports a data transfer speed of 11 Mbps. [Kane, 1]

Wi-Fi is part of the 802.11 group of standards (802.11a, 802.11b, and 802.11g) published by the IEEE (Institute of Electrical and Electronics Engineers) for wireless networking. All four standards use the Ethernet protocol and CSMA/CA for collision avoidance over Ethernet networks. The difference between 802.11 and 802.11b used for Wi-Fi is the modulation method. With 802.11, the phase-shift keying modulation method is used, whereas 802.11b uses *complementary code keying*. **Complementary code keying (CCK)** is a set of 64 (8-bit) code words used to encode data. The code words use unique mathematical properties allowing them to be correctly distinguished from one another even when they encounter heavy noise or multipath interference. CCK allows higher data speeds for wireless communications. [Search Networking, 1] [Webopedia, 1]

Most organizations that adopt Wi-Fi are concerned about security. The WEP encryption standard provides some security safeguards; however, to be fully secure, the LAN needs to provide a layered security defense (as discussed in Chapter 8) including VPN (Virtual Private Network), IPsec (Internet Protocol Security), a firewall, and a DMZ (demilitarized zone).

Bluetooth

Bluetooth (discussed in Chapter 1) is a short-range radio technology used by mobile phones, computers, and personal digital assistants (PDAs). Bluetooth provides built-in encryption and verification for security, and is used to simplify communications between mobile devices and the Internet. [Webopedia, 1]

Each device that uses Bluetooth technology requires a low-cost transceiver chip that is embedded on the logic board or is included on an add-in adapter card. The transceiver transmits and receives at the unused frequency band of 2.45 GHz. Each device has a unique 48-bit address that Bluetooth uses. The maximum range for transmission is 10 meters and the data transfer rate is 1 to 2 Mbps. [Search Networking, 1]

Bluetooth uses a master/slave relationship that supports one-to-one or one-to-many connections. The wireless connection between two or more Bluetooth devices allows changes in frequencies at fixed time intervals. The master determines the timing of the hopping intervals and the selection and sequence of channels used for transmission. Bluetooth strives to provide automatic avoidance of channels with interference and can be programmed to avoid specific channels using special management software. [Brown, 1]

Users enjoy Bluetooth technology because it makes their LAN connection mobile. An organization's employees benefit from this technology because they no longer have to be at their desks to retrieve files or papers. They can access the LAN through their PDA or mobile phone though a wireless connection using Bluetooth. Bluetooth uses a frequency-hopping spread spectrum radio technology, which allows it to communicate in areas such as airports and hospitals where there is significant electromagnetic interference. This technology works well for quick lookups to retrieve critical data. The transmission speed, however, is much slower than the 100 Mbps provided by a wired connection to the LAN.

Wireless Jamming

Wireless devices provide a truly mobile society with easy access methods to an organization's information. The question of security always looms in the background. In their effort to find a good universal solution, some organizations have tried wireless jamming to police their wireless communications.

Security organizations, law enforcement, and the military have adopted a variety of radio-frequency jamming technologies. These wireless jamming technologies can block calls and prevent signals from reaching phones. Although there are good reasons for blocking mobile device communications, many countries, including the United States, are reluctant to legalize wireless jamming. Some of the issues to be considered are jamming leakage, difficulty in isolating the range of blockage, and the telecommunications industry's opposition to legislation. In the United States, mobile devices are considered safety and security tools for medical and personal emergencies. Doctors, police, and fire rescue personnel use adjacent airwaves for their communications. Many see the airwaves as a public asset, and wireless jamming in most cases is seen as a socially irresponsible interference with that asset. Currently, there are no countries where phone jamming is "totally legal." [Wrolstad, 1]

1. What type of security do most mobile users want?
2. What encryption algorithm is used with WTLS?
3. How does SignText provide proof that someone has authorized a transaction?
4. How is WIM implemented in a cellular phone?
5. What is the purpose of the PKI portal used in WPKI security?

SATELLITE PHONES

Consultants, newspaper reporters, disaster relief workers, and telecommunication workers who travel to remote parts of the globe use satellite phones. Satellite phones are used to send and receive radio signals to and from geostationary satellites. Some satellite phones will work anywhere there is line of sight. This means, however, that the phone's antenna must be outside with an unobstructed view of most of the sky. Other satellite phones use non-directional antenna, which means it doesn't have to be pointed in any particular direction. Both types of satellite phones can be supplied with long antenna cable extensions so that they can be operated inside a building. For vehicle and maritime use, the satellite phone can use an optional automatic antenna, which points itself towards the satellite. [Orbit Research, 1]

Satellite phone communication is comprised of the satellite network, the ground network, and the satellite phone. The design of the satellite network enables voice and data communication to be routed anywhere in the world. Across very long distances, voice calls and data transmissions are relayed from one satellite to another until they reach the satellite that has line of sight with the satellite phone user.

On the ground is a **Land Earth Station (LES)**, which is basically a land base station that sends radio waves to and receives radio waves from the geostationary satellites (GEOs). The LES is connected to the traditional PSTN or an ISDN (Integrated Services Digital Network), and the communication method is established according to the type of call being made. [7E, 1]

Satellite services are offered in all four-ocean regions: Atlantic Ocean East Region (AOR-E), Indian Ocean Region (IOR), Pacific Ocean Region (POR), and Atlantic Ocean West Region (AOR-W). As these ocean regions overlap somewhat, a satellite phone user might be able to receive a working signal from two ocean region satellites. Satellite users can then choose the ocean region that offers them the strongest signal.

Satellite Phone Features

All satellite phones are not the same. Common features of a satellite phone, as shown in Figure 14.13, include voice, SMS, caller ID, voice mail service, position location, data transmission, and a digital facsimile. This particular satellite phone has two antennas. One is a cellular antenna used for standard cellular phone calls, while the other, located on the back of the unit, is the satellite antenna. Navigation options include scroll and smart keys. With this tri-mode satellite phone, the user can make satellite, digital, or analog calls. Other satellite phones are dual purposed and will work indoors in cellular mode when the user is within a cellular serviced area.

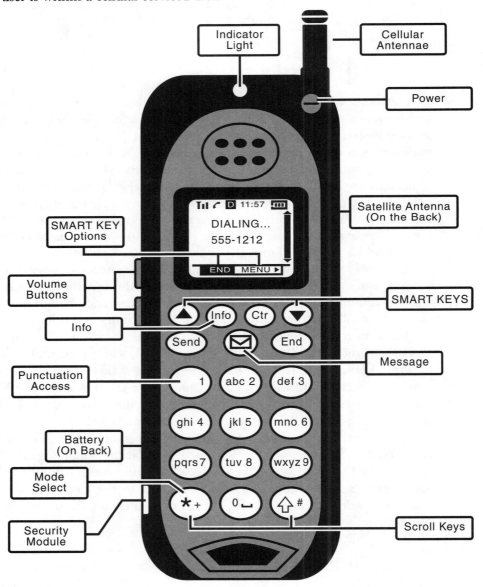

FIGURE 14.13 QUALCOMM Satellite Phone [Source: Qualcomm Globalstar, 1]

Satellite phones require cautious use, especially around television or radio. These phones can cause interference with the radio or TV signal. Regulatory agencies such as the FCC can prohibit use of these phones when interference cannot be eliminated.

Satellite versus Cellular Technology

Satellite phones look similar to and have some of the same features as a cellular phone. A clear distinction is made, however, in size, weight, line of sight, and cost. One of the main differences is the size of the antenna required. Satellite phones require a larger satellite antenna to receive satellite signals. When the satellite phone is used outdoors, the phone communicates with the geostationary satellite, which bounces the signal back down to the nearest station and then interconnects to local telephone systems.

A satellite phone call is placed by taking the following steps:

1. A satellite phone caller places the call via the satellite to one or more gateways.
2. The gateway routes the call to the existing phone network which is referred to as a cellular Public Land Mobile Network (PLMN) network.
3. The PLMN routes the call to the intended receiver. This completes the call.
4. Logging information such as call duration, service used, and service area used is reported to the service provider for billing purposes. [Qualcomm Globalstar, 1]

Many satellite phone manufacturers today offer dual- or tri-mode phones that provide service for both cellular and satellite communications.

Satellite Phone Roaming

Using a global air interface, a satellite phone user can roam to an area served by GSM or vice versa. This is commonly referred to as *satellite phone roaming*. **Satellite phone roaming** requires satellite phones to meet specific standards published by ANSI. These standards are specified as ANSI-41 and GSM-based satellite phones. A gateway, which is referred to as a mobile ground station, provides the ANSI-41 capability and works with a GSM MSC. These gateways have three satellite dish antennas, a switching station, and remote operating controls. The gateway is the termination point for network transmission and signaling. It receives transmissions from orbiting satellites, and processes calls and switches to the ground network. The gateway is connected to the PSTN via E1/T1 trunk lines. A gateway can service more than one country and is owned by the service provider. [Qualcomm Globalstar, 1] Figure 14.14 shows how the GSM MSC connects to a gateway that transmits to the satellite.

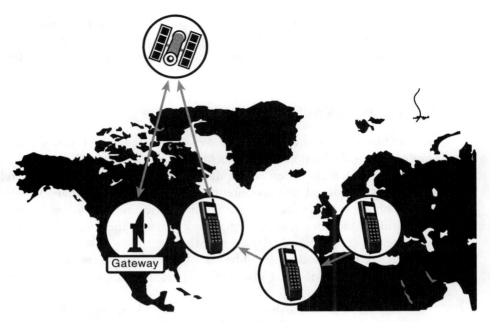

FIGURE 14.14 **Satellite Phone Roaming [Source: Qualcomm Globalstar, 2]**

The gateway includes support for both ANSI-41 and GSM capability. However, each type of phone only supports one of these standards. When a subscriber with a Dual-Mode GSM phone roams to North America, his or her phone will still operate through the gateway. When the gateway receives the signal from the satellite, it will be routed to the GSM MSC for processing. The phone will continue to operate using GSM protocols. Similarly, if a subscriber with an ANSI-41 tri-mode phone roams to Europe, the phone will operate using ANSI-41 protocols.

Portable Satellite Terminals

Portable satellite phones and terminals are sophisticated engineering devices that provide high-quality, static-free voice and data transmissions over a satellite network. These devices offer telephone, data, and video services in areas of the world where other everyday communication services do not exist. This offers users an environment where they can transmit and receive information from anywhere on Earth.

A **portable satellite terminal** acts as a powerful communication center. It provides simple reliable satellite communications from anywhere in the world. You can browse the Internet, check your e-mail, conduct video conferences, send a fax, or simply speak using a cordless phone. The satellite terminal uses geostationary satellites for high-quality long-distance geographic coverage. It provides a portable 64 Kbps/ISDN communications service. The transmit frequency is between 1,626.5 and 1,660.5 MHz, while the receive frequency is in the 1,525 to 1,559 MHz frequency. [NERA, 1]

Some portable satellite terminals also include a built-in cordless phone base station that can connect up to 12 cordless phones into a local phone network. It uses a 4.8 Kbps voice channel to allow for telephone conversations through the satellite connection. The entire terminal is modular and can fit in a laptop-type carrying case. The power source for the unit is a long-life, built-in Lithium-ion battery.

Portable satellite terminals are often used by news agencies and the military in war zones to provide telephone communications across the globe. Using a combination of satellite phones and portable satellite terminals, news reporters can broadcast and transmit live video of the events as they happen. The equipment can be moved easily between locations; however, it requires properly trained personnel to operate and troubleshoot transmission problems.

TOPIC review — Satellite Phones

1. What type of signals are transmitted and received by satellite phones?
2. How do satellite phone calls reach the PSTN?
3. What is the main difference between satellite and cellular phones?
4. What is the purpose of the gateway used for roaming satellite phones?
5. What is the power source for a portable satellite terminal?

CHAPTER SUMMARY

Wireless communication uses electromagnetic waves to transmit information over the airwaves. Some wireless devices are fixed while others are mobile or portable. Wireless communication requires a regional division of areas used for transmission frequencies. Mobile devices can support either analog or digital transmission. Analog mobile devices use conversion chips to translate incoming and outgoing analog signals to digital. Digital mobile devices have digital signal processors that perform signal calculations at high speed.

Mobile e-commerce allows users to transact business from mobile handheld devices. Mobile carriers have built a wireless infrastructure to support always-on access and a high-speed connection to the Internet. Levels of mobile communication include voice communication, mobile information, and e-commerce. Many different types of wireless technologies (GSM, GPRS, EDGE, I-Mode, IXRTT, 3G, and UMTS) are being used today to provide for mobile telephone systems. They all use the electromagnetic spectrum to transmit through the airwaves.

The electromagnetic radiation spectrum is the complete range of wavelengths from radio waves to light. The spectrum includes power, telephone, radio waves, microwaves, infrared, ultraviolet, X-rays, and gamma rays. Frequency is measured in hertz, megahertz, gigahertz, and terahertz. Digital signals are only represented in kilohertz. Frequency ranges go from low to high; different frequency ranges are dedicated to different applications such as submarines, marine navigation, radio, TV, cell and PCS phones, and satellite.

Cellular radio equipment provides frequency bands for wireless voice communication. Cellular phones contact a base station to establish a channel to transmit over. Frequency reuse allows radio channels to be reused to provide for more than one conversation at a time. When a cellular phone user travels, handovers are used to switch calls to stronger-frequency channels from a different cell. The MTSO establishes a connection between the wireless communications and the land-based phone system. Mobile phones have numbers (ESN, MIN, SID) used to provide unique identification for each phone.

Frames, slots, and channels are used to organize digital information. The frame carries the conversation or data along with error detection and correction bits. Multiplexing techniques are used to provide time slots for several calls allowing them to occupy one channel. Wireless multiplexing techniques (FDMA, TDMA, CDMA) provide different methods to provide multiple access for analog and digital transmissions.

Wireless standards and protocols have been published to standardize the way that wireless devices are used for transmission. The protocol stack, WAP, has several elements (WAE, WSP, WTP, WTLS, WDP, Bearers) to enable communication between Web servers and mobile phones.

Wireless security provides for secure communication to keep wireless voice and data transmissions private and confidential. Wireless security techniques are designed to provide security between the base station and the wireless device. Wireless security techniques (WTLS, SignText, WIM, WPKI) all use different methods to provide strong security for wireless communications. Other wireless technologies (Wi-Fi and Bluetooth) provide broadband access to the Internet from conference rooms, airport lounges, or libraries. Bluetooth provides built-in encryption and verification for security.

Satellite phones are used by workers who need access for voice and data services from remote locations anywhere in the world. Satellite phones are used to send and receive radio signals to and from geostationary satellites. Satellite phones either use line-of-sight or non-directional antennae to transmit to the satellite. Some satellite phones have a special cellular antenna allowing them to be used inside of a building. Gateways are used on the ground to provide a termination point and to process calls and switch them over to the PSTN. Portable satellite terminals are used frequently by news agencies and the military to provide for telephone and video conferencing through reliable satellites from anywhere in the world.

CHAPTER REVIEW QUESTIONS

(This quiz also can be printed from the Encore! CD that accompanies this book. File name—Chap14review.)

Circle a letter (a-d) for each question. Choose only one answer for each.

1. Cell phone technology is considered a form of:
   a. laser.
   b. infrared.
   c. radio.
   d. microwave.

2. The use of mobile devices to interact and transact business over the Internet is called:
   a. unified e-commerce.
   b. messaging e-commerce.
   c. wireless e-commerce.
   d. mobile e-commerce.

3. What is the 3G service designed for high-quality broadband information for e-commerce and entertainment services?
   a. EDGE
   b. UMTS
   c. GPRS
   d. IXRTT

4. What organization in the United States tightly controls RF transmission?
   a. EIA
   b. IEEE
   c. FCC
   d. ANSI

5. The base station communicates to the cell phone through a:
   a. block.
   b. circuit.
   c. channel.
   d. band.

6. The multiplexing technique used with digital cellular telephone communication is called:
   a. TDMA.
   b. FDMA.
   c. CDMA.
   d. WDMA.

7. The next generation of communication and the least expensive mode of wireless communication is:
   a. GPS.
   b. AMPS.
   c. WASP.
   d. SMS.

8. Data is presented to a WAP gateway in what format?
   a. SMSC
   b. HTTP
   c. XML
   d. FTP

9. What is used to provide a digital signature to WAP applications?
   a. WTLS
   b. WIM
   c. SignText
   d. API

10. Satellite phones are used to send and receive radio signals anywhere there is a:
    a. portal.
    b. line of sight.
    c. antenna.
    d. base station.

Circle the correct letter (A-E) that corresponds to the descriptions below. Choose only one answer for each.

   A. GSM
   B. WTP
   C. I-Mode
   D. D-AMPS
   E. MTSO

11. A B C D E   Supports Web browsing and e-mail, and allows users to execute banking and stock transactions from their mobile phones.

12. A B C D E   A digital mobile phone system that has become the de facto wireless telephone standard in Europe.

13. A B C D E   A cellular system's main mobile switching center.

14. A B C D E   Element of the WAP stack that acts like a traffic cop, keeping data flowing in a logical and smooth manner.

15. A B C D E   Divides the frequency bands available into one time slot at regular intervals.

A. LES
B. WPKI
C. Wi-Fi
D. 3G
E. WIM

16. A B C D E Encryption keys are processed and stored within it.

17. A B C D E An ITU specification for third-generation mobile communication technology.

18. A B C D E A security technique that brings the functions of PKI to wireless devices.

19. A B C D E Land base station that sends radio waves to and from geo-stationary satellites.

20. A B C D E A networking standard for WLANs in homes and offices.

INTERNET EXERCISES

1. Log on to the Internet and key the following URL:

   www.wapforum.org/what/WAPWhite_Paper1.pdf

   A. What protocols are supported by wireless devices in WAP 2.0?
   B. Does WAP 2.0 support 3G cellular?
   C. What are the major architectural components of WAP 2.0?
   D. Why doesn't WAP 2.0 require WAP gateways (proxy)?

2. Key the following URL:

   www.fcw.com/supplements/homeland/2002/sup1/hom-comm-03-25-02.asp

   A. How many United States Postal Service (USPS) branch offices use satellite connections as either their primary or backup communication method?
   B. Why has satellite technology become more attractive as a WAN service in recent years?
   C. How much increase in link time is attributed to TCP/IP framing, queuing, and switching?
   D. What types of workarounds are used to handle adverse weather conditions?

CONCEPT EXERCISES

Concept Narrative
(This narrative exercise also can be printed from the Encore! CD that accompanies this book. File name—Chap14connar.)

Fill in the blanks of the following narrative.

The _____ _____ _____ is used to store and process information needed for user identification and authentication. _____ keys are processed and stored within the WIM. This technique is used when performing _____ and application level security functions. In a cellular phone, WIM is implemented as the _____ _____ _____, which is a unique number that identifies the device. WIM requires the device to be tamper-resistant which means specific physical hardware is used so that the module cannot be tampered with.

WIM is targeted toward _____ _____ transactions. _____ devices that use WIM never expose their _____ keys outside the WIM. For that reason, WIM is a secure method that enables users to, for example, make mobile payments using a Visa card for goods and services. The introduction of secure payments via a mobile phone has initiated the development of new mobile e-commerce services and applications for the consumer.

Concept Table
(This table exercise also can be printed from the Encore! CD that accompanies this book. File name—Chap14contab.)

Read each statement carefully and choose the type of wireless multiplexing being described. Use only one "X" per statement.

STATEMENT	TYPES OF WIRELESS MULTIPLEXING		
	FDMA	TDMA	CDMA
1. A unique code is assigned to each call and spread over the available frequencies.			
2. Each call is on a separate frequency.			
3. Assigns each call a certain "slice of time" on a designated frequency.			
4. Used primarily for analog transmission.			

5. Uses spread spectrum technology to provide wider channels for mobile communication.			
6. Used with digital cellular telephone communication.			
7. A multiplexing technique used to allow several signals to occupy a single transmission channel.			
8. Voice data is converted to digital and is compressed.			
9. Voice channels are split into identical sections of bandwidth.			
10. The primary access technology for GSM used in Europe.			

Concept Picture

(This picture exercise also can be printed from the Encore! CD that accompanies this book. File name—Chap14conpic.)

In this exercise, look at the picture of the Secure Hosted Environment for a wireless device and label the missing elements.

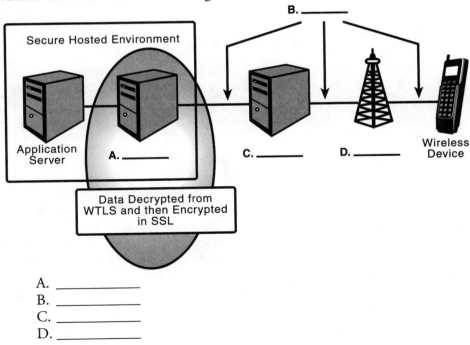

A. _____
B. _____
C. _____
D. _____

CASE STUDY

LANDMARK GREETINGS

Objective:

Investigate the use of wireless and satellite phone technologies to improve business resumption after a major disaster.

Company Profile:

Landmark Greetings is the world's largest maker of greeting cards. Today its greeting cards are sold to 16,000 retail outlets nationwide.

Current Situation:

Landmark Greetings recently suffered a major fire that burned down its main corporate office in St. Paul, Minnesota. The company has several unfilled greeting card orders and the entire inventory was wiped out in the fire. The company needs to restore business operations quickly. Many of the greeting card sales agents had offices in the corporate headquarters building and now are working out of their homes.

Business Information Requirements:

Landmark Greetings was able to locate an empty warehouse for rent a few blocks away. Even though the company suffered a great loss, it was able to salvage some of the publishing equipment and moved it to the new warehouse location. The company requested the IT department have information services available within five days.

Communication System Requirements:

A data communications link is required at the warehouse location to link to the Internet. The company needs its database information installed as soon as possible to find customer orders so the employees can notify the customers about the service disruption. Because the sales agents are now operating from their homes, the company decided the quickest way to restore service was to invest in mobile phones. They requested the IT department to set up a secure environment for wireless device access into the corporate e-mail system.

Information System Solution:

1. The company contacted its insurance company and ordered new servers and data communications equipment.
2. IT made an urgent request to the telecom service provider to have new data lines installed at the warehouse location within three days.
3. After securing a new site, the company wanted to get IT services up quickly. Luckily, the data was backed up on tape and the company requested the tapes from its off-site storage location. The company set up the database server and all of the data was recovered.
4. To accommodate the secure wireless access into the database and e-mail system, the company purchased additional services to set up a WAP gateway and application server. The company used WTLS transport to provide the security it required.
5. The IT department contracted for satellite services and purchased a few satellite phones for salesmen who had territories in mountainous areas. The satellite phones connected to the nearest satellite, and the dish antenna and VSAT hub were connected to the Internet so that salesmen could establish Web access for e-mail and simple database information.

Examine the configuration Landmark Greetings implemented as shown in Figure 14.15, and then answer the Study Questions that follow.

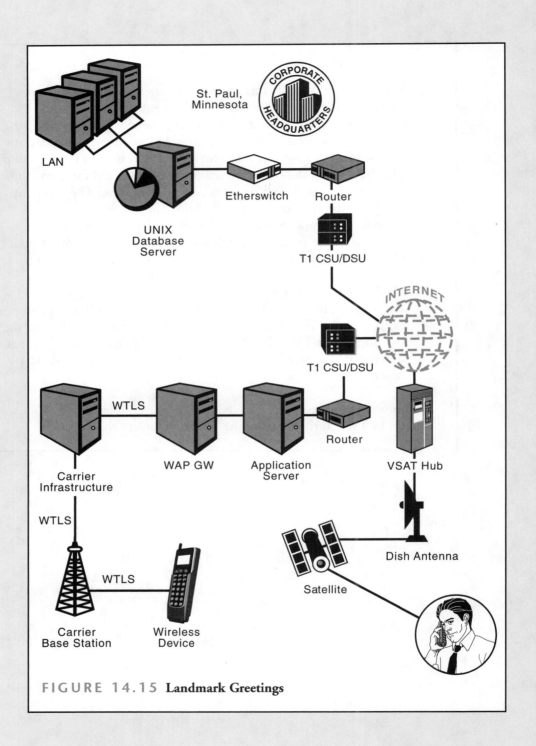

FIGURE 14.15 **Landmark Greetings**

CASE STUDY QUESTIONS

1. Do you think the company gave the IT department enough time to re-establish services?
2. Does the insurance company replace hardware and software?
3. How was the company able to recover the data into the database so quickly?
4. Do you think the company would be able to acquire the wireless hardware and get it installed and configured in 5 days?
5. Will the satellite phones be able to access users on the PSTN?

GROUP TERM PROJECT

Open and print the file *ProjectBudget* from the Encore! CD that came with this book. Consider the costs associated with the project. At this point, look into all of the resources (personnel, travel and after-support costs) required, and detail the costs for each of the eight locations. Next, gather the costs for each phase of the project and give a summary total for each phase. Finally, list the total costs for all hardware, software, and maintenance for the entire project. Provide a grand total for the entire project and compare the total to the proposed budget. If you are over budget, determine whether there are any opportunities to cut costs by using different equipment or software. If you are within the budget, then you have achieved the objectives of the project.

WAN PROJECT PLAN

BUDGET

**PROJECT
PLAN:**   **DATE:**

A.   **Resource Costs (People, Travel and After-Support Costs) per Location**

B.   **Cost for Each Phase**

C.   **Total Cost for Project (Hardware, Software, and Maintenance)**

CHAPTER TERMS

CHAPTER BIBLIOGRAPHY

Book, Magazine, Presentation Citations

Novell. *Networking Technologies*. Provo: Novell Education, 1995: 3-3.
Sheldon, Tom. *Encyclopedia of Networking and Telecommunications*. New York: Osborne/McGraw-Hill, 2001: 1-1447.

Web Citations

7E, "FAQs – Satphones," 7E Communications, <www.7e.com/content/faqs/faq_satphones.htm> (2002).

AIC, "Report of the Working Group 1," Asian Info Communications Council, www.aic.or.jp/conference/25th/PDF/Report%20of%20WG1.PDF> (23 April 2001).

Brain, Marshall and Jeff Tyson, "How Cell Phones Work," How Stuff Works, <www.howstuffworks.com/cell-phone.htm> (2002).

Brown, Bruce and Marge, "Bluetooth Real World, Part I," ExtremeTech, <www.extremetech.com/article2/0,3973,9259,00.asp> (2002).

Certicom, "Trustpoint JAVA," Certicom, <www.certicom.com> (2002).

ETI, "Server Assisted Wireless Public Key Infrastructure," E-Business Technology Institute, <www.eti.hku.hk/eti/web/p_s_wiress.html> (2002).

Farley, Tom, "Digital Wireless Basics: Mobile Phone History," Telecom Writing, <www.privateline.com/PCS/history.htm> (2002).

Hannigan, Brendan; Justin Bruton; Erin Roland; and Erin Zohar, "The Dawn of Mobile eCommerce," The Forrester Report, <www.forrester.com/ER/Research/Report/0,1338,7827,FF.html> (2001).

IEC, "Cellular Communications," International Engineering Consortium, <www.iec.org/> (2001).

ISN, "Security Watch," International Relations and Security Network, <www.isn.ethz.ch/infoservice/secwatch/> (2002).

Kane, Margaret, "Wi-Fi getting new security standard," CNET, <news.com.com/2102-1033-964046.html> (2002).

NERA, "Nera WorldCommunicator Portable Inmarsat M4," NERA Telecommunications, <www.satellite-phones-direct.com/m4_worldcomm.html> (2002).

Nokia, "Nokia Secure: Enabling the Mobile Internet," Nokia, <www.nokia.com/ipsecurity/whitepaper_form.html#wp> (2002).

Orbit Research, "Satellite Telephone," Orbit Research LTD, <www.orbitresearch.co.uk/docs/phonespec.html> (2002).

QUALCOMM Globalstar, "Products & Services," Globalstar USA, <www.globalstarusa.com/products/user_guides.shtml> (2002).

Search Networking, "I-mode," Search Networking, <www.searchnetworking.com/> (2002).

Search Networking, "CCK," Search Networking, <www.searchnetworking.com/> (2002).

Search Networking, "Bluetooth," Search Networking, <www.searchnetworking.com/> (2002).

Search Networking, "Radio Frequency," Search Networking, <www.searchnetworking.com/> (2002).

Search Networking, "GSM," Search Networking,
   (2002).

Search Networking, "EDGE," Search Networking,
   <www.searchnetworking.com> (2002)

Search Networking, "GPRS" Search Networking,
   <www.searchnetworking.com> (2002).

Tyson, Jeff, "How Wireless Internet Works," How Stuff Works,
   <www.howstuffworks.com/wireless-internet.htm> (2002).

UMTS, "Evolution to 3G/UMTS Services," UMTS Forum,
   , (2002)

Verisign, "Building an E-Commerce Trust Infrastructure," Verisign,
   <https://www.verisign.com/cgi-bin/
   clearsales_cgi/leadgen.htm?form_id=0045&toc=w110222810045000&emai
   l=> (2002).

WAP Forum, "WAP Architecture," Open Mobile Alliance,
   <www1.wapforum.org/tech/documents/WAP-210-WAPArch-20010712-
   a.pdf> (July, 2001).

Webopedia, "Bluetooth," Webopedia, <http:/www.webopedia.com> (2002).

Webopedia, "Cellular," Webopedia, <http:/www.webopedia.com> (2002).

Webopedia, "PCS," Webopedia, <http:/www.webopedia.com> (2002).

Webopedia, "3G," Webopedia, <http:/www.webopedia.com> (2002).

Webopedia, "SMSC," Webopedia, <http:/www.webopedia.com> (2002).

Webopedia, "HLR," Webopedia, <http:/www.webopedia.com> (2002).

Webopedia, "CCK," Webopedia, <http:/www.webopedia.com> (2002).

Whatis, "WEP," Tech Target,
   <searchsecurity.techtarget.com/sDefinition/0,,sid14_gci549087,00.html>
   (2002)

Whatis, "Electromagnetic Radiation Spectrum," Tech Target,
   (2002)

Wrolstad, Jay, "Wireless Jamming Debate Rages On," Wireless NewsFactor,
   (2002).

Ztango, "Corporate Overview," Ztango Wireless Media Services,
   (2002).

CHAPTER 15

GLOBAL WAN MANAGEMENT AND THE STATE OF THE WAN

CHAPTER OBJECTIVES

By the end of this chapter, you should understand these concepts:
- The five countries that contribute 69% of the world's telecommunications revenues
- The digital divide in developing countries
- Worldwide telecommunications trends
- Installation of miles of undersea fiber cabling to connect world regions together
- Co-location and Network Operations Centers (NOCs) for Web hosting and e-commerce applications
- The top 10 elements of a disaster recovery plan (DRP)
- IP routing extensions from the backbone
- Carrier outlook for simplified WAN
- Performance monitoring and optimization measurements

GLOBAL TELECOMMUNICATIONS

As organizations become more global, their end-to-end telecommunications needs expand to several countries. The five countries that use telecommunications most heavily are Japan, the United States, Germany, the United Kingdom, and France. In fact, these countries contribute 69% of the world's telecommunications revenues. [Jamison, 1-2] Multinational companies tend to locate their facilities in these countries, because line reliability and performance are stable. [Greenfield, 1]

As the pace of change and competitive dynamics continues to dominate in domestic and international markets, the major U.S. carriers have established high-speed international links to Europe, Asia Pacific, and South America. In addition, they have formed alliances with telcos in several countries to gain a global telecom competitive advantage.

A **digital divide** exists, however, in developing countries between those with and those without access to information and communication technologies. Incumbent telcos provide almost all of the local lines in these countries. Many telcos in Europe, Asia Pacific, and South America are legal monopolies, controlling pricing rates and access to the Internet. Global ISPs (Internet Service Providers) have been working in several countries to allow unmeasured (not tracking number of minutes online) access to the Internet, and have been successful so far in the United Kingdom, Germany, Hungary, Italy, South Korea, Sweden, and Switzerland. [Paltridge, 6]

Location is no longer relevant to voice communication worldwide. Today's telecommunications support information sharing and collaboration over long-haul telecommunications links daily. Telephone voice service is still growing in several countries overseas, and is being supplemented by growth in data, cellular, and satellite services. The following pages survey the state of growth in telecommunications and networks in different parts of the globe.

European Countries

E-commerce has pushed its way into Europe and wireless technology has hastened its deployment. Europe has several countries and they each adopt different telecom strategies and experience different rates of growth. The role of national governments has changed from that of supplier to that of a policy maker and regulator. Tariffs have been restructured and telephone service has expanded to include more mobile services in Europe. [Braunstein, 1] Data services are also growing as more countries install leased lines in most major cities to connect to the Internet. Internet access is driving significant investment in IP-based (Internet Protocol) networks for global e-commerce.

United Kingdom

The United Kingdom's fixed leased line business has grown slowly by 3.4% over the last 10 years. Both British Telecom and Cable & Wireless have expanded their cellular services. British Telecom (BT) is one of the world's leading providers of telecommunications and is one of the largest private sector companies in Europe. BT provides telecommunication services such as local, long distance, and international services that extend to 27 million exchange lines in the United Kingdom. BT has operations in more than 30 countries worldwide. In association with AT&T, BT has formed a joint partnership called Concert. This $10 billion venture is building an intelligent IP-based network for global e-commerce, global call centers, and Internet access. [List, 2]

Sweden

The Swedish carrier Telia has primarily invested its telecommunications dollars in Eastern and Western Europe. Fixed leased lines have been installed in Finland, Norway, Denmark, and the U.K. Sweden has had limited growth in telephone lines, at an annual rate of 1.3%, while telephone calls have been increasing at 2.8% a year. [Braunstein, 6]

Finland

Telecom Finland supports telephone services in Finland. Lately, its primary focus has been on cellular ventures abroad. Growth in telephone lines is limited to 2.4% while telephone calls have increased at 3.8% per year. [Braunstein, 6]

Denmark

Tele Danmark has considerable experience in cellular technologies and has recently invested heavily in cellular ventures in other countries. Tele Danmark opened up the home cellular market early in 1992. Telephone lines grow at the rate of 4.2% while telephone calls increase at the rate of 4% per year. [Braunstein, 6]

Germany

Deutsche Telecom has invested heavily in cellular ventures in Eastern Europe and Asia. Telephone lines have grown at the rate of 5% a year. The number of telephone calls has increased by approximately 7.1% annually. [Braunstein, 7]

France

France Telecom is primarily invested in cellular communications. They also distribute global mobile satellite services. Telephone lines have grown at a rate of about 3.4% a year while telephone calls have increased at a rate of 4.5%. [Braunstein, 7]

Spain

Telefonica participates with the Concert alliance for international business customers. It opened its cellular market to competition in 1985. Telephone lines have increased annually at 4.9% while telephone calls have increased by 5.2% per year. [Braunstein, 7]

Portugal

Portugal Telecom has invested primarily in the Portuguese-speaking world, serving its international customers with a Concert alliance. Telephone lines have increased dramatically at 10.1% while telephone calls have climbed by 17.7% per year. [Braunstein, 8]

Asia Pacific Countries

Investment in telecommunications in the Asia Pacific countries is concentrated in building intra-regional networks between several countries. Telecom providers in the Asia Pacific region are installing miles of undersea fiber to connect more countries to the Internet. Several countries are manufacturing telecom and video conferencing equipment and fiber-optic cabling.

Malaysia

Malaysia has successfully tested a desktop video-conferencing system on a satellite-based WAN. This service provides smooth full-motion video transmission in real time and without any time lags at a constant bandwidth of 250 Kbps. Malaysia plans to manufacture and market the product aggressively in 2003. [Ramadass, 1-2]

Singapore-Australia Joint Venture

The governments of Singapore and Australia have recently signed a telecommunications agreement to build an intra-regional connectivity network within the Asia Pacific region. They will establish a direct 4 Mbps Internet link between Singapore and Australia. The agreement aims to accelerate commercial and industry exchange, encourage IT investment, coordinate e-commerce policies and promote information exchange. [Pakrisamy, 1]

Singapore Telecom

Singapore Telecom plans, along with12 partners, to build a $1.6 billion underwater cable network. This underwater cable network will link Bangladesh, Egypt, France, India, Indonesia, Italy, Malaysia, Pakistan, Saudi Arabia, Singapore, Sri Lanka, and the United Arab Emirates. The project is planned to ease the expected bandwidth bottleneck anticipated between Asia and Europe. [Associated Press, 1]

SingTel Group

SingTel is the dominant provider of telecommunications services in Singapore and the second largest provider of long-distances services in Australia. SingTel also has 25 million mobile subscribers in Singapore, Australia, India, Indonesia, Philippines, and Thailand. In 2000, SingTel built the first private submarine cable system in the Asia Pacific. [SingTel, 1-4]

Vietnam

The Vietnam Post and Telecommunications Corp (VNPT) plans to increase the installation of phone lines from 2.5 to 6 per 100 people. NEC of Japan has secured 20% of the country's market for telephone exchange digital-switching systems, which cover 425,000 phone lines. In addition, Cable and Wireless of the U.K. plans to install 250,000 phone lines in Hanoi. A $12 million dollar factory is planned by Fujitsu Telecommunications of Japan to produce fiber-optic cables, telephone exchanges, microwave relay equipment, and network management tools. [Tran, 1-2]

Japan Telecom

For the past 15 years, Japan Telecom has been a major player in the Japanese telecommunications industry. Japan Telecom offers leased lines, local voice service, long-distance voice service, international voice service, narrow and broadband data service, and ISP service. In addition, the company offers an ATM (Asynchronous Transfer Mode) private leased-circuit service and has a Giga laser backbone service. The company's international circuits deploy diverse routing over various submarine cables and satellites to handle traffic in case of an outage. [Japan Telecom, 1]

China

China has launched an effort to reduce its high Internet fees to promote more Internet usage. Internet technology has been slow to catch on because Internet users in Beijing pay 34.8% of their monthly salaries for Internet use. Chinese-language Web sites are increasing at a fast rate. [Valigra, 1-2]

South American Countries

Recent liberalization of telecommunications and services in Central and South America has opened the doors to a great deal of investment. Heavy demand exists for telephone equipment and lines in South America. Before they can be adopted, manufacturers of telecom products must first meet a wide range of approval requirements and processes. [Jones, 1]

Some countries in Central and South America, such as Argentina, Brazil, and Chile, have formal approval processes. These countries have their own national standards and in-country testing requirements for all telecom products. Ecuador, Paraguay, and Peru also have national procedures and standards, but will accept foreign approvals. Countries in Central America such as El Salvador, Honduras, and Nicaragua will frequently review and validate FCC test reports and approval before approving an application. [Jones, 1]

There has been an increase in investment in deployment of undersea links in Central and South America. The Internet is the main catalyst for the surge in undersea construction. The installation of this cabling will be crucial to expanding ISP services in these countries. [Ruderman, 1]

In South America, Brazil and Argentina have the biggest population centers. Telecom providers have invested their efforts in the Atlantic coast since 75% of South America's traffic comes from Argentina and Brazil. Investment has increased in the Brazilian fiber optics industry as they predict more undersea development in South America over the next few years. [Ruderman, 1]

Brazil

Brazil recently opened its cellular market to foreign investors. Brazil expects to add 8 million new phone lines and 4 million cellular accounts in the next three years. [Bole, 1] Business-to-business e-commerce is soaring in Brazil and is expected to reach $5 billion by 2005. PSINet is buying up local companies and installing an infrastructure that will support the gigantic growth expected. [Ruderman, 1]

Argentina

Both Telfonica de Argentina and Telecom Argentina are focusing construction efforts on Buenos Aires. They are also constructing a corridor from the Atlantic coast to the Chilean border to provide a terrestrial ring. Within a year of its construction the Argentine Internet market is expected to gain significant momentum. [Ruderman, 1]

Mexico

Long-distance and metropolitan construction by new providers is opening up the Mexican telecom market. Network builders have been scrambling to provide connectivity and eliminate bandwidth bottlenecks. As many travelers flock to the Caribbean for vacation, demand for Internet addresses has grown. Consequently, Mexico has installed numerous high-speed connections to the Internet throughout the country. [Ruderman, 1]

Broadband Deployment Worldwide

Broadband connectivity has entered overseas telecom markets and some countries are way ahead of the United States in deployment. The growth of the Internet worldwide has brought large volumes of information to be transmitted electronically. New applications have emerged, such as full-motion video and CD-quality audio. Many countries have embraced broadband technology because it allows them to bundle convergence services to the residential market and increase their revenues significantly.

Table 15.1 lists the percentage of deployment of DSL (Digital Subscriber Lines), cable modems, and Fiber to the Home (FTTH) in 24 countries.

COUNTRY	DSL	CABLE MODEMS	FTTH	TOTAL
United Kingdom	.05	.03	0	.08
Spain	.12	.02	0	.14
Italy	.20	0	0	.20
Germany	.24	0	0	.24
Portugal	.01	.24	0	.25
New Zealand	.25	.02	0	.27
France	.11	.21	0	.32
Norway	.01	.34	0	.35
Australia	.05	.34	0	.39
Switzerland	.06	.38	0	.44
Japan	.01	.49	0	.50
Finland	.29	.29	0	.58
Iceland	.70	0	0	.70
Taiwan-China	.52	.48	0	1.00
Denmark	.49	.56	0	1.05
Sweden	.45	.62	.14	1.21
Belgium	.42	1.00	0	1.42
Netherlands	.09	1.58	0	1.67
Austria	.48	1.22	0	1.70
United States	.89	1.36	0	2.25
Canada	.48	3.01	0	3.49
Hong Kong	3.69	2.61	0	6.30
Singapore	3.23	4.82	0	8.05
Korea	5.88	3.32	0	9.20

TABLE 15.1 **Worldwide Broadband Deployment (% of Households)** [Source: Mitchell, 6]

Current trends appear to indicate substantial investment by Hong Kong, Singapore, and Korea in DSL broadband deployment. Cable modems have been increasing substantially in Belgium, Netherlands, Austria, Canada, Hong Kong, Singapore, and Korea. The bulk of the activity has been centered on building out broadband trunk capacity to residential customers. [Mitchell, 1-7]

Global Undersea Cabling

Global communications are enabled by the investment of telecommunication companies in transatlantic and transpacific undersea cabling and in satellites. Building cabling under the world's oceans costs millions and sometimes billions of dollars. Several cable installations have been constructed by large telcos either alone or in joint partnerships.

The links that have been constructed can deliver voice, data, and video at amazing speeds. In Table 15.2, statistics show performance of the Cable & Wireless worldwide network. Notice that the packet loss to all regions (Japan, Australia, Europe, the United Kingdom, and North America) is 0.00%. Latency for round-trip communications varies per region but in all cases latency does not exceed 256 milliseconds (ms).

REGION	JAPAN		AUSTRALIA		PAN EUROPE		UK		NORTH AMERICA	
	Latency (ms)	Loss (%)	Latency (ms)	Loss (%)	Latency (ms)	Loss (%)	Latency (ms)	Loss (%)	Latency (ms)	Loss (%)
Japan	8	0.00	-	-	256	0.00	-	-	101	0.00
Pan Europe	256	0.00	-	-	31	0.00	-	-	89	0.00
UK	-	-	-	-	-	-	-	-	82	0.00
North America	101	0.00	151	0.00	89	0.00	82	0.00	38	0.00

TABLE 15.2 **Cable & Wireless Global Internet Backbone, 2002 [Source: C & W, 1]**

Asia Pacific Internet Connections

Significant investment in Internet bandwidth has been made in the Asia Pacific region. International partnerships have enabled telecom companies to acquire resources and expand links to Asia. Multiple carriers have opened competition and interconnection to offer the right technology and access required to support Internet traffic between Asia and other countries. As they expand the deployment of telecommunications equipment and links, they enable their workforce to maintain a competitive advantage by offering Internet access to knowledge resources and collaborative sharing of information.

Several underwater fiber cables have been installed in the Asia Pacific region to support international voice and data communications. Asian Pacific countries have been quick to embrace a liberalization of technological, bureaucratic, and political constraints to provide services to multinational corporate customers. As the market expands, these less restrictive regulations will help lead to telecom products and services that will fuel further growth and promote commerce.

Worldwide Satellite Services

Satellite services are now available just about everywhere, providing for TV video and news broadcasts across the world. The investment being made in new satellite technologies is massive. Several large, financially stable firms have stepped through technological and financial hurdles to establish satellite connections to many regions throughout the world. [Braunstein, 11-12] These satellite systems are poised to provide wireless connections to user handsets worldwide.

This review of global telecommunications carriers and services makes apparent the abundant choices in establishing a global market presence. However, this increased globalization requires greater management and planning to ensure reliable communications across countries.

TOPIC *review* **Global Telecommunications**

1. Which countries generate 69% of the world's telecommunications revenue?
2. What is the digital divide?
3. Which country in Europe has sustained a dramatic increase in telephone lines and calling?
4. Which country in the Asia Pacific region is building a new $12 million dollar factory to produce fiber cables, telephone exchange, microwave relay equipment, and network management tools?
5. What is causing a massive investment in worldwide satellite services?

CO-LOCATION AND NETWORK OPERATION CENTERS

Co-location centers are designed to provide services for Web hosting and e-commerce applications. These centers offer customers a secure place for the physical location of their hardware and equipment without substantial capital investment in equipment. The **co-location center** provides a secure cage or cabinet for housing computer equipment, along with regulated power, dedicated Internet connection, security, and technical support. Often major co-location facilities also offer services to ensure high availability such as: cameras, fire detection and extinguishing devices, backup power generators, multiple connection feeds, and high security. International organizations use co-location centers to provide for several e-commerce Web sites distributed across the world.

Worldwide Co-location Centers

International organizations invest in co-location centers because they provide redundancy in services and equipment. The redundancy guarantees service will be always available for their global e-commerce business. For example, Internet connections within co-location facilities are usually provided by more than one ISP.

This offers alternate paths to the Internet should an ISP go down. They also provide connections for their customers to ATM and SONET (Synchronous Optical Network) links that are usually unaffordable for small or mid-sized organizations. The co-location center installs dense Wave Division Multiplexers (WDM) linked to SONET rings that provide speeds of OC12, OC48, or OC192. They also offer several OC-level international links to Europe, Latin America, South America, and Asia. These links alone are cost-prohibitive for most organizations.

Through private peering arrangements, the co-location center is able to provide connections to public exchanges such as MAE East, MAE West, and NAPs. In this way, an e-commerce site can offer customers an opportunity to reach it from anywhere they can connect to the Internet. [HerWebHost, 1] Some companies that offer Web hosting co-location centers have several constructed across the world. Figure 15.1 shows co-location centers in several countries. Backbones of various speeds connect the co-location centers together. With numerous network interconnects, a large organization can build several failover scenarios for disaster recovery.

The sites are connected in a redundant "mesh" configuration, which eliminates single points of potential fiber failures to ensure the uninterrupted flow of data, and with superior reliability and speed. [Exodus Communications, 5]

FIGURE 15.1 **Worldwide Co-location Centers [Exodus Communications, 5]**

Network Operations Centers

Co-location centers offer **Network Operations Centers (NOCs)** for the monitoring and supervising of equipment and personnel within the facility. A NOC is located centrally within the building. The NOC supplies the personnel needed to provide hardware and network troubleshooting, software updating and distribution, routers, domain name management, and performance monitoring as well as connections to other networks. The NOC is a secure room that typically has a large-screen TV displaying the network equipment being monitored. If a network device fails, a red light displayed on the screen notifies NOC engineers.

NOC engineers are experts in monitoring telecommunications links and WAN services, specializing in technologies such as ISDN (Integrated Services Digital Network), T-Carrier Lines, X.25, Frame Relay, and ATM. Senior technical personnel are also present to manage server and internetworking equipment (routers, switches, bridges, gateways, and firewalls). NOCs also staff network engineers who can troubleshoot network operating systems and Web hosting applications (Microsoft IIS and Apache). Some NOCs even provide operating system upgrades and software database services. NOCs are manned 24 hours a day, 7 days a week around the world. They strive to ensure the fastest resolution possible of any connectivity or network problem.

Co-location and NOCs minimize an organization's capital investment in telecommunications links, services, and networking hardware. For e-commerce sites, it's a real advantage to be able to connect to leading-edge technology and benefit from the latest software diagnostic techniques and the expertise of senior trained personnel. These organizations then avoid the cost of providing their own personnel and the thousands of dollars of investment in equipment. NOCs offer several service options that an organization can select from based on its dynamic requirements. In addition, each service is available at a reasonable monthly rate. This is made possible because NOC and co-location centers can, by distributing their services and costs to multiple customers, make the most of their investments in the latest technologies and telecommunications links.

TOPIC *review* **Co-Location and Network Operation Centers**

1. What services are provided by a co-location center?
2. What are the advantages of using a co-location center?
3. Are redundant and independent Internet connections to more than one ISP provided by a co-location facility?
4. What do NOCs provide?
5. What costs are avoided by using NOCs?

DISASTER RECOVERY

Most data center disasters are accidental and unexpected. Disasters can be caused by natural weather events such as hurricanes or earthquakes. Floods and fires also can render a data center useless in a matter of hours. These types of disasters prevent the continuation of normal business operations. All organizations regardless of size need to have a **disaster recovery plan (DRP)**. A DRP plan describes in detail how an organization should deal with a disaster. The goal is to minimize the effects of the disaster and resume mission-critical operations as quickly as possible. Sometimes a DRP is referred to as a **business continuity plan (BCP)** because it outlines how an organization should continue operations should a disaster occur.

Disaster recovery goes beyond simple data recovery. Appropriate planning should include a secondary site containing all of the same equipment as is housed in an organization's main data center. This strategy involves a substantial financial commitment by the organization because it must provide redundant equipment at each of the two locations. When considering a disaster recovery solution, there are two methods to choose from: outsourcing or building a secondary site. Outsourcing has the advantage of smaller up-front costs and the service provided is less expensive than actually building a second physical location. [Danielsson, 1]

Consideration should be given to the location of the secondary site. It is important not to locate it in the same hurricane corridor or earthquake disaster zone. Often, it is best to consider a location in another state. When a data center is located in a tower building and the organization chooses to outsource, it is important to select a different outsourcing company than other tenants in the building. Otherwise, if the entire building experiences a disaster, the outsourcing company might not be able to meet the agreement.

Another critical decision is how quickly the data services must be made available. For some organizations, a downtime period of three or four days can mean millions of dollars of revenue lost. Continuous availability requires mirroring data to two sites. This data has to travel across the WAN between the first and secondary site in real time. The data is written to drives at both locations at the same time. The right solution for an organization might be the inclusion of instant failover between sites, assuming the same data exists at both sites. The secondary site requires the same amount of disk space as the primary servers. Writing data over the WAN link requires substantial bandwidth between the two sites. A high availability solution can be expensive, but for mission-critical business operations it is a necessity.

Disaster Recovery within the United States

When an organization has sites dispersed across the United States, WAN links become its only source for data exchange between locations. These services are neither owned nor managed by the organization. Instead, service providers carry the responsibility of managing the data links for an organization. A good DRP will provide for redundant WAN links. Often, organizations use ISDN as the backup link.

In Figure 15.2, three locations are connected using a high-speed Frame Relay link. The core Frame Relay routers connect New York, Chicago, and Detroit together over the service provider's Frame Relay network. Between New York and Chicago is a 1.5 Mbps Frame Relay connection because the bulk of the business transactions occur between these two sites. Redundant links provided by ISDN routers are connected to the Local Exchange Carrier (LEC) and Interexchange Carrier (IXC) through the service provider's ISDN. An ISDN PRI (Primary Rate Interface) provides a 512 Kbps secondary backup link.

The Detroit site has a small sales office of 25 people whose data exchange requirements warrant a 256 Kbps Frame Relay link. An ISDN BRI (Basic Rate Interface) is used to provide a 128 Kbps backup link. Notice that the backup links are half the speed of the primary link. This often occurs because of cost considerations, where it is considered as a standby link with the purpose of providing services temporarily until the Frame Relay connection is available again.

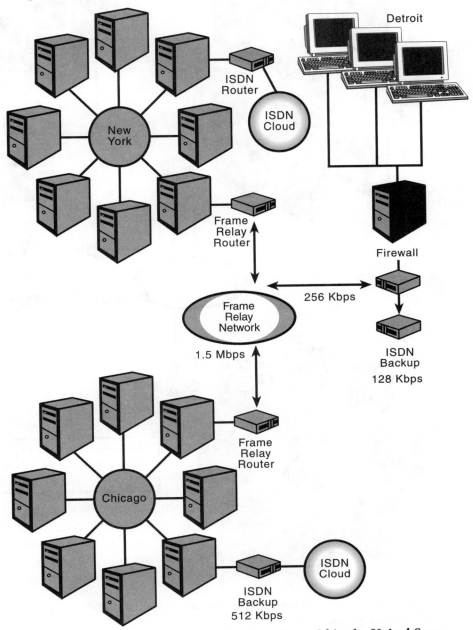

FIGURE 15.2 Disaster Recovery between Sites within the United States [Source: Winchester Systems, 1]

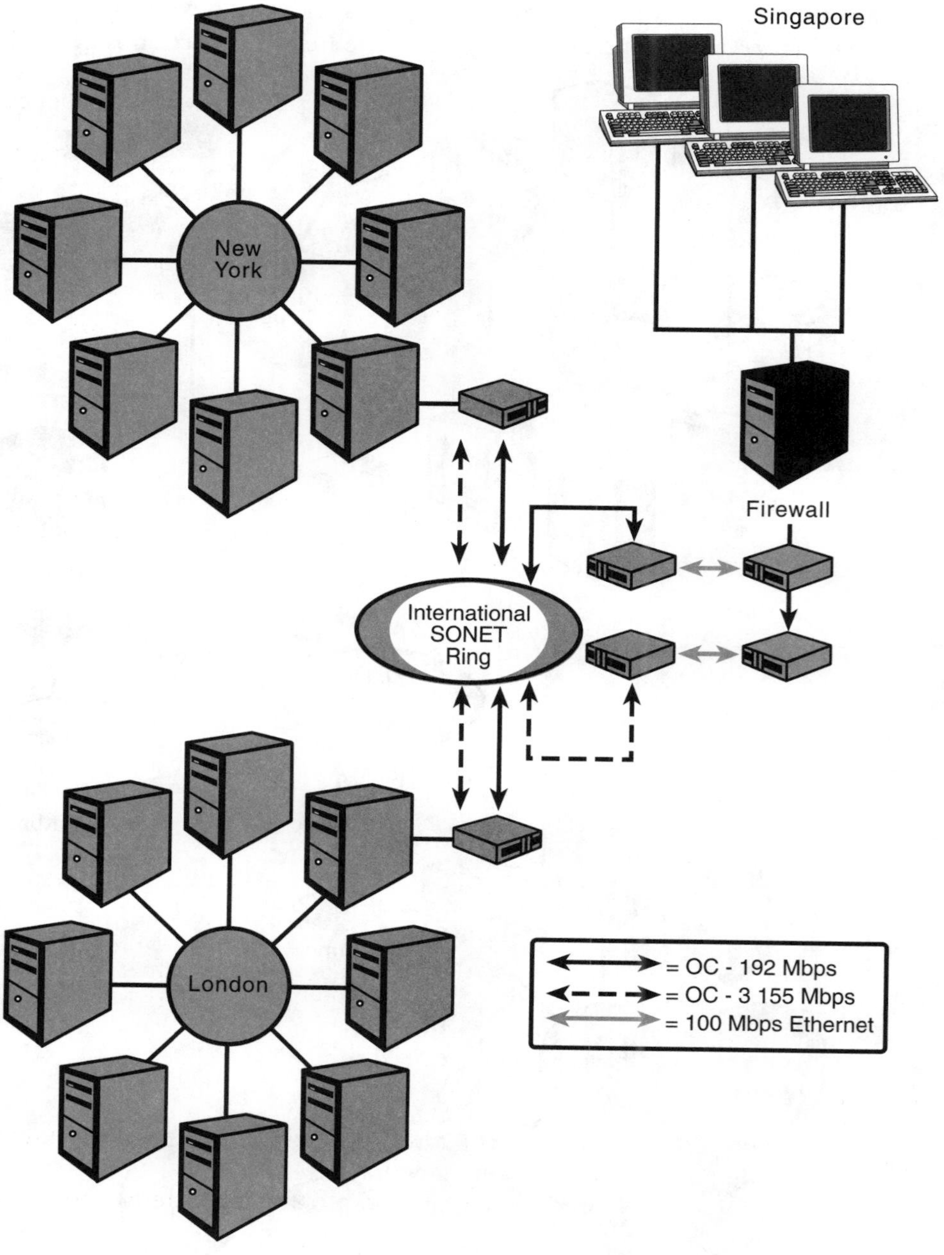
Singapore
New
York
Firewall
International
SONET
Ring
London
= OC - 192 Mbps
= OC - 3 155 Mbps
= 100 Mbps Ethernet

FIGURE 15.3 **Disaster Recovery between International Sites [Source: Winchester Systems, 1]**

Disaster Recovery between International Sites

Disaster recovery between international sites requires a greater investment because the bandwidth requirements are much higher. In Figure 15.3, three locations are connected over an ATM network: New York, London, and Singapore. Their present service provider has OC-192 (192 Mbps) SONET rings to their overseas locations. No other carrier service can offer the speed provided by SONET. Consequently, in this example, the organization has signed a SLA (Service Level Agreement) to provide backup ATM service to all locations over OC-3 (155 Mbps) because the organization cannot afford any network downtime. The SLA defines an immediate failover to the OC-3 connection should a disaster occur. In this case, contracting for half the speed of the primary link does not satisfy the organization's bandwidth, fault tolerance, or reliability requirements.

Top Ten Elements for Disaster Recovery Plan

Until recently, most organizations relied on daily tape backups for their recovery process. With the evolution of online businesses and e-commerce over the Internet, even temporary downtime can result in the loss of customers and thousands of dollars. Organizations can ready themselves for large-scale disasters by following a plan consisting of the 10 elements listed in Table 15.3.

1. Provide top management support and commitment to contingency planning objectives: • Tie the DRP to corporate objectives. • Establish the DRP as a critical business process.
2. Identify business-critical processes and supporting IT systems: • Identify core business processes. • Classify applications, databases, and required business continuity expected.
3. Perform a business impact analysis of mission-critical systems: • Analyze system downtime as a business operational loss. • Evaluate availability, recoverability, and security requirements for service restoration.
4. Classify priority levels of restoration of mission-critical and non-critical business systems: • Determine amount of bandwidth, time, and technical resources required to restore normal operations. • Establish enterprise recovery priorities for key systems and applications.
5. Examine application dependencies: • Analyze all application dependencies from the data source. • Identify lower profile components of application infrastructure.

TABLE 15.3 **Top 10 Elements of a Disaster Recovery Plan [Merryman, 1]**

6.	Test critical restore procedures in a real-time environment:
	• Test tape restores.
	• Have the end user community double check the data restored.
7.	Train regular staff to perform IT recovery without key personnel:
	• Cross train key management.
	• Cross train storage network, storage, system, backup, and database administrators.
8.	Review contracts with disaster recovery vendors:
	• Review SLAs on facilities.
	• Check equipment maintenance contracts.
	• "Hot Spare" equipment.
9.	Demand "restore performance" from disaster recovery vendors:
	• Perform surprise audit of disaster recovery vendor.
10.	Exercise the DRP on a limited scale to provide practice for emergency procedures. Identify single points of failure in the IT infrastructure:
	• Design redundancy into equipment, operating systems, databases, middleware, and applications.
	• Design for redundant power, cooling, telecommunications links, and personnel to accomplish the recovery.

TABLE 15.3 **Top 10 Elements of a Disaster Recovery Plan [Merryman, 1],** **continued**

If an organization cannot afford to fund a secondary site on its own, several alternatives and degrees of disaster recovery are available from recovery service providers. The most basic service is system recovery. This service provides outsourced tape-backup and restoration arrangements. The outsourcing company stores redundant backup copies at geographically dispersed data centers. Usually, the outsourcing agreement specifies a time frame of 48 hours for a complete restoration of services. However, for some companies, this amount of downtime has the potential of putting them out of business permanently.

For an organization such as a stock exchange, even a couple hours of downtime during prime stock trading hours can severely affect its operations. In this case, high availability services are required. There are several degrees of high availability. The top level of service guarantees an organization can be back up and running in anywhere from a few minutes to a couple of hours. A **data mirroring** system provides duplication of production data to physically separate target systems hosted at a data center.

Between the two sites, a SONET ring provides the bandwidth required to mirror data over the WAN. In case of a disaster, the secondary site fails over to the mainframe and the service is restored without any data loss. However, this type of DRP is expensive, costing more than $1 million. [Baltazar, 1]

Another option for DRP offers the same type of equipment at both the primary and secondary sites. If an organization has servers running UNIX and SAP at the primary site, this option provides for the leasing of equipment, storage capacity, and space at a secondary location. This is the most expensive recovery service option because it provides for data processing at both locations. Load balancers are used to offer parallel processing by delegating tasks equally to both sites. [Baltazar, 1]

DRPs and services are more than just insurance policies; they provide business preservation. Whatever the choice for disaster recovery, it is vital that the technology, bandwidth, and business continuity chosen match the organization's operations requirements. An appropriate DRP can guarantee 100% continuous business operations providing that the organization is willing to fund it.

TOPIC *review* **Disaster Recovery**

1. What type of consideration should be given to the location of the secondary site in a DRP?
2. What is required to provide for continuous availability?
3. What has been the usual method for the recovery process for most organizations?
4. What are the alternatives if your organization cannot fund a secondary site for disaster recovery?
5. What is meant by degrees of high availability?

THE STATE OF THE WAN

Applications are driving bandwidth growth and technologies are responding quickly to meet the need for more bandwidth. Still, availability, access, and economics remain the decision factors used to determine the appropriate WAN service for each location. Buying trends are moving certain technologies to the forefront. Frame Relay will continue to evolve and be used as a cost-effective method for long-haul networks. The use of native ATM might increase slightly, but LANE (LAN Emulation) using IP over ATM will continue to dominate. There will be less use of dial-up over POTS (Plain Old Telephone Service) and more use of dial VPNs (Virtual Private Networks) for remote access. Companies that do not already have an extensive WAN infrastructure will adopt site-to-site VPNs . There will be an increase in the use of MPLS (Multiprotocol Label Switching) and QoS (Quality of Service) between ISPs and phone company switches to manage services and large volumes of information. More companies will consider the deployment of Voice over IP (VoIP) as the technology matures to provide clearer connections and remain cost-effective. There will be an increase in e-learning, storage, and video applications at the WAN edge. [Metzler, 4]

Public and Private WAN Services

Today's networking environment is considered a hybrid of co-existing public and private WAN services. For public IP services, there is a perceived assumption that running applications over the public Internet is unreliable. ISPs have not yet been able to offer meaningful IP SLAs for their customers. It has been difficult to find a single performance management system capable of validating the performance of multiple ISPs that would allow an organization to determine whether or not their present SLA was being met.

Private IP services grow when organizations need to provide tighter security. Private IP VPNs are revitalizing traditional data services. New robust networks, as those shown in Figure 15.4, provide IP-aware Frame Relay and ATM services. These are emerging as the best technologies to use for private site-to-site connections.

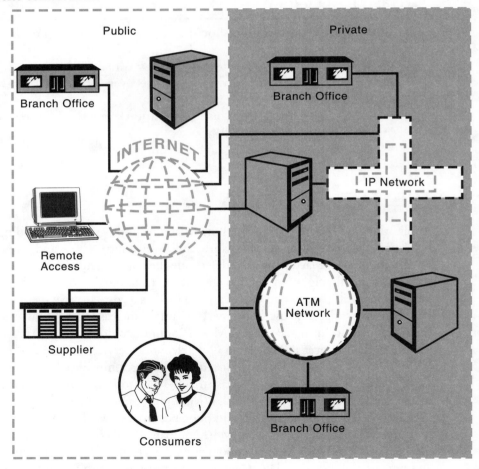

FIGURE 15.4 **Today's Wide Area Network [Source: Visual Networks, 1]**

Many organizations are trying out IP VPNs in their smaller sales offices, as IP VPN is more cost effective than IP Frame or ATM technologies. However, there is no visibility into performance of IP VPN over the Internet. Increased use of IP VPN will require performance guarantees (no CIR [Committed Information Rate] for IP VPN) like those provided by Frame Relay. Without them, organizations will continue to be concerned about security and management of IP VPNs. [Visual Networks, 2]

IP Routing

WANs have now embraced the architectural foundation provided by IP routing for applications and services. As shown in Figure 15.5, it is now evident that IP handles all layers of the network (backbone, edge, and end node access). The IP architecture allows for the scale and reach required for global networks. Global networks can gain speed for IP over a carrier's transport and optical infrastructure using ATM and SONET. The IP architecture provides for such applications as business-to-business (B2B) marketplaces, application hosting, and content networking. MPLS applies intelligence to bandwidth management. Carriers are able to offer IP QoS because MPLS provides levels of priority for different services. Running IP over ATM and SONET has enabled global networks to become adaptable, flexible, and device independent. MPLS is the enabling technology that facilitates network convergence in today's networks. [Cisco, 1] [Qwest, 3]

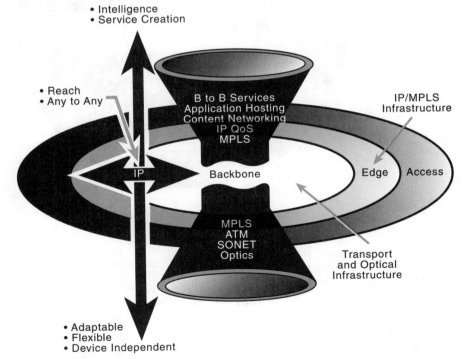

FIGURE 15.5 **IP Routing Architecture for the WAN [Source: Cisco, 1]**

Carrier Outlook for Simplified WAN

Carriers envision a simplified WAN for the future. As illustrated in Figure 15.6, organizations' buying patterns have centered around four main services (Frame Relay, private leased lines, VPN, and ATM). Convergence is now required for voice, video, data, and storage. Universal access requires redirecting users to content based on service metrics. Service providers plan to package and offer the best technology choice for core WAN services. Buyer preferences for usability are now driving WAN evolution. In the near future, a single box at an organization's site might provide all WAN services. The progression toward convergence means organizations will have to rely on their carrier to be their WAN technologist and guide them toward the right service for their applications. [Qwest, 4]

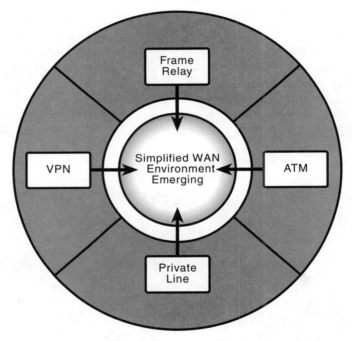

FIGURE 15.6 **A Simplified WAN** [Source: Qwest, 1]

Carrier Service Paradigm

Many carriers are now staffed with highly skilled technical people who can manage the components of the network infrastructure. As Figure 15.7 illustrates, enterprise expenditures will continue to rise and the service provider (carrier) engagement will provide more services from component (device) to final solution. The service paradigm has evolved to include network access, PVC (permanent virtual circuit)/tunnel connections, CPE (customer premise equipment) fault management, firewalls, intrusion detection systems (IDS), and remote access. For service providers to meet this challenge, they will have to streamline service activation, improve the efficiency of their operations, and focus on services that will add value for WANs. [Qwest, 4-5]

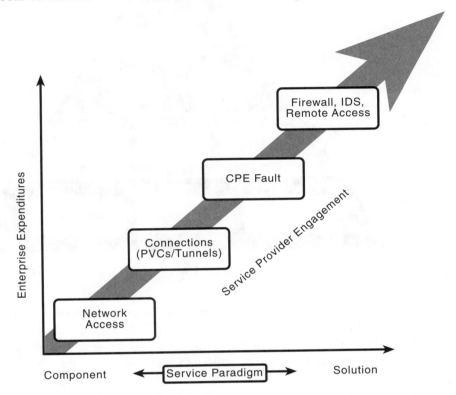

FIGURE 15.7 **Carrier Service Paradigm [Source: Qwest, 2]**

Future of Remote Access

Extending safe and secure computing to remote users requires serious attention by their organizations. IT departments provide devices and protect access through encryption, authentication, and security policies. However, laptops are not the only remote access device anymore. Mobile workers are requiring access to e-mail from PDAs (personal data assistants) and cell phones also. The challenge is to build a hierarchy of value within an organization. As shown in Figure 15.8, four layers are required for secure remote access: network, security, management, and policy. The network layer provides for dial-up, wireless, and broadband access to the enterprise. IT departments employ VPNs, firewalls, and antivirus software to filter and manage the security layer. Services require monitoring, reporting, and billing management. [Fiberlink, 3]

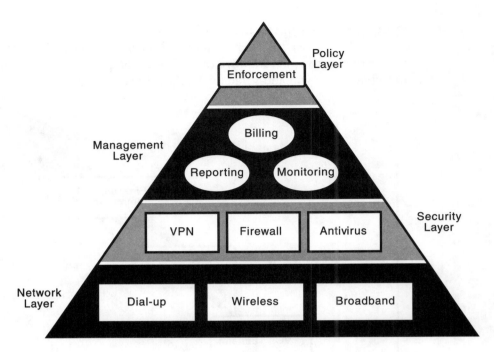

FIGURE 15.8 **WAN Management Layers** [Source: Fiberlink, 1]

Users and businesses desire maximum flexibility that allows them to make connections anywhere and anytime. The trick is to strike a balance between convenience and privacy. Security is not always convenient. The key to enforcing security policies is obtaining support from upper management. Sometimes this requires punitive actions for infractions. The proposed value has to be weighed against the cost of lost data attributed to unauthorized network intrusions. Software that provides policy management is well worth the investment because it provides for security protection. A layered security plan for remote access is the only effective approach for protecting company information assets.

Performance Monitoring and Optimization

Performance monitoring leads to the optimization of services over the WAN. **Performance management** is the ongoing analysis of network capacity requirements that ensures an organization has enough bandwidth to meet its business initiatives. It takes into account any upcoming changes in the application environment and predicts growth trends in network use. Analysis requires a baseline metric that measures changes in performance. **Baselining** is any analysis method that compares changes in actual data against a historical value (value over time).

Performance monitoring is used to measure the following:

- **Services Provided**. Measures end-to-end performance and service quality for carrier's availability and performance.
- **Services Used**. Monitors transport technologies and protocols to determine compliance with SLAs.
- **Capacity Planning**. Measures percentage of bandwidth used and how much delay there is in transporting data through the carrier.
- **Network Use**. Measures how the use of the network is changing. It may be necessary to track HTML or TCP/IP traffic on carrier's backbone links.
- **Network Health**. Monitors for the number of errors or the packet loss ratio on a WAN link. [Carden, 1]

The question is what needs to be monitored—the entire network, a site, or a PVC over the Frame Relay network? Is network delay or latency defined as site to site or from POP to POP (point of presence)? Is delay measured as an average over a day, a week, or a month? How is round trip delay time measured? Do carriers provide statistics to base the measurements from? [Metzler, 8] Round trip delay time averages are as follows:

- Between sites in the United States: 60 ms
- Between sites in the United States and Western Europe: 90 ms
- Between sites in the United States and Eastern Europe: 120 ms

The measurements are difficult to obtain without a tool that grants the administrator visibility into the carrier's network. In Figure 15.9, a network monitoring system is illustrated. The configuration requires a monitoring device, a database, and a console to view analysis information. This monitoring system allows for real-time performance monitoring of private IP networks. [Metzler, 8]

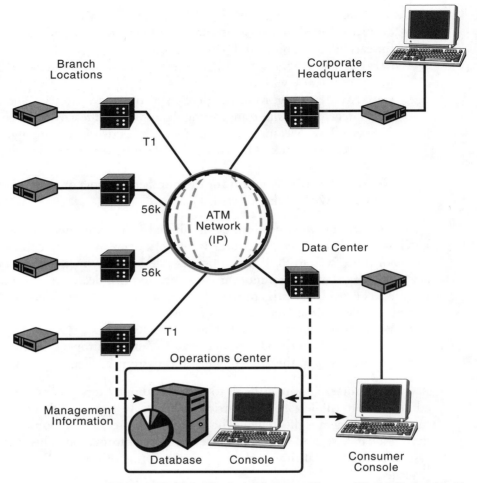

FIGURE 15.9 **Circuit UpTime Analysis Elements [Source: Visual Networks, 3]**

As shown in Figure 15.10, an IP Circuit Summary View provides visibility into site-to-site circuit throughput and performance. If an organization uses multiple protocols, the throughput per protocol is listed. It also can provide a list of the top five talkers over a site-to-site connection and percentage bandwidth they are using. This tool can verify the connectivity and availability of a carrier's service.

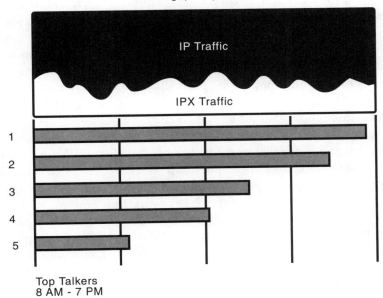

Site 1
Throughput by Protocol

IP Traffic

IPX Traffic

Top Talkers
8 AM - 7 PM

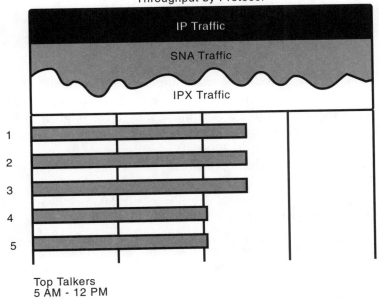

Site 2
Throughput by Protocol

IP Traffic

SNA Traffic

IPX Traffic

Top Talkers
5 AM - 12 PM

FIGURE 15.10 **IP Circuit Analysis Summary** [Source: Visual Networks, 5]

The application of an **IP Circuit Analysis** system offers the information needed for measuring latency, round trip delay time, and packet loss. The database provides a method for capturing historical information, which can be used to correlate end user usage and peak periods over time. The most important advantage is that the administrator can measure the throughput of the circuit and compare it to the SLA to verify the carrier's performance.

Some network monitoring tools allow for visibility into public IP networks. These tools can measure IP VPN and broadband connections and report on their throughput. With network intelligence built in, performance can be measured to the end user desktop. A customer service representative can deploy on-demand tests for measuring dial and broadband IP service performance.

Several telecommunications companies have started to offer management software for capacity planning and diagnostic tools to enable customers to monitor their network needs and uptime. Sprint, for example is offering a reporting tool that for a small charge, assists customers in monitoring network availability, packet loss, and throughput. In addition, Bell South has purchased a tool called "Visual IP InSight" to enable detection of network performance issues in their dial and DSL infrastructure. This software provides performance visibility at the service destination across all public IP services, including dial, broadband (DSL, cable, and fixed wireless) as well as dedicated (T1, T3, VPN) Internet access. Key performance metrics allow for measurement of availability, latency, packet loss, throughput, and time to download.

The Future of the WAN

Widespread convergence of entertainment, telephony, and data, voice, and video will characterize the future of the WAN for the next several years. Use of the Internet in the office and at home is expected to grow to 1 billion by 2004. Worldwide e-commerce revenues were $272 billion in 2000 and are expected to grow to $1,685 billion in 2003. Wireless access to the Internet is now affordable and easy to use through cellular phones and Palm Pilot type devices. [Plunkett, 14]

Many miles of fiber-optic cable have been laid worldwide to push thousands of times more data and voice across the continents. Enabling the Internet has resulted in the installation of over 54 million miles of land-based fiber-optic cable and 116,000 miles of undersea fiber cable worldwide. [Plunkett, 18] This fiber infrastructure has provided the Internet with the capacity for delivering massive quantities of digitized content. The globalization of business now happens instantly and business owes it all to the investments made in fiber and satellite networks.

Satellite transmission of television signals has also increased to offer new overseas outlets for TV programs, both live and in syndication. Video and digital compression are being used to reduce the amount of bandwidth required for transmission. Network news channels are being broadcasted using satellite phones, and transmission devices deliver up-to-the-minute news from remote locations all over the world. Information can now be shared globally and high-speed access to this information is always available. Continued research in science and technology will influence the shape of the WAN of the future, which will offer intelligent services, performance, and an evolutionary infrastructure.

TOPIC *review* **The State of the WAN**

1. What is driving bandwidth growth for WANs?
2. What are the best technologies to use for private site-to-site connections?
3. What has enabled carriers to provide adaptable, flexible, and device independence for global networks?
4. What is baselining?
5. What is performance monitoring used to measure?

CHAPTER SUMMARY

Today information exchange happens daily between countries all over the world. Surprisingly, 69% of the world's telecommunications revenue is supported by only a handful of countries (Japan, United States, Germany, France, and United Kingdom). Global carriers have invested heavily over the last few years in equipment and fiber links to provide for multinational networks. Voice telephone service is continuing to grow in several countries overseas.

In Europe, e-commerce and mobile wireless services are expanding. Portugal has seen a dramatic increase of 10% in telephone lines and 17.7% in telephone calls. In the Asia Pacific region, Singapore Telecom is installing massive amounts of undersea fiber cable. Large-scale factories are being built in Vietnam to provide for the production of fiber-optic cables, telephone exchanges, and microwave relay equipment. There is a heavy demand for telephone equipment and lines in South America. Eight South American countries (Argentina, Bolivia, Brazil, Chile, Colombia, Ecuador, Peru, and Venezuela) participated in the World Trade Organization's liberalization pact. This recent liberalization has opened the doors for foreign investment. Restrictive application procedures are required in most South American countries to obtain approval to construct undersea cabling, lay telephone lines, and market telecommunications equipment.

Many organizations that participate in the e-commerce marketplace have contracted with co-location facilities to house their computer equipment. These facilities provide NOCs with strict security, fire suppression, backup power generators, multiple Internet connections, temperature control, and power. Telecom companies have also entered into the co-location business and have deployed their own co-location centers worldwide. With high-bandwidth inter-connections, a multinational company can build several failover scenarios for disaster recovery.

Disaster recovery requires a plan that details how an organization should organize and deal with unexpected disasters. It outlines how an organization should continue operations and is often called a business continuity plan. Some organizations choose to build an entire secondary site with redundant equipment to support their disaster recovery efforts. Others contract with outsourcing disaster recovery providers who offer leased equipment, high-bandwidth connections for data mirroring, and complete restoration of service within the contracted time limit.

Bandwidth growth, availability, access requirements, and economics are driving the state of the WAN today. The networking environment worldwide is a hybrid of public and private WAN services. IP routing has become the foundation for all layers of the network (backbone, edge, and end node access). MPLS technology has enabled traffic management for convergence of voice, data, and video. Universal access worldwide has required carriers to be able to direct users to content based on service metrics. Buyer preferences for usability are now driving WAN evolution.

Users and businesses desire flexibility in making connections anywhere at any time. Providing security involves a trade-off between convenience and privacy. Four layers (network, security, management, and policy) are required to provide secure remote access. Performance management is required to optimize services over the WAN. Depending on what is being monitored, a network monitoring system will allow analysis for real-time information.

The Internet and multinational companies have escalated the use of the WAN. Miles of fiber-optic cable are being laid to provide more links and reduce bottlenecks. In addition, satellite services are being offered across the continent. Massive quantities of digitized content for entertainment, telephony, data, voice, and video are increasing the capacity requirements of WANs. Research in science and technology will influence and direct the evolutionary infrastructure of the WAN.

CHAPTER REVIEW QUESTIONS

(This quiz also can be printed from the Encore! CD that accompanies this book. File name—Chap15review.)

Circle a letter (a-d) for each question. Choose only one answer for each.

1. Substantial investment has occurred in Hong Kong, Singapore, and Korea in:
   a. ISDN.
   b. FTTH.
   c. asynchronous modems.
   d. DSL.

2. Liberalization of telecommunication services has opened the doors to investment in:
   a. China.
   b. United Kingdom.
   c. Central and South America.
   d. Vietnam.

3. This organization provides a secure cage or cabinet for housing computer equipment along with a dedicated Internet connection, security, and technical support.
   a. ISP
   b. co-location center
   c. BCP center
   d. NOC

4. When you outline how an organization should continue operations if a disaster occurs, you are writing a _____ plan.
   a. DRP
   b. ISP
   c. NOC
   d. BCP

5. A DRP can guarantee 100% continuous business operations providing an organization is willing to provide:
   a. daily tape backups.
   b. funding.
   c. a redundant site.
   d. load balancers.

6. What are the three decision factors used to determine the appropriate WAN service for each location?
   a. Alternate, agreement, and economics
   b. Accumulate, availability, and economics
   c. Availability, access, and economics
   d. Attention, access, and politics

7. What are the four main services provided by a simplified WAN?
   a. Cable modems, VPN, private leased lines, and ATM
   b. Frame Relay, private leased lines, VPN, and ATM
   c. ISDN, VPN, ATM, and SONET
   d. DSL, VPN, ATM, and SONET

8. The key to enforcing security policies is obtaining support from:
   a. Engineering management.
   b. IT management.
   c. Human Resource management.
   d. Upper management.

9. What are the four layers required for secure remote access?
   a. Network, security, management, and disaster recovery
   b. Management, policy, security, and redundancy
   c. Network, security, management, and policy
   d. Management, policy, firewall, and virus protection

10. The future of the WAN for the next several years will be characterized by:
    a. convergence of entertainment, telephony, data, voice, and video.
    b. convergence of telephony and data only.
    c. convergence of voice and video only.
    d. convergence of telephony, entertainment, voice, and video.

Circle the correct letter (A-E) that corresponds to the descriptions below. Choose only one answer for each.

   A. NOC
   B. Baselining
   C. DRP
   D. Performance management
   E. Digital divide

11. A B C D E   Any analysis method that compares changes in actual data against a historical value.

12. A B C D E   Personnel who provide hardware and network troubleshooting, software management, and performance monitoring.

13. A B C D E   Analysis of network capacity requirements to ensure an organization has enough bandwidth to meet business initiatives.

14. A B C D E   Separation between those with and without access to information and communication technologies in developing countries.

15. A B C D E   Describes in detail how an organization should deal with a disaster.

     A. Network health
     B. IP circuit analysis
     C. Data mirroring system
     D. Co-location center
     E. Capacity planning

16. A B C D E   Offers information needed to measure latency, round trip delay time, and packet loss.

17. A B C D E   Provides services for Web hosting and e-commerce applications.

18. A B C D E   Provides duplication of production data to physically separate target system.

19. A B C D E   Monitor for the number of errors or the packet loss ration on a WAN link.

20. A B C D E   Measures percentage of bandwidth used and how much delay there is in transporting data through the carrier.

INTERNET EXERCISES

1. Log on to the Internet and key the following URL:

   homepage.mac.com/michaelmino/PhotoAlbum3.html

   Select the map entitled Underwater Cable Routes, Japan. List the four primary countries in the region where underwater cable routes are concentrated.

   A. _____
   B. _____
   C. _____
   D. _____

2. Key the following URL:

http://stat.qwest.net/index_flash.html

Look across bottom menu bar and select <u>point to point</u>.

From the pull down menu that appears, select Los Angeles and Hong Kong

Look at the preformance statistics for the last 90 days and answer the questions below.

(1) What is the performance for FTP?
(2) What is the performance for HTTP?
(3) How long is the latency?
(4) What is the packet loss percentage?

CONCEPT EXERCISES

Concept Narrative
(This narrative exercise also can be printed from the Encore! CD that accompanies this book. File name—Chap15connar.)

Fill in the blanks of the following narrative.

When there is a data center disaster, it is most often accidental and unexpected. Disasters can be caused by natural weather events like hurricanes or earthquakes. Floods and _____ also can render a data center useless in a matter of hours. These types of disasters prevent the continuation of normal business operations. All organizations regardless of size need to have a _____ _____ _____ (DRP). A DRP describes in detail how an organization should deal with a disaster. The goal is to minimize the effects of the disaster and resume mission-critical operations as quickly as possible. Sometimes a DRP is referred to as a _____ _____ _____ (BCP) because it outlines how an organization should continue operations should a disaster occur.

Disaster recovery goes beyond simple data recovery. Appropriate planning should include a _____ _____ containing all of the same equipment as is housed in an organization's main data center. This strategy involves a substantial financial commitment by the organization because they must provide redundant equipment at each of the two locations. When considering a disaster recovery solution, there are two methods to choose from: outsourcing or building of a secondary site. Outsourcing has the advantage of smaller up-front costs and the service provided is less expensive than actually building a second physical location.

Consideration should be given to the location of a secondary site. It is important not to locate it in the same _____ corridor or earth-quake disaster zone. Often it is best to consider a location in another state. It is important when a data center is located in a tower building and the organization chooses to outsource to select a different outsourcing company than other tenants in the building. Otherwise, if the entire building experiences a disaster, the outsourcing company might not be able to meet the agreement.

Concept Table
(This table exercise also can be printed from the Encore! CD that accompanies this book. File name—Chap15contab.)

Read each statement carefully and choose the type of performance monitoring being described. Use only one "X" per statement.

STATEMENT	TYPES OF PERFORMANCE MONITORING		
	BASELINING	CAPACITY PLANNING	NETWORK HEALTH
1. Takes into account any upcoming changes in the application environment.			
2. Measures end-to-end performance and service quality for a carrier.			
3. Compares changes in actual data against a historical value.			
4. Measures percentage of bandwidth used and the amount of delay in transporting data through the carrier.			
5. Monitors the number of errors or packet loss ration on a WAN link.			
6. Requires a monitoring device, a database, and a console to view analysis information.			

7. Allows for real time monitoring of private IP networks.			
8. Provides a list of the top five talkers and percentage of bandwidth they are using.			
9. The database provides historical information of end user usage.			
10. Measures latency, round trip delay time, and packet loss.			

Concept Picture

(This picture exercise also can be printed from the Encore! CD that accompanies this book. File name—Chap15conpic.)

In this exercise, look at the picture of the emerging Simplified WAN Environment and label the missing elements.

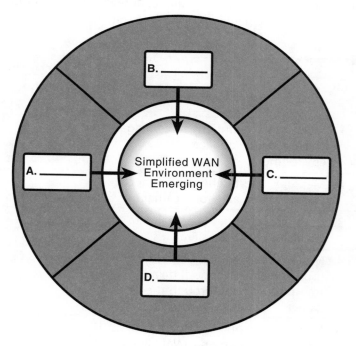

A. _____
B. _____
C. _____
D. _____

CASE STUDY

OCEAN VIEW PICTURES

Objective:

Learn how software decisions made for a new database system can influence the design of the data communications network. Determine the best WAN design for telecommunications links for the company.

Company Profile:

Ocean View Pictures is located in Hollywood, California. The company has produced thousands of movies and television pictures over the years. Several films and other programs have been distributed to companies overseas.

Current Situation:

Ocean View Pictures needs a client-server database system to keep track of licensing information and to preserve the records pertaining to 33,000 movies and television programs. All of this information has been gathered in the past on paper or over the telephone. The company has never been able to collect all of the information required for a complete analysis of its licensing and distribution worldwide.

Business Information Requirements:

Ocean View Pictures executives require an information system that will help them plan the distribution cycle of a movie or a TV show for theatrical release, pay-per-view, or on video cassette. The sales people need to have querying capability from anywhere so they can gather information about how long a movie has been in release, its language, and its consumer rating. They also need to determine what type of usage fees have been charged to the company, actors, and directors.

Communication System Requirements:

Currently, the corporate product database resides on a mainframe. Several independent LANs need to be connected to each other to share information. The IT department wants to purchase a Frame Relay network to link the company's domestic sales offices in New York City and London, England to the new database system. The users will still need to access historical information residing on the mainframe.

1. A dual processor UNIX system is used for the new database system.
2. Sales people in New York and London can access the database over the Web and execute queries from the database. They are able to find out how long a movie has been in release, its consumer rating, and the languages available. They can also query for usage fees charged to the company, actors, and directors.
3. When they need historical information, they query the UNIX server and it sends a Structured Query Language (SQL) command to the mainframe to retrieve the information requested.
4. The new database system is designed with over 100 predefined tables to simplify the queries for the users.
5. They purchased Frame Relay links to connect their sales office in New York and London.

Examine the new Frame Relay network developed for Ocean View Pictures shown in Figure 15.11, and then answer the Study Questions that follow.

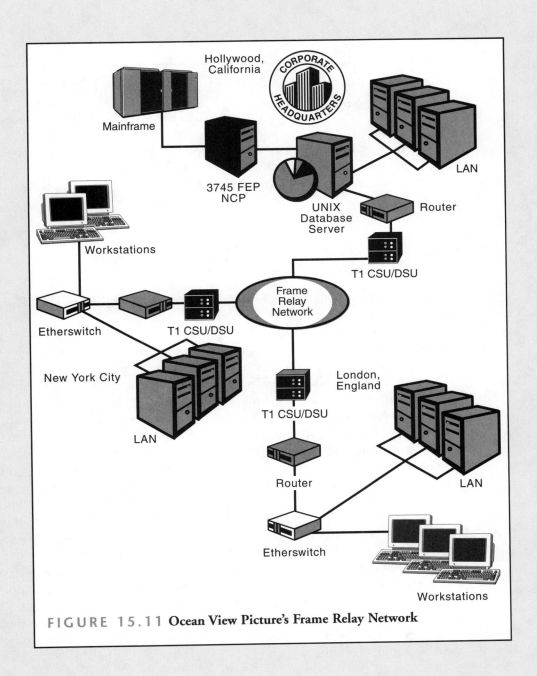

FIGURE 15.11 **Ocean View Picture's Frame Relay Network**

1. Why do you think the company decided to allow the salespeople to access the database over the Web?
2. Why can't the salespeople directly access the mainframe for the historical information?
3. Why do you think the company selected Frame Relay for the WAN links?
4. Does this WAN design provide for secure transmission over the Web?
5. What would the company need to add to its WAN design to make it more secure?

GROUP TERM PROJECT

Open and print the files *GroupReview* and *Summary* from the Encore! CD that came with this book.

In this part of the group project, there are two forms: the Group Review and the Post Project Summary. The Group Review provides for a walk-through of the project, which is typically performed two weeks prior to implementation. The purpose of the walk-through is to review the entire project and determine if there are any missing elements that would delay or postpone the implementation. There are three roles for participants: facilitator, recorder, and reviewer. The facilitator sets the format for the walk-through discussion and designates who will present each part of the project. The recorder records all the reviewers' comments under the comments/recommendations column. Reviewers discuss each part of the project and make recommendations for improvement.

The second form, Post Project Summary, is used to collect all group members' comments about issues they may have encountered during the project. For example, they may have had difficulty finding pricing for particular WAN services. Group members should pretend they have accomplished the implementation, providing details about what happened at each of the eight locations. For example, at the London site, equipment may have arrived damaged and, as a result, the installation team has had to arrange for replacement equipment locally. The purpose of this form is to serve as a planning tool for future implementations. It provides the opportunity to determine corrective actions to be used for future projects.

WAN PROJECT PLAN

GROUP REVIEW

Project Name: **Date of Review:**

Role	Participant's Name	Comments/Recommendations
Facilitator		
Recorder		
Reviewer 1		
Reviewer 2		
Reviewer 3		
Reviewer 4		
Reviewer 5		

WAN PROJECT PLAN
POST PROJECT SUMMARY

PREPARED BY:	**DATE:**

Comments/Recommendations

I.

II.

III.

IV.

V.

CHAPTER TERMS

baselining   802

BCP   791

capacity planning   803

co-location center   788

data mirroring   796

digital divide   780

DRP   791

IP Circuit Analysis   806

Network Health   803

NOCs   790

performance management   802

CHAPTER BIBLIOGRAPHY

Book, Magazine, Presentation Citations

Metzler,Jim, and Cisco & Fiber Link. *State of the WAN: Fine-Tuning Your Wide Area Infrastructure.* Southborough: Network World Seminars & Events, 2002: 1,4,8.

Plunkett, Jack. *Major Trends Affecting the Infotech Industry.* Houston: Plunkett Research, 2001-2002: 14, 18.

Web Citations

Associated Press, "Singapore Telecom Plans $1.6B Cable," Newsday, <asia.news.yahoo.com/bizcty/sg/> (4 September 2002).

Baltazar, Henry, "Outsourcing Degrees of Disaster Recovery," eWeek, <www.eweek.com/print_article/0,3668,a=10021,00.asp> (5 March 2001).

Braunstein, Yale; Meheroo Jussawalla; and Stephen Morris, "Comparative Analysis of Telecommunications Globalization," University of San Francisco, <www.usfca.edu/fac-staff/morriss/PTC.html> (1999).

Bole, Kristen, "Telecom industry surges to wire South America, San Francisco Business Times, <http://www.bizjournals.com/sanfrancisco/stories/1997/05/26/focus4.html> 23 May 1997.

Carden, Philip, "Network Baselining and Performance Management," Network Computing, <www.nwc.com/shared/printArticle.jhtml?article=/netdesign/base7.htmlandpub=nwc> (2002).

C & W, "C & W Global Internet Backbone (AS3561) SLA Performance Statistics," Cable and Wireless, <www.sla.cw.net/> (2002).

Danielsson, Matt, "Disaster Recovery: Are you prepared?" SAP News and Analysis, <searchsap.techtarget.com/oritinalContent/0,289142,sid21_gci803737,00.html> (2002).

Exodus Communications, "Internet Data Centers," Cable and Wireless Internet Services, <www.exodus.net/global_infrastrucute/index.html> (2002).

HerWebHost, "The Only Web Host You'll Ever Need," Her Web Host, <www.herwebhost.com/network.html> (2002).

Jamison, Mark, "Emerging Patterns in Global Telecommunications Alliances and Mergers," University of Florida, <bear.cba.ufl.edu/centers/ciber/workingpapers/JamMergP.html> (2002).

Japan Telecom, "Welcome to Japan Telecom Co., LTD." Japan Telecom, <www.japan-telecom.co.jp/English/aboutus/main.html> (2002).

Jones, Helen, "Central and South American Approvals: Green Light or Red Tape?," Compliance Engineering, <www.ce-mag.com/archive/01/Spring/Jones.html> (2001).

List, Barry, "British Telecommunications Honored in Operations Research Award," <www.informs.org/Press/Edelman1999c.html> (17 May 1999).

Matthews, Julian, "Malaysia Develops Multipoint Video-Conferencing System," NEA—News from Asia Pacific, <www.nikkeibp.com/nea/apr99/napapr/malay.html> (April 1999).

Merryman, John, "Top ten business continuity elements," Systems Management Newsletters, <searchsystemsmanagement.techtarget.com/tip/1,289483,sid20_gci818368,00.html> (02 April 2002).

Mino, Michael, "Telegeography Maps of the World," TeleCom Maps, <homepage.mac.com/michaelmino/PhotoAlbum3.html> (2002).

Mitchell, Brian, "Global top 24 countries ranked by total broadband deployments as of December 2000, expressed as number of digital subscriber line (DSL), cable modem and fiber-to-the-home subscribers per 100 inhabitants," Rural Telecommunications, <www.ruraltelecom.org/> (November 2001).

Pakrisamy, R. "Singapore, Australia Set up IT Joint Ventures," NEA, <http://www.nikkeibp.com/nea/apr99/napapr/sing.html> News from Asia Pacific. 1999.

Paltridge, Sam, "Local Access Pricing and the International Digital Divide," OTI, <www.isoc.org/oti/articles/1000/paltridge.html> (1999).

Qwest, "This is Riding the Light," Qwest Communications, <www.qwest.com> (2002).

Ramadass, Suresh, "Malaysia Develops Multipoint Video-Conferencing System," NEA, <http://www.nikkeibp.com/nea/apr99/napapr/malay.html> News from Asia Pacific. 1999.

Ruderman, Kurt, "America's Network," Diveo, <www.diveo.net/html/ar1034.html> (1 August 2000).

SingTel, "SingTel is committed to bringing the best of global communications to its customers in the Asia Pacific and beyond," SingTel, <home.singtel.com/about_singtel/company_profile/default.asp> (2002).

Tran, David, "Telecom Industry to Grow Despite Economic Downturn," NEA—News from Asia Pacific, <www.nikkeibp.com/nea/apr99/napapr/nam.html> (April 1999).

Valigra, Lori, "Chinese Sites Gain Momentum on Internet," NEA—News from Asia Pacific, <www.nikkeilp.com/nea/apr99/napaper/usa.html> (April 1999).

Visual Networks, "Solutions Overview," Visual Networks, <www.visualnetworks.com/products> (2002)

Winchester Systems, "Disaster Recovery," Winchester Systems, <www.winsys.com/products/disaster-recovery.php> (2002).

GLOSSARY

3G An ITU specification for third generation mobile communication technology. Designed to work with GSM, TDMA, and CDMA. Bandwidth speeds vary based on whether the mobile device is stationary or moving. When the mobile device is stationary, it is capable of transmitting at 384 Kbps. When the mobile device is in a moving vehicle, the bandwidth speed is 128 Kbps.

10BaseT Twisted-pair cabling that uses two wires at a transmission frequency of 10 MHz.

100BaseT4 Twisted-pair cabling that uses eight wires at a transmission frequency of 100 MHz.

100BaseTX Twisted-pair cabling that uses four wires at a transmission frequency of 100 MHz.

AAL ATM adaptation layer. Combined with the ATM layer, it corresponds to the data link layer of the OSI model. Defines a process for converting information from upper layers into ATM cells. Prepares user data for conversion into cells and segments the data into 48-byte cell payloads.

ABR Available Bit Rate. An ATM service category. Provides a guaranteed minimum capacity. Also allows data to be bursted at higher capacities when the network is free.

access The path over which you are connected to the PSTN or the Internet.

access box A small box, also called a station protector, usually located in the basement or on an outside wall of your home

access concentrators This device provides a central point for the connection of communication devices. Also routes IP traffic to local Ethernet ports.

access control A field in the SIP2 cell header that can carry request bits that indicate bids for the cell on the bus going from the switch to the CPE device.

access router A mid-sized router that supports three or four LAN and WAN interfaces, and also supports three or fewer network end user protocols.

access switches A programmable digital system, which supports POTS and Internet service.

access tandem A special switch used to concentrate all trunks from the central office to an interexchange carrier's POP (point of presence).

accounting Tracks the usage of resources for billing purposes.

AD Analog/Digital Converter. A device that converts analog signals to digital; the opposite of modems.

address screening A security feature implemented by SMDS that allows a subscriber to establish a VPN, and then excludes unwanted traffic. If an address is disallowed, the data unit is not discovered.

ADM Add/Drop Multiplexing. Used by SONET to provide interconnection of both telephone and data switches. Provides interfaces between different network signals and SONET signals.

ADSL Asymmetrical Digital Subscriber Line. Asymmetric technology in which the data rate of downstream data is much higher than the upstream.

advanced authentication Some users are granted access from the Internet to selected hosts in a private network. This access is granted based on advanced authentication such as digital certificates with a CA.

AFI A field in the ATM address format. Identifies the type and format of the address based on the authority that provides the address (E.164, ICD, or DCC).

alerts Notifications to administrators of potential trouble or security threats.

algorithm A procedure defined to proceed step-by-step to perform an operation.

amplitude Strength of a sine wave.

amplitude modulation AM. Two different voltage levels of a tone are used to indicate the 0 and 1 states.

AMPS Advanced Mobile Phone Service. A standard system widely used with FDMA for analog signal cellular telephone service. The predominant cellular technology used in the United States today.

analog This signal can have many values within a certain range and is represented as waveforms. Used to transmit information over the telephone lines.

analog switch A single connection is set up between two phone lines in the network. A connection is established and lasts for the duration of the call. The call takes a separate electrical path through the switch for each call as it is placed. This path is also known as a circuit.

ANSI American National Standards Institute. The primary organization for fostering the development of technology standards in the United States.

API Applications programming interface. A set of routines, protocols, and tools used for building software applications. The application programmers write an API to make requests and process replies with the operating system or database application.

application gateway Service is provided by processes that maintain complete TCP connection state and sequencing. Often re-addresses traffic so that it appears to have originated from the firewall, rather than the internal host.

applications software Database programs that provide the rules for the business process, logical flow of transactions, electronic catalog, pricing, and reporting information.

APS Automatic Protect Switching. Used by SONET to allow protected mode rings to take over in the event of a service disruption.

area A group of routers within logically defined network segments. Each area is uniquely identified by an area address.

ARPA Advanced Research Projects Agency. Used the TCP/IP protocol to test the viability of packet-switching networks.

ARPAnet Advanced Research Projects Agency Network. A packet-switching network used in the 1970s to link computer systems together between the defense department, universities, and government research laboratories.

ASCII Developed by ANSI to represent English characters as series of 0s and 1s.

ASM Application server model. A three-tier application architecture. Consists of client presentation through a Web browser, application or business logic, and data and resources provided by a database.

ASP Application Service Provider. Model that provides and manages software services over the WAN from a central data center.

ASR Aggregation service routers. Routers used to increase fault tolerance at the IP network's edge. ASRs are more reliable because they deliver a hot-standby processor, line card, and port-by-port protection.

asynchronous Start/stop transmission. Sends 10 bits: 8 bits of data, 1 start bit, and 1 stop bit.

ATM Asynchronous Transfer Mode. A high-speed, connection-oriented switching and multiplexing technology capable of transmitting voice, video, and data. Used to connect LANs to other LANs.

ATM Forum An international, non-profit organization formed to expand and advance the use of Asynchronous Transfer Mode (ATM) technology.

ATM layer Combined with AAL, it corresponds approximately to the data link layer of the OSI model. Responsible for establishing, maintaining, and terminating VCs over a physical link. Generally controls passing cells through the ATM network.

ATM multiplexing Asynchronous Transfer Mode multiplexing. A multiplexing technique used for ATM. Each user or device can use time slots on demand as these become available.

ATM switch High-end carrier-class switch that can transmit significant amounts of voice, data, video, and image traffic.

auctions Provide for the purchase and sale of surplus inventory, used capital equipment, discontinued goods, and perishable items.

authentication The process of verifying an identity claimed by or for a system entity.

authorization Specifies the level of access permitted to applications and data on the network.

autonomous system A collection of networks under common administration that share a universal routing strategy. Autonomous systems are separated into areas.

backbone A high-speed network structure that connects several locations together.

back-end systems Database and transaction servers, which can exist on a mainframe or a large UNIX server.

band A specific range of frequencies in the RF spectrum.

bandsplitting Splits the line data rate and bandwidth into smaller data rates. Each channel shares a data rate that is divided equally among them.

bandwidth The information-carrying capacity of a communications channel.

baseband Used to transmit digital signals in Ethernet LANs.

baselining Any analysis method that compares changes in actual data against a historical value (value over time).

BAsize Buffer Allocation Size. A field in a SIP3 PDU. Contains buffer allocation size.

batch processing A batch of requests is stored and then executed all at one time.

baud The speed or data rate of transmission.

Baudot The 5-bit code designed for telegraph systems.

B channel Bearer channel. Carries a single digitized voice call or can be used as a data channel.

BCP Business Continuity Plan. Another term for Disaster Recovery Plan (DRP).

Be Committed burst size. A minimum sustained rate at which the Frame Relay provider agrees to transfer data. Also the maximum size of a single traffic burst.

bearer An element of the WAP stack. Can be any of the existing technologies that wireless providers use, as long as the information is provided at the WDP level to interface WAP with the bearer.

BECN Backward Explicit Congestion Notification. Can be used to notify the user that congestion was experienced in the opposite direction of the frame carrying the FECN indication.

BEtag Beginning-end Tag. A field in a SIP3 PDU. Forms an association between first and last segments of a segmented SIP Level 3 PDU.

BGP Border Gateway Protocol. An Internet protocol used between ISPs. The groups of routers share routing information to establish loop-free routes between ISPs.

binary digit Represents one of only two numbers: 0 or 1.

bipolar encoding A special bit-translation pattern embedded into a digital signal. Uses positive and negative voltages to represent digital information.

B-ISDN Broadband-Integrated Services Digital Network. Standard developed to handle voice, video, and data applications within the same transmission. Can provide on-demand, reserved, or permanent services as stipulated in a contract between the service provider and the organization.

bits Binary digits used by computers to store information.

bit-stuffing The addition of extra bits. Often required for asynchronous traffic to enable it to handle individual data streams and to multiplex up to higher rates.

bit synchronization The control of the timing clocks critical for accurate transmission and reception of data.

bit time A common interval for bit signals for use with synchronous devices.

block cipher A type of cipher in which the cryptographic key and algorithm are applied to a block of data, usually 64 bits at once, rather than one bit at a time.

BLSR Bi-directional Line Switched Ring. A SONET architecture used for disaster recovery. A four-fiber, bidirectional, line-switched SONET ring. Two fibers are used to carry traffic while the other two fibers are on standby or protect mode.

Bluetooth A radio frequency standard used for wireless transmission to computers, cell phones, mice, and keyboards.

BOC Bell Operating Company. Telephone company in a given geographic area that provides local telephone service. The original 22 Bell Operating Companies were created by the AT&T divestiture in 1983.

border router A router that provides information about all of its internal routes to other border routers belonging to the other autonomous systems.

boundary router Acts as the primary switching agent for the devices located at the spoke-end of a star topology WAN. The devices can be remote bridges, routers, or low-end routers.

bridge Device that can filter and forward packets by MAC address. Provides for the creation of a single "logical" LAN longer than any one cable segment.

bridge taps A line is joined into an existing unused local loop left behind by a former customer. Bridge taps can cause signal distortion especially in T1 lines.

broadband Data to be transmitted is sent using a carrier signal such as a sine wave. More than one signal can be sent on the same wire.

broadcast A one-to-many signal transmission.

buffer Holding area in memory that captures incoming data in a multiplexer.

burst excess The maximum number of bits that the network agrees to transfer during any time interval.

burst modulation A burst is a set of bits, bytes, or characters grouped together and transmitted.. The data is modulated by converting it from digital to analog signals in order to transmit over a telephone wire. At the receiver, a device converts (demodulates) the received signals back to digital to obtain the data.

bursty LAN traffic that consumes high bandwidth for a short period of time.

BUS Broadcast Unknown Server. Responsible for handling broadcast, multicast, and initial unicast frames sent from a LANE client.

cable modem Modems that connect a computer to the cable network. Data transfer rates of 40 Mbps downstream and 2.5 Mbps upstream.

cabling The communication wire used to connect equipment in a network.

CAC Connection admission control. A procedure used by an ATM switch to determine whether it can provide the services required by the connection.

call accepted packet Packet issued when a call is accepted by the destination DTE.

call request packet Packet sent by the calling (source) DTE that includes the address of the destination DTE.

CAP Competitive Access Provider. Carriers that built their own metropolitan SONET rings and offered private metropolitan or wide area networking services to businesses that could bypass the incumbent carriers.

capacity planning Measures percentage of bandwidth used and how much delay there is in transporting data through the carrier.

carrier The local or long-distance telecommunication service provider that offers a range of data communication services.

carrier signal A specific frequency signal in an analog communication channel that is modulated to carry information.

Carterphone Decision This established the right of telephone company subscribers to connect their own equipment to the public telephone network, providing that the equipment was not harmful to the network.

CAT4 Twisted-pair cable with a transmission frequency of 20 MHz. Often used in Token-Ring networks.

CAT5E Cable has more twists in Category 5 and has higher quality manufacturing to minimize crosstalk. Transmission frequency reaches 200 MHz.

CAT6 Cable transmission frequency reaches 200 MHz. Uses specially designed components to reduce delay.

CAT7 Cable transmission frequency reaches 600 MHz. Each pair is individually shielded. The cable jacket is also shielded.

Category 5 (CAT5) Predominant cable installed in all new buildings with four twisted pairs, and a transmission frequency up to 100 MHz. The maximum distance is 100 meters with 8 twists per foot.

CBR Constant Bit Rate. An ATM service category. Specifies a fixed bit rate so that data can be sent in a steady stream. Provides service for voice and video traffic.

CCK Complementary code keying. A set of 64 8-bit code words used to encode data used with the 802.11 standard published by the IEEE for wireless networking.

CDMA Code Division Multiple Access. A wireless multiplexing technique in which a unique code is assigned to each call and spread over the available frequencies.

CDV Cell Delay Variation. Greatest amount of jitter allowed. Specified by CBR at connection setup.

cell A formatted packet that uses a fixed cell length data unit.

cell splitting A technique used to prevent compromised service as a result of the cell-phone carrier's area becoming full of users. Allows a single area to be split into smaller ones. Cities can be split into as many areas as necessary to provide acceptable service levels.

cellular Communications systems that divide a geographic region into sections, called cells.

cellular telephony Originally developed by scientist Don Ring of Bell Labs. He discovered wireless technology allowing frequencies to be reused for wide-range systems. Today, it is known as cellular radio technology, which offers a new way of providing mobile telephone service.

centralized processing All of the programs and software were executed in a central computer called a mainframe. The clients used terminals without any memory or disk storage.

channel A communications circuit between two or more devices.

character coding The encoding of characters.

character synchronization A sync character is used to synchronize a block of information and identify the boundaries of the characters.

character translation Also known as code conversion, which is required when character codes do not match between sender and receiver.

CIDR Classless Inter-Domain Routing. A new IP addressing scheme that allows a single IP address to be used to designate several unique IP addresses.

The purpose of CIDR is to reduce the size of routing tables and offer more IP addresses available within an organization.

CIR Committed Information Rate. A minimum sustained rate at which a Frame Relay provider agrees to transfer data.

circuit A wire that carries a single channel such as a telephone call.

circuit switch Sets up a dedicated communication channel between two end systems.

cladding A thin layer that surrounds the fiber core of a fiber-optic cable.

class Used to organize levels or layers of the DIT.

clear confirmation packet Packet issued by the remote DTE in acknowledgement of a clear request packet.

clear request packet Packet issued by the receiving DTE when it wants to terminate a call.

CLEC Competitive Local Exchange Carrier. A telephone company that competes with the already established local telephone company. Distinguishes new or potential competitors from the Local Exchange Carrier (LEC).

clients The PCs or workstations on which users run applications.

client-server An architecture in which program logic is distributed between client and server systems. Servers are distributed and can communicate with one another to provide services to clients.

CLLM Consolidated Link Layer Management. Mechanism defined by ANSI that reserves DLCI number 1023 on a Frame Relay interface for sending messages back to the source.

CLNP Connectionless Network Service Protocol. An OSI Connectionless Network Service that provides connectionless datagram services like IP, but it is only used over OSI networks.

clock Device that synchronizes the state of the signal characteristic.

CLP Cell Loss Priority. Determines whether cells should be dropped if extreme network congestion occurs.

clustering Provides for two or more computers to use multiple storage devices and redundant interconnections to form a single system.

CMTS Cable Modem Termination System. A data-switching system specifically designed to route data from many cable modem users simultaneously.

CO Central Office. A telephone company local office that has switching equipment that can switch calls locally or to long-distance service providers.

coating A layer of plastic that surrounds the core and cladding to reinforce the fiber core.

coaxial cable Primary cable used by cable television industry for multimedia and streaming video transmissions into TVs.

codec Coder/decoder. Device used to perform analog-to-digital conversion and digital-to-analog functions within a single chip.

codes A set of rules for manufacturers of computer equipment to follow ensuring their equipment is compatible.

collaboration Provides for electronic sharing of information. Electronic collaboration presently includes corporate instant messaging, white boarding, group discussions, and live document collaboration.

co-location center Offers its customers another secure place for the physical location of their hardware and equipment besides in their own offices. Provides a secure cage or cabinet for housing computer equipment, along with regulated power, dedicated Internet connection, security, and technical support.

communication server Universal managed PC platforms for network communication services.

community Web sites designed to feature industry-specific content and community information. They often offer buyers and sellers the latest news, editorial, market information, job listings, and so on.

component load balancing A technique used to distribute components within the application across servers.

compression Reduces the size of the data and saves usage costs on WAN links.

computing architecture The design and placement of servers, databases, backup devices, and telecommunications links.

congestion Slows traffic down and occurs when there are too many transmissions over the network.

connectionless protocol A protocol used for datagram delivery that does not require any connection setup or release between sender and receiver.

connection-oriented Requires connection establishment and release for asynchronous request/response interactions.

consumer satellite service Wireless satellite services to the home. Signals are delivered to and from the ISP through the satellite service.

container objects Upper layer objects that contain other objects.

content encryption service engine A product that identifies the sensitive data field and re-encrypts it using a 3DES or RSA public key.

control fields Fields used to direct the frame to the destination.

convergence A dynamic routing process used during the routing table update process. Describes the state of agreement of router tables between all routers in the network.

Convergence Age The age when entertainment, telephony, computerized data, voice, and video will be completely integrated. The appeal of the Convergence Age is that access is always on.

cookie A message given to a Web client browser by a Web server.

core A single continuous strand of glass or plastic.

counter-rotating Traffic flow in optical fiber rings. Two signal paths are provided, going in opposite directions.

CPE Customer premise equipment. Data communications equipment owned by the company and located on-site at one or more of the company's locations.

CRC Cyclic redundancy check. This error method uses an algorithm that counts the bits in the packet to ensure that all bits are accounted for.

C/R Field Command/ Response Field. Bits relating to congestion information stored if the network is experiencing congestion or several sources contend for the same bandwidth.

CRM Customer Relationship Management. A database that keeps track of customer service requirements and summarizes product purchases.

CSU Channel Service Unit. A device that connects with the digital communication line and provides a termination for the digital signal.

CSU/DSU Channel Service Unit/Digital Service Unit. A device that connects with the digital communication line and provides termination for the digital signal.

Cut Through The switch only reads destination addresses to pass frames quickly over the backbone. Greater speed is achieved by foregoing the error-checking process.

DA Destination Address. A field within an FDDI data frame. FDDI destination address is 6 bytes long. Contains unicast (singular), multicast (group), or broadcast (every station) address.

daemon A process that runs in the background of a UNIX server. Performs a specified operation at predefined times or in response to certain events.

D-AMPS Digital-Advanced Mobile Phone Service. Another name given to the Interim Standard I-136. Divides the frequency bands available into one time slot at regular intervals.

dark fiber The dark strands of fiber cable that are unused at the time of installation.

DAS Dual Attachment Station. A station is referred to as dual attachment because it is capable of connecting to both FDDI rings.

data A field within an FDDI data frame. Contains information destined for an upper-layer protocol or control information.

database A collection of information organized as an electronic filing system with fields, records, and files.

database driver Translates the application's queries into commands that the database can understand and execute.

database gateway An intermediate device or server that accepts connections from clients using one set of APIs and network protocols to another remote site using a completely different set of APIs and protocols.

data codes Represent information as electrical signals composed of combinations of 0s and 1s.

data encryption Protects data from mischievous hackers. Changes readable information into a scrambled mess of data, which can only be opened by using the proper encryption key.

datagrams In IP, the message is organized into packets.

data mirroring Provides duplication of production data to physically separate target systems hosted at a data center.

Datapak Network A packet-switched public network in the Nordic countries, provides operational control and monitoring of the X.25 network backbone.

data warehousing A database of transaction logs used for offline analysis on the number and types of orders received.

DBMS Database management system. A collection of programs used to enable a client to communicate with the database to store, modify, and extract information.

DBS Direct Broadcast Satellite. Provides digital TV broadcasting directly to users who have satellite dish equipment.

DCC Data Country Code. Address format designed to be used with private ATM networks. Administered by ANSI.

DCE   Data communications equipment. Provides a connection for the DTE into a communications network. Typically a modem or other communication device.

D channel   Channel is used for call establishment and signaling.

DCS   Digital cross connect. A piece of equipment that provides flexible connections between the termination points of devices used in SONET.

DDoS   Distributed Denial of Service. An attack against one or more servers. Using client-server technology, a master program initiates an attack on hundreds or thousands of agent programs.

DE   Discard Eligibility. Allows the network to determine which frames can be discarded under congestion situations.

decoder   Converts information back to its original form for the receiver.

decrypt   To convert data back to plain text so it can be read.

demodulator   The part of a modem's circuitry that converts analog signals back to digital form.

DEMUX   Combines data from multiple channels and puts it back into its original form.

DEN   Directory Enabled Applications. Supported by eDirectory. Integrates policy and directory services into an authoritative, distributed, intelligent repository of information.

DES   Data Encryption Standard. A widely used method of data encryption in which both the sender and receiver must know and use the same private key.

Diffie-Hellman   A key agreement algorithm used by two parties to agree on a shared secret key.

digiboard   A board with multiple serial ports.

digital   Signals in which each pulse is a signal element represented by a binary digit.

digital certificate   A certificate is issued in the form of an electronic "credit card" that establishes a user's credentials for conducting transactions over the Web.

digital circuits   Lines used for data transmission, which span several miles. Repeaters are placed at regular intervals to maintain the signal strength. Data is sent in square waveform without modulation.

digital divide   Separation between those with and those without access to information and communication technologies in developing countries.

digital signal   The binary digits are represented as electrical pulses in which each pulse is a signal element.

digitized   Any kind of information that has been converted to digital information.

diplexer   Provides upstream and downstream signals through the same tuner in a cable modem.

direct focus   An e-business model made up of only the supplier and manufacturer.

directory server   A server can be used to manage extranet user-authentication, create access control, set up user preference, and centralize user management.

directory service   A network service that identifies all resources on a network and makes them accessible to users and applications.

discovery   A task of eDirectory. Enables a user or application to browse the contents of the directory. Responsible for assigning characteristics to people and resources, establishing relationships, updating changes, and optimizing searches for them within the directory.

dish antenna   Known as a "dish," consists of an active element (that is, horn antenna) and a reflector.

distance vector algorithm   When a router uses this algorithm, it receives the entire contents of neighboring router tables.

distortions   A signal's frequency is shifted either higher or lower, which distorts the signal.

distributed computing environment   An environment in which computing and data exchange is distributed over a system of distributed computers.

distributed database   Databases are stored across two or more computer systems. The database system keeps track of which server the data is located on and the users are not aware that the database has been distributed.

distributed processing   A method in which both the client and the server execute part of the process. The business logic is split between the client and server.

DIT   Global Directory Information Tree. A hierarchical naming model used to represent countries, organizations, and localities.

DLCI   Data Link Connection Identifier. A number of a PVC or SVC that tells Frame Relay how to route the data.

DMZ   Demilitarized zone. An area behind the firewall, which is accessible from the Internet.

DNS   Domain Name System. A distributed database system used to perform address/name resolution on behalf of client applications. DNS servers maintain databases of domains and hosts for device identification.

DNS namespace Identifies the structure of the domains that are used to form a complete domain. The name assigned to a domain or computer relates to its position in the namespace.

domain A group of computers and devices on a network that are administered as one unit with common rules and procedures.

domain trees Hierarchical structures in which domains are combined.

DoS Denial of Service. An attack designed to render a computer or network incapable of providing normal services.

downstream The data flowing from the CMTS to the cable modem.

DQDB Data Queue Dual Bus. A data link communication protocol compatible with LANs and FDDI. Specifies a topology composed of two unconnected fiber-optic buses, in which each bus operates independently of the other.

DRP Disaster Recovery Plan. Describes in detail how an organization should deal with a disaster.

DSL Digital Subscriber Line. A technology that provides high-speed data transmissions over the "last mile" to the home or office.

DSL Forum This forum encourages the development of a global mass market for Digital Subscriber Line (DSL) broadband over existing copper telephone wire infrastructures.

DSPs Digital signal processors. Standard processors, used in echo cancellation, which share process time in a circuit within a channel or across channels. They provide a maximum of 128 ms of cancellation.

DSU Digital Service Unit. A device that converts signals from bridges, routers, and multiplexers into bipolar digital signals.

DTE Data terminal equipment. The source or destination of data in a communication connection. Can be a terminal, PC, mainframe, mini, or printer.

DUAL Diffusing-Update Algorithm. Used to determine the least cost route to a destination. EIGRP consults a DUAL finite-state machine for route computations that have been advertised by its neighbors.

dual-homed gateway A type of firewall that completely blocks IP traffic between the Internet and the private network. Uses a host system with two network interfaces and IP-forwarding capabilities disabled.

dual homing A fault-tolerance technique used with FDDI for critical devices such as routers or mainframe hosts. Provides additional redundancy for maintaining operation of the FDDI network. A router or DAS is connected to two concentrator ports on the FDDI concentrator.

DWDM Dense Wavelength Division Multiplexing. Each signal carried over optical fiber has its own separate light wavelength.

DX Directory exchange record. Used to point to a host performing the directory service for a domain rather than an e-mail service. Specifies a protocol for retrieving directory information as well as the host name.

DXI Data exchange interface. A method used when non-ATM equipment is used to transmit packets rather than cells to the ATM interface.

dynamic routing Router table is updated with addresses and network paths automatically.

E1 Transmission link that provides multiplexed, multichannel, point-to-point communication in Europe. Provides 30 Bearer (B) channels and 2 (D) data channels.

E.164 A public networking scheme similar to telephone numbering. Administered by the ITU.

E.164 NSAP E.164 Network Service Access Point. Address format defined by the ATM Forum. Is another version of E.164, however the ATM Forum does not administrate it.

EA Extended Address. Makes it possible to extend the header field to support DLCI addresses of more than 10 bits.

EBCDIC Extended Binary-Coded Decimal Interchange Code. Used for synchronous communications in mainframe computers.

echo cancellation Device used to remove echoes from conversations on voice-grade lines by subtracting the echo before it reaches the user.

echoes The reflection of energy back to its source. Three types of echoes are transmitter echo, receiver echo, and singing echo.

e-commerce Conducting traditional business operations such as selling and purchasing products. Also includes collaborating with members and suppliers over the Internet.

ED End Deliminator. A field within an FDDI data frame. Contains unique symbols that indicate the end of the frame.

EDGE Enhanced Data GSM Environment. An enhanced version of the GSM for mobile wireless service. Transmits at 384 Kbps and can support delivery of multimedia content to other mobile phone users.

eDirectory A full-service directory lays the foundation for capturing, storing, organizing, and leveraging important identity information.

EFCI Explicit Forward Congestion Indicator. ATM uses Resource Management (RM) cells to provide information concerning congestion and notification when transmission needs to be slowed down.

eHub Uses a spoke-and-wheel concept in which the hub is typically a large company at the center and the spokes are its suppliers.

EIA Electronics Industries Association. Includes organizations that together have agreed upon certain data transmission standards. This should not be confused with the Electronics Industries Alliance (also EIA), which is an alliance of trade organizations that lobbies in the interest of manufacturing companies who produce electronics-related devices and equipment.

ELAN Emulated LAN. An ELAN using bridging software to provide translation to ATM.

electromagnetic radiation spectrum The complete range of wavelengths of electromagnetic radiation. Spectrum represents "from DC to light," beginning with the longest radio waves and extending through visible light.

electronic collaboration People can display documents online and discuss the contents via e-mail or video conference.

e-mail virus Attaches itself to e-mail messages. Replicates itself by automatically mailing itself to everyone in the user's e-mail address book.

ENIAC Electronic Numerical Integrator and Computer. This was the first operational electronic digital computer built in 1945.

encoder Used to convert the information transmitted by the sender.

encryption Translation of data into a secret code.

endless loop Cycle that never ends.

end office Same as the central office (CO).

enterprise focus An e-business model detailing the supply chain from supplier to manufacturer to retailer.

ERP Enterprise Resource Planning. Systems used to facilitate the exchange of data among corporate divisions and unify key business processes within the organization. ERP unites major business

processes, such as order processing, general ledger, payroll, and production.

ESI End System Identifier. A field in the ATM address format. Identifies a unique device within the specified network. Designates the 48-bit MAC address, as administered by the Institute of Electrical and Electronic Engineers (IEEE).

ESN Electronic Serial Number. A code inside a mobile phone. A unique 32-bit number programmed into the phone when it is manufactured.

Ethernet 10BaseT A system developed by the IEEE that supports multiproduct and multivendor equipment.

exchanges Provides a market for commodities with high price volatility. They provide for the purchase and sale of natural gas, electricity, and telecommunications bandwidth.

export policies Rules that are distributed across the network to other routers.

extension header Replaced the optional fields defined in IPv4.

exterior routing Routing between autonomous systems.

extranet An organization's intranet is extended to users outside the company to share information with business partners and customers.

failover The system redirects user requests immediately to the secondary backup system that duplicates the operations of the primary system.

fast packet A packet transmitted without any error-checking points along the route.

fat client The bulk of the data-processing operation is performed at the client itself.

fault tolerance The capability of a system to respond quickly to an unexpected hardware or software failure. Fault tolerance is often achieved through redundancy.

FC Frame Control. A field within an FDDI data frame. Indicates the size of the address fields and whether the frame contains asynchronous or synchronous data.

FCC Federal Communications Commission. Functions as a regulatory authority for radio, television, wire, satellite, and cable communications within the United States.

FCS Frame Check Sequence. A field within an FDDI data frame. The source station fills the field with a calculated CRC value dependent on the frame contents.

FDDI Fiber Distributed Data Interface. A high-speed backbone technology with a dual-ring topology using fiber-optic cable to transmit light pulses to convey information between stations.

FDDI concentrator A device used to integrate FDDI stations into an FDDI network.

FDM Frequency Division Multiplexing. For dividing available bandwidth into separate carrier frequencies and then modulating data onto the carriers to create circuits.

FDMA Frequency Division Multiple Access. A wireless multiplexing technique where each call is on a separate frequency.

FECN Forward Explicit Congestion Notification. Can be used to notify the user that congestion was experienced in the same direction of the FECN indication.

fiber-optic cable The cabling favored for high-speed data communications.

field A pattern of bits that have a specific meaning to be interpreted by the router. Fields added to the data field are used to deliver control information.

filters Rules that a network engineer specifies in the firewall configuration to either allow or disallow different types of packets, IP addresses, or domain names.

FINDS Flexent Intelligent Network Determination System. A low-cost phone feature that allows a network to more accurately calculate a cell-phone handset's position.

firewall A gateway that restricts and controls the flow of traffic between networks.

five-nines Measurement of reliability that translates to up to five minutes of downtime per year.

fixed wireless Devices that are connected to the Internet using special modems in homes and offices.

forest Formed by creating multiple domains in a tree.

fractional T1 A sub channel of a full T1 line.

FRAD Frame Relay Assembler/Disassembler. A communications device that breaks a data stream into frames for transmission. It encapsulates outgoing data packets and decapsulates incoming packets.

frame A logical grouping of information that is formatted as a continuous series of bits, which are grouped together to form a single unit of data.

frame builder Multiplexes the information from the CSU/DSU into an aggregate stream for transmission over the line.

Frame Relay circuit table The virtual circuit is identified by an interface index and the corresponding DLCI. Virtual circuits associated with the same Frame Relay interface attachment are combined in one table.

Frame Relay data-link management interface table Contains data-link connection management interface parameters of a Frame Relay interface attachment.

Frame Relay Forum A non-profit organization focused on promoting the acceptance and implementation of Frame Relay.

Frame Relay header Contains the DLCI, FECN, and BECN bits and other information.

frame switching Services for frames provided at the first two layers of the OSI model.

frequency Rate at which voltages change.

frequency modulation Represents the frequency of signal changes based on binary input.

frequency reuse Radio channels have to be reused to provide for more than one conversation at a time. Requires a group of radio channels to be assigned to each cell within a small geographic area. Each cell is assigned a group of channels that is completely different from neighboring cells.

FS Frame Status. A field within an FDDI data frame. Allows the source station to determine whether an error occurred. Also identifies where the frame was recognized and copied by a receiving station.

FSK Frequency Shift Keying. Used with FM; only two frequencies are transmitted.

FTTH Fiber to the Home. From the CO, a trunk fiber-optic cable is extended to carrier remote terminals and then split into eight separate cables that extend to clusters of homes.

full-duplex Channel supports bi-directional flow of data.

full-service directory An LDAP-enabled, directory-based identity management system used to centralize management of user identities, access privileges, and other network resources. Lays the foundation for capturing, storing, organizing, and leveraging important identity information.

gateways Most frequently used to provide for protocol conversion.

GBR Guaranteed Bit Rate. An ATM service category. Allows users to send at any rate up to the PCR while the network is only committed to send at the MCR.

GC   Global Catalog. A server that contains a full replica of all objects in the directory for its host domain. Also contains a partial replica of all objects contained in the directory of every other domain in the forest.

geographic load balancing   Enables disaster recovery on a global scale, bypassing regional interruptions of service automatically. If one regional server cluster suffers failure due to an earthquake, flood, or other natural disaster, server clusters in other regions of the country or the world are available to take over the processing.

geostationary   A high orbit satellite that orbits at 22,300 miles (42,162 kilometers) above Earth.

GFC   Generic Flow Control. Provides logical functions, such as identifying multiple stations that share a single ATM interface. Used to control congestion on the user interface.

GFR   Guaranteed Frame Rate. An ATM service category which allows users to send at any rate up to the peak cell rate while the network is only committed to send at the minimum cell rate.

G. Lite   A "jump start" technology that is meant to deliver DSL to the greatest number of users as fast as possible.

GPRS   General Packet Radio Service. A packet-based wireless communication service that provides continuous connection to the Internet for mobile phone and computer users. Can transmit at data rates from 56 Kbps to 114 Kbps.

GSM   Global System for Mobile Communication. A digital mobile telephone system that has become the de facto wireless telephone standard in Europe. Operates at either 900 MHz or 1,800 MHz frequency band.

guard band   Separates the channels in FDM to prevent interference between adjacent channels.

H.323   Defined as an operability standard for voice and multimedia applications over the Internet. Addresses VoIP vendor equipment incompatibility with the help of gateways and gatekeepers. Does not address encoding, prioritization, or security.

hacker   Someone who tries to break into computer systems.

half-duplex   Channel allows data to pass in both directions but only one direction at a time.

HALO   High Altitude Long Operation. FAA certified aircraft that provides the hub for a WAN.

handover   Designed to manage communication when a cellular phone user travels from one cell to another during a call. Because adjacent areas do not use the same radio channel, a call needs to be transferred from one radio channel to another when a user crosses the line between adjacent cells.

handshaking   A data conversation between a DTE and a DCE to determine whether it is okay to send or receive signals.

hash algorithm   The key in public key encryption uses a hash value to compute a base input number for encryption.

hash value   A value computed from a base input number. A summary of the original value.

HDLC   High-level data link control.

HDSL   High Speed DSL. Delivers data symmetrically at T1 data rates of 1.544 Mbps.

HE   Header Extension. A field in a SIP3 PDU. Contains the SMDS version number.

Head-End center   Head office of cable network in which multiple CMTS and connections are provided to the Internet.

header   A field added to the beginning of a message. Each header field contains all of the fields used to perform the function of a specific protocol. The header field also contains instructions about the length of the packet, packet number, synchro-nization, protocol, destination, and source addressing.

head-of-line blocking   The piling up of packets behind the first packet while it waits for access to a resource that is busy.

HEC   Header Error Control. Used to provide forward error correction. Information is sent in the cell that can be used to fix errors. It first calculates a checksum on the first 4 bytes of the header. If there is a single bit error, HEC can correct it and preserve the cell rather than discard it.

HEL   Header Extension Length. A field in a SIP3 PDU. Indicates the number of 32-bit words in the Header Extension field.

Hertz   Used to measure frequency; represented in cycles per second.

HFC   Hybrid Fiber-Coax network. A CATV network that includes fiber-optic and coaxial cable. Fiber-optic cable from the cable company to near the home and coaxial cable into the home.

HIPPI   High Performance Parallel Interface. An ANSI standard developed in 1990 used to physically connect devices at short distances and high speeds.

HLPI   Higher-layer Protocol Identifier. A field in a SIP3 PDU. Indicates the type of protocol encapsulated in the information field.

HLR Home location register. Used to find the home location of a roaming customer. After receiving a request, it responds to the SMSC with the subscriber's status.

HNU Home Network Unit. A device to provide a connection for the consumer's TV, computer, and telephone.

HO-DSP High-Order Domain Specific Part. A field in the ATM address format. Combines the routing domain (RD) and the area identifier (AREA) of the NSAP addresses. Provides a flexible, multilevel addressing hierarchy for prefix-based routing protocols.

Homing Chain The hierarchy of switching systems used to route phone traffic.

hop The distance between the local router and its neighbor is assigned a value that is referred to as a hop.

horn antenna The antenna resembles an acoustic horn. Used for transmission and reception of microwave signals.

hosting platform The hardware and application software used to manage an organization's business activities.

host name A name that is used to identify the user, application, or workstation. Each host is recognized by a unique software address called an IP address.

hot standby controllers Secondary cards are installed in the large edge router to provide for restoration of service in case of a network fault.

HTML Hypertext Markup Language. An authoring language used to format documents and provide links to graphics, audio, and video files to create Web pages.

HTTP HyperText Transfer Protocol. A set of rules for exchanging files (text, graphic images, sound, video, and multimedia files) on the World Wide Web. Specifies the actions for browser requests and Web responses to various commands.

HTTP request HyperText Transfer Protocol request. A specially formatted request used to retrieve a Web page from a Web server application program.

hub A central device used to concentrate connections from workstations into a LAN.

hub supplier Receives updates from a supplier server. The hub supplier is considered a hybrid because it holds a read-only replica (consumer server) and a change log (supplier server).

IAB Internet Architecture Board. Oversees the technical evolution of the Internet. This organization supervises the Internet Engineering Task Force (IETF).

IANA Internet Assigned Numbers Authority. The first organization to coordinate the assignment of official IP addresses and domain names.

ICANN Internet Corporation for Assigned Names and Numbers. The U.S. government and IANA turned over IP address allocation to private-sector authorities and formed ICANN.

ICD International Code Designator. Address format administered by the British Standards Institute and designed for bar codes and library codes. Identifies particular international organizations. Not originally intended for network addressing.

ICI Intercarrier interface. A method used in establishing an interface through an ATM network where traffic is sent across intermediate networks.

ICP A competitive Local Exchange Carrier. Can own the local loop, SONET, cable TV, and wireless systems. It provides voice, data, Internet access, Web hosting, co-location services, and infrastructure outsourcing.

IDEA International Data Encryption Algorithm. Used by RSA version of PGP to generate a short key for an entire message and RSA to encrypt the short key.

identity information A summary of information on people, applications, and resources contained in incompatible directories and databases.

IDSL ISDN DSL. Allows for the use of existing ISDN card technology for data only. Used in areas where users are too far from the local CO.

IEEE Institute of Electrical and Electronics Engineers. Described as "the world's largest technical professional society." Promotes the development and application of electro-technology and allied sciences. Has fostered the development of standards that have become nationally and internationally accepted.

IETF Internet Engineering Task Force. Defines standard Internet operating protocols, such as TCP/IP. The Internet Society and the Internet Architecture Board act as supervisors.

iFolder Enables users to access personal files from anywhere at any time.

ILEC Incumbent Local Exchange Carrier. A U.S. telephone company that provided local service when the Telecommunications Act of 1996 was enacted. ILECs include the former Bell Operating Companies (BOCs).

I-Mode A packet-based mobile phone service introduced in Japan in 1999. Provides color and video transmission to the mobile phone user. Supports Web-browsing and e-mail and allows users to execute banking and stock transactions from their mobile phones.

impairment tolerance Refers to a certain accepted amount of errors, distortions, or echoes.

import policies Policies are designed to accept routing information.

Info+Pad Information+Padding. A field in a SIP3 PDU. Contains an encapsulated SMDS SDU and padding that ensures the field ends on a 32-bit boundary.

Information Age A period from 1800-1970 when information became very important and easy to obtain. In the Information Age, information was more valuable than money and natural resources.

information field Holds the actual data being transmitted (the "payload"). It can hold from 262 to 1,600 or more octets equivalent to a byte. For router traffic, this includes the RFC 1490 protocol header and the actual data packet.

infrared The region in the electromagnetic spectrum that falls between radio waves and visible light.

instant messaging Allows a person to "chat" with another user who is online at the same time.

intellectual property Web content that is classified as an intangible company asset.

interdomain Routing between autonomous systems, also called exterior routing.

interfaces Used to connect devices together. Hardware interfaces are the wires, plugs, connectors, and sockets that are used to provide communication between devices. Interfaces are often called ports.

InterLATA Telephone and data services provided between LATAs by an Interexchange Carrier (IXC).

Internet Age The current age. The goal is universal access to information and communications services using the Internet. This is designed to permit any user ready access to a set of independent networks that are interlinked as a single, uniform network.

Internet Society An international non-profit organization that acts as a leader in guiding the ethics and moral conscience of the Internet. This group supports the Internet Architecture Board (IAB).

internetwork Formed when a router is used to connect two or more LANS together.

InterNIC Internet Network Information Center. IANA established the center and delegated responsibility to them for managing the top-level domain names (.com, .org, .net).

intradomain Interior routing protocols that provide routing within a domain.

IntraLATA Telephone and data services provided within a LATA.

intranet A private network built within an enterprise network used by the organization's employees only.

intrusion An instance of someone trying to break into or misuse a computer system.

intrusion-detection system A system that performs system monitoring for activities by users and number of attempted logins. The statistics gathered are continually updated and correlated to determine whether a series of actions constitutes a potential intrusion.

IP address Each host on the Internet is recognized by a unique software address called an IP address. This address is represented in dotted decimal notation (142.121.86.132).

IP Circuit Analysis System that offers the information needed for measuring latency, round trip delay time, and packet loss.

IP datagram Data is encapsulated in a datagram to carry it across a network

IPng Next generation of IP also known as IPv6.

IPP Internet Printing Protocol. A new standard provides for easy network setup for printers; enables users to print using IP over the Internet.

iPrint Provides reliable secure printing capabilities using SSL encryption.

IPsec A set of protocols used to support secure exchange of packets at the IP layer of the TCP/IP suite.

IP spoofing A method used by hackers to redirect customers to a fake Web site where they collect and process orders. With spoofing, a system attempts to illicitly impersonate another system by using its IP address.

IPv4 IP protocol version 4. Uses a 32-bit addressing scheme for IP addresses.

IPv6 Internet Protocol version 6. With it, the IP address is lengthened from 32 to 128 bits. Also includes extensions that allow a packet to specify a mechanism for authenticating its origin for ensuring privacy and data integrity over the Internet.

IRTF Internet Research Task Force. A task force assigned within the Internet Society that defines and researches network technology for the Internet.

IR Wireless Infrared Radiation Wireless. Devices that use infrared radiation to convey data. They can function for limited-range communication.

ISDN BRI Basic Rate Interface. Consists of two digital circuits (64 Kbps each) for home or small business use.

ISDN PRI Primary Rate Interface. Consists of 24 digital circuits (64 Kbps) each for corporate ISDN use.

ISO International Organization for Standardization. A worldwide federation of national standards bodies with representatives from some 100 countries.

ISO 3166 A standard that specifies appropriate country codes for every country in the world.

ISP Internet Service Provider. Provides connections into the Internet for home users and businesses.

ISUP ISDN User Part. Messages that are used to set up, manage, and release trunk circuits that carry voice calls between CO switches.

IT Information Technology. Includes all forms of technology used to create, store, exchange, and use information. Includes both telephony and computer technology.

ITC Independent Telephone Company. Also called a nonincumbent telephone company. These operate in noncompetitive areas that are not covered by the RBOCs.

ITU International Telecommunications Union. An impartial, international organization within which governments and the private sector work together to coordinate the operation of telecommunications networks.

IXC Interexchange Carrier. A public long-distance telephone company that provides connections between Local Exchange Carriers (LECs) in different geographic areas.

IXRTT A one-carrier radio transmission technology. A high-capacity voice and data solution that operates at 1.25 MHz and provides a significant increase in speed to 144 Kbps. Offers an increase in RF capacity to enable more connections for simultaneous users.

jack A connection on a wall where you plug in a telephone.

jitter A phase variation with frequency components greater than or equal to 10 Hz.

join request Requests a connection to the LAN emulation server (LES).

join response The LAN emulation server responds to the join request and allows transmission to occur.

Kerberos Assigns a unique key to enable two parties to exchange private information across an open network.

key A variable that is combined with an algorithm.

Kingsbury Agreement Stipulates that AT&T should divest its holdings of Western Union, stop acquisition of other telephone companies, and permit other telephone companies to interconnect.

L2F Layer 2 Forwarding Protocol. Developed by Cisco systems. Independent of IP; able to interface with Frame Relay or ATM.

L2TF Layer 2 Tunneling Protocol. Merges the best features of PPTP and L2F. Can interface with X.25, Frame Relay, or ATM.

LAN Local Area Network. Most LANs connect workstations and printers together to allow sharing of organization data.

LANE LAN Emulation. A standard developed by the ATM Forum to give stations attached via ATM the same bit-passing capability as is required on an Ethernet or Token Ring LAN. Primary function is to emulate a LAN on top of an ATM network.

LAN emulation client End node (workstation or network device) that performs data forwarding and address resolution, as well as several control functions. Each LAN emulation client maintains LANE software.

LAPB Manages communication and packet framing between DTE and DCE.

LAPF Link Access Procedure for Frame-Mode Bearer Services. Provides the data link control for Frame Relay networks.

laser Light-based technology operates on low power levels.

last mile The wired connection from a telephone company's central office to its customers' telephones at their homes and businesses. Also referred to as the "local loop."

LATA Local Access and Transport Area. A geographic area covered by one or more local telephone companies.

latency Time delay between when a frame reaches the input port and leaves through the output port on a switch.

layer A level of user or network functions arranged in a hierarchy. The OSI model has seven layers.

Layer 3 switch These switches are generally used in networks that have changing traffic patterns and multiple network segments in larger networks.

Layer 4 switch A multilayer switch that has powerful network processors. These switches can classify traffic based on policies and rules that are defined for security reasons.

LCI Logical Channel Identifier. Used in virtual-circuit packet switching. A number provided by a telco for input into an organization's router table. Establishes the routers for each packet to the destination address.

LCN Logical Channel Number. Same as LCI.

LDAP Lightweight Directory Access Protocol. A set of protocols for accessing information directories. Operates over TCP, which enables it to provide services over the Internet. LDAP has simpler functions than X.500 and it streamlines coding/decoding of directory requests.

LDP Label Distribution Protocol used in MPLS. The label information identifies the path that the packet will follow to its destination.

leaf objects An end object such as a user, server, or printer that cannot contain other objects.

leased line A permanent telephone connection between two points set up by a telecommunications carrier.

LEC Local Exchange Carrier. A U.S. public telephone company that provides local telephone service.

LECID A unique identifier assigned to a LAN emulation client.

LECS LAN emulation configuration server. Provides configuration information about each network.

LEO Low Earth Orbit satellite. In orbit approximately 400 to 1,000 miles from Earth.

LER Label Edge Router that specifies a label identifier. The information contained in the label specifies destination, bandwidth, delay, and QOS metrics. In an MPLS network, LERs are placed at the perimeter.

LES Land Earth Station. Basically, a land base station that sends radio waves to and receives radio waves from the geostationary satellites (GEOs). Is connected to the traditional PSTN or an ISDN, and the communication method is established according to the type of call being made.

line An element of the overhead in STS-1. The physical path between the SONET hub, switch, or multiplexer in the carrier network. Allows any STS-n signal between any number of STS-n multiplexers.

line/modem Combines function of a line driver and a modem together in one card.

line of sight Transmits information from one point to another in a straight line.

link state Algorithm in which each router sends only the section of its routing table that describes the state of its own links. Also known as the shortest path first.

LLC Logical Link Control. A sublayer within the data link layer that controls frame synchronization, flow control, and error checking.

LMI Local Management Interface. Features handle information exchanges between the network and the router (or other network device). Provides the router with status and configuration information on the PVCs that are active at that time.

load balancing Distributes processing and communications actions evenly across a computer network.

local echo cancellation Telcos use active devices that suppress singing echo, or feedback, on the phone network.

local loop A pair of wires that are connected from the subscriber's telephone to the local central office (CO).

location discovery Used with SMDS, the SMDS router reads the source address in the header of the packet and determines whether the station is upstream or downstream on the two buses.

logical ID swapping A technique in which each ATM switch is responsible for changing the logical ID of one link to a different logical ID on another link as a cell passes through it.

LSA Link State Announcement. Sends an announcement to its neighbor routers whenever there is an update to the network.

LSP Label Switched Path. The pathway that is defined through the telco provider network.

LSR Label Switch Router. Placed at the core of the telco provider or ISP network, it is a device used to switch and place outgoing labels on packets.

MAC Media Access Control. A unique address inscribed on a NIC to identify it to an Ethernet network.

MAE Metropolitan Area Exchange. A major center in the United States where traffic is switched between ISPs.

MAN Metropolitan Area Network. Connects users over a high-speed backbone optical network used to share networking resources within a region that spans an entire city.

Manchester Encoding scheme in which the signal change always occurs in the middle of a bit.

MCR Minimum Cell Rate. A small amount of guaranteed bandwidth that is probably just enough to keep an application running.

media gateway A functional element of IP telephony networks. Used to terminate voice calls on inter-switch trunks from the PSTN. Compresses the voice signals, separates them into packets, and then delivers the compressed voice packets to the IP network.

media gateway controller A functional element of IP networks. Used to handle the registration and management of controller resources at the media gateways. Often called a soft switch because vendors use off-the-shelf computer platforms. Exchanges ISUP messages with CO switches using a signaling gateway.

MEO Middle Earth Orbit satellite. In orbit 8,000 miles from Earth.

mesh topology A point-to-point connection is established between all locations.

Message Authentication Code A programming encryption code appended to a cookie.

message ID A field in a SIP2 cell header. The same ID is used for all segments of a given Level 3 PDU.

message queuing Messages are exchanged between client and server regarding events, requests, and replies.

metadirectory A centralized service that stores and integrates identity information from multiple application-specific directories in an organization. Often described as a directory of directories.

metaframe Allows multiple sessions to be supported through one processor card in a communications server.

metric A number used as a standard of measurement for each link on a network.

MIB Management Information Base. Describes a set of objects that can be managed using SNMP.

microwave Electromagnetic energy having a frequency higher than 1 GHz.

middleware Used to connect two otherwise separate applications together. Passes data between them using querying and messaging techniques.

MIN Mobile Identification Number. A code inside a mobile phone. A 10-digit number derived from the phone number.

mirroring Requires two hard drives in a server that is configured to have data written to them simultaneously. If one drive fails, the other drive has all of the same data on it and takes over immediately.

MNP Microcom Network Protocol. Provides error-correction capabilities for the communications session. MNP requires implementation in modems at each end of a telecommunications link.

mobile e-commerce Enables users to communicate, interact, and transact business over the Internet through the use of mobile handheld devices.

mobile information Level of mobile communication in which mobile users can contact the office to retrieve priority e-mails. Instant messaging extended to provide two-way messaging for mobile phones. Another feature allows access to yellow pages information for phone numbers and street addresses. Mobile carriers have established partnerships with AOL and Yahoo! to provide content designed for mobile phone users.

mobile voice communications Level of mobile communication in which standard voice service is offered with connections established to land lines to communicate with regular phone users.

mobile wireless Devices that are used from motorized moving vehicles such as automobiles, buses, trains, and boats.

modem A device or program that enables a computer to transmit data over telephone lines.

Moore's Law The law states that capacity and power double every 18 months while costs go down in networking and telecom equipment.

Morse code A character code in which long and short tones are used to represent characters.

MPC Multiprotocol clients. The edge devices that generate ATM traffic when MPOA is used.

MPEG Motion Picture Expert Group. A working committee that defines industry standards for digital video systems. The standards specify data compression and decompression processes and how they are delivered on digital broadcast systems.

MPLS Multiprotocol Label Switching, used to build virtual circuits across IP networks.

MPOA Multiprotocol over ATM. Enables devices in different ELANs to communicate without the need to travel hop-by-hop. Only the first few frames between devices pass through routers. The path taken by these frames becomes the default path. After a few frames follow the default path, the MPOA devices discover the NSAP address of the destination device and then build a direct connection for subsequent frames in the flow.

M ports Master ports. Used to connect stations or additional concentrators into an FDDI network.

MPS Multiprotocol servers. Inter-ELAN routers that assist the MPCs in discovering how to build a direct connection to the destination end station.

MPTP Micro Payment Transfer Protocol. Defined for the transfer of payments through the services of a common broker. Designed for small payment amounts and for use in interactive applications. An asynchronous protocol that allows most of the processing to occur offline.

MTSO Mobile Telephone Switching Office. A cellular system's main mobile switching center. Located at the CO, it includes the MSC as well as field monitoring and the relay stations used to switch calls from cell sites to the PSTN.

multidrop Split usage of a single dedicated line.

multimode fiber Several wavelengths of light are used in the fiber core. Different wavelengths of light travel at different speeds through the fiber.

multiplexing Allows a single line to support multiple voice or data channels.

multipoint A connection that has many point-to-point connections and multidrop connections integrated into one large network.

Multiprotocol Router This device can support multiple protocols for user data. The router can route information by protocol.

multi-threaded application A thread is a semi-process that has its own stack, and executes a given piece of code. Multi-threaded means several operations can be carried out in parallel, and events can be handled immediately as they arrive (for example, if one thread handles a user interface, and another thread handles database queries, a heavy query requested by the user can be executed, and still respond to user input at the same time).

MUX Means to multiplex. Also is an acronym used for multiplexer. Splits data or voice out to multiple channels.

MX Mail exchange record. Provides mapping from a domain name to the name of one or more hosts performing mail service for that domain.

NAP Network Access Points. Determines how traffic is routed over the Internet backbone. Also provides switching facilities that select the path for sending data to its next destination, which might be another NAP.

narrowband Sender and receiver tune into a fixed frequency band. Used for radio broadcasts.

NAT Network Address Translation. Security technique that is used to protect IP addresses inside an organization's network. Uses private IP addresses inside the network that are mapped, through a router or firewall, to public IP addresses that are published to the Internet.

National ISDN Council Formed to support the development and resolve the technical and policy issues of ISDN services nationwide.

network carriers Same as bearers.

Network Control Information A field in a SIP2 cell header. Indicates whether the PDU contains information.

Network Health Monitors for the number of errors or the packet loss ratio on a WAN link.

network policy A policy specific to the firewall that defines the rules used to permit access to a private network. Can permit any service unless it is expressly denied or deny any service unless it is expressly permitted.

NEXT Near End Crosstalk. This specification exhibits signal interference from one wire pair that adversely affects another wire pair.

next generation mega networks Future networks that will combine semiconductor development with fiber photonics, ultra-dense WDM, and OA to deliver an all-optical network.

NIC Network interface card. An adapter that is inserted in the workstation to provide connections to Ethernet, Token Ring, and other types of networks.

NID Network Interface Device. A device used to connect loop facilities to inside wiring.

NNI Network-to-Network Interface. A method used in establishing an interface through an ATM network where all traffic travels between ATM devices within the same network.

NOCs Network Operations Centers. Offered by co-location centers for the monitoring and supervising of equipment and personnel within the facility. Supplies the personnel needed to provide hardware and network troubleshooting, software updating and distribution, routers, domain name management, and performance monitoring, as well as connections to other networks.

NRZ1 Non-return to zero. A change in voltage indicates a binary 1.

NSAP address Network service access point address. The location of the logical point between the network and transport layers of the OSI model. Defined by a network service provider.

NSIF Network and Services Integration Forum. Provides an open industry forum organized to discuss strategies for the integration and delivery of end-to-end multi-technology services.

NT1 Network Termination device. Connects the four-wire subscriber wiring to the conventional two-wire local loop.

NT2 A device typically found in a digital PBX, which is capable of performing concentration services.

OA Optical Amplification. Boosting of an optical signal without any conversion of the light into an electrical signal.

object A single entry in the DIT.

OC Optical Carrier. Designation used to specify the speed of transmission for digital signals. Signal rates range from OC-1 at 51.84 Mbps to OC-768 at 40 Gbps.

OC-768 Optical Carrier-768. Supports rates of 40 Gbps on a fiber-optic carrier. Uses DWDM (Dense Wavelength Division Multiplexing) to carry multiple channels of data over a single optical fiber. Currently the fastest Synchronous Optical Network (SONET) rate for data transmission.

ODBC Open Database Connectivity. Used to provide access to all data from any application regardless of which DBMS is handling the data. Inserts a middle layer called a database driver between an application and the database.

OEC Optical electrical converter. A device used to split the signal into the services needed by the consumer.

omni directional Signals are broadcast in all directions at once to guarantee wide coverage.

online catalogs Paper-based catalogs of multiple vendors (suppliers) that are digitized to provide product information and provide buyers with a way to place orders over the Internet.

ONU Optical network unit. Provides fan-out connections to subscribers. The connections can be coaxial, twisted-pair, fiber-optic, or wireless.

OPS Open Profiling Standard. Allows users to control how much personal information they want to share with a Web site.

optical bypass switches Used to eliminate failed stations from a ring to prevent ring segmentation. Switches have mirrors that pass light from the ring directly to the DAS during normal operation. If a DAS experiences a power loss, the optical bypass switch passes the light through itself by using internal mirrors to maintain the ring's integrity.

optical switch A switch that enables signals in optical fibers to be selectively switched from one circuit to another.

OSI A seven-layer model that has a different purpose at each layer. The layers are arranged in a hierarchy with the top being layer 7 and the bottom layer 1.

OTN Optical Transport Network. Operates in the optical domain and uses an optical channel, which is much larger than current Time Division Multiplexed (TDM) networks. Optical channels are frequency slots that provide for transmission and routing of client signals.

OU Organizational unit. A container object that can be designated as states, cities, divisions, or departments within an organization.

outsourcing An arrangement in which one company provides services for another company that could have been provided by in-house staff.

overhead Refers to the control information in a SONET frame.

P3P Used to control the amount of personal information users share with Web sites. Often called "privacy on the Internet assistant."

PA Preamble. A field within an FDDI data frame. Provides a unique sequence that prepares each station for an upcoming frame.

Pacific Telecom Council An international, non-profit organization dedicated to promoting the beneficial use of telecommunications in the Pacific hemisphere.

packet A piece of a message to be transmitted. Contains the data and the destination address of the recipient user.

packet filtering Packets are analyzed against a set of filters. If a packet is okay with the filter, it is sent to the intended receiver. If the packet violates one of the filters, it is discarded.

packet layer A piece of a message transmitted over a packet switching network. The framework for sending and receiving packets is defined by the OSI model. The message is formatted as a packet at layer 3, the network layer, and then it is routed over the packet switching network.

packet number A number identifies each packet and puts it in sequence to comprise a message.

packet switch Switches developed to connect low-speed data users to corporate data networks. Designed to handle variable bit rates of burst data transmission.

PAD Packet assembler/disassembler. Device performs three primary functions: buffering, packet assembly, and packet disassembly.

parallel Transmission method in which each bit of a character travels on its own wire. All 8 bits are sent at once.

parallel processing Provides for simultaneous use of more than one processor (CPU) to execute a program.

parity Used in error detection. A bit is added to make the total number of bits transmitted either an even or odd number.

partitioning Cuts NDS database into smaller pieces. A partition is stored on a server at each location. Used in replication model for Novell Netware 6 Directory Services and eDirectory.

partner focus Involves an online collaborative system, called a Web store, which integrates the supplier, manufacturer, and retailer into a private marketplace. Participating suppliers and buyers are specified by the market maker, with buying/selling activities limited to those participating in the marketplace.

path An element of the overhead in STS-1. Part of the payload envelope for STS-1, carrying information from end-to-end.

payload The body or data of the packet.

payload CRC Payload cyclic redundancy check. A trailer field in a SIP2 cell. Contains a CRC value used to detect errors in segment type, message ID, segmentation unit, and payload length.

payload unit A trailer field in a SIP2 cell. Indicates how many bytes of a Level 3 PDU are actually in the segmentation unit field. If the Level 2 cell is empty, this field is populated with 0s.

PBX Private branch exchange. A telephone switch located on the premises of a company.

PCM Pulse Code Modulation. Digital scheme for transmitting analog data.

PCR Peak Cell Rate. A maximum data rate negotiated by CBR at connection setup to be supported without cell loss.

PCS Personal Communication Services. Services that offer personal service and extended mobility.

PDA Personal Digital Assistant. A small mobile hand-held device that provides computing and information storage for personal and business use.

peering agreement Rules for traffic exchange between ISPs.

peer-to-peer topology A single interconnection is provided for each location. The dedicated circuits are leased from a service provider.

performance management The ongoing analysis of network capacity requirements that ensures an organization has enough bandwidth to meet its business initiatives. Takes into account any upcoming changes in the application environment and predicts growth trends in network use.

perimeter security Perimeters exist at points where the private network meets the interface to the public Internet. Perimeter security is traditionally provided by a firewall.

personal profile A profile that gives users much finer control over the use of their personal information. Users are able to define what information a specific site is or is not be provided.

PGP Pretty Good Privacy. Used to encrypt and decrypt e-mail over the Internet.

phase Amount of lag or acceleration between sine waves at the same frequency.

phase modulation A set frequency that shifts its phase in response to the data being transmitted.

PHY Physical Layer Protocol. Standard specification for FDDI. Defines data encoding/decoding procedures, clocking requirements, and framing.

PIC Primary Interchange Carrier. A code used to find the long-distance carrier you have chosen. The switch looks up the PIC code for your number and then connects it to a long-distance switch or POP for your long distance carrier.

PKI Public Key Infrastructure. This standard uses public key cryptography for encrypting and decrypting messages or data over the Internet. Public and private keys are created simultaneously using the same algorithm.

PKI portal Software that uses databases and directories to store and distribute certificates and their status. Is essentially a security-protocol converter that translates wireless PKI protocols to and from Internet protocols.

plenum The space above the ceiling used for air circulation in heating and air conditioning systems.

PLCP Physical Layer Convergence Protocol. Sublayer of SIP1. Formats the 53-byte cells for delivery across the network.

PLP Packet layer procedures. A procedure for packets used in X.25 at the network layer to establish and manage the connection setup and disconnection.

plug A modular plastic piece at the end of a cable called an RJ-11 connector. The contacts inside the RJ-11 must align exactly with the contacts inside the jack to provide the final connection.

PMD Physical Layer Medium. Standard specification for FDDI. Defines the characteristics of the medium. Includes the fiber-optic link, power levels, bit error rates, optical components, and connectors.

PON Passive Optical Network. A single fiber provides service to multiple customers. Passive implies that the system does not require power or active electronic components between the service provider and customer.

POP Point of presence. A place where communications services are available to subscribers.

port An interface on a computer or other data communications device to which you can connect to another device.

portable satellite terminal Acts as a powerful communication center to provide simple reliable satellite communications from anywhere in the world. Users can browse the Internet, check e-mail, conduct video conferences, send a fax, or simply speak over it using a cordless phone.

portable wireless Battery-powered wireless devices, such as cellular phones and PDAs, which travel with the user from office to home to vehicle.

POTS Plain Old Telephone Service. The analog telephone service that runs over copper twisted-pair wires and is based on the original Bell telephone system.

PPP Point-to-Point Protocol. The protocol used to establish dial-up Internet connections between users and an Internet point of presence (POP).

PPTP Point-to-Point Tunneling Protocol. Used to ensure messages transmitted from one VPN node to another are secure.

prefix Used with CIDR, it is added at the end of an IP address with a slash followed by a number. A special mask indicates how many bits in the address represent the network prefix.

premise wiring A uniform, structured wiring system designed to support multivendor products and environments. Includes telecommunication wiring for telephone and computer outlets in a building.

privacy policy A policy that specifically states the penalties for intrusion.

private connections Full 24 channel T1 lines that are private and dedicated solely to one organization.

private key A secret key that is known only to the two people that exchange messages. Used to encrypt and decrypt messages.

private key encryption A type of encryption in which a single key is used and known only to the two people that exchange the message.

Private NAP NAPs that are privately owned by a particular ISP. They typically bypass the public Internet POPs.

private network Only authorized users can access this network. Privacy is maintained throughout the internal network within an organization.

processor card A card, which has a CPU, memory, serial communications ports, Ethernet, audio, and video built in. Replaces the functions of a standalone PC.

protocol A set of rules that govern data communication.

protocol analyzer A device used to capture packet transmission and track the communication process from source to destination. The protocol analyzer examines (decodes) all of the fields in the frame.

protocol data unit An element (unit) of data that uses an agreed-upon format (protocol) to transmit data between two devices.

protocol stack A set of network protocol layers that work together. Also called a protocol suite.

proxy service Makes network requests on behalf of workstation users. A server is set up and configured through software to manage network requests to other servers. The proxy server protects the servers inside the firewall from intrusion.

PSK Phase shift keying. Modulation in which the phase of the carrier signal is shifted to represent digital data. It is used to encode two or three bits at a time. At intervals of $1/4$, $1/2$, or $3/4$ of its period, it shifts the period of the wave. The shift occurs in relation to the preceding wave period.

PS-NEXT Power-Sum Near End Crosstalk is the official TIA standard for backbone cables with more than four pairs.

PSE Packet-Switching Exchange. Switches located throughout a carrier's network.

PSTN Public Switched Telephone Switch. The transmission components, switching equipment, and facilities for maintenance equipment and billing systems.

PT Payload Type. Indicates the type of payload—either user, network, or management information—in the payload portion of the cell.

PTT Pre-Negotiated Target Time. Coordinated for the arrival of transmission prior to transmission.

public connection Business partners, overseas sites, home workers, and remote workers are connected over the Internet.

public key A value provided by a designated authority to be applied with a private key to encrypt messages and digital signatures.

public key encryption A type of encryption in which a public key is used to encrypt data and another private key is used to decrypt.

PVC Permanent virtual circuit. A continuously dedicated virtual circuit. Used for frequent and regular data transfers.

Q.922 standard A standard adhered to by Frame Relay that stipulates that protocols must encapsulate their data units within a Q.922 Annex A frame.

Q.931 standard A standard followed by ISDN that specifies control signaling and how connections are set up between the user and the network.

QAM Quadrature Amplitude Modulation. A method of modulating digital signals using four phase states to code two digital bits per phase shift.

QoS Quality of service. Offers a guaranteed service that defines in advance the transmission and error rates for LANs, WANs, and the Internet.

QPSX Queued-Packet Distributed Switch. A distributed queuing algorithm used in SMDS that manages access to each bus. Allows nodes or users to place data traffic in a queue for later transmission onto a bus.

RAIN Reliable Array of Independent Nodes. A software clustering technology originally developed by the California Institute of Technology and NASA.

RBOC Regional Bell Operating Company. A regional U.S. telephone company that was created by the AT&T divestiture in 1983. Also referred to as the "Seven Baby Bells."

RD Routing domains. Defined in lookup tables in the ATM switch. Used for traffic management to provide for an effective way to allocate bandwidth capacity.

read-write replicas Replicas that can be written to and that contain master copies of the directory.

real time Visual and audio communications that occur immediately.

Reed Solomon A 2-D error-correction code that derives the correction information by applying two different mathematical formulas on the same data. Reed Solomon codes are particularly effective in correcting large-scale burst errors.

refraction The bending of light that occurs as the light passes through the fiber-optic cable.

relationship A task of eDirectory. Responsible for building associations between people, network devices, network applications, and information on the network.

reliability The amount of time a network is available or unavailable. Measured as a percentage of uptime and network availability.

remote access The ability to access a computer or a network from a remote distance.

remote control Software enables a user to take control of a dedicated PC or server residing on the corporate network.

remote node Attaches the remote PC to the LAN over a dial-up connection. Allows for file sharing and data transfer.

repeaters Devices that regenerate signals and pass them to other network segments. They receive, amplify, and retransmit packets.

replica A redundant copy of a directory database.

replication The process of making a replica (copy) of the database on another database server.

replication topology The placement of the supplier and consumer servers in the network.

replication traffic Network traffic generated by the interaction and replication process between supplier and consumers.

Resource Definition Framework Uses a vocabulary and a standard data format for expressing personal information with OPS for electronic purchases.

RFC Request for Comment. Used by standards and forums to request input to proposed standards.

RFC 2052 Defines SRV records.

RG-59U The coaxial cable is constructed as 22 AWG stranded wire with 100% braided shield. Provides high-quality video, sound, and pictures to connect to your TV, VCR, DSS satellite box, home stereo system, and computer sound cards.

ring A ring is a network topology that forms a path in the shape of a ring. Each device is attached along the same signal path to two other devices.

Information flow may be either unidirectional or bidirectional. Some common ring networks for WANs are FDDI, SMDS, and SONET.

ring topology Topology built with dedicated circuits and constructed in such a way that each location is connected to two other locations. The physical layout of the WAN forms a complete ring.

RJ-11 The wiring that provides the electrical contact for your telephone.

RJ-11 interface Registered jack with four (two-pair) wires to connect to the telephone.

RJ-45 interface Registered jack with eight (four-pair) wires to connect to Ethernet and DSL.

RM Resource Management. A cell used to provide information concerning congestion and notification in an ATM network. (See EFCI.)

root Lies at the top of the hierarchical naming tree structure.

rotation time Amount of time it takes a signal to propagate around the ring in a ring-based network.

Router Packet Filtering Uses routers and packet filtering to grant or deny access. Can either grant or deny access by source address (host) or by port (service).

routers Intelligent, high-level internetworking devices that, on their own, can determine the best path through a network. A router forms the boundary between one network and another.

router table A database of information about an organization's network. Collects information about addresses of other routers and node addresses of devices (computers and printers) attached to the network.

routing algorithm A formula used by routers to determine how to process and forward packets.

routing domains Sets of routers that use the same routing code, administrative rules, and values for metrics. Inside a routing domain, there can be one or more areas.

routing policies Rules used to allocate network resources such as bandwidth, QOS, and firewalls according to defined business policies.

routing switch fabric Used to switch cells within a switch. Self-routing and can manage the flow of ATM cells through the switch.

RPC Remote procedure call. A type of protocol that allows a program on one computer to execute a program on a server computer.

RPR Resilient Packet Ring. A network topology currently being developed as a new standard for fiber-optic rings. The standard will specify access protocol and physical layer interfaces to enable high-speed data transmission in a fiber-optic ring topology.

RQ Request Counter. Counter used in SMDS. Placed on each bus to keep an accurate count of the number of data requests not reserved by downstream nodes.

RSA Version of PGP. Requires a licensing fee.

RSA algorithm Uses a combination of public and private keys for encrypting data. Used by nearly everyone for encryption and authentication because it is the encryption method for popular Web browsers.

RS-232 The most commonly and frequently used interface cable for serial communication with DCE.

RS-422 Standard interface used for serial communications and designed to replace the RS-232 standard. RS-422 has since been superseded by RS-423.

RS-449 Usually used with synchronous transmissions to employ serial binary data interchange.

RS-485 Used for serial multipoint communications. With an RS-485 connection, one computer can control many different devices.

RS-530 Uses the same mechanical connector as the RS-232 but supports higher data rates. Used to transmit serial binary, asynchronous, or synchronous data at rates ranging from 20 Kbps to 2 Mbps.

RTP Reliable Transport Protocol. Used to guarantee ordered delivery of all packets to its neighbors.

RXD Indicates that data communication can be received. Data is moved over pin 3 to receive (RXD) the data transmission.

RZ Return to zero. Voltage status of signal returns to 0 after a signal state.

SA Source Address. Identifies the single station that sent the frame.

SANS Security Administration, Networking, and Security. Published list of top 20 security flaws it had discovered.

SANS/FBI Top Twenty List Publication lists top 20 security flaws. Informs more than 156,000 security professionals, auditors, and system and network administrators of solutions found for security attacks.

SAS Single Attachment Station. Station/node that uses one cable to connect to the concentrator.

satellite phone roaming Using a global air interface, an ANSI-41 satellite phone user can roam to an area served by GSM or vice versa.

SAWPKI Server-Assisted Wireless Public Key Infrastructure. New version of WPKI. Used by mobile devices to contact a powerful server that is responsible for delegation of public key cryptographic processing.

schema The organization or structure of the database.

SCP Service Control Point. A signaling point in a SS7 network. A centralized database is used to determine how a call will be routed. A SCP sends a response to the origination SSP containing the routing number associated with the dialed number.

SCPC Single Channel Per Carrier. Links that connect local POP servers to Internet gateways.

SCR Sustained Cell Rate. Used to specify how long cells can be transmitted at the PCR rate.

screened host firewall Combines a packet-filtering router with an application gateway. This gateway is located on the protected side of the router.

screened subnet firewall Incorporates an intermediate perimeter network to shield the private network or intranet.

SCTP Stream Control Transmission Protocol. Allows for reliable transfer of signaling messages between signaling end points in an IP network.

SD Start Deliminator. A field within a FDDI data frame. Indicates the beginning of a frame by using a different signaling pattern than the rest of the frame.

SDH Synchronous Digital Hierarchy. International equivalent of SONET.

SDSL Symmetric Digital Subscriber Line. Symmetric bi-directional DSL that operates on one twisted-pair wire. Supports a bandwidth of 384 Kbps per channel using the same speed for upstream and downstream.

section An element of the overhead in STS-1. Handles the cable between adjacent network devices (regenerators).

security A task of eDirectory. Controls access to information in the directory. Allows for establishing rules and granting rights to users for various types of information.

security flaws Defects that attribute to the way a Web server passes uploaded data and can cause the software to misinterpret the size of large pieces of incoming data.

security monitoring Provides a staff of security experts who monitor security alerts generated by an organization's network. Security experts examine the audit log files from all devices (routers, firewalls, intrusion-detection systems, and servers) to verify whether an attack is real or a false alarm.

security policy A written set of procedures that protects the company's physical and information technology assets.

segmentation unit A field in a SIP2 cell header. Contains the data portion of the cell. If the Level 2 cell is empty, this field is populated with 0s.

segment type A field in a SIP2 cell header. Indicates whether the cell is the first, last, or middle cell from a segmented Level 3 PDU.

SEL Selector. A field in the ATM address format. Used for local multiplexing within end stations and has no network significance.

self-healing architecture Architecture in which, if the fiber is cut, transmissions are looped back onto a secondary fiber on both sides of the break and a new ring is then formed around the break.

sensors Servers used to watch all traffic.

serial Bits are sent one after another in a serial stream over one wire.

server clustering Data is written to both servers simultaneously, which means that the data on one server exactly matches the data on the other.

server farm A group of computers housed together in a single location.

servers Machines dedicated to managing processes, storing data, and controlling network traffic into and out of an application.

service provider A telephone company that provides local and long-distance voice and data services.

SET Secure Electronic Translation. Standard designed specifically to allow for secure credit card transactions over the Internet. Protects payment information confidentiality, provides cardholder authentication, and ensures the transmitted data integrity of payments.

SHDSL Symmetric high-speed Digital Subscriber Line. Designed to improve upon HDSL and SDSL. The upstream and downstream data rate is 2.3 Mbps.

S-HTTP Secure HyperText Transfer Protocol. A secure communications protocol designed to handle HTTP messages. Designed to send individual messages securely. Cannot be used to secure non-HTTP messages.

SID System Identification Code. A code inside a mobile phone. A unique five-digit number that is assigned by the FCC to each carrier.

signal Electrical voltage, current, or waves that carry information over an electronic circuit.

signaling gateway A functional element of IP telephony networks. Used to internetwork the signaling between switched-circuit and IP networks. Terminates SS7 signaling. Translates and relays messages over an IP network to a media gateway controller or another signaling gateway.

SignText A security technique used to provide a digital signature to WAP applications that require the capability to provide persistent proof that someone has authorized a transaction. Using WML, the SignText function executes a WML script that defines the use of a crypto API to provide the cryptography.

sigtran protocols A set of protocols defined by the IETF. Protocols specify a method for carrying SS7 over IP in VoIP networks.

silence suppression Used to monitor signals for voice activity so that when silence is detected for a specified length of time, the application informs the Packet Voice Protocol. Also prevents the encoder output from being transported across the network.

silica Silicon dioxide. A nonmetallic element used especially in alloys and electronic devices.

SIM Subscriber Identity Module. Implemented by WIM. A unique number that identifies the cellular phone.

SIM card Subscriber Identification Module card. Small, removable disk, on which GSM stores all of the connection data and identification numbers required to access a specific wireless service provider. When GSM users travel to different countries, they can switch to the SIM card, which grants them access to the service provider networks in the countries they travel to.

simplex Device supports the flow of data in one direction only.

sine waves Continuously varying electromagnetic waves.

single-mode fiber Can prevent wavelengths of light from overlapping and distorting data. Single-mode fiber has excellent linearity and dispersion behavior, which results in lower loss rates at high speeds.

Single Protocol Router Supports only one network protocol for user data. The entire network has to be set up to use only one protocol worldwide.

SIP SMDS Interface Protocol. A protocol based on the IEEE 802.6 standard for cell relay across MANs. Provides a connectionless service that allows the SMDS router to access the carrier's SMDS network.

SLA Service Level Agreement. A contract between a service provider and a customer. The SLA specifies the terms of the agreement and how much the customer will pay for those services.

slapd A daemon used by LDAP to handle connection management, access control, and protocol interpretation.

SLIP Serial Line Interface Protocol. Used to connect one TCP/IP system with another over a serial point-to-point communication line. IP packets are encapsulated into data link layer frames to travel across the serial link.

slurpd A daemon that provides replication services to update slave databases on other servers.

Smart Antenna Dedicated intelligent antennas that provide higher capacities for the radio frequency path to the base station. Used in wireless communications.

SMDS Switched Multimegabit Data Services. A WAN service designed for LAN interconnection through the PSTN that provides a high-speed packet-switch service for data exchange. Supports moderate bandwidth connections of between 1 and 45 Mbps.

SMS Short Message Service. Instant messaging for mobile phones. Short text messages can be transmitted to and from a mobile phone.

SMSC Short Message Service Center. After a message is sent, it is received by the SMSC. The SMSC passes the message through the network to the destination mobile device.

SMT Station Management. Standard specification for FDDI. Defines the FDDI station and ring configurations, initialization, scheduling, collection of statistics, fault isolation, and recovery. Also specifies ring control features such as station insertion and removal.

SMTP Simple Mail Transport Protocol. A simple protocol that controls the exchange of e-mail messages between two mail servers.

Smurf Attack A type of DDoS attack that uses the ping program with a forged address to continually ping one or more servers on a network. The forged address is overwhelmed by response traffic generated by the pings.

SNI Subscriber Network Interface. The interface between the CPE and carrier equipment in SIP.

SNS Satellite Network Service. Provides a link from the gateway to the consumer and used to transport data.

socket The combination of port and IP address. Packets flow across networks between sockets and end at the destination socket.

SONET Synchronous Optical Network. Provides for synchronous data transmission on optical media. Current line rates are approaching 20 Gbps.

SONET ADM/CC Synchronous Optical Network Add/Drop Multiplexing/Cross Connect. Uses add/drop multiplexers to cross connect between networks and offer customers bandwidth on demand.

source address validation A security feature implemented by SMDS. Verifies that the PDU source address is correctly assigned to the SNI from which it originated. Used to prevent address "spoofing."

Spanning Tree Algorithm An algorithm used to ensure that a packet cannot find itself in an endless loop in the network.

SPE Synchronous Payload Envelope. The actual payload transported in a SONET frame, and includes everything but the transport overhead.

splitter Used to convert a single outlet into a multiple outlet to accommodate two separate devices.

spokes The suppliers linked to the hub of an e-commerce eHub.

SQL Structured Query Language. A standard programming language used to get information from and into a database.

SRV records Service location resource records as defined in RFC 2052. They map the name of a service to the name of a server offering that service. Used to determine the IP addresses of domain controllers.

SS7 Signaling System 7. A telecommunications protocol used to offload PSTN data traffic congestion onto a wireless or wireline digital broadband network.

SSL Secure Sockets Layer. A secure negotiated session between the client browser and the Web server. Provides for authentication and confidentiality using digital certificates. Establishes a unique symmetric key called a session key, which is only used once for that specific session.

SSP Service Switching Point. A signaling point in a SS7 network. Sends signaling messages to other SSPs to set up, manage, and release voice circuits required to complete a call.

SST Spread Spectrum Technology. Signals are spread out over a very high frequency range, more than 200 times the bandwidth of the original signal.

Stacheldracht Launches a DoS attack using encrypted communication between the attacker and the master program. Also updates the agents automatically using the rcp (remote copy) UNIX command.

standards The written agreements that specifically define the rules, guidelines, or definitions of quality required to ensure that materials, products, processes, and services are appropriate for their purpose.

start bit The bit at the beginning of a character.

star topology This layout provides for multiple LANs to be connected through a central site.

stateful inspection Certain key parts of a packet are checked against a database of trusted information. Packets are monitored for specific characteristics. Stateful inspection tracks each connection through each interface of the firewall and makes sure it is valid.

static routing The router table is updated manually. User specifies addresses and routes.

STDM Statistical Time Division Multiplexing. A multiplexing method that constantly changes the allocation of time slots to accommodate the requests of the attached devices.

stop bit The bit at the end of the character.

storage The database structure for eDirectory. Enables a user to automatically control the type of data stored by applying classifications to the data structures.

store-and-forward Each and every packet is examined in its entirety. After it has been determined free of errors, the packet is sent to its destination.

STP Shielded Twisted Pair cable. STP cables are more expensive than unshielded cables and signals carried over them require more time to terminate.

stream cipher Type of cipher in which the cryptographic key and algorithm are applied to each binary digit in a data stream, one bit at a time.

strengthening fibers Fibers that are made of a substance called Kevlar, wire strands, or gel-filled sleeves. They protect against crushing forces and excessive tension during installation.

STS-1 Synchronous Transport Signal Level 1. A frame comprised of overhead and payload. The basic building block of the time-critical framing format used by SONET.

submarine cable Coaxial or fiber cable used to transmit information over bodies of water to replace or augment high frequency radio schemes.

subscriber The user or customer in a public-switched telecommunications network.

Supply chain management Links the buying, selling, shipping activities into an e-commerce system to run over the Internet.

SVC Switched virtual circuit. A temporary virtual circuit established and maintained only for the duration of a data transfer session.

switch These devices are used to alleviate network congestion. They divide a network into virtual LAN (VLAN) segments. Switches have the capability to dedicate more bandwidth to a port or a group of ports.

switch control point A module, or switch card, that implements cell switching capabilities and can handle an aggregate capacity of 3 Gbps.

symmetrical Equal bandwidth in upstream and downstream channels.

symmetric key encryption Encryption method in which the sender and receiver of a message share a single, common key to encrypt and decrypt the message.

synchronous Characters are sent as a stream of bits called data frames.

T1 A T carrier service that uses TDM (Time Division Multiplexing) techniques to transmit voice or data over digital trunk lines at 1.54 Mbps.

TA Terminal adapter. Allows a non-ISDN ready device to work over the ISDN connection.

tariff A record that describes prices, terms, and conditions of a telecommunications service offering. A tariff must be filed with either state or federal regulatory commissions.

TAXI Transport method named after the chipset created by Advanced Micro Devices for FDDI networks. Used for interfacing ATM networks with FDDI networks.

TC Telecommunications closet. A closet or room that houses all of the equipment associated with telecom links. Contains all WAN and LAN backbone and horizontal wiring for a building.

TCP/IP A suite of communications protocols used to connect hosts to the Internet.

TCP segment A packet of information that uses TCP to exchange data with its peers.

TDM Time Division Multiplexing. Supports data transmission through assigned time slots with guaranteed bandwidth.

TDMA Time Division Multiple Access. A wireless multiplexing technique that assigns each call a certain "slice of time" on a designated frequency.

TE1 An end-user ISDN terminal type 1 device, which connects to the ISDN line through a twisted pair four-wire digital link.

TE2 An ISDN terminal type 2 device that is used to connect to a terminal adapter.

telco The company that provides phone services to subscribers, also known as a local service provider.

Telecommunications Act 1996 An act enacted by the U.S. Congress that specifies laws that govern cable TV, telecommunications, and the Internet. The main purpose was to stimulate competition in telecommunication services.

teleconferencing Allows us to hold a conference, or group meeting, over an Internet connection.

Telemanagement Council A non-profit global organization assembled to provide leadership, strategic guidance, and practical solutions for improving the management and operation of communication services.

TELPAK Service introduced in the 1960s that created "electronic highways" between locations.

terminal emulation Software that allows a PC to act as a terminal device.

TFN Tribal Flood Network. Launches a DoS attack that can generate packets with a spoofed source IP address. The attacker accesses the master program and sends either a UPD, TCP, SYN, ICMP echo request flood, or an ICMP directed broadcast to all agent programs on several networked servers.

TFN2K Tribal Flood Network 2K. A more advanced version of TFN. Sends corrupt packets to cause a system to crash or become unstable. Can defeat router filters by spoofing IP source addresses to make packets appear to come from a neighboring router on the LAN.

thin client A browser based user interface is used that is free of application business logic.

throughput A guaranteed data speed measured in bits per second.

THT Token Holding Timer. Used to calculate the maximum length of time a station can hold a token to initiate asynchronous transmissions.

TIA Telecommunications Industry Association. An American standard for structured cabling systems.

tier topology Locations are connected in a star or ring formation at different levels.

time slot A physical dedicated path provided by a circuit switch. The user's information is transmitted in a specific time slot and only during that time slot using a method called synchronous transmission.

Tip The names for the two wires of a telephone line were derived from the electrical contacts on the original 1/4-inch telephone plug. The electrical contact is at the tip of the plug (used for Line +). The other is a ring just above it (used for Line -).

topology The layout of a LAN.

trailer A field appended to the end of the message that tells the network that it has reached the end of the packet. Also provides the control information used for error detection.

transaction processing A type computer processing in which the computer responds immediately to user requests.

translation table A table used by an ATM switch to manage cell transfer through the switch. Includes the incoming port number on the switch, the virtual connection ID, an outgoing port, and the virtual connection ID.

transport mode Only the data portion (payload) of each packet is encrypted.

Trinoo A complex DDoS program that uses master programs to automate the control of several agent programs. The agent programs then attack one or more servers by flooding the network with UDP packets.

Trojan Horse Virus that disguises itself and appears to the user as a normal computer program.

TRT Token Rotation Timer. A clock used to measure rotation time by timing the period between the receipt of the sender and encryption of the data.

trunk A line that carries multiple voice or data channels between two telephone exchange switching systems.

trusted domain Resource that contains all user accounts and their privileges.

trusting domain Resource that contains all the servers, printers, and workstations.

trust models Different levels of trust are defined for employees, customers, and business partners.

TSE Windows 2000 Terminal Services. Provides software applications so remote users can run software as a thin client through their browser.

TTL Time to Live. Controls how long a server will cache the IP address or other information.

TTRT Target Token Rotation Timer. Clock that calculates the operation of the MAC layer.

tuner Connects directly to the CATV outlet.

tunnel mode With this mode, both header and payload are encrypted.

tunneling protocol A secure tunnel created by a protocol that is used to transport data over the Internet. The protocol encrypts both the header and the data. Also requires a VPN device at the receiver end to decrypt each packet.

twisted pair The wiring used for telephone systems. Connected from the telephone switch to the wall jack where you plug in a phone and consists of two independent copper wires twisted around one another.

two-tier architecture The architecture is simply a client and a server. The user interface runs on the client and the database is stored on the server.

TXD Transmit. Data is moved over pin 2 to transmit data.

UBR Unspecified Bit Rate. An ATM service category. Does not guarantee any throughput levels.

U-int The U interface, also called the U-loop, represents the loop between your premises and the local telephone company's CO for an ISDN connection.

ultra-dense WDM A multiplexing technique that will someday greatly increase the number of messages that can be transmitted over a fiber connection.

UMTS Universal Mobile Telecommunications System. A worldwide broadband, packet-based service for mobile computer and phone users. Supports a roaming service that offers the same set of functions to and from any location. Designed as a 3G service for high-quality broadband information for e-commerce and entertainment services. Offers low-cost, high-capacity data rates as high as 2 Mbps when the mobile device is stationary. Support for global roaming is also included.

unbundled access Incumbent Local Exchange Carriers (LECs) offer separate services to CLECs for loops, subloops, NID, circuit switching, Interoffice Transmission Facilities, Signaling and Call-Related Databases, and Operations Support Systems.

UNE Unbundled network elements. Network services that are separated and granted to CLECs to access the local loop and to the subscribers connected on the other end.

unguided media Signals radiate freely. Signals are not carried over physical cables.

UNI User to Network Interface. The connection that exists between the user equipment and the ATM equipment.

unipolar Waveform of binary signals.

upstream The data flowing from the cable modem to the CMTS.

upstream band The frequency used to transmit data from the cable modem to the CMTS.

URL Uniform Resource Locator. Used to request a domain name to access a Web site.

USB Universal Serial Bus. A data communication standard for a peripheral bus that provides an interface for computer telephony devices.

USNs Update Sequence Numbers for each object. Using a time-based formula, it recognizes when an object has been created or modified.

UTP Unshielded twisted pair cable. Cable is not shielded and is subject to interference and crosstalk.

V.35 Designed to support high-speed serial connections at greater distances, and specifically for transmission between DTEs and DCEs over digital lines.

VAD Voice activation detection. A software application used in VoIP that allows a data network carrying voice traffic over the Internet to detect the absence of audio. Conserves bandwidth by preventing the transmission of silent packets over the network.

VBR Variable Bit Rate. An ATM service category. Provides a specified throughput capacity but, unlike CBR, data is not sent in a steady stream. Commonly used for voice and video conferencing.

VC Virtual channel. Similar to a virtual circuit, a channel that provides a fixed pathway or route between two points. A VC is set up across an ATM network whenever data transfer begins.

VCI Virtual Channel Identifier. Along with the VPI, it identifies the next destination of a cell as it passes through a series of ATM switches on the way to its destination. Specifies the virtual channel between users or between users and networks.

VC table Virtual Channel table. A lookup table within the ATM switch that maintains the output VP and VC to be used to send the cell.

VDSL Very High-Data-Rate Digital Subscriber Line. Asymmetric. The upstream data rate is 1.5- 2.3 Mbps. Downstream rate is 12.96 to 51.84 Mbps.

video conferencing A tool for communicating via audio, video, and data in real time.

video encoders Devices used to create the MPEG content in streaming video.

video servers Content repositories for images and information being streamed.

virtual channel connection (VCC) The connection from the source end user VCI to the destination end user VCI.

Virtual Channel ID The ID associated with a virtual channel.

virtual path connection (VPC) The connection from the source end user VPI to the destination end user VPI.

virus A small piece of software that attaches itself to a program. Each time the program runs, the virus runs too and then reproduces by attaching itself to other programs.

VLAN Virtual Local Area Network. Designed to logically define virtual segments or boundaries for workgroups or departments in a LAN.

VoIP Voice over Internet Protocol. Sends voice information in digital form as separate packets rather than over the traditional PSTN.

voltage Level of the polarity of a signal, which can be positive or negative.

VP Virtual path. A group of VCs used to tell the switch how to forward an ATM cell through the ATM network.

VPI Virtual Path Identifier. Used in combination with the VCI, it identifies the next destination of a cell as it passes through a series of ATM switches on the way to its destination. Used to distinguish VPs between users and in between users and networks.

VPN Virtual Private Network. A private data network that runs through a public telecommunications network or the Internet. Uses encryption and other security techniques to protect the privacy of data.

VP table Virtual Path table. A lookup table within the ATM switch that maintains a record of the VPs on each link.

VSAT Very Small Aperture Terminals. Contain an opening for the microwave beam that is very narrow.

VT Virtual tributary. A structure designed for transporting and switching payloads in a SONET frame. Allows slower speed services to be carried in the payload by putting them into separate VT containers.

WAE Wireless Application Environment. An element of the WAP stack that holds the tools that wireless Internet content developers use, including WML and WMLScript, a scripting language used in conjunction with WML.

WAN Wide Area Network. A geographically dispersed telecommunications network.

wander A phase variation at a rate of less than 10 Hz.

WAP Wireless Application Protocol. A set of communication protocols that standardize the way that wireless devices, such as cellular telephones and radio transceivers, can be used for Internet access.

WASP Wireless Access Service Provider. A service provider that supplies a high-speed connection to the Internet. The service provider connects to its nearest POP and is able to transmit and receive signals over the POP's connection to the Internet.

waveforms A graphical representation of a signal as a plot of amplitude versus time, that is, the shape of a wave.

wave guide Tubes used as a feeder between a microwave antenna and the equipment on the ground. Radio waves are channeled through a tube.

wavelength Distance between the beginning and end of a cycle.

WDM Wave Division Multiplexing. A Frequency Division Multiplexing (FDM) technique for fiber-optic cable in which multiple optical signal channels are carried across a single strand of fiber at different wavelengths of light.

WDP Wireless Datagram Protocol. An element of the WAP stack that works in conjunction with the network carrier layer. WDP makes it easy to adapt WAP to a variety of network carriers because the only change needed is to the information maintained at this level.

Web browsing Viewing of company or organization Web sites by the public where authentication is not necessary.

Web hosting Provides for storing, serving, and maintaining content files for one or more Web sites. Each Web site has its own domain name and set of e-mail addresses.

Web server A server that contains one Web site for all customers to access the application.

white boarding Uses a display screen, so that multiple users can write or draw on the screen and the people on the other end can both see and hear the ideas being presented.

Whois database A central database that contains information about the owner and name servers for each domain.

wideband Large capacity analog or digital circuits.

Wi-Fi A networking standard for WLANs in homes and offices. Provides broadband Internet access to PCs and laptops within a few hundred feet of a Wi-Fi base station or transmitter.

WIM WAP Identity Module. A security technique used to store and process information needed for user identification and authentication. Encryption keys are processed and stored within it.

wireless Methods of telecommunication that use electromagnetic waves to carry data and voice over the communication path.

Wireless Human A licensed band in the radio frequency spectrum, which operates from 2 GHz to 11 GHz. Also referred to as Wireless High Speed Unlicensed Metropolitan Area Network.

WML Wireless Markup Language. A programming language used to provide special text-only or low-graphics versions of a Web site for wireless mobile devices.

worm A small piece of software that uses computer networks and security holes to replicate itself.

WPKI Wireless Public Key Infrastructure. A security technique that brings the functions of PKI to wireless devices. Supports the standard PKI components: CAs, RAs, and end-entities. In addition to these components, WPKI defines a PKI portal.

WSP Wireless Session Protocol. An element of the WAP stack that determines whether a session between the device and the network will be connection-oriented or connectionless.

WTLS Wireless Transport Layer Security. An element of the WAP stack that provides many of the same security features found in the TLS part of

TCP/IP. Checks data integrity, provides encryption, and performs client and server authentication.

WTP Wireless Transaction Protocol. An element of the WAP stack that acts like a traffic cop, keeping the data flowing in a logical and smooth manner. Also determines that each transaction request will be classified as Reliable two-way, Reliable one-way, or Unreliable one-way. The WSP and WTP layers correspond to HTTP in the TCP/IP protocol suite.

X+ Carried Across Network Unchanged. A field in a SIP3 PDU. Ensures that the SIP PDU format aligns with the DQDB protocol format.

X.500 A global directory service framework defined by a set of international standards published jointly by the ISO and the ITU.

X.121 addressing scheme An ITU-T standard specification describing an addressing scheme used in X.25 networks.

X.21 bis A physical layer protocol used to define the electrical and mechanical procedures for using the physical medium. Supports point-to-point connections, synchronous full-duplex transmission at 19.2 Kbps over four-wire media.

INDEX